R BK 447.09 M3457N
NEW ENGLISH-FRENCH DICTIONARY OF SLANG
COLLOQUIALISMS /MAR
1 C1974 9.95 FV
3000 365315 30014
St. Louis Community College

S0-CPS-180

THE NEW ENGLISH–FRENCH DICTIONARY OF SLANG AND COLLOQUIALISMS

Uniform with this volume:

THE NEW FRENCH-ENGLISH DICTIONARY
OF SLANG AND COLLOQUIALISMS

Joseph Marks, M.A.

Revised and completed by
Georgette A. Marks and Albert J. Farmer

9 in. x 6 in., 255 pp., boards with jacket

THE NEW ENGLISH–FRENCH DICTIONARY OF SLANG AND COLLOQUIALISMS

by

GEORGETTE A. MARKS
Special Lecturer, University of Manchester

and

CHARLES B. JOHNSON, M.A.

A Sunrise Book E. P. DUTTON & CO., INC. *1975*

1-12-76

First published in the U.S.A. 1975
Dutton-Sunrise, Inc., a subsidiary of E. P. Dutton & Co., Inc.
Copyright © 1974 by Georgette A. Marks and Charles B. Johnson
All rights reserved. Printed in the U.S.A.

FIRST EDITION

10 9 8 7 6 5 4 3 2 1

No part of this publication may be reproduced or transmitted in any form or by any means, electronic or mechanical, including photocopy, recording, or any information storage and retrieval system now known or to be invented, without permission in writing from the publisher, except by a reviewer who wishes to quote brief passages in connection with a review written for inclusion in a magazine, newspaper or broadcast.

ISBN: 0-87690-149-6
Library of Congress Catalog Number: 74-32524

Published in Great Britain under the title:
Harrap's English-French Dictionary of Slang and Colloquialisms

THE NEW ENGLISH–FRENCH DICTIONARY OF SLANG AND COLLOQUIALISMS

FOREWORD

The present work is the second part (English-French) of *Harrap's French-English Dictionary of Slang and Colloquialisms* by Joseph Marks, and has been planned along the same lines. It is not intended only for the specialist. An ever-increasing number of French-speaking people travel in countries where English and American English are spoken; they like to be able to understand the man in the street, and are interested in English and American novels, plays and films. Our purpose is to enable them to cope with the English slang and colloquialisms they are likely to come across, and also to help English speakers to find the French equivalents of current words and expressions in non-standard English.

No dictionary can claim to be exhaustive. This one contains what is hoped to be a far-reaching and, at the same time, a judicious selection (subjective though it must be) of colloquial, popular and even vulgar words and phrases with appropriate French renderings. Admittedly some entries are rarely encountered outside certain contexts and *milieux*, but even so they are, we feel, of sufficient frequency to justify their inclusion.

Compiling a dictionary of slang may be regarded as a form of lexicographical heroism, for nothing is more subject to change than popular speech; at the same time, nothing is more succulent, vehement or picturesque. Plato, who did not care for the common people, nevertheless called them "my masters in language"; and Montaigne sought an approach to language "not so much delicate and well-groomed as vigorous, terse and concentrated, typical of the barrack-room rather than of pedantry". And so, however ephemeral some expressions may be, they have a span of life—a vogue—while others become common enough to pass into everyday language and literature.

In France, since the Second World War, a number of works, research studies and dictionaries have been devoted to *l'argot*, and, to take but one notable example, in the latest Supplement to the Robert dictionary it plays an important part. In Great Britain, on the other hand, linguists seem on the whole to disdain slang and there are very few, apart from Eric Partridge, who have spent many years of research on it. And yet slang has a long and fascinating history. As far back as in the reign of Elizabeth I, Thomas Harman, a worthy gentleman who set out to combat vagrancy, published a lexicon of vagabond terms. Dekker did likewise some fifty years later. Shakespeare, Beaumont and Fletcher, and Ben Jonson used beggars' cant in their plays. At length, in 1785, a certain Captain Francis Grose published his large *Classical Dictionary of the Vulgar Tongue*, more comprehensive than that of Hautel on the low French language which appeared in 1808. But who better to defend slang than G. K. Chesterton: "Good slang is the one stream of poetry which is constantly flowing. Every day some nameless poet weaves some fairy tracery of popular language. The world of slang is a kind of topsy-turvydom of poetry".

The origin of the word *slang* is obscure; it is supposed to have first applied to the language of nomads and gipsies, and it was not until the end of the eighteenth century that its meaning was broadened to include thieves' cant and the language of the underworld. The vocabulary of thieving and deception, of prostitution and sexual intercourse still figures among its richest elements. The secret language of criminals, tramps and beggars was known as *cant*—now understood as a mode of expression confined to members of a particular profession, trade, age-group or social stratum. *Jargon* is more restricted in that it is too technical in its terminology to be comprehensible to the uninitiated—i.e. to anyone outside the group in which it is spoken. As cant and jargon terms, in the course of time, filter through to a wider sector of the public they become known as *slang* or *popular language*.

At the other end of the spectrum are *colloquialisms*, words and expressions typical of everyday conversation but not regarded as being formal enough for "polite" conversation, business correspondence or the like. One of the major problems in the compilation of a dictionary of slang and colloquialisms is to determine which words and expressions are eligible for inclusion and which are to be omitted because they have reached the stage where they can rightly be regarded as "standard" or "approved" English. The problem is further complicated by the widespread use of figurative speech in English. The decision whether to include this or that word or expression must, in the end, be an arbitrary one, since there is no ultimate authority to which one can turn for guidance. One of the chief aims of this dictionary has been, so far as is possible, to elucidate a very broad range of terms, from the colloquial bordering on standard English to the very vulgar.

But not only does the dictionary contain a comprehensive cross-section of terms in use at the present time, but also a representative selection of those which, to the modern generation, will seem "dated"; yet they owe their place in this work to the fact that, over a period of time, they have established themselves sufficiently to find their way into the literature and other art-forms of this country and of other English-speaking countries. They are included, however, not only on account of their historical importance but also because such expressions have a habit of being reintroduced after a lapse of time, either for novel effect to a new generation or because the various alternatives tried are rejected in their favour. The fact is that, English being a living language, it is never static but for ever self-regenerating, and words are created and discarded practically every day—especially since the advent of mass-media.

Because of all these considerations it is very difficult to determine what is colloquial and what is popular or vulgar, but, to serve as a guide to the uninitiated, every head-word in the dictionary is followed by one of the following abbreviations:

F: = familiar; colloquial
P: = popular; slang
V: = vulgar
VV: = very vulgar; "taboo"

It is impossible to be squeamish, for the coarse, the violent and the obscene are part and parcel of popular expression. To call a spade a spade presents no problem nowadays. It is precisely when a spade is no longer a spade that the lexicographer's interest awakens. It may be added that the popular mentality was never greatly concerned with spades as such. It has moved in other fields, as has been noted above, with vigour and inventiveness, but with scant regard for social or moral conventions. We have not deemed it necessary to avoid printing in full English or French words that are often considered taboo.

The foreign student of English generally finds himself attracted by popular speech and is often tempted to use it, feeling that it gives the impression of a greater familiarity with the spoken language. But one has only to think of the many pitfalls *l'argot* offers in French—and not merely to foreigners—for one to be very cautious before attempting to use some of the expressions found in this dictionary. Slang, it should be remembered, is linked, even more than *l'argot,* not only with a particular *milieu* but often with specific circumstances. It is also characterized by forms of pronunciation and grammar peculiar to itself. Used "out of situation" and so away from its proper context it can appear ludicrous if not offensive.

In order to keep the work within a reasonable compass, a number of space-saving devices have been used. Where in an example a head-word is repeated in exactly the same form it is represented by the initial letter, though plural nouns or verb conjugations in which the form differs from the infinitive are written in full:

e.g. **stack** (*noun*) . . . **to have a s.** (*or* **stacks**) **of money,** être très riche*...
give (to) . . . don't g. me that! ne me raconte pas d'histoires!... **to know what gives,** être à la page. . .

Similarly, compound words appearing in examples are represented by the two initial letters:

e.g. **milk-train** (*noun*) . . . **to catch the m.-t.,** rentrer au petit matin.

This method of abbreviation also applies to the English compound verbs where the infinitive form remains intact in the example:

e.g. **doll up (to) . . . to d. oneself u.,** s'orner, se bichonner...

If, however, the form differs from the infinitive the components are given in full:

e.g. **doll up (to) . . . to get all dolled up,** se mettre sur son trente et un...

Irregular plural forms of nouns have been given only where it was felt they might present special difficulties for non-English users of the dictionary.

It should be noted that, for maximum convenience, the dictionary is arranged in strict alphabetical order; hence words which rightly belong together may be separated:

e.g. **goofball, goofed (up), goofer, go-off, go off, goof off.**

Entries labelled (*U.S.*) (Americanisms) or (*Austr.*) (Australianisms), though numerous, are restricted to such terms as would be unlikely to be understood in Great Britain in the context given. These labels are not used for words which have passed into English colloquial or popular usage, whatever their origin.

Popular language is so rich in synonyms that, in order to save space and avoid repetition, it has been decided to give the generic term followed by an asterisk (*e.g.* **mitt,** main*). The asterisk indicates that the word so marked is given as a head-word in the *Répertoire alphabétique de synonymes argotiques et populaires* at the end of the dictionary; there will be found a list of familiar and popular synonyms and closely related words from which a choice can be made. Most key-words in the dictionary itself are followed by one or more of these synonyms which approximate most closely in register. In the case of drugs (*drogues**) the reader is being referred to a wider group than the synonyms for a specific word.

To facilitate reference, nouns have normally been taken as key-words, and the first noun serves this purpose if a phrase contains two or more nouns (*e.g.* **like a dose of salts** will be found under **dose**). Cross-references are frequently given in cases where it was thought useful to do so.

The authors are indebted to all those who helped to make the publication of this dictionary possible: first and foremost to Mrs Jean Johnson, who provided the inestimable support of an understanding wife, and Mr David Marks, whose filial support was matched by his valuable collaboration; to Mr R. P. L. Ledésert, Director of the Modern Languages Department of Messrs Harrap, and to his wife Margaret—the Curies of lexicography—for their encouragement and help, and also to a number of his colleagues, especially Mr P. H. Collin, for their advice; to Mr F. White, whose knowledge and unflagging interest were extremely helpful; to Miss Gillian Seymour, who typed much of the material; and to everyone who, wittingly or unwittingly, contributed to this work.

G.A.M.
C.B.J.

AVANT-PROPOS

Cet ouvrage se présente comme la deuxième partie anglaise-française du *Harrap's French-English Dictionary of Slang and Colloquialisms* de Joseph Marks et a été conçu dans le même esprit. Il ne s'adresse pas seulement au spécialiste. Un nombre toujours croissant de touristes francophones voyagent dans les pays de langue anglaise et américaine; ils veulent comprendre l'homme de la rue et s'intéressent aux romans, aux pièces de théâtre, aux films anglais et américains. Notre but est de leur permettre d'assimiler les éléments populaires et argotiques de cette langue, et aussi d'aider l'anglophone curieux de la transposition en français des expressions courantes et vivantes de l'anglais non-académique.

Aucun dictionnaire ne peut prétendre être complet. Celui-ci veut présenter une sélection — personnelle peut-être — mais aussi étendue et judicieuse que possible de phrases et de mots familiers, populaires et même vulgaires et de leur équivalent en français. Certaines expressions sont peut-être rares et ne se rencontrent que dans certains contextes et certains milieux mais semblent cependant assez fréquentes pour justifier leur inclusion.

Présenter un dictionnaire d'argot est une sorte d'héroïsme lexicographique car rien n'est plus fluide, changeant, incertain que la langue populaire; mais rien non plus n'est aussi succulent, véhément et pittoresque. Platon, qui n'aimait pas le peuple, l'appelait cependant «mon maître de langue»; et Montaigne recherchait «un parler non tant délicat et peigné comme nerveux, court et serré, non pédantesque mais plutôt soldatesque.» Donc, même si certaines expressions sont éphémères, elles ont vécu et d'autres deviennent assez usuelles pour passer dans la langue de tous les jours et dans la littérature.

En France, depuis l'après-guerre, plusieurs ouvrages, études et dictionnaires ont été consacrés à *l'argot* et il est très caractéristique que le dernier Supplément du Dictionnaire de Robert lui fasse une large place. En Grande-Bretagne, au contraire, les linguistes semblent dédaigner le *slang* et il n'y a guère qu'Eric Partridge qui lui ait voué de longues années de recherches. Pourtant le slang a une longue et fascinante histoire. Dès le règne de la première Elizabeth, Thomas Harman, un digne homme qui voulait combattre le vagabondage, publia un lexique de sa langue. Dekker fit de même quelque cinquante années plus tard. Shakespeare, Beaumont et Fletcher, Ben Jonson employèrent le *cant* des mendiants dans leurs pièces. Enfin, en 1785, un capitaine Francis Grose publia un gros dictionnaire classique de la langue vulgaire plus compréhensif que celui d'Hautel sur le bas langage français qui parut à Paris en 1808. Mais qui peut mieux défendre le slang que G. K. Chesterton: «Le bon *slang* est un des ruisseaux de la poésie qui constamment s'écoule. Chaque jour quelque poète anonyme tisse quelque réseau féerique de la langue populaire. Le monde du *slang* est un royaume renversé de la poésie.»

L'origine du mot *slang* est obscure; on pense qu'il s'appliquait d'abord à la langue des nomades et des romanichels et ce ne fut qu'à la fin du dix-huitième siècle qu'il s'étendit à la langue de la pègre et du milieu. Le vocabulaire des voleurs et des escrocs, celui de la prostitution et des rapports sexuels lui procure encore ses plus riches éléments. Le langage secret des truands et des larrons d'autrefois s'appelait le *cant,* mot qui aujourd'hui désigne surtout le mode d'expression d'un métier, d'une profession, d'une génération ou d'une classe sociale. Le *jargon* a un sens plus restreint car il est trop technique pour être compris par le non-initié, c'est-à-dire quiconque n'appartient pas au groupe où on le parle. On peut donc dire qu'aujourd'hui le *slang* ou *langue populaire* couvre tous les termes de *cant* et de *jargon* qui se sont infiltrés dans un usage plus courant.

A l'autre bout de la gamme se trouve la langue familière et les locutions de la langue de tous les jours mais qu'on ne considère pas suffisamment convenables pour une conversation polie ou des rapports épistolaires. Un des grands problèmes de la composition d'un dictionnaire d'argot et de langue familière est de savoir déterminer quels termes peuvent y figurer et quels autres doivent être rejetés du fait qu'ils sont devenus de l'anglais «correct» et accepté. L'emploi en anglais du figuré et de la métaphore rend ce problème encore plus compliqué. Dans ce choix la décision finale ne peut être qu'arbitraire puisqu'on ne peut être guidé par aucun principe directeur. Autant que possible le but de ce dictionnaire a été de présenter un vaste déploiement de termes qui partent du familier touchant au correct, pour aller jusqu'à l'obscène et l'ordurier.

Ce dictionnaire contient non seulement un assortiment étendu de mots et expressions d'aujourd'hui mais aussi une sélection représentative de termes que les jeunes pourraient qualifier de «périmés». Ils ont leur place dans cet ouvrage car pendant un laps de temps ils ont vécu et ont pénétré dans l'expression littéraire orale ou écrite en Grande-Bretagne ou en Amérique. Et ce n'est pas seulement à cause de leur importance historique qu'ils ont été retenus, mais aussi parce qu'après un certain temps, souvent ils réapparaissent, sonnant neufs aux oreilles d'une nouvelle génération ou peut-être simplement exprimant mieux l'idée que ce qui les avait remplacés. L'anglais, parlé par tant de millions d'individus, est en vérité une langue vivante, jamais statique mais se renouvelant sans cesse; chaque jour des mots naissent et meurent, surtout depuis l'apparition du mass-media.

Du fait de toutes ces considérations il est donc fort difficile de déterminer le familier, le populaire, le vulgaire, mais pour guider le lecteur non averti chaque terme est suivi d'une des abréviations suivantes:

F pour familier
P pour populaire et argotique
V pour vulgaire et trivial
VV pour le très vulgaire, l'obscène, l'ordurier

Il est impossible de se montrer pudibond; le grossier, le violent et l'obscène font partie intégrante de l'expression populaire. On est habitué aujourd'hui à appeler les choses par leur nom: *un chat un chat, et Rolet un fripon,* mais c'est précisément quand un chat n'est plus un chat que l'intérêt du lexicographe s'éveille. D'ailleurs, la mentalité populaire a surtout tendance à broder sur le côté *fripon* avec vigueur et pittoresque sans se soucier des conventions sociales et morales. Il ne nous a donc pas semblé nécessaire d'éviter d'écrire en toutes lettres les mots anglais et français que certains déclarent tabous.

Quiconque apprend l'anglais semble attiré par le parler populaire et essaie de s'en servir, ayant ainsi l'impression qu'il se familiarise avec le langage courant du pays. Mais il suffit de penser à tous les traquenards que rencontre même le francophone s'il veut parler argot pour n'employer qu'avec beaucoup de précautions les expressions que l'on trouvera dans ce dictionnaire. Le *slang*, plus encore que l'*argot*, appartient non seulement à un milieu déterminé mais aussi dépend de circonstances précises. Il est accompagné d'une prononciation particulière et enrobé d'une grammaire spéciale. Si on le sort hors de son cadre et de son contexte normal, il devient grotesque et même choquant.

Afin que ce volume soit commode et maniable, on s'est servi de plusieurs moyens pour gagner de la place. Lorsque dans un exemple le mot de tête (ou entrée) est répété sans changement orthographique il est représenté par sa lettre initiale, mais les noms pluriel et les verbes conjugués dont la forme diffère de l'infinitif sont en toutes lettres:

ex. **stack** (*noun*) . . . **to have a s.** (*or* **stacks**) **of money,** être très riche*...
give (to) . . . **don't g. me that!** ne me raconte pas d'histoires!... **to know what gives,** être à la page...

De même, les mots composés qui se trouvent dans un exemple sont représentés par leurs deux lettres initiales:

ex. **milk-train** (*noun*) . . . **to catch the m.-t.,** rentrer au petit matin.

Cette méthode d'abréviation s'applique aussi aux verbes composés anglais lorsque la forme infinitive est conservée dans l'exemple:

ex. **doll up (to)** . . . **to d. oneself u.,** s'orner, se bichonner...

Mais si cette forme diffère de l'infinitif le verbe est alors donné en toutes lettres:

ex. **doll up (to)** . . . **to get all dolled up,** se mettre sur son trente et un...

Les pluriels irréguliers de certains noms ont été indiqués là où ils pourraient offrir quelques difficultés au lecteur non-anglais.

On remarquera aussi que, pour plus de commodité, ce dictionnaire est arrangé en suivant strictement un ordre alphabétique, ce qui explique pourquoi certains mots apparentés sont séparés les uns des autres:

ex. **goofball, goofed (up), goofer, go-off, go off, goof off.**

Les entrées indiquées (*U.S.*) (américanismes) ou (*Austr.*) (australienismes) sont assez nombreuses mais limitées à des termes qui seraient difficilement compris en Grande-Bretagne dans un contexte donné. Ces termes ne sont pas employés lorsque les mots, quelle que soit leur origine, sont passés dans la langue anglaise courante.

La langue populaire est si riche en synonymes que, pour économiser de la place et éviter les répétitions, il a été décidé de donner le terme générique suivi d'un astérisque (*ex.* **mitt,** main*). L'astérisque indique que le mot ainsi marqué figure comme entrée dans le *Répertoire alphabétique de synonymes argotiques et populaires* à la fin du dictionnaire, où l'on peut trouver une liste de synonymes et de termes apparentés et ainsi faire un choix. D'ailleurs, dans le corps du dictionnaire, ces entrées sont suivies d'un ou plusieurs synonymes qui semblent les plus proches de l'expression anglaise. Dans le cas des *drogues** le lecteur trouvera une liste plus complète de termes affiliés.

Pour faciliter l'emploi du dictionnaire, les noms sont pris comme mots-clefs dans une phrase. Si la phrase contient plus d'un nom c'est le premier nom qui sert de repère (*ex.* **like a dose of salts** se trouvera sous **dose**). Certains renvois peuvent aussi aider le lecteur à relier des expressions similaires.

Les auteurs tiennent à remercier tous ceux qui ont rendu possible la publication de ce dictionnaire.

Tout d'abord leurs proches: Mrs Jean Johnson qui apporta l'appui inestimable d'une épouse compréhensive, et Mr David Marks qui sut combiner le soutien filial à une collaboration précieuse.

Mr R. P. L. Ledésert, Directeur de la Section de Langues vivantes de la Maison Harrap et sa femme Margaret, les Curie de la Lexicographie, qui, avec générosité, prodiguèrent aide et encouragements.

Mr P. H. Collin et ses collaborateurs, dont les conseils furent fort appréciés.

Mr F. White qui allia connaissances et dévouement.

Miss G. Seymour, à qui l'on doit la dactylographie d'une grande partie du manuscrit.

Enfin tous les parents et amis qui ont, par leurs offrandes, contribué à cet ouvrage.

G.A.M.
C.B.J.

ABBREVIATIONS—ABRÉVIATIONS

abbr.	abbreviation	abréviation
adj.	adjective	adjectif
adv.	adverb; adverbial	adverbe; adverbial
attrib.	attributive	attributif
Austr.	Australianism	australienisme
av.	aviation	aviation
c.	circa	circa
cf.	refer to	conferatur
conj.	conjunction	conjonction
c.p.	catchphrase	locution populaire
euph.	euphemism	euphémisme
excl.	exclamation	exclamation
f	feminine	féminin
F:	familiar; colloquial	familier; style de la conversation
fig.	figurative(ly)	figuratif, figurativement
iron.	ironical(ly)	ironique(ment)
m	masculine	masculin
mf	masculine or feminine	masculin ou féminin
mil.	military	militaire
P:	popular; slang	expression populaire; argot
pej.	pejorative	sens péjoratif
pl.	plural	pluriel
p.p.	past participle	participe passé
prep.	preposition	préposition
pres. part.	present participle	participe présent
pr. noun	proper noun	nom propre
pron.	pronoun	pronom
qch.	something	quelque chose
qn	someone	quelqu'un
R.S.	Rhyming Slang	mots composés qui ont leur sens non pas en eux-mêmes mais dans le mot avec lequel ils riment

sing.	singular	singulier
s.o.	someone	quelqu'un
sth.	something	quelque chose
th.	theatre	théâtre
T.V.	television	télévision
U.S.	United States; Americanism	États-Unis; américanisme
V:	vulgar	trivial; vulgaire
VV:	very vulgar; "taboo"	très vulgaire; obscène; ordurier
W.W. II	Second World War	deuxième guerre mondiale
*	see Appendix	voir le Répertoire alphabétique de synonymes argotiques et populaires

PRONUNCIATION

The phonetics of every word listed are given, using the notation of the International Phonetic Association. Colloquial language and slang have a wide diversity of pronunciations which even have a tendency sometimes to produce a specialized form of expression. The best-known example is perhaps Cockney, the vernacular of Londoners, the features of which are too diverse to describe here. Moreover, the same words are pronounced in different ways in various English-speaking countries. Hence the task has not been an easy one, but the phonetics provided should at least serve as a useful—even if not an infallible—guide, particularly to non-English-speaking users of the work.

The following points call for special attention:

(1) Symbols appearing between round brackets, *e.g.* **empty** [ˈem(p)ti], show that there are alternative and equally acceptable pronunciations with or without the corresponding sound.

(2) Words such as **whip, whistle, white** have been shown with the optional initial h-sound [(h)wip, ˈ(h)wisl, (h)wait], though in practice the h is rarely sounded in colloquial or popular speech.

(3) Word-stress is indicated by a stress mark [ˈ] preceding the stressed syllable, *e.g.* **junky** [ˈdʒʌŋki], **connect** [kəˈnekt]. Secondary stress is not indicated.

(4) The sound [r] does not usually occur before consonants or before a pause; the italicized symbol [*r*] is used at the end of such words as **banger, door, here** [ˈbæŋə*r*, dɔː*r*, ˈhiə*r*] to show that the r-sound may occur there if, and only if, the following word in the phrase begins with a vowel and there is no intervening pause, as in **here and now** [ˈhiərəndˈnau].

TABLE OF PHONETIC SYMBOLS

VOWELS

[æ] bat, gander, **ack-ack**
[ɑː] cart, bar, nark, hoo-ha(a)
[e] get, jelly, dead
[i] bit, diddies, system, breeches, dimwitted
[iː] bee, peter, tea, spiel
[ɔ] hot, what, cough, Aussie
[ɔː] all, haul, rorty, jaw, war
[u] put, wool, pull
[uː] shoes, move, loo, jew
[ʌ] nut, bun, ton, some, cover, rough
[ə] china, goner, balon(e)y
[əː] burn, learn, herb, whirl

DIPHTHONGS

[ai] **ai**sle, h**igh**, k**i**te, fl**y**, h**y**po, b**uy**, **eye**

[au] d**ow**n, m**ou**se, kr**au**t

[ei] m**a**te, l**ay**, tr**ey**, b**ai**t, w**eigh**t

[ɛə] b**ear**, sp**are**, th**ere**, **airy**-f**airy**

[iə] qu**eer**, g**ear**, r**ea**l, h**ere**

[ɔi] b**oi**l, b**oy**

[ou] g**o**, sn**ow**, s**oa**p, d**o**pe, d**ough**

[uə] p**oor**, s**ure**

CONSONANTS

[b] **b**at, jo**b**, **b**oo**b**, gra**bb**ed

[d] **d**ab, ba**d**, un**d**er, gri**dd**le

[f] **f**at, **f**i**f**ty, ri**ff**, lau**gh**, rou**gh**, ele**ph**ants

[g] **g**a**g**, **gh**erkin, **gu**ide, a**g**ony, e**gg**

[h] **h**at, be**h**ind

[k] **c**at, a**ch**e, **k**itten, ma**k**e, plon**k**, qui**ck**, septi**c**

[l] **l**id, a**ll**, tumb**l**e, chise**l**, di**ll**y

[m] **m**ug, ra**m**, jis**m**, ja**mm**y

[n] **n**ab, bu**n**, te**nn**er, pa**n**cake, **kn**ob, **gn**ashers

[p] **p**an, na**p**, na**pp**er

[r] **r**at, a**r**ound, je**rr**y

[*r*] drive**r**, finge**r**, gea**r**
(*sounded only when final and carried on to the next word, as in* late**r** on)

[s] **s**au**s**age, **sc**ene, mou**s**e, sa**ss**y, **ps**ycho, whi**st**le, **c**ement

[t] **t**op, po**t**, ba**tt**er, **t**rip, **Th**ames

[v] **v**ine, e**v**er, ra**v**e, sa**vv**y

[z] **z**ip, qui**z**, bu**zz**, lou**s**y, pan**s**y, bree**z**e, bu**s**ine**ss**, egg**s**

[dz] re**ds**, o**dds**

[dʒ] **g**in**g**er, a**g**e, e**dg**e, **j**elly

[ks] e**x**tras, e**x**pect, a**cc**ident, mi**x**er

[kʃ] ru**cti**ons

[lj] mi**lli**on

[nj] o**ni**on

[tʃ] **ch**at, ha**tch**, sear**ch**, **ch**i**ck**, ri**ch**

[θ] **th**atch, too**th**, me**th**head

[ð] **th**at, **th**e, o**th**er, wi**th**

[ʃ] **sh**ark, di**sh**, **ch**assis, ma**ch**ine

[ʒ] u**s**ual

[ŋ] ba**ng**, si**ng**, co**n**k, a**n**chors

[ŋg] fi**ng**er, a**ng**le

SEMI-CONSONANTS

[j] **y**ack, **y**ob, c**u**te, p**u**trid, **u**sed, **eu**chre, f**ew**, q**ueue**

[w] **w**ad, **w**ind, s**w**ipe, a**w**ay

PRONONCIATION

Chaque entrée du dictionnaire est suivie de sa transcription phonétique pour laquelle on a employé les signes de l'Association phonétique internationale.

La langue populaire et le *slang* ont une prononciation extrêmement fluide et diversifiée, qui tend même quelquefois à en faire un langage particulier. Le plus connu est peut-être le *cockney* qui est la prononciation londonienne vulgaire, et il n'est pas question ici de le décrire. D'autre part, les mêmes mots sont prononcés différemment dans les pays si variés qui constituent le monde anglophone. Toutes ces considérations ont rendu notre tâche phonétique difficile, et notre but a été d'offrir un guide utile (et non infaillible) au lecteur étranger.

Il est quelques points sur lesquels nous nous permettons d'attirer l'attention:

(1) Les symboles mis entre parenthèses, *ex.* **empty** [ˈem(p)ti], indiquent qu'il y a deux prononciations possibles, avec ou sans ce symbole.

(2) Dans les mots tels que **whip, whistle, white** le h initial a été indiqué comme possible [(h)wip, ˈ(h)wisl, (h)wait], alors qu'en règle générale le h n'est jamais prononcé en anglais familier et populaire.

(3) L'accent tonique est indiqué par un accent [ˈ] précédant la syllabe accentuée, *ex.* **junky** [ˈdʒʌŋki], **connect** [kəˈnekt]. L'accent secondaire n'est pas indiqué.

(4) Le son [r] ne s'entend généralement pas devant une consonne ou devant une pause. On emploie le symbole en italique [*r*] à la fin des mots tels que **banger, door, here** [ˈbæŋə*r*, dɔː*r*, ˈhiə*r*] pour indiquer que le son de r peut se faire entendre dans le cas, et uniquement dans le cas, où le mot suivant dans la phrase commence par une voyelle sans qu'il y ait de pause, *ex.* **here and now** [ˈhiərəndˈnau].

TABLEAU DES SYMBOLES PHONÉTIQUES EN ANGLAIS

VOYELLES

[æ] bat, gander, ack-ack
[ɑː] cart, bar, nark, hoo-ha(a)
[e] get, jelly, dead
[i] bit, diddies, system, breeches, dimwitted
[iː] bee, peter, tea, spiel
[ɔ] hot, what, cough, Aussie
[ɔː] all, haul, rorty, jaw, war
[u] put, wool, pull
[uː] shoes, move, loo
[ʌ] nut, bun, ton, some, cover, rough
[ə] china, goner, balon(e)y
[əː] burn, learn, herb, whirl

DIPHTONGUES

[ai] **ai**sle, h**igh**, k**i**te, fl**y**, h**y**po
[aʊ] d**ow**n, m**ou**se, kr**au**t
[ei] m**a**te, l**ay**, tr**ey**, b**ai**t, w**eigh**t
[ɛə] b**ear**, sp**are**, th**ere**, **air**y-f**air**y
[iə] qu**eer**, g**ear**, r**ea**l
[ɔi] b**oi**l, b**oy**
[oʊ] g**o**, sn**ow**, s**oa**p, d**o**pe, d**ough**
[ʊə] p**oor**, s**ure**

CONSONNES

[b] **b**at, jo**b**, **b**oo**b**, gra**bb**ed
[d] **d**ab, ba**d**, un**d**er, gri**dd**le
[f] **f**at, **f**i**f**ty, ri**ff**, lau**gh**, rou**gh**, ele**ph**ants
[g] **g**a**g**, **gh**erkin, **gu**ide, a**g**ony, e**gg**
[h] **h**at, be**h**ind
[k] **c**at, a**ch**e, **k**itten, ma**k**e, plon**k**, qui**ck**, septi**c**
[l] **l**id, a**ll**, tumb**l**e, chise**l**, di**ll**y
[m] **m**ug, ra**m**, jis**m**, ja**mm**y
[n] **n**ab, bu**n**, te**nn**er, pa**n**cake, **kn**ob, **gn**ashers
[p] **p**an, na**p**, na**pp**er
[r] **r**at, a**r**ound, je**rr**y
[ʳ] drive**r**, finge**r**, gea**r**
(*prononcé seulement lorsqu'il est final et en liaison avec le mot suivant, ex.* late**r** on)
[s] **s**au**s**age, **sc**ene, mou**s**e, sa**ss**y, **ps**ycho, whi**st**le, **c**ement
[t] **t**op, po**t**, ba**tt**er, **t**rip, **Th**ames
[v] **v**ine, e**v**er, ra**v**e, sa**vv**y
[z] **z**ip, qui**z**, bu**zz**, lou**s**y, pan**s**y, bree**z**e, bu**s**iness, egg**s**

[dz] re**ds**, o**dds**
[dʒ] **g**in**g**er, a**g**e, e**dg**e, **j**elly
[ks] e**x**tras, e**x**pect, a**cc**ident, mi**x**er
[kʃ] ru**ct**ions
[lj] mi**lli**on
[nj] o**ni**on
[tʃ] **ch**at, ha**tch**, sear**ch**, **ch**i**ck**, ri**ch**
[θ] **th**atch, too**th**, me**th**head
[ð] **th**at, **th**e, o**th**er, wi**th**
[ʃ] **sh**ark, di**sh**, **ch**assis, ma**ch**ine, **s**ugar
[ʒ] u**s**ual
[ŋ] ba**ng**, si**ng**, co**n**k, a**n**chors
[ŋg] fi**ng**er, a**ng**le

SEMI-CONSONNES

[j] **y**ack, **y**ob, c**u**te, p**u**trid, **u**sed, **eu**chre, f**ew**
[w] **w**ad, **w**ind, a**w**ay

A

A [ei] (*abbr.*), *P:* **1.** (=*amphetamine*) amphétamine *f* (*drogues**). **2.** = **acid, 2.** **3. A. over T.** (=*arse over tip* (*or tit(s)*)), cul par-dessus tête; *cf.* **arse, 4.**

ab [æb], **A.B.** [ˈeiˈbiː] (*abbr.* = *abscess*), *P:* (*abcès causé par une piqûre avec aiguille non stérilisée ou par des drogues impures*) caramel *m*, fondant *m*, puant *m*; *cf.* **ABC, 3.**

ABC [ˈeibiːˈsiː] (*noun*). **1.** *F:* **(as) easy as ABC,** simple comme bonjour; *cf.* **easy[1], 6.** **2.** *F:* **the ABC of sth.,** le B.A. ba de qch. **3.** *P:* = **A.B.**

abdabs [ˈæbdæbz] (*pl. noun*), *P:* **to have the screaming a.,** piauler à la bit(t)ure, voir les rats bleus.

abo, Abo [ˈæbou] (*noun*) (*Austr.*), *F:* aborigène *mf.*

absoballylutely! [ˈæbsouˈbæliˈl(j)uːtli] (*excl.*), *F:* ça colle, Anatole! naturellement et comme de bien entendu!

absobloodylutely! [ˈæbsouˈblʌdiˈl(j)uːtli] (*excl.*), *P:* = **absoballylutely!**

abysmal [əˈbizməl] (*adj.*), *F:* d'une bêtise* noire, d'une ignorance crasse.

accident [ˈæksidənt] (*noun*), *F:* **to have an a.,** (*a*) avoir un avaro; (*b*) être pris d'un besoin pressant; s'oublier; **Guy has had an a.,** Guy a fait pipi dans sa culotte.

accidentally [æksiˈdentəli] (*adv.*), *F:* **a. on purpose,** exprès.

A.C.-D.C. (ac-dc, ac/dc) [ˈeisiːˈdiːsiː] (*adj.*), *P:* = **ambidextrous.**

ace[1] [eis] (*adj.*), *F:* **1.** excellent*, épatant, formid(able), super. **2.** (*a*) agréable; (*b*) généreux.

ace[2] [eis] (*adv. & excl.*), *F:* d'accord*, dac, O.K.

ace[3] [eis] (*noun*). **1.** *F:* as *m*, crack *m*. **2.** *F:* **to have an a. up one's sleeve,** avoir un as dans sa manche, avoir plus d'un tour dans son sac. **3.** *F:* **to hold all the aces,** avoir tous les atouts en main. **4.** (*U.S.*) *P:* billet* d'un dollar. **5.** *F:* (*a*) individu* loyal, bon, généreux; épée *f*; (*b*) individu* épatant. **6.** *P:* **on one's a.,** tout seul, seulabre. **7.** *P:* cigarette* de marijuana (*drogues**), reefer *m*, stick *m*. **8.** *F:* **to be aces with s.o.,** prendre qn pour un crack, ne voir que par qn.

ace[4] [eis] **(to),** *P:* **a. it!** ça suffit! c'est marre!

ace in [ˈeisˈin] **(to),** *P:* **1.** jouer des coudes, se faufiler en haut de l'échelle. **2. to a. i. on s.o.'s conversation,** piger la conversation de qn.

acid [ˈæsid] (*noun*), *P:* **1. to put the a. on, to come the a.,** la faire à la pose; **don't come the a. with me,** (*a*) ne fais pas le zouave; (*b*) ne jardine pas, ne te paye pas ma fiole. **2.** *P:* LSD *m* (*drogues**), sucre *m*; **a. freak, a. head,** habitué(e) du LSD, acidulé(e); **a. cube,** morceau *m* de sucre trempé dans du LSD (*cf.* **cubehead**); **a. funk,** dépression due au LSD, trouille acidulée.

ack-ack [ˈækˈæk] (*noun*), *F:* (*mil.*) défense antiaérienne, défense contre-avions (D.C.A.).

ackamaraka [ækəməˈrækə] (*noun*), *P:* **don't give me the (old) a.,** ne me bourre pas le crâne, ne me monte pas le cou (*ou* le coup).

ack-emma [ˈækˈemə] (*adv.*), *F:* (*mil.*) avant midi.

ackers [ˈækəz] (*pl. noun*), *P:* argent*, pésettes *f.pl.*

acquire [əˈkwaiər] **(to),** *F:* voler*, faucher, subtiliser.

act [ækt] (*noun*), *F:* **1. to put on an a.** (*or* **a big a.**), frimer. **2. to get in on the a.,** se mettre dans le bain. **3. to let s.o. in on the a.,** mettre qn dans le coup. *Voir aussi* **sob-act.**

actress [ˈæktris] (*noun*), *F:* **as the a. said to the bishop,** *c.p.*, comme dit l'autre.

ad [æd] (*abbr.*). **1.** *F:* (=*advertisement*) annonce *f*; **small ads,** petites annonces; *cf.* **advert. 2.** *P:* = **A.D.**

A.D. [ˈeiˈdiː] (*abbr.*) (=(*drug*) *addict*), *P:* drogué*, camé *m*, toxico *m*.

* L'astérisque indique que le mot marqué de ce signe figure comme entrée dans le Répertoire.

Adam [ˈædəm] (*pr. noun*), *F:* 1. **I don't know him from A.,** je ne le connais ni d'Ève ni d'Adam. 2. **the old A.,** le vieil Adam. 3. **A.'s ale,** eau*, Château-la-Pompe *m.* 4. **A. and Eve on a raft,** œufs servis sur du toast.

add up [ˈædˈʌp] (**to**), *F:* **it (just) doesn't a. u.,** cela n'a ni queue ni tête (*ou* ni sens ni raison).

adjourn [əˈdʒəːn] (**to**), *F:* (*a*) abandonner un travail; (*b*) passer autre part.

ad-lib[1] [ˈædˈlib] (*adj.*), *F:* (*a*) à volonté, à discrétion; (*b*) improvisé, impromptu.

ad-lib[2] [ˈædˈlib] (**to**), *F:* (*a*) dévider, palasser; (*b*) (*th.*) faire du texte, improviser.

ad-man [ˈædmæn] (*pl.* **ad-men**) (*noun*), *F:* agent *m* de publicité.

admirer [ədˈmaiərər] (*noun*), *F:* adorateur *m*, soupirant *m.*

adrift [əˈdrift] (*adv.*), *F:* 1. **to be (all) a.,** dérailler, perdre le nord. 2. **the button has come a.,** le bouton a lâché, le bouton est décousu. 3. **to be several hours a.,** avoir plusieurs heures de retard.

advert [ˈædvəːt] (*abbr.*) (=*advertisement*), *F:* annonce *f*; *cf.* **ad, 1.**

aer(e)ated [ˈɛər(i)eitid] (*adj.*), *P:* fâché, vexé; **don't get (all) a.,** ne prends pas la pique.

after [ˈɑːftər] (*prep.*), *F:* 1. **A. you, Claude. – No, a. you, Cecil,** *c.p.*, Après vous, Marquis. – Non, après vous, Prince. 2. **what are you a.?** qu'est-ce que tu cherches? où veux-tu en venir?

afters [ˈɑːftəz] (*pl. noun*), *F:* dessert *m.*

age [eidʒ] (*noun*), *F:* 1. **be (*or* act) your a.!** fais pas l'enfant! 2. **it took us an a. (*or* ages) to get here,** ça nous a pris un temps fou pour arriver ici; **I saw that film ages ago,** il y a une éternité que j'ai vu ce film. 3. (*a*) **the a. to catch 'em:** *voir* **bingo (17)**; (*b*) **my a.?:** *voir* **bingo (21)**. *Voir aussi* **awkward.**

aggravate [ˈægrəveit] (**to**), *F:* exaspérer, assommer, taper sur le système à (qn).

aggravating [ˈægrəveitiŋ] (*adj.*), *F:* exaspérant, assommant, crispant.

aggravation [ˈægrəˈveiʃ(ə)n] (*noun*), *F:* agacement *m*, exaspération *f.*

aggro[1] [ˈægrou] (*noun*), *P:* provocation *f*, discorde *f*; **to give s.o. the a. = to aggro s.o.**

aggro[2] [ˈægrou] (**to**), *P:* agacer, tracasser (qn); provoquer (qn); embêter (qn).

agin [əˈgin] (*prep. & adv.*), *F:* contre.

agony [ˈægəni] (*noun*), *F:* 1. **it was a.!** j'en ai bavé! 2. **to pile on the a.,** forcer la dose. 3. **a. column,** rubrique *f* des annonces personnelles.

agreeable [əˈgriːəbl] (*adj.*), *F:* **I'm a.,** je veux bien.

agro [ˈægrou] (*noun & verb*), *P:* = **aggro**[1, 2].

ahead [əˈhed] (*adv.*), *F:* 1. **to come out a.,** (*a*) être en pointe; (*b*) sortir en tête (de liste). 2. **to be one jump a.,** avoir de l'avance, avoir une longueur d'avance (sur qn). *Voir aussi* **go-ahead.**

aid [eid] (*noun*), *F:* **what's this (*or* that) in a. of?** à quoi ça rime?

ain't [eint], *P:* = *am not, is not, are not;* **a. got** = *has not (got), have not (got).*

air[1] [ɛər] (*noun*). 1. *F:* **to go (straight) up in the a.,** se mettre en colère*, se mettre en rogne. 2. *F:* **to float on (*or* tread on *or* walk on) a.,** nager dans le bonheur, être au septième ciel, voir les anges, voir la vie en rose; planer; voyager. 3. *F:* **to live on (fresh) a.,** vivre d'amour et d'eau fraîche, vivre de l'air du temps. 4. *F:* **to take the a.,** prendre le large. 5. *F:* **on the a.,** sur les ondes, en diffusion. 6. *P:* **to give s.o. the a.,** se débarrasser* de qn. 7. *P:* **airs and graces** (*R.S.* = *faces*), visages*. 8. *F:* **hot a.,** discours *m.pl.* vides, platitudes *f.pl.*; **that's all hot a.,** tout cela n'est que du vent. 9. *F:* **none of your airs!** pas tant de manières!; **to give oneself airs,** faire sa poire (anglaise).

air[2] [ɛər] (**to**), *P:* planter (là), plaquer (qn).

airy-fairy [ˈɛəriˈfɛəri] (*adj.*), *F:* vasouillard, du bidon.

aisle [ail] (*noun*). 1. *F:* **to walk down the a.,** se marier. 2. *P:* **that'll knock 'em (*or* have 'em rolling) in the aisles,** cela fera crouler la baraque; *cf.* **knock**[2] **(to), 5.**

akkers [ˈækəz] (*pl. noun*), *P:* = **ackers.**

alarming [əˈlɑːmiŋ] (*adv.*), *P:* **she carried on a.,** elle se démena comme une furie; **she went off at me (something) a.,** elle m'est tombée dessus (comme une furie).

Alec, alec(k) [ˈælik] (*noun*). 1. *F:* **smart**

* An asterisk indicates that the word so marked is included as a head-word in the Appendix.

a., finaud *m*, combinard *m*, plastronneur *m*, m'as-tu-vu *m*, je-sais-tout *m*. 2. (*Austr.*) *P:* dupe *f*, cavé *m*, navet *m*; *cf.* **bunny[1], 8.**

alf [ælf] (*noun*), *P:* mâle hétérosexuel.

alibi [ˈælibai] (*noun*), *F:* bonne excuse.

alive [əˈlaiv] (*adj.*), *F:* 1. **a. and kicking,** en pleine forme. 2. **look a.!** réveille-toi! secoue-toi! *Voir aussi* **dead-and-alive; Jack, 12.**

alky [ˈælki] (*noun*), *P:* 1. alcool*, gnôle *f*. 2. whisky *m* de mauvaise qualité *ou* de contrebande. 3. (*a*) alcoolique *mf*; (*b*) clochard* alcoolique.

all[1] [ɔːl] (*adv.*), *F:* 1. **to be a. for sth.,** en tenir pour qch., en être pour qch. 2. **to go a. out for sth.,** (*a*) être emballé par qch.; (*b*) mettre toute son énergie à faire qch., se donner corps et âme pour faire qch. 3. **that's him a. over,** c'est lui tout craché; je le reconnais bien là! 4. **to be a. in,** être fatigué*, être exténué. 5. **to be a. there,** avoir les yeux en face des trous; *voir aussi* **there, 2.** 6. **to be a. over s.o.,** faire de la lèche à qn. *Voir aussi* **all right; jump[2] (to), 11.**

all[2] [ɔːl] (*noun*), *F:* 1. **it's a. over** (*or* **up**) **with him,** (*a*) il est fichu, c'est le bout du rouleau pour lui; (*b*) il est liquidé; (*c*) il est pigé; *voir aussi* **up[2], 3.** 2. **I'm tired. – Aren't we a.?** Je suis fatigué.* – Et nous donc! 3. **a. but one:** *voir* **bingo** (89). *Voir aussi* **bugger-all; damn-all; fuck-all; know-all; sod-all; what-all.**

all-clear [ˈɔːlˈkliər] (*noun*), *F:* **to give the a.-c.,** donner le feu vert.

alley [ˈæli] (*noun*). 1. *F:* **that's right up my a.,** c'est tout à fait mon rayon; *cf.* **street, 2.** 2. *P:* **a. cat,** prostituée*, racoleuse *f*. *Voir aussi* **doodle-alley; tin-pan alley.**

allez oop! [ˈæliˈ(j)up, ˈæliˈ(j)uːp] (*excl.*), *F:* allez hop!

alligator [ˈæligeitər] (*noun*), *F:* **See you later, a.! – In a while, crocodile,** *c.p.*, A tout à l'heure, voltigeur! – A bientôt, mon oiseau.

all-nighter [ˈɔːlˈnaitər] (*noun*), *P:* 1. boum *f* du petit matin. 2. clille *m* de nuit. 3. session *f* (*parlement, etc.*) qui dure toute une nuit.

all-overish [ˈɔːlˈouvəriʃ] (*adj.*), *P:* **to be** (*or* **feel**) **a.-o.,** être patraque (*ou* tout chose).

all right[1] [ˈɔːlˈrait] (*adv.*), *F:* 1. d'accord*. 2. **it's a. r. for you, you don't have to get up early,** cela t'est bien égal, tu n'es pas obligé de te lever de bonne heure. 3. **don't worry about him, he's a. r.,** t'en fais pas pour lui. 4. **to see s.o. a.r.,** (*a*) veiller à ce que qn ait son dû, veiller à ce que qn ne soit pas lésé; (*b*) promettre de l'aide à qn, donner un coup de main à qn.

all right[2] [ˈɔːlˈrait] (*noun*), *P:* **a bit of a. r.,** une fille* séduisante, un beau petit lot.

all-time [ˈɔːlˈtaim] (*adj.*), *F:* sans précédent, inouï; **a.-t. high,** record le plus élevé. *Voir aussi* **great[3].**

almighty [ɔːlˈmaiti] (*adj.*). 1. *F:* formidable; **an a. crash,** un fracas de tous les diables. 2. *F:* **the a. dollar,** le dollar tout-puissant. 3. *P:* **God A.!** Bon Dieu de Bon Dieu!

alone [əˈloun] (*adj.*), *F:* 1. **to go it a.,** y aller d'autor. 2. **leave me a.!** laisse-moi tranquille!

Alphonse [ælˈfɔns] (*pr. noun*) (*R.S.* = *ponce*), *P:* souteneur*, Alphonse.

alright [ˈɔːlˈrait] (*adv.* & *noun*), *F:* = **all right,[1,2].**

also-ran [ˈɔːlsouræn] (*noun*), *F:* perdant *m*; **to be an a.-r.,** être dans les choux.

altogether [ˈɔːltəˈgeðər] (*noun*), *F:* **in the a.,** nu*, à poil.

ambidextrous [ˈæmbiˈdekstrəs] (*adj.*), *P:* ambivalent, qui marche à voiles et à vapeur.

ammo [ˈæmou] (*abbr.*) (=*ammunition*), *F:* munitions *f.pl.*

amscray [ˈæmˈskrei] (**to**) (*backslang* = *scram*), *P:* partir*, décamper, se débiner, se tailler.

amster [ˈæmstər] (*noun*) (*Austr.*), *P:* = **shill(aber).**

amy [ˈeimi] (*noun*), *P:* nitrite *m* d'amyle (*drogues*).

amy-john [ˈeimiˈdʒɔn] (*noun*), *P:* lesbienne*, gougnot(t)e *f*.

anchors [ˈæŋkəz] (*pl. noun*), *F:* **to put the a. on,** mettre les freins *m.pl.* (*ou* les ripans *m.pl.*).

ancient [ˈeinʃənt] (*adj.*), *F:* 1. **she's a.,** elle n'est pas de première jeunesse. 2. **that's a. history,** c'est du réchauffé.

angel[1] [ˈeindʒəl] (*noun*). 1. *F:* **you're an a.** (**to do that for me**), tu es un amour (de faire cela pour moi); **be an a. and . . .,** sois un amour,... 2. *F:* **you're no a.!**

* L'astérisque indique que le mot marqué de ce signe figure comme entrée dans le Répertoire.

ne te prends pas pour un enfant de chœur! tu n'es pas un prix de vertu! 3. *F:* **angels on horseback,** fricassée *f* d'huîtres au lard. 4. *P:* **white a.,** (*infirmière qui, à l'hôpital, fait passer des drogues à un toxicomane*) ange blanc. 5. *P:* (*a*) commanditaire *m* (*surtout* de théâtre); (*b*) (*U.S.*) commanditaire *m* d'un parti politique. 6. *P:* victime *f* d'un voleur *ou* d'un escroc. 7. *P:* pédéraste* qui tient le rôle de l'homme, rivette *f.* 8. *P:* cocaïne *f* (*drogues**), fée blanche. *Voir aussi* **hell, 15.**

angel[2] [ˈeindʒəl] (**to**), *P:* commanditer; (*th.*) bailler les fonds *m.pl.*

angel-face [ˈeindʒəlfeis], **angel-puss** [ˈeindʒəlpus] (*noun*), *F:* 1. (*terme d'affection*) ma toute belle. 2. gueule *f* d'amour, jolie frimousse.

angie [ˈeindʒi] (*noun*), *P:* = **angel**[1]**, 8.**

angle [ˈæŋgl] (*noun*), *F:* 1. **what's your a.?** (*a*) quel est ton point de vue?; (*b*) comment vois-tu la chose? 2. **to figure out an a.,** chercher moyen (de se tirer d'affaire). 3. **to know all the angles,** connaître la musique; la connaître dans les coins.

Anne [æn] (*pr. noun*), *F:* **Queen A.'s dead,** (*a*) ta combinaison passe; tu cherches une belle-mère?; *cf.* **Charl(e)y**[2]**, 2;** (*b*) c'est du réchauffé.

another [əˈnʌðər] (*pron.*), *F:* **tell me a.!** allez! va conter ça ailleurs!; **ask me a.,** tu me fais rigoler; et après?

answer [ˈɑːnsər] (*noun*), *F:* 1. **the a. to a maiden's prayer,** le mari rêvé. 2. **to know all the answers,** avoir réponse à tout, être un Monsieur Je-sais-tout.

answer back [ˈɑːnsəˈbæk] (**to**), *F:* **don't a. b.!** pas de rouspétance!

ante [ˈænti] (*noun*) (*U.S.*), *F:* **to up** (*or* **raise**) **the a.,** (*a*) forcer la mise (*poker*); (*b*) augmenter le prix, donner le coup de pouce, allonger le tir.

ante up [ˈæntiˈʌp] (**to**), *F:* payer*, les lâcher, cracher.

anti [ˈænti, *U.S.:* ˈæntai] (*adv. & prep.*), *F:* 1. **to feel a.,** avoir une âme de contestataire. 2. **to be a.** (*s.o. or sth.*), être contre, être de l'opposition.

antics [ˈæntiks] (*pl. noun*), *F:* **to be up to one's a. again,** rejouer les mêmes tours *m.pl.*

ants [ænts] (*pl. noun*), *F:* **to have a. in one's pants,** avoir la bougeotte, avoir le feu quelque part.

antsy [ˈæntsi] (*adj.*) (*U.S.*), *F:* énervé, agité, sur des charbons ardents, survolté.

any[1] [ˈeni] (*adj.*), *F:* 1. **a. more for a. more?** qui veut du rabiot? 2. **a. day,** n'importe quand; **I can do better than that a. day,** je peux faire mieux quand ça me chante.

any[2] [ˈeni] (*pron.*), *F:* 1. **he wasn't having a.,** il n'a pas marché; **I'm not having a.!** rien à faire! cela ne prend pas! 2. **a. to come,** (*turf*) report *m.* *Voir aussi* **without.**

anyhow [ˈenihaʊ] (*adv.*), *F:* 1. **to feel all a.,** se sentir tout chose. 2. **to do sth. all a.,** faire qch. à la six-quatre-deux.

Anzac [ˈænzæk] (*noun*), *F:* soldat* australien ou néo-zélandais.

apart [əˈpɑːt] (*adj.*), *P:* déboussolé, désorienté.

ape[1] [eip] (*adj.*) (*U.S.*), *P:* 1. époustouflant, formid(able). 2. **to go a.,** (*a*) perdre les pédales; (*b*) se déchaîner. 3. **to go a. over s.o.,** s'enticher (*ou* se toquer) de qn.

ape[2] [eip] (*noun*), *F:* **you big a.!** grosse brute! espèce de gorille!

apology [əˈpɔlədʒi] (*noun*), *F:* **an a. for . . .,** un vague semblant d'excuse pour...

apple [ˈæpl] (*noun*), *P:* 1. **apples (and pears)** (*R.S.* = *stairs*), escalier *m.* 2. (*U.S.*) individu*, type *m*, mec *m*; **smooth a.,** individu* suave, girofle *m*; **wise a.,** jeune effronté; **square a.,** (*a*) cave *m*; (*b*) individu* qui ne se drogue pas. 3. (*U.S.*) **to polish the a.,** (*a*) flatter*, faire de la lèche; *cf.* **apple-polish (to); apple-polisher;** (*b*) agir comme si on était occupé. *Voir aussi* **toffee.**

apple-cart [ˈæplkɑːt] (*noun*), *F:* **to upset s.o.'s a.-c.,** chambarder les plans de qn.

apple-pie[1] [ˈæplˈpai] (*attrib. adj.*), *F:* 1. **a.-p. bed,** lit *m* en portefeuille. 2. **in a.-p. order,** en ordre parfait, soin-soin.

apple-pie[2] [ˈæplˈpai] (*noun*), *F:* **as American as a.-p.,** amerloc comme l'oncle Sam.

apple-polish [ˈæplˈpɔliʃ] (**to**) (*U.S.*), *P:* flatter*, lécher les bottes à (qn); *cf.* **apple, 3.**

* An asterisk indicates that the word so marked is included as a head-word in the Appendix.

apple-polisher [ˈæplˈpɔliʃər] (*noun*) (*U.S.*), *P:* flatteur *m*, lèche-bottes *m*.
apple-sauce [ˈæplˈsɔːs] (*noun*) (*U.S.*), *P:* **1.** bêtise*, foutaise *f*, bidon *m*. **2.** flatterie *f*, pommade *f*.
apple-tree [ˈæpl-triː] (*noun*), *P:* **to fall off the a.-t.**, (*d'une fille*) perdre sa virginité, voir le loup, casser sa cruche.
appro [ˈæprou] (*abbr.*) (= *approval*), *F:* **on a.**, à condition, à l'essai.
apron-strings [ˈeiprən-striŋz] (*pl. noun*), *F:* **tied to mother's a.-s.**, dans les jupons de sa mère.
arf [ɑːf] (*adj.* & *adv.*), *P:* = **half.**
arf-an'-arf [ˈɑːfənˈɑːf] (*adv.* & *noun*), *P:* = **half and half** (*voir* **half**[1], **5**; **half**[2]).
arge [ɑːdʒ] (*noun*), *P:* argent *m* (*métal*), blanc *m*, blanquette *f*.
argie-bargie [ˈɑːdʒiˈbɑːdʒi] (*noun*), *F:* = **argy-bargy.**
argle-bargle [ˈɑːglˈbɑːgl] (**to**), *F:* discutailler; discuter le coup.
argufy [ˈɑːgjuːfai] (**to**), *P:* discuter le bout de gras.
argy-bargy [ˈɑːdʒiˈbɑːdʒi] (*noun*), *F:* chicane *f*, prise *f* de bec.
aris [ˈæris] (*noun*), *P:* = **Aristotle.**
Aristotle [æriˈstɔtl] (*noun*) (*R.S.* = *bottle*), *P:* bouteille *f*.
arm [ɑːm] (*noun*). **1.** *F:* **to chance one's a.**, tenter le coup. **2.** *P:* **to put the a. on s.o.**, mettre le grappin sur qn. **3.** (*U.S.*) *P:* **on the a.**, (*a*) à crédit, à la gagne, à croum(e); (*b*) gratuit*, gratis, à l'œil. *Voir aussi* **short**[1], **3**; **shot**[2], **3**; **strong-arm**[1, 2].
army [ˈɑːmi] (*noun*), *P:* **1. . . . you and whose a.?** (*réponse à une menace de coups*), toi et qui encore? **2. the (old) a. game,** escroquerie*, coup *m* d'arnac. *Voir aussi* **Fred.**
around [əˈraund] (*adv.*), *F:* **I've been a. (a bit),** je connais la vie, j'ai roulé ma bosse.
arse [ɑːs] (*noun*), *V:* **1.** cul*. **2. Twenty-five, my a.! She's forty if she's a day,** Vingt-cinq ans je t'en fiche, elle a quarante ans et mèche! **3. he doesn't know whether he's on his a. or his elbow,** (*a*) il ne sait pas où il en est; (*b*) c'est un vrai cul. **4. to go a. over tip** (*or* **tit(s)**), faire tête à cul; *cf.* **A. over T. 5. to sit on one's a. (and do nothing),** ne pas se manier le cul. **6. you can kiss my a.! you can stick it up your a.!** tu peux te le mettre au cul!; *voir aussi* **shove (to)**; **stick**[2] **(to)**, **3**. **7. a. about face,** sens devant derrière. **8. to be out on one's a.**, être flanqué (*ou* foutu) à la porte. **9. to shag one's a. off,** (*a*) coïter* fréquemment, bourriquer à gogo; (*b*) se vanner à la bourre. **10. to work one's a. off,** travailler* dur, en foutre un coup. *Voir aussi* **ass**[1]; **kick**[1], **5** (*b*); **lead**[1], **4**; **pain** (*c*); **short-arse**; **split-arse**; **tear-arse.**
arse about (*or* **around**) [ˈɑːsəˈbaut, ˈɑːsəˈraund] (**to**), *V:* traîner son cul; **don't go arsing about in there!** ne va pas te mêler là-dedans! va pas faire le con là-dedans!
arse-bandit [ˈɑːsbændit] (*noun*), *V:* pédéraste*, lopart *m*, enculé *m*.
arse-crawl [ˈɑːs-krɔːl] (**to**), *V:* lécher le cul à qn.
arse-crawler [ˈɑːs-krɔːlər] (*noun*), *V:* lèche-cul *mf*.
arse-crawling [ˈɑːs-krɔːliŋ] (*noun*), *V:* la lèche.
arse-creep [ˈɑːs-kriːp] (**to**), *V:* = **arse-crawl (to).**
arse-creeper [ˈɑːs-kriːpər] (*noun*), *V:* = **arse-crawler.**
arse-creeping [ˈɑːs-kriːpiŋ] (*noun*), *V:* = **arse-crawling.**
arsehole [ˈɑːs(h)oul] (*noun*), *V:* **1.** anus*, anneau *m*, troufignon *m*. **2. pissed as arseholes,** bourré à zéro, rond comme une bille.
arse-kisser [ˈɑːs-kisər] (*noun*), *V:* = **arse-crawler.**
arse-lick [ˈɑːs-lik] (**to**), *V:* = **arse-crawl (to).**
arse-licker [ˈɑːs-likər] (*noun*), *V:* = **arse-crawler.**
arse-licking [ˈɑːs-likiŋ] (*noun*), *V:* = **arse-crawling.**
arse-man [ˈɑːsmæn] (*noun*), *V:* = **arse-bandit.**
arse up [ˈɑːsˈʌp] (**to**), *V:* **1.** mettre en désordre, chambouler; foutre en l'air. **2.** abîmer*, amocher.
artillery [ɑːˈtiləri] (*noun*), *P:* **1. (light) a.**, attirail *m* de camé. **2.** revolver*; couteau*; armes *f.pl.* à main.
arty [ˈɑːti] (*adj.*), *F:* **to be a.**, se piquer de talent artistique.
arty-crafty [ˈɑːtiˈkrɑːfti] (*adj.*), *F:* artiste, bohème.

* L'astérisque indique que le mot marqué de ce signe figure comme entrée dans le Répertoire.

arvo [ˈɑːvou] (*noun*) (*Austr.*), *F:* après-midi *m ou f*.

ashes [ˈæʃiz] (*pl. noun*). 1. *F:* **the A.**, trophée symbolique remporté par l'Angleterre ou l'Australie après leurs jeux de cricket. 2. (*U.S.*) *P:* **to get one's a. hauled,** coïter*, tirer un coup. *Voir aussi* **green**[1], 1.

ask [ɑːsk] (**to**). 1. *P:* **to a. for it,** chercher des embêtements *m.pl.*; **you asked for it!** tu l'as cherché! tu l'as voulu!; **you're asking for it, and you'll get it if you're not careful!** tu me cherches, et tu vas me trouver! 2. *P:* **a. yourself!** raisonne-toi un peu! 3. *F:* **a. a silly question and you'll get a silly answer,** *c.p.*, à question idiote, réponse idiote. *Voir aussi* **another.**

ass[1] [æs] (*noun*) (*U.S.*), *V:* 1. = **arse.** (*Pour tous les composés de* **ass** *voir* **arse.**) 2. **piece of a.,** (*a*) coït*, partie *f* de jambes en l'air; (*b*) femme* (*péj.*), gonzesse *f*, fendue *f*. 3. (*parfois*) vulve*. 4. **on one's a.,** dans la gêne, dans le besoin. 5. **to do sth. a. backwards,** (*a*) faire qch. à rebours, brider l'âne par la queue; (*b*) faire un micmac. 6. **to have one's a. in a sling,** avoir le cafard, broyer du noir, être au sixième dessous. 7. (**big**) **a. man,** coureur *m* de jupons, cavaleur *m*. *Voir aussi* **green-ass; kiss-ass; lead**[1], 4; **ream out** (**to**); **shit-ass; suckass.**

ass[2] [ɑːs, æs] (*noun*), *P:* (**you**) **silly a.!** espèce d'idiot!

assy [ˈæsi] (*adj.*) (*U.S.*), *P:* 1. radin; entêté; vil; méchant. 2. (fond de pantalon) reluisant.

aste [eist] (**to**) (*Austr.*), *P:* **to a. it,** se tenir tranquille, s'appliquer.

at [æt] (*prep.*), *F:* **where it's a.,** où ça boume, où ça ronfle.

attababy! [ˈætəbeibi] (*excl.*), *F:* vas-y, petit!

attaboy! [ˈætəbɔi] (*excl.*), *F:* vas-y, fiston! vas-y, Toto!

attagirl! [ˈætəgəːl] (*excl.*), *F:* vas-y, fifille! vas-y, Nénette!

attic [ˈætik] (*noun*), *F:* **to be queer in the a.,** être fou*, yoyoter de la mansarde; *cf.* **bat**[1], 5.

aunt, Aunt [ɑːnt] (*noun*). 1. *F:* **my A. Fanny!** quelle bonne blague! et ta sœur! 2. *F:* **A. Jane,** W.C.*, goguenots *m.pl.* 3. *F:* **A. Sally,** jeu *m* de massacre. 4. *P:* (*a*) patronne* d'un bordel, taulière *f*, mère-maquerelle, mère-maca *f*; (*b*) vieille prostituée*, tarte *f*, tarderie *f*, fromage *m*. 5. *P:* vieux pédéraste*, tante *f*, tata *f*, tantouse *f*. 6. *P:* **A. Emma,** morphine *f* (*drogues**). 7. *P:* **Aunt Maria** (*R.S.* = *fire*), feu *m*, conflagration *f*. *Voir aussi* **Bob**[2].

auntie[1], **aunty**[1] [ˈɑːnti] (*noun*), *P:* pédéraste* qui prend de l'âge, tata *f*.

Auntie[2], **Aunty**[2] [ˈɑːnti] (*noun*), *F:* **A.** (**Beeb**), la BBC (British Broadcasting Corporation).

Aussie[1] [ˈɔsi] (*adj.*) (*abbr.* = *Australian*) *F:* Australien.

Aussie[2] [ˈɔsi] (*noun*) (*abbr.* = *Australian*), *F:* Australien *m*, kangourou *m*.

away [əˈwei] (*adv.*), *F:* 1. (*euph.*) en prison*, au bloc. 2. **well a.,** ivre*, pompette, parti. 3. **he's well a.,** le voilà lancé, il est bien parti (*ou* bien en train). *Voir aussi* **have** (**to**), 1, 2, 3.

awful [ˈɔːful] (*adj.*), *F:* terrible, affreux; détestable; **an a. bore,** (*a*) (*d'une chose*) qch. d'assommant (*ou* de canulant); (*b*) (*d'une personne*) casse-burettes *m*, casse-pieds *m*; **he's an a. bore,** il est terriblement rasoir; **a. weather,** un temps de chien (*ou* de cochon). *Voir aussi* **god-awful.**

awfully [ˈɔːfli] (*adv.*), *F:* **that's a. nice of you,** c'est tout plein gentil de votre part; **I'm a. glad about it,** j'en suis ravi; **thanks a.,** merci mille fois; **a. funny,** drôle comme tout.

awkward [ˈɔːkwəd] (*adj.*), *F:* **the a. age,** l'âge ingrat.

A.W.O.L. [ˈeiˈdʌbljuːˈouˈel, ˈeiwɔl] (*abbr.* = *absent without leave*) (*mil.*), *F:* absent sans permission, avec fausse-perm(e).

ax[1] [æks] (*U.S.*), **axe**[1] [æks] (*noun*), *F:* 1. **to get the a.,** passer au couperet, se faire vider. 2. **to give s.o. the a.,** se débarrasser* de qn, sacquer, vider, balancer qn. 3. **to have an a. to grind,** prêcher pour son saint. 4. **the a.,** coupe *f*, réduction *f* dans un budget; diminution *f* de personnel. *Voir aussi* **battle-axe.**

ax[2] [æks] (*U.S.*), **axe**[2] [æks] (**to**), *F:* **to a. expenditure,** faire des coupes *f.pl.* sombres dans le budget; **to a. s.o.,** porter la hache à qn.

* An asterisk indicates that the word so marked is included as a head-word in the Appendix.

B

b [biː] (*abbr.*), *P:* **1.** = **bloody.** **2.** =**bastard.** **3.** Benzédrine *f* (*marque déposée*). **4.** **B flats,** poux*, punaises *f.pl.*, morpions *m.pl.*

babbling [ˈbæbliŋ] (*adj.*), *F:* **b. brook,** jacteuse *f*, tapette *f*, pie *f* borgne.

babe [beib] (*noun*), *P:* **1.** pépée *f*, poupée *f*, poule *f*; petite amie; **hello b.!** bonjour poupée! salut beauté (*ou* bébé)! **2.** **a hot b.,** une chaude de la pince, une chaude lapine, bandeuse *f*, tendeuse *f*.

baboon [bəˈbuːn] (*noun*), *F:* **he's a great b.,** c'est une espèce d'armoire à glace, c'est un vrai orang-outan.

baby[1] [ˈbeibi] (*attrib. adj.*). **1.** *F:* **b. doll,** bonbonnière *f*, poupée *f*, bébé *f*; *voir aussi* **baby-doll.** **2.** *P:* **b. elephant,** femme* grosse, bonbonne *f*; **to walk around like a b. elephant,** marcher comme un chien dans un jeu de quilles.

baby[2] [ˈbeibi] (*noun*). **1.** *P:* = **babe, 1.** **2.** *P:* **a hot b.** = **a hot babe** (**babe, 2**). **3.** *P:* un homme*, un mec, un dur. **4.** *F:* **to be left holding the b.,** porter le chapeau, payer les pots cassés, être le dindon de la farce. **5.** *F:* **that's my b.,** c'est ma création, c'est mon blot. **6.** *F:* **that's your b.,** c'est ton business (*ou* tes oignons *m.pl.*); débrouille-toi tout seul. **7.** *P:* **to (nearly) have a b.,** (*a*) avoir peur*, chier dans son froc, être dans tous ses états; (*b*) être en colère*, être à cran. **8.** *P:* marijuana *f* (*drogues**), douce *f*. *Voir aussi* **bathwater; cry-baby; jelly-baby; scare-baby.**

baby-doll [ˈbeibi-dɔl] (*attrib. adj.*), *F:* **b.-d. pyjamas,** mini-pyjama *m*.

baby-juice [ˈbeibi-dʒuːs] (*noun*), *P:* sperme*, jus *m* de cyclope, purée *f*.

baby-kisser [ˈbeibi-kisər] (*noun*), *F:* député *m* en période électorale.

baby-snatcher [ˈbeibi-snætʃər] (*noun*), (*a*) *F:* kidnappeur *m*, -euse *f*; (*b*) *P:* vieux marcheur, vieux barbeau.

baccy [ˈbæki] (*noun*), *F:* tabac*, pétun *m*.

bach[1] [bætʃ] (*noun*), *F:* **1.** (=*bachelor*) célibataire *m*, vieux garçon. **2.** (*Austr.*) baraque *f*, cambuse *f*.

bach[2] [bætʃ] (**to**), *F:* **to b. it,** mener une vie de célibataire, vivre en vieux garçon.

bachelor [ˈbætʃələr] (*attrib. adj.*), *F:* **b. flat,** garçonnière *f*; **b. girl,** (*a*) jeune fille* indépendante, pucelle *f* de la première heure; (*b*) vieille fille, laissée pour compte.

back[1] [bæk] (*adj.*). **1.** *F:* **to take a b. seat,** être la cinquième roue du carrosse; *voir aussi* **backseat.** **2.** *F:* **the b. end,** automne *m*; *voir aussi* **back-end.** **3.** *P:* **b. door,** anus*, trou *m* de balle. *Voir aussi* **fed up,** (*a*).

back[2] [bæk] (*noun*). **1.** *F:* **to have one's b. up,** être en colère*; **to get s.o.'s b. up,** mettre qn en colère*, prendre (*ou* frotter) qn à rebrousse-poil, braquer qn. **2.** *P:* **get off my b.!** fous-moi la paix! **3.** *F:* **to be on s.o.'s b.** (**about sth.**), (*a*) tomber sur le dos (*ou* le râble) de qn; (*b*) talonner qn. **4.** *F:* **you scratch my b. and I'll scratch yours,** passe-moi la rhubarbe, je te passe le séné; *cf.* **backscratcher.** **5.** *F:* **to put one's b. into sth.,** donner un coup de collier, en mettre un coup. **6.** *F:* **to break one's b.,** se fatiguer, s'échiner. **7.** *F:* **to have one's b. to the wall,** avoir le dos au mur, tirer ses dernières cartouches, être acculé dans ses derniers retranchements. **8.** *F:* **the b. of beyond,** la brousse, en plein bled, au diable vauvert; **he lives at the b. of beyond,** il habite au delà des poules. **9.** *F:* **to be (laid) on one's b.,** (*a*) être malade*, être mal fichu; (*b*) être faible, être impuissant. **10.** *F:* **to break the b. of sth.,** faire le plus dur de qch. **11.** *P:* **she earns her living on her b.,** elle fait l'horizontale. *Voir aussi* **greenback; greybacks; piggyback; shellback.**

backasswards [bækˈæswədz] (*adv.*) (*U.S.*), *P:* = **ass backwards** (**ass**[1], **5**).

backbone [ˈbækboun] (*noun*), *F:* courage *m*, persévérance *f*, cran *m*.

* L'astérisque indique que le mot marqué de ce signe figure comme entrée dans le Répertoire.

backchat[1] [ˈbæktʃæt] (*noun*), *F:* **1.** (*a*) insolence *f*; (*b*) réplique cinglante. **2.** (*th.*) baratin *m* d'acteur.

backchat[2] [ˈbæktʃæt] (**to**), *F:* répliquer.

back down [ˈbækˈdaun] (**to**), *F:* caler, caner, lâcher pied.

back-end [ˈbækend] (*noun*), *F:* **she looks like the b.-e. of a bus,** c'est une mocheté. *Voir aussi* **back**[1], **2.**

backfire [ˈbækˈfaiər] (**to**), *F:* rater, mal tourner, faire fausse route.

backhanded [ˈbækˈhændid] (*adj.*), *F:* **b. compliment,** compliment *m* à double tranchant.

backhander [ˈbækˈhændər] (*noun*), *P:* **1.** revers *m* de main, baff(r)e *f*, torgnole *f*. **2.** graissage *m* de patte, pot-de-vin *m*.

backlash [ˈbæklæʃ] (*noun*), *F:* retour *m* de flamme, effet *m* de boumerang.

back-number [ˈbæknʌmbər] (*noun*), *F:* **1.** objet démodé. **2.** croulant *m*, périmé *m*.

back off [ˈbækˈɔf] (**to**), *P:* **b. o.!** fiche-moi la paix!

back out [ˈbækˈaut] (**to**), *F:* **1.** se dédire, se dérober, se défiler. **2.** sortir d'une position difficile, faire marche arrière.

back-pedal [ˈbækˈpedl] (**to**), *F:* faire marche arrière, faire machine arrière.

backroom [ˈbækru:m] (*attrib. adj.*), *F:* confidentiel, secret; **b. boy,** (*a*) technicien employé à des recherches secrètes; (*b*) = **boffin.**

backscratcher [ˈbæk-skrætʃər] (*noun*), *F:* flatteur *m* (*flatter**), lèche-cul *m*, lèche-bottes *m*, lécheur *m*; *cf.* **back**[2], **4.**

backscratching [ˈbæk-skrætʃiŋ] (*noun*), *F:* flagornerie *f*.

back-scuttle [ˈbæk-skʌtl] (**to**), *V:* pratiquer la pédérastie active sur (qn) (*coït* anal*); aller aux fesses de (qn), encaldosser.

backseat [ˈbæksi:t] (*attrib. adj.*), *F:* **b. driver,** passager *m* donnant des conseils au chauffeur.

backside[1] [ˈbæksaid] (*attrib. adj.*), *P:* **b. special,** spé *m*, spécial *m*.

backside[2] [ˈbækˈsaid] (*noun*), *F:* = **behind.**

backslang [ˈbæk-slæŋ] (*noun*), *F:* verlan *m*, code *m* verlan.

backslapper [ˈbæk-slæpər] (*noun*), *F:* **to be a b.,** être à tu et à toi avec qn.

backslapping [ˈbæk-slæpiŋ] (*noun*), *F:* bruyante démonstration d'amitié.

backstairs [ˈbæk-stɛəz] (*attrib. adj.*), *F:* **b. influence,** protection *f* en haut lieu; **he succeeded through b. influence,** il est arrivé à coups de piston; **b. gossip,** cancan *m* de domestiques; **b. politics,** intrigues *f.pl.* politiques, politique *f* de sous-main.

backtrack [ˈbæk-træk] (**to**). **1.** *F:* (*a*) rebrousser chemin; (*b*) faire marche arrière, se dégonfler, se défiler, caner. **2.** *P:* = **back up (to), 2** (*b*).

backtracker [ˈbæk-trækər] (*noun*), *F:* caneur *m*.

back-up [ˈbækʌp] (*noun*). **1.** *F:* appui *m*, soutien *m*, aide *f*. **2.** *P:* (*a*) piqûre *f* (dans une veine déjà gonflée); (*b*) poussette *f*. **3.** *P:* enculage (hétérosexuel).

back up [ˈbækˈʌp] (**to**). **1.** *F:* **to b. s.o. u.,** seconder qn, prendre (*ou* porter) les patins pour qn. **2.** *P:* (*a*) dilater la veine avant une piqûre de drogues; gonfler; (*b*) aspirer le sang dans la seringue pendant une piqûre; (*c*) faire poussette. **3.** *F:* faire marche arrière.

backward [ˈbækwəd] (*adj.*), *F:* **he's not b. in coming forward,** il n'est pas le dernier à se pousser, il n'a pas froid aux yeux.

backwards [ˈbækwədz] (*adv.*), *F:* **1. to lean over b. for s.o.,** se mettre en quatre pour qn, faire son possible pour aider qn; *cf.* **fall (to), 3. 2. to know sth. b.,** comprendre qch. parfaitement, savoir (*ou* connaître) qch. par cœur.

backwoodsman [ˈbækwudzmən] (*noun*), *F:* **1.** rustre *m*, rustaud *m*, péquenaud *m*. **2.** un Pair qui fréquente peu la Chambre des Lords.

bacon [ˈbeikən] (*noun*), *F:* **1. to bring home the b.,** (*a*) faire bouillir la marmite, gagner sa croûte (*ou* son bifteck); (*b*) remporter le pompon. **2. to save one's b.,** sauver sa peau (*ou* ses côtelettes *f.pl.*). *Voir aussi* **bonce.**

bad[1] [bæd] (*adj.*). **1.** *F:* **that's too b.!** (*a*) dommage! manque de pot!; (*b*) tant pis pour lui (eux, *etc.*)! **2.** *F:* **a b. lot** (*or* **'un** *or* **hat** *or* **egg**), sale* individu, canaille *f*, salaud *m*. **3.** *F:* **to turn up like a b. penny,** se présenter comme un mauvais sou; venir comme un cheveu (*ou* des cheveux) sur la soupe. **4.** *F:* **that's not b.!** c'est pas de la gnognot(t)e! **5.** *F:* **in b. shape** (*or* **in a b. way**), mal

* An asterisk indicates that the word so marked is included as a head-word in the Appendix.

parti, en fichu état. 6. *F:* **to give sth. up as a b. job,** laisser tomber qch. 7. *F:* **to have a b. time of it,** passer un mauvais moment (*ou* quart d'heure). 8. *F:* **to make it b. for s.o.,** (*a*) jouer un mauvais tour à qn; (*b*) en faire baver à qn. 9. *F:* **he's as b. as they make 'em** (*or* **as they come**), il est mauvais comme une teigne. 10. *F:* **b. form,** mauvaises manières; ce qui ne se fait pas. 11. *P:* **b. news,** facture *f*, note *f*, addition *f* (*surtout* dans une boîte de nuit). 12. *P:* excellent*, super, terrible.

bad² [bæd] (*adv.*) (=*badly*), *P:* mal; **to have it b. for s.o.,** aimer* qn, être épris de qn.

bad³ [bæd] (*noun*), *F:* 1. **to go to the b.,** être sur la mauvaise pente, mal tourner, tourner au sur. 2. **to the b.,** en arriérages, en moratoire.

baddie, baddy [ˈbædi] (*noun*), *F:* 1. vaurien*, affreux *m*, canaille *f*. 2. (*film, pièce de théâtre*) le vilain, le méchant; *cf.* **goodies, 2.**

badge [bædʒ] (*noun*), *P:* quantité de drogues insuffisante pour le prix payé.

badger [ˈbædʒər] (*noun*). 1. (*Austr.*) *P:* reçu maquillé, quittance maquillée. 2. *P:* **the b. game,** (*a*) moyens employés pour compromettre un homme avec une femme pour lui tirer de l'argent; (*b*) escroquerie*, chantage *m*; tromperie *f*, duperie *f* dans un but personnel ou politique. 3. (*U.S.*) *F:* habitant *m* de l'état de Wisconsin.

bad-looking [ˈbædˈlukiŋ] (*adj.*), *F:* **she's not b.-l.,** elle n'est pas mal, c'est un beau petit lot.

bad-mouth [ˈbædmauθ] (**to**) (*U.S.*), *F:* dire du mal de (qn, qch.), casser du sucre sur le dos de (qn).

bag¹ [bæg] (*noun*). 1. *P:* **(old) b.,** femme* (*péj.*); vieille pouffiasse, mocheté *f*. 2. *P:* **overnight b.,** baise-en-ville *m*. 3. *F:* **b. of wind,** (*a*) vantard*, hâbleur *m*; (*b*) bavard*, baratineur *m*. 4. *F:* **there's bags of it,** il y en a en abondance*, il y en a à gogo, il y en a une charibotée. 5. *F:* **it's in the b.,** c'est dans le sac, c'est du tout cuit. 6. *F:* **the whole b. of tricks,** tout le Saint-Frusquin. 7. *V:* **b. (of tricks),** testicules*, bijoux *m.pl.* de famille. 8. *F:* **she's a b. of bones,** elle est maigre*, elle n'a que la peau et (*ou* sur) les os. 9. *F:* **bags of mystery,** saucisses *f.pl.*, bifteck *m* de pan(n)é. 10. *P:* parachute *m*, pépin *m*. 11. (*pl.*) *F:* pantalon*, falzar(d) *m*. 12. (*U.S.*) *P:* **to have** (*or* **tie**) **a b. on,** (*a*) faire la bombe, faire ribote; (*b*) être ivre*, être en ribote. 13. *P:* humeur *f*, état *m* d'esprit; **to have sad bags,** être triste sur les bords. 14. (*U.S.*) *P:* occupation *f*, marotte *f*, dada *m*. 15. (*U.S.*) *P:* milieu social, entourage *m*, ambiance *f*, clique *f*, groupe *m*. 16. *P:* provision *f* de drogues d'un usager; plaquette *f*. 17. *P:* **the bottom of the b.,** (*a*) la dernière ressource; (*b*) atout gardé en réserve. 18. *F:* **to be left holding the b.** = **to be left holding the baby** (**baby²**, 4). 19. *P:* **to empty the b.,** vider son sac. 20. *P:* **to give s.o. the b.** = **to give s.o. the sack** (**sack¹**, 1). 21. (*U.S.*) *P:* **to set one's b.,** tout mettre en œuvre pour avoir un poste politique *ou* une promotion. 22. *P:* (*a*) capote (anglaise); (*b*) pessaire *m* en caoutchouc, calotte *f*. 23. *F:* **it's not my b.** = **it's not my scene** (**scene**, 7). *Voir aussi* **cat, 12; fag, 2** (*c*); **fleabag; gasbag; haybag; moneybags; nosebag; ragbag; ratbag; scumbag; shagbag.**

bag² [bæg] (**to**), *P:* 1. arrêter*, agrafer. 2. mettre le grappin sur (qch.). 3. voler*, piquer, chauffer. 4. descendre, piffer (un avion). 5. **b.** (*or* **bags**) **I the first go!** pour bibi (*ou* mézigue) le premier tour!

baggage [ˈbægidʒ] (*noun*), *F:* 1. fille* effrontée, garce *f*, gisquette *f*. 2. prostituée*, chamelle *f*.

bagged [bægd] (*adj.*) (*U.S.*), *P:* ivre*, blindé, chargé.

bagman [ˈbægmæn] (*noun*), *P:* 1. commis voyageur *m*. 2. fourgueur *m* de drogues.

bag-snatcher [ˈbæg-snætʃər] (*noun*), *F:* piqueur *m* (*ou* faucheur *m*) de sacs à main.

bail out [ˈbeilˈaut] (**to**), *P:* **to b. s.o. o.,** (*a*) aider qn à remonter le courant; (*b*) tendre une main secourable à qn.

bait [beit] (*noun*), *P:* (*a*) homme beau et efféminé qui attire, malgré lui, les pédérastes*; un Antinoüs; (*b*) femme belle mais masculine; une Diane chasseresse. *Voir aussi* **dream-bait; jail-bait.**

* L'astérisque indique que le mot marqué de ce signe figure comme entrée dans le Répertoire.

baksheesh [ˈbækʃiːʃ] (*noun*), *P:* bakchich(e) *m.*

baldheaded [ˈbɔːldˈhedid] (*adv.*), *P:* **to go for s.o., sth., b.,** foncer sur qn, qch., tête baissée, ne pas y aller de main morte.

baldie, baldy [ˈbɔːldi] (*noun*), *P:* personne chauve*, tête *f* de veau.

ball[1] [bɔːl] (*noun*). **1.** *F:* **to be on the b.,** (*a*) être là pour un coup; (*b*) être dans le coup, savoir nager, être sous la gouttière; (*c*) être malin*, être dégourdi. **2.** *P:* **to have (oneself) a b.,** se goberger, s'en payer une tranche, se marrer. **3.** *F:* **to play b. with s.o.,** coopérer avec qn, être de mèche avec qn, être en tandem avec qn, faire le chemin à deux. **4.** *F:* **to set the b. rolling,** mener la danse (*ou* le branle). **5.** *P:* pilule *f ou* portion *f* d'une drogue; *cf.* **goofball, 3, 4, 5; speedball. 6.** *F:* **b. of fire,** individu* du tonnerre; *cf.* **fireball. 7.** *P:* **b. and chain,** épouse*, boulet *m.* **8.** *F:* **the b. is in your court,** c'est à votre tour, c'est maintenant votre initiative. **9.** *P:* **that's the way the b. bounces,** c'est comme ça et pas autrement, voilà d'où vient le vent; *cf.* **cookie, 2; mop; onion, 1. 10.** *V:* testicule*, bille *f*, balloche *f*; *cf.* **ballock**[1], **1; balls.** *Voir aussi* **chalk, 4; eight, 2; fly-ball; oddball**[2]**; pat-ball; pinball; screwball**[2]**; snowball**[1].

ball[2] [bɔːl] (**to**). **1.** *P:* = **to have (oneself) a ball (ball**[1], **2). 2.** *V:* coïter* avec (une femme), égoïner, bourrer. *Voir aussi* **jack, 6; snowball**[2] **(to).**

ball-breaker [ˈbɔːl-breikər], **ball-buster** [ˈbɔːl-bʌstər] (*noun*) (*U.S.*), *P:* tâche *f* extrêmement difficile, casse-gueule *m*; *cf.* **balls, 10.**

balling out [ˈbɔːliŋˈaut] (*noun*), *P:* engueulade *f*, savon *m.*

ballock[1] [ˈbɔlək] (*noun*), *V:* **1.** testicule*, balloche *f.* **2. to drop a b.,** s'attirer des crosses *f.pl.*, s'emmouscailler. *Voir aussi* **ballocks**[1].

ballock[2] [ˈbɔlək] (**to**), *V:* réprimander*, enguirlander, engueuler.

ballocking [ˈbɔləkiŋ] (*noun*), *V:* **to get a b.,** recevoir un abattage (*ou* une engueulade).

ballock-naked [ˈbɔləkˈneikid] (*adj.*), *V:* nu*, à poil, le cul à l'air.

ballocks[1] [ˈbɔləks] (*pl. noun*), *V:* **1.** testicules*, balloches *f.pl.* **2. b. (to you)!** mon cul! **3. to make a b. of sth.,** faire cafouiller qch., foutre la pagaille. *Voir aussi* **ballock**[1].

ballocks[2] [ˈbɔləks] (**to**), *V:* **1.** esquinter, bousiller. **2. to be** (*or* **get**) **ballocksed,** se faire contrer ; *cf.* **ballock**[2] **(to).**

ball-off [ˈbɔːlɔf] (*noun*), *V:* branlage *m*; **to have a b.-o.,** se masturber*, se branler.

ball off [ˈbɔːlˈɔf] (**to**), *V:* = **to have a ball-off.**

balloon [bəˈluːn] (*noun*), *F:* **1. when the b. goes up . . .,** quand on découvrira le pot aux roses... **2.** ballon *m* d'essai.

balloon-head [bəˈluːnhed] (*noun*), *F:* individu bête*, ballot *m*, baluchard *m.*

ball out [ˈbɔːlˈaut] (**to**), *P:* injurier*, enguirlander (qn).

balls [bɔːlz] (*pl. noun*), *V:* **1.** testicules*, couilles *f.pl.* **2. to have s.o. by the b.,** avoir qn à la pogne. **3. to get one's b. chewed off,** se faire réprimander*, en prendre pour son grade; *voir aussi* **chew off (to). 4. b. (to you)!** mon cul!; espèce de couillon! **5. b. to that!** tête de con!; con à ressort! **6. it's all** (*or* **a load of**) **b.,** c'est de la couille (*ou* des couilles) en barre. **7. what b.!** quelle connerie!; quelle couillonnade! **8. it's cold enough to freeze the b. off a brass monkey,** ça caille; il fait un froid de canard; on se les gèle. **9.** (*U.S.*) courage *m*, cran *m.* **10. to break one's b.,** se casser les couilles; *cf.* **ball-breaker. 11.** = **balls-up.**

balls-ache [ˈbɔːlzeik] (*noun*), *V:* **you give me (the) b.-a.,** tu me casses les couilles, tu me fais mal aux couilles.

ballsey [ˈbɔːlzi] (*adj.*) (*U.S.*), *P:* agressif, impulsif, emplumé.

balls-up [ˈbɔːlzʌp] (*noun*), *V:* **to make a (right) b.-u. of it,** en faire une couillonnade (*ou* une connerie).

balls up [ˈbɔːlzˈʌp] (**to**), *V:* embrouiller, chambouler, bousiller.

ball up [ˈbɔːlˈʌp] (**to**). **1.** *V:* = **balls up (to). 2.** *P:* **to be (all) balled up,** être embrouillé, vasouiller.

bally [ˈbæli] (*adj.*), *F:* (*euph. pour* **bloody**) satané, sacré.

ballyhoo [ˈbæliˈhuː] (*noun*), *F:* **1.** grosse publicité, battage *m*, tamtam *m.* **2.** mensonge*, bourrage *m* de crâne, boniment *m.*

* An asterisk indicates that the word so marked is included as a head-word in the Appendix.

balmy [ˈbɑːmi] (*adj.*), *P:* = **barmy.**

balon(e)y [bəˈlouni] (*noun*), *F:* bêtises*, sornettes *f.pl.*; **b.!** c'est du bidon! *Voir aussi* **load, 2.**

bam [bæm] (*noun*), *P:* **1.** amphétamine *f* (*drogues**). **2.** mélange *m* de stimulant et de calmant (*drogues*).

bambalacha [ˈbæmbəˈlɑːtʃə] (*noun*), *P:* marijuana *f* (*drogues**), bambalouche *f.*

bamboo [bæmˈbuː] (*noun*), *P:* pipe *f* à opium, bambou *m*; **to suck the b.,** tirer sur le bambou; **b. puffer,** tireur *m* de dross.

bamboozle [bæmˈbuːzl] (**to**), *F:* duper*, empaumer, embobeliner, embobiner.

banana [bəˈnɑːnə] (*noun*). **1.** *V:* **to have one's b. peeled,** coïter*, arracher un copeau. **2.** *F:* **b. shot,** (*football*) balle *f* en courbe. **3.** *F:* **I haven't just come in on the b. boat,** je ne suis pas de la dernière couvée; je ne suis pas tombé de la dernière pluie. **4.** (*U.S.*) *F:* comédien *m*, acteur *m* burlesque; **top b.,** vedette *f*; **second b.,** acteur *m* de second rôle.

bananas [bəˈnɑːnəz] (*adj.*), *P:* fou*, maboul, toqué.

band [bænd] (*noun*), *F:* **Big B.,** grand orchestre de jazz comportant vingt éléments. *Voir aussi* **one-man.**

bandit [ˈbændit] (*noun*), *F:* **one-armed b.,** machine *f* à sous. *Voir aussi* **arse-bandit; beef-bandit.**

bandwagon [ˈbændwægən] (*noun*), *F:* **to jump** (*or* **climb** *or* **hop**) **on the b.,** prendre le train en marche, se mettre du côté du manche.

bandy-chair [ˈbændi-tʃɛər] (*noun*), *F:* **to make a b.-c.,** faire la chaise.

bang[1] [bæŋ] (*adj.*), *F:* **the whole b. lot** (*or* **shoot**), tout le tremblement, le train et l'arrière-train.

bang[2] [bæŋ] (*adv.*), *F:* **1. to arrive b. on time,** arriver pile (*ou* recta). **2. to be caught b. to rights,** être pris sur le fait, être pris en flagrant délit; *cf.* **dead**[2], **8** (*b*). *Voir aussi* **slap-bang(-wallop); wallop**[1].

bang[3] [bæŋ] (*noun*). **1.** *P:* coït*, partie *f* de jambes en l'air; **gang b.,** coït* d'une femme avec plusieurs hommes; dérouillage *m* en bande. **2.** *F:* coup*, gnon *m.* **3.** *F:* accrochage *m*, avaro *m.* **4.** *F:* **to go with a b.,** aller comme sur des roulettes, gazer. **5.** *P:* **I got a real b. out of it,** ce truc m'a remué les boyaux. **6.** *P:* **to have a b. at sth.,** tenter (*ou* risquer) le coup. **7.** *P:* **b.** (**in the arm**), piquouse *f*; **to give oneself a b.,** se charger. **8.** *P:* impression *f* de plénitude qui suit une injection intraveineuse de drogue; flash *m.* **9.** (*Austr.*) *P:* bordel*, claque *m. Voir aussi* **whizz-bang.**

bang[4] [bæŋ] (**to**). **1.** *P:* battre*, cogner, encadrer (qn). **2.** *P:* coïter* avec (une femme), envoyer en l'air. **3.** *F:* tamponner, entuber (une voiture). **4.** *F:* **to b. into s.o.,** se taper dans qn. **5.** *P:* piquouser.

banger [ˈbæŋər] (*noun*). **1.** *F:* voiture*, guimbarde *f.* **2.** *F:* saucisse *f*, bifteck *m* de pan(n)é. **3.** *P:* queutard *m*, bourriqueur *m.* **4.** *F:* mensonge* énorme, bateau *m.*

bang-on [ˈbæŋˈɔn] (*adv.*), *F:* **b.-o.!** recta!; **it's b.-o.,** c'est au poil, c'est extra.

bangster [ˈbæŋstər] (*noun*), *P:* piquouseur *m*, chevalier *m* de la poussette.

bang-up [ˈbæŋʌp] (*adj.*), *F:* excellent*, soin-soin, du tonnerre; **a b.-u. meal,** un repas à tout casser, de la grande bouffe; *cf.* **slap-up.**

banjax [ˈbændʒæks] (**to**), *P:* démolir, bousiller, foutre en l'air.

banjo [ˈbændʒou] (*noun*), *P:* **1.** miche de pain coupée en deux formant un grand sandwich. **2.** nourriture* volée aux cuisines de prison. *Voir aussi* **Irish**[1], 4.

bankroll [ˈbæŋkroul] (*attrib. adj.*), *P:* **b. man,** qn qui finance une affaire de jeu; directeur *m* d'une salle de jeux, bouleur *m.*

bar [bɑːr] (*noun*). **1.** *F:* **to be behind bars,** être emprisonné*, être derrière les barreaux *m.pl.*, être bouclé. **2.** *P:* billet* d'une livre. **3.** *V:* **to have a b.** (**on**), être en érection*, avoir la trique. *Voir aussi* **handlebar; nosh-bar.**

barber [ˈbɑːbər] (**to**), *P:* **to b. a joint,** voler* dans une chambre alors que qn y dort, grincher à l'endormage.

barbs [bɑːbz] (*pl. noun*) (*abbr.* = *barbiturates*), *P:* barbituriques *m.pl.* (*drogues**), barbitos *m.pl.*

bare-arsed [ˈbɛərˈɑːst], *U.S.:* **bare-ass(ed)** [ˈbɛərˈæs(t)] (*adj.*), *P:* nu*, le cul à l'air, en Jésus.

bareback [ˈbɛəbæk] (*adv.*), *P:* **to ride b.,** cracher dans le bénitier, jouer sans blanc.

* L'astérisque indique que le mot marqué de ce signe figure comme entrée dans le Répertoire.

barf [bɑːf] (**to**) (*U.S.*), *P:* vomir*, dégueuler.

bar-fly [ˈbɑːflai] (*noun*), *F:* **1.** pilier *m* de bistrot. **2.** ivrogne* qui se fait offrir des tournées.

barge in [ˈbɑːdʒˈin] (**to**), *F:* **1. to b. i. on a party,** (*a*) arriver en trouble-fête; (*b*) arriver en pique-assiette. **2. to b. i. on s.o.'s conversation,** mettre son grain de sel. **3. to b. i. where you're not wanted,** piétiner les bégonias, marcher sur les plates-bandes de qn.

barge into [ˈbɑːdʒˈintu] (**to**), *F:* **to b. i. s.o.,** se taper dans qn, bousculer qn, entrer dans qn.

barge out [ˈbɑːdʒˈaut] (**to**), *F:* partir* en claquant la porte.

barge-pole [ˈbɑːdʒpoul] (*noun*), *F:* **I wouldn't touch it with a b.-p.,** je ne le prendrais pas avec des pincettes *f.pl.*

bar-girl [ˈbɑːgəːl] (*noun*), *P:* hôtesse *f*, entraîneuse *f*.

bar-happy [ˈbɑːˈhæpi] (*adj.*) (*U.S.*), *F:* (légèrement) ivre*, éméché.

bark [bɑːk] (**to**), *F:* **1.** tousser bruyamment. **2. to b. up the wrong tree,** se mettre le doigt dans l'œil (jusqu'au coude), tirer sur ses propres troupes. *Voir aussi* **dog**[1], **7.**

barker [ˈbɑːkər] (*noun*), *P:* revolver*, pétard *m*, flingue *m*.

barmy [ˈbɑːmi] (*adj.*), *P:* fou*, toqué, loufoque; **to put on the b. stick,** faire le cinglé.

barn [bɑːn] (*noun*), *F:* **1. it's a b. of a place,** c'est une grande baraque (*ou* un vrai hangar); **it's like a b. in here,** c'est ouvert à tout vent, c'est comme chez Frisco et Cie. **2. were you born** (*U.S.:* **raised**) **in a b.?** t'es né sous les ponts?

Barnaby Rudge [ˈbɑːnəbiˈrʌdʒ] (*pr. noun*) (*R.S.* = *judge*), *P:* juge *m*, gerbier *m*.

barnet [ˈbɑːnit] (*noun*), *P:* = **Barnet Fair.**

Barnet Fair [ˈbɑːnitˈfɛər] (*pr. noun*) (*R.S.* = *hair*), *P:* cheveux*, tiffes *m.pl.*

barney[1] [ˈbɑːni] (*noun*), *P:* **1. a (bit of a) b.,** querelle*, prise *f* de bec, accrochage *m*. **2.** arrangement *m* malhonnête, entourloupette *f*.

barney[2] [ˈbɑːni] (**to**), *P:* discuter le bout de gras.

baron [ˈbærən] (*noun*). **1.** *P:* prisonnier *m* qui a de l'argent, du tabac, *etc.*; baron *m*; *cf.* **snout, 2. 2.** *F:* magnat *m*, gros bonnet (de l'industrie, *etc.*).

barrack-room [ˈbærək-ruːm] (*attrib. adj.*), *F:* **b.-r. lawyer,** chicaneur *m*, râleur *m*, mauvais coucheur, emmerdeur *m*.

barrel[1] [ˈbærəl] (*noun*), *P:* **1. to be over a b.,** être dans le pétrin (*ou* dans la merde). **2. to get** (*or* **have**) **s.o. over a b.,** avoir qn dans sa poche (*ou* à sa pogne). **3. to make a b.,** gagner des mille et des cents. *Voir aussi* **scrape**[2] **(to), 1.**

barrel[2] **(ass)** [ˈbærəl(æs)] (**to**) (*U.S.*), *P:* aller vite*, rouler à plein tube, gazer.

barrelhouse [ˈbærəlhaus] (*noun*) (*U.S.*), *P:* cabaret *m* populaire dans un quartier noir.

barrelled up [ˈbærəldˈʌp] (*adj.*), *P:* ivre*, bit(t)uré.

barrow [ˈbærou, ˈbærə] (*noun*). **1.** *P:* **to fall right into** (*or* **land right in**) **one's b.,** tomber tout frit (*ou* tout rôti), tomber dans le bec. **2.** *F:* **b. boy,** marchand *m* à la sauvette, estampeur *m*.

base [beis] (*noun*), *F:* **1. he won't even make first b.,** il claquera au départ. **2. he went b. over apex,** il a fait une belle culbute; *cf.* **arse, 4.**

bash[1] [bæʃ] (*noun*), *P:* **1.** coup*, châtaigne *f*. **2. to have a b. at sth., to give sth. a b.,** tenter le coup (*ou* sa chance).

bash[2] [bæʃ] (**to**), *P:* **1.** battre*, cogner. **2. to b. it** = **to hit the bottle (bottle**[1], **1**). *Voir aussi* **bishop; square-bash (to).**

basher [ˈbæʃər] (*noun*), *P:* cogneur *m*, pugiliste *m*, raton *m*, chasseur *m*; *cf.* **pak(k)i-basher; queer-basher; spud-basher; square-basher.**

bash in [ˈbæʃˈin] (**to**), *P:* **to b. i. s.o.'s face,** abîmer le portrait à qn.

bashing [ˈbæʃiŋ] (*noun*), *P:* **1.** coup(s)*, peignée *f*, raclée *f*, trempe *f*. **2. the platoon took a b.,** la section se fit amocher. *Voir aussi* **pak(k)i-bashing; queer-bashing; spud-bashing; square-bashing.**

bash on [ˈbæʃˈɔn] (**to**), *P:* **to b. o. (regardless),** aller envers et contre tout.

bash out [ˈbæʃˈaut] (**to**), *P:* **to b. o. a tune,** tapoter un air.

bash up [ˈbæʃˈʌp] (**to**), *P:* battre*, filer une avoine à (qn).

basinful [ˈbeisnful] (*noun*), *P:* **1. to**

* An asterisk indicates that the word so marked is included as a head-word in the Appendix.

have (had) a b., en avoir marre, en avoir ras le bol. **2. O.K., I'll have a b.**, O.K., je veux!

basket [ˈbɑːskit] (*noun*), *P:* **1.** (*euph. pour* **bastard**) vaurien*, salaud *m.* **2.** = **bread-basket.** *Voir aussi* **fruit-basket.**

bastard [ˈbɑːstəd, ˈbæstəd] (*noun*), *V:* **1.** vaurien*, fils *m* (*ou* fan *m*) de pute, canaille *f.* **2. that's a b.**, ça c'est couille; quelle mouscaille! quel emmerdement!

bat[1] [bæt] (*noun*), **1.** *P:* **an old b.**, (*a*) une vieille bique; (*b*) (*U.S.*) prostituée*, grue *f.* **2.** *F:* **like a b. out of hell,** vite*, comme un zèbre. **3.** *F:* **right off the b.**, illico-presto. **4.** *P:* réjouissances*, noce *f*, bombe *f*; **to be on the** (*or* **a**) **b.**, faire la nouba. **5.** *F:* **to have bats in the belfry** (*or* **attic**), être fou*, avoir une araignée au plafond, yoyoter de la mansarde.

bat[2] [bæt] (**to**). **1.** *P:* battre*, frapper, rosser. **2.** *F:* **he didn't b. an eyelid,** il n'a pas sourcillé (*ou* pipé). **3.** *F:* **to b. first,** tirer le premier. *Voir aussi* **sticky, 4.**

bat along [ˈbætəˈlɔŋ] (**to**), *P:* aller vite*, filer à pleins gaz, rouler à tout berzingue.

bat around [ˈbætəˈraund] (**to**), *F:* **to b. an idea a.**, tournicoter une idée.

batch [bætʃ] (**to**), *F:* **to b. it** = **to bach it (bach**[2] **(to)).**

bathwater [ˈbɑːθ-wɔːtər] (*noun*), *F:* **to throw the baby out with the b.**, envoyer tout promener, balancer le manche après la cognée.

bats [bæts] (*adj.*), *P:* **1.** fou*, timbré; **to go b.**, devenir fou*, perdre la boule. **2. to be b. about s.o., sth.**, aimer* (*ou* être toqué de) qn, qch.

batter[1] [ˈbætər] (*noun*), *P:* **to be on the b.**, (*a*) racoler*, aller aux asperges, faire le tapin; (*b*) = **to be on the bat (bat**[1]**, 4)**; (*c*) être échappé de prison*, déballonner de la taule. *Voir aussi* **belt**[2] **(to), 4.**

batter[2] [ˈbætər] (**to**), *P:* mendier*, taper qn (*argent*), faire la manche.

batter on [ˈbætəˈrɔn] (**to**), *P:* se batailler, piocher de l'avant.

battleaxe [ˈbætl-æks] (*noun*), *F:* femme* (*péj.*), harpie *f*, dragon *m.*

battledress [ˈbætldres] (*noun*), *F:* pyjama *m.*

battler [ˈbætlər] (*noun*), *P:* bagarreur *m*, battant *m*, chercheur *m* de cognes.

batty [ˈbæti] (*adj.*), *P:* = **bats, 1, 2.**

bawling out [ˈbɔːliŋˈaut] (*noun*), *P:* = **balling out.**

bawl out [ˈbɔːlˈaut] (**to**), *P:* = **ball out (to).**

bayonet [ˈbeiənit] (*noun*), *P:* pénis*, arbalète *f*; **to have b. practice,** coïter*, tirer un coup.

bazooka [bəˈzuːkə] (*noun*), *P:* **1.** pénis*, arbalète *f.* **2.** (*pl.*) seins*, doudounes *f.pl.*

bazookaed [bəˈzuːkəd] (*adj.*), *P:* coulé, sabordé, bousillé.

bazooms [bəˈzuːmz] (*pl. noun*), *P:* = **bazookas (bazooka, 2).**

beach [biːtʃ] (*noun*), *F:* **1. to be on the b.**, être sur le sable, être à la côte. **2. you're not the only pebble on the b.**, tu n'es pas unique dans ton genre; t'es pas l'oiseau rare.

beak [biːk] (*noun*), *P:* **1.** magistrat *m* (du commissariat de police), chat *m*, curieux *m.* **2.** nez* (crochu), pif *m*, tarin *m.* *Voir aussi* **stickybeak.**

beam [biːm] (*noun*), *F:* **1. on the b.**, (*a*) sur la même longueur d'ondes; (*b*) dans la bonne direction, sur la bonne route. **2. to be off the b.**, (*a*) ne pas comprendre, ne rien piger, être sur une autre longueur d'ondes; (*b*) faire fausse route, changer de cap. **3. to be broad in the b.**, être joufflu du pétard.

beam-ends [ˈbiːmˈendz] (*pl. noun*), *F:* **to be on one's b.-e.**, être pauvre*, être dans la dèche.

bean [biːn] (*noun*). **1.** *P:* tête*, caboche *f.* **2.** *F:* **old b.**, mon vieux pote, ma vieille branche. **3.** *F:* **he hasn't a b.**, il n'a pas le sou*, il n'a pas un radis. **4.** *F:* **it's not worth a b.**, cela ne vaut pas chipette (*ou* tripette). **5.** *F:* **he knows how many beans make five,** c'est un malin*, il en connaît un rayon. **6.** *F:* **to spill the beans,** (*a*) vendre (*ou* éventer) la mèche, vider son sac; (*b*) avouer*, manger le morceau. **7.** *F:* **to be full of beans,** (*a*) être d'attaque; (*b*) être plein d'entrain, péter le feu. **8.** *P:* Benzédrine *f* (*marque déposée*) (*drogues**). **9.** *P:* **jolly beans,** amphétamine *f* (*drogues**). **10.** (*U.S.*) *P:* (*péj.*) un Mexicain. *Voir aussi* **string-bean.**

beano [ˈbiːnou] (*noun*), *F:* réjouissances*, bamboula *f.*

* L'astérisque indique que le mot marqué de ce signe figure comme entrée dans le Répertoire.

bean-pole [ˈbiːnpoul], **bean-stick** [ˈbiːn-stik] (*noun*), *F:* (*d'une personne*) une grande perche, une asperge (montée).

bear [bɛər] (*noun*) (*U.S.*), *P:* **1.** femme laide*, mocheté *f*, tartignole *f*. **2.** qch. de très difficile*, duraille *f*. *Voir aussi* **sore, 2.**

beard [ˈbiəd] (*noun*), *V:* = **beaver, 2.**

bear-garden [ˈbɛəgɑːdn] (*noun*), *F:* foire *f*, pétaudière *f*; **to turn the place into a b.-g.,** mettre le désordre partout, foutre la pagaille.

beat[1] [biːt] (*adj.*), *F:* **1.** (**dead**) **b.,** très fatigué*, claqué, vanné. **2.** découragé, lessivé, vidé. **3.** **the b. generation,** la génération beat (*ou* sacrifiée). *Voir aussi* **downbeat; off-beat; upbeat.**

beat[2] [biːt] (*noun*). **1.** *P:* beatnik *m*. **2.** *F:* (*jazz*) temps fort de la mesure, le beat. **3.** *F:* **that's off my b.,** ce n'est pas mon rayon. **4.** *V:* **to have a b. on,** être en érection*, avoir le gourdin. *Voir aussi* **deadbeat.**

beat[3] [biːt] (**to**). **1.** *P:* **to b. it,** s'enfuir*, se tirer; **now then, b. it!** file! décampe! fiche le camp! débine-toi! **2.** *F:* **that beats everything** (*or* **the band**), c'est le comble, c'est plus fort que de jouer aux bouchons. **3.** *F:* **can you b. it!** ça alors! **4.** *F:* **it beats me,** cela me dépasse. *Voir aussi* **dummy, 5; meat, 4.**

beat off [ˈbiːtˈɔf] (**to**), *V:* se masturber*, s'en battre une.

beat-up [ˈbiːtʌp] (*adj.*), *F:* **a b.-u. old car,** une vieille voiture*, tacot *m*.

beat up [ˈbiːtˈʌp] (**to**), *F:* **1.** battre*, rosser. **2.** **to b. it u.,** mener une vie de patachon, faire les quatre cents coups.

beaut[1] [bjuːt] (*adj.*) (*Austr.*), *F:* beau*, bath.

beaut[2] [bjuːt] (*noun*) (=*beauty*). **1.** *F:* qch. de beau*; **she's a b.!** quelle belle poupée! **2.** *F:* coup bien envoyé par un boxeur. **3.** *P:* **two** (*or* **a pair of**) **beauts,** seins*, une paire de rotoplots *m.pl.*

beaver [ˈbiːvər] (*noun*). **1.** *F:* barbe*, barbouze *f*. **2.** (*U.S.*) *V:* (*d'une femme*) poils *m.pl.* du pubis, le barbu. *Voir aussi* **eager.**

bed[1] [bed] (*noun*), *F:* **1.** **b. of roses,** la vie de château; **it's not a b. of roses,** c'est pas tout miel. **2.** **you got out of** (*U.S.:* **you got up on**) **the wrong side of the b. this morning,** tu t'es levé du pied gauche ce matin. **3.** **b. and breakfast:** *voir* **bingo** (**26**). *Voir aussi* **breakfast; feather-bed.**

bed[2] [bed] (**to**), *P:* **to b. s.o.,** coïter* avec qn; **she's all right for bedding,** c'est une bonne baiseuse.

bed down [ˈbedˈdaun] (**to**), *F:* se coucher*, se bâcher.

bed-house [ˈbedhaus] (*noun*) (*mainly U.S.*), *P:* bordel*, boxon *m*.

bed-sit [ˈbedˈsit] (*noun*) (=*bed-sitter*), *F:* garni *m*, meublé *m*.

bedworthy [ˈbedwəːði] (*adj.*), *P:* belle de nuit, prix *m* de Diane.

bee [biː] (*noun*), **1.** *F:* **he thinks he's the b.'s knees,** il ne se prend pas pour de la petite bière (*cf.* **cat, 8**). **2.** *P:* **bees and honey** (*R.S.* = *money*), argent*, flouse *m*, fric *m*. **3.** *F:* **to have a b. in one's bonnet,** (*a*) être un peu fou*, avoir une araignée au plafond; (*b*) avoir une idée fixe. **4.** *P:* **to put the b. on s.o.,** taper qn (*argent*). *Voir aussi* **bird, 7; queen, 3.**

Beeb [biːb] (*noun*), *F:* **the B.** = **Auntie**[2].

beef[1] [biːf] (*noun*). **1.** *F:* **to have plenty of b.,** être fort* comme un bœuf, être costaud. **2.** *P:* réclamation *f*, rouspétance *f*. *Voir aussi* **corned beef.**

beef[2] [biːf] (**to**), *P:* grogner*, rouspéter, ronchonner.

beef-bandit [ˈbiːfbændit] (*noun*), *V:* = **arse-bandit.**

beefcake [ˈbiːfkeik] (*noun*), *F:* pin-up masculin; *cf.* **cheesecake.**

beefer [ˈbiːfər] (*noun*), *P:* rouspéteur *m*.

beef up [ˈbiːfˈʌp] (**to**), *P:* corser (qch.).

been [biːn] (*p.p.*), *P:* **he's b. and gone and done it!** il en a fait de belles! il a fait du joli! *Voir aussi* **has-been.**

beer [biər] (*noun*), *P:* **to go on the b.,** boire*, picoler.

beer-up [ˈbiərʌp] (*noun*), *P:* beuverie *f* de bière.

beer up [ˈbiərˈʌp] (**to**), *P:* boire* de la bière en grande quantité.

beetle-crushers [ˈbiːtl-krʌʃəz] (*pl. noun*), *F:* grosses chaussures*, écrase-merde *m.pl.*; *cf.* **crushers.**

beetle off [ˈbiːtlˈɔf] (**to**), *F:* partir*, déguerpir, se déhotter.

beezer[1] [ˈbiːzər] (*adj.*), *F:* = **spiffing.**

beezer[2] [ˈbiːzər] (*noun*), *P:* **1.** nez*, blair *m*. **2.** visage*; tête*, fiole *f*.

beggar [ˈbegər] (*noun*) (*euph. pour*

* An asterisk indicates that the word so marked is included as a head-word in the Appendix.

bugger), *F:* individu*; **silly b.!** espèce d'imbécile (*ou* d'abruti)!; **poor b.!** pauvre diable!

beggar-my-neighbour [ˈbegəmiˈneibər] (*noun*) (*R.S.* = *Labour* (*Exchange*)), *P:* **on the b.-m.-n.,** au chômage.

begorra! [biˈgɔrə] (*excl.*), *F:* nom d'un chien!

behind [biˈhaind, bəˈhaind] (*noun*), *F:* fesses*; postérieur *m*; **to sit on one's b. (and do nothing),** ne pas se manier le cul; **he does nothing but sit on his b.,** il ne bouge pas d'une semelle.

be-in [ˈbiː(j)in] (*noun*), *F:* réunion *f* d'individus pour participer à des activités spontanées.

bejesus![1] [biˈdʒiːzəs, biˈdʒeizəs] (*excl.*), *F:* = **begorra!**

bejesus[2] [biˈdʒiːzəs, biˈdʒeizəs] (*noun*), *P:* **to knock the b. out of s.o.,** battre* qn comme plâtre, envoyer dormir qn.

belch [beltʃ] (**to**), *P:* avouer*, dégorger.

bell [bel] (*noun*), *F:* **1. it rings a b.,** ça me dit quelque chose. **2. pull the other one** (=*leg*), **it's got bells on,** *c.p.*, à d'autres! cela ne prend pas! *Voir aussi* **dumb-bell.**

bell-bottoms [ˈbelbɔtəmz] (*pl. noun*) (=*bell-bottomed trousers*), *F:* pantalon* à pattes d'éléphant.

bell-hop [ˈbelhɔp] (*noun*) (*U.S.*), *F:* garçon *m* d'hôtel.

bell-rope [ˈbelroup] (*noun*), *V:* pénis*, berdouillette *f*.

belly [ˈbeli] (*noun*), *F:* ventre*, panse *f*, bedaine *f*; **my b. thinks** (*or* **is beginning to think**) **my throat's cut,** j'ai faim*, j'ai l'estomac dans les talons. *Voir aussi* **yellow-belly.**

belly-ache[1] [ˈbeli-eik] (*noun*), *F:* mal *m* au ventre.

belly-ache[2] [ˈbeli-eik] (**to**), *P:* grogner*, réclamer, ronchonner, rouspéter; **he's always belly-aching,** il râle toujours.

belly-acher [ˈbeli-eikər] (*noun*), *P:* râleur *m*.

belly-aching [ˈbeli-eikiŋ] (*noun*), *P:* rouspétance *f*.

belly-button [ˈbelibʌtn] (*noun*), *F:* nombril *m*, bouton *m* du milieu.

belly-flop [ˈbeliflɔp] (*noun*), *F:* **to do a b.-f.,** (*natation*) faire un plat (ventre).

bellyful [ˈbeliful] (*noun*), *P:* **to have (had) a b.,** (*a*) en avoir une gavée, en être gavé, en avoir tout son soûl; (*b*) en avoir assez*, en avoir marre, en avoir ras le bol; *cf.* **gutful.**

belly-laugh[1] [ˈbelilɑːf] (*noun*), *F:* rigolade *f*, marrade *f*; **it's a b.-l.,** c'est très amusant*, c'est bidonnant (*ou* boyautant).

belly-laugh[2] [ˈbelilɑːf] (**to**), *F:* se tordre de rire*, se bidonner, se boyauter.

belly-wash [ˈbeliwɔʃ] (*noun*), *F:* bibine *f*, vinasse *f*.

belt[1] [belt] (*noun*). **1.** *P:* **to give s.o. a b.,** battre* qn, donner (*ou* filer) une raclée à qn. **2.** *F:* **to hit s.o. below the b.,** donner un coup bas à qn. **3.** *F:* **to tighten one's b.,** se serrer la ceinture, se l'accrocher. **4.** *F:* **to have sth. under one's b.,** (*a*) avoir mangé*, avoir qch. dans le fusil; (*b*) avoir une réussite à son acquis. **5.** *P:* coït*, baisage *m*. **6.** *P:* bang *m* aux anges. **7.** *P:* **(endless) b.,** fille* *ou* femme* de mœurs faciles. **8.** *P:* **to have a b. at sth.,** s'attaquer à qch., tenter l'aventure. *Voir aussi* **bracket.**

belt[2] [belt] (**to**). **1.** *P:* attaquer*, violenter (qn), sauter dessus. **2.** *P:* battre*, filer une rossée à (qn). **3.** *P:* coïter* avec (qn), bourrer, bourriquer. **4.** *V:* **to b. one's batter,** se masturber*, se taper sur la colonne. **5.** (*U.S.*) *P:* **to b. the grape,** boire* abondamment, picoler, siroter.

belt around [ˈbeltəˈraund] (**to**), *P:* **1.** voyager, circuler. **2.** faire bombance.

belting [ˈbeltiŋ] (*noun*), *P:* **1.** volée *f* de coups*, raclée *f*, dérouillée *f*. **2.** défaite écrasante.

belt off [ˈbeltˈɔf] (**to**), *P:* s'enfuir*, se carapater, se tirer.

belt out [ˈbeltˈaut] (**to**), *P:* **1.** gueuler, brailler, beugler (une chanson). **2. to b. o. a tune** = **to bash out a tune.**

belt up [ˈbeltˈʌp] (**to**), *P:* se taire*, la boucler.

bend[1] [bend] (*noun*), *P:* **1.** (*a*) **to go round the b.,** devenir fou*, perdre la boule, déménager, piquer le coup de bambou; (*b*) **that kid drives me round the b.,** ce gosse me rend fou*; **I'm driven round the b. by her incessant chatter,** son bavardage incessant me fait perdre la boule. **2. to go on a b.** = **to go on a bender (bender, 1).**

bend[2] [bend] (**to**), *F:* **1. to b. the rules,**

* L'astérisque indique que le mot marqué de ce signe figure comme entrée dans le Répertoire.

faire un passe-droit. 2. **to b. over backwards to please s.o.,** se mettre en quatre pour qn. 3. **to catch s.o. bending,** surprendre qn en mauvaise posture. 4. **to b. to it,** faire qch. contre son gré, rechigner. *Voir aussi* **bent**[1]; **elbow,** 6.

bender [ˈbendər] (*noun*), *P:* 1. **to go on a b.,** faire la noce (*ou* la bringue); *cf.* **hell-bender.** 2. **to be on one's benders** (=*bended knees*), (*a*) être très fatigué*, être sur les genoux *m.pl.* (*ou* sur les rotules *f.pl.*); (*b*) être dans le pétrin, être foutu. 3. pédéraste*, emmanché *m. Voir aussi* **mind-bender.**

bennie, benny [ˈbeni] (*noun*), *P:* (*a*) Benzédrine *f* (*marque déposée*) (*drogues**), bennie *f*; (*b*) cachet *m* de Benzédrine.

bent[1] [bent] (*adj.*), *P:* 1. pauvre*, fauché. 2. **a b. copper,** un flic véreux. 3. (*U.S.*) **b.** (**out of shape**), déraisonnable, dérangé. 4. drogué*, camé. 5. homosexuel.

bent[2] [bent] (*noun*), *P:* pédéraste*, travesti *m.*

benz [benz] (*noun*) (*abbr.* = *Benzedrine*), Benzédrine *f* (*marque déposée*) (*drogues**); *cf.* **bennie.**

berk [bəːk] (*noun*), *P:* individu bête*, gourde *f*, tourte *f*, cornichon *m.*

bernice [ˈbəːnis] (*noun*), **bernies** [ˈbəːniz] (*pl. noun*), *P:* cocaïne *f* (*drogues**), topette *f.*

berth [bəːθ] (*noun*). 1. *F:* **to give s.o. a wide b.,** passer au large de qn. 2. *P:* **soft** (*or* **safe**) **b.,** emploi *m* pépère, planque *f*, filon *m.*

bet [bet] (**to**), *F:* 1. **you b.!** pour sûr! tu parles! (il) y a des chances! 2. **I b. you don't!** chiche (que tu ne le feras pas)! 3. **b. you I will!** chiche (que je le fais)! 4. **I'll b. you anything you like,** j'en mettrais ma tête à couper (*ou* ma main au feu). 5. **you can b. your boots** (*or* **your bottom dollar**), tu peux y aller; **I'll b. my boots** (*or* **my bottom dollar**) **that...,** je mettrais ma tête à couper que..., je vous parie la lune que ..., je te fous mon billet que..., chiche que... 6. **I b.!** je t'en fiche mon billet! 7. **want to b.?** tu t'alignes? *Voir aussi* **sweet**[1], 2.

better [ˈbetər] (*adj.*), *F:* **b. half,** épouse*, moitié *f.*

betty [ˈbeti] (*noun*), *P:* passe-partout *m*, crochet *m*, rossignol *m.*

betwixt [biˈtwikst] (*adv.*), *F:* **b. and between,** ni chèvre ni chou; mi-figue, mi-raisin.

bevvy [ˈbevi] (*noun*), *P:* un pot, un verre (de bière, vin, *etc.*); **we had a b. in the bar,** on a été boire un coup (*ou* siffler un verre) au bistrot.

b. f., B. F. [ˈbiːˈef] (*abbr.*), *F: euph. pour* **bloody fool** (*voir* **bloody**[1]).

B.-girl [ˈbiːgəːl] (*noun*), *P:* = **bar-girl.**

bhang [bæŋ] (*noun*), *P:* **baby b., b. ganjah,** marijuana *f* (*drogues**).

bi [bai] (*adj.*) (=*bisexual*), *P:* = **ambidextrous.**

bib [bib] (*noun*), *F:* **best b. and tucker,** beaux vêtements*; **in one's best b. and tucker,** sur son trente et un, tiré à quatre épingles.

bible-basher [ˈbaiblbæʃər], **bible-puncher** [ˈbaibl-pʌntʃər] (*noun*), *F:* évangéliste *m* de carrefour, prêcheur agressif.

biddy [ˈbidi] (*noun*), *F:* 1. jeune fille*, femme*. 2. servante *f*, femme de chambre, cambreline *f*, bonniche *f*. 3. **an old b.,** une vieille poule, une chipie. 4. **red b.,** vin* rouge de mauvaise qualité, gros *m* rouge, décapant *m*, casse-pattes *m*. 5. (*U.S.*) poule *f* (*oiseau*). 6. (*Austr.*) institutrice *f*, maîtresse *f* (d'école).

biff[1] [bif] (*noun*), *F:* coup*, gnon *m*, beigne *f.*

biff[2] [bif] (**to**), *F:* **to b. s.o.,** battre* qn, flanquer un gnon à qn; **to b. s.o. on the nose,** abîmer le portrait à qn, encadrer qn.

big[1] [big] (*adj.*), *F:* 1. **b. noise** (*or* **bug** *or* **cheese** *or* **gun** *or* **pot** *or* **shot**), grosse légume, grossium *m*, gros bonnet, ponte *m*. 2. **b. pot,** (*a*) = **big noise** (**big**[1], 1); (*b*) = **pot**[1], 2 (*a*). 3. **he has b. ideas,** il voit grand. 4. **he earns b. money,** il gagne gros. 5. **what's the b. idea?** à quoi ça rime? 6. **the b. time,** le haut de l'échelle; **to be in the b. time,** être en haut de l'échelle, être parmi les huiles, tenir le haut du pavé. 7. **to give s.o. a b. hand,** applaudir qn à tour de bras (*ou* à tout rompre). 8. **b. mouth,** vantard*, gueulard *m*, grande gueule. 9. **b. stiff,** (*a*) gros bêta; (*b*) individu prétentieux*, gros plein de

* An asterisk indicates that the word so marked is included as a head-word in the Appendix.

soupe. 10. **B. Brother,** le grand Frère. 11. **b. man,** le cerveau, la grosse tête. 12. **Mr B.,** le grand manitou, le gros bonnet. 13. **b. talk,** grande gueule. 14. **b. top,** (*a*) grande tente d'un cirque; (*b*) (vie *f* de) cirque *m*. 15. (*U.S.*) **B. House,** prison*, grande marmite. *Voir aussi* **bloke,** 3; **chief,** 1; **stick**[1], 2; **way**[2], 2.

big[2] [big] (*adv.*), *F:* 1. **to talk b.,** faire l'important, battre la grosse caisse. 2. **to come** (*or* **go**) **over b.,** boumer, réussir. 3. **to hit it b.,** mettre du foin dans ses bottes, attraper le haut de l'échelle.

big-bellied [ˈbigˈbelid], **big-gutted** [ˈbigˈgʌtid] (*adj.*), *P:* ventru, pansu, gros du bide.

biggie, biggy [ˈbigi] (*noun*), *F:* = **bigwig.**

big-head [ˈbighed] (*noun*), *P:* 1. bouffi *m*, enflé *m*. 2. gros plein de soupe.

big-headed [ˈbigˈhedid] (*adj.*), *P:* prétentieux*, vaniteux, suffisant.

big-note[1] [ˈbigˈnout] (*attrib. adj.*) (*Austr.*), *F:* **b.-n. man,** richard *m*, rupin *m*.

big-note[2] [ˈbigˈnout] (**to**) (*Austr.*), *F:* louanger, porter (qn) aux nues, empommader.

big-time [ˈbigˈtaim] (*adj.*), *F:* 1. **b.-t. operator,** gros trafiquant. 2. **b.-t. racketeer,** chef *m* de bande, caïd *m*; *cf.* **small-time.** *Voir aussi* **big**[1], **6.**

big-timer [ˈbɪgˈtaimər] (*noun*), *F:* 1. = **big noise** (**big**[1], 1); **to be a b.-t.,** être sur la lancée; *cf.* **small-timer.** 2. joueur (pour de l'argent) professionnel.

bigwig [ˈbigwig] (*noun*), *F:* personnage important, gros bonnet, grosse légume.

bike [baik] (*noun*). 1. *F:* bicyclette *f*, vélo *m*; *cf.* **push-bike.** 2. *F:* motocyclette *f*, moto *f*, pétrolette *f*. 3. (*Austr.*) *P:* cavaleuse *f*, Marie-couche-toi-là *f*.

bilge [bildʒ], (*noun*) *P:* 1. bêtise*, foutaise *f*, eau *f* de bidet, sornette *f*. 2. **to talk b.,** dire des bêtises*, sortir des foutaises. 3. boisson *f* insipide, pipi *m* de chien (*ou* de chat *ou* de singe), pissat *m* d'âne.

bilge-water [ˈbildʒwɔːtər] (*noun*), *P:* = **bilge, 3.**

bill [bil] (*noun*). 1. *F:* (*a*) **top of the b.,** tête *f* d'affiche; (*b*) **to top the b., to be top of the b.,** être en vedette; (*c*) **it tops the b.,** c'est le comble. 2. *F:* **to draw up a stiff b.,** saler la note. 3. *F:* **to stick it on the b.,** laisser monter l'addition; **stick it on the b.!** collez ça sur la note! 4. *F:* **to fit** (*or* **fill**) **the b.,** remplir toutes les conditions, faire l'affaire. 5. *P:* nez*, pif *m*, blair *m*. *Voir aussi* **foot**[2] **(to), 2.**

billet [ˈbilit] (*noun*), *F:* **to get a safe b.,** s'embusquer.

Billingsgate [ˈbiliŋzgeit] (*pr. noun – marché aux poissons de Londres*), *P:* 1. langage *m* de poissarde. 2. **B. pheasant,** gendarme*, sauret *m*.

billio [ˈbiliou] (*noun*), *F:* = **billy-ho.**

Billjim, billjim [ˈbildʒim] (*noun*), *F:* Australien *m*.

billy [ˈbili] (*noun*). 1. *P:* mouchoir*, blave *m*. 2. (*Austr.*) *F:* (*a*) (=*billy-can*) gamelle *f*, bouilloire *f* (à thé); (*b*) eau*, flotte *f*.

billy-ho [ˈbilihou] (*noun*), *F:* **to go like b.-h.,** (*a*) aller vite*, foncer à tout berzingue; (*b*) gazer à bloc.

bim [bim] (*noun*), *P:* agent* de police, flic *m*.

bin [bin] (*noun*), *P:* = **loony-bin.**

bind [baind] (*noun*), *F:* 1. (*d'une personne*) crampon *m*, casse-pieds *m*. 2. (*d'une chose*) scie *f*; **it's an awful b.,** quelle corvée! 3. **to be in a bit of a b.,** être dans le pétrin.

binder [ˈbaindər] (*noun*), *F:* 1. coup *m* de l'étrier. 2. = **bind, 1, 2.** *Voir aussi* **highbinder; spellbinder.**

bindle [ˈbindl] (*noun*) (*U.S.*), *P:* 1. baluchon *m*. 2. cornet *m* de stups. 3. **b. stiff,** (*a*) clochard*, clodo(t) *m*; (*b*) drogué*, camé *m*, toxico *m*.

bing [biŋ] (*noun*), *P:* 1. = **bindle, 2.** 2. piquouse *f*. 3. **b. room,** trou *m* à came. 4. (*U.S.*) cachot *m* (de prison), mitard *m*.

binge [bindʒ] (*noun*), *F:* réjouissances*, bombe *f*, ribouldingue *f*; **to go on the b.,** faire la ribouldingue; **to be on the b.,** faire une virée.

bingo [ˈbiŋgou] (*noun*), sorte de loto public. *Les termes suivants sont employés dans ce jeu:* **Kelly's eye** *or* **Little Jimmy** *or* **Willie's whatsit** = **1; buckle my shoe** *or* **dirty old Jew** *or* **Little Boy Blue** *or* **one little duck** = **2; dearie me!** = **3; knock at the door** = **4; Jack's alive** = **5; Tom Mix** = **6; lucky seven**

* L'astérisque indique que le mot marqué de ce signe figure comme entrée dans le Répertoire.

= 7; one fat lady = 8; doctor's orders = 9; Downing Street = 10; legs eleven = 11; one doz. = 12; unlucky for some = 13; she's lovely *or* **never been kissed = 16; the age to catch 'em = 17; key of the door** *or* **my age? = 21; all the twos** *or* **dinky-doo** *or* **two little ducks** *or* **toodle-oo = 22; bed and breakfast** *or* **half-a-crown = 26; you 're doing fine = 29; all the threes** *or* **feathers = 33; dirty whore = 34; all the steps = 39; life begins = 40; life's begun = 41; all the fours** *or* **droopy-drawers** *or* **open the door = 44; half-way = 45; bulls-eye** *or* **bung-hole = 50; all the varieties** *or* **Heinz = 57; Brighton line = 59; old-age pension = 65; clickety-click = 66; any way round = 69; was she worth it? = 76; crutches** *or* **sunset strip** *or* **walking-sticks = 77; two fat ladies = 88; all but one** *or* **nearly there** *or* **spot below = 89; top of the shop** *or* **as far as we go = 90; bingo!** jeu! gagné!

bint [bint] (*noun*), *P:* 1. femme*, gonzesse *f*. 2. petite amie, poule *f*.

bird [bəːd] (*noun*). 1. *F:* individu*, type *m*, oiseau *m*, moineau *m*; **who's that old b.?** qu'est-ce que c'est que ce vieux type? 2. *F:* (*a*) fille*, gamine *f*; (*b*) petite amie, poule *f*, souris *f*; (*c*) pépée *f*. 3. *F:* **to get the b.**, se faire siffler. 4. *F:* **to give s.o. the b.**, (*a*) envoyer promener qn, envoyer qn au bain (*ou* sur les roses); (*b*) (*th.*) huer qn, siffler qn. 5. *P:* **to do b.**, faire de la prison*, faire du trou (*ou* de la taule); **first b.**, première fois en prison*. 6. *F:* **it's (strictly) for the birds,** c'est seulement pour les cruches, c'est de la roupie de sansonnet. 7. *F:* **the birds and the bees,** éléments sexuels de base, l'histoire *f* du chou. 8. *P:* **red birds = reds (red**[2], **5).** *Voir aussi* **dicky-bird; dolly-bird; early; feather**[1], **1; gallows-bird; home-bird; jail-bird; jay-bird; lovebird; night-bird; snowbird; whirly-bird; yardbird.**

bird-brain [ˈbəːdbrein] (*noun*), *F:* 1. individu bête*, crâne *m* de piaf. 2. = **scatterbrain.**

bird-brained [ˈbəːdbreind] (*adj.*), *F:* 1. bête*. 2. = **scatterbrained.**

bird-cage [ˈbəːdkeidʒ] (*noun*), *P:* 1. cellule *f* de prison*, cellote *f*. 2. dortoir *m* dans un asile de nuit.

bird-fancier [ˈbəːdfænsiər] (*noun*), *P:* juponnard *m*, coureur *m* de filles, dragueur *m* de mines.

birdie [ˈbəːdi] (*adj.*), *P:* fou*, dingue, givré.

birdie-powder [ˈbəːdi-paudər] (*noun*), *P:* mélange *m* d'héroïne et de morphine (*drogues**).

bird-lime [ˈbəːdlaim] (*noun*) (*R.S.* = *time*), *P:* 1. **how's the b.-l.?** quelle heure est-il? 2. = **bird, 5.**

birdlimed [ˈbəːdlaimd] (*adj.* & *p.p.*) (*Austr.*), *P:* condamné pour le crime d'un autre, gerbé sans fleurs.

bird's-eye [ˈbəːdzai] (*noun*), *P:* 1. dix grammes de drogue. 2. chiffe *f* de came.

bird-watcher [ˈbəːdwɔtʃər] (*noun*), *P:* = **bird-fancier.**

bird-wood [ˈbəːdwud] (*noun*), *P:* cigarettes* de marijuana (*drogues**).

birk [bəːk] (*noun*), *P:* = **berk.**

birthday [ˈbəːθdei] (*noun*), *F:* 1. **to be in one's b. suit** (*U.S.:* **clothes**), être nu*, être à poil, être en Jésus. 2. (*sports*) **to have a b.**, avoir un bon match, avoir un jour de fête.

biscuit [ˈbiskit] (*noun*), *F:* **to take the b.**, avoir le pompon; **you take the b.**, à toi le pompon.

biscus [ˈbiskəs] (*noun*) (*Austr.*), *P:* **in the b.**, dans le pétrin, dans de mauvais draps.

bish[1] [biʃ] (*noun*), *F:* bévue*, bourde *f*, gaffe *f*.

bish[2] [biʃ] (**to**), *F:* gaffer, faire une bourde.

bishop [ˈbiʃəp] (*noun*), *V:* **to flog** (*or* **bash**) **the b.**, se masturber*, se secouer le bonhomme. *Voir aussi* **actress.**

bit[1] [bit] (*adj.*), *F:* (*th.*) **a b. part,** un rôle secondaire, une panne; **a b. player,** un figurant.

bit[2] [bit] (*noun*). 1. *P:* **a nice b. of stuff** (*or* **crackling** *or* **fluff** *or* **skirt**), un beau petit lot, un prix de Diane. 2. *F:* **a b. much,** (*a*) un peu cher*; (*b*) un peu exagéré, dépassant la dose; **it was all a b. of a laugh really,** c'était plutôt une rigolade; **he's a b. of a liar,** il est menteur sur les bords. 3. (*U.S.*) *F:* **two bits,** pièce *f* de 25 cents; *voir aussi* **two-bit.** 4. (*U.S.*) *P:* condamnation* à la prison, purge *f*. 5. *F:* **to do a b. of fishing,** taquiner le goujon (*ou* l'ablette *f*); **a b. of news,** une nouvelle. 6. *P:* activité *f*,

* An asterisk indicates that the word so marked is included as a head-word in the Appendix.

ligne *f* de conduite. 7. *F:* **to be thrilled to bits,** être ravi (*ou* rayonnant); exulter. *Voir aussi* **side,** 1, 2; **spare**[2]; **stray; threepenny-bits; trey-bits.**

bitch[1] [bitʃ] (*noun*), *P:* 1. femme* (*péj.*), salope *f*, ordure *f*, chameau *m*, chipie *f*. 2. pédéraste* cancanier. 3. plainte *f*, rouspétance *f*. 4. tâche *f ou* chose *f* désagréable, saloperie *f*. 5. **to be (as) drunk as a fiddler's bitch,** être saoul comme une bourrique. *Voir aussi* **s.o.b.,** 2; **son-of-a-bitch.**

bitch[2] [bitʃ] (**to**), *P:* 1. grogner*, rouspéter, bougonner, râler. 2. tromper*, entuber, rouler (qn); **to b. s.o. out of sth.,** roustir qn à propos de qch. 3. = **bitch up (to).**

bitchiness [ˈbitʃinis] (*noun*), *P:* méchanceté *f*, saloperie *f*, coup *m* en vache.

bitch up [ˈbitʃˈʌp] (**to**), *P:* saboter, bousiller (qch.).

bitchy [ˈbitʃi] (*adj.*), *P:* moche, rosse, vache.

bite[1] [bait] (*noun*). 1. *P:* **to put the b. on s.o.,** (*a*) emprunter* à qn; (*b*) faire chanter qn. 2. *F:* **to have a b. to eat,** manger* un morceau, casser la croûte. *Voir aussi* **cherry,** 2; **fleabite.**

bite[2] [bait] (**to**). 1. *F:* (*fig.*) se faire avoir, mordre à l'hameçon. 2. *F:* **I've been badly bitten** (*fig.*), (*a*) j'ai été roulé; (*b*) on m'a mis dedans. 3. *F:* **what's biting you?** quelle mouche te pique? qu'est-ce qui te prend? 4. *P:* **to b. s.o. for money,** taper qn. *Voir aussi* **dust**[1], 4.

bite off [ˈbaitˈɔf] (**to**), *F:* 1. **to b. s.o.'s head o.,** injurier* qn, rembarrer qn. 2. **to b.o. more than one can chew,** avoir les yeux plus grands que le ventre.

bitsy-witsy [ˈbitsiˈwitsi] (*noun*), *F:* **a b.-w.,** un peu*, un chouia.

bitter-ender [ˈbitərˈendər] (*noun*), *F:* jusqu'auboutiste *mf*; *cf.* **end,** 3.

bitty [ˈbiti] (*adj.*), *F:* (livre, pièce, *etc.*) décousu, hétéroclite, de bric et de broc.

bivvy [ˈbivi] (*noun*), *P:* 1. bière *f*; *cf.* **bevvy.** 2. **to have a b.,** tailler une bavette, faire un brin de causette.

biz [biz] (*noun*), *P:* **the b.** (=*the business*), le bis(e)ness, le truc. *Voir aussi* **show-biz.**

blab (off) [ˈblæb(ˈɔf)] (**to**), *P:* 1. révéler un secret, lâcher le morceau. 2. bavarder*, jacter, papoter.

black[1] [blæk] (*adj.*). 1. *F:* **a b. mark,** un mauvais point. 2. **b. spot,** (*a*) *F:* endroit dangereux; (*b*) *P:* fumerie *f* d'opium. 3. *P:* **b. stuff,** opium *m* (*drogues**), noir *m*. 4. *P:* **b. and white,** amphétamine *f* (*drogues**), durophet *m*, bonbon *m*; *voir aussi* **bomber** (*a*); **minstrel.** 5. **b. and tan,** (*a*) *F:* panaché *m* de bière brune et blonde; (*b*) *P:* amphétamine *f* (*drogues**), rouquine *f*; (*c*) *F:* **B. and Tans,** milice chargée de l'ordre en Irlande (*c.* 1920). 6. *F:* **B. Maria,** car* de police, panier *m* à salade, poulailler ambulant. 7. *F:* **b. diamonds,** (*a*) charbon *m*; (*b*) truffes *f.pl.* *Voir aussi* **book**[1], 2; **dog**[1], 19; **velvet,** 2.

black[2] [blæk] (*noun*). 1. *F:* nègre*, bougnoul *m*. 2. *F:* **to put up a b.,** faire une gaffe. 3. *P:* chantage *m*; **to put the b. on s.o.,** faire du chantage. 4. *F:* **in the b.,** à l'actif *m* de qn. 5. *F:* **in b. and white,** en noir et blanc.

black[3] [blæk] (**to**), *F:* = **blacklist (to).**

blackbirding [ˈblækbəːdiŋ] (*noun*), *P:* trafic *m* d'esclaves noirs.

blackbirds [ˈblækbəːdz] (*pl. noun*), *P:* esclaves noirs.

blackie [ˈblæki] (*noun*), *P:* = **black**[2], 3.

blackleg[1] [ˈblækleg] (*noun*), *F:* briseur *m* de grèves, renard *m*, jaune *m*, traître *m*.

blackleg[2] [ˈblækleg] (**to**), *F:* faire le briseur de grèves.

blacklist [ˈblæklist] (**to**), *F:* mettre sur la liste noire.

black-out [ˈblækaut] (*noun*), *F:* 1. évanouissement *m*. 2. (*a*) panne *f* d'électricité; (*b*) camouflage *m* des lumières.

black out [ˈblækˈaut] (**to**), *F:* 1. s'évanouir*, tomber dans le cirage. 2. être en panne d'électricité, se trouver dans le noir.

blag [blæg] (**to**), *P:* voler*, chiper, chaparder.

blah(-blah) [ˈblɑː(ˈblɑː)] (*noun*), *F:* bla-bla(-bla) *m*, baratin *m*.

blank [blæŋk] (*noun*), *F:* **to draw a b.,** faire chou blanc.

blankety(-blank) [ˈblæŋkiti(ˈblæŋk)] (*adj. & noun*), *F:* *euph. pour* **damn(ed), bloody,** *etc.*

blank out [ˈblæŋkˈaut] (**to**), *F:* = **black out (to),** 1.

* L'astérisque indique que le mot marqué de ce signe figure comme entrée dans le Répertoire.

blarney[1] [ˈblɑːni] (*noun*), *F:* flatterie *f*, cajolerie *f*, boniment *m*.

blarney[2] [ˈblɑːni] (**to**). **1.** *F:* flatter*, cajoler, bonimenter. **2.** (*U.S.*) *P:* crocheter une serrure.

blast[1] [blɑːst] (*noun*), *P:* **1.** réjouissances*, boum *f*. **2.** = **bang**[3], **7. 3.** longue bouffée de cigarette* de marijuana. **4.** effet puissant d'une drogue, flash *m*. **5.** attaque verbale, engueulade *f*, déblatérage *m*; **to put the b. on s.o.,** critiquer* qn, dénigrer, débiner qn.

blast[2] [blɑːst] (**to**), *P:* **1.** (*sports*) battre à plate(s) couture(s). **2.** avoir des injections de drogues, se piquouser; **to b. a joint** (*or* **a stick**), fumer la marijuana, tirer sur un stick. **3. b. (it)!** zut!; **b. you!** va au diable!; **damn and b.!** bordel de Dieu!

blasted [ˈblɑːstid] (*adj.*), *P:* **1.** = **damned. 2.** drogué*, chargé, envapé.

blasting [ˈblɑːstiŋ] (*noun*), *P:* **to give s.o. a b.,** réprimander* qn, passer une bonne engueulade à qn.

blast off [ˈblɑːstˈɔf] (**to**), *P:* **1.** s'enfuir*, décamper, mettre les bouts. **2. to b.o. at s.o.,** donner le bal à qn.

blather[1] [ˈblæðər] (*noun*), *F:* bêtises*, fadaises *f.pl.*

blather[2] [ˈblæðər] (**to**), *F:* dire des bêtises*, dire des inepties *f.pl.*

blazes [ˈbleiziz] (*pl. noun*), *F:* **1. go to b.!** allez au diable! va te coucher! **2. what the b....,** que diable... **3. to run like b.,** courir très vite*, comme si on avait le feu au derrière.

bleat [bliːt] (**to**), *P:* gémir, geindre, ronchonner.

bleeder [ˈbliːdər] (*noun*), *P:* **1. poor b.!** pauvre bougre! **2. wait till I catch the little b.!** le petit morveux ne perd rien pour attendre!

bleeding [ˈbliːdiŋ, ˈbliːdn] (*adj.*), *P:* = **bloody**[1, 2].

bleep out [ˈbliːpˈaut] (**to**), *F:* **to b. sth. o.,** laisser échapper une bourde.

blessed [ˈblesid] (*adj.*), *F:* **what a b. nuisance!** quel fichu contretemps!; **that b. boy!** ce sacré gamin!; **the whole b. day,** toute la sainte journée.

blest [blest] (*p.p.*), *F:* **well I'm b.!** par exemple!; **I'm** (*or* **I'll be**) **b. if I know,** que le diable m'emporte si je le sais.

blether [ˈbleðər] (*noun & verb*) (*Scottish*), *F:* = **blather**[1, 2].

blew [bluː] (**to**), *P:* = **blue**[3] (**to**).

blighter [ˈblaitər] (*noun*), *F:* individu*, type *m*, zèbre *m*; **poor b.!** pauvre hère! pauvre diable!; **you lucky b.!** veinard!; **you b.!** espèce de fripouille!

Blighty [ˈblaiti] (*noun*) (*mil.*), *F:* l'Angleterre *f*, retour *m* au foyer.

blimey! [ˈblaimi] (*excl.*), *P:* zut alors!; *cf.* **cor!** (*b*); **gorblimey!**

blimp [blimp] (*noun*) (*aussi:* **Colonel Blimp**), *F:* vieille culotte de peau.

blind[1] [blaind] (*adj.*). **1.** *F:* **b. date,** rendez-vous* (*ou* rancart *m*) fantôme (*ou* à l'aveuglette). **2.** *P:* = **blinders.** *Voir aussi* **eye, 13.**

blind[2] [blaind] (*noun*). **1.** *F:* couverture*, couverte *f*, couvrante *f*. **2.** *P:* = **blinder,2. 3.** *P:* **to put the blinds on s.o.,** mettre un bandeau sur les yeux de qn.

blind[3] [blaind] (**to**), *P:* **1.** jurer, sacrer. **2.** conduire avec insouciance; **b. and brake driver,** chauffard *m*.

blinder [ˈblaindər] (*noun*), *P:* **1.** jeu époustouflant. **2.** réjouissances*, bamboche *f*.

blinders [ˈblaindəz] (*adj.*), *P:* (**Harry**) **b.,** complètement ivre*, rétamé, blindé.

blink [bliŋk] (*noun*), *F:* **on the b.,** qui ne marche pas, qui foire (*ou* débloque), qui fait des siennes.

blinkers [ˈbliŋkəz] (*pl. noun*), *F:* yeux *m.pl.* (*œil**), quinquets *m.pl.*

blinking [ˈbliŋkiŋ] (*adj.*), *F:* *euph. pour* **bloody**[1, 2].

blister [ˈblistər] (*noun*), *P:* **1.** sommation *f*, faf(f)iot *m* à promont. **2.** prostituée*, pute *f*. *Voir aussi* **skin**[1], **11.**

blithering [ˈbliðəriŋ] (*adj.*), *F:* **b. idiot,** bougre *m* d'idiot, connard *m*.

blob [blɔb] (*noun*), *F:* zéro *m*; **to score a b.,** ne pas marquer de points.

block [blɔk] (*noun*), *P:* **1.** tête*, caboche *f*; **to knock s.o.'s b. off,** battre* qn, rentrer dans le chou (*ou* dans le lard) à qn. **2. to do one's b.,** se mettre en colère*, se mettre en rogne. **3.** (*a*) cornet *m* de morphine; (*b*) boulette *f* de hachisch (*drogues**). **4. to put the blocks on,** serrer la vis. **5. to put the b. on sth.,** mettre un frein à qch. *Voir aussi* **chip**[1], **6.**

blockbuster [ˈblɔkbʌstər] (*noun*), *P:* **1.** bombe très puissante, marmite *f*. **2.** coup *m* de poing très puissant, direct

* An asterisk indicates that the word so marked is included as a head-word in the Appendix.

m. 3. réussite *f* fantastique, coup *m* de Trafalgar.

blocked [blɔkt] (*adj.*), *P:* drogué*, chargé.

bloke [blouk] (*noun*), 1. *F:* individu*; **a good b.**, un brave type, un bon zigue. 2. *F:* **the B.**, (*Marine*) le Patron. 3. *P:* **big b.**, cocaïne *f* (*drogues**).

blood [blʌd] (*noun*). 1. *F:* **to be after s.o.'s b.**, vouloir la peau de qn. 2. *F:* **to get s.o.'s b. up**, mettre qn en colère*, faire fulminer qn. 3. *F:* **to have one's b. up**, être en colère*, voir rouge. 4. *F:* **to make s.o.'s b. run cold**, glacer le sang à qn. 5. *F:* **it makes my b. boil**, ça me fait voir rouge. 6. **to sweat b.**, suer sang et eau, travailler* dur, bûcher, turbiner. 7. *P:* = **soul-brother.** *Voir aussi* **Nelson.**

bloody[1] [ˈblʌdi] (*adj.*), *P:* sacré, satané, fichu, foutu; **you b. fool!** bougre *m* d'idiot! bon sang d'imbécile!; **to play the b. fool**, faire le con; **stop that b. row!** assez de chahut!; **they're all the b. same**, c'est du pareil au même; **the b. limit**, la fin des haricots. *Voir aussi* **Mary**, 4.

bloody[2] [ˈblʌdi] (*adv.*), *P:* vachement, bougrement; **How do you feel? – B!** Comment ça va? – Vachement mal!; **not b. likely!** pas de danger! non mais chez qui!; **it's b. hot!** qu'est-ce qu'il fait chaud!

bloody-minded [ˈblʌdimaindid] (*adj.*), *P:* pas commode; **a b.-m. fellow**, un mauvais coucheur.

bloody-mindedness [ˈblʌdiˈmaindidnis] (*noun*), *P:* sale caractère *m*, caractère de cochon, disposition *f* peu commode.

bloomer [ˈbluːmər] (*noun*), *F:* bévue*, gaffe *f*, bourde *f*.

blooming [ˈbluːmiŋ, ˈbləmin] (*adj. & adv.*), *F:* *euph. pour* **bloody**[1, 2].

blot out [ˈblɔtˈaut] (**to**), *P:* tuer*, effacer, dézinguer (qn).

blotto [ˈblɔtou] (*adj.*), *F:* complètement ivre*, rétamé, noir.

blow [blou] (**to**). 1. *F:* *euph. pour* **blast**[2] (**to**), 3; **b. the expense!** je me moque de la dépense!; **b. me!** zut alors!; **well I'm blowed!** j'en bave! j'en reste comme deux ronds de flan!; *cf.* **blest.** 2. *F:* **generous be blowed, he's as mean as they come,** généreux? mon œil! il est radin comme tout. 3. *P:* = **buzz off (to).** 4. *P:* (s)chnouffer, prendre une reniflette; **to b. hay** (*or* **a stick**), fumer de la marijuana, tirer sur un stick. 5. *F:* **to b. one's own trumpet** (*U.S.:* **horn**), se vanter, se faire mousser, s'envoyer des fleurs. 6. *P:* (*a*) dénoncer*, balanstiquer (qn); (*b*) révéler un secret, éventer la mèche. 7. *P:* exposer publiquement un scandale, lâcher les grandes orgues. 8. *V:* faire un coït* buccal à (qn), sucer, pomper. 9. *P:* bousiller, saboter, louper; **we should have won but we blew it,** on aurait dû gagner mais on a tout loupé; **to b. a chance,** louper l'occasion. 10. *P:* = **blue**[3] (**to**). 11. *P:* se masturber*, se faire mousser. 12. *P:* **to b. down s.o.'s ear,** donner un tuyau à qn. 13. *P:* **blown pack,** paquet *m* de cigarettes vide. 14. *F:* **to b. hot and cold,** souffler le chaud et le froid, n'être ni chair ni poisson. 15. *P:* **to b. one's mind,** (*a*) = **to blow one's top** (**top**[1], 2); *cf.* **cool**[3], **2; fuse; gasket;** (*b*) être profondément ému; **b. your mind!** branche-toi!; (*c*) s'effondrer sous l'émotion. *Voir aussi* **gaff, 3; lid, 2; stack, 2; tank, 1.**

blowens [ˈblouənz] (*noun*), *P:* = **bobtail.**

blower [ˈblouər] (*noun*), *P:* téléphone*, ronfleur *m*, tube *m*; **to get on the b. to s.o.,** passer un coup de fil à qn. *Voir aussi* **mind-blower.**

blow in [ˈblouˈin] (**to**), *P:* 1. = **blue**[3] (**to**), 1, 2. 2. arriver* en coup de vent, s'amener à l'improviste.

blow-job [ˈblouˈdʒɔb] (*noun*), *V:* coït* buccal, taillage *m* de plume.

blow off [ˈblouˈɔf] (**to**), *P:* 1. péter*, cloquer. 2. **to b. one's mouth o.,** parler* trop, dégoiser, dévider. *Voir aussi* **steam, 1.**

blow-out [ˈblou-aut] (*noun*), *F:* 1. gueuleton *m*, ripaille *f*; **to have a good b.-o.,** manger* abondamment, se taper la cloche, s'en mettre plein le fusil. 2. éclatement *m* de pneu. 3. (*électricité*) **there's been a b.-o.,** les plombs *m.pl.* ont sauté.

blow out [ˈblouˈaut] (**to**), *P:* rejeter, envoyer paître (qn).

blow over [ˈblouˈouvər] (**to**), *F:* se passer, se dissiper.

blow-through [ˈblouθruː] (*noun*), *V:*

* L'astérisque indique que le mot marqué de ce signe figure comme entrée dans le Répertoire.

to have a b.-t., coïter*, foutre un coup de brosse.

blow-up ['blou-ʌp] (*noun*), *F:* **1.** (accès *m* de) colère*. **2.** agrandissement *m* de photo.

blow up ['blou'ʌp] (**to**), *F:* **1.** se mettre en colère*, exploser. **2.** réprimander*, sonner les cloches à (qn). **3.** agrandir (une photographie), faire un agrandissement. **4.** survenir, arriver.

blub [blʌb] (**to**), *F:* pleurer*, chialer, pleurnicher.

blubberhead ['blʌbəhed] (*noun*), *F:* individu bête*, baluchard *m*, gourde *f*.

bludge[1] [blʌdʒ] (*noun*) (*Austr.*), *P:* **to have a b.**, (*a*) se reposer, tirer sa flemme; (*b*) travailler lentement, flânocher.

bludge[2] [blʌdʒ] (**to**) (*Austr.*), *P:* flâner, fainéanter, traîner, battre l'asphalte, flemmarder.

bludger ['blʌdʒər] (*noun*) (*Austr.*), *P:* **1.** fainéant *m*, flemmard *m*, batteur *m* de pavé. **2.** souteneur*, mangeur *m* de brioche. **3.** agent* de police, cogne *m*, flic *m*.

blue[1] [blu:] (*adj.*). **1.** *F:* (*a*) sale*, osé, cochon; (*b*) **b. film** (*or* **movie**), film bleu. **2.** *F:* **to scream** (*or* **yell**) **b. murder,** crier* (*ou* gueuler) au charron. **3.** *F:* **once in a b. moon,** la semaine des quatre jeudis; tous les 36 du mois. **4.** *F:* mélancolique, triste, cafardeux; *cf.* **devil**[1], **23**. **5.** *P:* **b. ruin,** alcool*, tord-boyaux *m*. **6.** *F:* **true b.,** (*en politique*) Conservateur, de la droite. *Voir aussi* **funk**[1], **1**; **velvet, 1**.

blue[2] [blu:] (*noun*). **1.** *P:* (*drogues*) la bleue; **double b.,** mélange *m* d'amphétamine et de barbiturique; **French b.,** cachet *m* d'amphétamine et de barbiturique; (*pl.*) bleues *f.pl.*; préparation artisanale d'amphétamines; **heavenly blues,** graines *f.pl.* de volubilis (employées comme drogues); *cf.* **pearly gates. 2.** *F:* **to turn up out of the b.,** arriver* à l'improviste, venir comme un cheveu sur la soupe. **3.** *F:* **to have the blues,** avoir le cafard, broyer du noir. **4.** *P:* = **bluebottle. 5.** (*pl.*) *F:* chant *m* populaire négro-américain; **country blues,** forme primitive du *blues*, blues rural. **6.** (*Austr.*) *P:* une perte, qch. de paumé.

blue[3] [blu:] (**to**), *P:* **1. to b. one's money,** dépenser*, bouffer son argent. **2. he blued his lot,** il a tout paumé, il a mangé la ferme.

blue-arsed ['blu:'ɑ:st] (*adj.*), *P:* **to rush around like a b.-a. fly,** se manier le popotin.

bluebottle ['blu:bɔtl] (*noun*), *P:* agent* de police, flic *m*, poulet *m*.

blue-eyed ['blu:aid] (*adj.*), *F:* innocent, candide; **to be s.o.'s b.-e. boy,** être le chouchou (*ou* le favori) de qn.

bluenose ['blu:-nouz], **bluenoser** ['blu:-nouzər] (*noun*), *F:* **1.** (*U.S.*) habitant *m* de l'est des États-Unis. **2.** (*Canada*) habitant *m* de la Nouvelle-Écosse.

bluey ['blu:i] (*noun*), *P:* = **French blue** (**blue**[2], **1**).

b.o., B.O. ['bi:'ou] (*abbr.* = *body odour*), *F:* odeur corporelle.

bo [bou] (*noun*) (*U.S.*), *F:* **1.** clochard*, chemineau *m*, clodot *m*. **2.** jeune garçon, gosse *m*. **3.** homme*, camarade *m*, Jules.

boat [bout] (*noun*). **1.** *F:* **to push the b. out,** (*a*) payer* une tournée; (*b*) partir* en virée. **2.** *F:* **to miss the b.,** passer à côté, manquer le coche. **3.** *F:* **to be in the same b.,** être sur le même bateau, être logé(s) à la même enseigne, être du même convoi. **4.** (*pl.*) *F:* grandes chaussures*, bateaux *m.pl.* **5.** *P:* (*R.S.* = *boat-race* = *face*) visage*. **6.** *P:* **the** (**little**) **man in the b.,** clitoris*, bouton *m* (de rose), clicli *m*. *Voir aussi* **dream-boat; gravy, 1; pig-boat; rock**[2] (**to**), **2**.

bob[1] [bɔb] (*noun*), *F:* cinq pence; **ten b.,** cinquante pence. *Voir aussi* **fly-bob.**

Bob[2] [bɔb] (*pr. noun*), *P:* **B.'s your uncle** (**and Fanny's your aunt**), ça y est, ça roule, c'est dans le sac.

bobbish ['bɔbiʃ] (*adj.*), *F:* en forme.

bobby ['bɔbi] (*noun*), *F:* agent* de police, flic *m*.

bobby-dazzler ['bɔbi-dæzlər] (*noun*), *F:* **1.** qch. de voyant (*ou* de clinquant *ou* de tapageur). **2.** fille* tape-à-l'œil.

bobbysock ['bɔbisɔk] (*noun*), *F:* socquette *f*.

bobbysoxer ['bɔbisɔksər] (*noun*), *F:* fille* dans le vent, fille à l'âge ingrat.

bo-bo ['boubou] (*noun*), *P:* marijuana *f* (*drogues**), kif *m*; *cf.* **bush, 3**.

bobtail ['bɔbteil] (*noun*), *P:* femme* atteinte de maladie vénérienne (*malade**), nazicotée *f*, plombée *f*, pourrie *f*.

* An asterisk indicates that the word so marked is included as a head-word in the Appendix.

bob up [ˈbɔbˈʌp] (**to**), *F:* apparaître, émerger, surgir.

bod [bɔd] (*noun*), *F:* individu*; **an odd b.**, un drôle de type; **a few odd bods,** quatre pelés et un tondu.

bodge[1] **(-up)** [ˈbɔdʒ(ʌp)] (*noun*), *F:* gâchis *m*, cafouillage *m*.

bodge[2] **(up)** [ˈbɔdʒ(ˈʌp)] (**to**), *F:* gâcher, cafouiller.

bodgie [ˈbɔdʒi] (*noun*) (*Austr.*), *P:* jeune voyou *m*.

bodywork [ˈbɔdiwəːk] (*noun*), *P:* = **shelf-kit.**

boffin [ˈbɔfin] (*noun*), *F:* scientifique *m* qui fait de la recherche.

bog [bɔg] (*noun*), *P:* **1.** W.C.*, goguenots *m.pl.*, chiottes *f.pl.* **2. to make a b. of sth.**, cafouiller qch., gâcher qch.; **what an awful b.!** quelle belle gaffe!

bogey, bogie [ˈbougi] (*noun*), *P:* **1.** policier* en civil, perdreau *m*. **2.** agent* de police, poulet *m*.

bogue [boug] (*adj.*), *P:* (*a*) en manque de drogues; (*b*) souffrant du sevrage de drogues.

bog-up [ˈbɔgʌp] (*noun*), *P:* = **bog, 2.**

bog up [ˈbɔgˈʌp] (**to**), *P:* = **bodge**[2] **(up) (to).**

bogy [ˈbougi] (*noun*), *P:* = **bogey, 1, 2.**

bohunk [ˈbouhʌŋk] (*noun*) (*U.S.*), *P:* **1.** immigrant *m* d'Europe centrale. **2.** individu bête* et gauche, empoté *m*, patate *f*.

boil[1] [bɔil] (*noun*), *F:* **to go off the b.**, perdre son enthousiasme, se dégonfler.

boil[2] [bɔil] (**to**), *P:* **go (and) b. your head!** va te faire voir! *Voir aussi* **blood, 5.**

boiled [bɔild] (*adj.*), *P:* ivre*, rétamé. *Voir aussi* **hard-boiled; shirt, 5.**

boiler [ˈbɔilər] (*noun*). **1.** *P:* vieille femme* (*péj.*), vieille poule, rombière *f*. **2.** *F:* poule *f* au pot. *Voir aussi* **pot-boiler.**

boiling [ˈbɔiliŋ] (*noun*), *P:* **the whole b.,** (*a*) toute la bande*; (*b*) tout le bazar, toute la ribambelle, tout le tremblement; *cf.* **caboodle; shebang, 1; shoot**[1], **1; shooting-match.**

boilout [ˈbɔilaut] (*noun*), *P:* déchargeage *m* (cure de toxicomane).

boing! [bɔiŋ] (*excl.*), *F:* boum (badaboum)! pan! vlan!

boko [ˈboukou] (*noun*), *P:* grand nez*, tarin *m*.

bollock [ˈbɔlək] (*noun & verb*), *V:* = **ballock**[1,2].

bollocking [ˈbɔləkiŋ] (*noun*), *V:* = **ballocking.**

bolon(e)y [bəˈlouni] (*noun*), *F:* = **balon(e)y.**

bolshie, bolshy[1] [ˈbɔlʃi] (*adj.*), *F:* **1.** bolcho, communo, communard. **2.** = **bloody-minded.**

bolshie, bolshy[2] [ˈbɔlʃi] (*noun*), *F:* = **commie**[2].

bomb [bɔm] (*noun*). **1.** *F:* **to cost a b.,** coûter cher*, coûter les yeux de la tête. **2.** *F:* **to make a b.,** gagner* beaucoup d'argent, faire du fric, tomber sur un champ d'oseille. **3.** *F:* **to go like a b.,** ronfler, gazer, boumer. **4.** (*U.S.*) *P:* échec*, fiasco *m*, four *m*. **5.** (*Austr.*) *F:* vieille voiture*, guimbarde *f*. *Voir aussi* **sex-bomb; stink-bomb.**

bombed (out) [ˈbɔmd(ˈaut)] (*adj.*), *P:* = **stoned** (*b*).

bomber [ˈbɔmər] (*noun*), *P:* (*a*) **black b.,** bonbon *m* (*drogues*); **brown b.** = **black and tan** (*b*) (*voir* **black**[1], **5**); (*b*) cigarette* de marijuana (*drogues**), reefer *m*.

bombita [bɔmˈbiːtə], **bombito** [bɔmˈbiːtou] (*noun*), *P:* amphétamine *f* pour injection (*drogues**).

bombshell [ˈbɔmʃel] (*noun*), *F:* **1. a blonde b.,** une blonde, un coup de foudre. **2. the news was a b.,** la nouvelle tomba comme une bombe.

bonaroo [ˈbɔnəˈruː] (*adj.*) (*U.S.*), *P:* excellent*, foutral, du tonnerre, bolide.

bonce [bɔns] (*noun*), *P:* tête*, caboche *f*; **bacon b.,** une andouille.

bone[1] [boun] (*noun*). **1.** *F:* **to make no bones about sth.,** ne pas y aller par quatre chemins. **2.** *F:* **to pick a b. with s.o.,** chercher querelle* à qn, chercher noise (*ou* des noises) à qn; **to have a b. to pick with s.o.,** avoir maille à partir avec qn. **3.** *F:* **to have a b. in one's leg,** avoir la cosse. **4.** *V:* **to have a b.,** être en érection*, bander. **5.** (*pl.*) *F:* dés*; **to roll the bones,** pousser les bobs *m.pl.* **6.** *P:* **pick the bones out of that!** va en tirer quelque chose! extirpe ce que tu peux! *Voir aussi* **dry, 1; marrow-bones; sawbones.**

bone[2] (boun] (**to**), *P:* **1.** voler*, chiper. **2.** (*U.S.*) ennuyer*, barber, canuler

* L'astérisque indique que le mot marqué de ce signe figure comme entrée dans le Répertoire.

(qn). 3. **to b. (up on) a subject,** piocher (*ou* potasser *ou* bûcher) un sujet. 4. interroger (un suspect), cuisiner.

bonehead ['bounhed] (*noun*), *F:* ignorant *m*, tête *f* de bois, bûche *f*.

bone-on ['bounɔn] (*noun*), *V:* = **hard-on;** *cf.* **bone**[1], 4.

bone-orchard ['boun-ɔːtʃəd], **bone-park** ['bounpɑːk] (*noun*), *P:* cimetière* parc *m* des cronis *m.pl.*

boner ['bounər] (*noun*). 1. *F:* bévue*, bourde *f*, gaffe *f*. 2. *V:* = **bone**[1], 4.

bone-rattler ['bounrætlər], **bone-shaker** ['bounʃeikər] (*noun*), *F:* vieille voiture*, tape-cul *m*.

bone-yard ['bounjɑːd] (*noun*), *P:* = **bone-orchard.**

bonk[1] [bɔŋk] (*noun*), *F:* coup*, gnon *m*.

bonk[2] [bɔŋk] (**to**), *F:* **to b. s.o. on the head,** donner un coup* (*ou* un gnon) sur le crâne de qn, assommer qn.

bonkers ['bɔŋkəz] (*adj.*), *P:* **stark raving** (*or* **staring**) **b., Harry b.,** fou* à lier, archifou.

bonzer ['bɔnzər] (*adj.*) (*Austr.*), *F:* excellent*, sensas(s), super.

boo [buː] (*noun*), *P:* marijuana *f* (*drogues**), kif *m*.

boob[1] [buːb] (*noun*). 1. *F:* (*a*) individu bête*, ballot *m*; (*b*) individu crédule, gogo *m*, nave *m*, gobe-mouches *m*. 2. *F:* bévue*, gaffe *f*, boulette *f*. 3. (*pl.*) *P:* = **boobies (booby, 2).**

boob[2] [buːb] (**to**), *F:* faire une bévue* (*ou* une gaffe *ou* une boulette).

booboo ['buːbuː] (*noun*). 1. *F:* = **boob**[1], 2. 2.(*pl.*) *P:* testicules*, clopinettes *f.pl.*

booby ['buːbi] (*noun*). 1. *F:* = **boob**[1], 1. 2. (*pl.*) *P:* seins*, doudounes *f.pl.*

booby-hatch ['buːbihætʃ] (*noun*), *P:* maison *f* de fous, cabanon *m*.

boodle ['buːdl] (*noun*), *P:* butin*, fade *m*, taf(fe) *m*.

boodler ['buːdlər] (*noun*) (*Austr.*), *P:* homme (politique) qui se pousse, arriviste *m*.

boofhead ['buːfhed] (*noun*) (*Austr.*), *F:* individu bête*.

boogie ['buːgi] (*noun*) (*U.S.*) (*pej.*), *P:* nègre*, bougnoul(l)e *m*.

book[1] [buk] (*noun*), *F:* 1. **to throw the b. at s.o.,** donner la peine maximum à qn, saper qn au maxi; **he got the b. thrown at him,** il a attrapé le maxi. 2. **to be in s.o.'s good books,** être dans les petits papiers de qn; **to be in s.o.'s bad** (*or* **black**) **books,** ne pas être en odeur de sainteté auprès de qn. 3. **it suits my b.,** ça me va, ça me botte. 4. **to make a b.,** organiser un sweepstake, *etc.* *Voir aussi* **cook**[2] **(to), 2; turn-up, 1.**

book[2] [buk] (**to**), *F:* 1. **to b. s.o.,** (*a*) farguer qn; (*b*) mettre un P.V. (procès-verbal) à qn. 2. **to get booked,** (*a*) se faire farguer; (*b*) coller un biscuit; (*c*) (*sports*) recevoir un avertissement.

bookie ['buki] (*noun*), *F:* book *m*.

book in ['buk'in] (**to**), *F:* s'inscrire à l'arrivée.

book out ['buk'aut] (**to**), *F:* s'inscrire au départ.

booky ['buki] (*noun*), *F:* = **bookie.**

boong [buŋ] (*noun*) (*Austr.*), *F:* aborigène *mf*.

boost [buːst] (**to**), *P:* voler* à l'étalage (*ou* à la détourne).

booster ['buːstər] (*noun*), *P:* 1. fourgue *m*. 2. voleur* à l'étalage (*ou* à la détourne), voleur* des grands magasins. 3. **b. (pill),** cachet *m* d'amphétamine (*drogues**), survolteur *m*.

boot [buːt] (*noun*). 1. *P:* **to give s.o. the (order of the) b.,** congédier* qn, mettre (*ou* flanquer) qn à la porte; **to get the b.,** être congédié*, se faire sa(c)quer. 2. *P:* **an old b.,** femme* (*péj.*), une vieille bique. 3. *P:* bang *m*. 4. *P:* **to put the b. in,** donner (*ou* filer *ou* flanquer) un coup de pied vicieux; *cf.* **boot-boy.** 5. *P:* **a boots and shoes,** un défoncé. 6. *F:* **to be too big for one's boots,** péter plus haut que son derrière. 7. *P:* **to splash one's boots,** uriner*, lancequiner. 8. *P:* **a new set of boots,** quatre pneus de voiture neufs. 9. *F:* **like old boots,** avec vigueur *f*, d'attaque. 10. *F:* **to lick s.o.'s boots,** lécher les bottes *f.pl.* (*ou* les pieds *m.pl.* *ou* les genoux *m.pl.*) de qn; *cf.* **boot-licker.** *Voir aussi* **bet (to), 5; bovver-boots; slyboots.**

boot-boy ['buːtbɔi] (*noun*), *P:* jeune gouape *f* qui se bat à coups de chaussures.

bootleg ['buːtleg] (**to**), *F:* faire la contrebande de l'alcool *ou* des boissons alcooliques.

bootlegger ['buːtlegər] (*noun*), *F:* contrebandier *m* de boissons alcooliques.

* An asterisk indicates that the word so marked is included as a head-word in the Appendix.

bootlicker [ˈbuːtlikər] (*noun*), *F:* lèche-bottes *m*, lèche-cul *m*.
boot out [ˈbuːtˈaut] (**to**), *P:* se débarrasser* de (qn), sacquer, vider, virer (qn).
booze[1] [buːz] (*noun*), *P:* alcool*, cric *m*; **to be on the** (*or* **to hit the**) **b.**, boire* beaucoup, picoler, bit(t)urer.
booze[2] [buːz] (**to**), *P:* = **to be on the booze.**
boozed (up) [ˈbuːzd(ˈʌp)] (*adj.*), *P:* ivre*, saoul.
boozer [ˈbuːzər] (*noun*), *P:* **1.** ivrogne*, poivrot *m*. **2.** café*, bistrot *m*, troquet *m*.
booze-up [ˈbuːzʌp] (*noun*), *P:* bringue *f*, bamboche *f*, bordée *f*.
boozing [ˈbuːziŋ] (*noun*), *P:* ivresse*, soûlerie *f*, bit(t)ure *f*.
boozy [ˈbuːzi] (*adj.*), *P:* ivrogne, soûlard, riboteur; **a b. evening,** un soir de nouba (*ou* de cuite).
bo-peep [ˈbouˈpiːp] (*noun*) (*R.S.* = *sleep*), *P:* dodo *m*.
boracic[1]]bəˈræsik, ˈbræsik] (*adj.*) (*R.S.* = *boracic lint* = *skint*): *voir* **skint.**
boracic[2] [bəˈræsik, ˈbræsik] (*noun*), *P:* = **ackamaraka.**
born [bɔːn] (*p.p.* & *adj.*), *F:* **1. never in all my b. days,** au grand jamais. **2. I wasn't b. yesterday,** je ne suis pas né d'hier, je ne suis pas tombé de la dernière pluie, je ne suis pas de la dernière couvée. *Voir aussi* **one, 7.**
borrow [ˈbɔrou] (**to**), *F:* **to live on borrowed time,** vivre sur le rabiot.
bosh [bɔʃ] (*noun*), *F:* bêtises*, boniments *m.pl.*, sornettes *f.pl.*
boss[1] [bɔs] (*adj.*) (*U.S.*), *P:* = **groovy.**
boss[2] [bɔs] (*noun*), *F:* patron*, singe *m*, boss *m*.
boss[3] [bɔs] (**to**), *P:* **1.** mener, diriger; **to b. the show** (*or* **the outfit**), contrôler, conduire, être le manitou de l'affaire, tenir la barre, faire marcher la machine, faire la pluie et le beau temps. **2.** vouloir tout diriger, faire preuve d'autorité. **3.** bâcler, saboter, louper.
boss about [ˈbɔsəˈbaut] (**to**), **boss around** [ˈbɔsəˈraund] (**to**), *F:* **to b. s.o. a.,** mener qn par le bout du nez, faire marcher qn.
boss-eyed [ˈbɔsaid] (*adj.*), *P:* qui louche,* qui boite des calots.
boss-man [ˈbɔsmæn] (*noun*), *F:* = **boss**[2].
bossy [ˈbɔsi] (*adj.*), *P:* autor(itaire); **he's (too) b.,** c'est un Monsieur Jordonne.
bossy-boots [ˈbɔsi-buːts] (*noun*), *F:* individu* autoritaire, grand manitou.
bot [bɔt] (*noun*), *F:* = **bottom**[2], **1.**
bottle[1] [ˈbɔtl] (*noun*), *P:* **1. to hit** (*or* **be on**) **the b.,** caresser la bouteille, pomper à la bouteille. **2. black b.** = **knockout drops** (*voir* **knockout**[1], **1**). *Voir aussi* **bluebottle; milk-bottles; titty-bottle.**
bottle[2] [ˈbɔtl] (**to**), *P:* taper (qn) à coups de bouteille.
bottled [ˈbɔtld] (*adj.*), *P:* ivre*, plein comme une bourrique.
bottle-holder [ˈbɔtlhouldər] (*noun*), *P:* assistant *m* d'un boxeur.
bottle-nose [ˈbɔtlnouz] (*noun*), *P:* nez* rouge, betterave *f*, pif communard.
bottler [ˈbɔtlər] (*noun*), *P:* = **palm-tree;** *cf.* **square-wheeler.**
bottle-washer [ˈbɔtlwɔʃər] (*noun*): *voir* **cook**[1], **2.**
bottom[1] [ˈbɔtəm] (*adj.*), *F:* **to bet one's b. dollar,** risquer le paquet; *voir aussi* **bet (to), 5.**
bottom[2] [ˈbɔtəm] (*noun*), *F:* **1.** fesses*, derrière *m*, dédé *m*. **2. bottoms up!** videz vos verres! cul sec! à la pomponnette! *Voir aussi* **bell-bottoms; heap, 2** (*b*); **rock**[1], **4; scrape**[2] **(to), 1.**
botty [ˈbɔti] (*noun*), *F:* **1.** = **bottom**[2], **1. 2.** biberon *m*. *Voir aussi* **smack-botty.**
bounce [bauns] (**to**). **1.** *P:* congédier*, flanquer (qn) à la porte (du cabaret, *etc.*), vider. **2.** *F:* **to b. a cheque,** renvoyer un chèque sans provision (chèque en bois).
bouncer [ˈbaunsər] (*noun*), *P:* **1.** videur *m*. **2.** chèque *m* en bois. **3.** (*pl.*) seins*, globes *m.pl.*, rotoplots *m.pl.*
bovver-boots [ˈbɔvəˈbuːts] (*pl. noun*), *P:* chaussures* des **boot-boys.**
bovver-boy [ˈbɔvəbɔi], **bovvie** [ˈbɔvi] (*noun*), *P:* = **boot-boy.**
bowler-hat[1] [ˈbouləˈhæt] (*noun*), *F:* **to give s.o. his b.-h.** = **to bowler-hat s.o.**
bowler-hat[2] [ˈbouləˈhæt] (**to**), *F:* renvoyer (qn) à la vie civile, limoger (qn).
bowl over [ˈboulˈouvər] (**to**), *F:* **1.** épater, sidérer. **2.** chambouler.
bowser [ˈbauzər] (*noun*) (*Austr.*), *F:* poste *m* d'essence.
bow-sow [ˈbausau] (*noun*), *P:* drogues*, stups *m.pl.*
bow-window [ˈbouˈwindou] (*noun*), *F:*

* L'astérisque indique que le mot marqué de ce signe figure comme entrée dans le Répertoire.

ventre* protubérant, bedaine *f*, brioche *f*.

box[1] [bɔks] (*noun*). 1. *V:* vagin*, boîte *f* à ouvrage; **to go down for a b. lunch,** faire un coït* buccal. 2. *F:* poste *m* de télé; **what's on the b.?** qu'est-ce qu'il y a à la télé?; *cf.* **goggle-box; idiot-box.** 3. *F:* barre *f* (de témoins). 4. *F:* (*football*) zone *f* de pénalisation. 5. *P:* cercueil*, boîte *f* à dominos; **to go home in a b.,** mourir*, partir les pieds en avant. 6. *P:* coffre-fort *m*, coffiot *m*. 7. *P:* **to make a b. of** = **box up (to).** *Voir aussi* **brain-box; domino-box; jack-in-the-box; saucebox; soapbox; squeezebox; think-box.**

box[2] [bɔks] (**to**), *F:* **to b. clever,** faire le malin, bien manœuvrer.

boxed [bɔkst] (*adj.*), *P:* 1. (*a*) ivre*, rétamé à l'alcool; (*b*) drogué*, camé. 2. emprisonné*, bloqué, bouclé, coffré.

box up [ˈbɔksˈʌp] (**to**), *F:* bousiller, gâcher, saboter, louper.

boy![1] [bɔi] (*excl.*), *F:* 1. **oh b.! b. oh b.!** chouette alors! 2. **b., did she tear me off a strip!** mes enfants! qu'est-ce qu'elle m'a passé!

boy[2] [bɔi] (*noun*), *F:* **hello, old b.!** salut, vieille branche (*ou* vieux pote)! *Voir aussi* **backroom; barrow, 2; boot-boy; bovver-boy; bum-boy; corner-boy; doughboy; glamour-boy; jay-boy; J-boy; jewboy; job, 15; K-boy; lover-boy; old-boy; playboy; sandboy; wide, 1.**

boyo [ˈbɔijou] (*noun*), *P:* fiston *m*, mon gars.

bra [brɑː] (*noun*) (*abbr.* = *brassière*), *F:* soutien(-gorge) *m*, soutien-loloches *m*.

bracelets [ˈbreislits] (*pl. noun*), *F:* menottes*, bracelets *m.pl.*, cadènes *f.pl.*

bracer [ˈbreisər] (*noun*), *F:* coup *m* de fouet; **to have an early-morning b.,** tuer le ver.

bracket [ˈbrækit] (*noun*), *P:* **to give s.o. a belt up the b.,** abîmer le portrait à qn. *Voir aussi* **upper**[1]**, 2.**

braille [breil] (*noun*), *P:* **a (bit of) b.,** renseignement*, rancard *m*, tuyau *m*.

brain[1] [brein] (*noun*), *F:* 1. individu de grande intelligence, grosse tête. 2. **to be the brains of the outfit,** être le ressort de la machine. 3. **to have s.o., sth., on the b.,** être obsédé par qn, qch., l'avoir sur le ciboulot. *Voir aussi* **bird-brain; featherbrain; lame-brain; scatter-brain.**

brain[2] [brein] (**to**), *F:* battre*, rosser, assommer, bourrer de coups*.

brain-box [ˈbreinbɔks] (*noun*), *F:* crâne *m*; **to have a b.-b.,** en avoir dans le ciboulot.

brain-drain [ˈbreinˈdrein] (*noun*), *F:* fuite *f* (*ou* exode *m*) des cerveaux, émigration *f* des savants.

brain-storming [ˈbreinstɔːmiŋ] (*noun*), *F:* remue-méninges *m*.

brainy [ˈbreini] (*adj.*), *F:* intelligent, calé, débrouillard.

brass[1] [brɑːs] (*attrib. adj.*), *F:* **b. tacks,** faits *m.pl.*, réalités essentielles; **to get down to b. tacks,** se concentrer sur l'essentiel, s'en tenir aux faits. *Voir aussi* **balls, 8.**

brass[2] [brɑːs] (*noun*), 1. *P:* argent*, pépettes *f.pl.*, pognon *m*. 2. *P:* toupet *m*, culot *m*. 3. *F:* **top b.,** (*mil.*) les galonnards *m.pl.* 4. *P:* prostituée*, roulure *f*, tapin *f*; *cf.* **half-brass.**

brassed off [ˈbrɑːstˈɔf] (*adj.*), *P:* de mauvaise humeur, de mauvais poil.

brass-hat [ˈbrɑːsˈhæt] (*noun*) (*mil.*), *F:* galonné *m*, galonnard *m*.

brass up [ˈbrɑːsˈʌp] (**to**), *P:* payer*, abouler, casquer.

brassy [ˈbrɑːsi] (*adj.*), *P:* effronté, culotté.

bread [bred] (*noun*). 1. *P:* (*a*) argent*, galette *f*, blé *m*; (*b*) salaire *m*, gages *m.pl.* 2. *P:* **to be on the b. line,** claquer du bec, danser devant le buffet. 3. *F:* **that's his b. and butter,** c'est son gagne-pain, c'est avec ça qu'il gagne sa croûte.

bread-and-butter [ˈbredən(d)ˈbʌtər] (*attrib. adj.*), *F:* 1. **b.-a.-b. issues,** (*politique*) le prix du bifteck. 2. **b.-a.-b. letter,** lettre *f* de remerciement (*ou* de château). *Voir aussi* **bread, 3.**

bread-basket [ˈbredbɑːskit] (*noun*), *F:* ventre*, bedaine *f*, brioche *f*; **to get one in the b.-b.,** recevoir un coup* dans le gésier.

break[1] [breik] (*noun*), *F:* 1. **a lucky b.,** de la chance*, coup *m* de pot; *cf.* **tough**[1]**, 4.** 2. **to give s.o. a b.,** (*a*) mettre qn à l'essai, donner sa chance à qn; (*b*) tendre la perche à qn. 3. récréation *f*; **a b. for lunch,** une pause pour le déjeuner. 4. évasion *f* de prison*, décarrade *f*.

* An asterisk indicates that the word so marked is included as a head-word in the Appendix.

break[2] [breik] (**to**), *F:* **to b. even,** rentrer dans son argent* (*ou* sa galette), faire ses frais, retomber sur ses pattes. *Voir aussi* **neck**[1], **9.**

breakfast [ˈbrekfəst] (*noun*), *V:* **to have b. in bed,** faire un coït* buccal. *Voir aussi* **bingo (26); hell, 13.**

break-in [ˈbreikin] (*noun*), *F:* cambriolage *m*, cambriole *f*, casse *m*, fric-frac *m*.

break-out [ˈbreikaut] (*noun*), *F:* = **break**[1], **4.**

break up [ˈbreikˈʌp] (**to**), *F:* **1. b. it u.!** arrêtez de vous battre! arrêtez de vous disputer! **2. that's right, b. u. the happy home!**, *c.p.*, faites chauffer la colle!

breather [ˈbriːðər] (*noun*), *F:* moment *m* de répit (*ou* de repos); **to go out for a b.,** sortir prendre l'air.

breeches [ˈbritʃiz] (*pl. noun*), *F:* **1. to wear the b.,** porter la culotte. **2. to be too big for one's b.** = **to be too big for one's boots (boot, 6).** *Voir aussi* **fussy-breeches.**

breeze[1] [briːz] (*noun*), *P:* **1.** (*a*) **to get the b. up,** avoir peur*, avoir la trouille; (*b*) **to put the b. up s.o.,** faire peur* à qn, ficher la frousse à qn. **2. there was a bit of a b. when he got home,** il y a eu du grabuge (*ou* de la houle) quand il est rentré. **3. it was a b.,** c'était facile, c'était l'enfance de l'art. *Voir aussi* **shoot**[2] **(to), 7.**

breeze[2] [briːz] (**to**), *P:* = **breeze off (to).**

breeze in [ˈbriːzˈin] (**to**), *F:* **1.** entrer en coup de vent. **2.** gagner (une course) dans un fauteuil.

breeze off [ˈbriːzˈɔf] (**to**), *F:* partir*, se barrer, se débiner.

breezy [ˈbriːzi] (*adj.*), *F:* **(all) bright and b.,** plein d'entrain (*ou* d'attaque).

brekker [ˈbrekər] (*noun*), *F:* (*langage enfantin*) petit déjeuner.

brick [brik] (*noun*), *F:* **1. he's been a (real) b.,** c'est le meilleur des potes. **2. to drop a b.,** faire une bévue*, lâcher le pavé dans la mare. *Voir aussi* **come down (to), 3; drop**[2] **(to), 1; goldbrick**[1]**; wall, 5, 6, 7.**

bride [braid] (*noun*), *P:* **1.** fille*, gamine *f*, môme *f*. **2.** la petite amie, la nénette.

bridge [bridʒ] (*noun*) (*Austr.*), *P:* boniment *m* plausible, bonne excuse.

bridgewater [ˈbridʒwɔːtər] (*noun*) (*Austr.*), *P:* objet truqué, article falsifié.

Brighton line [ˈbraitnˈlain], *F:* *voir* **bingo (59).**

bring-down [ˈbriŋdaun] (*noun*), *P:* qn *ou* qch. qui a un effet déprimant, rabat-joie *m*.

bring down [ˈbriŋˈdaun] (**to**), *P:* déprimer, attrister, rendre cafardeux; **he looked really brought down,** il avait l'air d'avoir un cafard noir. *Voir aussi* **brought down; house, 3.**

bring up [ˈbriŋˈʌp] (**to**), *P:* = **back up (to), 2.**

brinkmanship [ˈbriŋkmənʃip] (*noun*), *F:* la politique du bord de l'abîme.

briny [ˈbraini] (*noun*), *F:* **the b.,** l'océan *m*, la Grande Tasse, la Grande Baille.

bristlers [ˈbrisləz] (*pl. noun*), *P:* seins*, rondins *m.pl.*, nénés *m.pl.*

Bristol-fashion [ˈbristəl-fæʃən] (*adv.*), *F:* **(ship-shape and) B.-f.,** parfait en tout, nec plus ultra, parfaitement comme il faut.

Bristols, bristols [ˈbristəlz] (*pl. noun*) (*R.S.* = *Bristol City's* = *titties*), *P:* **(pair of) b.,** seins*, nichons *m.pl.*; *cf.* **fit**[2]**, 4; tale, 3; threepenny-bits; trey-bits.**

broad [brɔːd] (*noun*), *P:* **1.** (*U.S.*) (*a*) fille*, femme*, gonzesse *f*; (*b*) prostituée*, grue *f*. **2.** (*pl.*) cartes* à jouer; **to fake the broads,** truquer les cartes, maquiller les brèmes.

broadsman [ˈbrɔːdzmən] (*pl.* **broadsmen**) (*noun*), *P:* tricheur* aux cartes, empalmeur *m*, biseauteur *m*.

brodie, brody [ˈbroudi] (*noun*) (*U.S.*), *P:* **1.** échec*, four *m*, fiasco *m*; balourdise *f*, gaffe *f*. **2. to throw** (*or* **do**) **a b.,** tomber en digue-digue.

broke [brouk] (*adj.*), *F:* **1. to be b.** (*or* **stony b.** *or* **dead b.** *or* **flat b.**), être pauvre*, être sans un (sou); **to be b. to the wide,** être fauché (comme les blés). **2. to go for b.,** risquer tout, risquer le paquet.

broker [ˈbroukər] (*noun*), *P:* trafiquant *m*, fourgue *m*.

brolly [ˈbrɔli] (*noun*), *F:* **1.** parapluie*, pépin *m*, riflard *m*. **2.** parachute *m*, pépin *m*.

bronco [ˈbrɔŋkou] (*noun*) (*U.S.*), *F:* cheval non dressé.

bronco-buster [ˈbrɔŋkou-bʌstər] (*noun*) (*U.S.*), *F:* cowboy qui dresse les chevaux.

* L'astérisque indique que le mot marqué de ce signe figure comme entrée dans le Répertoire.

broth [brɔθ] (*noun*), *F:* **a b. of a boy,** (*irlandais*) un rude gars, un fameux gaillard.

brought down [ˈbrɔːtˈdaun] (*p.p.* & *adj.*), *P:* déprimé après le flash des drogues. *Voir aussi* **bring down (to).**

brown [braun] (*adj.*), *P:* **to be done b.,** se faire entuber, être chocolat.

brown-hatter [ˈbraunˈhætər] (*noun*), *V:* pédéraste*, tante *f*, tantouse *f*.

brown-nose [ˈbraun-nouz] (**to**), *V:* lécher le cul à (qn).

brown off [ˈbraunˈɔf] (**to**), *P:* décourager (qn); **to be browned off,** avoir le cafard, broyer du noir.

bruiser [ˈbruːzər] (*noun*), *F:* pugiliste *m*, boxeur *m*, cogneur *m*.

Brum [brʌm] (*pr. noun*), *F:* (habitant *m* de) Birmingham.

brumby [ˈbrʌmbi] (*noun*) (*Austr.*), *F:* = **bronco.**

brunch [brʌntʃ] (*noun*), *F:* petit déjeuner et déjeuner ensemble.

brush [brʌʃ] (*noun*). **1.** *P:* = **brush-off, 1. 2.** (*Austr.*) *P:* fille*, jeune femme*, mistonne *f*. **3.** *F:* moustache*, balai *m*. **4.** *V:* pubis féminin, barbu *m*. *Voir aussi* **tar² (to); tar-brush.**

brush-off [ˈbrʌʃɔf] (*noun*), *F:* **1.** rebuffade *f*, soufflet *m*; **to give s.o. the b.-o.** = **to brush s.o. off (brush off (to),** (*a*), (*b*)). **2.** coup *m* de balai.

brush off [ˈbrʌʃˈɔf] (**to**), *F:* **to b. s.o. o.,** (*a*) snob(b)er qn, faire un affront à qn; (*b*) se débarrasser* de qn, laisser choir qn, larguer qn.

bubbies [ˈbʌbiz] (*pl. noun*), *P:* seins*, nichons *m.pl.*

bubble [ˈbʌbl] (**to**), *P:* = **squeak² (to).**

bubble-and-squeak [ˈbʌblən(d)ˈskwiːk] (*noun*). **1.** *F:* mauvaise nourriture*, réchauffé *m*. **2.** *P:* (*R.S.* = *Greek*) un Grec. **3.** *P:* (*R.S.* = *beak* = *magistrate*): *voir* **beak, 1.**

bubbly [ˈbʌbli] (*noun*), *F:* (vin *m* de) champagne *m*, champ(e) *m*, roteuse *f*; *cf.* **champers.**

bubbly-jock [ˈbʌbli-dʒɔk] (*noun*), *F:* dindon *m*.

bubs [bʌbz] (*pl. noun*), *P:* = **bubbies.**

buck¹ [bʌk] (*noun*). **1.** *P:* **old b.,** (*a*) vieux birbe; (*b*) insolence *f*. **2.** (*U.S.*) *F:* dollar *m*; **fast b.,** argent* obtenu rapidement, facilement et sans scrupule, fric *m* de tripotage. **3.** *F:* **to pass the b.,** faire porter le chapeau.

buck² [bʌk] (**to**), *F:* **to b. (against),** résister (à), s'opposer (à); ruer dans les brancards.

bucked [bʌkt] (*adj.*), *F:* ragaillardi, content; enchanté, fier.

buckaroo, bucker(oo) [ˈbʌkər(ˈuː)] (*noun*) (*U.S.*), *F:* cowboy *m*.

bucket [ˈbʌkit] (*noun*), *F:* **1. to kick the b.,** mourir*, lâcher la rampe, casser sa pipe. **2. it's raining buckets,** il pleut à seaux (*ou* à torrents).

bucket down [ˈbʌkitdaun] (**to**), *F:* **it's bucketing down = it's raining buckets (bucket, 2).**

buckle [ˈbʌkl] (**to**), *P:* **1. b. my shoe:** *voir* **bingo (2). 2.** (*Austr.*) arrêter*, ceinturer, cravater.

bucko [ˈbʌkou] (*adj.*), *P:* (*a*) vantard, bravache, fanfaron; (*b*) crâneur, crosson.

buckshee¹ [ˈbʌkˈʃiː] (*adj.*), *F:* gratuit*, gratis, à l'œil.

buckshee² [ˈbʌkˈʃiː] (*noun*), *F:* **1.** rabiot *m*, rabe *m*. **2.** de la resquille, de l'affure.

buck up [ˈbʌkˈʌp] (**to**), *F:* **1.** (*a*) remonter le moral à (qn); (*b*) se ravigoter. **2.** se dépêcher*, se grouiller.

bud [bʌd] (*noun*), *F:* **1.** (*U.S.*) = **buddy, 1. 2. to nip sth. in the b.,** tuer (*ou* étouffer) qch. dans l'œuf.

buddy [ˈbʌdi] (*noun*), *F:* **1.** ami*, copain *m*, pote *m*; **they're great buddies,** ils sont comme cul et chemise. **2.** associé *m*, assoce *m*.

buddy-buddy [ˈbʌdi-bʌdi] (*adj.*), *F:* **to be b.-b.,** être amis comme cochons, s'entendre comme des larrons en foire.

buff [bʌf] (*noun*), *F:* **in the b.,** tout nu*, à poil.

buffalo [ˈbʌfəlou] (**to**) (*U.S.*), *F:* intimider, bluffer, entortiller, entourlouper (qn).

bug¹ [bʌg] (*noun*). **1.** *F:* écoute clandestine. **2.** *F:* enthousiaste *m*, mordu *m*. **3.** *F:* **a b. in the machine,** accroc *m*, pépin *m*. **4.** *P:* **b. doctor,** psychiatre *m*. **5.** *F:* obsession *f*, marotte *f*. **6.** *F:* microbe *m* *ou* bactérie *f* (*rhume, infection*). **7.** (*U.S.*) *P:* **to have a b. on,** être de mauvaise humeur, être de mauvais poil. **8.** (*U.S.*) *P:* (*a*) = **hot rod (hot, 22)**; (*b*) chauffeur *m* d'un bolide de course. **9.** *P:* **love bugs = crabs** (*voir* **crab¹, 2). 10.** *F:* **as snug as a b. in a**

* An asterisk indicates that the word so marked is included as a head-word in the Appendix.

rug, *c.p.*, tranquille comme Baptiste. *Voir aussi* **big**[1], **1; doodle-bug; fire-bug; jitterbug; litter-bug.**

bug[2] [bʌg] (**to**). **1.** *F:* installer des écoutes clandestines dans (une salle, *etc.*), sonoriser. **2.** *P:* **to b. s.o.,** ennuyer* qn, empoisonner qn. **3.** (*U.S.*) *P:* faire un examen psychologique *ou* psychiatrique à (qn).

bug-eyed [ˈbʌgaid] (*adj.*), *F:* **1. to be b.-e.,** (*a*) avoir les yeux* en boules de loto; (*b*) ouvrir les yeux* comme des portes cochères. **2. b.-e. monster,** monstre *m* atomique.

bugger[1] [ˈbʌgər] (*noun*), *V:* **1. don't play silly buggers with me!** ne te paye pas ma tête! ne fais pas l'idiot avec moi! **2. I don't give** (*or* **care**) **a b.,** je m'en fous (comme de l'an quarante). **3. that's a b.!** ça, c'est couillon! **4. you silly b.!** espèce de couillon! **5. you dirty little b.!** sale petite lope! **6. poor b.!** pauvre bougre!

bugger[2] [ˈbʌgər] (**to**), *V:* **1. b. him!** (*or* **he can go and b. himself**), qu'il aille se faire foutre. **2.** (*a*) faire échouer, faire avorter; (*b*) = **bugger up** (**to**); **it's buggered,** c'est foutu. **3. well I'm buggered!** j'en rote des ronds de chapeau! ça m'en bouche un coin!

bugger about (*or* **around**) [ˈbʌgər-əˈbaut, ˈbʌgərəˈraund] (**to**), *V:* **1.** traîner (la savate), flâner, flânocher. **2.** balocher, feignasser, se la couler (douce). **3.** avoir la main baladeuse; **to b. a. with s.o.,** peloter qn. **4. to b. s.o. a.,** faire tourner qn en bourrique.

bugger-all [ˈbʌgəˈrɔːl] (*noun*), *V:* rien*, des clous, que dalle.

buggeration![1] [ˈbʌgəˈreiʃən] (*excl.*), *V:* tonnerre de Dieu! bordel de Dieu!

buggeration[2] [ˈbʌgəˈreiʃən] (*noun*), *V:* **1.** fouterie *f.* **2.** emmerdement *m.*

buggered [ˈbʌgəd] (*adj.*), *V:* fatigué*, foutu. *Voir aussi* **bugger**[2] (**to**), **3.**

bugger off [ˈbʌgəˈrɔf] (**to**), *V:* partir*, foutre le camp.

bugger up [ˈbʌgəˈrʌp] (**to**), *V:* bousiller, saboter, cochonner, louper.

buggery [ˈbʌgəri] (*noun*), *V:* **1. can she cook? can she b.!** et quant à la cuisine? que dalle!; et pour la bouffe? mon cul! **2.** (**all**) **to b.,** complètement, jusqu'au trognon, en brise-tout. **3. like b.,** (*a*) bougrement, à corps et à cris, sadiquement; (*b*) certainement pas; comme mon cul! comme la peau!

bugging [ˈbʌgiŋ] (*noun*), *F:* installation *f* de microphones clandestins.

buggy [ˈbʌgi] (*adj.*), *P:* **1.** fou*, timbré, louftingue. **2.** névrosé, malade des nerfs, détraqué.

bug-house[1] [ˈbʌghaus] (*adj.*) (*U.S.*), *P:* = **bugs.**

bug-house[2] [ˈbʌghaus] (*noun*), *P:* asile *m* de fous, maison *f* de dingues, cabanon *m.*

bug-hunter [ˈbʌghʌntər] (*noun*), *F:* entomologiste *mf.*

bugle [ˈbjuːgl] (*noun*), *P:* nez*, pif *m*, blair *m.*

bugler [ˈbjuːglər] (*noun*) (*Austr.*), *F:* **1.** bavard*, baratineur *m*, jacasseur *m.* **2.** vantard*, fanfaron *m*, crâneur *m*, crosseur *m.*

bug out [ˈbʌgˈaut] (**to**) (*U.S.*), *P:* **1.** se dégonfler, retirer ses marrons du feu. **2.** s'enfuir*, déguerpir, foncer dans le brouillard.

bugs [bʌgz] (*adj.*) (*U.S.*), *P:* fou*, cinglé, dingo.

bug-trap [ˈbʌgtræp] (*noun*), *P:* lit*, pucier *m.*

build-up [ˈbildʌp] (*noun*), *F:* campagne *f* publicitaire, battage *m*, tam-tam *m.*

bulge [bʌldʒ] (*noun*), *F:* **the battle of the b.,** la bataille du bide, la lutte pour la ligne.

bull [bul] (*noun*), *P:* **1.** policier*, condé *m*, bourre *m*; *cf.* **fly-bull. 2.** = **bullshit**[1], **1,2. 3. b. and cow** (*R.S.* = *row*) querelle*. *Voir aussi* **rag**[1], **4; shoot**[2] (**to**), **7.**

bulldagger [ˈbul-dægər] (*noun*), *P:* = **bull-dyke.**

bulldoze [ˈbuldouz] (**to**), *F:* brutaliser (qn) (pour lui faire faire qch.).

bull-dyke [ˈbuldaik] (*noun*), *P:* lesbienne* qui tient le rôle de l'homme, vrille *f*; *cf.* **dyke.**

bullet [ˈbulit] (*noun*), *P:* **1.** capsule *f* de drogues. **2. to give s.o. the b.,** (*a*) se débarrasser* de qn, sacquer qn, virer qn; (*b*) refuser d'avoir affaire à qn, couper les ponts avec qn.

bullion-fringe [ˈbuljənˈfrindʒ] (*noun*), *F:* = **scrambled eggs** (**egg, 4**).

bullseye [ˈbulzai] (*noun*), *F:* *voir* **bingo** (**50**).

bullshine [ˈbulʃain] (*noun*), *F:* *euph. pour* **bullshit**[1], **1.**

* L'astérisque indique que le mot marqué de ce signe figure comme entrée dans le Répertoire.

bullshit[1] [ˈbulʃit] (*noun*), *P:* **1.** service-service *m.* **2.** bêtises*, boniments *m.pl.*, sornettes *f.pl.*; **b. artist** = **bullshitter, 1,2. 3.** propos peu importants, balivernes *f.pl.*, bagatelles *f.pl.*

bullshit[2] [ˈbulʃit] (**to**), *P:* baratiner, dévider, jaspiner.

bullshitter [ˈbulʃitər] (*noun*), *P:* **1.** baratineur *m*, jaspineur *m.* **2.** esbrouffeur *m*, plastronneur *m.*

bully[1] [ˈbuli] (*adj.*), *F:* **1.** (*U.S.*) fameux, épatant, bœuf. **2. b. for you!** bravo!

bully[2] [ˈbuli] (*noun*), *P:* souteneur*, maquereau *m*, Alphonse.

bum[1] [bʌm] (*adj.*) (*U.S.*), *F:* laid*, piètre, misérable, moche; **b. steer,** faux renseignement*, tuyau crevé. *Voir aussi* **kick**[1], **3.**

bum[2] [bʌm] (*noun*), *P:* **1.** fesses*, postérieur *m.* **2.** qui paresse*, fainéant *m*, crossard *m*; **ski b.**, qn qui passe ses journées à skier, et ne travaille pas; fana *mf* du ski. **3.** (*U.S.*) (*a*) clochard*, chemineau *m*; (*b*) purotin *m.* *Voir aussi* **touch-your-bum.**

bum[3] [bʌm] (**to**), *P:* **1.** emprunter* (qch.), taper (qn). **2. to b. a lift,** se faire emmener en voiture; **to b. a dinner off s.o.,** se faire payer à dîner par qn. **3.** vivre aux crochets de qn. **4.** = **bum around** (**to**), **1, 2. 5.** vivre en clochard*, faire le clodo(t).

bum around [ˈbʌməˈraund] (**to**) (*mainly U.S.*), *P:* **1.** paresser*, fainéanter. **2.** flânocher, traîner son cul.

bum-boy [ˈbʌmbɔi] (*noun*), *P:* pédéraste*, enculé *m.*

bumf [bʌmf] (*noun*) (=*bum-fodder*), *F:* **1.** papier *m* hygiénique, torche-cul *m.* **2.** paperasserie *f.* **3.** papillons *m.pl.*, tracts *m.pl.*

bum-fodder [ˈbʌmfɔdər] (*noun*), *P:* = **bumf, 1.**

bum-freezer [ˈbʌmfriːzər] (*noun*), *P:* pet-en-l'air *m*, rase-pet *m.*

bum-hole [ˈbʌm(h)oul] (*noun*), *V:* anus*, anneau *m*, rond *m.*

bummer[1] [ˈbʌmər] (*adj.*), *P:* bousillé.

bummer[2] [ˈbʌmər] (*noun*), *P:* **1.** bousillage *m.* **2.** fainéant *m*, écornifleur *m*, mendigot *m.* **3.** désappointement *m*, déception *f*, sale expérience *f.* **4.** mauvais voyage à la drogue. **5.** = **brown-hatter.**

bummy [ˈbʌmi] (*adj.*), *P:* sale*, cracra, merdeux.

bumper [ˈbʌmpər] (*adj.*), *F:* excellent*, formid(able), à tout casser.

bumph [bʌmf] (*noun*), *F:* = **bumf.**

bump off [ˈbʌmpˈɔf] (**to**), *F:* assassiner*, but(t)er, zigouiller.

bum-rubber [ˈbʌmrʌbər] (*noun*), *P:* pédéraste*, pédé *m.*

bum-sucker [ˈbʌmsʌkər] (*noun*), *P:* lèche-cul *m*, lécheur *m.*

bun [ˈbʌn] (*noun*). **1.** *P:* **to have a b. in the oven,** être enceinte*, avoir un polichinelle dans le tiroir. **2.** (*U.S.*) *P:* **to have a b. on,** (*a*) être ivre*, être saoul; (*b*) être défoncé (par les drogues). **3.** *F:* **to take the b.** = **to take the biscuit.** *Voir aussi* **currant-bun.**

bunce [bʌns] (*noun*), *F:* affure *f*, bénef *m.*

bunch [bʌntʃ] (*noun*). **1.** *F:* **a b. of idiots,** une bande* d'idiots. **2.** *P:* **a b. of fives,** main*, pince *f*, pogne *f.* *Voir aussi* **honeybunch; pick.**

bunco [ˈbʌŋkou] (**to**), *P:* rouler (qn) au jeu (*surtout* aux cartes).

bundle [ˈbʌndl] (*noun*). **1.** *F:* grande somme d'argent*, une liasse, un paquet; **to make a b.**, faire sa pelote. **2.** *P:* une belle fille*, une bath pépée, un beau petit lot. **3.** *P:* **to have a b.**, coïter*, se mélanger. **4.** *F:* **to go a b.**, parier gros, y mettre beaucoup d'argent* (*ou* le paquet). **5.** *P:* **I don't go a b. on that,** ça ne m'emballe pas, ça ne me botte pas. **6.** *F:* **a b. of nerves,** un paquet de nerfs.

bung[1] [bʌŋ] (*noun*), *P:* (*a*) pourboire*, bouquet *m*; (*b*) graissage *m* de patte.

bung[2] [bʌŋ] (**to**), *P:* **1.** jeter*, envoyer dinguer. **2.** donner*, abouler, allonger. **3.** payer*, les abouler, les allonger, arroser.

bung-ho! [ˈbʌŋˈhou] (*excl.*), *F:* **1.** au revoir! ciao! salut! **2.** à la tienne!

bung-hole [ˈbʌŋ(h)oul] (*noun*). **1.** *V:* anus*, anneau *m.* **2.** *F:* *voir* **bingo (50).**

bunhead [ˈbʌnhed] (*noun*), *F:* individu bête*, pomme *f*, tourte *f.*

bunk [bʌŋk] (*noun*). **1.** *F:* = **bunkum. 2.** *P:* **to do a b.**, s'enfuir*, filer, déguerpir.

bunk off [ˈbʌŋkˈɔf] (**to**), *P:* = **to do a bunk** (**bunk, 2**).

bunkum [ˈbʌŋkəm] (*noun*), *F:* bêtises*, fariboles *f.pl.*; **that's (all) b.!** tout ça c'est

* An asterisk indicates that the word so marked is included as a head-word in the Appendix.

des histoires *f.pl.* (*ou* des balivernes *f.pl. ou* du bidon)!

bunk-up [ˈbʌŋkʌp] (*noun*). **1.** *V:* **to have a b.-u.,** coïter*, coucher avec qn. **2.** *P:* **to give s.o. a b.-u.,** (*a*) faire la courte échelle à qn, aider qn dans une escalade; (*b*) pistonner qn.

bunny[1] [ˈbʌni] (*noun*). **1.** *P:* hôtesse *f*, entraîneuse *f*. **2.** *P:* femme* de petite vertu. **3.** *P:* prostituée* pour lesbiennes*, chatte *f* jaune. **4.** *P:* prostitué mâle pour pédérastes*, chien *m* jaune. **5.** *F:* lapin *m*, Jeannot Lapin. **6.** (*U.S.*) *F:* **lost b.,** ahuri *m*; **helpless b.,** abruti *m*. **7.** *P:* bavardage *m*, déblatérage *m*, bavette *f*. **8.** (*Austr.*) *P:* = **Alec, 2.** *Voir aussi* **dumb, 1** (*b*); **jungle, 3.**

bunny[2] [ˈbʌni] (**to**), *P:* = **rabbit**[2] **(to).**

bunny-fuck [ˈbʌni-fʌk] (**to**), *VV:* coïter* avec rapidité, fourailler à la une.

bunter [ˈbʌntər] (*noun*), *P:* prostituée*, radeuse *f*.

burk(e) [bəːk] (*noun*), *P:* = **berk.**

burl [bəːl] (*noun*) (*Austr.*), *F:* **to give sth. a b., to have a b. at sth.,** faire un essai à qch., tenter le coup.

burn[1] [bəːn] (*noun*), *P:* **1.** (*a*) cigarette*, cibiche *f*; **to twist a b.,** rouler une cigarette*; (*b*) cigarette* de marijuana (*drogues**), joint *m*. **2.** (*Austr.*) allumette *f*, bûche *f*, soufrante *f*.

burn[2] [bəːn] (**to**), *P:* **1.** (*a*) escroquer*, arnaquer, empiler; (*b*) voler*, barboter, chaparder. **2.** avoir une grosse déception. **3.** (*U.S.*) être exécuté par électrocution. **4.** (*a*) se mettre en colère*, fulminer; (*b*) mettre en colère*, mettre en boule. **5.** aller vite*, foncer, gazer. **6.** attraper *ou* donner une maladie vénérienne (*malade**), être fadé (*ou* faisandé *ou* nazicoté). **7.** fumer*, brûler, bouffarder.

burned out [ˈbəːndˈaut] (*p.p. & adj.*), *P:* **1.** fatigué*, pompé, flapi. **2.** ennuyé*, embêté, assommé. **3.** défoncé.

burnese [bəːˈniːz] (*noun*), *P:* = **bernice.**

burn-up [ˈbəːnʌp] (*noun*), *P:* **to have a b.-u.,** lutter de vitesse en auto *ou* en moto; *cf.* **burn up (to), 2.**

burn up [ˈbəːnˈʌp] (**to**), *P:* **1.** être très en colère*, voir rouge. **2. to b. u. the road,** aller très vite*, brûler le pavé (*ou* la route); *cf.* **burn-up.**

burp[1] [bəːp] (*noun*), *F:* rot *m*, soupir *m* de Bacchus.

burp[2] [bəːp] (**to**), *F:* roter, avoir une fuite de gaz.

burp-gun [ˈbəːpgʌn] (*noun*), *P:* mitraillette*, sulfateuse *f*, moulinette *f*.

burton [ˈbəːtn] (*noun*), *F:* **to go for a b.,** disparaître, s'évanouir (dans la nature); (*av.*) faire un trou dans l'eau; (*mil.*) mourir*; être manquant, être porté disparu.

bus [bʌs] (*noun*), *F:* **1.** (*a*) véhicule motorisé; (*b*) avion *m*, coucou *m*; tacot *m*. **2. to miss the b.,** manquer le coche, rater l'occasion. *Voir aussi* **back-end.**

bush [buʃ] (*noun*). **1.** *V:* mousse *f*, gazon *m*, fourrure *f*. **2.** (*Austr.*) *P:* fille* *ou* jeune femme*, gonzesse *f*. **3.** *P:* **bo-bo** (*or* **righteous**) **b.,** marijuana *f* (*drogues**), foin *m*. **4.** *F:* **b. telegraph,** téléphone *m* arabe. *Voir aussi* **mulberry-bush.**

bushed [buʃt] (*adj.*), *P:* **1.** désorienté, interdit. **2.** fatigué*, vanné, fourbu.

bushel and peck [ˈbuʃələn(d)ˈpek] (*noun*), *P:* (*R.S.* = *neck*) cou*.

bushwa(h) [ˈbuʃwɑː] (*noun*) (*U.S.*), *P:* = **bunkum.**

bush-whacker [ˈbuʃwækər] (*noun*) (*Austr.*), *F:* qn qui habite au fin fond du bled.

business [ˈbiznis] (*noun*). **1.** *F:* **to mean b.,** prendre les choses au sérieux, ne pas rigoler. **2.** *F:* **to do one's b.,** déféquer*, débourrer. **3.** *F:* **what a b.!** quelle affaire! **4. the b.,** (*a*) *P:* (i) traitement brutal; (ii) assassinat *m*, buttage *m*; (iii) réprimande *f*, savon *m*; (*b*) *V:* (i) pénis*, tracassin *m*; (ii) vagin*, didi *m*; (iii) coït*, truc *m*; (*c*) *P:* le business; (*d*) *P:* attirail *m* de camé; (*e*) *P:* poussette *f*. **5.** *F:* **what he paid for it is nobody's b.,** Dieu seul sait ce qu'il l'a payé. *Voir aussi* **funny**[1], **2.**

busk [bʌsk] (**to**). **1.** *F:* (*musiciens*) (*a*) jouer dans les rues; (*b*) improviser. **2.** (*th.*) *F:* jouer dans une troupe ambulante. **3.** *P:* vendre des livres obscènes à la sauvette.

busker [ˈbʌskər] (*noun*). **1.** *F:* (*a*) musicien *m* qui joue dans les rues; (*b*) improvisateur *m*. **2.** *F:* comédien

* L'astérisque indique que le mot marqué de ce signe figure comme entrée dans le Répertoire.

ambulant. 3. *P:* fourgueur *m* de livres obscènes.

busman [ˈbʌsmən] (*noun*), *F:* **to take a b.'s holiday,** faire du métier en guise de congé ou de loisirs.

bust[1] [bʌst] (*adj.*), *F:* **1.** cassé, esquinté. **2.** (*a*) sans le sou, dans la purée; (*b*) **to go b.,** faire faillite, boire un bouillon.

bust[2] (bʌst] (*noun*), *P:* **1.** (*th.*) fiasco *m*, four *m*. **2.** bamboche *f*, bringue *f*, bordée *f*. **3.** faillite *f*, binelle *f*. **4. to do a b.,** s'évader de prison, sauter le mur. **5.** rafle *f* de police.

bust[3] [bʌst] (**to**), *P:* **1.** casser (un sergent, un racket, *etc.*). **2.** (*a*) prendre sur le fait (*ou* en flagrant délit); (*b*) arrêter*, agrafer. **3.** battre*, frapper, rosser. *Voir aussi* **gut; shit**[4] **(to), 3.**

buster [ˈbʌstər] (*noun*), *P:* **1.** homme* fort*, malabar *m*, costaud *m*. **2.** = **whopper, 1, 2.** *Voir aussi* **ball-buster; blockbuster; bronco-buster; jaw-buster.**

bust in [ˈbʌstˈin] (**to**), *P:* **1.** entrer en coup de vent. **2. to b. s.o.'s face i.,** casser la figure* à qn, abîmer le portrait à qn. **3. to b. i. on s.o.,** arriver* comme un chien dans un jeu de quilles. **4. to b. i. on s.o.'s conversation,** s'injecter dans la conversation.

bust open [ˈbʌstˈoupən] (**to**), *P:* **to b. o. a safe,** casser un coffre-fort.

bust out [ˈbʌstˈaut] (**to**), *P:* **1.** s'évader, en jouer un air. **2. she's busting out all over,** elle a des seins* plantureux, il y a du monde au balcon.

bust-up [ˈbʌstʌp] (*noun*), *F:* **1.** querelle*, attrapade *f*. **2.** rupture *f*, mallette et paquette *f*; **they've had a b.-u.,** ils ont rompu.

bust up [ˈbʌstˈʌp] (**to**). *F:* **1.** esquinter (une pièce de machine, *etc.*). **2.** rompre (une amitié), briser (un mariage).

busty [ˈbʌsti] (*adj.*), *F:* avec une poitrine proéminente, avec de l'avant-scène, mamelue.

busy [ˈbizi] (*noun*), *P:* agent* *ou* inspecteur *m* de la Sûreté; policier*.

butchers [ˈbutʃəz] (*noun*) (*R.S.* = *butcher's hook* = *look*), *P:* coup d'œil*; **to give sth. a b., to take a b. at sth.,** regarder* qch., reluquer qch.

butt [bʌt] (*noun*) (*U.S.*). **1.** *F:* fesses*, derrière *m*. **2.** *P:* (*a*) **dusty b.,** trois pouces et le cul tout de suite; (*b*) mocheté *f* de trottoir, (vieux) passe-lacet.

butter [ˈbʌtər] (*noun*), *F:* **to look as though b. wouldn't melt in one's mouth,** faire la Sainte-Nitouche, faire la sucrée, ne pas avoir l'air d'y toucher. *Voir aussi* **bread, 3; bread-and-butter.**

buttercup [ˈbʌtəkʌp] (*noun*), *P:* pédéraste*, joconde *f*.

butterfingers [ˈbʌtəfiŋgəz] (*noun*), *F:* malagauche *mf*, malapatte *mf*; **to have b., to be a b.,** avoir la main malheureuse, être brise-tout.

butterflies [ˈbʌtəflaiz] (*pl. noun*), *F:* **to have b. (in the tummy),** avoir peur*, avoir les jetons.

butter up [ˈbʌtəˈ(r)ʌp] (**to**), *F:* flatter*, pommader, embobiner, passer à la pommade.

button[1] [ˈbʌtn] (*noun*). **1.** *P:* menton *m*, bichonnet *m*. **2.** *V:* clitoris*, bouton *m*. **3.** *F:* **on the b.,** à point, recta. *Voir aussi* **belly-button; panic, 2.**

button[2] [ˈbʌtn] (**to**), *P:* **b. your mouth** (*or* **lip**)**!** (ferme) ton bec!

buttoned up [ˈbʌtndˈʌp] (*p.p. & adj.*), *P:* **1.** peu communicatif, constipé. **2.** cadenassé. **3. it's all b. u.,** c'est dans le sac (*ou* dans la poche).

buttonhole [ˈbʌtnhoul] (**to**), *F:* agrafer, cramponner (qn).

buy[1] [bai] (*noun*), *F:* achat *m*; **a good b.,** une bonne occase.

buy[2] [bai] (**to**). **1.** *F:* (*a*) **(go on,) I'll b. it,** vas-y, déballe!; je donne ma langue au chat; (*b*) **I'll b. that,** je marche, je suis d'acc. **2.** *P:* **he bought it** (*or* **a packet**), il a écopé.

buyer [ˈbaiər] (*noun*), *P:* receleur*, fourgue *m*.

buzz[1] [bʌz] (*noun*). **1.** *F:* bruit *m*, on-dit *m*. **2.** *F:* **to give s.o. a b.,** donner (*ou* passer) un coup de fil à qn. **3.** *P:* plaisir violent, transport *m*, animation *f*, émoi *m*.

buzz[2] [bʌz] (**to**). **1.** *F:* **to b. s.o.** = **to give s.o. a buzz (buzz**[1]**, 2). 2.** *P:* voler* à la tire (*ou* à la fourche *ou* à la fourchette). **3.** *F:* (*d'un avion ou d'une voiture*) coller (un autre avion ou une autre voiture). **4.** *P:* être aux anges. **5.** *P:* essayer d'acheter des drogues*, bibeloter.

buzzing [ˈbʌziŋ] (*noun*), *P:* interroga-

* An asterisk indicates that the word so marked is included as a head-word in the Appendix.

toire* sévère (par la police), blutinage *m*, cuisine *f*.

buzz off [ˈbʌzˈɔf] (**to**), *F:* s'enfuir*, décamper, filer, se tailler; **b.o.!** débarrasse! de l'air!

bye(-bye)! [ˈbai(ˈbai)] (*excl.*), *F:* salut! ciao!

bye-byes [ˈbaibaiz] (*pl. noun*), *F:* (*langage enfantin*) dodo *m*; **to go to b.-b.,** aller faire dodo.

* L'astérisque indique que le mot marqué de ce signe figure comme entrée dans le Répertoire.

C

C, c [siː] (*abbr.* = *cocaine*), *P:* (**big**) **c.**, cocaïne *f* (*drogues**).

cabbage [ˈkæbidʒ] (*noun*), *P:* argent*, galette *f*; *cf.* **kale; lettuce.**

cabbage-head [ˈkæbidʒhed] (*noun*), *F:* individu bête*, gourde *f.*

cabbie, cabby [ˈkæbi] (*noun*), *F:* **1.** cocher *m*, collignon *m.* **2.** chauffeur *m* de taxi*, rongeur *m.*

caboodle [kəˈbuːdl] (*noun*), *F:* **the whole (kit and) c.**, tout le Saint-Frusquin, tout le bataclan; *cf.* **boiling; shebang,[1]; shoot[1], 1; shooting-match.**

cack[1] [kæk] (*noun*), *P:* étron*, caca *m.*

cack[2] [kæk] (**to**), *P:* déféquer*, caguer, faire caca.

cackhanded [ˈkækˈhændid] (*adj.*), *F:* balourd, empoté.

cackle [ˈkækl] (*noun*), *P:* **cut the c.!** assez bavardé! assez jacté!

cacky [ˈkæki] (*adj.*), *P:* merdeux.

cactus [ˈkæktəs] (*noun*), *P:* mescaline *f* (*drogues*), cactus *m* du Mexique.

cadet [kəˈdet] (*noun*), *P:* nouvel initié à la drogue.

cadge[1] [kædʒ] (*noun*), *F:* **he's always on the c.**, c'est un tapeur chronique (*ou* professionnel).

cadge[2] [kædʒ] (**to**), *F:* emprunter*, repasser le burlingue; **to c. a thousand francs from s.o.**, taper (*ou* torpiller) qn de mille francs.

cadger [ˈkædʒər] (*noun*), *F:* tapeur *m*, torpilleur *m.*

cadging [ˈkædʒiŋ] (*noun*), *F:* tapage *m*, relance *f.*

cadie [ˈkeidi] (*noun*), *P:* chapeau*.

cafe [kæf, keif], **caff** [kæf] (*noun*), *P:* café* (*débit*), troquet *m.*

cag(e)y [ˈkeidʒi] (*adj.*), *F:* malin*, futé; **to play c.**, se boutonner, jouer serré.

cahoot(s) [kəˈhuːt(s), kɑːˈhuːt(s)] (*noun*), *F:* **to be in c. with s.o.**, être de mèche (*ou* en cheville) avec qn; **to go c. with s.o.**, partager avec qn.

Cain [kein] (*pr. noun*), *P:* **1. to raise C.**, faire du bruit*, gueuler au charron. **2. C. and Abel** (*R.S.* = *table*), table *f.*

cake [keik] (*noun*), **1.** *F:* **a piece of c.**, du gâteau, du nanan. **2.** *F:* **that takes the c.**, c'est le comble (*ou* le bouquet). **3.** (*U.S.*) *P:* **to grab a piece of c.**, coïter*, faire un carton. **4.** *F:* **you can't have your c. and eat it, you can't eat your c. and have it,** on ne peut pas être et avoir été, on ne peut pas avoir le drap et l'argent. *Voir aussi* **beefcake; cheesecake; cup-cakes; fruitcake; hot, 18; pancakes.**

cakehole [ˈkeik(h)oul] (*noun*), *P:* bouche*, bec *m*; **shut your c.!** ferme ça! la ferme!

cake-walk [ˈkeik-wɔːk] (*noun*), *F:* **1.** = **piece of cake (cake, 1); it's a c.-w.**, c'est dans le sac. **2.** cake-walk *m* (*danse*).

calaboose, calaboosh [kæləˈbuːs, kæləˈbuːʃ] (*noun*), *P:* prison*, bloc *m*, violon *m.*

calf [kɑːf] (*noun*), *P:* **1.** cinquante pence; *cf.* **cow, 4. 2. in c.** = **in pig (pig[1], 5).**

call [kɔːl] (*noun*), *F:* **1. to pay a c.**, uriner*, aller faire sa petite commission. **2. it was a close c.**, il était moins une.

call down [ˈkɔːlˈdaun] (**to**) (*U.S.*), *F:* réprimander*, attraper.

calling-down [ˈkɔːliŋˈdaun] (*noun*) (*U.S.*), *F:* attrapade *f*, savon *m*; **to get a c.-d.**, être réprimandé*, recevoir un savon, en prendre pour son grade.

camp[1] [kæmp] (*adj.*), *F:* **1.** affecté, poseur. **2.** répugnant, véreux, à l'estoc. **3.** chichiteux. **4.** gommeux, gandin. **5.** rococo, vieux jeu. **6.** tartavelle, tocard. **7.** (*a*) efféminé; (*b*) homosexuel; (*c*) lesbienne.

camp[2] [kæmp] (*noun*), *F:* manières efféminées (*souvent* d'homosexuel), tantouserie *f.*

camp[3] [kæmp] (**to**), *P:* être pédéraste* *ou* lesbienne*, être de la bague *ou* de la maison tire-bouton.

* An asterisk indicates that the word so marked is included as a head-word in the Appendix.

camp about [ˈkæmpəˈbaʊt] (**to**), *F:* faire des simagrées *f.pl.*

camp up [ˈkæmpˈʌp] (**to**), *F:* **to c. it u.,** (*a*) jouer la comédie; (*b*) se montrer efféminé, faire la persilleuse; (*c*) prendre part à une partouse (*ou* à une surboum); (*d*) avoir une liaison homosexuelle; passer un week-end en pédale.

can[1] [kæn] (*noun*). **1.** *P:* prison*, bloc *m;* **to be in the c.,** être emprisonné*, être bloqué; **to put s.o. in the c.,** mettre qn dedans, fourrer qn au bloc. **2.** *F:* **in the c.,** en boîte. **3.** *F:* **to carry the c. (for s.o.),** écoper pour qn, porter le chapeau. **4.** *F:* pot *m,* chope *f,* chopotte *f.* **5.** *P:* (*a*) opium *m* (*drogues**), noir *m;* (*b*) deux grammes de n'importe quelle drogue. **6.** (*U.S.*) *P:* W.C.*, pissotière *f.* **7.** (*U.S.*) *P:* fesses*, montre *f;* **to kick s.o. in the c.,** botter les fesses* à qn. **8.** (*U.S.*) *P:* voiture*, auto *f,* bagnole *f.* **9.** (*U.S.*) (*pl.*) *P:* seins*, boîtes *f.pl.* à lait. *Voir aussi* **oil-can.**

can[2] [kæn] (**to**). **1.** *P:* emprisonner*, fourrer dedans. **2.** *P:* se débarrasser* de (qn), sacquer, flanquer à la porte. **3.** *F:* enregistrer (de la musique, *etc.*), mettre en conserve; *cf.* **canned, 2. 4.** *P:* **c. it!** ferme ça! *Voir aussi* **shitcan (to).**

canapa [ˈkænəpə] (*noun*), *P:* canapa *f,* marijuana *f* (*drogues**).

canary [kəˈnɛəri] (*noun*), *P:* dénonciateur*, chevreuil *m.,* donneur *m.*

cancer-stick [ˈkænsə-stik] (*noun*), *P:* cigarette*, cibiche *f.*

candle [ˈkændl] (*noun*), *F:* bougie *f* (*automobile*). *Voir aussi* **Roman, 1.**

candy [ˈkændi] (*noun*). **1.** *P:* (*drogues*) (*a*) cocaïne *f,* bigornette *f;* (*b*) hachisch *m;* (*c*) cube sucré de LSD; (*d*) drogues* en général; **c. man,** fourgueur *m* de drogues. **2.** (*U.S.*) *F:* bonbons *m.pl.,* friandises *f.pl.;* **like taking c. from a child** (*or* **blind man**), comme si on lui retirait la nourriture de la bouche. *Voir aussi* **needle-candy; nose-candy; rock-candy.**

cane[1] [kein] (*noun*), *P:* pince-monseigneur*, rossignol *m. Voir aussi* **varnish**[2] **(to).**

cane[2] [ˈkein] (**to**), *P:* **to c. s.o.,** (*a*) faire payer* trop cher à qn, fusiller qn; (*b*) battre qn à plate(s) couture(s).

canful [ˈkænful] (*noun*), *P:* **to have (had) a c.,** être ivre*, avoir une cuite.

caning [ˈkeiniŋ] (*noun*), *F:* victoire *f* facile (*ou* les doigts dans le nez).

canned [kænd] (*adj.*). **1.** *P:* (*a*) ivre*, saoul; (*b*) drogué*, camé. **2.** *F:* **c. music,** musique *f* en conserve (*disques, bandes, cassettes, etc.*). **3.** (*U.S.*) *P:* balancé, viré.

canoe [kəˈnuː] (*noun*), *F:* **to paddle one's own c.,** mener seul sa barque, voler de ses propres ailes.

canoodle [kəˈnuːdl] (**to**), *F:* (se) bécoter, (se) peloter.

canoodling [kəˈnuːdliŋ] (*noun*), *F:* pelotage *m,* mamours *m.pl.*

Canuck [ˈkænʌk] (*noun*), *F:* Canadien français.

cap[1] [kæp] (*noun*), *P:* capsule *f* de narcs. *Voir aussi* **Dutch**[1], **3; feather**[1], **2; Red-cap; thinking-cap.**

cap[2] [kæp] (**to**), *P:* **1.** ouvrir *ou* consommer une capsule de narcotique. **2.** acheter des narcotiques.

caper [ˈkeipər] (*noun*). **1.** *F:* (*a*) escapade *f,* farce *f;* (*b*) affaire*, fric-frac *m.* **2.** *P:* **. . . and all that c.,** entourloupe et compagnie. **3.** *P:* truc *m,* ficelle *f.*

carat [ˈkærət] (*noun*), *F:* **a twenty-two c. chap,** un vrai de vrai.

carcase, carcass [ˈkɑːkəs] (*noun*), *F:* **plant your c. there!** assieds-toi! pose ton pont arrière!; **drag your c. over here!** radine! amène ta viande!; **move your c.!** (*a*) bouge-toi! remue ta graisse!; (*b*) débarrasse!

card [kɑːd] (*noun*), *F:* **1.** drôle d'individu*, drôle de numéro (*ou* de phénomène). **2. to get one's cards,** être renvoyé, se faire virer; **to give s.o. his cards,** renvoyer qn, virer qn. **3. to put one's cards on the table,** jouer cartes sur table. **4. it's on the cards,** c'est du possible (*ou* probable). **5. to show one's cards,** abattre son jeu. **6. house of cards,** château *m* de cartes. **7. to play one's trump c.,** jouer sa meilleure carte (*ou* son atout); **to hold the trump c.,** avoir les atouts en main. **8. to throw in one's cards,** abandonner la partie. *Voir aussi* **mark**[2] **(to), 1.**

cardy [ˈkɑːdi] (*noun*) (*abbr.* = *cardigan*), *F:* paletot *m* de laine, cardigan *m.*

carpet[1] [ˈkɑːpit] (*noun*). **1.** *F:* **on the c.** (=*under consideration*), sur le tapis. **2.** *F:* **to put s.o. on the c.,** tenir qn sur

* L'astérisque indique que le mot marqué de ce signe figure comme entrée dans le Répertoire.

la sellette. 3. *P:* trois mois de taule. *Voir aussi* **dirt**[1], **4; red**[1], **2.**

carpet[2] [ˈkɑːpit] (**to**), *F:* **to c. s.o.** = **to put s.o. on the carpet (carpet**[1], **2).**

carpetbagger [ˈkɑːpitbægər] (*noun*) (*U.S.*), *F:* candidat parachuté, aventurier *m* politique.

carrier [ˈkæriər] (*noun*), *F:* contact *m*, intermédiaire *m* (pour les drogues).

carrot(s) [ˈkærət(s)], **carrot-top** [ˈkærəttɔp] (*noun*), *F:* rouquin *m*, poil *m* de carotte, poil *m* de brique.

carry [ˈkæri] (**to**), *F:* **1.** avoir en magasin. **2.** avoir, posséder de la drogue. **3. to c. s.o.**, garder du bois mort. **4. he's had as much as he can c.**, il a son compte, il en a tout son soûl.

carryings-on [ˈkæriiŋzˈɔn] (*pl. noun*), *F:* simagrées *f.pl.*, pitreries *f.pl.*

carry off [ˈkæriˈɔf] (**to**), *F:* **to c. it o. (well)**, bien s'en tirer, réussir le coup.

carry-on [ˈkæriˈɔn] (*noun*), *P:* **what a c.-o.!** quel cirque! quelle comédie!

carry on [ˈkæriˈɔn] (**to**), *F:* **1.** continuer, persister, aller jusqu'au bout; **c. o. regardless!** continue envers et contre tout! **2. to c. o. with s.o.**, fréquenter qn, sortir avec qn, flirter. **3. don't c. o. like that!** ne fais pas l'idiot! *Voir aussi* **alarming.**

cart [kɑːt] (*noun*), *F:* **to land s.o. (right) in the c.**, mettre qn dans le pétrin. *Voir aussi* **apple-cart; dog-cart.**

cart about [ˈkɑːtəˈbaut] (**to**), *F:* trimbal(l)er (qn, qch.).

cartload [ˈkɑːtloud] (*noun*), *F:* **a c. of trouble**, toute une accumulation de malheurs.

cart off [ˈkɑːtˈɔf] (**to**). **1.** *F:* **to get carted off to hospital**, être transbahuté à l'hôpital*. **2.** *P:* **c. yourself o.!** fiche le camp!

cartwheel [ˈkɑːt-wiːl] (*noun*). **1.** *F:* **to do a c.**, faire un tonneau (*ou* une roue). **2.** *P:* = **brodie, 1. 3.** (*pl.*) *P:* amphétamines *f.pl.* (*drogues**), topette *f.*

carve-up [ˈkɑːvʌp] (*noun*), *P:* **1.** escroquerie*, arnaquage *m*. **2.** distribe *f.*

carve up [ˈkɑːvˈʌp] (**to**), *P:* **1.** massacrer, charcuter (qn). **2.** partager, décarpiller.

carzy [kɑːzi] (*noun*), *P:* = **karzy.**

Casanova [ˈkæsəˈnouvə] (*noun*), *F:* Casanova *m*, cavaleur *m*, godilleur *m*.

case[1] [keis] (*noun*). **1.** *F:* **he's a hard c.**, c'est un dur, c'est une mauvaise tête. **2.** *P:* **to go c. with s.o.**, coïter* avec qn, godiller avec qn. **3.** *P:* casse *f*, fric-frac *m*; **to have** (*or* **do**) **a c.**, voler*, faire un fric-frac. *Voir aussi* **nut-case.**

case[2] [keis] (**to**), *P:* **1. to c. s.o.**, coïter* avec qn, godiller avec qn. **2. to c. a joint**, aller examiner une maison, *etc.*, avant de la cambrioler*; faire une ballade au fric-frac. **3.** guetter*, broquer, se rencarder. **4. to get cased**, être inculpé (*ou* fargué).

cash in [ˈkæʃˈin] (**to**). **1.** *P:* **to c. i. one's chips**, mourir*, lâcher la rampe, poser sa chique. **2.** *F:* **to c. i. on sth.**, tirer profit de qch.

cast-iron [ˈkɑːstˈaiən] (*adj.*), *F:* **1. c.-i. case**, affaire *f* inattaquable. **2. c.-i. constitution (will**, *etc.*), santé *f* (volonté *f*, *etc.*) de fer; **c.-i. stomach**, estomac *m* d'autruche (*ou* de fer); **c.-i. alibi**, alibi *m* irréfutable.

cast-offs [ˈkɑːstɔfs] (*pl. noun*), *F:* **1.** vieux vêtements*, vieilles frusques. **2.** laissés-pour-compte *m.pl.*

casual [ˈkæzjuəl] (*noun*), *F:* **1.** client *m* de passage. **2.** (*pl.*) mocassins *m.pl.*, chaussures* pour tout aller.

cat [kæt] (*noun*). **1.** *P:* (*a*) qn qui est de l'avant-garde en musique, art ou littérature; (*b*) qn qui s'habille à la dernière mode, minet *m*. **2.** *P:* musicien *m* de jazz; *voir aussi* **hot, 7. 3.** *P:* homme*, zèbre *m*. **4.** *P:* coureur *m* de jupons. **5.** *F:* **an old c.**, femme* (*péj.*), une vieille chipie. **6.** *P:* chapardeur *m*, chipeur *m*. **7.** (=*cat-o'-nine-tails*) *F:* fouet *m*, chat *m* à neuf queues. **8.** *F:* **he thinks he's the c.'s whiskers** (*or* **pyjamas**), il ne se prend pas pour de la crotte; *cf.* **bee, 1. 9.** *F:* **to lead a c. and dog life**, vivre comme chien et chat. **10.** *F:* **to play c. and mouse with s.o.**, jouer au chat et à la souris avec qn. **11.** *F:* **to be raining cats and dogs**, pleuvoir des hallebardes. **12.** *F:* **to let the c. out of the bag**, éventer la mèche. **13.** *P:* pédéraste*, pédoque *m*. *Voir aussi* **copycat; fraidy; hell-cat; hep-cat; holy, 1; piss**[1], **5; scaredy-cat; she-cat; shoot**[2] **(to), 6; wildcat.**

catch[1] [kætʃ] (*attrib. adj.*), *F:* **1. a c. question**, une question-piège. **2. a snappy c. answer**, une réponse bien envoyée (*ou* désinvolte).

* An asterisk indicates that the word so marked is included as a head-word in the Appendix.

catch[2] [kætʃ] (*noun*). **1.** *F:* (=*love-conquest*) prise *f*, chopin *m*. **2.** *P:* pédéraste* qui tient le rôle de femme, chouquette *f*.

catch[3] [kætʃ] (**to**), *F:* **1. c. me doing that!** pas de danger qu'on m'y prenne! **2. you'll c. it!** tu en prendras pour ton grade! **3. caught napping,** pris au pied levé (*ou* au dépourvu *ou* sans vert). **4. the age to c. 'em:** *voir* **bingo** (**17**). *Voir aussi* **cold**[2], **1**; **packet, 1.**

catch on [ˈkætʃˈɔn] (**to**), *F:* **1.** comprendre, piger, entraver. **2.** prendre, être en vogue (*ou* dans le vent).

catch out [ˈkætʃˈaut] (**to**), *F:* **1.** prendre en défaut. **2.** coincer.

cathouse [ˈkæthaus] (*noun*), *P:* **1.** bordel*, claque *m*, boxon *m*. **2.** (*U.S.*) = **barrelhouse.**

cat-lap [ˈkætlæp] (*noun*), *F:* bibine *f*, jus *m* de chaussette (*ou* de serpillière).

cat-lick [ˈkætlik] (*noun*), *F:* bout *m* de toilette.

catty [ˈkæti] (*adj.*), *F:* rosse, vache.

cauliflower [ˈkɔli-flauər] (*noun*), *F:* **1. c. ear,** oreille *f* en chou-fleur. **2.** trèfle *f* (*cartes*), herbe *f* à la vache.

caution [ˈkɔːʃ(ə)n] (*noun*), *F:* **a c.,** un drôle de numéro, un phénomène; **she's a (proper) c.,** elle est formid(able).

cave-man [ˈkeivmæn] (*noun*), *F:* grosse brute; **c.-m. stuff,** brutalités *f.pl.*

cazz [kæz] (*adj.*), *F:* (=*casual*) **in a very c. voice,** sans avoir l'air d'y toucher; **c. clothes,** vêtements* de sport.

Cecil, cecil [ˈsesl, ˈsisl] (*noun*), *P:* cocaïne *f* (*drogues**), cécile *m*. *Voir aussi* **after, 1.**

cee [siː] (*noun*), *P:* cocaïne *f* (*drogues**), la c.

ceiling [ˈsiːliŋ] (*noun*), *F:* **to go through** (*or* **hit**) **the c.,** se mettre en colère*, sortir de ses gonds, monter à l'échelle.

cement [siˈment] (*noun*), *P:* (=*illicit narcotics*) ciment *m*.

century [ˈsentʃuri, ˈsentʃəri] (*noun*), *P:* cent livres sterling.

cert [səːt] (*abbr.* = *certainty*), *F:* **it's a (dead) c.,** c'est du nougat, c'est du tout cuit, c'est affiché; (*courses aux chevaux*) c'est un gagnant sûr.

certifiable [səːtiˈfaiəbl] (*adj.*), *F:* bon pour le cabanon.

cha [tʃɑː] (*noun*), *F:* = **char, 1.**

chain-gang [ˈtʃeingæŋ] (*noun*), *P:* = **daisy chain** (*voir* **daisy**[2], **6**).

chair [ˈtʃɛər] (*noun*), *F:* **1.** (*U.S.*) chaise *f* électrique; **to go to the c.,** être grillé. **2. c. warmer,** rond-de-cuir *m*, gratte-papier *m*. **3. to be in the c.,** (*au café*) être celui qui offre une tournée. *Voir aussi* **bandy-chair.**

chalk [tʃɔːk] (*noun*). **1.** *F:* **better by a long c.,** de bien loin le meilleur; **not by a long c.,** il s'en faut de beaucoup. **2.** *F:* **they're like** (*or* **as different as**) **c. and cheese,** c'est le jour et la nuit. **3.** *P:* amphétamine *f* (*drogues**), topette *f*. **4.** *P:* **ball** (*or* **penn'orth**) **of c.** (*R.S.* = *walk*), promenade *f*.

chalk up [tʃɔːkˈʌp] (**to**). **1.** *F:* porter sur l'ardoise. **2.** *P:* **to c.u. a score** = **score**[2] (**to**), **1, 2.**

champ[1] [tʃæmp] (*noun*) (*abbr.* = *champion*), *F:* as *m*, crack *m*.

champ[2] [tʃæmp] (**to**), *F:* ronger son frein.

champers [ˈʃæmpəz] (*noun*), *F:* (vin *m* de) champagne *m*, champ(e) *m*.

champion[1] [ˈtʃæmpjən] (*adj.*), *F:* (**proper**) **c.,** excellent*, de première, impec; *voir aussi* **gate-crasher.**

champion[2] [ˈtʃæmpjən] (*adv.*), *F:* excellemment, soin-soin.

chancer [ˈtʃɑːnsər] (*noun*), *F:* risque-tout *m*, tête brûlée.

chancy [ˈtʃɑːnsi] (*adj.*), *F:* chanceux, glandilleux.

change [tʃeindʒ] (*noun*), *F:* **you won't get much c. out of him,** tu n'en tireras pas grand-chose, tu perds tes peines avec lui. *Voir aussi* **ring**[2] (**to**), **2.**

chant [tʃɑːnt] (**to**), *P:* chanter* dans les rues, pousser la goualante.

chap [tʃæp] (*noun*), *F:* individu*, type *m*; **he's a queer c.,** c'est un drôle de bonhomme; **hello, old c.!** salut, vieux pote (*ou* vieille branche)!

char [tʃɑːr] (*noun*), *F:* **1.** thé *m*; **a cup of c.,** une tasse de thé. **2.** (=*charwoman*) femme de ménage, torche-pot *m*.

character [ˈkæriktər] (*noun*), *F:* drôle d'individu*, un numéro.

charas [tʃæˈræs], **charash** [tʃæˈræʃ] (*noun*), *P:* cannabis *m*, marijuana *f* (*drogues**), dagga *m*.

charge [tʃɑːdʒ] (*noun*), *P:* **1.** marijuana *f* (*drogues**). **2.** piquouse *f*; **to go on the c.,** se camer. **3.** plaisir *m*, émotion *f*; **to get a c. out of sth.,** tirer plaisir de

* L'astérisque indique que le mot marqué de ce signe figure comme entrée dans le Répertoire.

qch., s'en payer une tranche; **I got a c. out of it,** ça m'a fait quelque chose. *Voir aussi* **depth-charge.**

charged (up) [ˈtʃɑːdʒd(ˈʌp)] (*p.p. & adj.*), *P:* drogué*, bourré, camé; **to get c.,** se camer.

charl(e)y[1], **charlie** [ˈtʃɑːli] (*adj.*), *P:* qui a peur*, flubé, foireux.

Charl(e)y[2], **charl(e)y, Charlie, charlie** [ˈtʃɑːli] (*noun*), *P:* **1. a right** (*or* **proper**) **C.,** un vrai gugusse. **2. C.'s dead,** ton jupon passe; tu pavoises; *cf.* **Anne** (*a*). **3.** (*pl.*) seins*, roberts *m.pl.* **4.** (*pl.*) testicules*, balloches *f.pl.* **5.** cocaïne *f* (*drogues**); **C. coke,** un Jules de la c. **6. race-horse C.,** morphine *f* (*drogues**). **7.** lesbienne*, gouchotte *f.* **8.** (*U.S.*) un blanc (*terme employé par les nègres*). **9.** (*U.S.*) un dollar. *Voir aussi* **good-time, 2.**

charms [tʃɑːmz] (*pl. noun*), *F:* seins*, appas *m.pl.*, doudounes *f.pl.*

chart [tʃɑːt] (*noun*), *F:* **1.** arrangement musical (*par ex.* pour orchestre de jazz). **2. to be in the charts,** être au palmarès, être dans le hit-parade.

charver [ˈtʃɑːvər] (*noun*), *V:* coït*, tringlage *m*; **to have a c.,** coïter*, tringler.

chase [tʃeis] (**to**), *F:* (**go**) **c. yourself!** va te faire fiche!

chase around [ˈtʃeisəˈraund] (**to**), *F:* **to c. a. after women,** courir les filles (*ou* les jupons).

chaser [ˈtʃeisər] (*noun*), *F:* **1.** rince-cochon *m*, rince-gueule *m.* **2.** lettre *f* qui fait suite à une autre. *Voir aussi* **petticoat-chaser; skirt-chaser; woman-chaser.**

chassis [ˈʃæsi] (*noun*), *F:* (*d'une femme*) châssis *m*, académie *f.*

chat [tʃæt] (*noun*), *P:* **1.** = **backchat**[1], **1** (*a*). **2.** pou*, galopard *m.*

chat up [ˈtʃætˈʌp] (**to**), *F:* baratiner; **to c. u. a bird,** faire du rentre-dedans (*ou* du gringue) à une fille*, faire du rambin à une fille*.

cheapjack [ˈtʃiːpdʒæk] (*noun*), *F:* camelot *m*, batousard *m.*

cheapskate [ˈtʃiːp-skeit] (*noun*), *F:* **1.** avare*, grippe-sou *m.* **2.** vaurien*, bon-à-rien *m.*

cheat [tʃiːt] (**to**) (*U.S.*), *F:* cocufier, doubler, faire porter des cornes (à).

cheaters [ˈtʃiːtəz] (*pl. noun*), *F:* **1.** = **falsies, 2. 2.** lunettes*, berniches *f.pl.*

check! [tʃek] (*excl.*), oui*, d'acc! banco!

check in [ˈtʃekˈin] (**to**), *F:* = **book in (to).**

check out [ˈtʃekˈaut] (**to**). **1.** *P:* mourir*, déposer le bilan, plier bagage. **2.** *F:* = **book out (to). 3.** *P:* partir*, filer. **4.** *F:* se vérifier. **5.** *F:* **to c. s.o., sth., o.** = **to check up on s.o., sth.**

checks [tʃeks] (*pl. noun*), *P:* **to hand in one's c.,** mourir*, dévisser son billard.

check-up [ˈtʃekʌp] (*noun*), *F:* **1.** (*personne*) contrôle *m*, examen médical. **2.** (*mécanique*) révision *f.*

check up [ˈtʃekˈʌp] (**to**), *F:* **to c. u. on s.o., sth.,** se rencarder sur qn, qch.

cheek[1] [tʃiːk] (*noun*), *F:* toupet *m*, culot *m*; **he's got plenty of c.** (*or* **a hell of a c.** *or* **the c. of the devil**), il a un culot monstre, il en a un souffle; **c.!** (*or* **the c. of him,** *etc.*!), quel culot! ce culot!; **don't give me any of your c.!** (ne) te fiche pas de moi!; **it's a damned c.!** c'est se fiche(r) du monde!

cheek[2] [tʃiːk] (**to**), *F:* se payer la tête de (qn), dire des impertinences à (qn), manquer de respect à (qn), faire l'insolent avec (qn).

cheeky [ˈtʃiːki] (*adj.*), *F:* effronté, culotté, soufflé.

cheerio! [ˈtʃiəriˈou] (*excl.*), *F:* **1.** = **cheers! 2.** à bientôt! bon courage! ciao!

cheers! [tʃiəz] (*excl.*), *F:* (*a*) à la bonne vôtre! à la tienne (Étienne)!; (*b*) (*parfois*) merci.

cheerybye! [ˈtʃiəriˈbai] (*excl.*), *F:* au revoir! salut!

cheese [tʃiːz] (*noun*). **1.** *P:* **big c.,** lourdaud *m*, butor *m*, rustre *m*; *voir aussi* **big**[1], **1. 2.** *P:* **old c.,** du réchauffé. **3.** *P:* **hard c.!** pas de chance*! pas de pot! quelle guigne! **4.** *P:* **c. and kisses** (*R.S.*) = **missis. 5.** *F:* **say c.!** souriez! regardez le petit oiseau! *Voir aussi* **chalk, 2.**

cheesecake [ˈtʃiːzkeik] (*noun*), *F:* pin-up *f.*

cheesed (off) [ˈtʃiːzd(ˈɔf)] (*p.p. & adj.*), *P:* **to be** (*or* **feel**) **c.,** avoir le cafard, en avoir marre.

cheese it [ˈtʃiːzit] (**to**), *P:* partir*, se calter; **c. i.!** ça va! barca! fiche le camp!

cheesy [ˈtʃiːzi] (*adj.*), *P:* miteux, à la manque, toc.

chef [ʃef] (*noun*), *P:* **1.** opium *m* (*drogues**),

* An asterisk indicates that the word so marked is included as a head-word in the Appendix.

boue verte. 2. (*dans une fumerie d'opium*) chef *m*, caïd *m*.

cherry [ˈtʃeri] (*noun*). 1. *P:* virginité *f*, pucelage *m*, fleur *f*, primeur *f*, coquille *f*, coquillage *m*; **to lose one's c.**, perdre sa fleur; **to pick a girl's c.**, déflorer une fille. 2. *F:* **to take two bites at the c.**, **to have another bite at the c.**, s'y prendre à deux fois, y remordre.

cherry-ripe [ˈtʃeriˈraip] (*noun*) (*R.S.*), *P:* (*a*) (=*pipe*) pipe *f*; (*b*) (=*tripe*) bêtises*, sornettes *f.pl*.

chest [tʃest] (*noun*), *F:* **to get sth. off one's c.**, déballer ce qu'on a sur le cœur, vider son sac. *Voir aussi* **close**[2]; **hair, 5.**

chestnut [ˈtʃesnʌt] (*noun*). 1. *F:* histoire rabâchée, rengaine *f*, blague éventée. 2. (*pl.*) *P:* seins*, pelotes *f.pl*. 3. (*pl.*) *P:* testicules*, olives *f.pl*.

chesty [ˈtʃesti] (*adj.*), *F:* 1. délicat des bronches. 2. (*U.S.*) vaniteux, faraud.

chevy (chase) [ˈtʃevi(ˈtʃeis)] (*noun*) (*R.S.* = *face*), *P:* visage*, bouille *f*.

chew [tʃuː] (**to**), *P:* **to c. the fat** (*or* **the rag**), bavarder*, jacter, discuter le bout de gras, ragoter. *Voir aussi* **bite off (to), 2.**

chewbacon [ˈtʃuː-beikən] (*noun*), *F:* paysan*, cul-terreux *m*.

chew off [ˈtʃuːˈɔf] (**to**), *F:* **to c. s.o.'s head** (*U.S.:* **ears**) **o.**, réprimander* qn, passer un savon à qn. *Voir aussi* **balls, 3.**

chew out [ˈtʃuːˈaut] (**to**) (*U.S.*), *P:* = **ball out (to)**; **to get (one's ass) chewed out,** se faire engueuler.

chew over [ˈtʃuːˈouvər] (**to**), *F:* **to c. it o.**, réfléchir, ruminer.

chi [tʃai] (*noun*), *F:* = **char, 1.**

chichi [ˈʃiːʃiː] (*adj.*), *F:* chichiteux, collet monté.

chick [tʃik] (*noun*), *F:* 1. enfant*, môme *mf*. 2. fille*, poulette *f*. 3. (*U.S.*) **to play c.** = **to lay chickie** (*voir* **chickie**). *Voir aussi* **head, 12.**

chickabiddy [ˈtʃikəbidi] (*noun*), *F:* cocotte *f*.

chicken[1] [ˈtʃikin] (*adj.*), *P:* poltron, capon; *cf.* **chicken**[2], **4; to turn c.** = **chicken out (to).**

chicken[2] [ˈtʃikin] (*noun*). 1. *F:* **she's no (spring) c.!** c'est pas un poulet de grain! 2. *F:* **to get up with the chickens,** se lever avec les poules. 3. *F:* **to count one's chickens before they are hatched,** vendre la peau de l'ours (avant de l'avoir tué). 4. *P:* poltron*, caneur *m*, dégonfleur *m*, flubard *m*, froussard *m*, poule mouillée. 5. *P:* mineur(e), gamin(e), poulet *m* de grain, poulette *f*; **to have a c. dinner,** faire l'amour avec un(e) mineur(e), déplumer le poulet. 6. *F:* **when the chickens come home to roost,** quand arrivera le règlement des comptes, au moment venu de la rétribution.

chicken-feed [ˈtʃikinfiːd] (*noun*), *F:* 1. quelques sous*, mitraille *f*. 2. rien*, des clopinettes *f.pl.*; **it's just c.-f.**, c'est de la gnognot(t)e.

chicken-hearted [ˈtʃikinˈhɑːtid] (*adj.*), *F:* **to be c.-h.**, avoir du sang de poulet (*ou* de navet).

chicken out [ˈtʃikinˈaut] (**to**), *P:* se dégonfler.

chicken-roost [ˈtʃikinruːst] (*noun*) (*th.*), *F:* poulailler *m*; *cf.* **pigeon-roost.**

chickie [ˈtʃiki] (*adv.*) (*U.S.*), *F:* **to lay c.**, faire le guet, arçonner, faire le gaffe.

chief [tʃiːf] (*noun*). 1. *F:* **the (big white) c.**, le patron*, le grand manitou. 2. *P:* **the c.**, (*a*) LSD *m* (*drogues**); (*b*) mescaline *f* (*drogues*).

chill [tʃil] (*noun*), *P:* 1. **to put the c. on s.o.**, battre froid à qn, faire la frime à qn. 2. (*U.S.*) **to have the chills,** avoir peur*, avoir la tremblote.

chimbley [ˈtʃimbli] (*noun*), *F:* (=*chimney*) cheminée *f*, bouffardière *f*.

chime in [ˈtʃaimˈin] (**to**), *F:* couper la parole, placer son mot, mettre son grain de sel.

chimney [ˈtʃimni] (*noun*), *F:* **to smoke like a c.**, fumer comme un pompier.

chin [tʃin] (*noun*), *F:* 1. **to take it on the c.**, encaisser un sale coup, ne pas se laisser abattre. 2. **c. up!** du courage! tiens bon!; **to keep one's c. up,** tenir bon, tenir le coup.

china [ˈtʃainə] (*noun*), *P:* ami(e)*, pote *m*, copain *m*, copine *f*.

Chinaman [ˈtʃainəmən] (*noun*), *P:* 1. **to have a C. on one's back,** souffrir des symptômes du sevrage de drogues. 2. **not to have a C.'s chance (in hell),** ne pas avoir l'ombre d'une chance.

chin-chin! [ˈtʃinˈtʃin] (*excl.*), *F:* 1. au revoir! adieu! 2. à la vôtre! à la tienne!

* L'astérisque indique que le mot marqué de ce signe figure comme entrée dans le Répertoire.

chinfest [ˈtʃinfest] (*noun*), *P:* = **chinwag**[1].

chink[1] [tʃiŋk] (*noun*), *P:* argent*, fric *m.*

Chink[2] [tʃiŋk] (*noun*), *P:* Chinois *m*, Chinoise *f*, Chinetoc *m.*

chinky, Chinky [ˈtʃiŋki] (*adj.*), *P:* chinois, chinetoque; **c. nosh,** nourriture* chinoise, bouffe *f* chinetoque.

chin-music [ˈtʃinmju:zik] (*noun*), *P:* = **chinwag**[1].

chino [ˈtʃainou] (*noun*), *P:* Chinois *m* fourgueur *m* de drogues.

chintzy [ˈtʃintsi] (*adj.*), *F:* rococo.

chinwag[1] [ˈtʃinwæg] (*noun*), *P:* bavette *f*, causette *f*.

chinwag[2] [ˈtʃinwæg] (**to**), *P:* bavarder*, jaboter, tailler une bavette.

chip[1] [tʃip] (*noun*). **1.** *P:* cinq pence. **2.** *P:* **to be in the chips,** être plein aux as. **3.** *F:* **he's had his chips,** il est cuit (*ou* fichu). **4.** *F:* **when the chips are down,** quand les dés sont jetés, en cas de coup dur. **5.** *F:* **to have a c. on one's shoulder,** chercher la bagarre (*ou* des crosses *f.pl.*). **6.** *F:* **he's a c. of(f) the old block,** c'est bien le fils de son père. **7.** *P:* **to hand out the chips,** donner* de l'argent* avec largesse, abouler le fric. *Voir aussi* **cash in** (**to**), **1; chips.**

chip[2] [tʃip] (**to**), *P:* **1.** faire l'insolent, se payer la tête de (qn). **2.** chiner, blaguer, charrier (qn).

chip at [ˈtʃip-æt] (**to**), *P:* critiquer*, bêcher, éreinter (qn, qch.).

chip in [ˈtʃipˈin] (**to**), *P:* **1.** payer* sa part. **2.** placer son mot, y aller de son grain de sel.

chipper[1] [ˈtʃipər] (*adv.*), *P:* **to feel c.,** être en forme.

chipper[2] [ˈtʃipər] (*noun*), *P:* bavardage *m*, commérages *m.pl.*, jacasserie *f*.

chippy[1] [ˈtʃipi] (*adj.*), *P:* **1.** aride, fade, sans intérêt, barbant. **2.** patraque, mal fichu.

chippy[2] [ˈtʃipi] (*noun*), *P:* **1.** (*a*) prostituée*, grue *f*, radeuse *f*; (*b*) allumeuse *f*, dragueuse *f*. **2.** receveuse *f* d'autobus. **3.** (*a*) (= *mild narcotic*) herbe *f* (*drogues*); (*b*) usager *m* de drogues à faibles doses et par intervalle. **4.** menuisier *m*, copeau *m*.

chippy[3] [ˈtʃipi] (**to**), *P:* prendre des drogues* irrégulièrement ou pour se montrer initié, barboter dans la came.

chips [tʃips] (*noun*), *P:* = **chippy**[2], **4.**

chirpy [ˈtʃə:pi] (*adj.*), *F:* gai, de bonne humeur.

chirrupy [ˈtʃirəpi] (*adj.*), *F:* éveillé, joyeux, bavard.

chisel[1] [ˈtʃiz(ə)l] (*noun*), *P:* escroquerie*, filouterie *f*, sale coup *m*.

chisel[2] [ˈtʃiz(ə)l] (**to**), *P:* voler*, rouler, carotter (qn); **to c. a fiver out of s.o., to c. s.o. out of a fiver,** taper qn d'un gros faffiot.

chiseller [ˈtʃiz(ə)lər] (*noun*), *P:* escroc*, carotteur *m*.

chiselling [ˈtʃiz(ə)liŋ] (*noun*), *P:* escroquerie*, resquille *f*.

chit [tʃit] (*noun*), *F:* petit enfant*, bout *m* de zan.

chiv[1] [ʃiv] (*noun*), *P:* **1.** couteau*, surin *m*. **2.** rasoir*, rasibe *m*.

chiv[2] [ʃiv] (**to**) (*p.p.* **chiv(v)ed** [ʃivd]), *P:* **1.** taillader, larder, suriner (qn). **2.** marquer, faire la croix des vaches à (qn).

chive [ʃiv] (*noun & verb*), *P:* = **chiv**[1,2].

chive-man [ˈ(t)ʃivmæn, ˈtʃaivmæn], **chive-merchant** [ˈ(t)ʃivmə:tʃənt, ˈtʃaivmə:tʃənt] (*noun*), *P:* surineur *m*.

chivey [ˈʃivi] (*noun*), *P:* = **chiv**[1], **1, 2.**

chiv(v)y up (*or* **along**)[ˈ tʃiviˈʌp, əˈlɔŋ)] (**to**), *F:* relancer, poursuivre, harceler (qn).

chock-a-block [ˈtʃɔkəˈblɔk] (*adj.*), *F:* plein à craquer, archi-plein, plein comme un œuf.

chocker [ˈtʃɔkər] (*adj.*). **1.** *F:* = **chock-a-block.** **2.** *P:* **to be c.,** en avoir assez*, en avoir marre; *cf.* **dead**[2], **5.**

chock-full [ˈtʃɔkˈful] (*adj.*), *F:* = **chock-a-block.**

chocolate [ˈtʃɔklit] (*noun*), *P:* **c. lover** = **dinge queen** (*voir* **queen, 2**); *cf.* **coal-burner.**

choke [tʃouk] (*noun*), *P:* = **chok(e)y, 2.**

choked [tʃoukt] (*p.p. & adj.*), *P:* **1.** déçu, chocolat. **2.** = **chocker, 2.**

choke off [ˈtʃoukˈɔf] (**to**), *F:* envoyer balader (qn).

choker [ˈtʃoukər] (*noun*), *P:* **that's a c.,** ça vous la bouche.

chok(e)y [ˈtʃouki] (*noun*), *P:* **1.** barrière *f* de péage. **2.** prison*, clou *m*. **3.** mitard *m*, trou *m*.

choo-choo [ˈtʃu:tʃu:] (*noun*), *F:* (*langage enfantin*) teuf-teuf *m*.

* An asterisk indicates that the word so marked is included as a head-word in the Appendix.

chook(ie) [ˈtʃuːk(i)] (*noun*) (*Austr.*), *F:* poule *f*, poulet *m*.

choosy [ˈtʃuːzi] (*adj.*), *F:* chipoteur.

chop[1] [tʃɔp] (*noun*), *P:* 1. (*a*) **to give s.o. the c.**, se débarrasser* de qn, sacquer qn; *cf.* **sack**[1], 1; (*b*) **he's for the c.!** qu'est-ce qu'il va prendre! son affaire est bonne! 2. **to smack s.o. round the chops**, donner une bonne claque à qn. 3. nourriture*, fricot *m*. *Voir aussi* **lamb**, 1; **lick**[2] **(to)**, 3; **slobber-chops.**

chop[2] [tʃɔp] **(to)**. 1. *P:* guillotiner, raccourcir. 2. *P:* pendre*, béquiller; *cf.* **top**[2] **(to)**. 3. *P:* (*sports*) donner un coup de pied dans les jambes de (qn). 4. *F:* **to c. and change**, changer d'idée comme de chemise.

chop-chop [ˈtʃɔpˈtʃɔp] (*adv.*), *F:* vite*, presto, dare-dare; **c.-c.!** dépêchez*-vous! vite!

chop down [ˈtʃɔpˈdaun] **(to)**, *F:* **to c. s.o. d. (to size)**, faire descendre qn d'un cran, rapetisser qn.

chophouse [ˈtʃɔphaus] (*noun*), *F:* restaurant chinois, gargot(t)e *f* chinetoque.

chopper [ˈtʃɔpər] (*noun*). 1. *V:* pénis*, défonceuse *f*. 2. *P:* mitraillette*, moulinette *f*. 3. *P:* hélicoptère *m*, battoir *m*, moulin *m*. 4. (*pl.*) *P:* dents*, croquantes *f.pl.* 5. *P:* vieille voiture* reprise pour une neuve. 6. *P:* (*a*) moto modifiée, sans chrome; (*b*) mini-vélo *m*.

chop-up [ˈtʃɔpʌp] (*noun*), *P:* partage *m* d'un butin, décarpillement *m*.

chouse [ˈtʃauz] **(to)**, *P:* **to c. sth. out of s.o.**, carotter qch. à qn.

chow [tʃau] (*noun*), *F:* nourriture*, mangeaille *f*, boustifaille *f*; **c. time**, l'heure *f* de la bouffe.

chowderhead [ˈtʃaudəhed] (*noun*) (*U.S.*), *F:* = **chucklehead.**

Christ [kraist] (*pr. noun*), *P:* 1. **C. (Almighty)!** bon Dieu (de bon Dieu)! Christi! 2. **for C.'s sake!** pour l'amour de Dieu! *Voir aussi* **Jesus (Christ)!**

Christmas-tree [ˈkrisməs-triː] (*noun*), *P:* drinamyl *m* (*drogues**), arbre *m* de Noël.

chromo [ˈkroumou] (*noun*) (*Austr.*), *P:* 1. fille*, môme *f*; femme*, gonzesse *f*. 2. fille *ou* femme facile (*ou* de petite vertu).

chronic[1] [ˈkrɔnik] (*adj.*), *F:* insupportable, empoisonnant.

chronic[2] [ˈkrɔnik] (*adv.*), *P:* à haute dose; **I've got guts-ache something c.**, j'ai un mal de ventre carabiné; **she went off at me something c.**, elle m'a fait une scène du tonnerre.

chronic[3] [ˈkrɔnik] (*noun*), *P:* drogué*, toxico(mane) *mf*.

chubb in [ˈtʃʌbˈin] **(to)**, *P:* boucler, enfermer, coffrer (un prisonnier, *etc.*); *cf.* **miln (to); unchubb (to).**

chuck[1] [tʃʌk] (*noun*), *P:* 1. nourriture*, bectance *f*. 2. **c. habit**, gavage *m*. 3. **c. horrors**, dégoût *m* de la nourriture pendant le sevrage de drogues. 4. **to give s.o. the c.**, se débarrasser* de qn, balancer qn.

chuck[2] [tʃʌk] **(to)**. 1. *F:* jeter*, lancer (qch.). 2. *P:* se débarrasser* de (qn), envoyer dinguer (qn). 3. *P:* (*a*) manger*, bouffer; (*b*) se gaver. 4. *F:* **c. it!** en voilà assez*! ça va comme ça! 5. *P:* **to get chucked**, être acquitté, être défargué. *Voir aussi* **dummy**, 4.

chuck about (*or* **around**) [ˈtʃʌkəˈbaut, ˈtʃʌkəˈraund] **(to)**, *F:* 1. **to c. one's money a.**, jeter son argent* par les fenêtres, gaspiller son argent*. 2. **to c. one's weight a.**, faire l'important, faire valoir son autorité, faire du volume (*ou* de l'esbrouf(f)e *f*).

chucker-out [ˈtʃʌkəˈraut] (*noun*), *F:* videur *m*.

chuck in [ˈtʃʌkˈin] **(to)**, *F:* 1. **to c. i. one's job**, lâcher son travail* (*ou* son boulot). 2. **to c. it i.**, y renoncer, quitter la partie, lâcher les dés.

chucklehead [ˈtʃʌklhed] (*noun*) (*U.S.*), *F:* individu bête*, andouille *f*.

chuckleheaded [ˈtʃʌklhedid] (*adj.*) (*U.S.*), *F:* bête*, bas de plafond.

chuck out [ˈtʃʌkˈaut] **(to)**, *F:* se débarrasser* de (qn), flanquer (qn) à la porte, balancer, vider (qn).

chuck up [ˈtʃʌkˈʌp] **(to)**. 1. *F:* = **chuck in (to)**, 1, 2. 2. *F:* **to c. s.o. u.**, lâcher qn, plaquer qn (comme une crêpe). 3. *P:* vomir*, dégobiller.

chuff [tʃʌf] (*noun*), *P:* 1. nourriture*, la soupe, le rata; *cf.* **honk (to)**, 1. 2. anus*, anneau *m*. 3. fesses*, postérieur *m*.

chuffed [tʃʌft] (*adj.*), *F:* **to be c.**, (*a*) être ravi(e), être aux anges; (*b*) en

* L'astérisque indique que le mot marqué de ce signe figure comme entrée dans le Répertoire.

avoir assez*, en avoir marre (*ou* ras le bol); (*c*) être furibard (*ou* furax).

chum [tʃʌm] (*noun*), *F:* **1.** ami*, pote *m.* **2. you've said it, c.!** comme de juste (*ou* tout juste), Auguste! *Voir aussi* **have (to), 4.**

chummy [ˈtʃʌmi] (*adj.*), *F:* amical, bon copain.

chump [tʃʌmp] (*noun*). **1.** *P:* tête*, caboche *f*; **off one's c.**, fou*, timbré, loufoque. **2.** *F:* **a (silly) c.**, un individu bête*, un nigaud, une cruche.

chum up [ˈtʃʌmˈʌp] (**to**), *F:* copiner.

chunder [ˈtʃʌndər] (**to**) (*Austr.*), *P:* vomir*, dégueuler.

chunks [tʃʌŋks] (*pl. noun*), *P:* hachisch *m* (*drogues**), griffs *m.pl.*

chunky [ˈtʃʌŋki] (*adj.*), *F:* **1.** trapu. **2.** (*ameublement*) encombrant, lourdaud. **3. c. jewellery,** bijoux *m.pl.* mastoc.

chunner [ˈtʃʌnər] (**to**), *P:* grogner*, radoter.

churchy [ˈtʃəːtʃi] (*adj.*), *F:* calotin, tala; **c. old women,** vieilles punaises de sacristie.

churchyard [ˈtʃəːtʃjɑːd] (*attrib. adj.*), *F:* **a c. cough,** une toux de déterré (*ou* qui sent le sapin).

churn out [ˈtʃəːnˈaut] (**to**), *F:* produire beaucoup de (qch.), confectionner en quantité.

chute [ʃuːt] (*noun*). **1.** *P:* **up the c.,** (*d'une personne*) bête*, navet, con(n)asse. **2.** *P:* **to go up the c.** = **to go up in smoke** (**smoke**[1], **1**). **3.** *F:* (=*parachute*) parachute *m*, pépin *m.*

chyack [ˈtʃaijæk] (**to**), *P:* se montrer très insolent envers (qn), narguer (qn).

cig(gy) [ˈsig(i)] (*noun*), *F:* cigarette*, cibiche *f.*

cinch [sintʃ] (*noun*), *F:* certitude *f*; **it's a c.,** (*a*) c'est certain, c'est couru d'avance, c'est du tout cuit; (*b*) c'est facile; **she's a c.,** c'est une femme facile.

circs [səːks] (*pl. noun*) (*abbr.* = *circumstances*), *F:* **in** (*or* **under**) **the c.,** dans ce cas-là.

circus [ˈsəːkəs] (*noun*). **1.** *F:* le cirque, une rigolade. **2.** = **brody, 2.** *Voir aussi* **Piccadilly Circus.**

cissy [ˈsisi] (*noun*), *F:* **1.** femmelette *f*, chiffe(niolle) *f* **2.** poltron*, vessard *m*, poule mouillée.

civvies [ˈsiviz] (*pl. noun*), *F:* **in c.,** en civelot, en bourgeois; (*police*) en pékin. *Voir aussi* **civvy**[2].

civvy[1] [ˈsivi] (*adj.*), *F:* civil, pékin; **in c. street,** dans le civil.

civvy[2] [ˈsivi] (*noun*), *F:* bourgeois *m*, civil *m. Voir aussi* **civvies.**

clack[1] [klæk] (*noun*), *P:* caquet *m*; **stop your c.!** tais*-toi, la ferme! ferme ça! ferme ton clapet!

clack[2] [klæk] (**to**), *P:* bavarder*, caqueter, jacasser.

clackety-clack [ˈklækətiˈklæk] (*noun*), *F:* caquetage *m*, jacasserie *f*; *cf.* **yackety-yack.**

clamp-down [ˈklæmpdaun] (*noun*), *F:* contrainte *f*, vissage *m*, étouffage *m.*

clamp down [ˈklæmpˈdaun] (**to**), *F:* contraindre par la force; **to c. d. on sth., s.o.,** serrer la vis à qch., qn, visser qch., qn.

clamps [klæmps] (*pl. noun*), *F:* **to put the c. on sth., s.o.** = **to clamp down on sth., s.o.**

clam up [ˈklæmˈʌp] (**to**), *F:* se taire*, la boucler.

clanger [ˈklæŋər] (*noun*), *F:* **to drop a c.,** faire une bévue*.

clanked [klæŋkt] (*adj.*) (*U.S.*), *P:* **1.** fatigué*, éreinté. **2.** déprimé, cafardeux.

clap [klæp] (*noun*), *P:* blennorragie*, gonorrhée *f*, chaude-pisse *f*, coulante *f.*

clapped out [ˈklæptˈaut] (*p.p. & adj.*). **1.** *P:* atteint de maladie vénérienne (*malade**), nazicoté. **2.** *F:* fatigué*, avachi.

clapper [ˈklæpər] (*noun*), *F:* **1.** langue*, clapette *f.* **2. to go like the clappers,** filer comme un zèbre.

claret [ˈklærət] (*noun*), *P:* sang *m*, résiné *m*; **to have one's c. tapped,** saigner du nez*, pavoiser.

class(y) [ˈklɑːs(i)] (*adj.*), *F:* (*a*) chic, bon genre; (*b*) beau*, badour; **to be c.,** avoir de la classe.

clean [kliːn] (*adj.*), *F:* **1. to be c. (as a whistle),** (*a*) être tout beau (*ou* tout propre); (*b*) être sans condamnation*, être blanc; (*c*) être pauvre*, être à blanc; (*d*) être sans arme; (*e*) ne pas prendre de drogues, être sur le blanc. **2. to make a c. breast of it,** tout avouer*, se mettre à table. **3. to come c.,** avouer*, lâcher le paquet. *Voir aussi* **nose, 3; sweep**[1], **3.**

* An asterisk indicates that the word so marked is included as a head-word in the Appendix.

cleaners ['kli:nəz] (*pl. noun*), *P:* **to take s.o. to the c.,** mettre qn à sec.

clean-out ['kli:naut] (*noun*), *F:* lessive *f*, coup *m* de balai.

clean out ['kli:n'aut] (**to**), *F:* **to c. s.o. o.,** prendre l'argent* à qn, lessiver qn; **to get cleaned out,** perdre son argent*, être rincé, boire un bouillon, se faire plumer.

clear[1] [kliər] (*adj.*), *F:* **it's (as) c. as mud,** c'est la bouteille à l'encre, c'est clair comme du jus de boudin (*ou* de chique).

clear[2] [kliər] (*noun*), *F:* (*a*) **to be in the c.,** (i) être tiré d'affaire (*ou* sorti de l'auberge); (ii) être blanc (*ou* défargué); (*b*) **to put s.o. in the c.,** (i) tirer qn d'affaire; (ii) défarguer qn. *Voir aussi* **all-clear.**

clear off ['kliər'ɔf] (**to**), *F:* partir*, prendre le large (*ou* la tangente); **c. o.!** file! fiche le camp! décampe!

clear-out ['kliəraut] (*noun*): **to have a c.-o.,** (*a*) *F:* faire du triage, désencombrer; (*b*) *P:* déféquer*, déflaquer.

clear out ['kliər'aut] (**to**), *F:* **1.** = **clear off (to). 2. to c. s.o. o. of sth.,** débarrasser qn de qch., nettoyer qn.

cleavage ['kli:vidʒ] (*noun*), *F:* (*a*) naissance *f* des seins*; (*b*) décolleté très ouvert.

cleft [kleft] (*noun*), *V:* vagin*, crac *m*, fente *f*.

clever-clever ['klevəklevər] (*adj.*), *F:* malin*, débrouillard.

cleverclogs ['klevəklɔgz], **cleverguts** ['klevəgʌts] (*noun*), *P:* = **clever Dick (dick, 3).**

click [klik] (**to**), *F:* **to c. with s.o.,** (*a*) sympathiser (*ou* accrocher) avec qn; (*b*) faire une touche.

clickety-click ['klikəti'klik], *F: voir* **bingo (66).**

cliffhanger ['klifhæŋər] (*noun*), *F:* (*film*) drame-feuilleton *m*; suspense *m*.

climb [klaim] (**to**), *P:* coïter* avec (une femme), chevaucher. *Voir aussi* **bandwagon.**

clinch [klintʃ] (*noun*), *F:* embrassade *f*, étreinte amoureuse, enlacement *m*.

clincher ['klintʃər] (*noun*), *F:* argument définitif; **that's a c.,** (*a*) ça lui a fermé le bec; (*b*) c'est le mot de la fin.

clinger ['kliŋər] (*noun*), *F:* crampon *m*.

clink [kliŋk] (*noun*), *P:* prison*, violon *m*; **to be in c.,** faire de la grosse caisse; **to put s.o. in c.,** mettre qn au bloc; **to go to c.,** être emprisonné*, être fourré au bloc.

clinker ['kliŋkər] (*noun*), *P:* **1.** coup*, gnon *m*. **2.** mensonge*, crac *m*. **3.** vieille voiture*, tacot *m*. **4.** type *m ou* chose *f* formidable.

clip[1] [klip] (*noun*), *F:* **1.** coup*, beigne *f*, taloche *f*. **2.** pas *m* rapide.

clip[2] [klip] (**to**). **1.** *F:* flanquer une taloche à (qn). **2.** *P:* voler*, écorcher, plumer, estamper (qn). **3.** *P:* aller à vive allure (*ou* à toute bride).

clip-game ['klipgeim] (*noun*), *P:* filouterie *f*.

clip-joint ['klipdʒɔint] (*noun*), *F:* boîte *f*, tripot *m*, maison *f* tire-pognon.

clipper ['klipər] (*noun*), *F:* individu *ou* chose remarquable, du tonnerre.

clippie ['klipi] (*noun*), *F:* receveuse *f* d'autobus.

clit [klit] (*noun*), *V:* clitoris*, clicli *m*.

cloak-and-dagger ['klouk(ə)n'dægər] (*attrib. adj.*), *F:* de cape et d'épée.

clobber[1] ['klɔbər] (*noun*), *P:* vêtements*, frusques *f.pl.*, hardes *f.pl.*

clobber[2] ['klɔbər] (**to**), *P:* **1.** battre*, matraquer, rosser; **to get clobbered,** être rossé, se faire arranger. **2.** écraser, battre à plate(s) couture(s).

clobbering ['klɔbəriŋ] (*noun*), *P:* **to give s.o. a c.,** donner une rossée à qn.

clock[1] [klɔk] (*noun*). **1.** *P:* visage*, poire *f*. **2.** *F:* **to beat the c.,** arriver* avant l'heure. **3.** *F:* **round the c.,** vingt-quatre heures sur vingt-quatre; **to sleep round the c., to sleep the c. round,** faire le tour du cadran.

clock[2] [klɔk] (**to**), *P:* **1.** battre*, calotter (qn), abîmer le portrait à (qn). **2.** guetter*, mater, gaffer (qn).

clock up ['klɔk'ʌp] (**to**), *F:* **to c. u. the miles,** rouler vite*, avaler les kilomètres.

clock-watcher ['klɔkwɔtʃər] (*noun*), *F:* tire-au-flanc *m*.

clod [klɔd] (*noun*), *F:* = **clodhopper, 1.**

clod-crushers ['klɔdkrʌʃəz] (*pl. noun*), *P:* = **clodhoppers (clodhopper, 3).**

clodhopper ['klɔdhɔpər] (*noun*), *P:* **1.** paysan*, plouc *m*. **2.** déguingandé *m*. **3.** (*pl.*) grosses chaussures*, tatanes *f.pl.*

clogging ['klɔgiŋ] (*noun*) (*football*), *F:* jeu déloyal, barbouillage *m*.

* L'astérisque indique que le mot marqué de ce signe figure comme entrée dans le Répertoire.

cloghead [ˈklɔghed] (*noun*), *P:* individu bête*, gourde *f.*
clomp about [ˈklɔmpəˈbaut] (**to**), *F:* = **clump about (to).**
clonk[1] [klɔŋk] (*noun*), *P:* coup*, ramponneau *m*; **to fetch s.o. a c.,** filer un ramponneau à qn.
clonk[2] [klɔŋk] (**to**), *P:* battre*, frapper; **to c. s.o. one,** filer un gnon à qn; **to c. s.o. on the head,** assommer qn, envoyer dormir qn.
clonk about [ˈklɔŋkəˈbaut] (**to**), *F:* = **clump about (to).**
close[1] [klous] (*adj.*), *P:* excellent*, foutral. *Voir aussi* **shave.**
close[2] [klous] (*adv.*), *F:* **to play it c. (to the chest),** y aller mollo, jouer serré.
close-fisted [ˈklousˈfistid] (*adj.*), *F:* avare*, radin, dur à la détente.
clot [klɔt] (*noun*), *F:* personne bête*, clope *m*, cave *m*; **you clumsy c.!** espèce d'empoté! **what a c.!** qu'est-ce qu'il trimbal(l)e!
cloth-ears [ˈklɔθ-iəz] (*noun*), *F:* sourd*, dur *m* de la feuille.
clothes-horse [ˈklouðzhɔːs] (*noun*), *P:* femme* tape-à-l'œil, mannequin ambulant.
cloth-head [ˈklɔθhed] (*noun*), *F:* = **clot.**
cloud [klaud] (*noun*), *F:* **1. to have one's head in the clouds,** être dans la lune. **2. to be (up) in the clouds,** être aux anges. **3. to be on c. nine,** être au septième ciel.
cloud-cuckoo-land [ˈklaudˈkukuːlænd] (*noun*), *F:* pays *m* des rêves, pays des Châteaux en Espagne.
clout[1] [klaut] (*noun*). **1.** *F:* coup*, calotte *f*; **to give (*or* fetch) s.o. a c.,** filer une calotte à qn. **2.** *V:* vagin*, motte *f. Voir aussi* **dishclout.**
clout[2] [klaut] (**to**), *F:* filer une calotte à (qn).
clover [ˈklouvər] (*noun*), *F:* **to be in c.,** être comme un coq en pâte.
club [klʌb] (*noun*). **1.** *F:* **to join the c.,** s'acoquiner avec qn. **2.** *P:* **to join the (pudding) c.,** être enceinte*.
cluck [klʌk] (*noun*), *P:* **dumb c.,** individu bête*, gourde *f*, cruchon *m.*
clue [kluː] (*noun*), *F:* **he hasn't a c.,** (*a*) il n'a pas la moindre idée; (*b*) il n'est bon à rien.
clueless [ˈkluːlis] (*adj.*), *F:* **1.** qui est dans le noir (*ou* dans le brouillard). **2.** qui n'a pas trouvé le joint.
clue up [ˈkluːˈʌp] (**to**), *F:* **to c. s.o. u.,** mettre qn sur la piste (*ou* au parfum *ou* à la page); **to be clued up,** être au parfum; **to get clued up,** se faire rencarder.
clump[1] [klʌmp] (*noun*), *F:* coup*, beigne *f.*
clump[2] [klʌmp] (**to**), *F:* battre*, tabasser (qn).
clump about [ˈklʌmpəˈbaut] (**to**), *F:* marcher lourdement.
clunk [klʌŋk] (*noun & verb*), *P:* = **clonk**[1,2].
clunkhead [ˈklʌŋkhed] (*noun*) (*U.S.*), *P:* = **chucklehead.**
clutch up [ˈklʌtʃˈʌp] (**to**) (*U.S.*), *F:* s'énerver, se monter le ciboulot.
cly [klai] (*noun*), *P:* poche*, fouille *f.*
coal-burner [ˈkoulbəːnər] (*noun*), *P:* = **dinge queen** (*voir* **queen, 2**); *cf.* **chocolate.**
coalie, coaly [ˈkouli] (*noun*), *F:* charbonnier *m*, carbi *m.*
coast along [ˈkoustəˈlɔŋ] (**to**), *F:* **1.** aller en roue libre. **2.** se la couler douce, ne pas se fouler.
coasting [ˈkoustiŋ] (*noun*). **1.** *F:* (*d'une personne, d'un véhicule*) marche *f* en roue libre. **2.** *P:* état *m* d'animation dû à la drogue, bang *m.*
cob [kɔb] (*noun*), *P:* miche *f* de pain* (*en prison*), demi-boule *f.*
cobber [ˈkɔbər] (*noun*) (*Austr.*), *F:* ami*, copain *m*, pote *m.*
cobbler [ˈkɔblər] (*noun*), *P:* faussaire *m*, homme *m* de lettres. *Voir aussi* **cobblers.**
cobblers [ˈkɔbləz] (*pl. noun*) (*R.S.* = *cobblers' awls* = *balls*), *P:* **it's a load of c.** = **it's all balls (balls, 6).**
cock [kɔk] (*noun*). **1.** *V:* (*a*) pénis*, queue *f*; (*b*) mâle (considéré sexuellement). **2.** *P:* bêtise*, coq-à-l'âne *m*; **to talk c.,** déconner; *voir aussi* **load, 2; poppycock. 3.** *P:* **all to c.,** de traviole. **4.** *P:* **well, old c.,** eh bien, mon colon!; **wotcher, c.!** comment ça gaze, ma vieille branche? **5.** *P:* **c. and hen** (*R.S.* = *ten*), billet* de dix livres; **half a c.,** billet* de cinq livres, un gros talbin. *Voir aussi* **half-cock.**
cock-a-hoop [ˈkɔkəˈhuːp] (*adj.*), *F:* fier comme Artaban.

* An asterisk indicates that the word so marked is included as a head-word in the Appendix.

cockalorum [kɔkəˈlɔːrəm] (*noun*), *F:* petit* individu plein de prétention, astèque plastronneur.

cockatoo(er) [ˈkɔkəˈtuː(ər)] (*noun*) (*Austr.*), *P:* compère *m* qui fait le guet, arçonneur *m*, gaffe *m*, gâfe *m*.

cocked [kɔkt] (*adj.*), *F:* **to knock sth. into a c. hat,** démantibuler qch.; **to knock s.o. into a c. hat,** (*a*) battre* qn à plate(s) couture(s), pulvériser qn; (*b*) abasourdir qn.

cocker [ˈkɔkər] (*noun*), *P:* = **cock, 4.**

cockeyed [ˈkɔkaid] (*adj.*), *P:* **1.** très bête*, noix, à la manque. **2.** ivre*, rétamé à bloc. **3.** de travers, de guingois. **4.** qui louche*, qui a un œil qui dit zut à l'autre. **5.** inexact, biscornu.

cock-handler [ˈkɔkhændlər], **cock-pusher** [ˈkɔkpuʃər] (*noun*), *V:* pédéraste*, empaffé *m*.

cock-shy [ˈkɔkʃai] (*adj.*), *V:* (*d'une femme*) qui a peur des rapports sexuels.

cock-sparrow [ˈkɔkˈspærou, ˈkɔkˈspærə] (*noun*). **1.** *F:* = **cockalorum. 2.** *P:* **wotcher, me old c.-s.!** = **wotcher, cock!** (**cock, 4**).

cock-stand [ˈkɔk-stænd] (*noun*), *V:* érection*, bandoche *f*, coliques cornues.

cock-sucker [ˈkɔk-sʌkər] (*noun*), *V:* **1.** pédéraste*, lope *f*. **2.** salaud *m*, fumier *m*. **3.** lèche-bottes *m*, lèche-cul *m*.

cock-sucking [ˈkɔk-sʌkiŋ] (*noun*), *V:* coït* buccal, prise *f* de pipe.

cock-teaser [ˈkɔk-tiːzər] (*noun*), *V:* = **prick-teaser.**

cock-up [ˈkɔkʌp] (*noun*), *V:* = **balls-up.**

cock up [ˈkɔkˈʌp] (**to**). **1.** *V:* = **balls up** (**to**). **2.** *F:* **to c. u. one's eyes,** faire des yeux de merlan frit.

cocky [ˈkɔki] (*adj.*), *F:* culotté, qui a du toupet; suffisant.

coco(a) [ˈkoukou] (**to**), *P:* **1.** (*R.S.* = *say so*) **I should c.!** et comment donc! tu parles! **2.** croire*, couper dedans; **you wouldn't c. it!** tu ne t'en fais pas la moindre idée!

cod [kɔd] (**to**), *P:* duper*, emmener (qn) en bateau, faire marcher (qn).

codger [ˈkɔdʒər] (*noun*), *F:* **1.** (drôle de) coco *m*. **2. old c.,** vieux décati.

cods [kɔdz] (*pl. noun*), *P:* testicules*, burettes *f.pl.*, burnes *f.pl.*

codswallop [ˈkɔdzwɔləp] (*noun*), *F:* **1.** bêtises*, tissu *m* d'âneries. **2.** bière *f* de mauvaise qualité, bibine *f*.

co-ed [ˈkouˈ(w)ed] (*noun*), *F:* élève *mf* d'une école mixte.

coffin [ˈkɔfin] (*noun*). **1.** (*U.S.*) *P:* mitard *m*, (s)chtard *m*. **2.** *F:* **c. nail,** cigarette*, cibiche *f*.

cog [kɔg] (**to**), *P:* tricher* (*surtout* aux dés), biseauter; **cogged dice,** dés* pipés.

coin [kɔin] (**to**), *F:* **to c. it, to be coining it,** devenir riche*, faire des affaires d'or, tomber sur un champ d'oseille.

coke [kouk] (*noun*). **1.** *F:* Coca-Cola *m* (*marque déposée*). **2.** *P:* cocaïne *f* (*drogues**), coco *f*; **c. fiend,** cocaïnomane *mf*, (s)chnouffé(e); **c. oven,** clandé *m*. *cf.* **charl(e)y**[2], **5.**

coked (up) [ˈkoukt(ˈʌp)] (*adj.*), *P:* drogué*, chargé, bourré (à la cocaïne).

cokehead [ˈkoukhed] (*noun*), *P:* = **coke fiend** (**coke, 2**).

cokernut [ˈkoukənʌt] (*noun*). **1.** *F:* (=*coco(a)nut*) noix *f* de coco. **2.** *P:* tête*, coco *m*.

cokey, cokie [ˈkouki], **cokomo** [kouˈkoumou] (*noun*), *P:* = **coke fiend** (**coke, 2**).

cold[1] [kould] (*adj.*), *F:* **1. to be out** (**stone**) **c.,** être dans les pommes; **to pass out c.,** s'évanouir*, tourner de l'œil; **to knock s.o. out c.,** mettre qn sur le tapis, étendre raide qn. **2. that leaves me c.,** ça me laisse froid. **3. to give s.o. the c. shoulder,** battre froid à qn, faire la tête à qn; *cf.* **cold-shoulder** (**to**). **4. c. feet,** peur*, frousse *f*; **to get c. feet,** caner, caponner. **5. c. fish,** pisse-froid *m*. **6.** (*a*) **c. potato** = **c. fish** (*voir* **5**); (*b*) **c. potatoes,** du réchauffé. **7. to put in c. storage,** (*a*) (*fig.*) mettre au frigidaire; (*b*) économiser*, mettre à gauche; (*c*) emprisonner*, mettre au bloc. *Voir aussi* **blood, 4; meat, 5; stone-cold; sweat**[1]**, 4; turkey, 1; water, 1.**

cold[2] [kould] (*noun*), *F:* **1. to catch a c.,** écoper. **2. to be left out in the c.,** être mis de côté, rester sur le carreau.

cold-shoulder [ˈkouldˈʃouldər] (**to**), *F:* battre froid à (qn), faire grise mine à (qn); *cf.* **cold**[1]**, 3.**

colin [ˈkɔlin] (*noun*), *P:* érection*, bambou *m*, trique *f*.

collar[1] [ˈkɔlər] (*noun*), *F:* **to get one's c. felt** (*or* **touched**), être arrêté*, se faire alpaguer. *Voir aussi* **dog-collar; hot, 5; white-collar.**

* L'astérisque indique que le mot marqué de ce signe figure comme entrée dans le Répertoire.

collar² [ˈkɔlər] (**to**), *F:* **1.** arrêter*, cravater. **2.** (*a*) plaquer; (*b*) saisir, pincer, mettre la main sur (qn, qch.).

collywobbles [ˈkɔliwɔblz] (*pl. noun*), *F:* **to have the c.,** (*a*) avoir des borborygmes *m.pl.*; (*b*) avoir la diarrhée*, avoir la chiasse.

colour [ˈkʌlər] (*noun*), *F:* **let's see the c. of your money,** prouve que tu as de l'argent*; où est l'auréole de ton Saint-Fric? *Voir aussi* **horse¹, 3; off⁴, 1.**

column-dodger [ˈkɔləmˈdɔdʒər] (*noun*), *F:* tire-au-flanc *m*; *cf.* **to dodge the column** (**dodge²** (**to**), **1**).

combo [ˈkɔmbou] (*noun*), *P:* orchestre *m* de jazz.

comb-out [ˈkoumaut] (*noun*), *F:* ratissage *m*.

come¹ [kʌm] (*noun*), *P:* sperme*, jus *m*.

come² [kʌm] (**to**). **1.** *P:* avoir un orgasme*, jouir, juter. **2.** *F:* **as dim** (*or* **daft**) **as they c.,** bête* comme ses pieds. **3.** *F:* **you'll get what's coming to you!** tu ne perds rien pour attendre! **4.** *F:* **to c. it (a bit) strong,** exagérer*, y aller fort, attiger (la cabane). **5.** *P:* **to c. it over s.o.,** faire la loi à qn. **6.** *P:* **don't (you) c. it with me!** charrie pas avec moi! **7.** *F:* **to c. over funny** (*or* **queer**), se sentir tout chose. *Voir aussi* **acid, 1; clean, 3; soldier¹, 3; think¹.**

come-back [ˈkʌmbæk] (*noun*), *F:* **1. to make a c.-b.,** se remettre sur pied, se retaper, se refaire. **2.** réplique pertinente *ou* pleine de sel.

come-down [ˈkʌmdaun] (*noun*). **1.** *F:* **what a c.-d.!** quelle dégringolade! quelle douche! **2.** *P:* retour *m* à l'état hors drogue, descente *f*.

come down [ˈkʌmˈdaun] (**to**). **1.** *F:* revenir à l'état hors drogue, redescendre. **2.** *V:* **to c. d. on s.o.** = **eat (to), 7;** *cf.* **go down (to), 5. 3.** *F:* **to c. d. on s.o. (like a ton of bricks),** réprimander* qn, enguirlander qn. **4.** *F:* **to c. d. in the world,** déchoir, descendre plusieurs échelons. *Voir aussi* **peg¹, 2** (*b*).

comedy [ˈkɔmidi] (*noun*), *F:* **cut the c.!** finie la comédie!

come-hither [ˈkʌmˈhiðər] (*adj.*), *F:* **a c.-h. look,** les yeux* doux, œillade* en lousdoc.

come off [ˈkʌmˈɔf] (**to**), *P:* **1.** = **come² (to), 1. 2. c. o. it!** (*a*) change de disque! arrête ton char!; (*b*) pas tant de manières!

come-on [ˈkʌmɔn] (*noun*), *P:* **to give s.o. the c.-o.,** encourager les avances sexuelles de qn.

come on [ˈkʌmˈɔn] (**to**), *P:* **1.** commencer à ressentir les effets d'une drogue, partir. **2.** flirter, faire des avances. **3. to c. o. (a bit)** = **to come it (a bit) strong** (**come²** (**to**), **4**).

come up [ˈkʌmˈʌp] (**to**), *F:* gagner, affurer; **to c. u. on the horses,** gagner aux courses; prendre un paquet aux courtines.

come-uppance [ˈkʌmˈʌpəns] (*noun*), *F:* coup *m* de caveçon; **to get one's c.-u.,** recevoir un coup de caveçon, se faire dire ses quatre vérités.

comfy [ˈkʌmfi] (*adj.*) (=*comfortable*), *F:* confortable, douillet. *Voir aussi* **nice and . . .**

comic [ˈkɔmik] (*adj.*), *F:* **c. cuts,** (*a*) bandes dessinées; (*b*) bille *f* de clown, gugusse *m*; (*c*) rapport confidentiel.

commercial [kəˈməːʃəl] (*noun*), *P:* **to have a right old c.,** faire du bruit*, faire du barouf.

Commie¹, commie [ˈkɔmi] (*adj.*), *F:* communiste, bolcho, communo.

Commie², commie [ˈkɔmi] (*noun*), *F:* communiste *mf*, communo *m*.

common [ˈkɔmən] (*noun*), *F:* sens commun, du chou.

compree [ˈkɔmˈpriː] (*verbal form*), *F:* compris, pigé.

con¹ [kɔn] (*noun*). **1.** *F:* (=*convict*) taulard *m*; *cf.* ex. **2.** (*U.S.*) *P:* pédéraste*, lope *f*. **3.** *F:* escroquerie*, carottage *m*; **c. game,** combine *f* louche, attrape-couillons *m*; **c. man** (*or* **artist**), escroc*, arnaqueur *m*, estampeur *m*. *Voir aussi* **pro, 3.**

con² [kɔn] (**to**), *F:* escroquer*, empaumer (qn); **to c. s.o. into doing sth.,** entortiller qn.

conchie, conchy [ˈkɔntʃi] (*noun*), *F:* (=*conscientious objector*) objecteur *m* de conscience.

confab [ˈkɔnfæb] (*noun*), *F:* bavette *f*, causette *f*; **there's a family c. going on,** toute la famille est en train de conférer.

confab(ulate) [kənˈfæb(juleit)] (**to**), *F:* bavarder*, tailler une bavette; conférer.

* An asterisk indicates that the word so marked is included as a head-word in the Appendix.

conflab ['kɔnflæb] (*noun*), *F:* = **confab.**

Congo Mataby ['kɔŋgou'mætəbi] (*noun*), *F:* cannabis *m* (*drogues**).

conk[1] [kɔŋk] (*noun*), *P:* **1.** nez*, pif *m.* **2.** tête*, caboche *f,* ciboulot *m.* **3.** coup*, gnon *m.*

conk[2] [kɔŋk] (**to**), *P:* **to c. s.o.,** flanquer un gnon à qn, matraquer qn.

conker ['kɔŋkər] (*noun*). **1.** *F:* marron *m* d'Inde. **2.** (*pl.*) *F:* jeu *m* de marrons. **3.** (*pl.*) *P:* argent*, flouze *m.* **4.** (*pl.*) *P:* testicules*, olives *f.pl.*

conk out ['kɔŋk'aut] (**to**). **1.** *F:* tomber en rade, claquer, caler. **2.** *P:* s'évanouir*, tomber dans les pommes. **3.** *P:* mourir*, caner, cadancher.

Connaught ranger ['kɔnɔːt'reindʒər] (*noun*) (*R.S.* = *stranger*), *P:* inconnu *m,* étranger *m.*

connect [kə'nekt] (**to**), *P:* **1.** faire un boum. **2.** faire une touche. **3.** acheter des drogues.

connection [kə'nekʃ(ə)n], **connector** [kə'nektər], **connexion** [kə'nekʃ(ə)n] (*noun*), *F:* contact *m,* inter *m,* fourgue *m.*

conshie, conshy ['kɔnʃi] (*noun*), *F:* = **conchie, conchy.**

contract ['kɔntrækt] (*noun*), *P:* engagement *m* à tuer* qn, dessoudage *m;* **to have a c. on s.o.,** s'être engagé à tuer* qn.

coo! [kuː] (*excl.*), *F:* tiens! mazette! c'est pas vrai!

cook[1] [kuk] (*noun*). **1.** *P:* = **chef, 2. 2.** *F:* **to be head** (*or* **chief**) **c. and bottle-washer,** être l'homme à tout faire, être le lampiste (*ou* le sous-fifre en chef).

cook[2] [kuk] (**to**). **1.** *F:* **what's cooking?** quoi de neuf? qu'est-ce qui se mijote? qu'est-ce qui se goupille? **2.** *F:* **to c. the books,** trafiquer (*ou* tripoter *ou* cuisiner *ou* maquiller) les comptes *m.pl.* **3.** *F:* **to c. s.o.'s goose,** faire son affaire à qn, régler son compte à qn. **4.** *P:* = **cook up** (**to**), **2** (*b*).

cooked [kukt] (*adj.*). **1.** *F:* très fatigué*, exténué. **2.** *F:* **to be c.,** (*d'une personne*) cuire dans son jus. **3.** *P:* = **cooked up.**

cooked up ['kukt'ʌp] (*adj.*), *P:* drogué*, camé. *Voir aussi* **cook up** (**to**), **2.**

cooker ['kukər] (*noun*). **1.** *F:* (=*cooking apple*) pomme *f* à cuire. **2.** *P:* = **cookie, 4.**

cookie ['kuki] (*noun*). **1.** *F:* **that's the way the c. crumbles** = **that's the way the mop flops** (*voir* **mop**). **2.** *P:* cocaïne *f* (*drogues**), coco *f.* **3.** *P:* toxico *m,* cocaïnomane *mf.* **4.** *P:* = **chef, 2. 5.** (*U.S.*) *F:* individu*, type *m.* **6.** *P:* **hot c.** = **hot babe** (**babe, 2**). **7.** (*U.S.*) *V:* = **cooze, 2.**

cook up ['kuk'ʌp] (**to**). **1.** *F:* **to c. u. an excuse,** combiner une excuse. **2.** *P:* (*a*) cuire (de l'opium); (*b*) dissoudre une drogue à la chaleur avant la piqûre. *Voir aussi* **cooked up.**

cool[1] [kuːl] (*adj.*). **1.** *F:* détendu, relax. **2.** *F:* beau*, bath; bien, satisfaisant. **3.** *F:* **a c. £1000,** £1000 au minimum. **4.** *F:* distant, peu abordable, peu émotif, cool. **5.** *F:* passionnant, palpitant. **6.** *F:* dans le vent, avant-garde. **7.** (*jazz*) *F:* sobre (dans l'expression musicale), cool; *cf.* **hot, 7. 8.** *P:* **to be c.,** (*drogués*) planer calmement.

cool[2] [kuːl] (*adv.*), *F:* **to play it c.,** ne pas s'énerver, y aller la tête froide.

cool[3] [kuːl] (*noun*), *F:* **1. to keep one's c.** = **to play it cool** (**cool**[2]). **2. to lose** (*or* **blow**) **one's c.,** se mettre en colère*, piquer une crise. **3.** le cool (*type de jazz*).

cool[4] [kuːl] (**to**), *F:* **to c. it,** se relâcher, se calmer; **c. it!** ne t'emballe pas! laisse courir! *Voir aussi* **heel, 3.**

cooler ['kuːlər] (*noun*), *P:* **1.** prison*, taule *f,* tôle *f.* **2.** mitard *m,* (s)chtard *m.*

coon [kuːn] (*noun*), *P:* **1.** nègre*, bougnoule *m.* **2.** individu*, mec *m.*

co-op ['kou(w)ɔp] (*noun*), *F:* (=*co-operative stores*) société coopérative, coopé *f.*

coop [kuːp] (*noun*), *P:* prison*; **to fly the c.,** s'évader*, (se) calter.

coot [kuːt] (*noun*). **1.** *P:* individu bête*, gourde *f.* **2.** *F:* **bald as a c.,** chauve* comme un genou (*ou* un œuf *ou* une bille).

cootie ['kuːti] (*noun*), *P:* pou*, morbac *m.*

cooty ['kuːti] (*adj.*), *P:* pouilleux, plein de poux*.

cooze [kuːz], **coozie** ['kuːzi] (*noun*) (*U.S.*), *V:* **1.** coït*, coup *m* de tringle. **2.** vulve*, baba *m.* **3.** femelle *f,* bout *m* de con.

cop[1] [kɔp] (*noun*). **1.** *F:* = **copper, 1; speed** (*or* **courtesy**) **c.,** motard *m; cf.* **fly-cop. 2.** *P:* **it's a fair c.,** on est fait,

* L'astérisque indique que le mot marqué de ce signe figure comme entrée dans le Répertoire.

rien à dire. 3. *P:* **no (great) c., not much c.,** sans valeur, pacotille. 4. (*Austr.*) *P:* (bon) filon, affure *f.*

cop² [kɔp] **(to),** *P:* 1. arrêter*, pincer (qn); **to get copped,** se faire pincer. 2. **to c. it,** (*a*) écoper; (*b*) être réprimandé*, recevoir un savon. 3. affurer, agricher. 4. **to c. hold of sth.,** choper, attraper (le bout de qch.). 5. obtenir *ou* acheter des drogues, se fournir. *Voir aussi* **dose,** 1; **needle¹,** 1 (*c*); **packet,** 1; **spike¹,** 2.

copilot [ˈkouˈpailət] (*noun*), *P:* Benzédrine *f* (*marque déposée*) (*drogues**), topette *f.*

cop out [ˈkɔpˈaut] **(to),** *P:* 1. se retirer, se dégager. 2. se désolidariser, s'esquiver. 3. éluder (une question, *etc.*). 4. ne pas tenir une promesse. 5. vendre la mèche, lâcher le paquet. 6. avouer*, accoucher, déballonner.

copper [ˈkɔpər] (*noun*). 1. *P:* agent* de police, flic *m.* 2. *P:* **to come c.,** devenir indicateur* de police, y aller du coup de casserole. 3. *F:* gros sou*.

copper-nob [ˈkɔpənɔb], **copper-top** [ˈkɔpətɔp] (*noun*), *P:* rouquin(e), poil *m* de carotte.

cop-shop [ˈkɔp-ʃɔp] (*noun*), *P:* commissariat *m* de police, burlingue *m* de quart.

cop-wagon [ˈkɔpwægən] (*noun*), *P:* = **Black Maria.**

copycat [ˈkɔpikæt] (*noun*), *F:* **to be a c.,** faire le singe; **c.!** perroquet!.

cor! [kɔːr] (*excl.*), (*a*) *F:* ça alors!; **c., she's a smasher!** bon Dieu, ce qu'elle est bath!; **c. love a duck!** grands dieux!; (*b*) *P:* **c. blimey! = gorblimey!**

corked [kɔːkt] (*adj.*), *P:* ivre* mort.

corker [ˈkɔːkər] (*noun*), *F:* 1. (*a*) individu* formidable; (*b*) une belle fille. 2. gros mensonge*, bourrage *m* de crâne. 3. **that's a c.,** ça vous la bouche, ça vous en bouche un coin.

corking [ˈkɔːkiŋ] (*adj.*), *F:* excellent*, foutral, formid(able).

corky [ˈkɔːki] (*adj.*), *F:* plein d'allant, éveillé, animé.

corn [kɔːn] (*noun*), *F:* 1. vieille rengaine. 2. vieux jeu. 3. guimauve *f.* 4. **to step** (*or* **tread**) **on s.o.'s corns,** toucher qn à l'endroit sensible, marcher sur les pieds de qn; froisser qn. *Voir aussi* **popcorn.**

corned beef [ˈkɔːn(d)ˈbiːf] (*noun*), *P:* (*R.S.* = *thief*) voleur*; *cf.* **tea-leaf.**

corner [ˈkɔːnər] (*noun*), *F:* (*a*) part *f*, portion *f*; **to pay one's c.,** payer* sa part; (*b*) part *f* de butin*, fade *m.* *Voir aussi* **cut³ (to), 7, 8; hole-and-corner.**

corner-boy [ˈkɔːnəbɔi] (*noun*), *P:* batteur *m* de pavé, traîne-cul *m*, traîne-lattes *m.*

cornhole¹ [ˈkɔːnhoul] (*noun*) (*U.S.*), *V:* anus*, trou *m* de balle.

cornhole² [ˈkɔːnhoul] **(to)** (*U.S.*), *V:* empaffer (*coït* anal*).

cornholer [ˈkɔːnhoulər] (*noun*) (*U.S.*), *V:* pédéraste*, qui est de la bague.

corn-stalk [ˈkɔːn-stɔːk] (*noun*) (*U.S.*), *F:* (*d'une personne*) grande perche.

corny [ˈkɔːni] (*adj.*), *F:* 1. banal, rebattu. 2. vioque. 3. à l'eau de rose.

'cos [kɔz] (*conj.*), *F:* (=*because*) parce que, pasque, bicause.

cosh¹ [kɔʃ] (*noun*), *F:* matraque *f*, assommoir *m*, cigare *m.*

cosh² [kɔʃ] **(to),** *F:* matraquer, assommer (qn).

cost [kɔst] **(to),** *F:* **I can get it but it'll c. you,** je peux l'avoir mais ça sera chérot (*ou* ça ira chercher loin).

cotics [ˈkɔtiks] (*pl. noun*) (=*narcotics*), *P:* drogues*, narcs *m.pl.*

cotton¹ [kɔtn] (*noun*), *P:* 1. amphétamines *f.pl.* (*drogues**). 2. tout ce qui est saturé d'une drogue qui peut être inhalée; **c. freak,** drogué* par inhalation.

cotton² [kɔtn] **(to),** *F:* **to c. to s.o.,** être attiré par qn, avoir qn à la bonne.

cotton on [ˈkɔtnˈɔn] **(to),** *F:* 1. comprendre, piger, entraver. 2. **I can't c. o. to him,** sa tête ne me revient pas, ça ne biche pas avec lui.

cotton-picking [ˈkɔtnˈpikiŋ] (*adj.*) (*U.S.*), *F:* 1. commun, vulgaire. 2. sacré, satané. 3. gnognot(t)eux, navet.

cotton-wool [ˈkɔtnˈwul] (*noun*), *F:* **to wrap s.o. in c.-w.,** mettre qn dans du coton, garder qn sous cloche.

couch [kautʃ] (*noun*), *F:* **casting c.,** lit *m* par où doit passer une actrice pour avoir un rôle.

couch-doctor [ˈkautʃdɔktər] (*noun*), *F:* psychanalyste *mf.*

cough-drop [ˈkɔfdrɔp] (*noun*), *F:* 1. dur *m* à cuire. 2. drôle *m* de numéro.

cough up [ˈkɔfˈʌp] **(to),** *F:* 1. payer*,

* An asterisk indicates that the word so marked is included as a head-word in the Appendix.

cracher, abouler. 2. parler*, dévider, dégoiser.

count [kaunt] (*noun*), *F:* **to be out for the c.**, (*a*) avoir son compte, aller au tapis, être K.O.; (*b*) être profondément endormi.

counter [ˈkauntər] (*noun*), *F:* **to sell sth. under the c.**, vendre qch. en cachette. *Voir aussi* **under-the-counter.**

count in [ˈkauntˈin] (**to**), *F:* **you can c. me i.**, je marche, je suis partant.

count out [ˈkauntˈaut] (**to**), *F:* **you can c. me o.**, je ne marche pas, je ne suis pas partant.

county [ˈkaunti] (*adj.*), *F:* (*a*) **the c. set,** l'aristocratie provinciale, la haute bourgeoisie provinciale; (*b*) qui appartient au beau monde.

courage [ˈkʌridʒ] (*attrib. adj.*), *P:* **c. pills,** comprimé *m* d'héroïne (*drogues**).

cove [kouv] (*noun*), *F:* individu*; **a queer c.**, un drôle de pistolet.

Coventry [ˈkɔvəntri] (*noun*), *F:* **to send s.o. to C.**, mettre qn en quarantaine.

cover[1] [ˈkʌvər] (*noun*), *F:* couverture*, couverte *f*, prétexte *m*.

cover[2] [ˈkʌvər] (**to**), *P:* 1. accepter un pari. 2. faire un pari, parier, mettre une mise.

cover-girl [ˈkʌvəgəːl] (*noun*), *F:* pin-up *f*, cover-girl *f*.

cover up [ˈkʌvərˈʌp] (**to**), *F:* **to c. u. for s.o.,** couvrir qn, prendre les patins pour qn.

cow [kau] (*noun*). 1. *P:* **an (old) c.**, femme* (*péj.*), une vieille bique, une vache. 2. *P:* **poor c.!** pauvre pute! 3. (*Austr.*) *P:* loquedu *m*, teigne *f*; **it's a fair c.**, que c'est moche!; **he's a fair c.**, qu'il est moche! 4. *P:* une livre sterling; **a c. and calf,** une livre cinquante pence; *cf.* **calf,** 1. 5. *F:* **till the cows come home,** dans la semaine des quatre jeudis, jusqu'à la Saint-Glinglin, quand les poules auront des dents, jusqu'à plus soif. *Voir aussi* **bull,** 3; **holy,** 1; **moo-cow.**

cow-juice [ˈkaudʒuːs] (*noun*), *F:* lait *m*, lolo *m*.

cow-poke [ˈkaupouk], **cow-puncher** [ˈkaupʌntʃər] (*noun*) (*U.S.*), *F:* cowboy *m*.

cozzer [ˈkɔzər] (*noun*), *P:* policier*, condé *m*.

cozzy [ˈkɔzi] (*noun*), *P:* = **karzy.**

crab[1] [kræb] (*noun*), *P:* 1. grognon *m*, rouscailleur *m*; **she's an old c.**, elle est une vieille emmerdeuse (*ou* râleuse). 2. (*pl.*) poux* du pubis, morpions *m.pl.*

crab[2] [kræb] (**to**), *P:* 1. grogner*, râler. 2. **to c. the act** (*or* **deal**), mettre des bâtons dans les roues.

crabber [ˈkræbər] (*noun*), *P:* grognon *m*, rouspéteur *m*.

crack[1] [kræk] (*noun*). 1. *V:* vagin*, fente *f*, crac *m*. 2. *F:* blague *f*, vanne *f*. 3. *F:* **to have a c. (at sth.)**, tenter le coup (*ou* sa chance). 4. *F:* **to have a c. at s.o.**, (*a*) filer une taloche à qn; (*b*) se moquer* de qn; *cf.* **wisecrack**[1]. *Voir aussi* **paper**[2] (**to**), 2; **whip**[1], 1.

crack[2] [kræk] (**to**). 1. *P:* filer un coup* à (qn). 2. *F:* **to get cracking,** (*a*) commencer, embrayer; (*b*) aller vite*, se grouiller. 3. *F:* craquer, flancher. 4. **to c. it,** (*a*) *F:* réussir, l'avoir belle; (*b*) *P:* (*d'un homme*) coïter*, avoir réussi un exploit amoureux, tringler. *Voir aussi* **crib**[1], 1; **nut**[1], 6; **whip**[1], 4.

crack down [ˈkrækˈdaun] (**to**), *F:* 1. **to c. d. on s.o.**, (*a*) tomber sur le paletot à qn; (*b*) serrer la vis à qn. 2. **to c. d. on sth.**, mettre le frein à qch.

cracked [krækt] (*adj.*), *P:* fou*, fêlé.

cracker [ˈkrækər] (*noun*), *F:* 1. mensonge*, craque *f*. 2. **she's a c.**, elle est formid(able). *Voir aussi* **crib-cracker; whipcracker.**

crackerjack[1] [ˈkrækədʒæk] (*adj.*), *F:* excellent*, formid(able), sensas.

crackerjack[2] [ˈkrækədʒæk] (*noun*), *F:* 1. as *m*, crack *m*. 2. du tonnerre.

crackers [ˈkrækəz] (*adj.*), *P:* fou*, cinglé.

cracking [ˈkrækiŋ] (*adj.*), *F:* 1. **to be in c. form,** être en pleine forme. 2. **at a c. pace,** très vite*, en quatrième vitesse.

crackle [ˈkrækl] (*noun*), *P:* billets*, gros faf(f)iots *m.pl.*

crackling [ˈkrækliŋ] (*noun*), *P:* **a nice bit of c.**, une croquignole, un prix de Diane.

crack on [ˈkrækˈɔn] (**to**), *F:* 1. faire semblant, frimer. 2. faire savoir, répandre, semer la nouvelle (que...); **don't c. o.!** ne crache pas le morceau!

crackpot [ˈkrækpɔt] (*adj. & noun*), *F:* fou*, fada (*m*), louf(oque) (*m*).

cracksman [ˈkræksmən] (*noun*), *P:* cambrioleur*, casseur *m*.

* L'astérisque indique que le mot marqué de ce signe figure comme entrée dans le Répertoire.

crack-up [ˈkrækʌp] (*noun*), *F:* 1. accident *m* d'avion très sérieux. 2. dépression nerveuse.
crack up [ˈkrækˈʌp] (**to**), *F:* 1. vanter, pommader, porter aux anges. 2. prendre un coup de vieux, craquer. 3. flancher, se détraquer, s'effondrer. 4. faire une dépression nerveuse.
cradle [ˈkreidl] (*noun*), *F:* **to rob the c.**, les prendre au berceau.
cradle-robber [ˈkreidl-rɔbər], **cradle-snatcher** [ˈkreidl-snætʃər] (*noun*), *F:* = **baby-snatcher** (*b*); *cf.* **cradle.**
crafty [ˈkrɑːfti] (*adj.*), *F:* **to have a c. smoke,** en griller une en loucedoc. *Voir aussi* **arty-crafty.**
crank up [ˈkræŋkˈʌp] (**to**), *P:* piquer, pousser.
cranky [ˈkræŋki] (*adj.*), *P:* 1. malade*, patraque. 2. mal boumé.
crap[1] [kræp] (*noun*), *V:* 1. étron*. 2. bêtise*; **don't give me that c.**, ne me sers pas ces conneries. 3. **it's a lot** (*or* **load**) **of c.**, tout ça c'est de l'eau de bidet. 4. **full of c.**, fort en gueule. 5. héroïne *f* (*drogues**) de qualité inférieure. *Voir aussi* **shoot**[2] **(to)**, 7.
crap[2] [kræp] (**to**), *V:* 1. déféquer*, chier. 2. **don't c. about like that!** fais pas le con!
craphouse [ˈkræphaus], **crapper** [ˈkræpər] (*noun*), *V:* W.C.*, chiottes *f.pl.*, goguenots *m.pl.*
crappy [ˈkræpi] (*adj.*), *V:* sale*, cracra, dégueulasse.
crash [kræʃ] (**to**), *P:* 1. = **gate-crash (to)**. 2. roupiller, pioncer, en écraser.
crashed [kræʃt] (*adj.*) (*U.S.*), *P:* ivre*, rétamé.
crashing [ˈkræʃiŋ] (*adj.*), *F:* **c. bore,** casse-pieds *m* (*ou* raseur *m*) de première classe.
crash-out [ˈkræʃaut] (*noun*), *F:* = **break**[1], 4; *cf.* **break-out.**
crash-pad [ˈkræʃpæd] (*noun*), *P:* asile *m* temporaire.
crate [kreit] (*noun*), *F:* 1. coucou *m*, zinc *m*. 2. vieille voiture*, tacot *m*.
crawl [krɔːl] (**to**), *F:* 1. s'aplatir, faire des courbettes *f.pl.*; **to c. round s.o.,** ramper devant qn; **to c. all over s.o.,** faire de la lèche. 2. **the place was crawling with police,** l'endroit grouillait de policiers*. *Voir aussi* **arse-crawl (to); pub-crawl**[2] **(to).**
crawler [ˈkrɔːlər] (*noun*), *F:* 1. lécheur *m* de bottes. 2. = **pub-crawler.** 3. tortillard *m*. *Voir aussi* **arse-crawler.**
crazy [ˈkreizi] (*adj.*), *F:* 1. **are you c.?** t'es pas fou*? 2. terrible, formid(able). 3. enthousiaste, fervent, passionné. *Voir aussi* **man-crazy; sex-crazy; woman-crazy.**
crazyhouse [ˈkreizihaus] (*noun*), *P:* maison *f* de fous, asile *m* de dingues.
cream[1] [kriːm] (*noun*), *P:* sperme*, blanc *m*, jus *m*. *Voir aussi* **ice-cream.**
cream[2] [kriːm] (**to**) (*U.S.*), *P:* 1. battre*, filer une raclée à (qn). 2. tuer*, repasser, descendre (qn). 3. éjaculer*, cracher son venin; **to c. one's jeans,** juter dans son froc.
cream off [ˈkriːmˈɔf] (**to**), *P:* faire jouir (qn).
creampuff [ˈkriːmˈpʌf] (*noun*), *P:* 1. amusette *f*, qch. de facile. 2. femmelette *f*, mollasson *m*.
crease[1] [kriːs] (*noun*), *V:* = **crack**[1], 1.
crease[2] [kriːs] (**to**), *P:* 1. tuer*, effacer (qn). 2. assommer, aplatir (qn). 3. ennuyer*; **you c. me,** tu me cours. 4. **to feel creased,** (*a*) être déprimé (*ou* cafardeux); (*b*) être fatigué* (*ou* vanné). 5. **you c. me!** tu me fais tordre de rire!
create [ˈkriːeit] (**to**), *P:* faire une scène, grogner*, rouscailler; *voir aussi* **hell,** 3.
creature [ˈkriːtʃər] (*noun*). 1. *F:* femme* (*péj.*), créature *f*, femelle *f*. 2. *P:* **the c.,** whisky *m*, scotch *m*.
creek [kriːk] (*noun*), *F:* **to be up the c.** (*or V:* **up shit c.**) **(without a paddle),** être embêté (*ou* emmouscaillé); *V:* être dans les emmerdements *m.pl.*
creep[1] [kriːp] (*noun*). 1. *F:* vaurien*, salaud *m*, fripouille *f*. 2. *F:* lèche-bottes *m*, lèche-cul *m*, flagorneur *m*. 3. *P:* chapardeur *m*, chipeur *m*. *Voir aussi* **creeps.**
creep[2] [kriːp] (**to**). 1. *F:* ramper (devant les grands), s'aplatir. 2. *P:* **c. away and die!** fous-moi le camp! va te faire fiche! *Voir aussi* **arse-creep (to).**
creeper [ˈkriːpər] (*noun*). 1. *F:* = **creep**[1], 2. 2. *P:* monte-en-l'air *m*. 3. (*pl.*) *F:* espadrilles *f.pl.* *Voir aussi* **arse-creeper; jeepers!**
creeps [kriːps] (*pl. noun*), *F:* **he gives me the c.,** il me fait peur*, il me donne la chair de poule; **it gives me the c.,** ça me met les nerfs en pelote.
creepy-crawly[1] [ˈkriːpiˈkrɔːli] (*adj.*), *F:*

* An asterisk indicates that the word so marked is included as a head-word in the Appendix.

c.-c. feeling, (*a*) fourmillement *m*; (*b*) chair *f* de poule.

creepy-crawly[2] [ˈkriːpiˈkrɔːli] (*noun*), *F:* vermine *f*; insecte *etc.* rampant.

cretin [ˈkretin] (*noun*), *F:* individu absolument bête*, crétin *m*.

cretinous [ˈkretinəs] (*adj.*), *F:* (remarque, *etc.*) bête* (*ou* crétine).

crib[1] [krib] (*noun*). **1.** *P:* = **pad**[1], **1**; **to crack a c.,** cambrioler*, faire un fric-frac, casser un coffiot; *voir aussi* **crib-cracker. 2.** *F:* antisèche *f*. **3.** *P:* rouspétance *f*.

crib[2] [krib] (**to**). **1.** *F:* tricher, bidocher. **2.** *P:* voler*, chaparder. **3. to c. at sth.,** tiquer sur qch., regimber.

crib-cracker [ˈkribkrækər] (*noun*), *P:* cambrioleur*, casseur *m*; *voir aussi* **crib**[1], **1.**

crib-cracking [ˈkribkrækiŋ] (*noun*), *P:* cambriolage *m*, casse(ment) *m*.

cricket [ˈkrikit] (*noun*), *F:* **it's not c.,** c'est pas de jeu.

crikey! [ˈkraiki] (*excl.*), *F:* **c. (Moses)!** mince alors! fichtre! mazette!

crimp [krimp] (*noun*), *F:* **to put a c. in s.o.'s style,** couper les effets à qn.

cripes! [kraips] (*excl.*), *F:* = **crikey!**

croak [krouk] (**to**), *P:* **1.** tuer*, descendre (qn), liquider (qn). **2.** mourir*, cronir, cadancher.

croaker [ˈkroukər] (*noun*), *P:* docteur *m*, toubib *m*; **right c.,** toubib à la gauche.

crock[1] [krɔk] (*noun*). **1.** *P:* (*a*) pipe *f* à opium, bambou *m*; (*b*) fourneau *m* (de pipe). **2.** *F:* **old c.,** (*a*) vieille voiture*, tacot *m*, bagnole *f*; (*b*) croulant *m*, vieux birbe, vieux jeton. **3.** *F:* cheval*, rosse *f*, carne *f*. **4.** (*U.S.*) *F:* individu* peu sympathique, arsouille *m*, sale coco *m*. **5.** (*U.S.*) *P:* **c. of shit,** (*a*) mensonges*, boniments *m.pl.*; (*b*) menteur *m*, bourreur *m* de crâne, fumiste *m*.

crock[2] [krɔk] (**to**), *F:* **to get crocked,** (*a*) se blesser*, s'amocher; (*b*) s'enivrer, se (faire) rétamer.

crockery [ˈkrɔkəri] (*noun*), *F:* dentier *m*, tabourets *m.pl.*

crock up [ˈkrɔkˈʌp] (**to**), *F:* **1.** tomber malade*, se décatir. **2.** blesser*, abîmer, amocher.

crocky [ˈkrɔki] (*adj.*), *F:* abîmé, claqué.

crocodile [ˈkrɔkədail] (*noun*), *F:* élèves marchant deux à deux, en rang(s) d'oignons (*ou* à la queue leu-leu). *Voir aussi* **alligator.**

crombie [ˈkrɔmbi] (*noun*), *P:* pardessus*, lardingue *m*.

cronk[1] [krɔŋk] (*adj.*) (*Austr.*), *F:* **1.** = **crook**[1], **2. 2.** camelote, tocard. **3.** défavorable, adverse, anti.

cronk[2] [krɔŋk] (*noun*), *F:* **old c.** = **old crock** (**crock**[1], **2** (*a*)).

crook[1] [kruk] (*adj.*). **1.** *P:* malhonnête, louche. **2.** (*Austr.*) *F:* malade*, patraque. **3.** (*Austr.*) *F:* **to go c. at s.o.,** se mettre en colère* contre qn, fulminer contre qn.

crook[2] [kruk] (*noun*), *F:* **1.** escroc*, arnaqueur *m*. **2.** voleur*, doubleur *m*, faiseur *m*.

cropper [ˈkrɔpər] (*noun*), *F:* **to come a c.,** (*a*) tomber*, prendre une pelle, ramasser une bûche; (*b*) tomber sur un bec, faire un bide.

crop up [ˈkrɔpˈʌp] (**to**), *F:* survenir à l'improviste, surgir.

cross[1] [krɔs] (*noun*), *P:* **on the c.,** malhonnêtement, en filouterie. *Voir aussi* **white**[1], **1.**

cross[2] [krɔs] (**to**), *F:* **1.** tromper*, trahir, posséder (qn); *cf.* **double-cross (to). 2. to c. one's heart,** jurer ses grands dieux; **c. my heart (and hope to die),** (*enfants*) croix de bois, croix de fer (, si je meurs j'irai en enfer).

crotch [krɔtʃ] (*noun*), *P:* **1.** vulve*, cramouille *f*. **2. c. crickets** = **crabs** (*voir* **crab**[1], **2**).

crow [krou] (*noun*). **1.** *P:* guetteur *m*, gaffeur *m*. **2.** *P:* prêtre*, corbeau *m*, ratichon *m*. **3.** *F:* **old c.,** femme* (*péj.*), vieille bique, vieux trumeau. **4.** (*U.S.*) *F:* **to eat c.,** avaler des couleuvres. *Voir aussi* **Jim Crow.**

crowd[1] [kraud] (*noun*), *F:* bande*, équipe *f*, soce *f*.

crowd[2] [kraud] (**to**), *P:* casser les pieds à (qn), s'en prendre à (qn), chercher noise à (qn).

crown [kraun] (**to**), *F:* **1.** flanquer un coup* à la tête de (qn), assommer (qn). **2. and to c. everything . . .,** le comble c'est...

crow's-feet [ˈkrouzfiːt] (*pl. noun*), *F:* pattes *f.pl.* d'oie (sur le visage).

crud [krʌd] (*noun*), *P:* **1.** = **turd, 2. 2. Bombay cruds,** diarrhée*, riquette *f*.

* L'astérisque indique que le mot marqué de ce signe figure comme entrée dans le Répertoire.

cruiser [ˈkruːzər] (*noun*), *P:* prostituée*, marcheuse *f*, péripaticienne *f*.

crumb [krʌm] (*noun*), *P:* vaurien*, salaud *m*.

crumbs! [krʌmz] (*excl*.), *F:* = **crikey!**

crummy [ˈkrʌmi] (*adj*.), *F:* sale*, miteux.

crump [krʌmp] (*noun*), *P:* gros obus, (grosse) marmite.

crumpet [ˈkrʌmpit] (*noun*). **1.** *V:* vulve*, framboise *f*; **to have a bit of c., to have** (*or* **get**) **one's c.,** coïter*, se farcir (*ou* s'envoyer) une femme*. **2.** *P:* **she's a nice bit of c.,** c'est une môme bath. **3.** *F:* tête*, caboche *f*; **off one's c.,** fou*, maboul, loufoque; (*Austr*.) **to bow the c.,** plaider coupable, se péter bon (*ou* propre), larguer le blanc.

crunch [krʌntʃ] (*noun*), *F:* **the c.,** le moment critique; **when it comes to the c....,** quand on est au pied du mur...

crush [krʌʃ] (*noun*), *F:* **1.** béguin *m*; **to have a c. on s.o.,** aimer* qn, en pincer pour qn. **2.** boum surpeuplée, moutonnaille *f*.

crushers [ˈkrʌʃəz] (*pl. noun*), *F:* grosses chaussures*, godasses *f.pl.*; *cf.* **beetle-crushers; clod-crushers.**

crust [krʌst] (*noun*), *F:* **1. the upper c.,** la haute, le gratin, le dessus du panier. **2. to be off one's c.,** être fou*, être parti du ciboulot. **3. to have plenty of c.,** être très culotté.

crutch [krʌtʃ] (*noun*). **1.** *P:* béquille *f* (*allumette fendue qui permet de fumer une cigarette de marijuana jusqu'au bout*). **2.** (*pl*.) *F: voir* **bingo (77).**

cry-baby [ˈkrai-beibi] (*noun*), *F:* chialeur *m*, pleurnicheur *m*.

cry off [ˈkraiˈɔf] (**to**), *F:* lâcher les dés, caner.

cry out [ˈkraiˈaut] (**to**), *F:* **for crying out loud!** c'est le bouquet!

crystal [ˈkristəl] (*adj*.), *F:* **to gaze into the c. ball,** prédire l'avenir, lire dans le marc du café (*ou* dans la boule de cristal).

crystals [ˈkristəlz] (*pl. noun*), *P:* méthédrine cristallisée (*drogues**).

C.T., c.t. [ˈsiːˈtiː] (*abbr*.), *P:* = **cock-teaser;** *cf.* **P.T.**

cube [kjuːb] (*noun*), *P:* **1.** un gramme de hachisch *m*, un cube; *voir aussi* **acid, 2. 2.** (*pl*.) dés*, bouts *m.pl.* de sucre, doches *m.pl.*, bobs *m.pl.*

cubehead [ˈkjuːbhed] (*noun*), *P:* consommateur *m* de morceaux de sucre imprégnés de LSD.

cuckoo [ˈkukuː] (*adj*.), *P:* fou*, loufoque.

cuddlesome [ˈkʌdlsəm], **cuddly** [ˈkʌdli] (*adj*.), *F:* bien capitonné(e), qu'on aimerait bichot(t)er, gentil(le) à croquer.

cuff [kʌf] (*noun*). **1.** *P:* **to buy sth. on the c.,** acheter qch. à crédit (*ou* à croume). **2.** *F:* **to say sth. off the c.,** dire qch. au pied levé, improviser. **3.** *F:* **for the c.,** confidentiel(lement), sous cape. **4.** *F:* (*pl*.) (=*handcuffs*) menottes*, bracelets *m.pl.* **5.** *P:* = **soul-brother.**

cum [kʌm] (*noun & verb*), *P:* = **come[1], come[2], 1.**

cunt [kʌnt] (*noun*), *VV:* **1.** vulve*, con *m*. **2.** femme* (*péj*.), fumelle *f*, garce *f*; **a nice bit of c.,** une gonzesse qui a du chien. **3. he's a prize** (*or* **first-class**) **c.,** il est archi-con.

cunt-lapper [ˈkʌnt-læpər] (*noun*), *VV:* brouteur *m* de cresson.

cunt-struck [ˈkʌnt-strʌk] (*adj*.), *VV:* queutard, porté sur la bagatelle.

cup [kʌp] (*noun*). **1.** *F:* **that's not my c. of tea,** (*a*) ça ne me dit rien, ce n'est pas à mon goût; (*b*) ce n'est pas dans mes cordes. **2.** *P:* **to have a c. of tea,** coïter* entre pédérastes* dans des toilettes publiques. **3.** *F:* **in one's cups,** dans les Vignes du Seigneur.

cup-cakes [ˈkʌpkeiks] (*pl. noun*), *P:* testicules*, croquignoles *f.pl.*, olives *f.pl.*

cuppa, cupper [ˈkʌpə] (*noun*), *F:* tasse *f* (*ou* bol *m*) de thé.

curfuffle [kəˈfʌfl] (*noun*), *F:* = **kerfuffle.**

curl up [ˈkəːlˈʌp] (**to**), *F:* **1. I just want to c. u. and die,** j'ai envie de tout lâcher (*ou* de tout planter là). **2. he simply curled up,** on l'aurait fait rentrer dans un trou de souris.

curly [ˈkəːli] (*noun*). **1.** *F:* frisé(e). **2.** *P:* **to have s.o. by the short and curlies,** avoir qn à sa merci (*ou* à sa pogne).

currant-bun [ˈkʌrəntˈbʌn] (*noun*) (*R.S.* = *son*), *P:* fils *m*.

curse [kəːs] (*noun*), *F:* **the c.,** menstrues*, argagnasses *f.pl.*

curtains [ˈkəːtnz] (*pl. noun*), *F:* **it'll be**

* An asterisk indicates that the word so marked is included as a head-word in the Appendix.

c. for you if . . ., votre compte est bon si...

curvaceous [kəːˈveiʃəs] (*adj.*), *F:* (*d'une femme*) bien balancée (*ou* carrossée *ou* capitonnée), plantureuse.

cushy [ˈkuʃi] (*adj.*), *F:* **a c. time** (*or* **number**), une planque, un filon; **to have a c. time (of it),** l'avoir pépère; **a c. life,** une vie pépère; **c. job,** prébende *f*, sinécure *f*.

cuss[1] [kʌs] (*noun*), *F:* **1.** individu*, client *m*; **an awkward c.,** un mauvais coucheur. **2. it's not worth a (tinker's) c.,** ça ne vaut pas un clou; *voir aussi* **tinker, 2.**

cuss[2] [kʌs] (**to**), *F:* **1.** sacrer, jurer. **2.** réprimander*, enguirlander (qn).

cussed [ˈkʌsid] (*adj.*), *F:* damné, sacré.

customer [ˈkʌstəmər] (*noun*), *F:* **1.** individu*, type *m*; **a queer c.,** un drôle de client (*ou* de numéro); **an awkward c.,** un type pas commode; *voir aussi* **rough**[1], **4; tough**[1], **2. 2.** (*de prostituée*) clille *m*.

cut[1] [kʌt] (*adj.*). **1.** *P:* (légèrement) ivre*, pompette, éméché; *cf.* **half-cut. 2.** *F:* **c. and dry** (*or* **dried**), tout fait, tout taillé.

cut[2] [kʌt] (*noun*), *F:* **1.** fade *m*, taf(fe) *m*; **to get one's c.,** prendre son fade, avoir sa gratte. **2. a c. above . . .,** un cran (*ou* un échelon) au-dessus de... **3. a short c. (to riches,** *etc.***),** un raccourci. **4.** (*cartes*) **to slip the c.,** faire sauter la coupe.

cut[3] [kʌt] (**to**). **1.** *P:* partir*; **to c. and run,** se tirer. **2.** *P:* adultérer, couper (une drogue). **3.** *F:* **to c. it fine,** (*a*) compter (*ou* calculer) trop juste; (*b*) ne pas laisser beaucoup de temps, arriver* à la dernière minute (*ou* tout juste). **4.** *F:* **to c. no ice (with s.o.),** demeurer sans effet. **5.** *F:* **to c. s.o. dead,** snober qn, tourner le dos à qn. **6.** *F:* **to c. a class,** sécher la classe. **7.** *F:* **to c. a corner,** (*auto*) prendre un virage à la corde. **8.** *F:* **to c. corners,** économiser*, couper un sou en quatre. **9.** *F:* **it cuts both ways,** c'est à double tranchant. **10.** *F:* **to c. a dash,** faire de l'épate. **11.** *F:* **to c. loose,** (*a*) s'évader*, se cavaler; (*b*) être déchaîné, mener une vie de patachon, envoyer son bonnet par-dessus les moulins. *Voir aussi* **cackle; comedy; rug, 1; throat, 2.**

cut-back [ˈkʌtbæk] (*noun*), *F:* **1.** retour *m* en arrière, flash-back *m*. **2.** économie *f* (sur les dépenses).

cut back [ˈkʌtˈbæk] (**to**), *F:* **1.** économiser*, mettre à gauche. **2.** revenir sur ses pas.

cut down [ˈkʌtˈdaun] (**to**), *F:* = **cut back (to), 1.** *Voir aussi* **size, 1.**

cute [kjuːt] (*adj.*), *F:* **1.** (*de personnes*) (*a*) charmant, gentil; **what a c. little baby!** quel mignon petit bébé!; (*b*) malin*, déluré; **he's a c. one,** il a le nez creux. **2.** (*de choses*) mignon, savoureux, délicat. **3. to play a c. trick on s.o.,** faire une entourloupette à qn.

cutey, cutie [ˈkjuːti] (*noun*), *F:* **1.** charmante jeune personne, mignonne poupée. **2.** petite maligne.

cut in [ˈkʌtˈin] (**to**), *F:* **to c. s.o. i.,** mettre qn dans le coup.

cut out [ˈkʌtˈaut] (**to**). **1.** *P:* = **cut**[3] **(to), 1. 2.** *F:* **c. it o.!** ça suffit! basta! rideau! **3.** *F:* **to have one's work c. o. (to do sth.),** avoir de la besogne sur les bras, avoir de quoi faire, avoir du pain sur la planche. **4.** *F:* **I'm not c. o. for that sort of work,** je ne suis pas taillé pour ce genre de travail. **5.** *F:* souffler la place à (qn), couper l'herbe sous les pieds de (qn). *Voir aussi* **fancy**[1], **4.**

cut-throat [ˈkʌtθrout] (*attrib. adj.*), *F:* **1. c.-t. competition,** concurrence acharnée. **2. c.-t. razor,** rasoir*, grattoir *m*, coupe-chou *m*.

cutty(-pipe) [ˈkʌti(paip)] (*noun*), *F:* pipe*, brûle-gueule *m*.

cut up [ˈkʌtˈʌp] (**to**), *F:* **1. to be** (*or* **feel**) **c. u.,** être démonté (*ou* affecté *ou* affligé). **2.** éreinter, mettre en morceaux (un livre, *etc.*). **3. to c. u. nasty** (*or* **rough** *or* **rusty** *or* **savage** *or* **ugly**), (*a*) se mettre en colère* (*ou* en rogne), se rebiffer, regimber; (*b*) mal prendre les choses, faire le méchant. **4. to c. u. rich,** mourir* riche*, claquer plein aux as.

cylinder [ˈsilindər] (*noun*), *F:* **to fire** (*or* **hit**) **on all cylinders,** (*a*) rouler très vite*, rouler à pleins tubes; (*b*) rouler comme un charme, tourner rond; **to miss on two cylinders,** avoir des ratés.

* L'astérisque indique que le mot marqué de ce signe figure comme entrée dans le Répertoire.

D

d [diː] (*abbr.* = *decent*), *F:* gentil, chic, chouette; **that's jolly d of you,** c'est joliment chic de ta part; *cf.* **decent, 1.**

D [diː] (*abbr.*), *P:* **1.** (=*LSD*) D *m*, acide *m* (*drogues**). **2.** (=*diamond*) diamant*, diame *m*. **3.** (=*detective*) agent* de la Sûreté. *Voir aussi* **D-racks.**

D.A. [ˈdiːˈei] (*abbr.* = *drug addict*), *P:* drogué*, toxico(mane) *mf*, camé *m*.

da [dɑː] (*noun*), *F:* père*, papa, daron *m*; *cf.* **dar.**

dab[1] [dæb] (*adj.*), *F:* capable, calé, fort(iche); **a d. hand** = **dab**[3], **4.**

dab[2] [dæb] (*adv.*), *F:* (**right**) **d. in the middle,** en plein dans le mille.

dab[3] [dæb] (*noun*). **1.** *F:* **a d.,** un peu*, une miette, un (petit) bout, un chouia. **2.** *F:* **poor d.!** pauvre type! pauvre diable! **3.** *F:* (petite) tape, tapette *f*, rampognon *m*. **4.** *F:* expert *m*, as *m*, épée *f*, crack *m*. **5.** (*pl.*) *P:* empreintes digitales; **to have one's dabs taken,** passer au piano; *voir aussi* **mug**[1], **1.** **6.** *F:* = **dash**[1], **2.**

dab[4] [dæb] (**to**), *F:* **to d. one's nose,** se poudrer le nez, faire un raccord.

dabble [ˈdæbl] (**to**), *F:* se droguer* irrégulièrement, (s)chnouffailler.

dabbler [ˈdæblər] (*noun*), *F:* drogué* par intermittence, toxico *m* du dimanche, (s)chnouffailleur *m*.

dab down [ˈdæbˈdaun] (**to**), *P:* donner* de l'argent*, les allonger, les abouler.

dabster [ˈdæbstər] (*noun*), *F:* = **dab**[3], **4.**

dad [dæd] (*noun*), *F:* **1.** père*, papa, daron *m*. **2.** un vieux, un pépère.

dad(d)a [ˈdædə] (*noun*), *F:* (*langage enfantin*) père*, papa, papy.

daddio [ˈdædiou] (*noun*), *P:* **1.** = **dad, 2.** **2.** chef *m* d'un groupe de beatniks, moré *m*.

daddle [ˈdædl] (*noun*), *P:* main*, paluche *f*, pince *f*.

daddy [ˈdædi] (*noun*), *F:* **1.** = **dad, 1.** **2. the d. of them all,** l'ancien, le maestro; **he's the d.** (**of them all**), il les coiffe tous. **3.** = **sugar-daddy.**

daffodil [ˈdæfədil] (*noun*), *P:* jeune homme* efféminé, minet *m*.

daffy [ˈdæfi] (*adj.*), *P:* **1.** (*a*) bête*, cruche; (*b*) fou*, timbré, toqué. **2. to be d. about s.o.** = **to be daft about s.o.** (**daft**[1], **2**).

daft[1] [dɑːft] (*adj.*), *F:* **1.** (**as**) **d. as a brush** (*or* **as they come** *or* **as they make 'em**), (*a*) bête* comme ses pieds; (*b*) fou* à lier. **2. to be d. about s.o.,** être toqué de qn. *Voir aussi* **plain.**

daft[2] [dɑːft] (*adv.*), *P:* **don't talk d.!** ne sors pas des inepties!

daftie, dafty [ˈdɑːfti] (*noun*), *P:* individu bête*, cruche *f*, crétin *m*.

dag [dæg] (*noun*) (*Austr.*), *F:* rigolo *m*, excentrique *m*.

dagga [ˈdægə] (*noun*), *P:* cannabis *m* (*drogues**), dagga *m*.

dagged [dægd] (*adj.*) (*U.S.*), *P:* ivre*, saoul.

dago [ˈdeigou] (*noun*), *P:* **1.** (*péj.*) métèque *m*. **2. d. red,** vin* rouge ordinaire, pivois *m*.

dairies [ˈdɛəriz] (*pl. noun*), *P:* seins*, boîtes *f.pl.* à lait, lolos *m.pl.*

daisy[1] [ˈdeizi] (*adj.*), *F:* excellent*, super; **a d. day,** une belle journée.

daisy[2] [ˈdeizi] (*noun*). **1.** *F:* qn *ou* qch. d'excellent* (*ou* d'épatant *ou* d'impec); **she's a d.,** c'est une perle; elle est bath. **2.** *P:* pot *m* de chambre, Jules. **3.** *F:* **to be kicking** (*or* **pushing**) **up the daisies,** être enterré, bouffer les pissenlits par la racine. **4.** (*pl.*) *P:* = **daisy roots** (*voir* **5**). **5.** *P:* **d. roots** (*R.S.* = *boots*), chaussures*, godillots *m.pl.* **6.** *P:* pédéraste*; **d. chain,** partouze *f* à la bague. **7.** *F:* **as fresh as a d.,** frais et rose (*ou* dispos). *Voir aussi* **knee-high; oops-a-daisy!; ups-a-daisy!; upsy-daisy!; whoops-a-daisy!**

dallop [ˈdɔləp] (*noun*), *F:* = **dollop.**

dam [dæm] (*noun*), *F:* **1.** = **damn**[3]. **2. that's water over the d.,** c'est de l'eau sous le pont.

damage [ˈdæmidʒ] (*noun*), *F:* **what's**

* An asterisk indicates that the word so marked is included as a head-word in the Appendix.

the **d.**? ça fait combien?; **to stand the d.**, payer* l'addition, régler la douloureuse.

damaged [ˈdæmidʒd] (*adj.*), *P:* **d. goods,** une ex-vierge, cruche cassée, branche défleurée, fille* qui a vu le loup.

dame [deim] (*noun*), *F:* femme*, baronne *f*, gonzesse *f*; *cf.* **dizzy, 2.**

damfool[1] [ˈdæmˈfu:l] (*adj.*), *F:* bête*, stupide, idiot.

damfool[2] [ˈdæmˈfu:l] (*noun*), *F:* individu bête*, sacré idiot, imbécile *m*, crétin *m*.

damfoolery [ˈdæmˈfu:ləri], **damfoolishness** [ˈdæmˈfu:liʃnis] (*noun*), *F:* sacrée imbécillité.

dammit! [ˈdæmit] (*excl.*), *F:* **1.** sacrebleu! nom d'un chien! sacristi! **2. it was as near as d.**, il était moins une; **as quick** (*or* **soon**) **as d.**, aussi sec, illico.

damn[1] [dæm] (*adj.* & *adv.*) = **damned**[1, 2].

damn![2] [dæm] (*excl.*) = **dammit!, 1**; *voir aussi* **damn**[4] **(to), 4, 5, 6.**

damn[3] [dæm] (*noun*), *F:* **I don't give** (*or* **care**) **a d.** (*or* **a tinker's d.** *or* **a tupp'ny d.**), je m'en moque pas mal, je m'en fiche (*ou* je m'en soucie) comme de ma première chemise (*ou* comme de colin-tampon); *cf.* **tuppenny.**

damn[4] [dæm] **(to)**, *F:* **1. d. you!** (*or* **you be damned!**), va te faire pendre! **2. well I'm** (*or* **I'll be**) **damned!** ça c'est (trop) fort! **3. I'll see him damned first!** qu'il aille au diable! **4. d. it!** zut! **5. d. and blast!** nom de Dieu! bordel (de Dieu)! **6. d. it all!** nom de nom! nom d'un chien!

damnable [ˈdæmnəbl] (*adj.*), *F:* maudit, exécrable.

damnably [ˈdæmnəbli] (*adv.*), *F:* diablement, bigrement.

damn-all [ˈdæmˈɔ:l] (*noun*), *F:* **he's doing d.-a.**, il ne fiche rien; **he's done d.-a. today,** il n'a fichu que dalle aujourd'hui, il n'a pas fichu un coup de la sainte journée.

damnation! [ˈdæmˈneiʃ(ə)n] (*excl.*), *F:* sacrebleu!; **d. take it!** le diable l'emporte!

damned[1] [dæmd] (*adj.*), *F:* **1.** sacré, satané. **2. what a d. nuisance!** quel empoisonnement! **3. he's a d. nuisance!** quel enquiquineur! **4. it's a d. shame!** c'est une sacrée honte! **5. a d. sight better than . . .**, bigrement mieux que..., fichtrement meilleur que...

damned[2] [dæmd] (*adv.*), *F:* **1.** diablement, bigrement, vachement; **it's d. hard,** c'est vachement difficile. **2. . . . and a d. good job!** ...et c'est pas malheureux! **3. he knows d. well he mustn't,** il sait pertinemment bien qu'il ne doit pas; *voir aussi* **damned-well. 4. you're d. right there!** là tu as joliment raison! **5. pretty d. quick!** au trot! et que ça saute! **6. it'll be d. useful,** ça va nous rendre rudement service.

damnedest [ˈdæmdist] (*noun*), *F:* **to do** (*or* **try**) **one's d.**, se décarcasser, travailler* d'achar.

damned-well [ˈdæmdˈwel, ˈdæmˈwel] (*adv.*), *F:* **1. it d.-w. serves you right!** c'est bougrement bien fait! **2. you can do what you d.-w. like!** fais ce que tu veux, je m'en fous!

damp [dæmp] (*noun*), *F:* **to keep the d. out,** boire* un alcool, se rincer le gosier, tuer le ver.

damper [ˈdæmpər] (*noun*), *F:* **1.** rabat-joie *m*. **2. to put the d. on sth.**, (*a*) donner un coup de frein à qch.; (*b*) refroidir l'enthousiasme, défriser qch. **3. to put the d. on s.o.**, faire taire* qn, boucler la trappe à qn, clouer le bec à qn.

dance [dɑ:ns, *U.S.:* dæns] (*noun*), *F:* **to lead s.o. a d.**, donner du fil à retordre à qn, en faire voir (des vertes et des pas mûres) à qn. *Voir aussi* **song, 1.**

dander [ˈdændər] (*noun*), *F:* **to get one's d. up,** se mettre en colère*, s'emballer.

dandruff [ˈdændrʌf] (*noun*), *P:* **walking d.**, poux*, morpions *m.pl.*

dandy[1] [ˈdændi] (*adj.*), *F:* excellent*, sensas, super, de première.

dandy[2] [ˈdændi] (*adv.*), *F:* excellemment; **to get along (just) d. with s.o.**, s'entendre épatamment avec qn.

dandy[3] [ˈdændi] (*noun*), *F:* chose excellente* (*ou* épatante).

dang[1] [dæŋ] (*noun*) (*mainly U.S.*), *F:* = **damn**[3].

dang[2] [dæŋ] **(to)** (*mainly U.S.*), *F:* = **damn**[4] **(to)**.

danglers [ˈdæŋgləz] (*pl. noun*), *V:* testicules*, balloches *f.pl.*

* L'astérisque indique que le mot marqué de ce signe figure comme entrée dans le Répertoire.

daphne ['dæfni] (*noun*) (*Austr.*), *P:* femme* hétérosexuelle.

dar [dɑ:r] (*noun*), *F:* père*, daron *m*; *cf.* **da.**

darb [dɑ:b] (*noun*) (*U.S.*), *P:* chose excellente* (*ou* remarquable).

darbies ['dɑ:biz] (*pl. noun*), *P:* **1.** menottes*, fichets *m.pl.*, bracelets *m.pl.* **2.** empreintes digitales, piano *m*.

Darby and Joan ['dɑ:biən(d)'dʒoun] (*pr. noun*). **1.** *F:* un vieux ménage; **D. and J. club,** club *m* du troisième âge. **2.** *P:* (*R.S.* = *telephone*) téléphone*, bigophone *m*. **3.** *P:* **on one's D. and J.** (*R.S.* = *alone*), seul(abre).

dare [dɛər] (**to**), *F:* **I d. you!** chiche!

dark[1] [dɑ:k] (*adj.*), *F:* **to keep it d.,** cacher*, étouffer; **keep it d.!** motus! *Voir aussi* **horse**[1], **1.**

dark[2] [dɑ:k] (*noun*). **1.** *F:* **to be in the d. about sth.,** ne pas être dans le coup. **2.** *P:* (*mil.*) **in the d.,** au cachot, à l'ombre. *Voir aussi* **shot**[2], **7.**

darkey, darkie, darky ['dɑ:ki] (*noun*) (*often pej.*), nègre*, moricaud *m*, bougnoul(l)e *m*.

darling ['dɑ:liŋ] (*adj.*), *F:* **that is d. of you!** c'est chou(ette) de ta part.

darn[1] [dɑ:n] (*adj. & adv.*), *F:* *euph. pour* **damned**[1,2]; *cf.* **darned.**

darn![2] [dɑ:n] (*excl.*), *F:* *euph. pour* **damn!**[2].

darn[3] [dɑ:n] (**to**), *F:* *euph. pour* **damn**[4] (**to**).

darnation! [dɑ:'neiʃ(ə)n] (*excl.*), *F:* *euph. pour* **damnation!**; *cf.* **tarnation!**

darned [dɑ:nd] (*adj. & adv.*), *F:* *euph. pour* **damned**[1,2]; *cf.* **darn**[1].

darnedest ['dɑ:ndist] (*noun*), *F:* *euph. pour* **damnedest.**

darry ['dæri] (*noun*), *P:* coup *m* d'œil, coup de sabords; **to have a d. at sth.,** regarder* qch., reluquer qch.

dash[1] [dæʃ] (*noun*), *F:* **1.** (=*dashboard*) tableau *m* (*ou* panneau *m*) de bord. **2.** tentative *f*, essai *m*; **to have a d. at sth.,** tenter le coup, risquer sa chance. *Voir aussi* **cut**[3] (**to**), **10.**

dash[2] [dæʃ] (**to**), *F:* partir* rapidement, filer, se débiner; **(I) must d.,** il faut que je file.

dash(ed) [dæʃ(t)] (*adj. & adv.*), *F:* *euph. pour* **damned**[1,2].

dasher ['dæʃər] (*noun*), *F:* **1.** (*a*) individu élégant*; (*b*) individu gommeux (*ou* miché). **2.** prétentieux *m*, crâneur *m*, épateur *m*. **3.** dragueur *m*.

date[1] [deit] (*noun*), *F:* **1.** individu bête*, cruche *f*, crétin *m*; **you soppy d.!** espèce de gourde! **2.** rendez-vous*, rambour *m*; **to break a d.,** poser un lapin. **3.** personne (du sexe opposé) avec qui on a rendez-vous*.

date[2] [deit] (**to**), *F:* **to d. s.o.,** donner rendez-vous* à qn, sortir régulièrement avec qn. *Voir aussi* **blind**[1], **1.**

daughter ['dɔ:tər] (*noun*) (*R.S.* = *quarter*), *P:* 25 livres sterling; **four and a d.,** £425.

day [dei] (*noun*), *F:* **1. that'll be the d.!** on fera une croix à la cheminée! **2. to name the d.,** fixer le jour du mariage. **3. to pass the time of d.,** bavarder*, jacasser, tailler une bavette. **4. to win the d.,** gagner, emporter le morceau. **5. to know the time of d.,** la connaître (dans les coins). **6. to call it a d.,** débrayer (à la fin de la journée), dételer. **7. to have seen better days,** avoir connu des jours meilleurs, être décati, avoir fait son temps. **8. it's not my d.,** aujourd'hui le sort est contre moi, rien ne tourne rond aujourd'hui. **9. I've had my d.,** mes beaux jours sont passés. **10. at the end of the d.,** à la fin, en fin de compte. *Voir aussi* **rainy-day.**

daylight[1] ['deilait] (*adj.*), *F:* **it's d. robbery!** c'est du vol manifeste! on est volé comme au coin d'un bois!

daylight[2] ['deilait] (*noun*), *F:* **1. to be able to see d.,** apercevoir la fin d'un long travail, commencer à en voir le bout, sortir du tunnel. **2. to knock** (*or* **beat** *or* **bash**) **the (living) daylights out of s.o.,** battre* qn comme plâtre, envoyer dormir qn.

dazzler ['dæzlər] (*noun*), *F:* **1.** diamant*, diame *m*, éclair *m*. **2.** une journée très ensoleillée, où le bourguignon tape. **3.** un(e) m'as-tu-vu; époustoufleur *m*, époustoufleuse *f*, qn qui en met plein la vue. *Voir aussi* **bobby-dazzler.**

dead[1] [ded] (*adj.*), *F:* **1. a d. loss,** (*a*) une nullité, un propre à rien; (*b*) une perte sèche; **a d. cert** (*or* **cinch**), une certitude absolue; **a d. liberty,** une sacrée audace; *cf.* **diabolical; to come to a d. stop,** s'arrêter pile, stopper net. **2. d. man** (*or* **'un** *or* **soldier** *or* **marine**), bouteille*

* An asterisk indicates that the word so marked is included as a head-word in the Appendix.

vide, cadavre *m*; *voir aussi* **soldier**[1], 2 (*b*). 3. **drop d.!** écrase! ta gueule! 4. **a d. duck,** une chose *ou* personne fichue, ruinée, finie; échec*, faillite *f*, four complet. 5. **d. from the neck up,** bête*, bouché à l'émeri. 6. **the d. spit of s.o.,** l'image crachée de qn; **he's the d. spit of his father,** c'est son père tout craché. 7. **d. to the world** (*or* **to the wide**), (*a*) ivre* mort, bourré à bloc; (*b*) profondément endormi, dans les bras de Morphée. 8. (*d'un moteur, etc.*) à plat, mort; **to go d.,** lâcher. 9. **to be waiting for d. men's shoes,** attendre la dépouille de qn. 10. **I wouldn't be seen d. with him,** à aucun prix je ne veux être vu(e) avec lui. 11. très fatigué*, claqué, crevé. 12. ennuyeux*, barbant, canulant. *Voir aussi* **Anne; Charl(e)y**[2], 2; **cut**[3] **(to)**, 5; **dead-and-alive; horse**[1], 4; **ringer,** 1; **set**[2].

dead[2] [ded] (*adv.*), *F:* 1. **d. broke,** archi-pauvre*, fauché, sans le sou. 2. **d. easy,** facile comme bonjour, bête comme chou. 3. **d. scared,** mort de peur*; **d. drunk,** ivre* mort. 4. **d. innocent,** innocent comme l'enfant qui vient de naître. 5. **d. chocker** (*or* **choked**), ennuyé* à mourir, en ayant ras le bol. 6. **d. chuffed,** (*a*) =**d. chocker** (*voir* 5); (*b*) aux anges. 7. **d. on,** dans le mille. 8. (*a*) **d. to rights,** absolument; (*b*) **to catch s.o. d. to rights,** prendre qn sur le fait (*ou* la main dans le sac), épingler qn sur le tas; *cf.* **bang**[2], 2. 9. **to be d. (set) against sth.,** être braqué (*ou* monté *ou* buté) contre qch.

dead-and-alive [ˈdedəndəˈlaiv] (*adj.*), *F:* **a d.-a.-a. place,** un endroit mort (*ou* triste *ou* sans animation), un trou, un bled.

dead-beat [ˈdedˈbiːt] (*adj.*), *F:* très fatigué*, épuisé, vanné.

deadbeat [ˈdedbiːt] (*noun*), *P:* 1. paresseux*, fainéant *m*, parasite *m*. 2. (*U.S.*) mauvais payeur, filou *m*.

dead-end [ˈdedˈend] (*adj.*), *F:* 1. **d.-e. job,** travail* (*ou* boulot *m*) sans avenir. 2. **d.-e. kid,** blouson noir.

deader [ˈdedər] (*noun*), *P:* cadavre*, croni *m*, refroidi *m*.

deadhead [ˈdedhed] (*noun*), *P:* 1. individu bête*, déplafonné *m*. 2. ennuyeux*, casse-pieds *m*, crampon *m*. 3. (*th.*) personne qui entre avec un billet de faveur.

deadly[1] [ˈdedli] (*adj.*), *F:* ennuyeux*, mourant.

deadly[2] [ˈdedli] (*adv.*), *F:* archi-, très; **d. dull,** mortellement ennuyeux*.

deadneck [ˈdednek] (*noun*), *P:* = **deadhead,** 1.

deadpan [ˈdedpæn] (*adj.*), *F:* (visage) impassible, de pierre, de marbre; **to give s.o. the d. treatment,** battre froid à qn.

deal [diːl] (*noun*). 1. *F:* **to clinch a d.,** s'assurer une vente, boucler une affaire; **to make a d.,** décrocher une affaire; **a new d.,** un nouveau départ; **a phoney** (*or* **rigged**) **d.,** une affaire véreuse; **to get the short end of the d.,** recevoir une petite partie des bénéfices, tenir le mauvais bout, n'avoir que les clopinettes; **dirty d.,** mauvais tour, **sale** coup *m*, vacherie *f*; *voir aussi* **raw**[1], 1; **square**[1], 1. 2. *F:* **big d.!** belle affaire! et mon œil!; **no d.!** pas mèche! rien à faire! 3. *P:* petite dose (d'une drogue).

dealer [ˈdiːlər] (*noun*), *F:* fourgueur *m* (de drogues), trafiquant *m*. *Voir aussi* **wheeler-dealer.**

dearie, deary [ˈdiəri] (*noun*), *F:* 1. (mon petit) chéri, (ma petite) chérie. 2. **(oh) d. me!** (*a*) mes enfants! douce Mère!; (*b*) *voir* **bingo** (3). *Voir aussi* **hello-dearie.**

death [deθ] (*noun*), *F:* 1. **to feel like d. (warmed up),** se sentir mortibus (*ou* fricassé); **to look like d. (warmed up),** avoir l'air cadavérique (*ou* d'un cadavre ambulant). 2. **to die the d.,** (*d'un acteur*) tomber à vide. 3. **to do sth. to d.,** faire qch. jusqu'à la lie (*ou* jusqu'à en vomir). 4. **to bore s.o. to d.,** faire mourir* qn d'ennui, barber qn jusqu'à la gauche. 5. **I'm frozen to d.,** je meurs de froid. *Voir aussi* **flog (to),** 3; **hang on (to),** 2; **sudden; tickle**[2] **(to),** 3.

deb (deb] (*abbr.* = *debutante*), *F:* débutante *f*.

debag [ˈdiːˈbæg] (**to**), *F:* déculotter.

debt [det] (*noun*), *F:* **to pay the last d.,** mourir*, avaler sa chique.

debug [ˈdiːˈbʌg] (**to**), *F:* 1. réparer, mettre au point, réviser. 2. désonoriser, neutraliser des micros clandestins.

debunk [ˈdiːˈbʌŋk] (**to**), *F:* déboulonner, dégonfler, faire descendre d'un cran.

* L'astérisque indique que le mot marqué de ce signe figure comme entrée dans le Répertoire.

decent [ˈdiːs(ə)nt] (*adj.*), *F:* **1.** passable, acceptable, correct; **a d. chap,** un brave type, un bon gars. **2. to be d.,** être habillé décemment, être convenable.

decently [ˈdiːs(ə)ntli] (*adv.*), *F:* généreusement, abondamment.

deck [dek] (*noun*). **1.** *F:* **to hit the d.,** (*a*) se lever du lit, se dépager, se dépieuter; (*b*) tomber à plat ventre. **2.** *F:* **to clear the decks,** tout préparer, se préparer à agir, être sur le point d'attaquer, faire le branle-bas. **3.** *F:* jeu *m* de cartes*; **to play with a stacked d.,** (*a*) jouer avec des cartes biseautées (*ou* maquillées); (*b*) avoir l'avantage sur qn, tenir le bon bout. **4.** *P:* (*a*) petite quantité de drogues, prise *f*, boulette *f*; (*b*) petite dose d'héroïne *ou* de cocaïne (*drogues**).

decker [ˈdekər] (*noun*), *P:* chapeau*, doulos *m*. *Voir aussi* **double-decker.**

decko [ˈdekou] (*noun*), *P:* = **dekko.**

deck out [ˈdekˈaut] (**to**), *F:* **to be all decked out,** être sur son trente et un, être tout flambé.

decoke [ˈdiːˈkouk] (**to**), *F:* décalaminer, décarburer.

decorators [ˈdekəreitəz] (*pl. noun*), *P:* **to have the d. in,** avoir ses menstrues*, repeindre sa grille en rouge; *cf.* **painter, 2.**

dee-jay (*noun*) (*abbr.* = *disc-jockey*), *F:* présentateur *m* de disques, disquaire *m*.

deep[1] [diːp] (*adj.*), *F:* **1.** malin*, fin, matois, retors. **2. to put sth. in the d. freeze,** mettre qch. au frigidaire, mettre qch. sur la planche. *Voir aussi* **end, 5, 13; jump**[2] **(to), 12.**

deep[2] [diːp] (*noun*), *P:* **to plough the d.** (*R.S.* = *to sleep*), dormir*, pioncer.

degree [diˈgriː] (*noun*), *F:* **1. to be** (*or* **feel**) **one d. under,** être légèrement malade*, être patraque, ne pas être dans son assiette. **2. third d.,** tortures *f.pl.* pour faire avouer*, cuisinage *m*; **to give s.o. the third d.,** cuisiner qn, griller qn.

dekko [ˈdekou] (*noun*), *P:* **let's have a d.!** fais-moi voir! juste un coup d'œil*!; **have** (*or* **take**) **a d. out of the window,** jette un coup d'œil* par la fenêtre.

delicate [ˈdelikət] (*adj.*), *F:* **to be in a d. condition,** être enceinte*, être dans une situation intéressante.

demo [ˈdemou] (*noun*), *F:* manifestation *f* politique, manif *f*.

demob[1] [ˈdiːˈmɔb] (*noun*) (*abbr.* = *demobilization*), *F:* libération *f* militaire, décarrade *f*, la quille; **to be due for d.,** être de la classe.

demob[2] [ˈdiːˈmɔb] (**to**) (*abbr.* = *demobilize*), *F:* libérer, décarrer, renvoyer dans ses foyers.

demolish [diˈmɔliʃ] (**to**), *F:* manger*, boulotter.

den [den] (*noun*), *F:* repaire *m*, clandé *m*.

dense [dens] (*adj.*), *F:* bête*, bouché.

dent [dent] (*noun*), *F:* **to make a d. (in sth.),** commencer à mordre.

depth-charge [ˈdepθtʃɑːdʒ] (*noun*), étouffe-chrétien *m*.

Derby Kel(l) *or* **Kelly** [ˈdɑːbiˈkel(i)] (*noun*) (*R.S.* = *belly*), *P:* ventre*, bide *m*.

dern [dəːn] (*adj.* & *adv.*), *F:* *euph. pour* **damned**[1,2]; *cf.* **darn.**

derry [ˈderi] (*noun*), *P:* baraque *f*, cambuse *f*.

deuce [djuːs] (*noun*). **1.** *F:* diable *m*; **to raise the d.** = **to raise the devil (devil**[1]**, 15). 2.** *F:* **to get the d.** = **to get the devil (devil**[1]**, 17). 3.** *F:* **to give s.o. the d.,** réprimander* qn, lessiver la tête à qn. **4.** *P:* deux livres sterling; (*U.S.*) deux dollars.

deuced[1] [djuːst] (*adj.*), *F:* satané, sacré.

deuced[2] [djuːst] (*adv.*), *F:* diablement, diantrement, bigrement.

devil[1] [ˈdevl] (*noun*), *F:* **1. I had the d. of a job** (*or* **the d.'s own job**) **to . . .,** c'était la croix et la bannière pour . . .; **it's the very d. to wake him up in the morning,** c'est la croix et la bannière pour le réveiller le matin. **2. he's an absolute d.!** il est infernal! **3. he's a d. with women,** il est terrible avec les femmes; il les tombe toutes. **4. who the d. are you?** qui, diable, êtes-vous?; **who the d. do you think you are?** pour qui, diable, te prends-tu? **5. how the d. . . .?** comment diable...? **6. go to the d.!** (allez) au diable! **7. poor d.!** pauvre hère! pauvre diable! **8. to send s.o. to the d.,** envoyer qn au diable (*ou* sur les roses). **9. to go to the d.,** mal tourner, tomber dans la mélasse, piquer une tête. **10. he has the d. of a temper,** il est mauvais coucheur, il a un caractère de cochon. **11. there'll be the d. to**

* An asterisk indicates that the word so marked is included as a head-word in the Appendix.

pay, ça nous (vous) coûtera cher (*ou* chaud); vous ne perdez rien pour attendre. 12. **be a d. and have another drink,** laisse-toi tenter (*ou* faire) et reprends un verre. 13. **to play the d. with sth.,** mettre la confusion dans qch., mettre la pagaille; **to play the d. with s.o.,** maltraiter qn, malmener qn, être chien (*ou* vache) avec qn. 14. **to work like the d.,** travailler* avec acharnement, trimer comme un nègre (*ou* un forçat). 15. **to raise the d.,** faire du bruit*, faire un potin du diable. 16. **to beat the d. out of s.o.,** battre* qn comme plâtre, secouer les puces à qn. 17. **to get the d.,** se faire réprimander* (*ou* enguirlander). 18. **give the d. his due,** à chacun son dû; rendons justice à... 19. **between the d. and the deep blue sea,** entre l'enclume et le marteau. 20. **the D.'s Bible** (*or* **playthings**), cartes* à jouer. 21. **to be a d.,** avoir le diable au corps. 22. **red devils** = **reds** (**red**[2], 5). 23. **blue devils,** le cafard, le bourdon.

devil[2] [ˈdevl] (**to**), *F:* **to d. the life out of s.o.,** tourmenter qn, faire suer qn, empoisonner qn.

devil-dodger [ˈdevldɔdʒər] (*noun*), *F:* prêtre*, ratichon *m.*

devilish(ly) [ˈdevliʃ(li)] (*adv.*), *F:* diablement, diantrement, extrêmement.

dewdrop [ˈdjuː-drɔp] (*noun*), *F:* la goutte au nez, chandelle *f.*

dex [deks], **dexie** [ˈdeksi], **dexo** [ˈdeksou], **dexy** [ˈdeksi] (*noun*), *P:* cachet *m* de dexamphétamine, dexo *m* (*drogues*); (*pl.*) amphétamines *f.pl.* (*drogues**).

dhobying [ˈdoubiːiŋ] (*noun*), *P:* lessive *f,* blanchissage *m,* savonnage *m.*

diabolical [daiəˈbɔlik(ə)l] (*adj.*), *F:* diabolique, satané, affreux, odieux; **it's a d. liberty!** c'est un sacré culot!

diabolically [daiəˈbɔlikli] (*adv.*), *F:* = **devilish(ly).**

dial(-piece) [ˈdaiəl(piːs)] (*noun*), *P:* visage*, museau *m,* margoulette *f,* bobine *f.*

dib [dib] (*noun*), *P:* 1. part *f,* fade *m.* 2. (*pl.*) argent*, fric *m;* **to have the dibs,** être riche* (*ou* bourré), avoir du fric, être au pèze.

dice[1] [dais] (*pl. noun*), *F:* 1. **no d.!** pas mèche! je ne marche pas! rien à faire! 2. **to throw in the d.,** lâcher les dés (*ou* la partie), jeter l'éponge, mettre les pouces.

dice[2] [dais] (**to**), *F:* (*automobiles*) se poursuivre, gratter; *cf.* **dicing; to d. with death,** faire la course à la mort, jouer avec la mort.

dicey [ˈdaisi] (*adj.*), *F:* hasardeux, au flanc; **it's a bit d.,** c'est du risqué, c'est pas du tout cuit.

dicing [ˈdaisiŋ] (*noun*), *F:* (*automobiles*) course *f* entre deux chauffeurs, grattage *m;* *cf.* **dice**[2] (**to**).

dick [dik] (*noun*), *P:* 1. pénis*, Charles-le-Chauve, Popaul *m.* 2. policier*, détective *m,* poulet *m,* bourre *m;* *cf.* **fly-dick.** 3. **clever D.,** un petit (*ou* gros) malin, affranchi *m.* 4. **dirty D.,** sale dégoûtant, sale coco *m.* 5. (*pl.*) poux*, morpions *m.pl.* 6. déclaration *f,* serment *m;* **to take one's d.,** prêter serment, salbiner. 7. **up to d.** = **up to scratch; to keep s.o. up to d.,** serrer les côtes à qn. 8. dictionnaire *m,* dico *m;* **to swallow the d.,** avoir avalé le dico. 9. (*U.S.*) **to buy the d.,** (*a*) s'attirer des ennuis, s'amocher; (*b*) mourir*, dévisser son billard. *Voir aussi* **Tom, 1.**

dickens [ˈdikinz], **the** (*noun*), *F:* 1. le diable. 2. **the d. of a noise,** un bruit* (*ou* un potin) du diable. 3. **it's the d. of a job,** c'est le diable à confesser. 4. **to give s.o. the d.** = **to give s.o. the deuce** (**deuce,** 3); **to get the d.** = **to get the devil** (**devil**[1], 17); **to raise the d.** = **to raise Cain** (**Cain,** 1).

dickey [ˈdiki] (*noun*), *F:* = **dicky**[2], 3.

dickory-dock [ˈdikəriˈdɔk] (*noun*), *P:* 1. (*R.S.* = *clock*) horloge *f,* toquante *f.* 2. (*R.S.*) = **cock, 1.**

dicky[1] [ˈdiki] (*adj.*), *F:* 1. malade*, patraque, pas dans son assiette; *cf.* **ticker, 1.** 2. déchard, frisant la faillite.

dicky[2] [ˈdiki] (*noun*). 1. *P:* = **dick, 1.** 2. *F:* = **dicky-bird, 1.** 3. *F:* plastron *m* (de chemise) mobile, bavoir *m* à liquette.

dicky-bird [ˈdikibəːd] (*noun*), *F:* 1. (*R.S.* = *word*) mot *m.* 2. oiseau *m,* zozio *m.*

dicky-dido [ˈdikiˈdaidou] (*noun*), *V:* vulve*, cramouille *f.*

dicky-dirt [ˈdikiˈdəːt] (*noun*) (*R.S.* = *shirt*), *P:* chemise *f,* liquette *f.*

* L'astérisque indique que le mot marqué de ce signe figure comme entrée dans le Répertoire.

dicy [ˈdaisi] (*adj.*), *F:* = **dicey.**

diddies [ˈdidiz] (*pl. noun*), *P:* seins*, nénés *m.pl.*

diddle [ˈdidl] (**to**). **1.** *F:* voler*. **2.** *F:* duper*, rouler, carotter (qn). **3.** *P:* coïter* avec (une femme), calecer. **4.** (*U.S.*) *P:* se masturber*, se branler. **5.** *F:* = **piddle**[2] (**to**).

diddle around [ˈdidl-əˈraund] (**to**), *P:* flânocher, baguenauder.

diddle away [ˈdidl-əˈwei] (**to**), *F:* **to d. a. one's time,** flâner.

diddler [ˈdidlər] (*noun*), *F:* **1.** voleur*. **2.** escroc*, carotteur *m*, estampeur *m*. **3.** bricoleur *m*, baguenaudeur *m*.

diddling [ˈdidliŋ] (*noun*), *F:* **1.** vol *m*, estampage *m*. **2.** escroquerie*

diddy [ˈdidi], **didekei, didikai** [ˈdidikai], **didlo** [ˈdidlou] (*noun*), *P:* romanichel *m*, romani *m*, rabouin *m*.

dido [ˈdaidou] (*noun*) (*U.S.*), *P:* farce *f*, niche *f*, frasque *f*, fredaine *f*. *Voir aussi* **dicky-dido.**

dig[1] [dig] (*noun*). **1.** *F:* fouilles *f.pl.* (archéologiques). **2.** *P:* **d. in the grave** (*R.S.* = *shave*), rasage *m*, raclage *m*. **3.** (*pl.*) *F:* logement*, garni *m*, crèche *f*. **4.** *F:* **to have a d. at s.o., to get a d. in at s.o.,** lancer (*ou* filer) un vanne (*ou* un coup de patte) à qn. **5.** *P:* piqûre *f*, piquouse *f*.

dig[2] [dig] (**to**). **1.** *F:* (*a*) **I d. that,** ça me plaît, ça me botte; (*b*) comprendre, piger, entraver (qch.). **2.** *F:* aimer*, gober (qn), avoir à la bonne. **3.** *P:* taper sur les nerfs (*ou* le système) à (qn). **4.** *P:* coïter* avec (une femme), piquer, bourrer. **5.** *F:* se moquer* de, bêcher, lancer des vannes à. **6.** *P:* faire gaffe, se débrider l'esgourde. **7.** *F:* travailler* dur, trimer, bosser. **8.** *F:* habiter*, crécher.

digger [ˈdigər] (*noun*). **1.** *F:* (*a*) Australien *m*; (*b*) Néo-zélandais *m*. **2.** (*pl.*) *P:* groupe de hippies qui veulent abattre le système capitaliste en donnant au lieu de vendre; les sapeurs *m.pl.* **3.** (*mil.*) *P:* **the d.,** trou *m*, taulerie *f*. **4.** (*pl.*) (*cartes*) *P:* pique *m*, croque-mort *m*, piche *m*. *Voir aussi* **gold-digger.**

diggings [ˈdigiŋz] (*pl. noun*), *F:* logement*, crèche *f*, carrée *f*.

dig in [ˈdigˈin] (**to**), *F:* **1.** manger*, s'empiffrer, bouffer. **2.** travailler* soigneusement. **3.** rester sur ses positions, ne pas broncher.

dig into [ˈdigˈintuː] (**to**), *F:* creuser (une question, *etc.*), pinocher.

digit [ˈdidʒit] (*noun*), *F:* **to extract the d.:** *euph. pour* **to pull one's finger out.** (**finger**[1], **2**).

digums [ˈdaigəms] (*pl. noun*), *P:* bouts *m.pl.* des seins*, fraises *f.pl.*

dig up [ˈdigˈʌp] (**to**), *F:* **where did you d. that u.?** d'où l'as-tu tiré? où l'as-tu déniché (*ou* pêché *ou* cueilli)?

dike [daik] (*noun*), *P:* **1.** W.C.*, chiottes *f.pl.*; **to do a d.,** déféquer*, aller à la débourre. **2.** = **dyke.**

dikey [ˈdaiki] (*adj.*), *P:* = **dykey.**

dildo [ˈdildou] (*noun*), *P:* gode(miché) *m*.

dill [dil] (*noun*) (*Austr.*), *P:* = **alec, 2.**

dilly[1] [ˈdili] (*adj.*), *F:* chouette, bath, mignon.

dilly[2] [ˈdili] (*noun*), *F:* **1. she's a d.,** elle est mignonne (à croquer). **2.** qch. de chouette. **3.** star *f*, as *m*, vedette *f*, starlette *f*.

dim [dim] (*adj.*), *F:* **1. to take a d. view of sth.,** avoir une piètre opinion de qch. **2. a d. type** (*or* **character**), (*a*) individu bête*, espèce d'idiot, buse *f*; (*b*) nullité *f*, mocheté *f*, perte sèche; *cf.* **come**[2] (**to**), **2.**

dime [daim] (*noun & attrib. adj.*) (*U.S.*), *F:* dîme *f* (dix cents); **d. novel,** roman feuilleton (*ou* de deux sous); **a d. a dozen,** qui ne vaut pas cher (*ou* deux sous *ou* pipette *ou* peau de balle); **d.-a-dance palace,** bal musette, bastringue *m*, guinche *f*.

dimmock [ˈdimək] (*noun*), *P:* argent*, artiche *m*.

dimp [dimp] (*noun*), *P:* mégot*, clope *m*.

dimwit [ˈdimwit] (*noun*), *F:* individu bête*, andouille *f*, ballot *m*.

dimwitted [ˈdimwitid] (*adj.*), *F:* bête*, bas de plafond, baluche.

dinch [dintʃ] (*noun*), *P:* = **dimp.**

din-dins [ˈdindinz] (*pl. noun*), *F:* (*langage enfantin*) repas *m*, dînette *f*.

dine out [ˈdainˈaut] (**to**), *F:* danser devant le buffet, claquer du bec, la sauter, manger avec les chevaux de bois.

ding [diŋ] (*noun*), *P:* **to have a d. with a girl,** fréquenter une fille, sortir avec une fille.

ding-dong [ˈdiŋdɔŋ] (*adj.*), *F:* **d.-d. battle,** lutte acharnée, luttanche *f*, pétard *m*.

* L'astérisque indique que le mot marqué de ce signe figure comme entrée dans le Répertoire.

dinge[1] [dindʒ] (*noun*), *P:* nègre* (*péj.*), bougnoule *m. Voir aussi* **queen, 2.**

dinge[2] [dindʒ] (**to**), *P:* amocher, esquinter, bosseler, cabosser.

dinger [ˈdiŋər] (*noun*), *P:* = **humdinger.**

dinghiyen [ˈdiŋgiˈjen] (*noun*), *P:* = **dripper.**

dingle-dangle [ˈdiŋglˈdæŋgl] (*noun*), *P:* pénis*, berdouillette *f*, queue *f.*

dingus [ˈdiŋ(g)əs] (*noun*), **1.** *F:* truc *m*, machin *m*, chose *f*, fourbi *m.* **2.** *P:* = **dripper.**

dinkum [ˈdiŋkəm] (*adj.*) (*Austr.*), *F:* **1.** **(fair) d.,** régulier, réglo, aux petits oignons, vrai de vrai. **2.** **the d. article,** (*a*) de l'authentique, du vrai; (*b*) l'homme qu'il faut. **3.** **a d. Aussie,** Australien *m* de naissance, kangourou *m.*

dinky [ˈdiŋki] (*adj.*), *F:* **1.** mignon, menu, joliet, croquignole. **2.** (*Austr.*) sûr et certain.

dinky-doo [ˈdiŋkiˈduː], *F:* *voir* **bingo (22).**

dinlow [ˈdinlou] (*noun*), *F:* = **dimwit.**

dip[1] [dip] (*noun*). **1.** *P:* voleur* à la tire (*ou* à la fourche *ou* à la fourchette). **2.** *P:* drogué*, camé *m*, toxico *m.* **3.** *P:* diphtérie *f.* **4.** *P:* individu bête*, nigaud *m*, ballot *m.* **5.** *F:* une petite baignade, une trempette. **6.** *F:* **lucky d.,** (*a*) loterie *f*; (*b*) au petit bonheur la chance. **7.** *P:* chapeau*, bada *m*, doulos *m.*

dip[2] [dip] (**to**), *P:* **1.** mettre en gage, mettre au Mont (de Piété) (*ou* chez ma tante). **2.** voler* à la tire (*ou* à la fourche *ou* à la fourchette). *Voir aussi* **lid, 1; wick, 2.**

dipper [ˈdipər] (*noun*), *P:* **1.** = **dip**[1], **1.** **2.** baptiste *m* (qui croit au baptême par immersion).

dippy [ˈdipi] (*adj.*), *P:* **1.** fou*, maboul, timbré, loufoque, dingo. **2.** **to be d. about s.o.,** être entiché de qn, avoir le béguin pour qn.

dipso [ˈdipsou] (*abbr.* = *dipsomaniac*), *F:* dipsomane *mf*, ivrogne*, soûlot *m*, poivrot *m.*

dirt[1] [dəːt] (*noun*). **1.** *F:* porno(graphie) *f*, obscénité *f*, cochonnerie *f.* **2.** *P:* ragots *m.pl.*, cancans *m.pl.*, potins *m.pl.*; **to dish out the d.,** ragoter, cancaner, potiner; **to throw d. at s.o.,** déblatérer contre qn, débiner qn, dauber sur qn; **to have the d. on s.o.,** savoir des choses peu relevées sur qn. **3.** *F:* **to treat s.o. like d.,** traiter qn plus bas que terre. **4.** *F:* **to sweep the d. under the carpet** (*U.S.:* **under the rug**), couvrir la vérité, tirer le rideau, mettre la lumière sous le boisseau. **5.** *F:* **to eat d.,** avaler son amour-propre, avaler des couleuvres. **6.** *P:* **to do d. on s.o., to do s.o. d.,** faire un sale coup (*ou* une crasse *ou* une vacherie) à qn; *cf.* **dirty**[2]. **7.** *P:* **yellow d.,** or*, jonc *m*, quart *m* de beurre. **8.** *P:* argent*, braise *f. Voir aussi* **dicky-dirt; grass**[1], **2.**

dirt[2] [dəːt] (**to**), *P:* duper*, rouler, carotter (qn).

dirt-cheap [ˈdəːtˈtʃiːp] (*adj. & adv.*), *F:* à vil prix, pour rien*, pour des prunes (*ou* des haricots).

dirt-track [ˈdəːttræk] (*attrib. adj.*), *P:* **d.-t. rider,** pédéraste* qui est de la bague (*ou* du zéro).

dirty[1] [ˈdəːti] (*adj.*). **1.** *F:* **to have a d. mind,** avoir l'esprit cochon (*ou* mal tourné); **how d.-minded she is!** comme elle est cochonne! **2.** *F:* **d. dog,** sale type *m*; **d. trick,** sale tour *m*; **d. weather,** sale temps *m*; **d. look,** sale coup *m* d'œil; **d. rat,** bordille *f.* **3.** (*a*) *F:* **he does the d. work,** il fait la grosse besogne, à lui la sale besogne; (*b*) **d. work at the crossroads,** (i) *F:* sale coup *m*, crasse *f*, saloperie *f*; (ii) *P:* coït*. **4.** *P:* (*intensif*) **a d. great lorry,** un camion maous(se); **a d. big suitcase,** une valise qui se pose là. **5.** *F:* **a d. old man,** un vieux barbeau, un vieux marcheur. **6.** *P:* (*a*) **d. old Jew:** *voir* **bingo (2)**; (*b*) **d. whore:** *voir* **bingo (34).** **7.** *F:* **a d. weekend,** un week-end de débauche. **8.** *P:* **d. money,** (*a*) argent* mal acquis, gratte *f*, tour *m* de bâton; (*b*) prime *f* (de travail). **9.** *F:* **to have a d. mouth,** parler comme un charretier, être mal embouché. **10.** *P:* (*jazz*) grinçant, agressif. *Voir aussi* **linen; mac**[2].

dirty[2] [ˈdəːti] (*noun*), *P:* **to do the d. on s.o.,** jouer un tour de cochon à qn, chier dans les bottes de qn; *cf.* **dirt**[1], **6.**

disappearing [disəˈpiəriŋ] (*adj.*), *F:* **to do a d. act,** (*a*) partir*, s'esquiver, jouer rip; (*b*) déménager à la cloche de bois.

dischuffed [ˈdisˈtʃʌft] (*adj.*), *P:* dé-

* An asterisk indicates that the word so marked is included as a head-word in the Appendix.

couragé, dégoûté, qui n'a pas le moral; *cf.* **chuffed,** (*b*).

disco [ˈdiskou] (*noun*), *F:* **1.** discothèque *f.* **2.** club *m* de discophiles.

dish[1] [diʃ] (*noun*). **1.** *F:* belle* fille; **what a d.!** quelle beauté! un vrai régal!; *cf.* **dishy. 2.** *P:* fesses*, arrière-boutique *f,* dédé *m.* **3.** *P:* visage*, fiole *f,* binette *f.*

dish[2] [diʃ] (**to**), *P:* **1.** enfoncer (ses adversaires), prendre de court, couper l'herbe sous le pied à (qn); **to be dished,** être coulé (*ou* enfoncé *ou* flambé). **2.** duper*, rouler (qn). **3.** confondre, dérouter, frustrer. **4.** (*U.S.*) bavarder*, potiner.

dishclout [ˈdiʃ-klaut] (*noun*), *P:* salope *f,* souillon *f.*

dish out [ˈdiʃˈaut] (**to**), *F:* **1. to d. o. money** (*or* **the lolly**), payer*, casquer (*ou* abouler *ou* cracher) de l'argent*. **2. to d. it o.,** réprimander*, faire une semonce, passer un savon. **3. to d. o. punishment,** (*d'un boxeur*) assener des coups* à son adversaire, envoyer les marrons. *Voir aussi* **dirt**[1], **2; porridge.**

dishrag [ˈdiʃræg] (*noun*), *F:* **to feel like a d.,** se sentir très fatigué*, être éreinté (*ou* sur les genoux).

dish up [ˈdiʃˈʌp] (**to**). **1.** *F:* bien arranger (*ou* trousser), pomponner, requinquer. **2.** *P:* **to be dished up,** être fatigué* (*ou* éreinté *ou* pompé *ou* à bout).

dishwater [ˈdiʃwɔːtər] (*noun*), *F:* **1.** lavasse *f;* bibine *f;* **to taste of d.,** (*nourriture*) sentir le graillon. **2. dull as d. = dull as ditchwater** (*voir* **ditchwater**).

dishy [ˈdiʃi] (*adj.*), *F:* qui a du chien; *cf.* **dish**[1], **1.**

dismals [ˈdizməlz] (*pl. noun*), *F:* **to have the d.,** broyer du noir, avoir le cafard.

distance [ˈdist(ə)ns] (*noun*), *F:* **to go the d.,** (*boxe, lutte*) aller à la limite.

ditch[1] [ditʃ] (*noun*), *F:* **1. to die in the last d.,** mourir* dans l'impénitence finale (*ou* à la dernière extrémité). **2. the D.,** (*a*) la Manche *ou* la mer du Nord; (*b*) Shoreditch (*banlieue-est de Londres*); **the big d.,** l'océan *m,* la Grande Tasse, la baille. *Voir aussi* **last-ditch.**

ditch[2] [ditʃ] (**to**), *F:* **1.** jeter par-dessus bord, larguer. **2. to d. a car,** (*a*) verser une automobile dans un fossé, la faire entrer dans les décors; (*b*) abandonner* une voiture, la larguer. **3. to d. a plane,** amerrir en catastrophe, faire un amerrissage forcé. **4.** (*a*) abandonner* (une femme, idée, *etc.*), plaquer, laisser tomber; (*b*) se débarrasser* de, sacquer, balancer. **5.** faire dérailler.

ditchwater [ˈditʃwɔːtər] (*noun*), *F:* **dull as d.,** ennuyeux* comme la pluie; **he's as dull as d.,** c'est un robinet d'eau tiède.

dither [ˈdiðər] (*noun*), *F:* **to be all of a d., to have the dithers,** être dans tous ses états, ne plus savoir où donner de la tête.

dithery [ˈdiðəri] (*adj.*), *F:* agité, nerveux, tout chose.

ditto[1] [ˈditou] (*noun*), *F:* **1.** un complet, un ensemble. **2. to say d.,** opiner du bonnet.

ditto[2] [ˈditou] (**to**), *F:* faire *ou* dire la même chose.

dive[1] [daiv] (*noun*), *F:* **1.** café*, bouge *m,* tripot *m,* gargote *f,* boui-boui *m.* **2. to take a d.,** (*a*) (*boxe*) se coucher; (*b*) faire le plongeon. *Voir aussi* **nose-dive**[1].

dive[2] [daiv] (**to**). **1.** *F:* **to d. into a shop,** s'engouffrer dans un magasin. **2.** *V:* **to d. (into the bushes) = muff**[2] **(to), 3;** *cf.* **pearl-dive (to).** *Voir aussi* **nose-dive**[2] **(to).**

divi [ˈdivi] (*noun*), *F:* = **divvy.**

divine [diˈvain] (*adj.*), *F:* excellent*, divin.

divvy [ˈdivi] (*noun*), *F:* intérêt *m,* divi(dende) *m,* fade *m.*

divvy up [ˈdiviˈʌp] (**to**), *F:* partager, aller au fade, faire la motte.

dizzy [ˈdizi] (*adj.*), *F:* **1. = scatter-brained. 2. a d. blonde,** une blonde tape-à-l'œil; **a d. dame,** une femme* bête*, cruche *f,* bourrique *f,* gourde *f.* **3. it's the d. limit,** c'est le comble, c'est la fin des haricots. **4. to go the d. round,** faire la noce (*ou* la bamboche), faire la tournée des grands-ducs.

D.J., d.j. [ˈdiːˈdʒei] (*abbr. = disc-jockey*), *F: voir* **dee-jay.**

do[1] [duː] (*noun*). **1.** *F:* réjouissances*, boum *f,* bombance *f.* **2.** *P:* filouterie *f,* sale tour *m,* attrape *f.* **3.** *F:* affaire(s) *f.* (*pl.*), événement *m.* **4.** (*pl.*) *F:* partage *m,* portion *f,* taf *m;* **fair d.'s,**

* An asterisk indicates that the word so marked is included as a head-word in the Appendix.

une juste part; **to give s.o. fair d.'s,** jouer franc jeu avec qn. **5.** *P:* réussite *f;* **to make a d. of sth.,** se bien tirer de qch. **6.** *P:* bataille *f* entre jeunes voyous; rififi *m. Voir aussi* **hair-do; shaky.**

do[2] [du:] (**to**). **1.** *P:* coïter* avec (qn), tomber, brosser (qn). **2.** *P:* sodomiser, caser, empaffer (*coït* anal*). **3.** *F:* **to d. sth. no one else can d. for you,** déféquer*, aller où le Roi va à pied. **4.** *P:* escroquer*, refaire; **to be** (*or* **get**) **done,** se faire avoir; *voir aussi* **eye, 5. 5.** *P:* cambrioler*, caroubler; *cf.* **drum, 1** (*b*). **6.** *P:* battre*, passer (qn) à tabac. **7.** *P:* arrêter*, épingler; **to get done,** se faire paumer (*ou* fabriquer). **8.** *F:* visiter; **to d. Venice,** faire Venise. **9.** *F:* **that'll d.,** ça suffit; **that'll d.!** assez!* c'est marre! classe! **10.** *F:* botter (qn); **he'll d. me,** il me va, ça fait mon blot. **11.** *F:* **that won't d.,** cela ne prend pas (*ou* ne passe pas). **12.** *F:* **have nothing to d. with it!** ne vous y frottez pas! **13.** *F:* **nothing doing!** rien à faire! **14.** *F:* **it (simply) isn't done, it's (simply) not done,** ça ne se fait pas, c'est pas canonique. **15.** *F:* **done!** d'accord!* dac! **16.** *F:* **that's done it! = that's torn it! (tear**[2] **(to)). 17.** *F:* **d. or die,** marche ou crève. *Voir aussi* **done** *et les verbes composés* **to do down, for, in, out, over, up, with, without.**

dobeying ['doubi:iŋ] (*noun*), *P:* = **dhobying.**

dob in ['dɔb'in] (**to**) (*Austr.*), *F:* trahir, vendre, moutonner (qn).

doc [dɔk] (*abbr.* = *doctor*), *F:* docteur *m,* toubib *m.*

dock[1] [dɔk] (*noun*), *F:* **in d.,** (*a*) à l'hôpital, à l'hosto; (*b*) (*d'une voiture*) au garage, en réparation. *Voir aussi* **dickory-dock.**

dock[2] [dɔk] (**to**), *F:* **to d. s.o.'s pay,** diminuer (*ou* rogner) le salaire de qn.

doctor[1] ['dɔktər] (*noun*), *F:* **1. just what the d. ordered,** exactement ce qu'il (me) faut. **2. d.'s orders:** *voir* **bingo** (**9**). *Voir aussi* **couch-doctor; horse-doctor.**

doctor[2] ['dɔktər] (**to**), *F:* **1.** châtrer, couper. **2.** frelater (vin, *etc.*), tripatouiller. **3.** truquer, maquiller (comptes).

doctor up ['dɔktər'ʌp] (**to**), *F:* raccommoder, remettre en état, rafistoler, retaper.

do-da ['du:dɑ:] (*noun*), *F:* = **doo-da.**

dodderer ['dɔdərər] (*noun*), *F:* (**old**) **d.,** vieux* gaga, croulant *m,* gâteux *m,* ramolli *m.*

doddle[1] [dɔdl] (*noun*), *F:* = **cinch.**

doddle[2] [dɔdl] (**to**), *F:* **to d. it,** gagner les doigts dans le nez, gagner dans un fauteuil.

dodge[1] [dɔdʒ] (*noun*), *F:* **1.** ruse *f;* **to be up to all the dodges,** connaître tous les trucs (*ou* toutes les ficelles), la connaître dans les coins. **2. a clever d.,** un bon truc, une astuce.

dodge[2] [dɔdʒ] (**to**), *F:* **1. to d. the column,** tirer au flanc, se défiler, couper à qch.; *cf.* **column-dodger. 2. to d. the draft,** (*a*) éviter d'être envoyé outre-mer, se défiler; (*b*) déserter, faire chibis à la grive; *cf.* **draft-dodger.**

dodger ['dɔdʒər] (*noun*): **artful d.,** (*a*) *F:* malin *m,* dégourdi *m,* débrouillard *m;* (*b*) *P:* (*R.S.* = *lodger*) locataire *mf. Voir aussi* **column-dodger; devil-dodger; draft-dodger.**

dodgy ['dɔdʒi] (*adj.*). **1.** *F:* **d. business,** affaire louche (*ou* douteuse *ou* qui sent mauvais). **2.** *P:* **d. grub,** nourriture* volée, boustifaille ratiboisée. **3.** *F:* difficile*, coton, duraille. **4.** *F:* malin*, débrouillard, roublard, madré.

dodo ['doudou] (*noun*), *F:* vieux* rabâcheur, vieux croûton; **old d.,** vieux* bonze (*ou* birbe), son-et-lumière *m;* **dead as a d.,** mort et enterré.

do down ['du:'daun] (**to**), *F:* l'emporter sur (qn), rouler (qn).

do for ['du:'fɔ:r] (**to**). **1.** *P:* tuer*, descendre, dégommer, zigouiller. **2.** *P:* faire le ménage pour (qn). **3.** *F:* **to be done for,** (*a*) être ruiné (*ou* fauché *ou* flambé *ou* fichu *ou* fini *ou* cuit); **he's done for,** ses carottes sont cuites; (*b*) être à la mort (*ou* foutu); (*c*) être fatigué* (*ou* pompé *ou* à bout de forces).

dog[1] [dɔg] (*noun*), *F:* **1. it's a d.'s life,** c'est une vie de chien. **2. to be dressed up** (*or* **got up**) **like a d.'s dinner,** être en grand tralala (*ou* sur son trente et un *ou* tout fringué). **3. to try (sth.) out on the d.,** utiliser comme cobaye. **4. to take a hair of the d. (that bit you),** reprendre du poil de la bête. **5. he doesn't stand a d.'s chance,** il n'a pas

* L'astérisque indique que le mot marqué de ce signe figure comme entrée dans le Répertoire.

l'ombre d'une chance. 6. **d.'s nose,** boisson *f* de bière et de gin. 7. (*pl.*) pieds*, nougats *m.pl.*; **to have dogs that bite** (*or* **barking dogs**), avoir mal aux pattes. 8. vaurien*, sale type *m*, fripouille *f*, canaille *f*. 9. **a gay d.**, un gai luron, un joyeux drille, un noceur. 10. **a sly d.**, un fin renard. 11. **the dogs,** courses *f.pl.* de lévriers. 12. **to go to the dogs,** mal tourner, aller à sa ruine. 13. **to be top d.**, être vainqueur, avoir le dessus. 14. **d. in the manger,** le chien du jardinier. 15. **hot d.**, hot dog *m*, (*saucisse chaude dans du pain*). 16. **let sleeping dogs lie,** ne réveillez pas le chat qui dort. 17. **to put on (the) d.**, faire le paon, en étaler, poser pour la galerie. 18. = **dog-end.** 19. **to have a black d. on one's back,** broyer du noir, avoir le bourdon, être au 36ème dessous. 20. **to see a man about a d.**, aller aux W.C.*, aller changer son poisson d'eau. 21. **to work like a d.**, travailler* dur, trimer. 22. **in a d.'s age,** il y a belle lurette (*ou* un bail *ou* une paye). 23. **to call off the dogs,** cesser les hostilités. 24. (*a*) pleutre *m*; (*b*) camelote *f*, gnognot(t)e *f*. 25. **there's life in the old d. yet,** il n'est pas près de sa fin, il a encore du ressort. 26. **spotted d.**, (*a*) chien *m* de Dalmatie; (*b*) pudding *m* aux raisins. *Voir aussi* **cat,** 9, 11; **dirty**[1], 2; **dumb,** 2; **hot,** 26; **hound-dog; shaggy-dog; sheep-dog; yard-dog.**

dog[2] [dɔg] (**to**), *F:* **to d. it,** négliger son travail, traîner les patins.

dog-cart [ˈdɔgkɑːt] (*noun*) (*Austr.*), *P:* = **trawler.**

dog-collar [ˈdɔgkɔlər] (*noun*), *F:* faux-col *m* d'ecclésiastique, col romain; **the d.-c. brigade,** le clergé, les prêtres*, la ratiche.

dog-end [ˈdɔgend] (*noun*), *F:* mégot*, clope *m*.

dog-fashion [ˈdɔgfæʃ(ə)n] (*adv.*), *P:* = **dogways.**

dog-fight [ˈdɔgfait] (*noun*), *F:* combat aérien; mêlée *f*.

doggie [ˈdɔgi] (*noun*), *F:* = **doggy**[2], 1.

doggo [ˈdɔgou] (*adv.*), *F:* caché*, planqué; **to lie d.**, faire le mort, se tenir peinard.

doggone [ˈdɔgɔn] (*adj.*) (*U.S.*): *euph. pour* **goddamned.**

doggy[1] [ˈdɔgi] (*adj.*), *F:* 1. amateur de chiens, père à chiens. 2. élégant*, flambard.

doggy[2] [ˈdɔgi] (*noun*), *F:* 1. chien*, chien-chien *m*, toutou *m*, azor *m*. 2. officier secondant un amiral.

dog-hole [ˈdɔghoul] (*noun*), *P:* logement* sale, piaule *f*, bouge *m*, porcherie *f*.

dog-house [ˈdɔghaus] (*noun*), *F:* **in the d.-h.**, mis de côté, en quarantaine, mal en cour.

dogie [ˈdoudʒi] (*noun*), *P:* héroïne *f* (*drogues**), cheval *m*.

do-gooder [ˈduːˈgudər] (*noun*), *F:* redresseur *m* de torts, dame patronesse.

dogsbody [ˈdɔgzbɔdi] (*noun*), *F:* subordonné(e), sous-fifre *m*, lampiste *m*.

dog-tag [ˈdɔgtæg] (*noun*), *F:* plaque *f* d'identité.

dog-tired [ˈdɔgˈtaiəd] (*adj.*), *F:* très fatigué*, crevé, claqué, fourbu, vanné.

dogways [ˈdɔgweiz] (*adv.*), *P:* **to have** (*or* **do**) **it d.**, coïter* par enculage, enculer (*coït* anal*).

do in [ˈduːˈin] (**to**), *P:* 1. tuer, assassiner*; **to d. oneself i.**, se suicider*, se buter, se flanquer en l'air. 2. fatiguer, éreinter; **done in,** très fatigué*, claqué. 3. démolir, saboter, bousiller. 4. dépenser*, claquer, bouffer (de l'argent*).

doing! [ˈdɔiŋ] (*excl.*), *F:* = **boing!**; *cf.* **doink!**

doings [ˈduiŋz] **the** (*pl. noun*), *F:* 1. machin *m*, truc *m*, fourbi *m*. 2. (*a*) raclée *f*, dérouillée *f*; (*b*) réprimande *f*, savon *m*, engueulade *f*. 3. tout le bataclan, tout le fourbi; **I've got the d.**, j'ai de quoi, j'ai ce qu'il faut.

doink! [dɔiŋk] (*excl.*), *F:* = **boing!**; *cf.* **doing!**

do-it-yourself [ˈduitjəˈself] (*noun*). 1. *F:* (*a*) bricolage *m*, la bricole; (*b*) attirail *m* de bricoleur. 2. *V:* masturbation *f*, branlage *m* maison.

do-it-yourselfer [ˈduitjəˈselfər] (*noun*), *F:* bricoleur *m*.

dojee, dojie [ˈdoudʒi] (*noun*), *P:* = **dogie.**

dokka [ˈdɔkə] (*noun*), *P:* cigarette*, cibiche *f*, sèche *f*.

doldrums [ˈdɔldrəmz] (*pl. noun*), *F:* **to be in the d.**, (*a*) avoir le cafard, broyer du noir; (*b*) être dans le marasme.

doll [dɔl] (*noun*), *F:* 1. fille* *ou* jeune

* An asterisk indicates that the word so marked is included as a head-word in the Appendix.

femme*, poupée *f*. 2. tête *f* de linotte, poupée *f*. *Voir aussi* **baby[1], 1; baby-doll.**

dollop [ˈdɔləp] (*noun*), *F:* morceau *m* informe, flanquée *f*, plâtrée *f*; **a good d. of jam,** une bonne tapée de confiture.

doll up [ˈdɔlˈʌp] (**to**), *F:* **to d. oneself u.,** se pomponner, se bichonner; **to get all dolled up,** se mettre sur son trente et un.

dolly[1] [ˈdɔli] (*adj.*), *F:* 1. **that's real d.!** c'est du nanan! 2. (*cricket, etc.*) **d. catch,** balle facilement prise de volée.

dolly[2] [ˈdɔli] (*noun*). 1. *F:* poupée *f*, pépée *f*. 2. *F:* = **dolly-bird, 1.** 3. *P:* méthadone *f* (dolophine) (*drogues*). 4. (*pl.*) *P:* seins*, rotoplots *m.pl.*

dolly-bird [ˈdɔlibəːd], **dolly-girl** [ˈdɔligəːl] (*noun*). 1. *F:* (belle) poupée, prix *m* de Diane. 2. *P:* fille facile, pépée *f*, nana *f*.

dolly-shop [ˈdɔliʃɔp] (*noun*), *P:* (*a*) officine *f* de prêteur sur gage; (*b*) boutique *f* de chiffonnier, friperie *f*.

dome [doum] (*noun*), *F:* tête*, caboche *f*, boule *f*. *Voir aussi* **double, 4; ivory.**

domino-box [ˈdɔminoubɔks] (*noun*), *P:* = **box of dominoes (dominoes, 3).**

dominoes [ˈdɔminouz] (*pl. noun*), *P:* 1. capsules *f.pl.* de durophet, dominos *m.pl.* (*drogues*). 2. **it's d. with** (*or* **for**) **him,** il est fichu (*ou* foutu). 3. dents* jaunies, dominos *m.pl.*; **box of d.,** bouche*, boîte *f*.

dona(h) [ˈdounə] (*noun*), *P:* la petite amie, sa régulière, sa particulière.

done [dʌn] (*adj.* & *p.p.*), *P:* = **done up, 1, 2.** *Voir aussi* **do[2] (to); frazzle, 1.**

done up [ˈdʌnˈʌp] (*adj.* & *p.p.*), *P:* 1. très fatigué*, crevé. 2. ruiné*, fauché, nettoyé. 3. (*a*) maquillée, emplâtrée; (*b*) habillé élégamment, bien fringué, tiré à quatre épingles. *Voir aussi* **do up (to).**

dong [dɔŋ], **donker** [ˈdɔŋkər] (*noun*), *V:* = **donkey, 5.**

donkey [ˈdɔŋki] (*noun*). 1. *F:* **to talk the hind leg off a d.,** être bavard* comme une pie, être un moulin à paroles. 2. *F:* **d. work,** travail *m* de routine. 3. *F:* **d.'s years,** une éternité, un bail, une paye; **d.'s years ago,** il y a belle lurette. 4. *F:* âne bâté, imbécile *mf*. 5. *V:* (gros) pénis*, gros bout; **to flog one's d.,** se masturber*, s'astiquer la colonne.

donnybrook [ˈdɔnibruk] (*noun*) (*U.S.*), *F:* querelle*, bagarre *f*, badaboum *m*, corrida *f*.

doo-da [ˈduːdɑː], **doodad** [ˈduːdæd], **doodah** [ˈduːdɑː] (*noun*), *F:* 1. truc *m*, machin *m*, fourbi *m*. 2. agitation *f*, énervement *m*; **to be all of a d.,** être aux cent coups, être démonté.

doodle [ˈduːdl] (*noun*), *P:* individu bête*, nouille *f*.

doodle-alley [ˈduːdlˈæli] (*adj.*), *P:* (*a*) qui a une case de vide, demeuré; (*b*) fou*, tapé, cinoque.

doodle-bug [ˈduːdlbʌg] (*noun*), *F:* 1. vieille voiture*, tacot *m*. 2. (*W.W.II*) bombe volante.

doofer [ˈduːfər] (*noun*), *P:* 1. moitié *f* de cigarette*, un ça suffit. 2. = **whatcha-(ma)callit.**

doohickey [ˈduːˈhiki] (*noun*) (*U.S.*), *F:* = **doo-da, 1.**

doojee [ˈduːdʒiː], **doojer** [ˈduːdʒər], **dooji** [ˈduːdʒiː] (*noun*), *P:* = **dogie.**

doojigger [ˈduːdʒigər] (*noun*) (*U.S.*), *F:* = **doo-da, 1.**

dooks [duːks] (*pl. noun*), *P:* = **dukes.**

doolally (tap) [ˈduːˈlæli(ˈtæp)] (*adj.*), *P:* = **doodle-alley.**

door [dɔːr] (*noun*), *F:* 1. **to show s.o. the d.,** mettre (*ou* flanquer) qn à la porte. 2. **you make a better d. than a window,** tu n'es pas transparent. 3. (*a*) **knock at the d.:** *voir* **bingo (4)**; (*b*) **key of the d.:** *voir* **bingo (21)**; (*c*) **open the d.:** *voir* **bingo (44).** *Voir aussi* **back[1], 3.**

doormat [ˈdɔːmæt, ˈdɔəmæt] (*noun*), *F:* individu* qui se laisse marcher dessus, paillasson *m*.

door-nail [ˈdɔːneil, ˈdɔəneil] (*noun*), *F:* **dead as a d.-n.,** mort et enterré.

doorstep [ˈdɔːstep, ˈdɔəstep] (*noun*), *F:* quignon *m* de pain.

do out [ˈduːˈaut] (**to**), *F:* 1. débarrasser, lessiver. 2. **to d. s.o. o. of sth.,** escroquer* qn, arnaquer, rouler, carotter qn, souffler qch. à qn.

do over [ˈduːˈouvər] (**to**). 1. *F:* recouvrir, retaper (peinture, *etc.*). 2. *P:* = **do[2] (to), 3.** 3. *P:* (*a*) voler* (qn); (*b*) tromper*, estamper (qn). 4. *P:* fouiller (un suspect).

dope[1] [doup] (*noun*). 1. *F:* (*a*) renseignement* (confidentiel *ou* préalable), tuyau *m*, tubard *m*; **the latest d.,** les dernières nouvelles, les derniers renseignements*; **to give s.o. the latest d.,** mettre qn à la page, affranchir qn; (*b*) renseignements* exacts; (*c*) faux renseignements*;

* L'astérisque indique que le mot marqué de ce signe figure comme entrée dans le Répertoire.

bourrage *m* de crâne; (*d*) tuyaux *m.pl.* sur les courses de chevaux; **d. sheet,** journal *m* hippique, le papier. **2.** *F:* **what a d. he is!** quel crétin (*ou* quelle nouille) que ce type! qu'il est bête*! **3.** *F:* potion *f*, remède *m*. **4.** *P:* essence *f*, jus *m*. **5.** *F:* doping *m* (administré à un cheval), dopage *m*. **6.** *P:* stup(éfiant) *m*, narc(otique) *m* (*drogues**); **d. hop,** défonce *f*, planète *f*; **d. fiend,** morphinomane *mf*, drogué*, toxico(mane) *mf*; **d. habit,** toxicomanie *f*; **d. peddler** (*or* **pedlar** *or* **merchant** *or* **runner**), fourgueur *m* de came, trafiquant *m* (en stupéfiants); **d. den,** fumerie *f* d'opium, repaire *m* de drogués*, clandé *m*; **to hit the d.,** se droguer*, se schnouffer; **to be on d.,** être un usager de drogues, marcher à la drogue; **d. racket,** trafic *m* de drogues; **d. ring,** bande* de trafiquants, flèche *f* de la came. **7.** (*U.S.*) *P:* = **dopehead.**

dope[2] [doup] (**to**). **1.** *F:* (*a*) administrer un narcotique à (qn), droguer, doper; (*b*) mêler un narcotique à (un verre de vin), narcotiser (une cigarette), doper; (*c*) **to d. oneself,** prendre des stupéfiants *m.pl.*, se droguer*; **doped (up) to the eyebrows,** schnouffé à bloc. **2.** *F:* doper (un cheval). **3.** *F:* ajouter de l'alcool à une boisson non alcoolisée, corser. **4.** *F:* calmer, tranquilliser. **5.** *P:* tromper*, refaire, rouler (qn).

dopehead [ˈdouphed] (*noun*), *P:* drogué*, camé *m*, toxico *m*.

dope out [ˈdoupˈaut] (**to**), *P:* (*a*) découvrir*, dénicher; (*b*) trouver le joint.

doper [ˈdoupər] (*noun*), *P:* = **dopehead.**

doperie [ˈdoupəri] (*noun*), *P:* = **dope den (dope**[1]**, 6).**

dopester [ˈdoupstər] (*noun*), *P:* **1.** = **dopehead. 2.** marchand *m* de tuyaux (*courses hippiques*), tuyauteur *m*, tubardeur *m*.

dope up [ˈdoupˈʌp] (**to**), *P:* (*a*) se droguer*, se camer; (*b*) droguer, schnouffer (qn).

dopey[1] [ˈdoupi] (*adj.*), *F:* **1.** bête*, bêta, empoté. **2.** abruti (de fatigue). **3.** stupéfié, hébété (par un narcotique); léthargique.

dopey[2], **dopie** [ˈdoupi] (*noun*), *P:* = **dopehead.**

dopium [ˈdoupiəm] (*noun*), *P:* opium *m* (*drogues**), op *m*, noir *m*.

dopy [ˈdoupi] (*adj. & noun*) = **dopey**[1,2].

do-re-mi [ˈdouˈreiˈmiː] (*noun*), *P:* argent*, pépettes *f.pl.*, picaillons *m.pl.*

dorm [dɔːm] (*abbr.* = *dormitory*), *F:* dortoir *m*, dorto *m*.

dose [dous] (*noun*). **1.** *P:* **to get** (*or* **catch** *or* **cop**) **a d.,** attraper une maladie* vénérienne, ramasser la chtouille, se faire poivrer (*ou* fader *ou* plomber *ou* nazicoter). **2.** *F:* **like a d. of salts,** comme une lettre à la poste.

dose up [ˈdousˈʌp] (**to**), *P:* contaminer (qn) avec une maladie* vénérienne, fader, poivrer, plomber (qn); **to be dosed up (to the eyebrows),** (*a*) souffrir d'une maladie* vénérienne, être (bien) poivré (*ou* fadé); (*b*) être drogué* (*ou* camé *ou* chargé) jusque-là.

dosh [dɔʃ] (*noun*), *P:* argent*, fric *m*, pèze *m*.

doss[1] [dɔs] (*noun*), *P:* **1.** lit* (dans une pension peu relevée), plumard *m* de garno (*ou* de bustingue). **2.** un somme, une dorme; **to do a d.,** dormir*, piquer un roupillon.

doss[2] [dɔs] (**to**), *P:* dormir*, pioncer.

doss down [ˈdɔsˈdaun] (**to**), *P:* **1.** se coucher*, se lâcher. **2.** arranger un lit de dépannage.

dosser [ˈdɔsər] (*noun*), *P:* **1.** clochard*, clodo *m*. **2.** drogué*, junkie *m*, camé *m*.

doss-house [ˈdɔshaus] (*noun*), *F:* asile *m* de nuit, dorme *m*, piaule *f* à clodos.

dot[1] [dɔt] (*noun*). **1.** *F:* **on the d.,** à l'heure, à pic, pile, recta. **2.** *P:* **off one's d.,** fou*, timbré. **3.** *F:* **in the year d.,** il y a longtemps; **it goes back to the year d.,** cela remonte au déluge, c'est antédiluvien. **4.** *P:* clitoris*, bouton *m*, grain *m* de café.

dot[2] [dɔt] (**to**). **1.** *P:* **to d. s.o. (one),** battre* qn, flanquer un gnon à qn. **2.** *F:* **to d. and carry one,** boiter (en marchant), béquiller, faire cinq et trois font huit, clopiner.

dottiness [ˈdɔtinis] (*noun*), *F:* toquade *f*, loufoquerie *f*, détraquage *m*.

dotty [ˈdɔti] (*adj.*), *F:* fou*, cinglé, tapé, toqué; **to go d.,** perdre la boule (*ou* la boussole).

double [ˈdʌbl] (*adj.*), *F:* **1. to do a d. take,** regarder* par deux fois. **2. d. talk,** propos *m.pl.* à endormir les gens,

* An asterisk indicates that the word so marked is included as a head-word in the Appendix.

double parler *m*. 3. **d. think,** croyance *f* au pour et au contre, double penser *m*. 4. **d. dome,** intellectuel *m*, mandarin *m*, grosse tête. 5. **to do the d. act,** se marier. *Voir aussi* **Dutch[3], 1.**

double-cross[1] [ˈdʌblˈkrɔs] (*noun*), *F:* entubage *m*, roustissure *f*.

double-cross[2] [ˈdʌblˈkrɔs] (**to**), *F:* tromper*, entuber, doubler.

double-crosser [ˈdʌblˈkrɔsər] (*noun*), *F:* faux jeton, entubeur *m*, fourbe *m*.

double-decker [ˈdʌblˈdekər] (*noun*), *F:* 1. autobus *m* à impériale. 2. sandwich *m* à deux étages.

double-quick [ˈdʌblˈkwik] (*adv.*), *F:* au pas de course, en cinq secs. *Voir aussi* **quick.**

double-sheet [ˈdʌblˈʃi:t] (**to**) (*U.S.*), *F:* = **short-sheet (to).**

double-tongued [ˈdʌblˈtʌŋd] (*adj.*), *F:* qui a deux paroles.

double up [ˈdʌblˈʌp] (**to**), *F:* 1. **to d. u.** (*or* **to be doubled up**) **with laughter, pain,** se tordre de rire*, de douleur, être plié en deux. 2. **to d. u. on a horse,** doubler la mise. 3. **to d. u. with s.o.,** partager une chambre avec qn.

douche [du:ʃ] (*noun*), *F:* surprise *f* désagréable, douche *f*.

dough [dou] (*noun*), *F:* argent*, galette *f*, fric *m*; **to be in the d.** (*or* **rolling in d.**), être riche*, rouler dans le fric, être bourré à bloc; **to throw one's d. around,** dépenser* sans compter, jeter son argent* par les fenêtres.

doughboy [ˈdoubɔi], **doughfoot** [ˈdoufut] (*noun*) (*U.S.*), *F:* soldat* (de 2ème classe) de l'infanterie américaine, biffin *m*, troufion *m*.

doughy [ˈdou(w)i] (*adj.*), *F:* 1. (teint) pâle, pâteux, de papier mâché. 2. riche*, galetteux, bourré aux as.

do up [ˈdu:ˈʌp] (**to**). 1. *P:* fatiguer, éreinter, crever. 2. *P:* battre*, arranger, tabasser. 3. *F:* raccommoder, remettre en état. 4. *F:* ficeler (un paquet), boutonner (un vêtement). *Voir aussi* **done up.**

dove [dʌv] (*noun*), *F:* qn qui s'oppose à la guerre, colombe *f*; *cf.* **hawk[1].**

do with [ˈdu:wið] (**to**), *F:* 1. supporter, tolérer, encaisser. 2. **I could d. w. a drink,** je prendrais bien un verre, un verre ne serait pas de refus.

do without [ˈdu:wiðˈaut] (**to**), *F:* se l'accrocher, se serrer la ceinture, se brosser, se taper.

down[1] [daun] (*adj.*), *F:* **d. drugs,** drogues tranquillisantes; *cf.* **up[1].**

down[2] [daun] (*adv.*), *F:* 1. **to be d. and out,** être très pauvre*, être dans la dèche (*ou* la mouise). 2. **to be d. on s.o.** = **to have a d. on s.o.** (**down[3], 1**). 3. **to be d. for the count,** (*a*) (*boxe*) être knock-out, être k.o.; (*b*) être ruiné*, être sur le pavé. 4. **to be d. on one's luck,** avoir de la malchance* (*ou* de la guigne *ou* la poisse). 5. **d. under,** aux antipodes. 6. **to be d.,** (*drogues*) redescendre, avoir la gueule de bois. *Voir aussi* **ground, 2; mouth, 2.**

down[3] [daun] (*noun*), *F:* 1. **to have a d. on s.o.,** avoir une dent contre qn, avoir qn dans le nez. 2. = **downer, 1, 2.**

down[4] [daun] (**to**), *F:* 1. faire tomber, descendre (qn), envoyer (qn) à terre. 2. boire*; **to d. a pint,** s'envoyer un coup, s'en jeter un derrière la cravate. 3. **to d. tools,** se mettre en grève. *Voir aussi* **dust[1], 3.**

down-and-out[1] [ˈdaunəndˈaut] (*adj.*), *F:* vrai; **a d.-a.-o. cad,** une canaille achevée; **a d.-a.-o. liar,** un fieffé menteur. *Voir aussi* **down[2], 1.**

down-and-out[2] [ˈdaunəndˈaut], **down-and-outer** [ˈdaunəndˈautər] (*noun*), *F:* fauchemane *m*, déchard *m*, bat-la-dèche *m*.

downbeat [ˈdaunbi:t] (*adj.*), *F:* calme, tête froide, sans avoir l'air d'y toucher; *cf.* **upbeat.**

downer [ˈdaunər] (*noun*), *F:* 1. tranquillisant *m*, sédatif *m*; *cf.* **up(per).** 2. situation déprimante, déconfiture *f*. *Voir aussi* **up-and-downer.**

downhill [ˈdaunhil] (*adv.*), *F:* **to go d.,** dégringoler, être sur le déclin (*ou* sur la mauvaise pente).

downie [ˈdauni] (*noun*), *P:* = **downer, 1.**

Downing Street [ˈdauniŋstri:t] (*pr. noun*), *F:* *voir* **bingo (10).**

downy[1] [ˈdauni] (*adj.*), *F:* malin*, marloupin, roublard.

downy[2] [ˈdauni] (*noun*), *P:* lit*, plumard *m*, pageot *m*.

doxy [ˈdɔksi] (*noun*), *F:* garce *f*, salope *f*, boudin *m*, pouffiasse *f*.

doz. [dʌz] (*noun*) (*abbr.* = *dozen*), *F:* **one d.:** *voir* **bingo (12).**

dozen [ˈdʌzn] (*noun*), *F:* 1. **a baker's**

* L'astérisque indique que le mot marqué de ce signe figure comme entrée dans le Répertoire.

d., treize à la douzaine. 2. **daily d.**, culture *f* physique. 3. **dozens of...**, une abondance* de..., une flop(p)ée de..., une tripotée de..., une tapée de ... *Voir aussi* **dime; nineteen; six,** 3.

dozy [ˈdouzi] (*adj.*), *F:* 1. abruti, endormi, demeuré. 2. paresseux*, flemmard, cossard.

dozy-arsed [ˈdouzi-ɑːst] (*adj.*), *P:* bête*; **d.-a. bastard,** cucul *m*, connasse *m*.

D-racks [ˈdiːræks] (*pl. noun*), *P:* cartes* à jouer.

draft-dodger [ˈdrɑːftdɔdʒər] (*noun*), *F:* tire-au-flanc *m*, insoumis *m*; (*mil.*) déserteur *m*; *cf.* **dodge**[2], 2.

drag[1] [dræg] (*noun*). 1. *F:* (*a*) vêtements* de travelo; **in d.**, en travelo; **d. queen,** travelo *m*; (*b*) boum *f* de travelo, partouse *f* de bague. 2. *F:* individu ennuyeux*, casse-pieds *m*, raseur *m*. 3. *P:* voiture*; camion *m*; **d. race,** course *f* de vieilles voitures*; *voir aussi* **hot,** 9. 4. *P:* (*a*) cigarette*, cibiche *f*, sèche *f*; *voir aussi* **spit,** 2; (*b*) bouffée *f* de tabac; **to take a d.**, tirer une bouffée; **give us a d.**, donne une bouffée; (*c*) bouffée *f* (*drogues*). 5. (*U.S.*) *P:* piston *m*, pistonnage *m*. 6. (*U.S.*) *P:* **the main d.**, la grand-rue.

drag[2] [dræg] (**to**), *F:* **to d. one's feet,** se faire tirer l'oreille, renâcler, marcher à contre-cœur.

drag-ass [ˈdrægæs] (**to**) (*U.S.*), *P:* 1. être abattu, être à plat. 2. partir*, se barrer, se carapater.

dragged out [ˈdrægdˈaut] (*adj.*) (*U.S.*), *P:* fatigué*, crevé, éreinté. *Voir aussi* **drag out (to).**

dragger [ˈdrægər] (*noun*), *P:* voleur* de voitures*, leveur *m* de bagnoles.

dragging [ˈdrægiŋ] (*noun*), *P:* (*a*) vol *m* de voitures*; (*b*) vol *m* à la roulotte.

draggy [ˈdrægi] (*adj.*), *P:* ennuyeux*, canulant, rasoir.

drag in [ˈdrægˈin] (**to**), *F:* amener (qch.) comme les cheveux sur la soupe.

dragnet [ˈdrægnet] (*noun*), *F:* rafle *f*, descente *f* de police, coup *m* de filet (*ou* de raclette), quadrillage *m*.

drag on [ˈdrægˈɔn] (**to**), *F:* tirer en longueur.

dragon [ˈdrægən] (*noun*). 1. *F:* (*personne féroce, chaperon sévère*) dragon *m*. 2. *F:* **d.'s teeth,** défenses *f.pl.* anti-tank. 3. *P:* **green d.**, amphétamine *f* (*drogues**), serpent vert; **to chase the d.**, avoir la toxicomanie, fonctionner à la drogue, marcher à la topette.

drag out [ˈdrægˈaut] (**to**), *F:* 1. éterniser, faire traîner. 2. **to d. sth. o. of s.o.,** extirper qn, délier la langue à qn. *Voir aussi* **dragged out.**

dragsman [ˈdrægzmən] (*noun*), *P:* voleur* de train.

drag up [ˈdrægˈʌp] (**to**). 1. *F:* **to d. u. s.o.'s past,** faire ressortir (*ou* déterrer) le passé de qn. 2. *P:* **where were you dragged up?** où as-tu été élevé? d'où sors-tu?; **dragged up,** élevé à la va-comme-je-te-pousse.

drain[1] [drein] (*noun*), *F:* 1. **to go down the d.**, échouer*, tomber dans le lac; **it's money down the d.**, c'est jeter l'argent* par les fenêtres. 2. **to laugh like a d.**, rire* de bon cœur, se boyauter, se bidonner, se tordre comme une baleine. 3. **up the d.**, (*a*) dans le pétrin, dans ses petits souliers; (*b*) dans le lac. *Voir aussi* **brain-drain.**

drain[2] [drein] (**to**), *F:* **to d. s.o. dry,** saigner qn à blanc, tondre la laine sur le dos à qn.

drainpipe [ˈdreinpaip] (*noun*), *F:* 1. individu* grand et mince, échalas *m*, asperge *f*, grande perche. 2. (*pl.*) (=*drainpipe trousers*) pantalon* étroit, tuyau *m* de poêle, fuseau *m*.

drape[1] [dreip] (*noun*), *F:* toilette tapageuse (*ou* outrée), grand tralala; **a set of drapes,** un complet, un ensemble.

drape[2] [dreip] (**to**), *F:* **to d. oneself,** se draper dans sa dignité, se carrer, poser pour la galerie.

drappie, drappy [ˈdræpi] (*noun*), *F:* **a wee d.**, un petit verre (*ou* un petit coup) d'alcool* (*ou* de gnôle).

drat [dræt] (**to**), *F:* (*a*) **d. the child!** sacré gosse! au diable ce gosse! maudit mioche!; (*b*) **d. (it)!** sacré nom! nom de nom! bon sang!

dratted [ˈdrætid] (*adj.*), *F:* maudit, sacré, satané.

draught [drɑːft] (*noun*), *F:* **to feel the d.**, être touché à mal par qch., le sentir passer.

draw[1] [drɔː] (*noun*), *F:* 1. **to be quick on the d.**, (*a*) être rapide à dégainer son arme, être rapide à la détente, avoir la détente facile; (*b*) piger au quart de tour, avoir de bonnes reprises.

* An asterisk indicates that the word so marked is included as a head-word in the Appendix.

2. to be slow on the d., (*a*) être lent à la détente; (*b*) avoir la comprenette lente (*ou* difficile).

draw[2] [drɔː] (**to**), *F:* **1.** être le point de mire. **2. to d. s.o.,** faire parler* qn, le travailler, lui tirer les vers du nez. **3.** taquiner, faire enrager (*ou* bisquer). **4. to d. it mild,** modérer ses propos, mettre de l'eau dans son vin. **5. to d. the long bow,** exagérer*, faire du pallas, cherrer dans les bégonias.

drawers [ˈdrɔːz] (*pl. noun*), *P:* culotte *f*; **to let one's d. down, to drop one's d.,** (*d'une femme*) permettre des rapports sexuels, laisser tomber la culotte. *Voir aussi* **droopy-drawers.**

dream[1] [driːm] (*attrib. adj.*), *F:* rêvé, de rêve; **to live in a d. world,** nager dans le bleu.

dream[2] [driːm] (*noun*). **1.** *F:* **she's a d.,** (*a*) c'est la femme rêvée; (*b*) elle est dans les nuages (*ou* dans la lune). **2.** *F:* **wet d.,** carte *f* (de France). **3.** (*pl.*) *P:* opium *m* (*drogues**); **d. wax,** opium *m* (*drogues**); **d. stick,** (*a*) bambou *m*, pipe *f* à rêves; (*b*) pilule *f* d'opium.

dream-bait [ˈdriːmbeit], **dream-boat** [ˈdriːmbout] (*noun*), *F:* = **dream**[2], **1** (*a*).

dreamer [ˈdriːmər] (*noun*), *P:* opiomane *mf*, noircicot *m*.

dream up [ˈdriːmˈʌp] (**to**), *F:* imaginer, inventer, gamberger.

dreamy [ˈdriːmi] (*adj.*), *F:* exquis, charmant.

dreck [drek] (*noun*), *P:* **1.** camelote *f*, gnognot(t)e *f*. **2.** clinquant *m*, tape-à-l'œil *m*.

dress down [ˈdresˈdaun] (**to**), *F:* **1.** battre*, filer une raclée à (qn). **2.** réprimander*, enguirlander, assaisonner (qn). *Voir aussi* **dressing-down.**

dressed [drest] (*p.p. & adj.*), *F:* **d. (fit) to kill,** élégant*, habillé sur son trente et un, en grand tralala, tiré à quatre épingles; *cf.* **dress up (to), 2.**

dress-house [ˈdreshaus] (*noun*), *P:* bordel*, maison bancale, boxon *m*.

dressing-down [ˈdresiŋˈdaun] (*noun*), *F:* **1.** volée *f* de coups*, raclée *f*. **2.** réprimande *f*, abattage *m*, savon *m*. *Voir aussi* **dress down (to).**

dress up [ˈdresˈʌp] (**to**), *F:* **1. all dressed up and nowhere to go,** laissé(e) pour compte (*ou* en plan). **2. dressed up to the nines** (*or* **to the teeth** *or* **to the knocker**) = **dressed (fit) to kill** (*voir* **dressed**). *Voir aussi* **dog**[1], **2.**

dressy [ˈdresi] (*adj.*), *F:* élégant*, chic, ridère.

dribs [dribz] (*pl. noun*), *F:* **in d. and drabs,** petit à petit, au compte-gouttes.

drift[1] [drift] (*noun*), *F:* **to catch the d.,** tenir (*ou* piger) le fil, entraver, saisir; **get the d.?** tu piges? tu saisis?

drift[2] [drift] (**to**), *F:* **1.** se laisser aller (à vau-l'eau *ou* à la dérive). **2.** baguenauder, flâner, flânocher.

drifter [ˈdriftər] (*noun*), *F:* personne qui se laisse aller, gnangnan *m*.

drill [dril] (*noun*), *F:* **to know the d.,** connaître les rouages *m.pl.* (*ou* la musique), s'y connaître. *Voir aussi* **pack-drill.**

drin [drin] (*noun*), *P:* comprimé *m* de Benzédrine (*marque déposée*) (*drogues**).

drink [driŋk] (*noun*), *F:* **the d.,** la mer, la Grande Tasse, la flotte.

drinkies [ˈdriŋkiz] (*pl. noun*), *F:* boissons *f.pl.*, consommations *f.pl.*

drip [drip] (*noun*), *F:* nouille *f*, empoté *m*.

dripper [ˈdripər] (*noun*), *F:* goutte-à-goutte *m* (*seringue faite avec un compte-gouttes et une épingle*).

drippy [ˈdripi] (*adj.*), *F:* **1.** bête*, empoté. **2.** fadasse, larmoyant, vieux jeu.

driver [ˈdraivər] (*noun*). **1.** *F:* **to be in the d.'s seat,** être en position de force, tenir les rênes, diriger les opérations. **2.** *P:* amphétamine *f* (*drogues**); *cf.* **truck-driver.** *Voir aussi* **backseat; nigger-driver; pile-driver; slave-driver.**

drizzle-puss [ˈdrizlpus] (*noun*) (*U.S.*), *F:* rabat-joie *m*, peau *f* de vache, vieux chameau.

drome [droum] (*noun*) (*=aerodrome*), *F:* aérodrome *m*, terrain *m* (d'aviation).

drongo [ˈdrɔŋgou] (*noun*) (*Austr.*), *F:* individu bête*, buse *f*.

droob [druːb] (*noun*) (*Austr.*), *F:* **1.** un chouia; **he didn't get a d.,** il n'a rien* eu, il n'a eu que dalle. **2.** = **drube.**

drool [druːl] (**to**), *F:* **to d. over sth., s.o.,** baver (d'admiration, de plaisir) sur qch., qn.

droop [druːp] (*noun*), *P:* **1.** = **drip. 2. brewer's d.,** affaissement *m* du pénis dû à l'alcool, le six heures de l'alcoolique.

* L'astérisque indique que le mot marqué de ce signe figure comme entrée dans le Répertoire.

drooper [ˈdruːpər] (*noun*), **1.** *F:* moustache* tombante, ramasse-miettes *m.* **2.** (*pl.*) *P:* seins* tombants, blagues *f.pl.* à tabac, pendants *m.pl.*, tétasses *f.pl.*

droopy-drawers [ˈdruːpidrɔː(ə)z] (*noun*), *P:* **1.** individu dont la culotte tombe, nu-fesses *f.* **2.** *voir* **bingo** (44).

drop[1] [drɔp] (*noun*). **1.** *P:* = **dropsy, 1, 2.** **2.** *F:* **at the d. of a hat,** tout de suite, illico. **3.** *P:* cache *f*, planque *f.* **4.** *P:* **to get the d. on s.o.,** sortir son arme (*ou* gagner de vitesse) avant l'adversaire; tenir qn à merci, tenir le bon bout. **5.** *F:* **a d. in the ocean,** une goutte d'eau dans la mer. **6.** *P:* **to have a d. in the eye,** être ivre*, avoir chaud aux plumes. **7.** *F:* petit verre d'alcool*, une goutte, un doigt, un fond de verre. **8.** *P:* **on the d.,** (achat *m*) à tempérament. *Voir aussi* **cough-drop.**

drop[2] [drɔp] (**to**). **1.** *F:* **to d. s.o. (like a hot potato** *or* **a hot brick),** abandonner* qn, lâcher qn, plaquer qn comme une crêpe. **2.** *F:* abattre, descendre (qn), envoyer (qn) à terre. **3.** *F:* (*comme cycliste*) semer. **4.** *P:* donner un pourboire*; **did he d.?** a-t-il lâché le pourliche? a-t-il donné la pièce? **5.** *P:* (*jeu*) perdre, paumer de l'argent*. **6.** *F:* **d. it!** c'est marre! arrête les frais! laisse tomber! **7.** *F:* **fit to d.,** très fatigué*, crevé, éreinté; **he's fit to d.,** il a (reçu) le coup de bambou. **8.** *F:* **to d. s.o. a line,** envoyer (*ou* mettre *ou* griffonner) un mot à qn. **9.** *F:* **to d. the matter, to let it d.,** laisser courir. **10.** *P:* prendre des pilules *f.pl.* (*ou* capsules *f.pl.*) par voie buccale. *Voir aussi* **brick, 2; clanger; mire; shit**[3]**, 2; stumer, 3.**

drop in [ˈdrɔpˈin] (**to**), *F:* **to d. i. on s.o.,** rendre visite à qn en passant, passer chez qn.

drop off [ˈdrɔpˈɔf] (**to**), *F:* **1.** s'endormir, piquer un roupillon, baisser la vitrine. **2.** baisser, décliner, être sur la pente. **3. to d. s.o. o.,** déposer qn (à un certain endroit).

drop-out [ˈdrɔpaut] (*noun*), *F:* **1.** qn qui refuse la société (*ou* le système), qn qui vit en marge de la société; hors-la-loi *mf.* **2.** qn qui se retire d'un jeu, *etc.*

drop out [ˈdrɔpˈaut] (**to**), *F:* **1.** refuser la société (*ou* le système), vivre en marge de la société. **2.** tirer son épingle du jeu, reprendre ses billes.

dropper [ˈdrɔpər] (*noun*). **1.** *F:* = **dripper.** **2.** *P:* passeur *m* de faux chèques, pastiqueur *m.* *Voir aussi* **name-dropper.**

dropsy [ˈdrɔpsi] (*noun*), *P:* **1.** pot-de-vin *m*, graissage *m* de patte, dessous-de-table *m.* **2.** pourboire*, pourliche *m*, pièce *f.*

dross [drɔs] (*noun*). *P:* argent*, fric *m*, pèze *m.*

drown [draun] (**to**), *F:* **1. to d. a drink,** mettre trop d'eau dans une boisson, inonder (*ou* noyer) une boisson. **2. to d. in a teacup,** se noyer dans un crachat (*ou* dans un verre d'eau). **3. to d. one's sorrows,** noyer ses chagrins.

drube [druːb] (*noun*) (*Austr.*), *F:* individu bête*, nouille *f.*

drum [drʌm] (*noun*). **1.** *P:* logement*, bocal *m*, cambuse *f*; **to have one's d. done,** (*a*) avoir une perquisition, avoir une descente dans sa piaule; (*b*) être cambriolé*, en être d'un baluchonnage; *cf.* **gaff, 1; screw**[2] **(to), 3.** **2.** *P:* un paradis pour les voleurs, un bon casse. **3.** *F:* **to beat the drums** (*or* **the big d.**) **for s.o.,** faire du battage pour qn, faire du tamtam, battre la grosse caisse pour qn. **4.** *P:* route*, antif(fe) *f*, ruban *m.*

drummer [ˈdrʌmər] (*noun*), *P:* commis voyageur, roulant *m*, hirondelle *f.*

drumming [ˈdrʌmiŋ] (*noun*). **1.** *F:* (*d'une auto*) ferraillement *m.* **2.** *P:* vol *m* après avoir sonné à la porte pour s'assurer qu'il n'y a personne, vol *m* au bonjour.

drumstick [ˈdrʌm-stik] (*noun*), *F:* **1.** pilon *m* (de poulet). **2.** (*pl.*) jambes* maigres, allumettes *f.pl.*, flûtes *f.pl.*; **d. cases,** pantalon*, fourreau *m*, fendard *m.*

drum up [ˈdrʌmˈʌp] (**to**), *F:* **1. to d. u. one's friends,** rassembler (*ou* réunir *ou* racoler) ses amis, battre le rappel de ses amis. **2. to d. u. business,** faire de la réclame, chauffer une affaire.

drunk [drʌŋk] (*noun*), *F:* **1.** ivrogne*, saoulard *m.* **2.** ivresse*, cuite *f*, soûlerie *f*, bit(t)ure *f*; ribote *f.*

dry [drai] (*adj.*). **1.** *F:* **to be d.,** avoir

* An asterisk indicates that the word so marked is included as a head-word in the Appendix.

soif*, avoir la pépie; **d. as a bone,** sec comme un clou. 2. *F:* **not d. behind the ears,** blanc-bec, morveux, qui a le lait qui sort du nez; *cf.* **wet**[1], 5. 3. *F:* **the d. facts,** les faits tout purs. 4. **d. run,** (*a*) *P:* coït* avec emploi d'un contraceptif, dérouillage *m* à sec; (*b*) *F:* (*th.*) répétition *f* d'essai; (*c*) *F:* (*av.*) manœuvre *f* d'essai. *Voir aussi* **drain**[2] (**to**); **high**[1], 2; **home,** 1; **suck** (**to**), 2.

dry out [ˈdraiˈaut] (**to**), *P:* 1. couver son vin, déboiser sa gueule, se dépoivrer. 2. se désintoxiquer (des drogues).

dry up [ˈdraiˈʌp] (**to**), *F:* 1. **d. u.!** tais-toi! (*se taire**), ferme-la! écrase! 2. (*th.*) oublier son rôle, sécher, avoir un trou.

D.T.'s [ˈdiːˈtiːz] (*pl. noun*), *F:* delirium *m* tremens, les rats bleus.

dub[1] [dʌb] (*noun*). 1. *F:* (*th.*) doublure *f*, double *m*. 2. (*U.S.*) *P:* nourriture*, boustifaille *f*. 3. (*pl.*) *P:* W.C.*, chiottes *f.pl.*

dub[2] [dʌb] (**to**), *F:* 1. **to d. for s.o.,** remplacer qn, suppléer qn. 2. **to d. s.o.,** qualifier qn, donner un sobriquet à qn. 3. **to d.** (**in**), doubler.

dubee [ˈd(j)uːbiː] (*noun*), *P:* cigarette* de marijuana (*drogues**), reefer *m*.

dub up [ˈdʌbˈʌp] (**to**), *P:* 1. enfermer (un prisonnier), boucler (la lourde sur...). 2. payer*, douiller, décher.

duby [ˈd(j)uːbiː] (*noun*), *P:* = **dubee.**

duchess [ˈdʌtʃis] (*noun*), *F:* 1. grande dame, marquise *f*. 2. **my old d.** = **my old Dutch** (**Dutch**[3], 2).

duck[1] [dʌk] (*noun*), *F:* 1. (*terme d'affection*) mon poulet, mon chou; *voir aussi* **ducks; ducky**[2]. 2. (**Lord**) **love a d.!** grands dieux! 3. **a sitting d.,** une cible facile. 4. **to behave like a dying d.** (**in a thunderstorm**), faire la carpe pâmée, faire des yeux de merlan frit. 5. **to have d.'s disease,** avoir le cul bas, traîner le derrière. 6. **lame d.,** (*a*) une épave, un(e) éclopé(e); **to help a lame d.,** aider un canard boiteux; (*b*) (*U.S.*) fonctionnaire public qui arrive à terme sans être réélu; (*c*) (*Bourse*) défaillant *m*, agent *m* en défaut; (*d*) bateau endommagé. 7. (*mil.*) véhicule *m* amphibie. 8. **it's like water off a d.'s back,** c'est comme si on chantait. 9. **to play ducks and drakes with one's money,** jeter son argent* par les fenêtres. 10. **like a d. takes to water,** comme un poisson dans l'eau. 11. **d.** (**egg**), zéro (pointé), chou blanc; **to break one's d.,** retrouver sa veine. 12. (*U.S.*) **to have** (*or* **throw**) **a d. fit,** se mettre en colère*, piquer une crise. 13. (*U.S.*) **d. soup,** qch. de très facile, du cousu-main, bête comme chou. 14. **a nice day for ducks,** beau temps pour les grenouilles. 15. **one little d.** (=2), **two little ducks** (=22): *voir* **bingo.** *Voir aussi* **dead**[1], 4; **fuck**[2] (**to**), 3; **knee-high.**

duck[2] [dʌk] (**to**), *F:* éviter (qn, qch.); *voir aussi* **duck out** (**to**); **scone.**

duckie [ˈdʌki] (*noun*), *F:* = **ducky**[2].

duck out [ˈdʌkˈaut] (**to**), *F:* **to d. o. of** (**doing**) **sth.,** s'esquiver, se tirer, se débiner, se dérober, sécher; *voir aussi* **duck**[2] (**to**).

ducks [dʌks] (*noun*), *F:* chéri(e), chou *m*; *voir aussi* **duck**[1], 1; **ducky**[2].

ducky[1] [ˈdʌki] (*adj.*), *F:* excellent*, très satisfaisant, chouette, bath.

ducky[2] [ˈdʌki] (*noun*), *F:* mon poulet, ma petite chatte, ma poupoule, ma cocotte, mon chou; **she's a dear little d.,** c'est un amour.

dud[1] [dʌd] (*adj.*), *F:* mauvais*, toc(ard), à la manque.

dud[2] [dʌd] (*noun*), *F:* 1. obus non éclaté. 2. échec*, four *m*, un(e)...à la manque. 3. faux billet; chèque *m* sans provision. 4. un raté, un zéro, une nullité, un cancre. 5. (*pl.*) vêtements*, frusques *f.pl.*, nippes *f.pl.*

dude [d(j)uːd] (*noun*) (*U.S.*), *F:* 1. gommeux *m*, miché *m*, freluquet *m*. 2. **d. ranch,** ranch-hôtel *m* de vacances (*ou* pour vacanciers).

dud up [ˈdʌdˈʌp] (**to**), *F:* 1. maquiller (la marchandise, la vérité, *etc.*). 2. se bichonner, se pomponner.

duff[1] [dʌf] (*adj.*), *F:* faux, truqué, à la manque, gnognot(t)eux; *voir aussi* **gen.**

duff[2] [dʌf] (*noun*). 1. *P:* dessert *m* (de prison). 2. *F:* pudding anglais. 3. *F:* poussière *f* de charbon. 4. *P:* agent* de police, flic *m*.

duff[3] [dʌf] (**to**), *F:* 1. (*golf, etc.*) cogner une balle de travers, louper une balle. 2. rater, bousiller, louper. 3. maquiller, camoufler. 4. truquer, frauder.

duffer [ˈdʌfər] (*noun*), *F:* individu bête*, cancre *m*; **a d. at maths,** une nullité en maths.

* L'astérisque indique que le mot marqué de ce signe figure comme entrée dans le Répertoire.

dugout [ˈdʌgaʊt] (*noun*), *P:* 1. drogué*, junkie *m.* 2. officier *m* à la retraite rappelé en service, rempilé *m*, naphtalinard *m.*

duke off [ˈdjuːkˈɔf] (**to**), *P:* filer en poussant l'adversaire.

dukes [djuːks] (*pl. noun*), *P:* mains*, poings *m.pl.*, paluches *f.pl.*, pognes *f.pl.*

dullsville [ˈdʌlzvil] (*noun*), *F:* comble *f* de la monotonie.

dumb [dʌm] (*adj.*). 1. (*a*) *F:* bête*, bouché, stupide; (*b*) *P:* **d. bunny** (*or* **cluck** *or* **jerk**), individu bête*, cruchon *m*, gourde *f*; (*c*) *F:* **to act** (*or* **play**) **d.**, faire l'idiot; (*d*) *F:* **d. blonde** (*or* **Dora**), blonde évaporée, bécasse *f*; *voir aussi* **plain.** 2. *F:* **d. dog,** personne *f* taciturne, bonnet *m* de nuit.

dumb-bell [ˈdʌmbel], **dumbhead** [ˈdʌmhed] (*noun*), *F:* individu bête*, baluche *f*, andouille *f.*

dumb-lick [ˈdʌmlik] (*noun*) (*U.S.*), *P:* vaurien*, canaille *f.*

dumbo [ˈdʌmbou], **dummox** [ˈdʌməks] (*noun*), *P:* = **dumb-bell.**

dummy [ˈdʌmi] (*noun*). 1. *P:* sourd-muet *m*, sourde-muette *f.* 2. *P:* un ballot, un empoté, un empaillé. 3. *P:* = **flash Harry** (**flash**[1], 1). 4. *P:* **to chuck a d.,** (*a*) s'évanouir*, tomber dans le cirage (*ou* dans les vapes); (*b*) simuler un évanouissement dans une foule pour faciliter le travail des pickpockets. 5. *V:* **to beat** (*or* **flog**) **the d.**, se masturber*, se secouer le bonhomme, se branler. 6. *P:* portefeuille*, lazingue *m.*

dummy up [ˈdʌmiˈʌp] (**to**), *P:* se taire*, boucler la trappe, la boucler.

dump[1] [dʌmp] (*noun*), *F:* 1. endroit *m* sordide, dépotoir *m*, taudis *m.* 2. gargote *f*, boui-boui *m*, bouge *m.* 3. **to be fit for the d.,** être bon pour la casse. 4. **to be (down) in the dumps,** avoir le cafard, être dans le cirage (*ou* dans le 36ème dessous).

dump[2] [dʌmp] (**to**), *F:* 1. abandonner*, larguer, laisser choir. 2. délaisser, planter, plaquer.

dumpling [ˈdʌmpliŋ] (*noun*). 1. *F:* patapouf *m*, pot *m* à tabac, bouboule *m.* 2. (*pl.*) *P:* seins*, rondins *m.pl.*

dun [dʌn] (*noun*), *P:* tueur *m* à gages, homme *m* de main.

dunk [dʌŋk] (*noun*), *F:* **to take a quick d.,** prendre un bain rapide, faire trempette.

dunno [dəˈnou] (=*don't know*), *P:* sais pas!

duros [ˈduːrɔs] (*noun*) (*U.S.*), *P:* marijuana *f* (*drogues**).

durries [ˈdʌriz] (*pl. noun*), *P:* amphétamines *f.pl.* (*drogues**), bonbons *m.pl.*

dust[1] [dʌst] (*noun*). 1. *F:* **you couldn't see him for d.,** il courait comme s'il avait le feu au derrière, il a filé comme l'éclair. 2. *P:* (*a*) (**foo-foo** *or* **happy** *or* **heaven** *or* **reindeer**) **d.,** narcotiques *m.pl.* en poudre, poudrette *f*; (*b*) **gold** (*or* **heaven**) **d.,** cocaïne *f* (*drogues**), coco *f*, talc *m*, neige *f.* 3. *P:* argent*, pépettes *f.pl.*, picaillons *m.pl.*; **to down the d.,** payer*, casquer, les allonger; **to raise the d.,** se procurer de l'argent*. 4. *F:* **to bite** (*or* **kiss**) **the d.,** mordre la poussière. 5. *F:* **to lick the d.,** s'aplatir, lécher les bottes à qn. 6. *F:* **to shake the d. off one's feet,** secouer la poussière de ses souliers. 7. *F:* **to throw d. in s.o.'s eyes,** jeter de la poudre aux yeux de qn. 8. *F:* **to make s.o. eat one's d.,** dépasser qn (*en véhicule ou au figuratif*), faire sentir ses gaz, faire la pige à qn. *Voir aussi* **kick up** (**to**), 2 (*b*); **stardust.**

dust[2] [dʌst] (**to**), *F:* **to dust s.o.'s jacket for him,** battre* qn, flanquer une raclée à qn, tanner le cuir à qn.

dustbin [ˈdʌs(t)bin] (*noun*), *P:* **d. lids** (*R.S.* = *kids*), enfants*, mioches *m.pl.*; *cf.* **godfer.**

duster [ˈdʌstər] (*noun*), *P:* 1. (=*knuckle-duster*) coup-de-poing américain, sortie *f* de bal. 2. (*Austr.*) (*pl.*) testicules*, roupignolles *f.pl.*

dusting [ˈdʌstiŋ] (*noun*), *F:* coups*, raclée *f*, tabassée *f*, trempe *f.*

dustman [ˈdʌs(t)mən] (*noun*), *F:* **the d.,** sommeil *m*, le marchand de sable; *cf.* **sandman.**

dust off [ˈdʌstˈɔf] (**to**), *F:* 1. **to d. s.o. o.,** abandonner* qn, se débarrasser* de qn, laisser qn en carafe. 2. **to d. sth. o.,** faire qch. rapidement, enlever un travail; bâcler, torcher qch.

dust-up [ˈdʌstʌp] (*noun*), *F:* bagarre*, coup *m* de chien.

dusty [ˈdʌsti] (*adj.*). 1. *F:* **not so d.,** pas si moche, pas tarte (du tout).

* An asterisk indicates that the word so marked is included as a head-word in the Appendix.

2. *F:* **to get a d. answer,** se faire rembarrer. *Voir aussi* **butt,** 2.

Dutch[1] [dʌtʃ] (*adj.*), *F:* 1. **D. courage,** courage puisé dans la bouteille *ou* dans les stupéfiants. 2. **D. auction,** enchère *f* au rabais, vente *f* à la baisse. 3. **D. cap,** pessaire *m,* capote anglaise. 4. **D. comfort,** consolation qui n'en est pas une, piètre consolation. 5. **to talk to s.o. like a D. uncle,** dire ses quatre vérités à qn. 6. **D. treat,** sortie *f* où chacun paye son écot, sortie en Suisse; *cf.* **Dutch**[2]. 7. **to do the D. act,** se suicider*, se faire sauter la caisse, se flanquer en l'air. 8. **to take D. leave,** filer à l'anglaise.

Dutch[2] [dʌtʃ] (*adv.*), *F:* **to go D.,** payer son écot; *cf.* **Dutch**[1], **6.**

Dutch[3] [dʌtʃ] (*noun*). 1. *F:* **to talk double D.,** baragouiner, parler une langue inintelligible; **that's double D. to me,** pour moi c'est de l'hébreu. 2. *F:* **my (old) D.,** mon épouse*, ma bourgeoise. 3. *F:* **that beats the D.!** c'est le comble! c'est le bouquet! 4. *P:* **to be in D.,** avoir de la malchance*, être dans le pétrin (*ou* dans la panade).

Dutchman [ˈdʌtʃmən] (*noun*), *F:* 1. **if that's so then I'm a D.,** si c'est ainsi j'y perds mon latin (*ou* je veux bien être pendu). 2. **to have a D.'s headache,** avoir la gueule de bois.

duty [ˈdjuːti] (*noun*), *F:* **to do one's d.,** déféquer*, faire sa grande commission.

dyke [daik] (*noun*), *P:* lesbienne*, gouine *f,* gousse *f*; *cf.* **bull-dyke; dike, 2.**

dykey [ˈdaiki] (*adj.*), *P:* lesbienne*, gavousse, aillée; *cf.* **dikey.**

dynamite [ˈdainəmait] (*noun*). 1. *P:* (*a*) stupéfiant très fort, dynamite *f*; (*b*) stupéfiant *m* de haute qualité; (*c*) marijuana *f* (*drogues**); (*d*) héroïne *f* (*drogues**). 2. *F:* **she's d.!** elle est explosive! 3. *F:* **don't touch it, it's d.!** n'y touche pas, c'est de la dynamite (*ou* c'est explosif *ou* c'est jouer avec le feu)!

* L'astérisque indique que le mot marqué de ce signe figure comme entrée dans le Répertoire.

E

eager ['iːgər] (*adj.*), *F:* **e. beaver,** bourreau *m* de travail*, turbineur *m*, bûcheur *m*; **to be an e. beaver,** faire du zèle.

ear [iər] (*noun*). **1.** *F:* **to be all ears,** être tout oreilles, être tout ouïe. **2.** *F:* **up to one's ears** (*in debt, etc.*), jusqu'au cou, par-dessus la tête; **up to one's ears in work,** accablé (*ou* débordé) de travail*. **3.** *F:* **to play it by e.,** jouer d'oreille, y aller d'instinct, voir venir, aller au pif(f)omètre. **4.** *P:* **to throw s.o. out on his e.,** se débarrasser* de qn, flanquer (*ou* foutre) qn dehors; **to get thrown out on one's e.,** se faire flanquer dehors. **5.** *F:* **to give s.o. a thick e.,** donner des coups* à qn, abîmer le portrait à qn, donner une paire de gifles *f.pl.* (*ou* de taloches *f.pl.*) à qn. **6.** *F:* **to pin s.o.'s ears back,** réprimander* qn, enguirlander qn, passer un savon à qn. *Voir aussi* **blow (to), 12; cloth-ears; dry, 2; flea, 2; pig¹, 4; wet¹, 5.**

earful ['iəful] (*noun*), *P:* **1.** tas *m*, tapée *f*, séquelle *f* (de nouvelles, potins, *etc.*). **2. to give s.o. an e.,** (*a*) réprimander* qn, enguirlander qn; (*b*) dire son fait à qn.

earhole ['iəroul] (*noun*), *P:* **to clip s.o. round the e.** = **to give s.o. a thick ear (ear, 5).** *Voir aussi* **plug¹, 2.**

early ['əːli] (*adj.*), *F:* **to be an e. bird,** se lever tôt (*ou* avec les poules).

earners ['əːnəz] (*pl. noun*), *P:* (*a*) argent*, pognon *m*; (*b*) aumônes *f.pl.*, truches *f.pl.*, trunes *f.pl.*

earth [əːθ] (*noun*), *F:* **1. to come back to e.,** revenir sur terre, (re)tomber des nues. **2. to cost the e.,** coûter cher*; **to pay the e. for sth.,** payer les yeux de la tête pour qch. **3. to be down to e.,** avoir les pieds sur terre, être terre à terre. **4. where on e....?** où diable...? où diantre...?; **why on e....?** pourquoi diable...? *Voir aussi* **end, 4.**

earthly¹ ['əːθli] (*adj.*), *F:* **no e. use,** sans aucune (*ou* la moindre) utilité, comme un cautère sur une jambe de bois; **for no e. reason,** à propos de bottes.

earthly² ['əːθli] (*noun*), *F:* **he hasn't an e.,** il n'a pas l'ombre d'une chance, il n'a pas la moindre chance (de réussir).

earwig ['iəwig] (*noun*), *F:* qn qui écoute aux portes, esgourdeur *m* de lourdes.

ease off ['iːz'ɔf] (**to**), *F:* se détendre, se relaxer, se relâcher.

East-ender ['iːst'endər] (*noun*), *F:* habitant *m* de la banlieue-Est de Londres, faubourien *m*.

easy¹ ['iːzi] (*adj.*), *F:* **1. to be on e. street,** être riche*, rouler sur l'or, être tombé sur un champ d'oseille. **2. e. money,** argent* gagné facilement, affure *f*, fleur *f*. **3. e. mark,** personne bête* et crédule, dupe *f*, jobard *m*, andouille *f*. **4. to take the e. way out,** (*a*) sortir par la première porte, ne pas s'en faire, s'en tirer à bon compte; (*b*) se suicider*, se déramer. **5. e. meat,** (*a*) individu* complaisant (*ou* facile *ou* de bonne composition); (*b*) adversaire peu dangereux, une bouchée (de pain). **6. e. as pie,** simple comme bonjour, bête comme chou, qui est du billard; *cf.* **ABC, 1. 7. e. rider,** souteneur*, mangeur *m* de brioche.

easy² ['iːzi] (*adv.*), *F:* **1. to take it e.,** ne pas se fouler la rate, en prendre à son aise; **take it e.,** (*a*) ne te tracasse* pas, ne t'en fais pas; (*b*) laisse-toi vivre. **2. e. now!** doucement! piano! **3. e. does it!** vas-y doucement (*ou* mou *ou* chouia)! **4. e. come, e. go,** vite gagné, vite perdu; ce qui vient avec le flot s'en retourne avec la marée. **5. go e. on it!** vas-y mollo (*ou* en peinard)!

easy-going ['iːzi'gouiŋ] (*adj.*), *F:* facile à vivre, du bois dont on fait les flûtes.

eat [iːt] (**to**). **1.** *F:* **what's eating him?** quelle mouche l'a piqué? qu'est-ce

* An asterisk indicates that the word so marked is included as a head-word in the Appendix.

qui le tracasse? qu'est-ce qui le turlupine? 2. *F:* **to e. one's words,** se rétracter, revenir sur ses paroles. 3. *F:* **to e. one's heart out,** se ronger le cœur, sécher sur pied. 4. *F:* **to e. s.o. out of house and home,** coûter plus qu'on est gros, ruiner qn. 5. *F:* **to e. out of s.o.'s hand,** manger dans la main de qn. 6. *F:* **to e. s.o.'s head off,** réprimander* qn, avaler qn. 7. *V:* sucer, brouter (qn) (*coït* buccal*). *Voir aussi* **dirt[1], 5.**

eatery [ˈiːtəri] (*noun*), *P:* café* (*débit*), bistroquet *m.*

eats [iːts] (*pl. noun*), *P:* nourriture*, boustifaille *f*; **an e. joint,** une gargote.

edge[1] [edʒ] (*noun*). 1. (*U.S.*) *P:* **to have an e.,** être légèrement ivre*, être parti (*ou* éméché). 2. (*Austr.*) *F:* **over the e.,** qui dépasse les limites.

edge[2] [edʒ] (**to**) (*Austr.*), *P:* **to e. it = to aste it.**

edged [edʒd] (*adj.*) (*U.S.*), *P:* ivre*, rétamé, blindé.

edgy [ˈedʒi] (*adj.*), *F:* crispé, ayant les nerfs en pelote (*ou* à fleur de peau).

educated [ˈedjukeitid] (*adj.*), *F:* malin*, marloupin.

egg [eg] (*noun*). 1. *F:* individu*, mec *m,* zigue *m*; **bad** (*or* **rotten**) **e.,** vaurien*, sale type *m,* bon à rien. 2. *F:* **good e.!** épatant! bravo! 3. *F:* **golden eggs,** gros bénéfices*, grosse gratte, beau velours. 4. *F:* (*mil.*) **scrambled eggs,** feuilles *f.pl.* de chêne, graine *f* d'épinards, sardines *f.pl.* 5. *F:* **as sure as eggs is eggs,** couru d'avance, aussi vrai qu'il fait jour, comme un et un font deux. 6. *F:* **don't put all your eggs in one basket,** ne mettez pas vos œufs dans le même panier. 7. *F:* **to teach one's grandmother to suck eggs,** apprendre aux vieux singes à faire la grimace. 8. *P:* **to lay an e.,** avoir un échec*, faire four. *Voir aussi* **nest-egg.**

egghead [ˈeghed] (*noun*), *F:* intellectuel *m,* mandarin *m,* grosse tête.

eight [eit] (*numeral adj. & noun*), *F:* 1. **to have one over the e.,** être ivre*, boire un coup de trop; *voir aussi* **one, 1.** 2. (*U.S.*) **to be behind the e. ball,** être en mauvaise posture (*ou* dans le pétrin *ou* mal en point).

eighteen-pence [ˈeitiːnˈpens] (*noun*) (*R.S. = (common) sense*), *P:* bon sens, sens commun, du chou; **ain't you got no e.-p.?** as-tu perdu la tête* (*ou* la boussole)?

elbow [ˈelbou] (*noun*), *F:* 1. **at one's e.,** à portée de la main. 2. **out at e.,** miteux, déguenillé, loqueteux. 3. **to rub elbows with s.o.,** fréquenter qn, s'acoquiner avec qn. 4. **e. room,** du champ, du large, les coudées franches. 5. **e. grease,** huile *f* de coude (*ou* de bras), énergie *f,* de la moelle. 6. **to bend** (*or* **lift**) **the e.,** boire*, lever le coude; **e. bender,** ivrogne*, picoleur *m*; **e. bending,** ivresse*, bit(t)ure *f,* cuite *f.* 7. **more power to your e.!** vas-y! bonne chance! la meilleure des chances! *Voir aussi* **arse, 3.**

elbow out [ˈelbouˈaut] (**to**), *F:* écarter, évincer, envoyer dinguer (qn); **to be elbowed out,** être délogé.

elephant [ˈelifənt] (*noun*). 1. *F:* **white e.,** possession inutile et coûteuse, éléphant blanc, attrape-poussière *m.* 2. *F:* **pink elephants,** rats bleus (vus par les alcooliques). 3. (*U.S.*) *P:* **to see the e.,** se rincer l'œil, s'en mettre plein les mirettes. 4. *P:* **she's seen the e.,** elle a vu le loup (*ou* la lune). *Voir aussi* **baby[1], 2.**

elephants [ˈelifənts] (*adj.*) (*R.S. = elephant's trunk = drunk*), ivre*.

elevenses [iˈlevnziz] (*pl. noun*), *F:* pause-café *f.*

'em [əm] (*pron.*), *F: = them*; *cf.* **daft[1], 1; lick[2] (to), 1** (*c*)**; make[2] (to), 2; pack in (to), 3; set up (to), 1; stick up (to), 2.**

empty [ˈem(p)ti] (*adj.*), *F:* **to feel e.,** avoir faim*, avoir un creux, claquer du bec.

end [end] (*noun*). 1. *P:* fesses*, l'arrière-train *m*; *cf.* **rear (end).** 2. *V:* pénis*, queue *f,* le (gros) bout; **to get one's e. in** (*or* **away**), coïter*, mettre la cheville dans le trou. 3. *F:* (*a*) **to the bitter e.,** jusqu'au bout des bouts; **to go on to the bitter e.,** boire le calice jusqu'à la lie; *cf.* **bitter-ender;** (*b*) **he's the (bitter) e.,** il est au-dessous de tout. 4. *F:* **to go to the ends of the earth (to do sth.),** se mettre en quatre, se démener, se donner un mal fou (pour faire qch.). 5. *F:* **to go off the deep e.,** (*a*) se mettre en colère*, sortir de ses gonds, piquer une crise, monter sur ses grands chevaux; (*b*) prendre les choses au

* L'astérisque indique que le mot marqué de ce signe figure comme entrée dans le Répertoire.

tragique, broyer du noir. **6.** *F:* **to keep one's e. up,** (*a*) résister, se défendre, tenir bon; (*b*) faire sa part, y mettre du sien. **7.** *F:* **at a loose e.,** désœuvré, traînant les patins, s'endormant sur le mastic; **to be at a loose e.,** se tourner les pouces, avoir du temps à perdre. **8.** *F:* **to make ends meet,** joindre les deux bouts, boucler son budget. **9.** *F:* **no e. of...,** une abondance* de..., une infinité (*ou* flopée *ou* tapée *ou* bardée) de...; **it'll do you no e. of good,** ça vous fera un bien fou (*ou* énormément de bien); **no e. of money,** un argent* fou; **he thinks no e. of himself,** il est prétentieux*, il se gobe, il s'en croit. **10.** *F:* **on e.,** (*a*) debout, tout droit; (*b*) sans relâche; **three weeks on e.,** trois semaines d'affilée. **11.** *F:* (*a*) **to get hold of the wrong e. of the stick,** prendre qch. à contre-sens, saisir le mauvais bout, comprendre de travers; (*b*) **to have the right e. of the stick,** être dans la bonne voie, tenir le bon bout. **12.** *F:* **to beat s.o. all ends up,** battre qn à plate(s) couture(s). **13.** *F:* **to be thrown in at the deep e.,** être mis en pleine eau, être tout de suite dans le bain. *Voir aussi* **back¹, 2; back-end; beam-ends; dead-end; dog-end; fag-end; jump² (to), 12; tab-end; tail-end.**

enders [ˈendəz] (*noun*), *P:* **to go e. with a woman, to have (Harry) e.,** coïter* avec une femme*, mettre une femme* au bout.

enemy [ˈenəmi] (*noun*), *F:* **the e.,** l'heure *f* qui tourne.

erk [əːk] (*noun*), *F:* conscrit *m*, bleu *m*, recrue *f*.

euchre [ˈjuːkər] **(to)**, *P:* duper*, entuber (qn); **to be euchred,** être dans le pétrin (*ou* dans une impasse).

even¹ [ˈiːvən] (*adj.*), *P:* **e. Steven** (*or* **Stephen**), quitte; **to call it e. Steven,** être quitte; **to go e. Steven,** aller fifty-fifty.

even² [ˈiːvən] (*adv.*), *F:* **to get e. (with s.o.),** se venger, aller à la rebiffe, rendre la pareille, attraper qn au tournant. *Voir aussi* **break² (to).**

evens [ˈiːvənz] (*pl. noun*), *F:* **to lay e.,** parier à égalité.

even up on [ˈiːvənˈʌp-ɔn] **(to)**, *F:* = **get even with (to)** (*voir* **even²**).

ever [ˈevər] (*adv.*), *F:* **1. e. so...,** tellement...; **e. so much,** beaucoup*, bougrement. **2. did you e.!** époustouflant! renversant!

ex [eks] (*prefix & noun*), *F:* ex(-mari, *etc.*); **ex-con,** ex-prisonnier *m*, relargué *m*, guéri *m*.

exhibition [eksiˈbiʃ(ə)n] (*noun*), *F:* **to make an e. of oneself,** faire la comédie, se donner en spectacle.

expect [eksˈpekt] **(to)**, *F:* **1.** penser, supposer; **I e. you're right,** tu as sans doute raison. **2. to be expecting,** être enceinte*, être dans une situation intéressante.

experience [eksˈpiəriəns, iksˈpiəriəns] (*noun*), *F:* voyage *m* (*drogues*).

extras [ˈekstrəz] (*pl. noun*), *F:* à-côtés *m.pl.*

extra-special [ˈekstrəˈspeʃ(ə)l] (*adj.*), *F:* excellent*, super, sensas(s).

eye [ai] (*noun*). **1.** *F:* **easy on the e.,** agréable à regarder (*ou* à l'œil), de quoi se rincer l'œil. **2.** *F:* **to have an e. for sth.,** s'y connaître, avoir l'œil américain (*ou* le coup d'œil). **3.** *F:* **all my e. (and Betty Martin),** bêtises*, foutaises *f.pl.*, balivernes *f.pl.* **4.** *F:* **my e.!** (*a*) mon œil! mon zob!; (*b*) mince alors! **5.** *P:* **to do s.o. in the e.,** duper* qn, empiler qn. **6.** *F:* **glad e.,** œillade*; **to give s.o. the (glad) e.,** faire de l'œil à qn, lancer des coups de châsse à qn. **7.** *F:* **to keep an e. on s.o.,** surveiller qn, avoir qn à l'œil. **8.** *F:* **to keep one's eyes open** (*or* **skinned**), allumer ses lampions, ouvrir l'œil et le bon, ne pas avoir ses yeux dans sa poche. **9.** *F:* **sheep's eyes,** des yeux de carpe pâmée. **10.** *F:* **to make eyes at s.o.,** couver qn des yeux, faire les yeux doux (*ou* en coulisse *ou* en tirelire). **11.** *F:* **to open s.o.'s eyes (to sth.),** éclairer la lanterne à qn, nettoyer les lucarnes à qn. **12.** *F:* **to see e. to e. (with s.o.),** être d'accord, voir du même œil. **13.** *F:* **to turn a blind e. (to sth.),** fermer les yeux (sur qch.). **14.** *F:* **to be up to the** (*or* **one's**) **eyes in sth.,** être plongé jusqu'aux yeux (*ou* pardessus les yeux *ou* jusqu'au cou); *cf.* **ear, 2. 15.** *F:* **a sight for sore eyes,** un régal pour les yeux. **16.** *F:* **there's more in this than meets the e.,** il y a quelque anguille sous roche. **17.** *F:* **to have eyes for s.o.,** aimer* qn, être entiché, avoir le pépin pour qn. **18.**

* An asterisk indicates that the word so marked is included as a head-word in the Appendix.

F: **to have an e. to the future,** avoir des visées d'avenir. **19.** *F:* **to have an e. to the main chance,** s'attacher à ses intérêts, viser au solide. **20.** *F:* **to see with half an e.,** voir du premier coup, sauter aux yeux. **21.** *F:* **private e.,** détective privé, fileur *m.* **22.** *F:* **to get one's e. in,** s'habituer à une situation, être rodé. **23.** *P:* **that's one in the e. for him!** il a été mouché de belle façon! **24.** *V:* **round e.,** anus*, œil de bronze. *Voir aussi* **bird's-eye; drop[1], 6; four-eyes; Kelly, 2; mud, 1; red-eye; shut-eye; slap[2], 1; snake-eyes.**

eyebrows [ˈai-brauz] (*pl. noun*), *F:* **he's hanging on by his e.,** il se maintient tout juste, il est sur la corde raide, il tient à un fil. *Voir aussi* **dose up (to); poxed (up).**

eye-eye! [ˈaiˈ(j)ai] (*excl.*), *P:* ouvre l'œil! fais gaffe!

eyeful [ˈaiful] (*noun*), *P:* **1.** jolie fille*, chouette pépée. **2. to get an e.,** voir qch. de très beau* (*ou* de très intéressant), se rincer l'œil, s'en mettre plein les mirettes.

eye-opener [ˈai(j)oup(ə)nər] (*noun*), *F:* **1.** révélation *f*, surprise *f*; **it was an e.-o. for me,** ça a déclenché mes clignotants. **2.** boisson forte prise à jeun, rince-cochon *m*, réveil-matin *m*.

Eyetie [ˈaiˈtai, ˈaitai] (*noun*), *P:* Italien *m*, rital *m*, macaroni *m*.

eyewash [ˈaiwɔʃ] (*noun*), *F:* **1.** flatterie *f*, bourrage *m* de crâne, frime *f*. **2.** baratin *m*, foutaise *f*, boniment *m*. **3.** explications *f.pl.* miton mitaine.

* L'astérisque indique que le mot marqué de ce signe figure comme entrée dans le Répertoire.

F

f.a. [ˈefˈei] (*abbr.*) = **fuck-all; sweet f.a.** (*or* **F.A.**) = **sweet fuck-all** *or* **sweet Fanny Adams (sweet**[1], 4).

fab(ulous) [ˈfæb(juləs)] (*adj.*), *F:* excellent*, fabuleux, sensas(s), du tonnerre.

face[1] [feis] (*noun*). **1.** *P:* **shut** (*or* **button up**) **your f.!** ferme ta boîte (*ou* ton clapet *ou* ta gueule)! **2.** *F:* **to have the f. to do sth.**, avoir le culot (*ou* l'audace *f ou* le toupet) de faire qch. **3.** *F:* **to show one's f.**, montrer (le bout de) son nez. **4.** *F:* **to feed one's f.**, manger*, s'empiffrer. **5.** *F:* **to paint one's f.**, se maquiller*, se badigeonner; *cf.* **face-paint.** *Voir aussi* **angel-face; fungus; laugh**[2] **(to), 2; pudding-face; pushface; slap**[2], **1; stare (to); turn-about-face.**

face[2] [feis] **(to)**, *F:* **1. let's f. it,** il faut regarder les choses en face. **2.** (*Austr.*) = **dud up (to), 1.** *Voir aussi* **music.**

face-ache [ˈfeiseik] (*noun*), *P:* tête *f* à claques; **hello, f.-a.!** salut, corniaud!

face-lift [ˈfeislift] (*noun*), *F:* (*a*) chirurgie *f* esthétique, lifting *m*; (*b*) (*fig.*) embellissement *m*, rénovation *f*, retapage *m.*

face off [ˈfeisˈɔf] **(to)**, *F:* tenir tête à qn.

face out [ˈfeisˈaut] **(to)**, *F:* **to f. it o.** = **to face the music** (*voir* **music**).

face-paint [ˈfeis-peint] (*noun*), *F:* badigeon *m*; *cf.* **face**[1], **5; war-paint.**

facer [ˈfeisər] (*noun*), *F:* **1.** coup* au visage, torgnole *f.* **2.** pépin *m*, tuile *f.* **3.** carte* (à jouer) qui baise.

face up [ˈfeisˈʌp] **(to)**, *F:* **to f. u. to s.o.**, affronter qn.

facings [ˈfeisiŋz] (*pl. noun*), *F:* **to put s.o. through his f.**, (*a*) éprouver le savoir de qn, voir ce qu'il a dans le crâne (*ou* dans le ventre); (*b*) injurier* qn comme il faut, dire son fait à qn.

factory [ˈfæktəri] (*noun*), *P:* **1.** = **artillery, 1. 2.** commissariat *m* de police. *Voir aussi* **glue-factory.**

fade [feid] **(to)**, *P:* s'enfuir*, s'éclipser, en jouer un air.

fag [fæg] (*noun*). **1.** *F:* cigarette*, sèche *f*, cibiche *f.* **2.** *P:* (*a*) pédéraste*, fiotte *f*, lope(tte) *f*; (*b*) homme efféminé, chouquette *f*; (*c*) **f. bag,** femme* qui recherche la compagnie des pédérastes*, fagoteuse *f.* **3.** *F:* **what a f.!** quelle corvée!

fag-end [ˈfægend] (*noun*), *F:* mégot*, clope *m.*

fageroo [fægəˈruː] (*noun*), *P:* = **fag, 1.**

fagged (out) [ˈfægd(ˈaut)] (*adj.*), *F:* très fatigué*, vanné, éreinté.

faggot [ˈfægət] (*noun*). **1.** *P:* pédéraste*, fagot *m.* **2.** *F:* **old f.**, vieille femme* (*péj.*), fumelle *f*, vieille pouffiasse.

fainites! [ˈfeinaits] (*excl.*), *F:* (*langage enfantin*) pouce!; *cf.* **pax!**

fair[1] [ˈfɛər] (*adj.*), *F:* **1. f. enough!** ça va! d'accord!* **2. it's f. and square,** c'est de bonne guerre (*ou* à la loyale). **3. it's a f. swindle,** c'est une pure escroquerie*, c'est un vrai (*ou* sacré) coup d'arnac. *Voir aussi* **cow, 3; do**[1], **4; middling; shake**[1], **3; whip**[1], **1.**

fair[2] [ˈfɛər] (*adv.*), *P:* très, bougrement; **I'm f. knackered,** je suis complètement à plat; **this f. stumped me,** du coup je n'ai su que répondre.

fair[3] [ˈfɛər] (*noun*), *F:* **to arrive the day after the f.**, arriver trop tard, manquer le coche.

fair-haired [ˈfɛəˈhɛəd] (*adj.*) (*U.S.*), *F:* = **blue-eyed.**

fair-looking [ˈfɛə-lukiŋ] (*adj.*), *F:* beau*, bath, badour.

fair-weather [ˈfɛəweðər] (*adj.*), *F:* **f.-w. friends,** amis *m.pl.* des beaux jours.

fairy [ˈfɛəri] (*noun*), *P:* **1.** pédéraste*, tapette *f*; **f. hawk** = **queer-basher; f. lady** (*or* **queen**), lesbienne*, vrille *f*, gougne(tte) *f.* **2.** (*football*) joueur ramollo, mou *m. Voir aussi* **airy-fairy.**

fairyland [ˈfɛərilænd] (*noun*), *P:* le monde des pédérastes*, les familles *f.pl.* tuyau de poêle, la pédale; *cf.* **pansyland.**

fake[1] [feik] (*adj.*), *F:* bidon, toc.

* An asterisk indicates that the word so marked is included as a head-word in the Appendix.

fake[2] [feik] (*noun*), *F:* **1.** = **faker. 2.** imposteur *m.*
fake[3] [feik] (**to**), *F:* **1.** cuisiner (des comptes, *etc.*), truquer. **2.** (*th.*) faire du texte.
faker [ˈfeikər] (*noun*), *F:* faisan *m*, estampeur *m.*
fall [fɔːl] (**to**), *F:* **1. to f. for a trick,** gober, tomber dans un piège. **2. to f. for s.o.,** se toquer de qn, s'amouracher de qn. **3. to f. all over oneself to please s.o.,** se mettre en quatre (*ou* en trente-six) pour plaire à qn; *cf.* **backwards, 1.**
fall down [ˈfɔːlˈdaun] (**to**), *F:* **1. to f. d. on a job,** échouer*, louper, faire la culbute (*ou* un four), foirer. **2. it's falling down,** ça flotte dur, ça dégringole à seaux.
fall-guy [ˈfɔːlgai] (*noun*), *F:* bouc *m* émissaire, âne *m* de moulin, dindon *m* de la farce, lampiste *m.*
fall through [ˈfɔːlˈθruː] (**to**), *F:* foirer; **it fell through at the last moment,** ça m'a claqué dans la main.
false [fɔls] (*adj.*), *F:* **f. money,** (*chèque, etc.*) cavalerie *f* de Saint Georges.
falsies [ˈfɔlsiz] (*pl. noun*), *F:* **1.** fausses dents*, râtelier *m*, clavier *m.* **2.** seins* artificiels, roberts *m.pl.* de chez Michelin, flotteurs *m.pl.*
family [ˈfæm(i)li] (*attrib. adj.*). **1.** *F:* **in the f. way,** enceinte*, cloquée, dans une situation intéressante. **2.** *P:* **f. jewels,** testicules*, bijoux *m.pl.* de famille, précieuses *f.pl.*
famished [ˈfæmiʃt], **famishing** [ˈfæmiʃiŋ] (*adj.*), *F:* **to be f.,** avoir très faim*, la crever, avoir la dent.
famous [ˈfeiməs] (*adj.*), *F:* excellent*, sensas(s), fameux.
famously [ˈfeiməsli] (*adv.*), *F:* fameusement, épatamment; **to get on f.,** s'entendre à merveille.
fan [fæn] (*noun*), *F:* fanatique *mf*, fan *m*, fana *m*, mordu *m*, emballé *m*; **f. club,** club *m* des fanas; **f. mail,** courrier *m* des admirateurs (*ou* des fanas).
fancy[1] [ˈfænsi] (*adj.*). **1.** *P:* **f. man,** (*a*) amant *m* de cœur, gigolo *m*; (*b*) souteneur*. **2.** *P:* **f. woman,** (*a*) prostituée*, mousmé(e) *f*; (*b*) maîtresse *f.* **3.** *P:* **f. pants,** coco *m*, joli-cœur *m.* **4.** *F:* **to cut out the f. stuff,** déblayer, élaguer; **cut out the f. stuff!** pas d'enjolivures, au fait!
fancy[2] [ˈfænsi] (*noun*), *P:* (*a*) = **fancy man (fancy**[1]**, 1)**; (*b*) = **fancy woman (fancy**[1]**, 2)**. *Voir aussi* **tickle**[2] **(to), 1.**
fancy[3] [ˈfænsi] (**to**), *F:* **1. f. (now)!** (*or* **f. that!**), figurez-vous ça! comme ça se trouve! **2. f. meeting you!** quelle bonne rencontre! quel hasard de vous rencontrer! **3. to f. oneself,** être infatué de sa petite personne, se gober, s'en croire, faire sa poire, croire que c'est arrivé. **4. a little of what you f. does you good,** *c.p.*, un chouia de ce qui ragaillardit, ça fait du bien par où ça passe. **5. do you f. her?** elle te dit?
fandangle [fænˈdæŋgl] (*noun*), *F:* oripeau *m*, clinquant *m*, broquille *f*, zinzin *m.*
fanny [ˈfæni] (*noun*). **1.** *V:* vagin*, minou *m*; **f. tickler,** lesbienne*, gouchotte *f.* **2.** (*U.S.*) *P:* fesses*, baba *m*, pétrousquin *m.* **3.** *P:* bêtises*, sornettes *f.pl.*; **a lot** (*or* **load**) **of f.,** un tas de foutaises. *Voir aussi* **aunt, 1; Bob**[2]**; sweet**[1]**, 4.**
fanzine [ˈfænziːn] (*noun*) (*U.S.*), *F:* magazine *m* des fans, fanzine *m.*
far [fɑːr] (*adv.*), *F:* **1. f. gone,** (*a*) fou* à lier; (*b*) ivre* mort; *cf.* **gone, 1. 2. as f. as we go:** *voir* **bingo (90).**
far-out [ˈfɑːrˈaut] (*adj.*), *F:* **1.** loufoque, branquignole. **2.** intellectuel, avant-garde. **3.** emballant, enthousiasmant. **4.** éloigné (de la réalité), perdu en soi. **5.** fervent du jazz *far-out* (jazz extra-moderne).
fart[1] [fɑːt] (*noun*), *V:* **1.** pet*, cloque *f*, vesse *f.* **2.** = **turd, 2. 3. I don't care a f.** (*or* **two farts**), je m'en bats l'œil, je m'en fiche comme de ma première chemise (*ou* culotte). **4. to stand as much chance as a f. in a wind-storm,** ne pas avoir la moindre chance de réussir, avoir autant d'effet que pisser dans la mer. **5. like a f. in a bottle,** agité, nerveux. *Voir aussi* **sparrow-fart.**
fart[2] [fɑːt] (**to**), *V:* péter*, cloquer, en écraser un.
fart(-arse) around (*or* **about**) [ˈfɑːt(ɑːs)əˈraund, əˈbaut] (**to**), *V:* **1.** traîner son cul. **2.** faire le con.
fart-catcher [ˈfɑːtkætʃər] (*noun*), *V:* pédéraste*, enculé *m.*
fart-hole [ˈfɑːt(h)oul] (*noun*), *V:* anus*, trou *m* de balle, troufignon *m.*
fast[1] [fɑːst] (*adj.*), *F:* dévergondé; **to**

* L'astérisque indique que le mot marqué de ce signe figure comme entrée dans le Répertoire.

lead a f. life, mener une vie de bâtons de chaise, faire les quatre cents coups. *Voir aussi* **buck**[1], **2; one, 4.**

fast[2] [fɑːst] (*adv.*), *F:* **to play f. and loose,** jouer double jeu.

fastie [ˈfɑːsti] (*noun*), *P:* cavaleur *m*, juponneur *m.*

fat[1] [fæt] (*adj.*). **1.** *P:* bête*, ballot, enflé, lourdaud. **2.** *P:* **a f. lot,** (*a*) abondance*, tas *m*, tapée *f*; (*b*) rien*, des clous, nix; **a f. lot of good that'll do you!** cela vous fera une belle jambe!; **a f. lot I care!** je m'en fiche pas mal! je m'en soucie comme de l'an quarante (*ou* comme de ma première chemise)!; **a f. lot you know about it!** comme si vous en saviez quelque chose!; **a f. lot of difference it makes to you!** pour ce que ça vous coûte! **3.** *P:* **a f. chance he's got!** il n'a pas l'ombre d'une chance. **4.** *F:* **a f. salary,** de gros appointements. **5.** *F:* **to cut up f.** = **to cut up rich** (**cut up** (**to**), **4**). **6.** *F:* **one f. lady** (=**8**), **two fat ladies** (=**88**): *voir* **bingo.**

fat[2] [fæt] (*noun*), *F:* **1.** (*a*) (*th.*) premier rôle, rôle en or; (*b*) bonne réplique, une percutante. **2. the f. is in the fire,** le feu est aux poudres; le torchon brûle. **3. to live off the f. of the land,** vivre grassement, mener la vie de château, vivre comme un coq en pâte. **4. to live on one's f.,** vivre sur ses réserves (*ou* sur sa graisse). *Voir aussi* **chew** (**to**); **puppy, 1.**

fathead [ˈfæthed] (*noun*), *F:* individu bête*, enflé *m*, empaqueté *m*, bas *m* de plafond.

fatheaded [ˈfæthedid] (*adj.*), *F:* bête*, ballot, baluchard.

fatso [ˈfætsou], **fatty** [ˈfæti] (*noun*), *P:* personne grosse*, bouboule *mf*, patapouf *m*, gravos(se) *m*(*f*), gros plein de soupe.

favourite (*U.S.:* **favorite**) [ˈfeiv(ə)rit] (*adj.*), *F:* excellent*, bœuf, chouette.

faze [feiz] (**to**) (*U.S.*), *F:* gêner (qn), casser les pieds à (qn), courir sur l'haricot (*ou* le haricot) à qn.

fear [ˈfiər] (*noun*), *F:* **no f.!** pas de danger! sois sans crainte!

fearful [ˈfiəful] (*adj.*), *F:* **1.** terrible, formidable; **f. bore,** emmerdeur *m*, emmerdement *m*, casse-pieds *m.* **2.** en abondance*; **a f. lot,** une tapée, une flopée.

fearfully [ˈfiəfəli] (*adv.*), *F:* terriblement, fichtrement, bigrement.

feather[1] [ˈfeðər] (*noun*). **1.** *F:* **birds of a f.,** du pareil au même, du même acabit (*ou* bateau *ou* bord). **2.** *F:* **a f. in one's cap,** une perle à sa couronne, un bon point. **3.** *F:* **in high f.,** en pleine forme, plein d'entrain. **4.** *F:* **to show the** (**white**) **f.,** laisser voir qu'on a peur*, caner, caler. **5.** *F:* **you could have knocked me down with a f.!** j'ai pensé tomber de mon haut! **6.** (*pl.*) *P:* lit*, plumard *m*; **to hit the feathers,** se coucher*, se plumer. **7.** *F:* **to make the feathers fly** = **to make the fur fly** (*voir* **fur**). **8.** (*pl.*) *F: voir* **bingo** (**33**).

feather[2] [ˈfeðər] (**to**), *F:* **to f. one's nest,** faire ses choux gras, faire sa pelote (*ou* son beurre), mettre du foin dans ses bottes.

feather-bed [ˈfeðəbed] (*noun*), *F:* traitement *m* de faveur, fromage *m.*

featherbrain [ˈfeðəbrein] (*noun*), *F:* individu bête*, tête *f* de linotte; **she's a f.,** c'est une petite évaporée.

featherbrained [ˈfeðəbreind] (*adj.*), *F:* bête*, à tête de linotte, écervelé, évaporé; **to be f.,** avoir une cervelle de moineau.

fed[1] [fed] (*adj.*), *P:* = **fed up.**

fed[2], **Fed** [fed] (*noun*) (*abbr.* = *Federal Agent*) (*U.S.*), *F:* **1.** fonctionnaire fédéral de l'ordre judiciaire. **2.** agent *m* de la Brigade fédérale des Stupéfiants.

fed up [ˈfedˈʌp] (*adj.*), *F:* (*a*) **to be f. u.** (**to the back teeth**), en avoir assez*, en avoir sa claque, en avoir ras le bol, en avoir (plus que) marre; (*b*) **I'm f. u. with him,** il me tape sur le système, il m'enquiquine, j'ai soupé de lui.

feed [fiːd] (*noun*), *F:* **to be off one's f.,** être malade*, n'être pas dans son assiette. *Voir aussi* **chicken-feed.**

feeding [ˈfiːdiŋ] (*adj.*), *P:* ennuyeux*, barbe, canulant.

feel[1] [fiːl] (*noun*), *P:* attouchement *m*, tripotage *m*, pelotage *m.*

feel[2] [fiːl] (**to**). **1.** *P:* caresser, peloter (une femme); aller aux renseignements, mettre la main au panier. **2.** *F:* **do you f. like it?** est-ce que cela te chante? est-ce que le cœur t'en dit?

feel up [ˈfiːlˈʌp] (**to**), *P:* = **feel**[2] (**to**), **1.**

feet [fiːt] (*pl. noun*): *voir* **foot**[1].

* An asterisk indicates that the word so marked is included as a head-word in the Appendix.

feeze[1] [fiːz] (*noun*) (*U.S.*), *P:* potin *m*, chichis *m.pl.*, histoires *f.pl.*
feeze[2] [fiːz] (**to**) (*U.S.*), *P:* en faire un plat, faire des histoires (*ou* des chichis *ou* des arias).
feisty [ˈfaisti] (*adj.*) (*U.S.*), *F:* hargneux, irritable, de mauvais poil.
feller [ˈfelər] (*noun*), *F:* (=*fellow*) (*a*) individu*, type *m*, mec *m*, coco *m*; (*b*) prétendant *m*, soupirant *m*, amoureux *m*.
fem [fem] (*noun*), *P:* **1.** femme*. **2.** lesbienne* (qui tient le rôle de la femme), gavousse *f*.
female [ˈfiːmeil] (*noun*), *F:* femme* (*péj.*), femelle *f*, fumelle *f*.
fence[1] [fens] (*noun*), *F:* **1.** receleur*, fourgueur *m*, lessiveur *m*. **2. to sit on the f.**, ménager la chèvre et le chou, nager entre deux eaux, ne pas se mouiller. **3.** (*Austr.*) **over the f.** = **over the edge** (**edge**[1], **2**).
fence[2] [fens] (**to**), *F:* receler, fourguer.
fencing [ˈfensiŋ] (*noun*), *F:* recelage *m*, fourgage *m*, lessivage *m*, fourgue *f*.
fest [fest] (*noun*), *F:* fête *f*, festival *m*, gala *m*; *voir aussi* **chinfest; eatfest; gabfest; popfest; slugfest.**
fetch[1] [fetʃ] (*noun*), *F:* ruse *f*, attrape *f*, truc *m*, attrape-couillons *m*.
fetch[2] [fetʃ] (**to**), *F:* séduire, emballer, taper dans l'œil. *Voir aussi* **clonk**[1]; **clout**[1], **1**; **one, 3.**
fetching [ˈfetʃiŋ] (*adj.*), *F:* beau*, chic, chouette.
fetch up [ˈfetʃˈʌp] (**to**), *F:* vomir*, refiler, dégobiller.
few [fjuː] (*pl. noun*), *F:* **to have (had) a f.**, être ivre*, avoir bu un coup de trop, avoir un verre dans le nez.
fib[1] [fib] (*noun*), *F:* mensonge*, craque *f*.
fib[2] [fib] (**to**), *F:* mentir*, en conter.
fibber [ˈfibər] (*noun*), *F:* menteur *m*, craqueur *m*.
fiddle[1] [ˈfidl] (*noun*), *F:* **1.** violon *m*, crincrin *m*, frémillon *m*. **2.** combine *f* (à la gomme); *cf.* **work**[2] (**to**), **1. 3.** fricotage *m*; **to be on the f.**, fricoter. **4. to be as fit as a f.**, se porter comme un charme. **5. to play second f.**, jouer en sous-fifre.
fiddle[2] [ˈfidl] (**to**), *F:* **1.** violoner, racler du violon. **2. to f. the income tax**, rouler le percepteur, maquiller sa feuille d'impôts. **3.** combiner, fricoter, trafiquer. **4.** barboter, écornifler.
fiddle about [ˈfidl-əˈbaut] (**to**), *F:* (*a*) aller et venir, traînasser, flânocher; (*b*) bricoler.
fiddle-arse about [ˈfidlˈɑːsəˈbaut] (**to**), *P:* = **fiddle about (to)**, (*b*).
fiddle-arsed [ˈfidl-ɑːst] (*adj.*), *P:* insignifiant, cucul, camelote.
fiddlede(e)dee! [ˈfidldi(ː)ˈdiː] (*excl.*), *F:* = **fiddlesticks!**
fiddle-faddle[1] [ˈfidlfædl] (*noun*), *F:* bêtise*, baliverne *f*.
fiddle-faddle[2] [ˈfidlfædl] (**to**), *F:* musarder, baguenauder, tatillonner, chercher midi à quatorze heures.
fiddler [ˈfidlər] (*noun*), *F:* **1.** racleur *m* de violon. **2.** fricoteur *m*, combinard *m*. **3.** écornifleur *m*, pique-assiette *m*. **4.** (*a*) baguenaudeur *m*; (*b*) bricoleur *m*.
fiddlestick [ˈfidl-stik] (*noun*), *F:* **1.** archet *m* (*ou* baguette *f*) de violon. **2.** un rien, un brin, une vétille.
fiddlesticks! [ˈfidl-stiks] (*excl.*), *F:* balivernes! quelle bêtise*! quelle blague!
fiddling[1] [ˈfidliŋ] (*adj.*), *F:* insignifiant; **f. queries**, questions oiseuses (*ou* futiles *ou* agaçantes).
fiddling[2] [ˈfidliŋ] (*noun*), *F:* **1.** raclage *m* de violon. **2.** combine *f*, fricotage *m*. **3.** écorniflage *m*, manche *f*. **4.** (*a*) baguenaudage *m*, tripotage *m*; (*b*) bricolage *m*.
fiddly [ˈfidli] (*adj.*), *F:* **a f. job**, un travail délicat, un sac de nœuds.
fidgets [ˈfidʒits] (*pl. noun*), *F:* **to have the f.**, avoir la bougeotte, ne pas tenir en place, être assis sur une pile électrique.
fiend [fiːnd] (*noun*), *F:* amateur passionné, fana *m*, emballé *m*, mordu *m*; **fresh-air f.**, pleinairiste *mf*, fervent du plein air; **sex f.**, coureur *m* de jupon, queutard *m*; **dope f.**, toxico(mane) *mf*, drogué*, morphinomane *mf*.
fierce [ˈfiəs] (*adj.*), *F:* affreux, détestable, épouvantable; **f. weather**, temps *m* de chien.
fifty-fifty [ˈfiftiˈfifti] (*adj. & adv.*), *F:* à parts égales, moitié-moitié, afanaf; **to go f.-f.**, se mettre de moitié; **a f.-f. chance**, une chance sur deux; *cf.* **half**[1], **5** (*b*).
fig[1] [fig] (*noun*). **1.** *V:* vagin*, figue *f*.

* L'astérisque indique que le mot marqué de ce signe figure comme entrée dans le Répertoire.

2. *F:* **I don't care a f.**, je m'en moque pas mal, je m'en fiche éperdument. 3. *F:* **full f.**, tenue *f* de soirée, queue de pie; **in full f.**, sur son trente et un.

fig[2] [fig] (**to**), *P:* doper (un cheval).

figure [ˈfigə] (**to**), *F:* 1. compter (sur qch.), penser; **they don't f. he'll live,** on ne pense pas le sauver. 2. **that figures,** ça va de soi, ça va sans dire. 3. **I f. that's O.K.**, ça m'a l'air régulier (*ou* O.K.), ça a l'air d'aller.

figure out [ˈfigərˈaʊt] (**to**), *F:* 1. calculer, supputer, chiffrer. 2. comprendre; **he can't f. it o.**, ça le dépasse. *Voir aussi* **angle, 2.**

file [fail] (*noun*), *P:* 1. malin *m*, roublard *m*, matois *m*. 2. tireur *m*, fourchette *f*.

fill-in [ˈfilin] (*noun*), *F:* 1. sommaire *m*, tuyautage *m*, mise *f* au courant. 2. suppléant *m*, intérim *m*, volant *m*.

fill in [ˈfilˈin] (**to**), *F:* 1. **to f. s.o. i. (on sth.)**, affranchir qn, mettre qn au courant (*ou* au parfum), faire le point pour qn. 2. faire le remplaçant; **to f. i. for s.o.**, suppléer, remplacer qn.

filly [ˈfili] (*noun*), *F:* jeune fille* fringante, jolie pouliche.

filter [ˈfiltər] (**to**), *P:* déserter, faire chibis à la grive.

filthy [ˈfilθi] (*adj.*), *F:* 1. (*a*) sale*, cradingue; **f. weather,** temps *m* de chien (*ou* de cochon), bougre *m* de temps; (*b*) **don't be f.!** ne sors pas d'ordures!; **you've got a f. mind,** tu es mal embouché. 2. riche*; **the f. rich,** les (sales) rupins, les pleins aux as, les cousus d'or. 3. (*sport*) **f. player,** joueur salaud. *Voir aussi* **lucre.**

fin [fin] (*noun*), *P:* 1. main*, pince *f*, patte *f*; **tip us your f.**, serre-moi la pince; on y va de cinq; *cf.* **flipper.** 2. bras*, aile *f*, nageoire *f*.

finagle [finˈeigl] (**to**), *F:* manigancer, resquiller; (*cartes*) renoncer.

finagler [finˈeiglər] (*noun*), *F:* manigancer *m*, fricoteur *m*, resquilleur *m*.

fine[1] [fain] (*adj.*), *F:* 1. chic, parfait; **it's all very f. but . . .**, tout cela est bien joli (*ou* bel et bien) mais... 2. **one f. day,** un beau matin, un de ces quatre matins.

fine[2] [fain] (*adv.*), *F:* 1. **I'm doing f.!** je me débrouille bien! 2. **you're doing f.:** *voir* **bingo** (29). *Voir aussi* **cut**[3] (**to**), 3.

finger[1] [ˈfiŋgər] (*noun*). 1. *P:* indicateur*, mouchard *m*, donneur *m*; **to put the f. on s.o.**, (*a*) balancer qn, enfoncer qn; (*b*) dénoncer* qn, donner qn (à la police), balanstiquer qn, cafarder qn. 2. *F:* **to pull one's f. out,** se secouer, se dégrouiller; **pull your f. out! finger(s) out!** secoue tes puces! 3. *F:* **to put one's f. on it** (*the real issue, etc.*), mettre le doigt dessus. 4. *P:* **fingers to you!** je t'emmerde!; *cf.* **fingers-up.** 5. *F:* **to have a f. in the pie,** (*a*) y être mêlé, y être pour quelque chose; (*b*) en être. 6. *F:* **to lay a f. on s.o.**, toucher qn, amocher qn. 7. *F:* **not to lift a f. (to help s.o.)**, ne pas se remuer, ne pas lever le petit doigt (pour aider qn). 8. *F:* **to twist s.o. round one's little f.**, entortiller qn, faire tourner (et virer) qn (en bourrique), faire de qn tout ce qu'on veut. 9. (*U.S.*) *P:* **to give s.o. the f.**, (*a*) faire une crasse à qn; (*b*) snober qn, bazarder qn; **she was giving me the polite f.**, elle me snobait, elle me donnait le signal du départ. 10. *F:* **to keep one's fingers crossed,** toucher du bois. 11. *F:* **to lift** (*or* **raise**) **the little f.**, boire*, lever le coude. 12. *P:* **f. artist,** lesbienne*, gouchotte *f*. *Voir aussi* **butterfingers; fruit-basket; green**[1], **5; sticky, 3; thumb, 1.**

finger[2] [ˈfiŋgər] (**to**). 1. *P:* (*a*) fouiller (qn); (*b*) dénoncer*, moucharder, balancer (qn). 2. *P:* **to f. sth.**, (*a*) chaparder, chiper, griffer qch.; (*b*) receler, fourguer qch. 3. *V:* **to f. oneself,** (*d'une femme*) se masturber*, s'astiquer le boilton.

finger-fuck[1] [ˈfiŋgəfʌk], **finger-job** [ˈfiŋgədʒɔb] (*noun*), *VV:* (*d'une femme*) masturbation *f*, gerbe *f*.

finger-fuck[2] [ˈfiŋgəfʌk] (**to**), *VV:* (*d'une femme*) (*a*) se masturber*; (*b*) mettre la main au panier.

fingers-up [ˈfiŋgəzˈʌp] (*noun*), *V:* geste *m* obscène de défi et de mépris.

finisher [ˈfiniʃər] (*noun*), *F:* knock-out *m*, coup* de la fin, coup d'assommoir.

fink[1] [fiŋk] (*noun*) (*mainly U.S.*), *P:* 1. briseur *m* de grèves, jaune *m*, faux frère, traître *m*. 2. clochard*, clodo *m*. 3. vaurien*, fripouille *f*, ordure *f*, fumier *m*; *cf.* **ratfink.** 4. détective privé, policier*, poulet *m*, perdreau *m*. 5. indicateur*, indic *m*, donneur *m*,

* An asterisk indicates that the word so marked is included as a head-word in the Appendix.

cafard *m.* **6.** des rossignols *m.pl.*, de la pacotille.

fink[2] [fiŋk] (**to**) (*mainly U.S.*), *P:* **1.** dénoncer* (à la police), cafarder, balancer. **2.** se dégonfler, se déballonner, foirer.

fire[1] [ˈfaiər] (*noun*), *F:* **1. between two fires,** entre deux feux. **2. to hang f.,** traîner, faire long feu. **3. to play with f.,** jouer avec le feu. **4. running f.,** feu roulant (de questions). **5. under f.,** sur la sellette. **6. where's the f.?** il y a le feu sur le pont? *Voir aussi* **sure-fire; Thames.**

fire[2] [ˈfaiər] (**to**), *F:* balancer, sacquer, dégommer (qn).

fire away [ˈfaiərəˈwei] (**to**), *F:* commencer (à parler), se lancer; **f. a.!** allez-y! dites toujours! à vous d'ouvrir le feu!

fireball [ˈfaiəbɔːl] (*noun*), *F:* = **ball of fire (ball**[1]**, 6).**

fire-bug [ˈfaiəbʌg] (*noun*), *F:* incendiaire *mf*, boutefeu *m.*

fire-eater [ˈfaiəriːtər] (*noun*), *F:* matamore *m.*

fire off [ˈfaiəˈrɔf] (**to**), *F:* lancer, décocher.

fire up [ˈfaiəˈrʌp] (**to**). **1.** *F:* se mettre en colère*, s'emporter, voir rouge. **2.** *P:* fumer la marijuana (*drogues**).

fire-water [ˈfaiəwɔːtər] (*noun*), *F:* alcool*, casse-gueule *m*, tord-boyaux *m.*

fireworks [ˈfaiəwəːks] (*pl. noun*), *F:* **1.** éclat *m* de colère, pétard *m*, grabuge *m.* **2. if you do that again there'll be f.!** si tu recommences, ça va barder (*ou* il y aura du grabuge)!

first [fəːst] (*adj.*), *F:* **I'll do it f. thing,** c'est ce que je ferai en premier; je le ferai avant tout.

first-class [ˈfəːstˈklɑːs], **first-rate** [ˈfəːstˈreit] (*adv.*), *F:* excellemment, au poil, de première; **it's going f.-c., f.-r.,** ça marche à merveille.

first-rater [ˈfəːstˈreitər] (*noun*), *F:* as *m*, crack *m.*

first-timer [ˈfəːstˈtaimər] (*noun*), *F:* prisonnier *m* pour la première fois, un nouveau de la lourde.

fish[1] [fiʃ] (*noun*). **1.** *F:* individu*, zèbre *m*; **a queer f.,** un drôle d'oiseau (*ou* de client); **a poor f.,** un paumé. **2.** *F:* **to cry stinking f.,** se dénigrer, se déprécier. **3.** *F:* **to feed the fishes,** (*a*) avoir le mal de mer, donner à manger aux poissons; (*b*) se noyer, boire le bouillon. **4.** *F:* **to have other f. to fry,** avoir d'autres chiens (*ou* chats) à fouetter. **5.** *F:* **to be like a f. out of water,** ne pas être dans son élément; **like a f. out of water,** comme un poisson hors de l'eau. **6.** *F:* **to drink like a f.,** boire* comme un trou (*ou* un tonneau). **7.** *P:* **a fresh f.,** (*a*) un nouveau, un bleu; (*b*) qn arrêté pour la première fois, un ramassé de preu. *Voir aussi* **cold**[1]**, 5; jellyfish; kettle, 2; tin**[1]**, 4.**

fish[2] [fiʃ] (**to**), *F:* **1.** aller à la pêche, tirer les vers du nez à qn; **to f. for compliments,** quêter des compliments. **2. to f. in troubled waters,** pêcher en eau trouble.

fish-bowl [ˈfiʃboul] (*noun*) (*U.S.*), *P:* = **tank, 2.**

fish-pond [ˈfiʃpɔnd], **fish-shop** [ˈfiʃʃɔp] (*noun*), *P:* vulve*, boîte *f* à ouvrage, bénitier *m.*

fish-tank [ˈfiʃtæŋk] (*noun*) (*U.S.*), *P:* = **tank, 2.**

fish-wrapper [ˈfiʃræpər] (*noun*), *F:* journal*, canard *m.*

fishy [ˈfiʃi] (*adj.*), *F:* douteux, louche, équivoque, véreux; **it looks f.,** ça ne dit rien de bon (*ou* rien qui vaille).

fist [fist] (*noun*), *P:* main*, pogne *f*, paluche *f. Voir aussi* **hand**[1]**, 2.**

fistful [ˈfistful] (*noun*), *F:* **a f. of money,** un tas d'argent*, le sac, flouze *m* à la pelle.

fit[1] [fit] (*adj.*), *F:* **are you f.?** es-tu prêt? tu te sens d'attaque? *Voir aussi* **dressed; drop**[2] **(to), 7; dump**[1]**, 3.**

fit[2] [fit] (*noun*). **1.** *F:* **to have** (*or* **throw**) **a f.,** (*a*) piquer une colère*, se mettre à cran; (*b*) avoir peur*, avoir les foies. **2.** *F:* **to have s.o. in fits,** faire rire* qn, faire boyauter qn, donner le fou-rire à qn. **3.** *P:* instance judiciaire qui peut être retournée contre un criminel; beurre *m.* **4.** *P:* **fainting fits** (*R.S.* = *tits*), seins*, tétons *m.pl.*; *cf.* **Bristols; tale, 3; threepenny-bits; trey-bits. 5.** *P:* attirail *m* de camé.

fit-out [ˈfitaut] (*noun*), *F:* attirail *m*, équipement *m*, barda *m.*

five [faiv] (*numeral adj. & noun*), *F:* **1. take f.!** arrêt buffet! dételez un peu! **2. to give f.,** en écraser cinq, y aller de cinq; *cf.* **bunch, 2.**

* L'astérisque indique que le mot marqué de ce signe figure comme entrée dans le Répertoire.

fiver ['faivər] (*noun*), *F:* (*a*) cinq livres *f.pl.* sterling; gros faffiot; (*b*) billet* de cinq livres *ou* de cinq dollars.
five-spot ['faivspɔt] (*noun*) (*U.S.*), *F:* **1.** billet* de cinq dollars. **2.** emprisonnement *m* de cinq années, cinq longes *f.pl.* (*ou* berges *f.pl.*). **3.** le cinq.
fix[1] [fiks] (*noun*). **1.** *P:* (*a*) le fixe, la piquouse, le joint; **to take a f.,** se piquer; (*b*) quantité *f* de drogue vendue en sac *ou* en paquet; fixe *m*. **2.** *P:* **the f.,** (*a*) pot-de-vin *m*, dessous-de-table *m*; (*b*) graissage *m* de patte (de la police, *etc.*). **3.** *F:* difficulté *f*, mauvais pas; **to be in a f.,** être dans une situation embarrassante; **to get into a f.,** se mettre dans le pétrin. **4.** *F:* éléments *m.pl.* et données *f.pl.* qui permettent de déterminer la position d'un bateau *ou* d'un avion.
fix[2] [fiks] (**to**). **1.** *F:* arranger, mettre en ordre. **2.** *F:* réparer, retaper, rabibocher. **3.** *F:* préparer, décider (d'un jour, d'une heure); **I'm fixing to go to London,** je compte aller à Londres. **4.** *F:* soudoyer, suborner. **5.** *P:* rendre la pareille à (qn); **I'll f. him!** je lui ferai son affaire! je l'aurai au tournant! **6.** *F:* **how are you fixed (for money)?** es-tu paré côté argent? **7.** *F:* **to f. a fight,** truquer un combat. **8.** *P:* s'injecter une drogue, avoir un fixe, faire une piquouse.
fixer ['fiksər] (*noun*), *P:* **1.** avocat* véreux, arrangeur *m*, faisan *m*. **2.** pourvoyeur *m* de drogues, fourgue(ur) *m*, porteur *m*.
fixings ['fiksiŋz] (*pl. noun*), *F:* fourniture *f*, équipement *m*, garniture *f*.
fixture ['fikstʃər] (*noun*), *F:* **1. to be a (permanent) f.,** (*d'une personne*) faire partie des meubles, être fixé en permanence. **2. I've got a full f. list,** j'ai un programme bien rempli. **3.** voiture* ventouse.
fix-up ['fiksʌp] (*noun*), *P:* = **fix**[1], **1.**
fix up ['fiks'ʌp] (**to**), *F:* **1. to f. u. accommodation for s.o.,** caser qn. **2. to f. s.o. u. with a job,** trouver un emploi à qn. **3. they got fixed up,** (*a*) ils se sont fait mettre en règle; (*b*) ils se sont casés. **4.** réparer, rapetasser, rafistoler.
fizz [fiz] (*noun*), *F:* champagne *m*, champ(e) *m*.
fizzer ['fizər] (*noun*), *F:* **1.** qch. d'excellent* (*ou* de super), du tonnerre. **2.** balle rapide lancée à toute vitesse. **3.** (*mil.*) **to be on a f.,** être consigné au rapport.
fizzle[1] ['fizl] (*noun*), *P:* **1.** échec*, bide *m*. **2.** raté *m*, fruit sec.
fizzle[2] ['fizl] (**to**), *F:* échouer*, se casser le nez, faire chou blanc.
fizzle out ['fizl'aut] (**to**), *F:* ne pas aboutir, finir en queue de poisson, foirer, s'en aller en eau de boudin.
flabbergast ['flæbəgɑːst] (**to**), *F:* épater; **I was flabbergasted,** j'en suis resté baba.
flabby ['flæbi] (*adj.*), *F:* avachi, mou comme une chique.
flag[1] [flæg] (*noun*). **1.** *F:* **to show the f.,** faire acte de présence, faire une apparition. **2.** *P:* faux nom*, blaze *m*, alias *m*. **3.** *F:* **to lower one's f.,** baisser pavillon. **4.** *F:* **to keep the f. flying,** tenir bon, se défendre. **5.** *P:* **to fly the f.,** avoir ses menstrues*, repeindre sa grille en rouge.
flag[2] **(down)** ['flæg('daun)] (**to**), *F:* arrêter (une voiture, *etc.*) au drapeau.
flag-pole ['flægpoul] (*noun*), *F:* = **beanpole.**
flag-wagger ['flægwægər], **flag-waver** ['flægweivər] (*noun*), *F:* **1.** cocardier *m*, chauvin *m*. **2.** signaleur *m*.
flag-wagging ['flægwægiŋ], **flag-waving** ['flægweiviŋ] (*noun*), *F:* le chauvinisme, la cocarde.
flake [fleik] (*noun*), *P:* cocaïne *f* (*drogues**), poudrette *f*.
flaked (out) ['fleikt('aut)] (*adj.*), *F:* = **flakers.**
flake out ['fleik'aut] (**to**), *F:* **1.** s'évanouir*, tourner de l'œil. **2.** être très fatigué*, avoir le coup de barre (*ou* de pompe).
flakers ['fleikəz] (*adj.*), *P:* **(Harry) f.,** très fatigué*, crevé, esquinté, claqué.
flam[1] [flæm] (*noun*), *F:* **1.** histoire *f*, chiqué *m*, trompe-l'œil *m*, salades *f.pl.* **2.** (*U.S.*) escroquerie*, arnaque *f*, blague *f*; *cf.* **flimflam**[1]. **3.** lèche-cul *m*, eau bénite (de cour).
flam[2] [flæm] (**to**), *F:* **1.** escroquer*, arnaquer, refaire, rouler; *cf.* **flimflam**[2] **(to)**. **2.** flirter avec (qn). **3.** se rebiffer.
flame [fleim] (*noun*), *F:* béguin *m*, flamme *f*; **an old f.,** une de mes anciennes (amours). *Voir aussi* **shoot down (to).**

* An asterisk indicates that the word so marked is included as a head-word in the Appendix.

flaming [ˈfleimiŋ] (*adj.*), *F:* (*a*) **a f. temper,** un caractère infernal; (*b*) **a f. row,** une querelle* du tonnerre, un barouf de tous les diables; (*c*) **a f. idiot,** un satané crétin, un imbécile achevé.

flannel[1] [ˈflæn(ə)l] (*noun*), *F:* flatterie *f,* huile (versée sur les rouages), pommade *f,* lèche *f,* eau bénite.

flannel[2] [ˈflæn(ə)l] (**to**), *F:* acheter les bonnes grâces de (qn); verser de l'huile sur les rouages, passer la pommade.

flanneller [ˈflænələr] (*noun*), *F:* flatteur *m,* bonimenteur *m,* lèche-bottes *m.*

flannelling [ˈflænəliŋ] (*noun*), *F:* = **flannel**[1].

flap[1] [flæp] (*noun*). **1.** *F:* affolement *m,* panique *f;* **to be in a f.,** être dans tous ses états; **to get into a f.,** paniquer, s'affoler. **2.** (*pl.*) *P:* oreilles*, pavillons *m.pl.,* anses *f.pl.*

flap[2] [flæp] (**to**), *F:* = **to get into a flap** (**flap**[1], **1**).

flapdoodle [ˈflæpˈdu:dl] (*noun*), *F:* bêtise*, bidon *m,* salades *f.pl.;* baratin *m.*

flapjaw [ˈflæpdʒɔ:] (*noun*), *F:* **1.** bavardage *m,* bavette *f,* papotage *m.* **2.** bavard*, jacteur *m,* tapette *f.*

flapper [ˈflæpər] (*noun*). **1.** *F:* jeune fille*, gamine *f,* loulou *f.* **2.** *P:* = **fin, 1;** *cf.* **flipper.**

flare-up [ˈflɛərʌp] (*noun*), *F:* (*a*) une colère bleue; (*b*) altercation *f,* scène *f;* (*c*) bagarre *, grabuge *m.*

flare up [ˈflɛəˈrʌp] (**to**), *F:* se mettre en colère*, s'emporter.

flash[1] [flæʃ] (*adj.*). **1.** *F:* voyant, tapageur; **F. Harry** (*or* **Jimmy**), Fredo l'Esbrouf(f)e, minet *m,* un m'as-tu-vu. **2.** *P:* contrefait, toc, bidon. **3.** qui est du milieu, de la pègre.

flash[2] [flæʃ] (*noun*). **1.** *F:* (*a*) épate *f,* esbrouf(f)e *f;* (*b*) clinquant *m,* tape-à-l'œil *m.* **2.** *F:* **a f. in the pan,** un feu de paille. **3.** *P:* le flash, le bang (des drogués); *cf.* **rush**[1]. **4.** *P:* argot* des voleurs, arguemuche *m* du milieu, jars *m.* **5.** *P:* œillade*, clin *m* d'œil, coup *m* de sabord. **6.** *F:* pensée-éclair *f,* idée-éclair *f.*

flash[3] [flæʃ] (**to**), *P:* **1.** arborer, étaler. **2.** crâner, plastronner. **3.** exhiber ses organes génitaux (*ou* ses parties *f.pl.*).

flasher [ˈflæʃər] (*noun*), *P:* qn qui exhibe ses parties *f.pl.;* satyre *m.*

flashy [ˈflæʃi] (*adj.*), *F:* (*a*) = **flash**[1], **1;** (*b*) qui jette du jus.

flat[1] [flæt] (*adj.*). **1.** *F:* net, catégorique; **that's f.!** c'est clair et net! c'est mon dernier mot! **2.** *P:* ruiné*, fauché, raide, à la côte. *Voir aussi* **spin, 1.**

flat[2] [flæt] (*adv.*), *F:* **1.** entièrement, tout à fait; **f. broke,** fauché comme les blés, grand schlem. **2.** exactement, au poil. **3.** carrément, catégoriquement. **4. to go f. out,** (*a*) se mettre en quatre; (*b*) aller bille en tête, mettre le paquet; (*c*) aller à fond de train (*ou* à plein gaz). **5. to fall f.** (**on its face**), (*a*) (*plaisanterie*) manquer son effet, rater; (*b*) (*pièce*) faire four. *Voir aussi* **nothing, 2.**

flat[3] [flæt] (*noun*). **1.** *P:* individu *m* bête*, nouille *f,* cave *m.* **2.** *F:* pneu *m* à plat.

flat-backer [ˈflætbækər] (*noun*), *P:* prostituée*, bourrin *m.*

flatfoot [ˈflætfʊt] (*noun*), *F:* agent* de police, poulet *m.*

flatfooted [ˈflætˈfʊtid] (*adj.*), *P:* **1.** bête*, lourdaud, pied, empoté. **2. to be caught f.,** être pris la main dans le sac, être piqué sur le tas.

flathead [ˈflæthed] (*noun*), *P:* = **flat**[3], **1.**

flatheaded [ˈflætˈhedid] (*adj.*), *P:* bête*, bas de plafond.

flatten [ˈflætn] (**to**), *F:* **1.** mettre (qn) knock-out, knockouter (qn). **2.** aplatir, déconcerter, déconfire (qn).

flattener [ˈflætnər] (*noun*), *F:* coup* d'assommoir, knock-out *m,* un K.O.

flattie, flatty [ˈflæti] (*noun*), *P:* **1.** = **flatfoot.** **2.** femme aux seins* plats, une planche à repasser.

flea [fli:] (*noun*), *F:* **1.** individu ennuyeux*, barbe *f,* crampon *m,* raseur *m.* **2. to send s.o. away with a f. in his ear,** secouer les puces *f.pl.* à qn, dire à qn ses quatre vérités.

fleabag [ˈfli:bæg] (*noun*), *P:* **1.** (*a*) sac *m* de couchage; (*b*) lit*, pucier *m;* (*c*) matelas *m.* **2.** pouilleux *m,* sac *m* à puces. **3.** mauvais cheval* de course, tocard *m,* bourrin *m,* bique *f.* **4.** = **fleapit,** (*a*).

fleabite [ˈfli:bait] (*noun*), *F:* un rien, une bagatelle, une vétille, une broutille.

flea-bitten [ˈfli:bitn] (*adj.*), *F:* sale*, pouilleux, miteux, craspouillard.

flea-house [ˈfli:haʊs] (*noun*), *P:* **1.** hôtel *m* borgne, hôtel des Trois Canards. **2.** = **fleapit** (*b*).

* L'astérisque indique que le mot marqué de ce signe figure comme entrée dans le Répertoire.

flea-market [ˈfliː-mɑːkit] (*noun*), *F:* marché *m* aux puces.
fleapit [ˈfliː-pit], **flea-trap** [ˈfliː-træp] (*noun*), *F:* (*a*) piaule *f*, taudis *m*, nid *m* (*ou* trou *m*) à puces, bouge *m*; asile *m* de nuit; (*b*) cinéma *m*.
fleece [ˈfliːs] (**to**), *F:* estamper, plumer, écorcher (qn).
flesh-peddler [ˈfleʃpedlər] (*noun*), *F:* **1.** souteneur*, mangeur *m* de blanc, maquereau *m*. **2.** prostituée*, marcheuse *f*, raccrocheuse *f*.
flick [flik] (*noun*), *F:* **1.** film *m*, ciné *m*, cinoche *m*. **2.** cinéma *m*; **to go to a f.** (*or* **to the flicks**), aller au cinetoche. *Voir aussi* **skin-flick.**
flier [ˈflaiər] (*noun*), *F:* **to take a f.**, (*a*) risquer le paquet; (*b*) tomber*, ramasser une bûche, prendre une pelle. *Voir aussi* **high-flier.**
flim [flim] (*noun*), *P:* **1.** billet* de cinq livres; *cf.* **flimsy, 2. 2.** cinq longes *f.pl.* (*ou* berges *f.pl.*) en taule.
flimflam[1] [ˈflimflæm] (*noun*) (*U.S.*), *F:* escroquerie*, filouterie *f*, entubage *m*.
flimflam[2] [ˈflimflæm] (**to**) (*U.S.*), *F:* escroquer*, filouter, entuber.
flimflammer [ˈflimflæmər] (*noun*) (*U.S.*), *F:* escroc*, entôleur *m*, filou *m*.
flimsy [ˈflimzi] (*noun*). **1.** *F:* papier-pelure *m*. **2.** *F:* billet* de banque, faf(f)iot *m*, faffe *m*. **3.** *P:* télégramme *m*, petit bleu.
fling [fliŋ] (*noun*), *F:* **1.** réjouissances*, bamboche *f*, foire *f*. **2.** boum *f*, coup *m* de bastringue, guinche *f*. **3. to take a f.**, tenter sa chance. **4. to have one's f.**, jeter sa gourme. **5. to have a f. at s.o.**, envoyer (*ou* lancer) un trait à qn.
flip[1] [flip] (*adj.*). **1.** *P:* impudent, désinvolte, culotté, qui a du toupet. **2.** *P:* mordu pour qch., qui en pince. **3.** *F:* **f. side (of a record)**, revers *m* (d'un disque).
flip[2] [flip] (*noun*). **1.** *F:* un petit tour, une virée (en auto, *etc.*). **2.** *P:* faveur *f*, gracieuseté *f*; **do me a f.**, fais-moi une fleur. **3.** *P:* rigolade *f*, bonne blague. **4.** *P:* fervent *m*, fana(tique) *mf*, mordu *m*. **5.** *P:* peur*, délire *m* des drogués.
flip[3] [flip] (**to**). **1.** *P:* s'emballer, tiquer, entraver. **2.** *P:* **to f. one's top** (*or* **lid** *or* (*U.S.*) **noodle** *or* **raspberry** *or* **wig**), être très en colère*, sortir de ses gonds, piquer une crise. **3.** (*U.S.*) *P:* rouler dans un train sans payer, brûler le dur. **4.** *P:* faire rire* (*ou* gondoler *ou* bidonner) (qn). **5.** *P:* emballer, botter (qn). **6.** *P:* **to f. one's lip,** (*a*) bavarder*, jacasser, baver; (*b*) dire des bêtises*, dégoiser, radoter. **7.** *F:* **to f. a coin,** jouer à pile ou face. **8.** *P:* faire une dépression émotive, être claqué. **9.** *P:* dénoncer*, bourdiller.
flip out [ˈflipˈaut] (**to**), *P:* = **freak out** (**to**), **1, 2, 3.**
flipper [ˈflipər] (*noun*), *P:* = **fin, 1.**
flipping [ˈflipiŋ] (*adj.*), *F:* satané, fichu; **it's a f. nuisance,** c'est un fichu embêtement.
flit[1] [flit] (*noun*). **1.** *F:* **to do a moonlight f.**, déménager à la cloche de bois. **2.** *F:* fuite *f*, enlèvement *m*. **3.** *P:* pédéraste*, lope *f*.
flit[2] [flit] (**to**), *F:* **1.** = **to do a moonlight flit** (**flit**[1], **1**). **2.** s'enfuir* (avec un amant, *etc.*), se faire enlever.
fliv [fliv] (*noun*), *P:* = **flivver, 1.**
flivver [ˈflivər] (*noun*), *P:* **1.** vieille voiture*, guimbarde *f*, tinette *f*. **2.** échec*, bide *m*, fiasco *m*, four *m*. **3.** supercherie *f*, farce *f*, fumisterie *f*, canular(d) *m*. **4.** porte-guigne *m*, porte-poisse *m*.
float[1] [flout] (*noun*), *P:* client qui sort pendant que le marchand cherche l'article; volant *m*.
float[2] [flout] (**to**), *P:* **to f. one,**(*a*) toucher un chèque; (*b*) prêter de l'argent*. *Voir aussi* **air**[1]**, 2.**
float about (*or* **around**) [ˈfloutəˈbaut, ˈfloutəˈraund] (**to**), *F:* **to f. names a.**, lancer des noms*.
floater [ˈfloutər] (*noun*), *F:* **1.** un prêt, argent* prêté *ou* emprunté*, tapage *m*, sonnage *m*. **2.** bévue*, faux pas, gaffe *f*, bourde *f*. **3.** (*a*) vagabond*, vacant *m*; (*b*) ouvrier itinérant.
floating [ˈfloutiŋ] (*adj.*) (*U.S.*), *F:* (*a*) ivre*, dans les vapes; (*b*) high, flippé par la drogue.
flog [flɔg] (**to**). **1.** *P:* bazarder, trafiquer, troquer, lessiver. **2.** *P:* voler*, barboter, choper. **3.** *F:* **to f. sth. to death,** éreinter qch.; **to f. s.o. to death,** matraquer qn; **to f. oneself to death,** se fatiguer à l'extrême, se crever. *Voir aussi* **bishop; donkey, 5; dummy, 5; horse**[1]**, 4.**
floor[1] [flɔːr, ˈflɔər] (*noun*). **1.** *F:* **to take the f.,** (*a*) ouvrir le bal; (*b*) prendre la

* An asterisk indicates that the word so marked is included as a head-word in the Appendix.

parole. 2. *F:* **to hold the f.,** tenir le crachoir. 3. *P:* **to be on the f.,** être pauvre*, être sur le pavé, traîner la savate. *Voir aussi* **wipe**[2] **(to), 1.**

floor[2] [flɔːr, ˈflɔər] **(to),** *F:* 1. terrasser (qn), envoyer (qn) à terre. 2. coller (un adversaire), réduire (qn) à quia, désarçonner (qn). 3. secouer (qn), laisser (qn) baba.

floorer [ˈflɔːrər, ˈflɔərər] *(noun), F:* une colle; **that's a f. for you!** ça te la coupe!

floosie, floosy, floozie, floozy [ˈfluːzi] *(noun) (mainly U.S.), P:* 1. une mémère, une fille* quelconque, une fille pot-au-feu. 2. aguicheuse *f*, cocotte *f*, mousmé(e) *f*. 3. prostituée*, roulure *f*.

flop[1] [flɔp] *(adv.), F:* 1. **to fall f.,** faire patapouf. 2. **to go f. = flop**[3] **(to), 1, 2.**

flop[2] [flɔp] *(noun).* 1. *F:* *(a)* échec*; *(b)* raté *m*, laissé *m* pour compte; four noir, chou blanc. 2. *P:* *(a)* asile *m* de nuit, abri *m*, guérite *f*; *(b)* lit*, bâche *f*, paddock *m*. *Voir aussi* **belly-flop.**

flop[3] [flɔp] **(to),** *F:* 1. échouer*, faire faillite, ramasser une veste. 2. s'affaisser, s'affaler; **to f. into an armchair,** s'effondrer dans un fauteuil. *Voir aussi* **mop, 1.**

flop about [ˈflɔpəˈbaut] **(to),** *F:* faire des sauts *m.pl.* de carpe.

flop-house [ˈflɔphaus] *(noun), P:* 1. hôtel *m* borgne (*ou* des Trois Canards). 2. asile *m* de nuit.

flop out [ˈflɔpˈaut] **(to),** *P:* s'évanouir*, tomber dans les pommes.

flopperoo [ˈflɔpəˈruː] *(noun) (U.S.), P:* **= flop**[2]**, 1.**

floppy [ˈflɔpi] *(adj.), F:* *(d'une personne)* mollasse, veule.

floral [ˈflɔːrəl] *(adj.), P:* **f. arrangement = daisy chain (daisy**[2]**, 6).**

flossie, flossy [ˈflɔsi] *(adj.), F:* *(a)* archi-élégant*, riflo, urf(e); *(b)* tape-à-l'œil.

flounder[1] [ˈflaundər] *(noun), P:* **f. (and dab)** *(R.S. = (taxi-)cab)*, taxi*.

flounder[2] [ˈflaundər] **(to),** *F:* cafouiller, patauger.

flower [ˈflauər] *(noun).* 1. *F:* **F. people,** enfants-fleur *m.pl.*; **F. power,** règne *m* de la fleur (*vocable hippy pour le retour à la nature*). 2. *(pl.) P:* menstrues*, carlets *m.pl.*, affaires *m.pl.* 3. *P:* pédéraste*, chouquette *f*. *Voir aussi* **wallflower.**

flowery (dell) [ˈflau(ə)ri(ˈdel)] *(noun)* *(R.S. = (prison) cell), P:* cellule *f* (de prison), bloc *m*, trou *m*; *cf.* **Peter (Bell) (peter, 2).**

flu [fluː] *(noun) (=influenza), F:* grippe *f*.

flue [fluː] *(noun).* 1. *V:* vagin*, cheminée *f*, bonbonnière *f*. 2. *V:* **you can stick it up your f.,** tu peux te le mettre quelque part; *cf.* **stick**[2] **(to), 3.** 3. *P:* *(R.S. = screw)* gardien* de prison, gaffe *m*, matuche *m*. 4. *(U.S.) F:* **to go up the f.,** échouer*, foirer.

fluence [ˈfluːəns] *(noun), F:* 1. influence délicate et subtile. 2. **to put the f. on s.o.,** *(a)* persuader qn; *(b)* hypnotiser qn.

fluey [ˈfluːi] *(adj.), F:* **to feel f.,** se sentir grippé; *cf.* **flu.**

fluff[1] [flʌf] *(noun).* 1. *F:* *(a)* jeune femme*, une jeunesse, mousmé(e) *f*; *(b)* **a nice piece** (*or* **bit**) **of f.,** un beau petit lot. 2. *F:* *(a)* cuir *m*, pataquès *m*; *(b)* boulette *f*. 3. *P:* **to give s.o. the f.,** remettre qn à sa place, snober qn, asseoir qn, rabattre le caquet à qn.

fluff[2] [flʌf] **(to),** *F:* 1. *(th.)* rater (*ou* louper) son entrée, bouler (son rôle). 2. saboter, bousiller, louper, rater.

fluff off [ˈflʌfˈɔf] **(to),** *P:* **to f. s.o. o. = to give s.o. the fluff (fluff**[1]**, 3).**

fluke[1] [fluːk] *(noun), F:* coup *m* de chance*, veine *f*, fion *m*, bol *m*, pot *m*.

fluke[2] [fluːk] **(to),** *F:* 1. avoir un coup de chance*, avoir une veine de cocu. 2. gagner par raccroc.

fluky [ˈfluːki] *(adj.), F:* 1. incertain, hasardeux. 2. par raccroc.

flummery [ˈflʌməri] *(noun), F:* 1. bêtises*, balivernes *f.pl.*, blagues *f.pl.*, sornettes *f.pl.* 2. flatterie *f*, boniment *m*, panade *f*, du plat.

flummox [ˈflʌməks] **(to),** *F:* démonter, épater, éberluer (qn).

flump[1] [flʌmp] *(noun), F:* coup sourd, plouf *m*, floc *m*.

flump[2] [flʌmp] **(to),** *F:* 1. tomber avec un bruit sourd, s'affaisser. 2. laisser tomber lourdement, flanquer par terre.

flunk [flʌŋk] **(to),** *F:* 1. se dérober, se défiler, tirer au flanc. 2. être recalé (*ou* collé *ou* étendu) à un examen. 3. recaler, coller, étendre.

flurry [ˈflʌri] *(noun), F:* **all in** (*or* **of**) **a f.,** en catastrophe.

* L'astérisque indique que le mot marqué de ce signe figure comme entrée dans le Répertoire.

flush[1] [flʌʃ] (*adj.*), *F:* riche*, plein aux as.

flush[2] [flʌʃ] (**to**), *P:* faire monter le sang dans une seringue hypodermique, rougir la poussette. *Voir aussi* **four-flush (to)**.

flute [flu:t], **fluter** [ˈflu:tər] (*noun*), *P:* pédéraste*, tapette *f*, lope(tte) *f*. *Voir aussi* **whistle**[1], **2**.

flutter [ˈflʌtər] (*noun*), *F:* **1. to be in a** (*or* **all of a**) **f.**, être tout chose, être dans tous ses états. **2. to have a f. on the gee-gees,** jouer aux courtines, avoir une petite flambée, faire le thunard.

fly[1] [flai] (*adj.*), *F:* **1.** malin*, roublard, mariole. **2.** agile, leste, preste.

fly[2] [flai] (*noun*), *F:* **1. there are no flies on him,** c'est un malin, il n'est pas né d'hier, il n'est pas tombé de la dernière pluie, il n'est pas manchot. **2.** (*sing. ou pl.*) braguette *f*. **3. a f. in the ointment,** une ombre au tableau, un cheveu (dans la soupe), un hic. **4.** (*Austr.*) **to have a f. at sth. = to have a stab at sth.** *Voir aussi* **bar-fly.**

fly[3] [flai] (**to**). **1.** *F:* **to f. in the face of sth.,** braver qch., tenir tête à qch., lancer un défi à qch. **2.** (*a*) *F:* **to f. high,** voler (*ou* voir *ou* viser) haut; (*b*) *P:* **flying high,** camé, envapé. **3. to let f.,** (*a*) *F:* lâcher une volée d'injures; (*b*) *P:* cracher*, glavioter; (*c*) *P:* uriner*, lâcher un fil (*ou* l'écluse). *Voir aussi* **coop; flag**[1], **4, 5; fur; handle, 1.**

fly-ball [ˈflaibɔ:l], **fly-bob** [ˈflaibɔb], **fly-bull** [ˈflaibul] (*noun*), *P:* policier* en civil, hambourgeois *m*, perdreau *m*.

fly-by-night[1] [ˈflaibainait, ˈflaibənait] (*adj.*), *F:* irréfléchi, évaporé.

fly-by-night[2] [ˈflaibainait, ˈflaibənait] (*noun*), *F:* **1.** déménageur *m* à la cloche de bois. **2.** évaporé *m*, huluberlu *m*, tête *f* de linotte, oiseau *m* des îles. **3.** noctambule *m*, oiseau *m* de nuit.

fly-cop [ˈflaikɔp], **fly-dick** [ˈflaidik], **fly-mug** [ˈflaimʌg] (*noun*), *P:* = **fly-ball.**

fly out [ˈflaiˈaut] (**to**), *F:* = **to fly off the handle (handle, 1)**.

fly-pitch [ˈflaipitʃ] (**to**), *F:* vendre à la sauvette, cameloter.

fly-pitcher [ˈflaipitʃər] (*noun*), *F:* camelot *m* à la sauvette.

fly-pitching [ˈflaipitʃiŋ] (*noun*), *F:* vente *f* à la sauvette.

fob [fɔb] (**to**), *P:* duper*, rouler, empiler, embobiner.

fob off [ˈfɔbˈɔf] (**to**), *F:* **to f. sth. o. on s.o.,** refarcir qch. à qn; **to get fobbed off with sth.,** se faire refiler qch.

fog [fɔg] (*noun*), *F:* **to be in a f.,** être dans le brouillard (*ou* le cirage), perdre les pédales.

fogey [ˈfougi] (*noun*), *F:* **(old) f.,** vieille baderne, croulant *m*, périmé *m*.

foggiest [ˈfɔgiist] (*adj.*), *F:* **I haven't the f. (idea)**, je n'ai pas la moindre idée.

fog up [ˈfɔgˈʌp] (**to**), *F:* brouiller (les cartes), embrouiller.

fogy [ˈfougi] (*noun*), *F:* = **fogey.**

fold (up) [ˈfould(ˈʌp)] (**to**), *F:* **1.** s'effondrer, lâcher, caner, se dégonfler. **2.** échouer*, faire faillite.

folks [fouks] (*pl. noun*), *F:* **1.** les gens, le populo, populmiche *m*. **2. (old) f.,** les parents*, les vieux, les dab(e)s *m.pl.*

folksy [ˈfouksi] (*adj.*), *F:* **1.** populo. **2.** folklore, campagnard, à la bonne franquette. **3.** sociable, populaire, sympa.

Follies [ˈfɔliz] (*pl. noun*), *P:* **the F.,** les Assises trimestrielles, les grands carreaux, les Assiettes *f.pl.*, les Assottes *f.pl.*; **to be weighed off at the F.,** être jugé aux Assises trimestrielles, passer aux Assiettes; *cf.* **weigh off (to).**

fooey! [ˈfu:i] (*excl.*), *F:* la barbe! flûte!

foo-foo [ˈfu:fu:] (*adj.*), *P:* **f.-f. dust:** *voir* **dust**[1], **2** (*a*); *cf.* **fu.**

fool[1] [fu:l] (*adj.*), *F:* bête*, idiot, imbécile; *cf.* **damfool**[1].

fool[2] [fu:l] (*noun*), *F:* **to play the f.** = **fool**[3] **(to), 1.**

fool[3] [fu:l] (**to**), *F:* **1.** faire le bête*, faire des bêtises*. **2. to f. s.o.,** (*a*) se payer la tête de qn; (*b*) escroquer* qn, empiler qn.

fool around [ˈfu:ləˈraund] (**to**), *F:* **1.** flânocher, lanterner, vadrouiller, baguenauder. **2.** taquiner, asticoter, faire enrager qn. **3.** flirter, faire des avances (*ou* les yeux doux) à qn.

foot[1] [fut] (*noun*) (*pl.* **feet**), *F:* **1. my f.!** quelle blague! et ta sœur! **2. to fall on one's feet,** (re)tomber sur ses pieds (*ou* pattes). **3. to find one's feet,** voler de ses propres ailes, (re)trouver son aplomb. **4. to have one f. in the grave,**

* An asterisk indicates that the word so marked is included as a head-word in the Appendix.

avoir un pied dans la tombe. **5. to put one's f. down,** faire acte d'autorité, mettre bon ordre, mettre le holà. **6. to put one's best f. forward,** (*a*) allonger le pas; (*b*) faire de son mieux. **7. to put one's f. in it,** mettre les pieds dans le plat; **he's always putting his f. in it!** il n'en rate pas une! **8. to put one's feet up,** se reposer, s'allonger, se relaxer, poser ses fesses. **9. to be carried out feet first,** mourir*, partir les pieds devant. **10. to be out on one's feet,** être très fatigué*, être à plat. *Voir aussi* **cold**[1], **4; crow's-feet; doughfoot; drag**[2] **(to); flatfoot; pussyfoot**[1]**; six, 1; sweep**[2] **(to), 1; tanglefoot.**

foot[2] [ˈfʊt] (**to**), *F:* **1.** donner un coup de pied* à (qn). **2. to f. the bill,** payer* la note, douiller, casquer, cigler, arroser la douloureuse. **3. to f. it,** marcher*, aller à pattes, arquer. *Voir aussi* **hotfoot (to); pussyfoot**[2] **(to).**

football [ˈfutbɔːl] (*noun*), *P:* mélange *m* de dextroamphétamine et amphétamine (*drogues**), football *m*.

footer [ˈfutər] (*noun*), *F:* **1.** le football. **2.** baby-foot *m*.

footle[1] [ˈfuːtl] (*noun*), *F:* bêtise*, fadaise *f*.

footle[2] [ˈfuːtl] (**to**), *F:* **1.** (*a*) traînasser, flemmarder, baguenauder; (*b*) bricoler. **2.** (*a*) faire des bêtises*; (*b*) dire des sornettes *f.pl.*, bavasser.

footless [ˈfutlis] (*adj.*) (*U.S.*), *F:* maladroit, impuissant, empoté, empaillé.

footling [ˈfuːtliŋ] (*adj.*), *F:* **1.** bête*, stupide. **2.** futile, insignifiant, négligeable. **3.** tatillon, mesquin, chichiteux.

footman [ˈfutmən] (*noun*), *F:* pédicure *m*.

footsies [ˈfutsiz] (*pl. noun*), *F:* = **footsy.**

foot-slog [ˈfut-slɔg] (**to**), *F:* marcher* péniblement, cheminer, se traîner, arquer, trimarder, battre le bitume.

foot-slogger [ˈfut-slɔgər] (*noun*), *F:* marcheur *m*, pousse-cailloux *m*; (*mil.*) biffin *m*.

footsy [ˈfutsi], **footums** [ˈfutəmz], **footy-footy** [ˈfutiˈfuti] (*noun*), *F:* **to play f. (with s.o.) (under the table),** faire du pied* à qn; *cf.* **kneesies; tootsy-footsy.**

foozle[1] [ˈfuːzl] (*noun*), *P:* **1.** coup raté. **2.** vieux tableau, vieille rombière, vieille barbe. **3.** parent*, dab(e) *m*.

foozle[2] [ˈfuːzl] (**to**), *P:* patauger, louper, bousiller, rater son coup.

for [fɔːr] (*prep.*), *F:* **to be f. it,** (*a*) être pour...; **I'm all f. it,** je suis pour, je suis partisan de cela, j'en suis très partisan; (*b*) être bon pour...; **you'll be f. it!** ton affaire est bonne! qu'est-ce que tu vas prendre!; *cf.* **what-for.**

fork [fɔːk] (*noun*), *P:* (*a*) main*, croche *f*, grappin *m*; (*b*) (*pl.*) doigts*, fourchettes *f.pl.*

fork out [ˈfɔːkˈaut] (**to**), *F:* payer*, les allonger, les aligner; **to f. o. again,** redouiller. *Voir aussi* **needful.**

fork up [ˈfɔːkˈʌp] (**to**), *F:* = **fork out (to).**

form [fɔːm] (*noun*), *F:* **1. good f.,** savoir-vivre *m*, bon ton; **bad f.,** mauvais genre, mauvais ton. **2.** casier *m* judiciaire, blase *m*, faffes *f.pl.*; **to have f.,** avoir ses faffes. **3. to be off f.,** ne pas tenir la forme, n'avoir pas la patate.

forrader [ˈfɔrədər] (*adv.*), *F:* plus en avant; **that doesn't get us any further f.,** ça ne nous avance pas.

fort [fɔːt] (*noun*), *F:* **to hold the f.,** garder la baraque.

forty [ˈfɔːti] (*numeral adj.*), *F:* **to have f. winks,** dormir*, faire un petit somme, piquer une ronflette (*ou* un roupillon).

forty-four (*noun*) (*R.S.* = *whore*), *P:* prostituée*, putain *f*.

forward [ˈfɔːwəd] (*noun*), *P:* amphétamine *f* (*drogues**).

fossick [ˈfɔsik] (**to**), *F:* **1.** fureter, fouiller, farfouiller. **2.** (*Austr.*) marauder dans les mines d'or.

fossil [ˈfɔsl] (*noun*), *F:* **1. (old) f.,** vieux birbe, un fossile, un périmé, un vestige. **2.** le vieux, le dab(e).

foul [faul] (*adj.*), *F:* **1.** dégueulasse, dégoûtant, infect. **2. to fall f. of s.o.,** se brouiller avec qn, se prendre de querelle* avec qn.

foul-mouth [ˈfaulmauθ] (*noun*), *F:* grossier personnage.

foul up [ˈfaulˈʌp] (**to**), *F:* amocher, bousiller, saloper; **to f. u. the works,** esquinter le mécanisme; **to f. u. s.o.'s plans,** faire louper (*ou* saboter) les projets de qn; **all fouled up,** (*a*) emberlificoté; (*b*) amoché; *voir aussi* **snafu.**

four-eyes [ˈfɔːraiz] (*noun*), *P:* qn qui porte des lunettes*, binoclard *m*, bésiclard *m*.

* L'astérisque indique que le mot marqué de ce signe figure comme entrée dans le Répertoire.

four-flush [ˈfɔːflʌʃ] (**to**), *P:* **1.** bluffer*, se gonfler, se monter le job. **2.** ne pas payer ses dettes, ne pas essuyer (*ou* laisser) une ardoise. **3.** écornifler, vivre aux crochets de qn.

four-flusher [ˈfɔːflʌʃər] (*noun*), *P:* vantard*, bluffeur *m*, chiqueur *m*.

four-letter [ˈfɔːletər] (*adj.*), *F:* **f.-l. word,** les cinq lettres, le mot de Cambronne (=merde), un gros mot.

fourpenny [ˈfɔːpni] (*adj.*), *P:* **to give s.o. a f. one,** donner un coup* de poing (*ou* un gnon *ou* un marron) à qn, filer une châtaigne maison à qn.

fox [fɔks] (**to**), *F:* (*a*) duper*, avoir, posséder, rouler (qn); (*b*) mystifier (qn).

frabjous [ˈfræbdʒəs] (*adj.*), *F:* pharamineux.

fracture [ˈfræktʃər] (**to**), *P:* **1. you f. me!,** (*a*) tu me fais tordre de rire*! tu me boyautes!; (*b*) tu m'écœures! tu me fais mal (aux tripes)! **2.** battre*, tabasser (qn).

fractured [ˈfræktʃəd] (*adj.*), *P:* ivre*, mâchuré, rétamé.

fraidy [ˈfreidi] (*adj.*), *F:* **to be a f. cat,** être un poltron* (*ou* un couard *ou* une poule mouillée), avoir peur*, avoir les jetons (*ou* les copeaux *ou* la colique).

frail[1] [freil] (*adj.*), *P:* **f. job,** (*a*) femme* de petite vertu, femme facile, nénette *f*, gonzesse *f*; (*b*) coït*, chique *f*, partie *f* de jambes en l'air.

frail[2] [freil] (*noun*), *P:* = **frail job** (**frail**[1] (*a*)).

frame[1] [freim] (*noun*), *P:* hétérosexuel *m* qui attire les homosexuels, une amorce; *cf.* **bait** (*a*).

frame[2] [freim] (**to**), *F:* **to f. s.o.,** farguer qn, faire porter le bada à qn, poser un gluau à qn, monter un coup contre qn.

frame-up [ˈfreimʌp] (*noun*), *F:* complot *m*, machination *f*, coup monté.

frat [fræt] (**to**), *F:* fraterniser.

frazzle [ˈfræzl] (*noun*). **1. to be done to a f.,** (*a*) *F:* être trop cuit, être carbonisé; (*b*) *P:* se faire empiler (dans les grandes largeurs). **2.** *F:* **to be worn to a f.,** être très fatigué*, être à plat (*ou* à bout *ou* rendu). **3.** *F:* **to beat s.o. to a f.,** battre* qn à plate(s) couture(s).

frazzled [ˈfræzld] (*adj.*), *P:* ivre*, blindé, qui a une cuite, noir.

freak[1] [friːk] (*adj.*), *F:* bizarre, fantaisiste, hors-circuit, hors-série.

freak[2] [friːk] (*noun*). **1.** *F:* drôle *m* de numéro, phénomène *m*, curiosité *f*. **2.** *P:* pédéraste*, lopette *f*. **3.** *P:* usager *m* d'un narcotique; *voir aussi* **acid,2.** **4.** *P:* fervent *m*, fana *m*, mordu *m*. **5.** *P:* hippy *m*.

freak out [ˈfriːkˈaut] (**to**), *P:* **1.** se dévergonder. **2.** devenir farfelu. **3.** perdre tout contrôle mental après l'usage de drogues; être défoncé.

freaky [ˈfriːki] (*adj.*), *F:* = **freak**[1].

Fred [fred] (*pr. noun*), *F:* **F. Karno's army,** cafouillis *m*, gâchis *m*, loufoquerie *f*.

Freddy [ˈfredi] (*noun*), *P:* comprimé *m* d'éphédrine (*drogues**), Freddie *m*.

free [friː] (*adj.*), *F:* **f., gratis and for nothing** (*or* **for f.**), gratuit*, gratis (pro Deo), pour la peau. *Voir aussi* **show**[1], **1.**

free-for-all [ˈfriːfərɔːl] (*noun*), *F:* mêlée générale, barouf *m*, corrida *f*, castagne *f*.

free-load [ˈfriːˈloud] (**to**) (*U.S.*), *P:* écornifler, écumer la marmite, vivre aux crochets de qn.

free-loader [ˈfriːloudər] (*noun*) (*U.S.*), *P:* parasite *mf*, écornifleur *m*, tapeur *m*.

free-loading [ˈfriːloudiŋ] (*noun*) (*U.S.*), *P:* vie *f* aux crochets des autres (*ou* de pique-assiette).

free-wheeling [ˈfriː(h)wiːliŋ] (*adj.*), *F:* **1.** qui dépense* sans compter, qui les fait valser. **2.** sans gêne, en roue libre.

freeze[1] [friːz] (*noun*), *P:* **to put the f. on s.o.** = **to put the chill on s.o.** (**chill, 1**). *Voir aussi* **deep**[1], **2.**

freeze[2] [friːz] (**to**), *F:* **1.** mettre en quarantaine, boycotter. **2.** (*a*) avoir peur*, avoir le sang qui gèle, se glacer; (*b*) être figé sur place, se figer. **3. it's freezing cold,** ça caille; *cf.* **balls, 8.**

freeze out [ˈfriːzˈaut] (**to**), *F:* (*a*) = **freeze**[2] (**to**), **1**; (*b*) supplanter (un rival), évincer (qn).

freeze-up [ˈfriːzʌp] (*noun*), *F:* **1.** gel *m* à pierre fendre. **2.** statue *f* de glace, frigorification *f*.

French[1] [frentʃ] (*adj.*). **1.** *F:* **F. kiss,** baiser lingual, patin *m*, saucisse *f*, langouse *f*. **2.** *F:* **F. letter** (*U.S.:* **F. safe**), capote anglaise, imperméable *m* à Popaul (*ou* Popol). **3.** *F:* **F. fries,** pommes frites. **4.** *F:* **to take F. leave,** filer à l'anglaise, brûler la politesse à qn. **5.** *V:* **the F. way,** coït* buccal, (*a*)

* An asterisk indicates that the word so marked is included as a head-word in the Appendix.

broutage *m*; (*b*) suçage *m*, taillade *f* de plume. *Voir aussi* **blue**[2], **1.**

French[2] [frentʃ] (*noun*), *F:* **that goddamned ... – pardon my F.!** ce sacré... – excusez mon latin!

french[3] [frentʃ] (**to**), *V:* faire un coït* buccal à (qn), prendre (qn) en poire.

frenchie, frenchy [ˈfrentʃi] (*noun*), *P:* = **French letter** (**French**[1], **2**).

fresh[1] [freʃ] (*adj.*), *F:* **1.** légèrement ivre*, gris, paf, parti. **2.** effronté; **don't get f. with me!** ne la ramène pas avec moi! **3.** bleu, en herbe; **young man f. down from university,** jeune homme frais émoulu de l'université. **4.** flirt(eur), coureur. *Voir aussi* **air**[1], **3.**

fresh[2] [freʃ] (*adv.*), *F:* **to be f. out of sth.,** être complètement vidé de qch.

fresher [ˈfreʃər] (*noun*), *F:* étudiant de première année, bizut *m*.

friar [ˈfraiər] (*noun*), *P:* **holy f.** (*R.S.* = *liar*), menteur *m*.

fridge [fridʒ] (*noun*) (*abbr.* = *refrigerator*), *F:* réfrigérateur *m*, frigo *m*.

frig[1] [frig] (*noun*), *V:* coït*, bourre *f*, tronche *f*.

frig[2] [frig] (**to**). **1.** *V:* coïter* avec (une femme), baiser, bourrer, troncher. **2.** (*U.S.*), *P:* escroquer*, carotter, baiser, entuber.

frigger [ˈfrigər] (*noun*). **1.** *V:* baiseur *m*, tringleur *m*, troncheur *m*. **2.** (*U.S.*) *P:* escroc*, empileur *m*, carotteur *m*.

frigging[1] [ˈfrigiŋ] (*adj.*), *P:* sacré, satané.

frigging[2] [ˈfrigiŋ] (*noun*). **1.** *V:* coït*, partie *f* de balayette, bourre *f*. **2.** (*U.S.*) *P:* escroquerie*, entubage *m*, filouterie *f*.

fright [frait] (*noun*), *F:* individu laid*, mocheté *f*, tarte *f*, caricature *f*, carnaval *m*.

frightful [ˈfraitful] (*adj.*), *F:* affreux, effroyable.

frightfully [ˈfraitfəli] (*adv.*), *F:* bougrement, fichtrement, vachement; **it's f. good of you,** c'est extrêmement aimable à vous; **I'm f. sorry,** mille excuses!

frill [fril] (*noun*), *P:* jeune fille* *ou* femme*, frou-frou *f*, mousmé(e) *f*, tartavelle *f*.

frippet [ˈfripit] (*noun*), *P:* = **talent.**

frisk [frisk] (**to**), *F:* fouiller (un suspect *ou* un local), barboter.

Fritz [frits] (*pr. noun*), *P:* Allemand*, fritz *m*, fridolin *m*, frizou *m*.

frog[1] [frɔg] (*noun*), *P:* **f.** (**and toad**) (*R.S.* = *road*), route*. *Voir aussi* **knee-high; pond, 2.**

Frog[2] [frɔg], **frog-eater** [ˈfrɔgiːtər], **Froggie, Froggy** [ˈfrɔgi] (*noun*), *P:* Français *m*, Fransquillon *m*.

front[1] [frʌnt] (*adj.*), *F:* **1. f. runner,** candidat *m* en tête, la tête de liste (*ou* de peloton), le major. **2. to have a f. seat,** être aux premières loges.

front[2] [frʌnt] (*noun*), *F:* **1.** couverture *f*, parapluie *m*, homme *m* de paille. **2.** culot *m*, toupet *m*. **3. to put on a f.,** faire le prétentieux*, crâner, faire de l'esbrouf(f)e. **4.t o put on a bold f.,** faire bonne contenance (*ou* figure). **5. to come to the f.,** émerger, percer, se pousser (en avant).

frost [frɔst] (*noun*), *F:* échec*, four *m* (complet *ou* noir), fiasco *m*, bouchon *m*.

frowst [fraust] (*noun*), *F:* **1.** renfermé *m*, odeur *f* de renfermé. **2.** qn qui se confine (*ou* qui aime ses quat' murs).

frowsty [ˈfrausti] (*adj.*), *F:* qui sent le renfermé.

frowsy, frowzy [ˈfrauzi] (*noun*), *F:* femme* mal torchée.

fruit [fruːt] (*noun*). **1.** *P:* pédéraste*, fagot *m*; **frozen f.,** pédéraste* frigide, fruit rafraîchi; **f. fly** = **fag bag** (**fag, 2** (*c*)). **2.** (*U.S.*) *P:* prostituée*, grue *f*, morue *f*. **3.** *F:* **hello, old f.!** salut, vieux pote (*ou* vieille branche)!

fruit-basket [ˈfruːtbɑːskit] (*noun*), *V:* vagin*, boîte *f* à ouvrage, bonbonnière *f*; **to have one's fingers in the f.-b.,** mettre la main au panier.

fruit-cake [ˈfruːtkeik] (*noun*). **1.** (*U.S.*) *P:* pédéraste*, tapette *f*. **2.** *F:* **nutty as a f.-c.,** fou* à lier, complètement dingue.

fruit-salad [ˈfruːtˈsæləd] (*noun*), *F:* **1.** rangée *f* de médailles et décorations, batterie *f* de cuisine, bananes *f.pl.* **2.** (*d'une machine à sous*) embrouillamini *m*.

fruity [ˈfruːti] (*adj.*). **1.** *F:* salace, épicé, pimenté, corsé. **2.** *F:* (voix) chaude, moelleuse. **3.** *P:* homosexuel, tapette. **4.** *P:* = **horny** (*b*).

fruity-pie[1] [ˈfruːtipai] (*adj.*), *P:* = **fruity, 3.**

fruity-pie[2] [ˈfruːtipai] (*noun*), *P:* = **fruit, 1.**

fry [frai] (**to**) (*U.S.*), *F:* (*a*) électrocuter

* L'astérisque indique que le mot marqué de ce signe figure comme entrée dans le Répertoire.

(qn) (dans la chaise), griller (qn); (*b*) être grillé (*ou* épuré). *Voir aussi* **fish[1], 4.**

fu [fu:] (*noun*), *P:* marijuana *f* (*drogues**); *cf.* **foo-foo.**

fuck[1] [fʌk] (*noun*), *VV:* **1.** coït*, baisage *m*, baisade *f*. **2. I don't give a f.,** je m'en fous et m'en contrefous. **3. what the f.!** quelle espèce de connerie! qu'est-ce que c'est que ce con! *Voir aussi* **finger-fuck[1]; honey-fuck(ing).**

fuck[2] [fʌk] (**to**), *VV:* **1.** (*a*) coïter*; (*b*) coïter avec (qn), baiser. **2. f. me!** [ˈfʌkˈmi:], mon cul! merde alors!; **f. you!** [ˈfʌkˈju:], **go f. yourself!** je t'emmerde! tiens mes deux! va te faire foutre! **3. f. a duck!** sacré nom de Dieu! **4. f. it!** [ˈfʌkit], (*a*) merde (alors)!; (*b*) c'est marre! change de disque! **5.** (*U.S.*) escroquer*, empiler, carotter, baiser. *Voir aussi* **bunny-fuck (to); finger-fuck[2] (to); honey-fuck (to).**

fuckable [ˈfʌkəbl] (*adj.*), *VV:* bonne à baiser.

fuck about (*or* **around**) [ˈfʌkəˈbaʊt, ˈfʌkəˈraʊnd] (**to**), *VV:* **1.** traîner son cul, couillonner. **2.** faire tourner (qn) en bourrique.

fuck-all [ˈfʌkˈɔ:l] (*noun*), *VV:* (**sweet**) **f.-a.,** rien*, peau de balle (et balai de crin), que dalle, des prunes; *cf.* **f. a.**

fucked (out) [ˈfʌkt(ˈaʊt)] (*adj.*), *VV:* fatigué*, foutu, rendu, vidé, vanné.

fucking[1] [ˈfʌkiŋ] (*adj.*), *VV:* **1.** sacré, satané, foutu. **2. what the f. hell!** Bon Dieu de merde! **3.** difficile*, coton, glandilleux. **4.** dégueulasse, dégueulbif. **5.** couillonnant, emmouscaillé. *Voir aussi* **motherfucking.**

fucking[2] [ˈfʌkiŋ] (*adv.*), *VV:* **it's f. cold,** il fait bougrement froid; **a f. awful film,** une vraie connerie de film; **it's a f. long way,** c'est vachement loin.

fucking[3] [ˈfʌkiŋ] (*noun*), *VV:* coït*, baisage *m*, dérouillage *m*, tronche *f*. *Voir aussi* **honey-fuck(ing).**

fuck off [ˈfʌkˈɔf] (**to**), *VV:* **1.** s'enfuir*, se tirer, se tailler, mettre les bouts; **f. o.!** va te faire foutre! **2.** se masturber*, se branler (la colonne), se tirer un coup. **3.** (*U.S.*) faire le con, déconner.

fuck over [ˈfʌkˈouvər] (**to**) (*U.S.*), *VV:* (*police*) fouiller, décarpiller (qn).

fuckster [ˈfʌkstər] (*noun*), *VV:* baiseur *m*, qn porté sur l'article (*ou* sur la bagatelle).

fuckstress [ˈfʌkstris] (*noun*), *VV:* baiseuse *f*, chaude *f* de la pince.

fuck up [ˈfʌkˈʌp] (**to**), *VV:* cochonner, massacrer, torcher, bousiller. *Voir aussi* **snafu.**

fuddy-duddy [ˈfʌdi-dʌdi] (*noun*), *F:* vieux croulant, vieux rococo, périmé *m*.

fudge [ˈfʌdʒ] (**to**) (*U.S.*). **1.** *F:* raconter des blagues *f.pl.* (*ou* des craques *f.pl.*). **2.** *V:* faire jouir au toucher, faire mousser.

fudge out [ˈfʌdʒˈaʊt] (**to**), *P:* caner.

fug [fʌg] (*noun*), *F:* forte odeur de renfermé, schlingage *m*.

full [ful] (*adj.*), *P:* **1.** ivre*, plein (comme une bourrique), rond. **2.** intoxiqué par la drogue, chargé, bourré. *Voir aussi* **chock-full.**

fume [fju:m] (**to**), *F:* se mettre en colère*, fumer, fulminer.

fuming [ˈfju:miŋ] (*adj.*), *F:* **to be in a f. temper,** être en colère*, être à cran (*ou* en rogne), voir rouge.

fun[1] [fʌn] (*attrib. adj.*), *F:* **it's the f. thing to do,** c'est la chose bath à faire; **f. clothes,** vêtements* psychédéliques.

fun[2] [fʌn] (*noun*), *F:* **1. like f.,** (*a*) pas du tout; (*b*) très vite*, à toute barre, en moins de deux. **2. f. and games,** (*a*) farces et attrapes; (*b*) grabuge *m*; (*c*) (toute la) musique.

funeral [ˈfju:nərəl] (*noun*), *F:* **that's your f.,** c'est votre affaire; mêle-toi de tes oignons; **it's not my f.,** ce n'est pas mon affaire, c'est pas mon rayon, c'est pas mes oignons.

fungus [ˈfʌŋgəs] (*noun*), *P:* (**face**) **f.,** barbe*, moustache*, poils *m.pl.* au menton.

funk[1] [fʌŋk] (*noun*), *F:* **1.** peur*, frousse *f*, trac *m*, trouille *f*; **to be in a** (**blue**) **f.,** avoir une peur* bleue, avoir la frousse (*ou* le trac); *voir aussi* **acid, 2. 2.** froussard *m*, trouillard *m*, mouilleur *m*.

funk[2] [fʌŋk] (**to**), *F:* **to f. it,** caner, se dégonfler, les mouiller.

funked out [ˈfʌŋktˈaʊt] (*adj.*), *P:* sous l'influence des drogues, chargé, défoncé.

funky [ˈfʌŋki] (*adj.*). **1.** *F:* froussard. **2.** *P:* bath, badour, jojo, chouctose, nickel. **3.** *P:* (*jazz*) manière virile de jouer les blues.

funny[1] [ˈfʌni] (*adj.*). **1.** *F:* **don't be f.**

* An asterisk indicates that the word so marked is included as a head-word in the Appendix.

ne fais pas l'imbécile (*ou* le zigoto)! **2.** *F:* **f. business,** affaire *f* louche, fricotage *m*; **none of your f. tricks! I don't want any f. business!** (*a*) pas de blagues! (*b*) je ne veux pas d'histoires! **3.** *F:* **I came over all f.,** je me suis senti tout chose. **4.** *P:* **f. farm,** asile *m* d'aliénés, maison *f* de loufoques.

funny[2] [ˈfʌni] (*noun*) (*pl.* **funnies**), *F:* **1. a f.,** plaisanterie *f*, blague *f*, rigolade *f*. **2.** (*pl.*) (*a*) bandes dessinées; (*b*) dessins animés.

fur [fəːr] (*noun*), *F:* **to make the f. fly,** (*a*) se battre* avec acharnement, se crêper le chignon; (*b*) se quereller avec fracas, tempêter.

furburger [ˈfəːbəːgər] (*noun*), *VV:* = **hairburger.**

furniture [ˈfəːnitʃər] (*noun*), *F:* **1. to be part of the f.** = **to be a (permanent) fixture (fixture, 1).** **2.** (*U.S.*) **a nice little piece of f.,** une fille* qui a du chien, un beau petit lot.

furphy [ˈfəːfi] (*noun*) (*Austr.*), *P:* fausse rumeur, clabaud *m*, canular(d) *m*.

fury [ˈfjuːri] (*noun*), *F:* **like f.,** (*a*) déchaîné, en (pleine) fureur; (*b*) très vite*, à toute pompe, à tout berzingue.

fuse [fjuːz] (*noun*), *F:* **to blow a f.,** se mettre en colère*, piquer une crise.

fuss [fʌs] (*noun*), *F:* chichis *m.pl.*, chinoiseries *f.pl.*; **to make a f.,** faire des arias; **it's nothing to make a f. about,** il n'y a pas de quoi fouetter un chat.

fusspot [ˈfʌspɔt], **fussy-breeches** [ˈfʌsi-britʃiz] (*noun*), *F:* individu* qui fait des histoires (*ou* des embarras), chichiteux *m*.

future [ˈfjuːtʃər] (*noun*). **1.** *F:* **there's no f. in it,** ça n'a pas d'avenir *m* (*ou* de débouchés *m.pl.*). **2.** *P:* testicules*, sac *m* à roupes.

futz[1] [fʌts] (*noun*), *V:* vagin*, fente *f*, chagatte *f*.

futz[2] [fʌts] (**to**) (*U.S.*), *V:* = **fuck**[2] **(to), 1.**

fuzz [fʌz] (*noun*), *P:* **1.** policier*, détective *m*, flic *m*, roussin *m*. **2.** la police*, flicaille *f*, rousse *f*. **3.** gardien* de prison, matuche *m*, maton *m*. **4.** (*U.S.*) Brigade fédérale des Stupéfiants.

fuzzled [ˈfʌzld] (*adj.*), *P:* ivre*, asphyxié, bit(t)uré, chargé.

* L'astérisque indique que le mot marqué de ce signe figure comme entrée dans le Répertoire.

G

G [dʒiː], *P:* **1. to put in the G,** (*a*) agir sur qn, serrer la vis (*ou* les pouces) à qn; (*b*) dénoncer*, cafarder, moutonner, moucharder, donner qn. **2.** = **grand.** *Voir aussi* **G-man.**

gab[1] [gæb] (*noun*). **1.** *P:* blabla *m*, jactage *m*. **2.** *F:* **to have the gift of the g.,** (*a*) avoir du bagout, savoir baratiner, avoir une bonne tapette; (*b*) savoir vendre sa salade. **3.** *P:* = **gob**[1], **1.**

gab[2] [gæb] (**to**), *P:* parler* trop, bavarder*, bavasser, blablater, jacter, jacasser, tenir le crachoir.

gabber [ˈgæbər] (*noun*), *P:* bavard*, baratineur *m*, jacteur *m*, tapette *f*.

gabby [ˈgæbi] (*adj.*), *P:* bavard, qui a la langue bien pendue.

gabfest [ˈgæbfest] (*noun*), *P:* bavette *f*, causette *f*.

gad, Gad [gæd] (*noun*), *F:* **by g.!** sacrebleu! sapristi! mes aïeux!

gad about [ˈgædəˈbaut] (**to**), *F:* **1.** vadrouiller, être par voies et par chemins (*ou* par monts et par vaux). **2.** courir le jupon, courir la prétentaine.

gadie [ˈgeidi] (*noun*), *P:* gadjé *m* (celui qui n'est pas bohémien ou manouche).

gaff [gæf] (*noun*), *P:* **1.** logement*, piaule *f*, taule *f*, crèche *f*; **they did him in his g.,** ils l'ont piqué dans sa piaule; *cf.* **drum, 1;** *voir aussi* **screw**[2] **(to), 3. 2. gambling g.,** maison *f* de jeu, tripot *m*. **3. to blow the g.,** vendre la mèche; **to blow the g. on s.o.,** dénoncer* qn, donner qn. **4.** (*U.S.*) **to stand the g.,** être brave, encaisser les coups durs, en avoir dans le ventre, être gonflé. **5.** = **guff. 6.** café-concert *m*, beuglant *m*.

gaffed [gæft] (*adj.*) (*U.S.*), *P:* **g. dice** = **shapes.**

gaffer [ˈgæfər] (*noun*), *F:* patron*, taulier *m*, singe *m*.

gag[1] [gæg] (*noun*), *F:* **1.** plaisanterie *f*, blague *f*, rigolade *f*. **2. to pull a g. on s.o.,** (*a*) mettre qn en boîte; (*b*) faire une entourloupe à qn. **3.** (*cinéma, etc.*) gag *m*.

gag[2] [gæg] (**to**), *F:* (*th.*) enchaîner.

gaga [ˈgɑːgɑː] (*adj.*), *F:* **1.** gaga. **2.** fou*, cinglé, timbré. **3. to go g. over s.o.,** s'enticher de qn, se toquer de qn.

gage [geidʒ] (*noun*) (*mainly U.S.*), *P:* **1.** whisky *m*, alcool* bon marché, tord-boyaux *m*. **2.** tabac*, cigarettes*, cigares*, chique *f*; **stick of g.,** cigarette* (tabac *ou* marijuana), la fume. **3.** marijuana *f* (*drogues**). **4. to get one's g. up,** (*a*) se mettre en colère*, sortir de ses gonds; (*b*) être ivre*, se piquer le nez, se bit(t)urer, avoir sa cuite.

gaged [geidʒd] (*adj.*) (*U.S.*), *P:* ivre*, bit(t)uré, noir, rond, schlass.

gal [gæl] (*noun*), *F:* jeune fille*, môme *f*, gonzesse *f*.

galah [ˈgɑːlə] (*noun*) (*Austr.*), *F:* individu bête*, buse *f*.

gall [gɔːl] (*noun*), *F:* culot *m*, toupet *m*.

gallows-bird [ˈgælouzbəːd] (*noun*), *F:* gibier *m* de potence.

galluses [ˈgæləsiz] (*pl. noun*), *P:* bretelles *f.pl.*

galoot [gəˈluːt] (*noun*), *P:* **1.** individu*, type *m*, mec *m*, client *m*. **2.** lourdaud *m*, empoté *m*, godiche *m*.

galumph [gəˈlʌmf] (**to**), *F:* caracoler, galoper lourdement.

gam[1] [gæm] (*noun*). **1.** *V:* = **gamaroosh**[1]. **2.** (*pl.*) *P:* jambes*, guibolles *f.pl.*, gambettes *f.pl.* **3.** (*U.S.*) *F:* bavette *f*, causette *f*.

gam[2] [gæm] (**to**). **1.** *V:* = **gamaroosh**[2] **(to). 2.** (*U.S.*) *P:* se vanter, esbrouffer, en installer. **3.** (*U.S.*) *P:* flirter.

gamaroosh, gamar(o)uche[1] [ˈgæməˈruːʃ] (*noun*), *V:* coït* buccal, suçage *m*, taillade *f* de plume.

gamaroosh, gamar(o)uche[2] [ˈgæməˈruːʃ] (**to**), *V:* faire un coït* buccal, sucer; faire minette, prendre la pipe, souffler dans la canne (*ou* dans le mirliton).

game[1] [geim] (*adj.*), *F:* **1. I'm g.!** dac! ça botte! je veux! **2.** crâne; **to be dead g.,** avoir beaucoup de courage, en avoir dans le ventre. **3.** = **gammy.**

game[2] [geim] (*noun*). **1.** *P:* **to be on the g.,** racoler* (*prostituée*), turfer, turbiner. **2.** *F:* **I know your little g.!** je vois votre manigance (*ou* votre petit jeu)! **3.** *F:* **to have the g. sewn up,** avoir la partie belle (*ou* en main), tenir le bon bout. *Voir aussi* **army, 2; badger, 2; clip-game; fun**[2], **2; play**[2] **(to), 2; sack**[1], **4; skin**[1], **5** (*a*)**; up**[2], **3.**

gamesmanship [ˈgeimzmənʃip] (*noun*), *F:* l'art *m* de gagner.

gammer [ˈgæmər] (*noun*), *F:* grand-mère, la vieille.

gammon[1] [ˈgæmən] (*noun*), *P:* bobards *m.pl.*, boniments *m.pl.*

* An asterisk indicates that the word so marked is included as a head-word in the Appendix.

gammon[2] [ˈgæmən] (**to**), *P:* **1.** duper*, monter un bateau à (qn), emmener (qn) en bateau. **2.** emberlificoter.

gammy [ˈgæmi] (*adj.*), *F:* boiteux, bancal, banban, béquillard.

gamp [gæmp] (*noun*), *F:* parapluie*, riflard *m*, pébroc *m*.

gander[1] [ˈgændər] (*noun*), *P:* **to have a g.**, jeter un coup d'œil,* bigler, zyeuter; **just take a g.!** mate-moi ça!

gander[2] [ˈgændər] (**to**), *P:* regarder*, lorgner, reluquer.

ganga [ˈgændʒər] (*noun*), *P:* marijuana *f* (*drogues**), gania *m*.

gangster [ˈgæŋstər] (*noun*), *P:* (*a*) marijuana *f* (*drogues**); (*b*) habitué(e) de la marijuana; (*c*) cigarette* de marijuana, reefer *m*, stick *m*.

gang up [ˈgæŋˈʌp] (**to**), *F:* **to g. u. on s.o.**, former équipe (*ou* se liguer) contre qn, s'acoquiner pour tomber qn.

ganjah [ˈgændʒɑː], **ganji** [ˈgændʒi] (*noun*), *P:* marijuana *f* (*drogues**); *cf.* **bhang; ganga; gunji.**

gannet [ˈgænit] (*noun*), *F:* goinfre*, bouffe-tout *m*, bec *m* à tout grain.

garbage [ˈgɑːbidʒ] (*noun*). **1.** *F:* camelote *f*, rossignols *m.pl.* **2.** *P:* boniments *m.pl.*, bobards *m.pl.*, bidon *m*. **3.** *P:* mauvaise nourriture*, ragougnasse *f*. **4.** *P:* drogue *f* de mauvaise qualité, foin *m*. **5.** *P:* résidu *m* après cuisson d'une drogue, fond *m* de culot. **6.** *P:* amphétamines *f.pl.* (*drogues**).

garbo [ˈgɑːbou] (*noun*) (*Austr.*), *F:* boueur *m*.

garden [ˈgɑːdn] (*noun*), *F:* **1. to lead s.o. up the g. path,** faire marcher qn, faire voir des étoiles en plein midi, emmener qn en bateau. **2. everything in the g. is lovely,** tout va comme sur des roulettes, tout baigne dans le beurre. *Voir aussi* **bear-garden.**

gas[1] [gæs] (*adj.*), *P:* **1.** excellent*, terrible, super. **2.** très amusant*, à crever de rire*, marrant, boyautant, astap.

gas[2] [gæs] (*noun*). **1.** *F:* bavardage *m* vide, palas(s) *m*, baratinage *m*, bidon *m*; **his talk is all g.**, il parle pour ne rien dire, tout ça c'est du vent. **2.** (*U.S.*) *F:* (=*gasoline*) essence *f*, jus *m*; **to step on the g.**, (*a*) appuyer sur le champignon, donner plein gaz; (*b*) se dépêcher*, se grouiller; **to run out of g.**, (*a*) être en panne d'essence (*ou* en manque de jus); (*b*) devenir fatigué* (*ou* vidé), être à bout de souffle. **3.** *P:* du tonnerre, qch. de foutral.

gas[3] [gæs] (**to**). **1.** *F:* bavarder*, baratiner, jacter. **2.** *P:* bonimenter, bourrer le crâne, avoir (qn) au baratin. **3.** *P:* entourlouper, épater, époustoufler.

gasbag [ˈgæsbæg] (*noun*), *F:* moulin *m* à paroles, beau parleur, phraseur *m*.

gash[1] [gæʃ] (*adj.*), *P:* de rechange, en surplus, en rab(iot). *Voir aussi* **lob**[1], **3.**

gash[2] [gæʃ] (*noun*). **1.** *P:* rab(iot) *m*. **2.** *P:* femme*, fendue *f*, fumelle *f*. **3.** *V:* vagin*, fente *f*, crevasse *f*; (*b*) coït*, giclée *f*.

gash-hound [ˈgæʃhaund] (*noun*), *P:* coureur *m* de jupons, chaud lapin.

gasket [ˈgæskit] (*noun*), *F:* **to blow a g.** = **to blow a fuse** (*voir* **fuse**).

gas-meter [ˈgæsmiːtər] (*noun*), *F:* **to lie like a g.-m.**, mentir* comme un arracheur de dents.

gasp [gɑːsp] (*noun*), *F:* **to be at one's last g.**, être à bout (*ou* au bout de son rouleau).

gasper [ˈgɑːspər] (*noun*), *P:* cigarette*, cibiche *f*, sèche *f*.

gassed [gæst] (*adj.*), *P:* **1.** ivre*, asphyxié, allumé. **2.** tordu de rire*, époustouflé, renversé.

gasser [ˈgæsər] (*noun*), *P:* **1.** baratineur *m*, fort *m* en gueule. **2.** une merveille, du bath, du badour. **3.** éteignoir *m*, vieux jeu, périmé *m*. **4.** rigolade *f*, franche marrade.

gassy [ˈgæsi] (*adj.*), *P:* **1.** bavard, baratineur, esbrouffeur. **2.** = **groovy.**

gas up [ˈgæsˈʌp] (**to**) (*U.S.*). **1.** *F:* se fournir d'essence, faire le plein. **2.** *P:* animer, exciter, stimuler, émoustiller.

gat [gæt] (*noun*) (*U.S.*), *P:* revolver*, pistolet *m*, calibre *m*.

gate-crash [ˈgeitkræʃ] (**to**), *F:* se rendre à une réception (*fête, etc.*) sans être invité, resquiller.

gate-crasher [ˈgeitkræʃər] (*noun*), *F:* passe-volant *m*, resquilleur *m*; **champion g.-c.**, roi *m* des resquilleurs.

gate-post [ˈgeitpoust] (*noun*), *F:* **between you and me and the g.-p.**, entre quat'zyeux, entre quat'murs, de toi z'à moi.

gauge [geidʒ] (*noun*), *P:* = **gage, 3.**

Gawd [gɔːd] (*noun*) (=*God*), *P:* **oh my G.!** ah mon Dieu!

* L'astérisque indique que le mot marqué de ce signe figure comme entrée dans le Répertoire.

gawk [gɔːk] (*noun*), *F:* **1.** godiche *mf.* **2. big g.**, grand escogriffe.

gawky [ˈgɔːki] (*adj.*), *F:* dégingandé.

gay[1] [gei] (*adj.*), *F:* **1. g. deceivers** = **falsies, 2. 2.** homosexuel, qui sent la pédale. *Voir aussi* **dog[1], 9.**

gay[2] [gei] (*noun*) (*Austr.*), *P:* = **alec, 2.**

gazump [gəˈzʌmp] (**to**), *F:* **1.** escroquer* en faisant monter le prix d'une propriété au dernier moment; faire valser les prix. **2.** escroquer*, carotter.

gazumper [gəːzʌmpər] (*noun*), *F:* escroc* en propriétés immobilières.

gear[1] [giər] (*adj.*), *P:* excellent*, du tonnerre, formid, bath.

gear[2] [giər] (*noun*). **1.** *F:* biens *m.pl.*, possessions *f.pl.*; *cf.* **marriage. 2.** *F:* attirail *m*, barda *m*, bataclan *m.* **3.** *F:* vêtements*, nippes *f.pl.*, frusques *f.pl.* **4.** *P:* attirail *m* de drogué*, la popote. **5.** *P:* butin*, rafle *f*, fade *m.* **6.** *F:* **to be in high g.**, être survolté, péter le feu; **to be in low g.**, ne pas être en forme, être déprimé. **7.** *P:* grand spectacle, gala *m.* **8.** (*Austr.*) *P:* fausses dents*, râtelier *m.*

geared up [ˈgiədˈʌp] (*p.p. & adj.*), *F:* **to be g. u. for sth.**, être fin prêt, être conditionné pour qch.

geck[1] [gek] (*noun*), *P:* = **git[2].**

geck[2] [gek] (**to**), *P:* zyeuter, filer un coup de sabord.

gee![1] [dʒiː] (*excl.*), *F:* **g.** (**whiz(z)**)! ah, dis donc! mince! bigre!

gee[2] [dʒiː] (*noun*), *P:* **1.** = **G, 1, 2. 2.** (*U.S.*) individu*, mec *m*; **front g.**, homme *m* de paille, couverture *f*; **a hip g.**, un mec à la coule; un pote, un régulier.

gee[3] [dʒiː] (**to**), *P:* voler*, chiper.

geed up [ˈdʒiːdˈʌp] (*adj.*), *P:* sous l'effet des drogues*, chargé, défoncé.

gee-er [ˈdʒiːər] (*noun*), *P:* cafardeur *m*, faiseur *m* de crosses, mauvais coucheur.

gee-gee [ˈdʒiːdʒiː] (*noun*), *F:* **1.** cheval*, dada *m.* **2. to follow the gee-gees**, jouer aux courtines, suivre les gails (*ou* les canassons). *Voir aussi* **flutter, 2.**

gee-up [ˈdʒiːʌp] (*noun*), *F:* = **gip, 2.**

gee up [ˈdʒiːˈʌp] (**to**). **1.** *F:* (*à un cheval*) **g. u.!** hue! au trot! **2. he gee-ed them up**, (*a*) *P:* il les a montés l'un contre l'autre; (*b*) *F:* il les a fait se dégrouiller. *Voir aussi* **geed up.**

Geez(e)! [dʒiːz] (*excl.*), *P:* bon Dieu! tonnerre de Dieu!; *cf.* **Jeeze!**

geezed up [ˈdʒiːzdˈʌp] (*adj.*), *P:* **1.** ivre*, bit(t)uré, blindé, rétamé. **2.** = **geed up.**

geezer [ˈgiːzər] (*noun*), *P:* **1.** (*a*) homme*, type *m*, mec *m*; (*b*) femme*, souris *f.* **2. an old g.**, (*a*) un vieux*, un vieux birbe (*ou* bonze); (*b*) une carabosse, une vieille rombière.

gefuffle [gəˈfʌfl] (*noun*), *F:* = **kerfuffle.**

gel [gel] (*noun*), *F:* = **gal.**

gelt [gelt] (*noun*), *P:* argent*, pognon *m*, soudure *f.*

gen [dʒen] (*noun*), *F:* renseignements*, tuyaux *m.pl.*; **duff g.**, faux renseignements, canard *m*, du bidon; **pukka g.**, renseignement* sûr, bon tuyau, tuyau increvable, de l'officiel, de l'authentique, bath rencard *m.*

genned up [ˈdʒendˈʌp] (*adj. & p.p.*), *F:* **to get g. u.**, se mettre au courant, se rencarder; **to be g. u.**, être rencardé, être à la page (*ou* dans le bain *ou* au parfum).

gent [dʒent] (*noun*) (=*gentleman*), *F:* **1.** un monsieur, un type bien. **2. to go to the gents**, aller aux W.C.*, aller chez les messieurs.

geography [dʒiˈɔgrəfi] (*noun*), *F:* **to show s.o. the g. of the house**, (*a*) faire le tour du propriétaire; (*b*) montrer les W.C.* à qn.

Geordie [ˈdʒɔːdi] (*noun*), *F:* originaire de la région de Tyneside.

George[1] [dʒɔːdʒ] (*pr. noun*), *F:* **1. by G.!** sapristi! mince alors! **2.** (*av.*) pilote *m* automatique, Georges *m.*

george[2] [dʒɔːdʒ] (**to**), *P:* émoustiller, échauffer, allumer (qn).

gerdoing! gerdoying! [gəˈdɔiŋ] (*excl.*), *F:* boum (badaboum)! pan! vlan!; *cf.* **doing!; kerdoing!**

gessein [geˈsiːn] (**to**), *P:* = **con[2] (to).**

gesseiner [geˈsiːnər] (*noun*), *P:* **1.** tout le bataclan, les cliques et les claques. **2.** (*Marine marchande*) poubelle *f*, boîte *f* à ordures.

gessump [geˈsʌmp] (**to**), *P:* voler*, barboter, empiler; emberlificoter; **to g. the gesseiner**, s'affurer, chauffer, faire une cambriole.

get [get] (**to**). **1.** *F:* comprendre; **I don't g. you**, je ne pige pas; **g. me?** tu y es? tu saisis? **2.** *F:* **I'll g. you for that!**

* An asterisk indicates that the word so marked is included as a head-word in the Appendix.

j'aurai ta peau, je t'aurai au tournant; **I've got him,** je le tiens. 3. *F:* **it gets me when . . .,** ça m'énerve (*ou* ça me crispe *ou* ça m'agace) lorsque... 4. *F:* **to g. it in the neck,** écoper, en prendre pour son grade (*ou* son compte), se faire aplatir. 5. *P:* **we got trouble** (*=we have trouble*), on a des ennuis; **I got rhythm** (*=I have rhythm*), j'ai du swing; (**you**) **got a light?** (*=do you have a light?*), t'as du feu? 6. *F:* **to g. ten years,** attraper (*ou* piger) dix berges. 7. *F:* **you've got me there,** tu m'as, tu me colles; je donne ma langue au chat. 8. *F:* émouvoir, secouer, emballer. 9. *F:* tuer*, bousiller, zigouiller. 10. *F:* arrêter*, épingler. 11. *F:* **to g. there,** réussir, arriver, se débrouiller; **not to g. anywhere,** n'aboutir à rien. 12. *F:* **to g. going,** (*a*) se dépêcher*, se magner, se dégrouiller; **g. going!** en route!; (*b*) se mettre au travail*, se mettre en branle. 13. *P:* **to g. behind it,** (*a*) (*drogues*) être défoncé, être high; (*b*) être possédé (par qch.).

get across [ˈgətəˈkrɔs] (**to**), *F:* (*a*) faire comprendre, faire piger, éclairer; (*b*) communiquer, faire passer la rampe.

get along [ˈgetəˈlɔŋ] (**to**), *F:* 1. **I must be getting along,** il faut que je m'en aille (*ou* que je me mette en route). 2. **g. a. with you!** (*a*) va te promener! débarrasse (le plancher)!; (*b*) vas-y voir! tu charries!; (*c*) je n'en crois rien; allons donc!; pour qui me prends-tu? 3. **to g. a. with s.o.,** bien s'entendre avec qn. 4. se défendre, pouvoir faire.

get around [ˈgetəˈraund] (**to**), *F:* 1. **it's getting around that . . .,** le bruit court que... 2. rouler sa bosse, circuler. 3. = **get round** (**to**). 4. **to g. a. to doing sth.,** arriver à faire qch. 5. circonvenir, surmonter (une difficulté, *etc.*).

get at [ˈget-æt] (**to**), *F:* 1. acheter, soudoyer, graisser la patte à (qn). 2. découvrir (la vérité, *etc.*). 3. **what are you getting at?** où voulez-vous en venir? 4. asticoter, chercher des crosses à (qn). 5. tripoter, tripatouiller, trifouiller.

get-at-able [ˈgetˈætəbl] (*adj.*), *F:* accessible, d'accès facile.

getaway [ˈgetəwei] (*noun*), *F:* évasion *f*, la belle, la cavale; **to make a g.,** s'éclipser, faire un plongeon; **g. car,** voiture* de fuite, bagnole *f* de cavale.

get away [ˈgetəˈwei] (**to**). 1. *F:* **g. a. (with you)!** (*a*) laisse tomber! fiche-moi la paix! barca!; (*b*) je ne mords pas! ça ne prend pas! 2. *F:* **to g. a. with it,** s'en tirer à bon compte; **he won't g. a. with it,** il ne l'emportera pas au paradis. 3. *F:* **there's no getting away from it,** il n'y a pas moyen d'en sortir. 4. *P:* **to g. it a.** = **to get it off** (**get off** (**to**), 4 (*b*)).

get by [ˈgetˈbai] (**to**), *F:* s'en tirer, en être quitte, s'en contenter.

get down [ˈgetˈdaun] (**to**), *F:* 1. **to g. s.o. d.,** irriter, déprimer, déconcerter qn; taper sur le système à qn, coller le cafard à qn; **what gets me down is . . .,** ce qui est cafardeux, c'est... 2. **to g. d. to it,** s'y mettre, en mettre un coup.

get off [ˈgetˈɔf] (**to**). 1. *F:* **to g. o. lightly,** s'en tirer à bon compte, bien s'en sortir. 2. *P:* **g. o.!** fous-moi la paix! arrête le char! 3. *F:* **to g. o. with s.o.,** faire une touche. 4. *V:* **to g. it o.,** (*a*) avoir un orgasme*, lâcher le jus; (*b*) coïter*, s'envoyer en l'air; (*c*) se masturber*, se branler. 5. *P:* se doper, s'enfoncer (avec la drogue). 6. *F:* **g. it o. your chest!** vide ton sac! 7. *F:* **to tell s.o. where to g.o.,** réprimander* sévèrement qn, dire à qn ses quatre vérités. 8. *P:* **to g. o. on sth.,** être transporté par qch.; **we got off on that music,** cette musique nous a remués (*ou* nous a secoué les entrailles *ou* nous a pris au ventre).

get on [ˈgetˈɔn] (**to**), *F:* **g. o. with you!** = **get along with you!** (**get along** (**to**), 2).

get on to [ˈgetˈɔntuː] (**to**), *F:* 1. découvrir*. 2. se mettre en rapport avec (qn), contacter (qn).

get-out [ˈgetaut] (*noun*), *F:* 1. esquive *f*, moyen *m* de sortie. 2. (*U.S.*) = **get-up,** 1.

get out [ˈgetˈaut] (**to**), *P:* **to g. o. from under** = **to find an out** (**out**[2]).

get over [ˈgetˈouvər] (**to**), *F:* **I can't g. o. it!** je n'en reviens pas, j'en reste baba!

get-rich-quick [ˈgetˈritʃˈkwik] (*adj.*), *F:* véreux; **g.-r.-q. plan,** projet *m* qui promet la lune.

get round [ˈgetˈraund] (**to**), *F:* cajoler,

* L'astérisque indique que le mot marqué de ce signe figure comme entrée dans le Répertoire.

enjôler; **you can't g. r. me like that,** tu ne m'auras pas comme ça.

get through [ˈgetˈθruː] (**to**). **1.** *F:* contacter, avoir la communication. **2.** *F:* **to g. t. to s.o.,** faire comprendre qch. à qn, faire piger qn. **3.** *F:* **to g. t. the month,** boucler son mois, joindre les deux bouts. **4.** *P:* obtenir des drogues*, se garnir, trouver la cheville (*ou* le joint *ou* le contact). **5.** *F:* **to g. t. some work,** abattre du travail*; **to g. t. a lot of money,** dépenser* beaucoup d'argent*, croquer beaucoup de fric.

get-together [ˈgettəgeðər] (*noun*), *F:* réunion amicale, retrouvaille *f.*

get together [ˈgettəˈgeðər] (**to**), *F:* **to g. it t.,** (*a*) se préparer à partir d'un endroit, prendre ses cliques et ses claques; (*b*) s'éclaircir les idées, éclairer sa lanterne.

get-up [ˈgetʌp] (*noun*), *F:* **1.** vêtements*, fripes *f.pl.*, nippes *f.pl.*, loques *f.pl.*, accoutrement *m.* **2.** tenue *f*, présentation *f.*

get up [ˈgetˈʌp] (**to**), *V:* **to g. it u.,** coïter*, s'envoyer en l'air.

get-up-and-go [ˈgetʌpən(d)ˈgou] (*adj.*), *F:* plein d'allant, plein d'entrain, dynamique.

ghastly [ˈgɑːstli] (*adj.*), *F:* abominable, hideux; **the weather's g.,** il fait un temps de chien; **what a g. woman!** quelle femme* abominable! quelle sale chipie!

gherkin [ˈgəːkin] (*noun*), *P:* pénis*, gourdin *m*, gourde *f* à poils; **to jerk one's g.,** se masturber*, se tirer son coup.

ghost [goust] (**to**), *F:* **to g. (for) s.o.,** remplacer qn, faire le nègre.

G.I. [ˈdʒiːˈai] (*abbr.*) (*U.S.*), *F:* **1.** (= *government issue*) ce qui vient de l'intendance militaire américaine. **2.** soldat* américain; **G.I. Joe,** le type du biffin américain pendant la deuxième guerre mondiale.

giddy up [ˈgidiˈʌp] (**to**), *F:* = **gee up (to), 1.**

gift [gift] (*noun*), *F:* qch. de pas difficile*, du beurre, du nougat.

gig¹ [gig] (*noun*) (*mainly U.S.*). **1.** *F:* joujou *m* quelconque, sucette *f.* **2.** *V:* anus*, rondibé *m*, trou *m*; **up your g.!** mon cul! **3.** *V:* vagin*, baba *m*, crac *m.* **4.** *F:* réjouissances*, surboum *f*, bamboche *f.* **5.** *F:* festival *m* de jazz. **6.** *F:* engagement *m* d'un soir (*th., jazz, etc.*). **7.** *P:* (*a*) vieille voiture*, guimbarde *f*; (*b*) bolide *m.* **8.** *P:* emploi* bouche-trou, placarde *f.* **9.** *P:* qn qui regarde* avec curiosité, reluqueur *m*, zyeuteur *m.* **10.** *P:* détective privé, condé *m.* **11.** *P:* (**prize**) **g.,** individu bête*, gourde *f*, crétin *m* de première. **12.** *F:* passe-temps *m*, dada *m*, hobby *m.*

gig² [gig] (**to**). **1.** (*U.S.*) *F:* jouer dans un groupe de jazz. **2.** *P:* regarder*, reluquer, zyeuter. **3.** (*Austr.*) *P:* taquiner, tourmenter, faire enrager (qn).

giggle [ˈgigl] (*noun*). **1.** *F:* **we did it (just) for a g.,** c'était pour rigoler. **2.** *F:* **we had a right g.,** on s'est tordu de rire*; **what a g.!** quelle bonne rigolade! **3.** *F:* **to get the giggles,** attraper un fou-rire. **4.** *P:* **g. smoke** (*or* **weed**), cigarette* de marijuana (*drogues**), joint *m*, stick *m*, reefer *m.* **5.** (*U.S.*) *F:* **g. water,** champagne *m.*

gigi [ˈʒiːʒiː] (*noun*) = **gig¹, 1, 2, 3.**

gills [gilz] (*pl. noun*), *P:* **to be stewed to the g.,** être complètement ivre*, avoir sa cuite, être bourré à bloc.

gimme [ˈgimi] (*abbr.*) (=*give me*), *F:* donne! aboule!; *cf.* **skin¹, 10.**

gimmick [ˈgimik] (*noun*), *F:* **1.** attrape *f*, tour *m*, combine *f*, astuce *f*, truc *m.* **2.** attrape-couillons *m*, truc *m* publicitaire. **3.** gadget *m*, truc *m*, machin *m.*

gimmickry [ˈgimikri] (*noun*), *F:* truquage *m.*

gimmicky [ˈgimiki] (*adj.*), *F:* rempli de trucs *m.pl.*

gin [dʒin] (*noun*), *P:* **1.** (*U.S.*) prostituée* nègre*, pépée cirée, frangine *f* bamboula. **2.** (*Austr.*) femme aborigène. **3.** cocaïne *f* (*drogues**).

ginger [ˈdʒindʒər] (*noun*), *F:* **1.** rouquin(e) *m(f)*, poil *m* de carotte. **2.** boisson gazeuse au gingembre. **3.** **to have (a lot of) g.,** avoir de l'entrain *m* (*ou* de l'allant *m ou* de l'abattage *m*). **4. g. group,** groupe *m* de pression. *Voir aussi* **stone-ginger.**

ginger up [ˈdʒindʒərˈʌp] (**to**), *F:* émoustiller, mettre de l'entrain dans, donner un coup de fouet à.

gink [giŋk] (*noun*), *P:* (*a*) (*terme de mépris pour un individu*) plouc *m*, rustre *m*, pataud *m*, drôle de parois-

* An asterisk indicates that the word so marked is included as a head-word in the Appendix.

sien *m*; (*b*) pauvre type *m*, couillon *m*, tartempion *m*, zigomar *m*.

gin-mill [ˈdʒinmil] (*U.S.*), **gin-palace** [ˈdʒinpæləs] (*noun*), *F:* bar *m* de basse classe, boui-boui *m*, bouge *m*, assommoir *m*.

ginormous [dʒaiˈnɔːməs] (*adj.*), *F:* colossal, maous(se), bœuf.

gip [dʒip] (*noun*), *F:* **1. to give s.o. g.**, tomber sur qn à bras raccourcis, tomber sur le paletot à qn. **2. my rheumatism is giving me g.**, mes rhumatismes me font voir trente-six chandelles.

giped [ˈgaiped] (*adj.*) (*mainly Scottish*), *P:* fou*, toqué, timbré.

gippo [ˈdʒipou] (*noun*), *P:* **1.** romanichel *m*, romani *m*, manouche *m*. **2.** (*mil.*) la soupe, le rata.

girl [gəːl] (*noun*), *P:* **1.** cocaïne *f* (*drogues**), fillette *f*, coco *f*. **2.** pédéraste*, chouquette *f*, tante *f*. **3. working g.**, prostituée*, persilleuse *f*, gagneuse *f*. *Voir aussi* **bar-girl; B-girl; cover-girl; dolly-girl; glamour-girl; playgirl; sweater-girl; yes-girl.**

girlie [ˈgəːli] (*noun & attrib. adj.*). **1.** *F:* fillette *f*, girl *f*; **g. show,** spectacle *m* de girls; **g. magazines,** presse *f* de charme.. **2.** *P:* (*mainly U.S.*) prostituée*, fille *f*.

git![1] [git] (*excl.*), *P:* file! fiche le camp! décolle!

git[2] [git] (*noun*), *P:* individu bête*, crétin *m*, con *m*.

give [giv] (**to**), *F:* **1. don't g. me that!** ne me raconte pas d'histoires! **2. to g. it to s.o.,** réprimander* qn, passer un savon à qn. **3. g. it all you've got!** faites le maximum! donne un (bon) coup de collier! **4. to know what gives,** être à la page (*ou* dans le vent *ou* à la coule). **5. what gives?,** (*a*) salut!; (*b*) qu'est-ce qui se fricote?; (*c*) quoi de neuf? *Voir aussi* **vocals.**

give-away[1] [ˈgivəwei] (*adj.*), *F:* **to sell sth. at a g. price,** vendre qch. à un prix défiant toute concurrence.

give-away[2] [ˈgivəwei] (*noun*), *F:* **1.** article sacrifié. **2. a (dead) g.,** geste *m* (mot, *etc.*) qui en dit long.

give over [ˈgivˈouvər] (**to**), *F:* renoncer à (qch.), dételer, remiser; **g.o., will you?** laisse tomber, veux-tu?

glad [glæd] (*adj.*), *F:* **g. rags,** les plus beaux vêtements* de sa garde-robe, des nippes *f.pl.* baths, les fourgues *f.pl.* du dimanche; **to put on one's g. rags,** se mettre sur son trente et un. *Voir aussi* **eye, 6.**

glamour-boy [ˈglæməbɔi] (*noun*), *F:* (*a*) séducteur *m*, joli cœur, jeune premier; (*b*) un beau mâle.

glamour-girl [ˈglæməgəːl] (*noun*), *F:* (*a*) ensorceleuse *f*, vamp *f*; (*b*) beau morceau, prix *m* de Diane.

glamour-puss [ˈglæməpus] (*noun*), *F:* pin-up *f*, ensorceleuse *f*.

glass[1] [glɑːs] (*adj.*), *F:* **to have a g. jaw,** (*d'un boxeur*) avoir la mâchoire en verre.

glass[2] [glɑːs] (*noun*), *P:* bimbeloterie *f*, verroterie *f*, strass *m*.

glass[3] [glɑːs] (**to**), *P:* taillader (qn) avec du verre cassé (dans une rixe).

glasshouse [ˈglɑːshaus] (*noun*), *P:* (*mil.*) prison* militaire, grosse lourde.

glassy-eyed [ˈglɑːsiˈaid], **glazed** [gleizd] (*adj.*), *F:* ivre*, blindé, blindezingue.

gleep [gliːp] (**to**), *P:* injurier*, agoniser (qn).

glims [glimz] (*pl. noun*), *P:* **1.** yeux*, quinquets *m.pl.*, lanternes *f.pl.* **2.** lumières *f.pl.*, ca(le)bombe *f*, calbiche *f*; **to douse the g.,** étouffer la cabombe. **3.** phares *m.pl.* (d'une voiture). **4.** lunettes*, bernicles *f.pl.*, carreaux *m.pl.*

glitch [glitʃ] (*noun*), *F:* **1.** (*a*) anicroche *f*, accroc *m*, hic *m*; (*b*) panne *f*, os *m* (*mécanique, etc.*). **2.** (*astronautique*) perturbations *f.pl.* atmosphériques.

globes [gloubz] (*pl. noun*), *P:* seins*, globes *m.pl.*, ballons *m.pl.*

glory [ˈglɔːri] (*noun*), *F:* **1. he's got the g.,** il tombe dans la bondieuserie. **2. to go to g.,** (*a*) mourir*; (*b*) se délabrer, dégringoler, aller à dame.

glory-hole [ˈglɔːrihoul] (*noun*), *F:* capharnaüm *m*, cagibi *m*.

glossies [ˈglɔsiz] (*pl. noun*), *F:* **the g.,** revues *f.pl.*, magazines *m.pl.*, les glossies *m.pl.*

glow [glou] (*noun*), *F:* **to have** (*or* **get**) **a g. on,** être légèrement ivre*, être gris (*ou* pompette *ou* éméché).

glue-factory [ˈgluːfæktəri], **glue-pot** [ˈgluːpɔt] (*noun*), *V:* vagin*, baveux *m*.

G-man [ˈdʒiːmæn] (*noun*) (*U.S.*), *F:* agent *m* du Deuxième Bureau américain.

* L'astérisque indique que le mot marqué de ce signe figure comme entrée dans le Répertoire.

gnashers [ˈnæʃəz] (*pl. noun*), *P:* dents*, croquantes *f.pl.*

go[1] [gou] (*adj.*), *F:* en bon ordre, O.K.; **all systems are g.,** on a le feu vert.

go[2] [gou] (*noun*), *F:* **1.** (*a*) **no g.! = no dice! (dice**[1], **1)**; (*b*) **it's no g.,** rien à faire, cela ne prend pas, c'est nib, c'est midi (sonné). **2. to have a g. at s.o.,** s'en prendre à qn, dire deux mots à qn. **3. to be always on the g.,** avoir la bougeotte, être toujours (*ou* tout le temps) sur la brèche, avoir toujours un pied en l'air; **it's all g.!** on n'a pas une minute à soi! **4. have a g.!** tente la chance!; **have another g.!** remets ça! **5. he's got no g. in him,** il n'a pas d'allant, il est ramollo. **6. to put some g. into it,** y mettre de l'entrain (*ou* de l'animation). **7. to give sth. a g.,** tenter le coup, s'attaquer à qch. **8. at one g.,** d'un seul coup (*ou* trait), tout d'une haleine. **9. to be all the g.,** faire rage, faire fureur. **10. (right) from the word g.,** dès le départ, tout au début. *Voir aussi* **bag**[2] **(to), 5; little, 1; touch**[1], **2.**

go[3] [gou] (**to**). **1.** *F:* **how goes it?** ça va-t-il comme vous voulez? **2.** *F:* **g. it!** lance-toi! fonce! **3.** *P:* **to be gone,** être défoncé, planer (*drogues*). *Voir aussi* **gone** *et les verbes composés* **to go along with, down, for, off, on, out, over, through, up.**

go-ahead[1] [ˈgouəhed] (*adj.*), *F:* **a g.-a. young man with g.-a. ideas,** un garçon entreprenant qui voit loin; un jeune loup.

go-ahead[2] [ˈgouəhed] (*noun*), *F:* **to get the g.-a.,** avoir le feu vert.

goalie [ˈgouli] (*noun*) (*=goalkeeper*), *F:* gardien *m* de but, goal *m.*

go along with [ˈgouəˈlɔŋwið] (**to**), *F:* accepter (qch.) en tout et pour tout; **I'll g. a. w. that,** je suis pleinement d'accord; **I can't g. a. w. that,** je ne suis pas d'accord; je ne marche pas.

goat [gout] (*noun*), *F:* **1. to get s.o.'s g.,** ennuyer* qn, déconcerter, irriter, ahurir qn; faire bisquer qn; **he gets my g.,** il me sort par les narines. **2. old g.,** vieux* birbe, vieille bique, vieille baderne.

gob[1] [gɔb] (*noun*), *P:* **1.** bouche*, gueule *f;* **to keep one's g. shut,** se taire*; **shut your g.!** la ferme! **2.** crachat*, glaviot *m,* mollard *m.* **3.** (*U.S.*) marin*, cachalot *m,* mataf *m.* **4. gobs of...,** une abondance* de..., une flopée (*ou* tapée) de...

gob[2] [gɔb] (**to**), *P:* cracher*, mollarder; *cf.* **gob**[1], **2.**

gobbledegook [ˈgɔbldiguːk] (*noun*), *F:* jargon *m,* charabia *m,* baragouin *m.*

gobble up [ˈgɔblˈʌp] (**to**) (*Austr.*), *P:* arrêter*, agrafer, coffrer (qn).

gobstruck [ˈgɔb-strʌk] (*adj.*), *P:* ahuri, abasourdi, estomaqué; **I'm g.!** je suis comme deux ronds de flan!

goby [ˈgoubi] (*noun*) (*=go-between*), *P:* messager *m,* matignon *m.*

go-by [ˈgoubai] (*noun*), *F:* **to give s.o. the g.-b.,** battre froid à qn, snober qn, faire grise mine à qn; **to give sth. the g.-b.,** dépasser qch., esquiver qch.

God, god [gɔd] (*noun*). **1.** *F:* **by G.!** (sacré) nom de Dieu! grands dieux!; **my G.!** bon Dieu (de bon Dieu)!; **G. Almighty!** Dieu Tout-Puissant!; **G. only knows,** Dieu seul le sait. **2.** *P:* **the G. man,** prêtre*, l'homme du bon Dieu, cureton *m.* **3.** (*th.*) *F:* **the gods,** le poulailler, la poulaille, le paradis, le paradou, les titis *m.pl. Voir aussi* **tin**[1], **3.**

god-awful [ˈgɔdˈɔːful] (*adj.*), *P:* répugnant, dégueulasse, puant, infect.

goddam [ˈgɔdæm], **goddamned** [ˈgɔdæmd] (*adj.*), *P:* sacré, satané; **this g. idiot,** ce sacré bon Dieu d'idiot.

goddammit! goddamnit! [ˈgɔdˈdæmit] (*excl.*), *P:* sacré nom (de nom)!

godfer [ˈgɔdfər] (*noun*) (*R.S. = God forbid = kid*), *P:* enfant*, gosse *mf,* môme *mf; cf.* **dustbin.**

God-forbid [ˈgɔdfəbid] (*noun*) (*R.S. = kid*), *P: =* **godfer.**

go down [ˈgouˈdaun] (**to**). **1.** *F:* (*a*) finir ses études universitaires; (*b*) partir en vacances. **2.** *F:* tomber malade*. **3.** *F:* **my dinner won't g. d.,** mon dîner a du mal à passer. **4.** *F:* **it goes down well with the public,** le public l'avale tout rond; **that won't g. d. with me,** ça ne prend pas avec moi. **5.** *V:* faire un coït* buccal; **to g. d. on s.o.,** manger, sucer, pomper qn; *cf.* **box**[1], **1; come down (to), 2.**

goer [ˈgouər] (*noun*), *P:* **1. she's a g.,** c'est une chaude de la pince, c'est une chaude lapine; elle en veut. **2.** expert *m,* calé *m,* fortiche *m.*

go for [ˈgoufɔːr, ˈgoufər] (**to**), *F:* **1. to**

* An asterisk indicates that the word so marked is included as a head-word in the Appendix.

g. f. s.o., rentrer dans le chou à qn, tomber sur le poil à qn. **2.** aller chercher, essayer d'obtenir. **3.** marcher pour, être entiché de; **I don't g. f. that,** cela ne m'emballe pas beaucoup.

go-getter [ˈgougetər] (*noun*), *F:* arriviste *m*, homme qui a les dents longues.

go-getting [ˈgougetiŋ] (*adj.*), *F:* opportuniste, ambitieux, arriviste.

goggle-box [ˈgɔglbɔks] (*noun*), *F:* télé *f*, boîte *f* à images, petit écran; *cf.* **box**[1], **2; idiot-box; idiot's lantern** (*voir* **lantern**).

goggle-eyed [ˈgɔglˈaid] (*adj.*), *F:* avec les yeux en boules de loto (*ou* qui sortent de la tête).

goggles [ˈgɔglz] (*pl. noun*), *P:* lunettes*, pare-brise *m.pl.*

going [ˈgouiŋ] (*noun*), *F:* **to get out while the g.'s good,** partir* pendant que c'est possible (*ou* que la voie est libre *ou* qu'on a le vent en poupe *ou* qu'on en a l'occase).

going-over [ˈgouiŋˈouvər] (*noun*), *F:* **1. to give s.o. a g.-o.,** (*a*) battre* qn, donner une raclée à qn; (*b*) réprimander* qn, attraper qn; (*c*) fouiller qn, faire la barbote à qn. **2.** fignolage *m*, révision *f*.

goings-on [ˈgouiŋzˈɔn] (*pl. noun*), *F:* conduite *f*, manège *m*, manigances *f.pl.*; **such g.-o.!** en voilà des façons!; **I've heard of your g.-o.,** j'en ai appris de belles sur vous.

gold [gould] (*noun*), *P:* **1.** argent*, pèze *m*, flouze *m*. **2.** (**Acapulco**) **g.,** marijuana *f* (*drogues**) de bonne qualité, gold *m*. *Voir aussi* **dust**[1], **2** (*b*).

goldbrick[1] [ˈgouldbrik] (*noun*) (*U.S.*), *P:* **1.** paresseux*, tire-au-flanc *m*, ramier *m*. **2.** une fille* tartignole.

goldbrick[2] [ˈgouldbrik] (**to**) (*U.S.*), *P:* **1.** paresser à son travail, tirer au cul (*ou* au flanc), se défiler. **2.** duper*, estamper (qn).

goldbricker [ˈgouldbrikər] (*noun*) (*U.S.*), *P:* **1.** = **goldbrick**[1], **1. 2.** escroc*, estampeur *m*.

gold-digger [ˈgoulddigər] (*noun*), *F:* croqueuse *f* de diamants, gigolette *f*.

golden [ˈgould(ə)n] (*adj.*), *F:* **1. g. disc,** disque *m* d'or (le millionième). **2. g. opportunity,** affaire *f* d'or, occasion rêvée. **3.** doré, beurre, en or. **4.** excellent*, superbe, doré sur tranche. *Voir aussi* **handshake.**

goldfish-bowl [ˈgouldfiʃboul] (*noun*), *F:* maison *f* de verre, place *f* publique.

goldmine [ˈgouldmain] (*noun*), *F:* situation lucrative, mine *f* d'or, filon *m*.

gollion [ˈgɔliən] (*noun*) (*Austr.*), *P:* crachat*, graillon *m*.

golly! [ˈgɔli] (*excl.*), *F:* (**by**) **g.!** mince alors! flûte! bigre!

goma [ˈgoumə] (*noun*), *P:* opium brut (*ou* vert), goma *m* (*drogues*).

gone [gɔn] (*adj.*), *P:* **1.** parti (sous l'influence de l'alcool* ou du hachisch, *etc.*); *cf.* **go**[3] (**to**), **3. 2.** du nanan, du cool. *Voir aussi* **far; go on** (**to**), **6.**

goner [ˈgɔnər] (*noun*), *F:* **1.** (*a*) type fini; (*b*) chose perdue. **2. almost a g.,** crevard *m*, crevetant *m*, qui a son compte.

gong [gɔŋ] (*noun*). **1.** *F:* médaille *f*, pastille *f*, banane *f*, méduche *f*. **2.** *P:* pipe *f* à opium, bambou *m*; **to kick the g. around,** tirer sur le bambou.

gonga [ˈgɔŋgə] (*noun*), *P:* anus*, anneau *m*, troufignon *m*; (**you can**) **stick it up your g.!** tu peux te le mettre (*ou* te le fourrer) quelque part!; *cf.* **stick**[2] (**to**), **3.**

gonif[1] [ˈgɔnif] (*noun*), *P:* **1.** voleur*, chapardeur *m*, barboteur *m*. **2.** pédéraste*, pédé *m*.

gonif[2] [ˈgɔnif] (**to**), *P:* voler*, chaparder, barboter.

gonna [ˈgɔnə], *P:* = *going to.*

goo [guː] (*noun*), *F:* **1.** sentimentalité excessive (*ou* à la guimauve *ou* à l'eau de rose). **2.** bouillabaisse *f*, ratatouille *f*, colle *f*. **3.** flatterie *f*, pommade *f*, lèche *f*. *Cf.* **gooey.**

good [gud] (*adj.*), *F:* **1. g. God** (*or* **Lord**)! bondieu! **2. g. heavens!** ciel! **3. g. grief!** zut alors! **4. g. gracious!** fichtre! **5. g. egg!** bath! super! bravo! *Voir aussi* **hiding, 1; job, 6, 7; no-good; thing, 9.**

goodies [ˈgudiz] (*pl. noun*), *F:* **1.** gourmandises *f.pl.*, du nanan. **2.** les bons, les bien-pensants; *cf.* **baddie, 2.**

goodish [ˈgudiʃ] (*adj.*), *F:* **1.** assez bon. **2. a g. while,** assez longtemps, une paie; **it's a g. way** (*or* **step**) **from here,** c'est à un bon bout de chemin d'ici.

goodness [ˈgudnis] (*noun & excl.*), *F:* **g.!** Dieu! bigre!; **g. me!** bonté divine!; **g. gracious** (**me**)! miséricorde!; **for g. sake!** pour l'amour de Dieu! **thank g.!**

* L'astérisque indique que le mot marqué de ce signe figure comme entrée dans le Répertoire.

Dieu merci!; g. (**only**) **knows what I must do,** Dieu sait ce que je dois faire. *Voir aussi* **honest-to-goodness.**

goodo! [ˈgudou] (*excl.*), *F:* chic alors! parfait! épatant!

goods [gudz] (*pl. noun*), *P:* **1. a nice bit of g.,** une fille* bien balancée, un beau petit châssis, une jolie poupée; *voir aussi* **damaged. 2. it's the g.,** c'est ce qu'il faut, ça tombe pile. **3. to deliver the g.,** remplir ses engagements, tenir parole. **4.** chose promise, chose due. **5. to have the g.,** être capable. **6.** preuves *f.pl.* de culpabilité; **to have the g. on s.o.,** tenir le bon bout contre qn. **7.** drogues* en général, stups *m.pl.*, came *f. Voir aussi* **sample** (**to**).

good-time [ˈgudˈtaim] (*adj.*), *P:* **1. g.-t. girl,** fille* rigolote (*ou* qui en prend une bosse). **2. g.-t. Charley,** (joyeux) viveur *m*, noceur *m*, bambocheur *m*.

goody [ˈgudi] (*noun*), *F: voir* **goodies.**

goody-goody[1] [ˈgudigudi] (*adj.*), *F:* bien-pensant; d'une vertu suffisante; **to be g.-g.,** faire le saint, faire sa Sophie, recevoir le bon Dieu sans confession.

goody-goody![2] [ˈgudiˈgudi] (*excl.*), *F:* chic de chic!

goody-goody[3] [ˈgudigudi] (*noun*), *F:* **he's a little g.-g.,** c'est un petit saint (de bois).

gooey [ˈguːi] (*adj.*), *F:* **1.** collant, visqueux, poisseux. **2.** mièvre, à l'eau de rose. *Cf.* **goo.**

goof[1] [guːf] (*noun*) (*mainly U.S.*). **1.** *F:* individu bête*, couillon *m*, cavé *m*, empoté *m*. **2.** *F:* fou *m*, timbré *m*. **3.** *F:* homme*, mec *m*, type *m*. **4.** *P:* drogué*, camé *m*, toxico *m*. **5.** *F:* bévue*, boulette *f*, gaffe *f*, bourde *f*.

goof[2] [guːf] (**to**). **1.** *F:* gaffer, faire une bourde (*ou* une boulette); *cf.* **goof off** (**to**), **1. 2.** *F:* se trahir, se vendre, se couper. **3.** *F:* rêvasser, être dans les nuages. **4.** *F:* duper*, endormir, engourdir (qn). **5.** *P:* rater (*ou* louper) une piquouse. **6.** *P:* se droguer*, se camer; *cf.* **goofed** (**up**).

goof at [ˈguːfˈæt] (**to**), *P:* regarder*, reluquer, mirer, mater.

goofball [ˈguːfbɔːl] (*noun*) (*mainly U.S.*), *P:* **1.** = **goof**[1], **1. 2.** individu* bizarre, drôle d'oiseau, drôle de paroissien. **3.** barbiturique *m* (*drogues**), schnouff *m*, balle *f* de copaille (*cf.* **ball**[1], **5**). **4.** marijuana *f* (*drogues**), kif *m*. **5.** (*a*) dose *f* de narcotique, boulette *f* de narcs, un fade; (*b*) mélange *m* de cocaïne et d'héroïne; panaché *m*; (*c*) mélange *m* de barbituriques et d'amphétamines. **6.** drogué*, camé *m*, toxico *m*. **7.** calmant *m*, tranquillisant *m*.

goofed (up) [ˈguːft(ˈʌp)] (*adj.*), *P:* sous l'influence d'un narcotique ou d'un barbiturique; bourré, chargé, défoncé; *cf.* **goof**[2] (**to**), **6.** *Voir aussi* **goof up** (**to**).

goofer [ˈguːfər] (*noun*), *P:* qn qui prend des pilules.

go-off [ˈgouˈɔf] (*noun*), *F:* **at the first g.-o.,** au premier coup, au départ.

go off [ˈgouˈɔf] (**to**), **1.** *F:* détériorer, s'abîmer, tourner. **2.** *F:* **to g. o. s.o.,** ne plus aimer* qn, ne plus en pincer, en revenir de qn. **3.** *F:* s'évanouir*, perdre connaissance. **4.** *P:* avoir un orgasme*, décharger, jouir. **5.** *F:* **how did it g. o.?** comment cela a-t-il tourné? comment cela s'est-il passé? *Voir aussi* **alarming; end, 5; rails.**

goof off [ˈguːfˈɔf] (**to**) (*U.S.*), *P:* **1.** faire une bévue*, gaffer, mettre les pieds dans le plat; *cf.* **goof**[2] (**to**), **1. 2.** traînasser, flemmarder, ne rien faire de ses dix doigts.

goof up [ˈguːfˈʌp] (**to**) (*mainly U.S.*), *P:* mal exécuter, rater, saboter, louper. *Voir aussi* **goofed** (**up**).

goofy [ˈguːfi] (*adj.*) (*mainly U.S.*), *F:* **1.** bête*, stupide, sot, gourde. **2. to be g. over s.o.,** être toqué de qn; **to be g. over sth.,** être enthousiasmé pour qch., être mordu pour qch.

goog [gug] (*noun*) (*Austr.*), *F:* **1.** œuf *m*. **2.** individu bête*, ballot *m*.

goo-goo [ˈguːguː] (*adj.*), *F:* **to make g.-g. eyes at s.o.,** faire les yeux doux à qn.

gook[1] [guk] (*adj.*) (*mainly U.S.*), *P:* du toc, de la camelote.

gook[2] [guk] (*noun*) (*mainly U.S.*), *P:* **1.** saleté*, saloperie *f*, crasse *f*. **2.** sauce ou assaisonnement visqueux; graille *f*. **3.** moricaud *m*, café *m* au lait.

gooky [ˈguki] (*adj.*) (*mainly U.S.*), *P:* gras, collant, poisseux.

gool(e)y [ˈguːli] (*noun*) (*pl.* **goolies**), *P:* **1.** (*pl.*) testicules*, pendeloques *f.pl.*, balloches *f.pl.* **2. to drop a g.,** faire une gaffe, gaffer.

goon [guːn] (*noun*). **1.** *F:* individu

* An asterisk indicates that the word so marked is included as a head-word in the Appendix.

bête* et grotesque, clown *m*, cornichon *m*, enflé *m*. **2.** (*U.S.*) *P:* anti-gréviste *m*, jaune *m*, renard *m*. **3.** (*U.S.*) *P:* gorille *m*, cogneur *m*, casseur *m* de gueules. **4.** (*U.S.*) *P:* un(e) laissé(e) pour compte, un hotu.

go on [ˈgouˈɔn] (**to**), *F:* **1. that's enough to g. o. with** (*or* **to be going on with**), voilà du pain sur la planche, assez pour le quart d'heure. **2. I don't g. much o. that,** ça ne me chante pas, je ne suis pas d'accord. **3. g. o.!**, (*a*) dis toujours!; (*b*) **g. o. (with you)!** à d'autres! n'en jetez plus! **4.** discuter le bout de gras; **she does g. o.!** impossible de lui boucler la trappe!; **to g. o. and on (about sth.)**, déblatérer (sur qch.). **5. to be going on for forty,** friser la quarantaine, aller sur ses quarante ans. **6. to be gone on s.o.,** aimer* qn, être entiché (*ou* pincé) de qn. **7.** = **go for (to), 3.**

goop [gu:p] (*noun*) (*mainly U.S.*), *F:* **1.** = **goof[1], 1. 2.** bêtise*, foutaise *f*, connerie *f*.

goose[1] [gu:s] (*noun*), *F:* **1.** individu bête*, oie *f*. **2. all his geese are swans,** tout ce qu'il fait tient du prodige. *Voir aussi* **cook[2] (to), 3.**

goose[2] [gu:s] (**to**), *P:* **1.** mignoter, faire des papouilles (*ou* des pattes d'araignée) à (qn). **2.** pincer les fesses* à (qn). **3.** duper*, faisander, pigeonner, englander (qn).

gooseberry [ˈguzb(ə)ri] (*noun*). **1.** *F:* **to play g.,** faire le chaperon, tenir le chandelier. **2.** *P:* les fils barbelés, les barbelouses *f.pl.* **3.** *P:* corde *f* à linge.

goosegog [ˈguzgɔg] (*noun*) (=*gooseberry*), *P:* groseille verte (*ou* à maquereau).

gooser [ˈgu:sər] (*noun*), *P:* pédéraste*, empapaouté *m*.

go out [ˈgoˈaut] (**to**), *F:* **to g. o. like a light,** s'évanouir*, tourner de l'œil, tomber dans les pommes.

go over [ˈgouˈouvər] (**to**), passer la rampe, faire son petit effet.

gope [goup] (**to**), *F:* regarder* fixement, zyeuter; béer, être bouche bée, bayer aux corneilles; **to g. at sth.,** regarder* qch. d'un air hébété.

gorblimey! [ˈgɔ:ˈblaimi] (*excl.*), *P:* zut de zut! sacré nom (de nom)!; *cf.* **blimey!**

gorgeous [ˈgɔ:dʒəs] (*adj.*), *F:* excellent*, super(be), terrible, bath.

gorilla [gəˈrilə] (*noun*). **1.** *F:* brute *f*, gorille *m*. **2.** *P:* gangster *m*, tueur *m*, malfrat *m*. **3.** *P:* mille livres sterling; *cf.* **monkey, 2.**

gormless [ˈgɔ:mlis] (*adj.*), *F:* bouché, gourde.

gosh! [gɔʃ] (*excl.*), *F:* **(by) g.!** mince! zut! bigre!

gospeller [ˈgɔspələr] (*noun*), *F:* **hot g.,** évangéliste outré, bigot *m* à tous crins.

go through [ˈgoˈθru:] (**to**). **1.** *F:* **he's gone through a lot,** il en a vu des vertes et des pas mûres. **2.** (*Austr.*) *P:* = **tommy (to).**

gotta [ˈgɔtə], *P:* **1.** (=*got to*) **when you've g. go you've g. go,** quand l'heure est venue il faut partir. **2.** (=*got a*) **you've g. lot to go through,** tu en verras des vertes et des pas mûres.

go up [ˈgouˈʌp] (**to**), *P:* s'envoyer en l'air, s'envoyer haut (*dû à la drogue*). *Voir aussi* **air[1], 1.**

gov [gʌv], **governor** [ˈgʌvnər], **the** (*noun*), *F:* **1.** le patron*, le singe; dirlot *m*. **2.** père*, le vieux, le paternel.

gow [gau] (*noun*), *P:* **1.** opium *m* (*drogues**), chandoo *m*. **2.** came *f*. **3.** cigarette* de marijuana, stick *m*, reefer *m*. **4.** le voyage (*expérience psychédélique*). **5.** = **cheesecake.** *Voir aussi* **hoosegow.**

gowed up [ˈgaudˈʌp] (*adj.*), *P:* **1.** drogué*, camé. **2.** survolté.

gowster [ˈgaustər] (*noun*), *P:* fumeur *m* de marijuana, amateur *m* de stick, pipeur *m*.

goy, Goy [gɔi] (*noun*), *F:* non-Juif *m*, Gentil *m*, goy(e) *m*.

grab[1] [græb] (*noun*), *P:* **1.** paye *f*, salaire *m*; **g. day,** jour *m* de paye, la Sainte-Touche. **2. up for grabs,** sur le marché, à vendre.

grab[2] [græb] (**to**). **1.** *P:* arrimer (qn, qch.). **2.** *F:* accrocher (qn), prendre (qn) aux entrailles. **3.** *F:* **how does that g. you?** qu'est-ce que tu en dis? **4.** *F:* **to g. a bite of sth. to eat,** avaler un casse-croûte (*ou* un morceau) (sur le pouce). **5.** *P:* arrêter*, agrafer, agriffer (qn).

grabber [ˈgræbər] (*noun*), *P:* **1.** qch. qui accroche. **2.** qn qui intéresse et stimule.

* L'astérisque indique que le mot marqué de ce signe figure comme entrée dans le Répertoire.

grade [greid] (*noun*), *F:* **to make the g.,** réussir, être à la hauteur.

graft [grɑːft] (*noun*). **1.** *F:* pot-de-vin *m*, graissage *m* de patte, gratte *f*, tour(s) *m* (*pl.*) de bâton. **2.** *F:* (**hard**) **g.,** travail*, boulot *m*, turbin *m*. **3.** *P:* logement* et nourriture*, pension *f*; **good g.,** bon gîte, bonne bouffe.

grafter [ˈgrɑːftər] (*noun*), *F:* **1.** tripoteur *m*, rapineur *m*, trafiquant *m*. **2.** politicien véreux, affairiste *m*, politicard *m*. **3.** bûcheur *m*, turbineur *m*, boulot *m*.

grand [grænd] (*noun*), *F:* (*a*) mille livres sterling; (*b*) (*U.S.*) mille dollars; un gros faf(f)iot.

grannie, granny [ˈgræni] (*noun*). **1.** *F:* grand-mère, mémé(e), mémère, bonne-maman. **2.** *P:* négoce légal qui couvre des activités condamnables; couvert *m*, couverture *f*, paravent *m*. **3.** *P:* **to strangle one's g.,** se masturber*, s'astiquer la colonne.

grapes [greips] (*pl. noun*), *P:* hémorroïdes *f.pl.*, grappillons *m.pl.*

grapevine [ˈgreipvain] (*noun*), *F:* renseignements* (de vive voix), téléphone *m* arabe.

grappler [ˈgræplər] (*noun*). **1.** *F:* lutteur *m*, catcheur *m*, tombeur *m*. **2.** (*pl.*) *P:* mains*, agrafes *f.pl.*, grappins *m.pl.*

grappling [ˈgræpliŋ] (*attrib. adj.*). **1.** *F:* **g. fan,** amateur *m* de lutte, fervent *m* du catch. **2.** *P:* **g. hooks** = **grapplers** (**grappler, 2**).

grass[1] [grɑːs] (*noun*), *P:* **1.** = **grasser.** **2.** (**dirt**) **g.,** marijuana *f* (*drogues**), thé vert. **3.** (*Austr.*) **to be on the g.** = **reign (to).**

grass[2] [grɑːs] (**to**), *P:* cafarder, moutonner; **to g. on s.o.,** dénoncer* qn.

grasser [ˈgrɑːsər] (*noun*), *P:* dénonciateur*, cafardeur *m*, mouton *m*, donneur *m*.

grasshopper [ˈgrɑːshɔpər] (*noun*), *P:* **1.** (*a*) usager *m* de la marijuana; (*b*) habitué(e) de la marijuana; *cf.* **grass**[1], **2.** **2.** (*R.S.* = *copper* = *policeman*) agent* de police, perdreau *m*. *Voir aussi* **knee-high.**

grassroots[1] [ˈgrɑːsˈruːts] (*adj.*), *F:* qui vient de la masse (*ou* d'en bas); **g. political movement,** mouvement *m* politique populaire; **g. democracy,** le populisme.

grassroots[2] [ˈgrɑːsˈruːts] (*pl. noun*), *F:* **1.** région *f* agricole, la brousse. **2.** le gros (de la troupe), la masse, la base (d'un parti, d'une société, *etc.*). **3.** raisonnements *m.pl.* de grosse caisse. **4.** fondation *f*, source *f*, base *f*.

grass-widow [ˈgrɑːsˈwidou] (*noun*), *F:* **1.** femme dont le mari est absent pendant un laps de temps. **2.** (*parfois*) femme séparée ou divorcée.

graveyard [ˈgreivjɑːd] (*attrib. adj.*), *F:* **1.** **a g. cough,** une toux qui sent le sapin. **2.** **g. shift,** équipe *f* (de travailleurs) de nuit.

gravy [ˈgreivi] (*noun*), *P:* **1.** bénéfice*, butin*, bénef *m*, affure *f*, gratte *f*; **the g. train** (*or* **boat**), l'assiette *f* au beurre, bon filon; **to ride the g. train,** taper dans l'assiette au beurre. **2.** l'Atlantique *m*, la Grande Tasse. **3.** **to dish out the g.** = **to dish out the porridge** (*voir* **porridge**).

grease[1] [griːs] (*noun*), *P:* **1.** (*a*) petit cadeau, glissage *m* de pièce, pommade *f*; (*b*) achat *m* de conscience, prix *m* du silence, amende *f*; *cf.* **palm-grease.** **2.** **g. monkey,** garagiste *m*, mécanicien *m*, mécano *m*.

grease[2] [griːs] (**to**). **1.** *P:* acheter, soudoyer; *voir aussi* **palm, 1.** **2.** *F:* **like greased lightning,** (rapide) comme l'éclair.

greaser [ˈgriːsər] (*noun*), *P:* **1.** soudoyeur *m*, graisseur *m*, chien couchant. **2.** (*U.S.*) (*péj.*) Mexicain *m*, Sud-Américain *m*, café au lait.

greasie, greasy[1] [ˈgriːsi] (*noun*), *P:* = **smarmer.**

greasy[2] [ˈgriːsi, griːzi] (*adj.*), *P:* **1.** flagorneur, lèche-bottes. **2.** **g. spoon,** bistrot *m*, gargote *f*.

great[1] [greit] (*adj.*), *F:* excellent*, terrible, du tonnerre; **it's g. to be alive,** c'est bon d'être au monde et d'y voir clair; **he's a g. guy,** (*a*) c'est un chic type; (*b*) c'est un type sensas(s); **he's g. at tennis,** il est fort(iche) au tennis. *Voir aussi* **gun**[1], **3, 4; shake**[1], **5.**

great[2] [greit] (*adv.*), *F:* **I feel g.,** je suis bien dans ma peau.

great[3] [greit] (*noun*), *F:* **he's one of the all-time greats,** il est un des grands de toujours (*ou* un des plus fameux de tous les temps).

greedy-guts [ˈgriːdigʌts] (*noun*), *P:* goinfre*, glouton *m*, (béni-)bouftou(t) *m*.

* An asterisk indicates that the word so marked is included as a head-word in the Appendix.

greefa ['gri:fə] (*noun*), *P:* cigarette* de marijuana *f* (*drogues**), reefer *m*, stick *m*.

greefo ['gri:fou] (*noun*), *P:* marijuana *f* (*drogues**), kif *m*, herbe *f*.

Greek[1] [gri:k] (*adj.*), *P:* **the G. way,** coït* anal, baisage *m* à la riche.

Greek[2] [gri:k] (*noun*), *F:* **it's all G. to me,** c'est de l'hébreu, c'est du chinois.

Greek[3] [gri:k] (**to**), *P:* pratiquer le coït* anal, casser coco.

green[1] [gri:n] (*adj.*). **1.** *P:* **g. mud** (*or* **ashes**), opium *m* (*drogues**), dross *m*, boue verte. **2.** *P:* **g. and blacks,** capsules *f.pl.* barbituriques, vert et noir. **3.** *F:* **to give s.o. the g. light,** donner le feu vert à qn. **4.** *F:* (*a*) novice, inexpérimenté; (*b*) crédule, naïf, béjaune, blanc-bec. **5.** *F:* **to have a g. thumb** (*or* **g. fingers**), être un habile jardinier, avoir la main verte. *Voir aussi* **dragon, 3.**

green[2] [gri:n] (*noun*), *F:* **do you see any g. in my eye?** tu ne m'as pas regardé? je ne suis pas né d'hier! *Voir aussi* **greens.**

green-ass ['gri:næs] (*adj.*) (*U.S.*), *P:* = **green**[1], **4** (*a*), (*b*).

greenback ['gri:nbæk] (*noun*), *F:* (*a*) billet* d'une livre sterling; (*b*) billet* de banque américain.

greenie ['gri:ni] (*noun*), *P:* **1.** novice *m*, bleu *m*, blanc-bec *m*, serin *m*. **2.** = **green dragon** (**dragon, 3**).

greens [gri:nz] (*pl. noun*). **1.** *F:* légumes verts. **2.** *P:* **to like one's g.,** être porté sur l'article (*ou* sur la bagatelle).

grefa ['gri:fə] (*noun*), *P:* = **greefo.**

gremlin ['gremlin] (*noun*), *F:* **1.** lutin *m* de malheur, pépin *m*, eau *f* dans le gaz. **2.** crampon *m*, casse-pieds *m*, enquiquineur *m*.

greta ['gri:tə] (*noun*), *P:* = **greefo.**

greybacks ['grei-bæks] (*pl. noun*), *P:* poux*, grains *m.pl.* de blé, mies *f.pl.* de pain.

griddle[1] ['gridl] (*noun*), *P:* (*th.*) cabotin *m*, théâtreux *m*.

griddle[2] ['gridl] (**to**), *P:* faire du théâtre ambulant, cabotiner.

griff(in) ['grif(in)] (*noun*), *F:* **the g.,** renseignement* utile, bon tuyau, bon rencart; **to get the g. on sth.,** être affranchi (*ou* mis à la page), s'être rencardé sur qch.

grift [grift] (**to**), *P:* escroquer*, empiler, estamper.

grifter ['griftər] (*noun*), *P:* escroc*, estampeur *m*, empileur *m*.

grill[1] [gril] (*noun*), *F:* **mixed g.** = **fruit-salad, 2.**

grill[2] [gril] (**to**), *F:* **to g. s.o.,** serrer les pouces *m.pl.* à qn (pour obtenir un aveu), cuisiner qn.

grilled [grild] (*adj.*) (*U.S.*), *P:* ivre*, noir, noircicot.

grim [grim] (*adj.*), *F:* mauvais*, désagréable, de mauvais augure; **things look g.,** ça la fout mal, ça s'annonce mal. *Voir aussi* **hang on** (**to**), **2.**

grind[1] [graind] (*noun*). **1.** *F:* travail* dur et monotone; **the daily g.,** la routine, le train-train quotidien, le métro-boulot-dodo; **to go back to the old g.,** reprendre le collier, se remettre au turbin. **2.** *F:* (*a*) course *f* difficile; (*b*) steeple *m*. **3.** *P:* coït*, fouraillage *m*, dérouillade *f*.

grind[2] [graind] (**to**). **1.** *F:* travailler* dur; trimer, bûcher, bosser. **2.** *P:* coïter*, fourailler, dérouiller. *Voir aussi* **axe**[1], **3.**

grinder ['graindər] (*noun*), *F:* **1.** **to put s.o. through the g.,** faire passer un mauvais quart d'heure à qn. **2.** (*pl.*) dents*, croquantes *f.pl.*, piloches *f.pl.*

grip[1] [grip] (*noun*). **1.** **to get a g. on oneself,** (*a*) *F:* se contenir, se retenir, se contrôler; (*b*) *V:* = **grip**[2] (**to**). **2.** *F:* **to lose one's g.,** perdre la tête (*ou* les pédales *f.pl.*), déménager.

grip[2] [grip] (**to**), *V:* se masturber*, se taper la colonne, se pogner.

gripe[1] [graip] (*noun*), *F:* **1.** plainte *f*, rouspétance *f*; **to have the gripes,** (*a*) = **gripe**[2] (**to**), **1**; (*b*) avoir la diarrhée* (*ou* la courante). **2.** geignard *m*, râleur *m*, bâton merdeux.

gripe[2] [graip] (**to**), *F:* **1.** grogner*, rouspéter, ronchonner, râler. **2.** ennuyer*, tourmenter, barber, raser (qn).

griper ['graipər] (*noun*), *F:* râleur *m*, rouspéteur *m*.

grit [grit] (*noun*), *F:* cran *m*, battant *m* ; *cf.* **sand.**

gritty ['griti] (*adj.*), *F:* qui est brave*, qui a du cran, qui a qch. dans le ventre.

grizzle ['grizl] (**to**), *F:* **1.** pleurnicher, geindre. **2.** grogner*, rouspéter.

* L'astérisque indique que le mot marqué de ce signe figure comme entrée dans le Répertoire.

grizzleguts [ˈgrizlgʌts], **grizzler** [ˈgrizlər] (*noun*), *F:* **1.** pleurnicheur *m*, chialeur *m*. **2.** geignard *m*, chignard *m*.

groaty [ˈgrouti] (*adj.*), *F:* = **grotty, 1.**

groggy [ˈgrɔgi] (*adj.*), *F:* **1.** un peu malade*, patraque, mal fichu. **2.** (*boxe*) groggy, sonné. **3.** ivre*, paf, éméché, parti. **4. a g. old table,** une vieille table bancale.

groin [grɔin] (*noun*), *P:* bande* noire de parieurs sur un champ de courses.

grooby [ˈgruːbi] (*adj.*), *F:* = **groovy.**

groove [gruːv] (*noun*), *F:* **1.** spécialité *f*, dada *m*, rayon *m*; **that's my g.,** ça, c'est mon blot. **2. it's a g.,** c'est chic. **3. in the g.,** en pleine forme, en plein boum; (*jazz*) (orchestre) donnant son plein, faisant des étincelles. **4. to get into a g.,** s'encroûter, être dans l'ornière, s'enroutiner.

groovy [ˈgruːvi] (*adj.*), *F:* excellent*, bath, en bon ordre.

grope [group] (**to**), *P:* (*a*) = **feel**[2] **(to), 1;** (*b*) palper les «parties» de qn sous ses vêtements.

grotty [ˈgrɔti] (*adj.*), *F:* **1.** laid*, moche, tocard, tarte. **2.** outré et inutile.

grouch[1] [grautʃ] (*noun*), *F:* **1.** ronchonnage *m*, rouspétance *f*. **2.** râleur *m*, ronchonneur *m*.

grouch[2] [grautʃ] (**to**), *F:* grogner*, râler, ronchonner.

groucher [ˈgrautʃər] (*noun*), *F:* = **grouch**[1]**, 2.**

ground [graund] (*noun*), *F:* **1. to run s.o. into the g.,** débiner, démolir qn. **2. that suits me down to the g.,** cela me convient parfaitement, ça me botte, ça fait mon affaire. **3. to get (a scheme,** *etc.*) **off the g.,** faire démarrer (un projet, *etc.*); **it'll never get off the g.,** cela ne verra jamais le jour, cela ne démarrera jamais. *Voir aussi* **stamping-ground.**

groupie [ˈgruːpi] (*noun*). **1.** *F:* fervente des pop-groups, groupette *f*. **2.** *P:* fille* qui fait l'amour en groupe, groupe-sexuelle.

grouse[1] [graus] (*noun*), *F:* **1.** grogne(rie) *f*, bougonnement *m*. **2.** rouscailleur *m*, marronneur *m*.

grouse[2] [graus] (**to**), *F:* grogner*, marronner, rouscailler.

grouser [ˈgrausər] (*noun*), *F:* = **grouse**[1]**, 2.**

grub [grʌb] (*noun*), *P:* **1.** nourriture*, boustifaille *f*, mangeaille *f*; **g. up!** la bouffe! la soupe! **2.** enfant sale*, petite vermine, petit morveux.

grubby [ˈgrʌbi] (*adj.*), *F:* sale*, pouilleux, cracra, crado; **g. hands,** mains douteuses.

gruel [ˈgruːəl] (*noun*), *F:* **1.** réprimande *f*, attrapade *f*, engueulade *f*, trempe *f*. **2. to give s.o. his g.,** (*a*) battre* qn (comme plâtre); (*b*) éreinter, échiner qn. **3. to take** (*or* **get**) **one's g.,** avaler sa médecine, encaisser.

gruelling [ˈgruːəliŋ] (*noun*), *F:* (*a*) passage *m* à tabac, dérouillée *f*, raclée *f*; (*b*) épreuve éreintante.

Grundy [ˈgrʌndi] (*pr. noun*), *F:* **not to care about Mrs. G., not to care what Mrs. G. says,** se moquer du qu'en-dira-t-on.

grunt-and-groan [ˈgrʌntən(d)ˈgroun] (*noun*), *F:* la lutte, le catch.

grunt-and-groaner [ˈgrʌntən(d)ˈgrounər] (*noun*), *F:* lutteur *m*.

grunter [ˈgrʌntər] (*noun*), *F:* porc *m*.

G-string [ˈdʒiː-striŋ] (*noun*), *F:* cache-sexe *m*, feuille *f* de vigne, cache-fri-fri *m*, cache-truc *m*.

gubbins [ˈgʌbinz] (*noun*), *F:* **1.** nourriture*, becquetance *f*. **2.** gadget *m*, bidule *m*, truc *m*, machin *m*. **3.** = **muggins.**

guess [ges] (**to**) (*mainly U.S.*), *F:* croire, penser; **I g. that . . .,** il y a des chances pour que...; **you're right, I g.,** oui, il me semble que vous avez raison.

guesstimate[1] [ˈgestimət] (*noun*), *F:* conjecture *f*, estimation bien pesée.

guesstimate[2] [ˈgestimeit] (**to**), *F:* estimer, évaluer soigneusement.

guest [gest] (*noun*), *F:* **be my g.!** c'est à vous! prends! emporte!

guff [gʌf] (*noun*), *F:* bêtise*, blague *f*, foutaise *f*.

guide [gaid] (*noun*), *P:* drogué* endurci qui entraîne les autres, guide *m* de neufs.

guinea [ˈgini] (*noun*), *F:* **it's a g. a minute,** c'est très amusant*, c'est impayable.

guiver[1] [ˈgaivər] (*noun*) (*Austr.*), *F:* baratin *m*; **to sling the g.** = **guiver**[2] **(to).**

guiver[2] [ˈgaivər] (**to**) (*Austr.*), *F:* baratiner, faire du baratin.

gum [gʌm] (*noun*), *F:* **by g.!** mince alors! *Voir aussi* **gum-tree.**

* An asterisk indicates that the word so marked is included as a head-word in the Appendix.

gump [gʌmp] (*noun*), *F:* individu bête*, nouille *f*, oie *f*.

gumption [ˈgʌm(p)ʃ(ə)n] (*noun*), *F:* débrouillardise *f*, entregent *m*; **to have g.**, avoir de la jugeot(t)e; **he's got plenty of g.**, c'est un débrouillard.

gumshoe [ˈgʌmʃuː] (*noun*) (*U.S.*), *F:* agent* de police habillé en civil, poulet *m*, ham(bourgeois) *m*, condé *m*.

gum-tree [ˈgʌmtriː] (*noun*), *F:* **up a g.-t.**, dans une impasse, dans le pétrin, dans de beaux draps.

gum up [ˈgʌmˈʌp] (**to**), *F:* **to g. u. the works**, encrasser les rouages, mettre des bâtons dans les roues.

gun[1] [gʌn] (*noun*). **1.** *P:* seringue *f* hypodermique, poussette *f*, lance *f*. **2.** *F:* **to jump the g.**, brûler le feu, marcher avant les violons. **3.** *F:* **to go great guns**, prospérer, faire boum. **4.** *F:* **to blow great guns**, (*du vent*) souffler en tempête (*ou* à décorner les bœufs). **5.** *F:* **to stick to one's guns**, soutenir son opinion, s'accrocher, tenir bon, ne pas en démordre. **6.** (*U.S.*) *P:* (*a*) voleur*, caroubleur *m*, casseur *m*; voleur à la tire; (*b*) bandit *m*, gangster *m*, malfrat *m*, porte-flingue *m*. **7.** *F:* **to give sth. the g.**, accélérer qch., mettre les gaz, mettre la gomme. **8.** *P:* **to get behind the g.**, risquer la prison* (*ou* la taule). *Voir aussi* **big**[1], **1**; **burp-gun**; **spike**[2] (**to**), **3**.

gun[2] [gʌn] (**to**), *F:* **to be (out) gunning for s.o.**, pourchasser qn pour se venger de lui, aller à la rebiffe.

gun down [ˈgʌnˈdaun] (**to**), *F:* fusiller, flinguer, descendre (qn).

gunge [gʌndʒ] (*noun*), *F:* saleté*, saloperie *f*, crotaille *f*.

gunji [ˈgʌndʒi], **gunny** [ˈgʌni] (*noun*), *P:* marijuana *f* (*drogues**), kif *m*; *cf.* **ganjah**.

gunsel [ˈgʌnzl] (*noun*) (*U.S.*), *P:* **1.** gangster *m*, malfrat *m*, dur *m*, poisse *m*. **2.** faux jeton, faux frère, bordille *f*. **3.** mignon *m*, giton *m*, lopette *f*. **4.** blanc-bec *m*, béjaune *m*, dadais *m*.

gunslinger [ˈgʌn-sliŋər] (*noun*), *F:* vaurien* armé, porte-flingue *m*.

gup [gʌp] (*noun*), *P:* potin *m*, ragots *m.pl.*, foutaise *f*, cancans *m.pl.*

gurk [gəːk] (**to**), *P:* roter, avoir une fuite de gaz.

gussie [ˈgʌsi] (*noun*) (*Austr.*), *P:* pédéraste*, lopaille *f*.

gut [gʌt] (*noun*), *P:* **to bust a g. to do sth.**, se sortir les tripes pour faire qch. *Voir aussi* **guts**; **rot-gut**.

gutful [ˈgʌtful] (*noun*), *P:* (*a*) ventrée *f*, gavée *f*; (*b*) **to have (had) a g.**, en avoir ras le bol, en avoir son compte; *cf.* **bellyful**.

gutless [ˈgʌtlis] (*adj.*), *P:* **to be g.**, être poltron, ne rien avoir dans le bide; **a g. character**, un type mou, un trouillard, une lavette.

gut-rot [ˈgʌt-rɔt] (*noun*), *F:* = **rot-gut**.

guts [gʌts] (*pl. noun*). **1.** *F:* **to have g.**, être brave*, avoir du cran (*ou* de l'estomac), en avoir dans le bide; **to lose one's g.**, perdre courage, avoir les foies *m.pl.*, ne pas en avoir dans le bidon. **2.** *P:* **to hate s.o.'s g.**, détester* qn, avoir qn dans le nez, ne pas pouvoir blairer qn. **3.** *V:* **to drop one's g.**, péter*, en lâcher un, vesser. **4.** *P:* **to knife s.o. in the g.**, éventrer qn, mettre les tripes à l'air à qn, crever la paillasse à qn. **5.** *P:* **put some g. into it!** mets-en un (bon) coup! magne-toi le train! dépêche! **6.** *P:* **to sweat one's g. out**, travailler* dur, en foutre un coup, se casser les reins, pisser du sang. **7.** *P:* **to heave** (*or* **spew**) **one's g. up**, vomir*, dégoupillonner. **8.** (*Austr.*) *P:* **to hold one's g.**, se taire*, poser sa chique. **9.** (*Austr.*) *P:* **to spill one's g.**, avouer*, vider son sac. **10.** *P:* **I'll have your g. for garters!** j'aurai ta peau! je me ferai un porte-monnaie avec tes couilles! **11.** *P:* du charnu, de l'étoffe *f*, de la substance. **12.** *P:* engrenages *m.pl.*, rouages *m.pl.*, boyaux *m.pl.*, entrailles *f.pl.* **13.** *P:* = **greedy-guts**. *Voir aussi* **cleverguts**; **grizzleguts**; **gut**; **worryguts**.

guts-ache [ˈgʌts-eik] (*noun*), *P:* **1.** mal *m* au ventre*. **2.** casse-pieds *m*, casse-burettes *m*.

gut-scraper [ˈgʌt-skreipər] (*noun*), *P:* racleur *m* de cordes, joueur *m* de crincrin.

gutsy [ˈgʌtsi] (*adj.*), *P:* **1.** percutant, qui a du cran (*ou* des entrailles *f.pl.*). **2.** goinfre*, goulu. **3.** passionné, jouisseur.

gutter [ˈgʌtər] (*noun*), *F:* **to be in the g.**, être dans la pauvreté* (*ou* dans le ruisseau *ou* sur la paille).

gutty [ˈgʌti] (*adj.*), *P:* **1.** qui prend aux entrailles (*ou* aux tripes), qui empoigne.

* L'astérisque indique que le mot marqué de ce signe figure comme entrée dans le Répertoire.

2. fondamental, substantiel, qui vient du tréfonds. 3. bolide, puissant.

gutzer ['gʌtsər] (*noun*) (*Austr.*), *P:* **to come a g.** = **to come a cropper** (**cropper** (*a*)).

guv [gʌv], **guv'nor** ['gʌvnər], **the** (*noun*), *F:* = **gov, governor, the.**

guy[1] [gai] (*noun*). 1. *F:* homme*, type *m*, loustic *m*, zigoto *m*; **a wise g.**, (*a*) un crâneur, un je-sais-tout; (*b*) un roublard, un mariol(e). 2. *P:* **to do a g.**, (*a*) = **slope off (to)**; (*b*) donner un faux nom*, filer le faux blaze (*ou* le faublas). *Voir aussi* **fall-guy; great**[1]; **right,** 3; **tough**[1], 1.

guy[2] [gai] (**to**), *P:* = **to do a guy** (**guy**[1], 2 (*a*)).

guzunder [gə'zʌndər] (*noun*), *F:* pot *m* de chambre, Jules *m*, Thomas *m*, Colin *m*.

gyp[1] [dʒip] (*noun*). 1. *F:* domestique dans un collège, larbin *m*. 2. *F:* = **gip,** 1, 2. 3. (*U.S.*) *P:* escroc*, filou *m*, carotteur *m*. 4. (*U.S.*) *P:* escroquerie*, tromperie *f*, arnaque *f*, carottage *m*. 5. *P:* **g. joint** = **clip-joint.**

gyp[2] [dʒip] (**to**) (*U.S.*), *P:* **to g. s.o.**, (*a*) escroquer* qn, tirer une carotte à qn, estamper qn, empiler qn; (*b*) écorcher qn; **to be gypped,** être pigeonné.

gyve [dʒaiv] (*noun*), *P:* cigarette* de marijuana (*drogues**), stick *m*, reefer *m*.

* An asterisk indicates that the word so marked is included as a head-word in the Appendix.

H

H [eitʃ] (*abbr.* = *heroin*), *P:* héroïne *f* (*drogues**), H *f.*

habit [ˈhæbit] (*noun*). **1.** *F:* usage *m* des drogues; **to kick the h.,** se décamer, lâcher le pied; **off the h.,** décamé, désintoxiqué. **2.** *P:* dose habituelle de drogues.

hack around [ˈhækəˈraund] (**to**), *F:* flâner, flânocher.

hack down [ˈhækˈdaun] (**to**), *F:* assaillir, faire des crocs-en-jambe *m.pl.* à (qn).

hacked (off) [ˈhækt(ˈɔf)] (*adj.*), *P:* **1.** en colère*, à cran. **2.** qui en a assez*, qui en a soupé.

haddock [ˈhædək] (*noun*), *F:* **limp h.,** main* molle et flasque.

hair [hɛər] (*noun*). **1.** *F:* **to get in s.o.'s h.,** irriter qn, taper sur les nerfs à qn. **2.** *F:* **to let one's h. down,** se laisser aller, ne pas faire de chichis. **3.** *P:* **keep your h. on!** calme-toi! ne t'emballe pas! **4.** *F:* **to split hairs,** couper les cheveux en quatre. **5.** *F:* **get some h. on your chest!** conduis-toi en homme! sors de tes langes! **6.** *P:* **to have s.o. by the short hairs** = **to have s.o. by the short and curlies** (**curly, 2**). *Voir aussi* **dog**[1], **4; long-hair**[2].

hairburger [ˈhɛəbəːgər] (*noun*) (*U.S.*), *VV:* vagin*, barbu *m.*

haircut [ˈhɛəkʌt] (*noun*), *P:* courte période en prison*.

hair-do [ˈhɛəduː] (*noun*), *F:* **I'm going to have a h.-d.,** je vais me faire coiffer.

hairpie [ˈhɛəˈpai] (*noun*) (*U.S.*), *VV:* = **hairburger.**

hairy [ˈhɛəri] (*adj.*), *P:* **1.** périlleux, épineux, provocateur. **2.** vieux*, passé, rengaine. **3.** piètre, miteux, moche.

half[1] [hɑːf] (*adv.*), *F:* **1. not h.!** et comment! tu peux y aller! tu parles! **2. she didn't h. laugh,** elle s'est bien tordue de rire. **3. you won't h. catch it!** qu'est-ce que tu vas prendre! **4. he hasn't h. changed,** il a drôlement décollé. **5.** (*a*) **h. and h.,** moitié-moitié; (*b*) **to go h. and h.,** faire (*ou* marcher) afanaf; *voir aussi* **fifty-fifty; half**[2]. **6. to be only h. there,** être un peu fou*, être toqué. *Voir aussi* **shift**[2] (**to**), **1.**

half[2] [hɑːf] (*noun*), *F:* **h. and h.,** panaché *m* de bière brune et blonde. *Voir aussi* **better; half**[1], **5.**

half-a-crown [ˈhɑːfəˈkraun] (*noun*), *F:* *voir* **bingo (26).**

half-assed [ˈhæfˈæst] (*adj.*) (*U.S.*), *V:* **1.** margoulin, sabreur, sabot. **2.** mal fait, torché, bousillé.

half-baked [ˈhɑːfˈbeikt] (*adj.*), *F:* **1.** inexpérimenté, blanc-bec. **2.** bête*, niais, bêta.

half-brass [ˈhɑːfˈbrɑːs] (*noun*), *P:* femme facile qui ne fait pas payer ses faveurs; *cf.* **brass**[2], **4.**

half-cock [ˈhɑːfˈkɔk] (*noun*), *F:* **to go off at h.-c.,** mal partir, mal démarrer.

half-cut [ˈhɑːfˈkʌt] (*adj.*), *P:* légèrement ivre*, gris; *cf.* **cut**[1], **1.**

half-inch [ˈhɑːfˈintʃ] (**to**) (*R.S.* = *pinch* = *steal*), *P:* voler*, chiper, chaparder.

half-iron [ˈhɑːfˈaiən] (*noun*), *P:* qn qui fréquente les homosexuels sans en être; *cf.* **iron hoof (hoof**[1], **2).**

half-pint [ˈhɑːfˈpaint], **half-portion** [ˈhɑːfˈpɔːʃən] (*noun*), *F:* petit* individu, personne insignifiante, demi-portion *f.*

half-screwed [ˈhɑːfˈskruːd], **-seas-over** [-ˈsiːzˈouvər], **-shaved** [-ˈʃeivd], **-shot** [-ˈʃɔt], **-slewed** [-ˈsluːd], **-snaped** [-ˈsneipt], **-sprung** [-ˈsprʌŋ] (*adj.*), *P:* légèrement ivre*, paf.

half-squarie [ˈhɑːfˈskwɛəri] (*noun*) (*Austr.*), *P:* fille* *ou* jeune femme* de petite vertu, Marie-couche-toi-là *f.*

half-stewed [ˈhɑːfˈstjuːd], **-under** [-ˈʌndər] (*adj.*), *P:* = **half-screwed.**

half-way [ˈhɑːfˈwei] (*adv.*), *F:* **1. to meet s.o. h.-w.,** couper la poire en deux. **2.** *voir* **bingo (45).**

halls [hɔːlz] (*pl. noun*), *F:* **the h.,** théâtres *m.pl.* vaudeville.

halvers [ˈhɑːvəz], **halvo(e)s** [ˈhɑːvouz] (*adv.*), *F:* **to go h.,** y aller moitié-

* L'astérisque indique que le mot marqué de ce signe figure comme entrée dans le Répertoire.

moitié.

ham[1] [hæm] (*adj.*), *F:* **1.** amateur. **2.** inférieur, de basse qualité; **h. joint,** gargote *f.*

ham[2] [hæm] (*noun*), *F:* **1. pure h.,** (*th.*) pièce pleine de clichés et d'emphase; cagnade *f.* **2.** acteur amateur. **3.** mauvais acteur, cabotin *m*, crabe *m.* **4.** radio-téléphoniste amateur.

ham[3] [hæm] (**to**), *F:* **1.** (*th.*) mal jouer un rôle, cabotiner. **2.** déclamer, jouer pour la galerie.

ham-fisted [ˈhæmˈfistid], **ham-handed** [ˈhæmˈhændid] (*adj.*), *F:* maladroit, empoté, lourdaud, balourd.

hammer [ˈhæmər] (**to**). **1.** *F:* (*Bourse*) déclarer (un agent) en défaut (*ou* défaillant). **2.** *F:* **to h. s.o. into the ground,** vaincre qn, battre qn à plate(s) couture(s), tailler qn en pièces. **3.** *P:* **to h. (and nail)** (*R.S.* = *trail*), traîner, suivre.

hammering [ˈhæməriŋ] (*noun*), *F:* **1.** volée *f* de coups*. **2.** (*sports*) défaite *f*, raclée *f.*

hammocks [ˈhæməks] (*pl. noun*), *P:* seins* opulents, balcons *m.pl.*

hammy [ˈhæmi] (*adj.*), *F:* outré, chargé, exagéré.

Hampton [ˈhæmptən] (*noun*) (= *Hampton Wick, R.S.* = *prick*), *V:* pénis*; **it gets on my H.,** ça me tape sur les couilles; *cf.* **wick, 1, 2.**

hand[1] [hænd] (*noun*), *F:* **1. to keep one's h. in,** conserver le pied à l'étrier. **2. to make money h. over fist,** gagner* beaucoup d'argent*, remuer (*ou* ramasser) du fric à la pelle, faire des affaires d'or. *Voir aussi* **big**[1], **7; dab**[1].

hand[2] [hænd] (**to**). **1.** *F:* **you've got to h. it to him!** devant lui, chapeau! **2.** *P:* **don't h. me that!** ne me raconte pas cela! ne me fais pas accroire cela! *Voir aussi* **sweet**[1], **3.**

handful [ˈhændful] (*noun*). **1.** *P:* condamnation* à cinq ans* de prison*, cinq longes *f.pl.* de taule. **2.** *P:* cinq livres sterling; **a couple of handfuls,** dix livres sterling. **3.** *F:* **to be a h.,** donner du fil à retordre, être une teigne.

hand-job [ˈhænd-dʒɔb] (*noun*), *V:* **to give s.o. a h.-j.,** masturber* qn, pogner qn.

handle [ˈhændl] (*noun*), *F:* **1. to fly off the h.,** se mettre en colère*, sortir de ses gonds. **2. to have a h.,** avoir un titre, avoir un nom à charnière. **3.** nom* de famille, prénom *m*, surnom *m*, blaze *m.*

handlebar [ˈhændlbɑːr] (*attrib. adj.*), *F:* **h. moustache,** moustache* à la gauloise, bacchantes *f.pl.* en guidon.

hand-me-downs [ˈhændmidaunz] (*pl. noun*), *F:* vêtements* usagés *ou* bon marché; frusques *f.pl.*; décrochez-moi-ça *m*; *cf.* **reach-me-downs.**

hand-out [ˈhændaut] (*noun*), *F:* **1.** prospectus *m*, circulaire *m* publicitaire. **2.** aumône *f*, charité *f.*

handshake [ˈhændʃeik] (*noun*), *F:* **golden h.,** cadeau *m* d'adieu, indemnité *f* de départ.

handsome [ˈhænsəm] (*adv.*), *F:* **to come down h.,** être généreux, être large.

hang[1] [hæŋ] (*noun*), *F:* **1. to get the h. of sth.,** saisir le truc pour faire qch.; **when you've got the h. of things,** quand vous serez au courant. **2. I don't give a h.,** je m'en moque, je m'en fiche, je m'en fous; **it's not worth a h.,** cela ne vaut pas tripette.

hang[2] [hæŋ] (**to**), *F:* **h. it!** flûte! mince alors!; **h. the expense!** = **blow the expense!** (**blow** (**to**), **1**). *Voir aussi* **hung.**

hang about (*or* **around**) [ˈhæŋəˈbaut, ˈhæŋəˈraund] (**to**), *F:* **1.** flâner, flânocher, rôdailler; **to keep s.o. hanging a.,** faire (*ou* laisser) poireauter qn. **2. to h. a. s.o.,** fréquenter qn, se coller à qn.

hanger-on [ˈhæŋəˈrɔn] (*pl.* **hangers-on**) (*noun*), *F:* **1.** dépendant *m*, parasite *m.* **2.** crampon *m*, pique-assiette *m.*

hang on [ˈhæŋˈɔn] (**to**). **1.** *F:* (*a*) attendre*; **h. o.!** une seconde! un moment!; (*b*) poireauter. **2.** *F:* **to h. o. like grim death,** s'agrafer, se cramponner, s'accrocher. **3.** *F:* tenir bon. **4.** (*U.S.*) *P:* **to h. one o.,** s'enivrer, se piquer le nez.

hang-out [ˈhæŋaut] (*noun*), *F:* **1.** logement*, chez-soi *m.* **2.** rendez-vous*, lieu *m* de réunion; repaire *m* de gangsters.

hang out [ˈhæŋˈaut] (**to**), *F:* **1. to h. o. for sth.,** réclamer, contester qch. **2.** habiter*, crécher, nicher; **where do you h. o.?** où perchez-vous?

hangover [ˈhæŋouvər] (*noun*), *F:* **to have a h.,** avoir la gueule de bois, avoir mal aux cheveux.

hang-up [ˈhæŋʌp] (*noun*), *F:* **1.** ennui

* An asterisk indicates that the word so marked is included as a head-word in the Appendix.

mental, trouble *m* psychique. **2.** dada *m*, combine *f*. **3.** embêtement *m*, enquiquinement *m*, scie *f*.

hang up [ˈhæŋˈʌp] (**to**), *F:* **1.** (*téléphone*) raccrocher (l'appareil). **2. he wants to h. u. his hat,** il a envie de se marier. **3. to h. s.o. u. = to stand s.o. up.** *Voir aussi* **hung up.**

hankie, hanky [ˈhæŋki] (*noun*) (= *handkerchief*), *F:* mouchoir*, blave *m*.

hanky-panky [ˈhæŋkiˈpæŋki] (*noun*), *F:* **1.** supercherie *f*, tour *m* de passe-passe, coup fourré. **2.** (*a*) adultère*, carambolage *m* en douce; (*b*) flirt *m*. **3.** manigance *f*.

happen[1] [ˈhæp(ə)n] (*adv.*), *F:* peut-être; **h. he will, h. he won't,** peut-être bien que oui, peut-être bien que non.

happen[2] [ˈhæp(ə)n] (**to**), *F:* **it's all happening,** tout est en marche, tout roule.

happen along [ˈhæp(ə)nəˈlɔŋ] (**to**), *F:* arriver* au hasard, entrer en passant.

happenings [ˈhæp(ə)niŋz] (*pl. noun*), *F:* drogues*, narcotiques *m.pl.*, came *f*.

happenstance [ˈhæp(ə)nstæns] (*noun*) (*U.S.*), *F:* événement fortuit.

happy [ˈhæpi] (*adj.*), *F:* **1.** légèrement ivre*, paf. **2. h. days!** à la bonne vôtre! *Voir aussi* **bar-happy; dust**[1], **2** (*a*); **shag-happy; slap-happy; trigger-happy.**

hard[1] [hɑːd] (*adj.*). **1.** *F:* **a drop of the h. stuff,** une goutte d'alcool*, un petit coup de gnôle. **2.** *F:* **h. drugs,** drogues toxiques majeures (opiacés et cocaïne); *cf.* **soft**[1], **4. 3.** *F:* **h. lines,** malchance*, guigne *f*, poisse *f*; *cf.* **cheese, 3. 4.** *F:* **h. tack,** biscuits *m.pl.* de marin. **5.** *F:* **h. sell,** battage *m* publicitaire, vente *f* au sabot; *cf.* **soft**[1], **5. 6.** *F:* **to play h. to get,** faire la difficile, faire la Sainte-Nitouche. **7.** *P:* excellent*, super. *Voir aussi* **hat, 6.**

hard[2] [hɑːd] (*noun*). **1.** *P:* (=*hard labour*) travaux forcés; **fifteen years' h.,** quinze longes *f.pl.* des durs. **2.** *V:* = **hard-on.**

hard-baked [ˈhɑːdˈbeikt] (*adj.*), *F:* endurci, dur(aille).

hard-bitten [ˈhɑːdˈbitn] (*adj.*), *F:* = **hard-boiled, 2.**

hard-boiled [ˈhɑːdˈbɔild] (*adj.*), *F:* **1.** malin*, coriace; **a h.-b. businessman,** un homme d'affaires consommé. **2.** dur (à cuire). **3.** peu susceptible.

hard-liner [ˈhɑːdˈlainər] (*noun*), *F:* **1.** intransigeant *m* (en politique), dur *m* (d'un parti). **2.** toxicomane majeur (opium et dérivés).

hard-on [ˈhɑːdɔn] (*noun*), *V:* **to have a h.-o.,** être en érection*, bander.

hard up [ˈhɑːdˈʌp] (*adj.*), *F:* pauvre*, dans la gêne, dans la dèche, fauché; **to be h. u.,** tirer le diable par la queue.

hardware [ˈhɑːdwɛər] (*noun*), *F:* armes *f.pl.*, outils *m.pl.*

hare[1] [hɛər] (*noun*), *F:* **1.** plan *m ou* projet *m* impraticable. **2. to raise a h.,** donner un nouveau tour à la discussion.

hare[2] **(off)** [ˈhɛər(ˈɔf)] (**to**), *F:* s'enfuir*, se sauver à toutes jambes; **to h. back home,** regagner la maison à toutes jambes.

Harley [ˈhɑːli] (*noun*), *P:* **a H.,** un club.

harnessed [ˈhɑːnist] (*adj. & p.p.*), *F:* **to get h.,** se marier, sauter le fossé.

harp[1] [hɑːp] (*noun*), *F:* un Irlandais. *Voir aussi* **jew's-harp.**

harp[2] [hɑːp] (**to**), *F:* **he's always harping on the same string,** il récite toujours la même litanie; il rabâche toujours la même chose.

Harry [ˈhæri] (*pr. noun*). **1.** *F:* **old H.,** le diable; **it's giving me old H.,** cela me fait un mal du diable. **2.** *F:* **to play old H. with s.o.,** engueuler, enguirlander qn. **3.** *P:* **H. preggers = preggers,** *q.v.*; **H. blinders = blinders; H. bonkers = bonkers,** *etc. Voir aussi* **flash**[1], **1; Tom, 1.**

has-been [ˈhæzbiːn] (*noun*), *F:* **1.** individu* vieux-jeu; vieux ramolli; **he's a h.-b.,** il est déchu (*ou* démodé); **it's better to be a h.-b. than a never-was,** il vaut mieux ne plus être que n'avoir jamais été. **2.** chose périmée (ayant perdu son utilité).

hash[1] [hæʃ] (*adj.*), *P:* formid(able), super, cool.

hash[2] [hæʃ] (*noun*), *F:* **1.** nourriture*, boustifaille *f*, bectance *f*. **2.** (*U.S.*) nouvelles *f.pl.*, potins *m.pl.*, cancans *m.pl.* **3.** hachisch *m* (*drogues**). **4.** pagaille *f*, embrouillamini *m*, gâchis *m*; **to make a h. of it,** bousiller l'affaire. **5.** du rebattu, du rabâché. **6. to settle s.o.'s h.,** (*a*) régler son compte à qn; (*b*) rabattre le caquet à qn.

* L'astérisque indique que le mot marqué de ce signe figure comme entrée dans le Répertoire.

hash[3] [hæʃ] (**to**), *F:* gâcher, bousiller, bâcler.

hashery [ˈhæʃəri], **hash-house** [ˈhæʃhaʊs] (*noun*), *F:* gargote *f.*

hash over [ˈhæʃˈouvər] (**to**) (*U.S.*), *F:* discuter, ramener, rabâcher.

hash-slinger [ˈhæʃsliŋər] (*noun*), *F:* **1.** mauvaise cuisinière, Marie-graillon *f.* **2.** serveur *m* de gargote, loufiat *m.* **3.** marmiton *m*, coq *m*, gargot *m.*

hash-up [ˈhæʃʌp] (*noun*), *F:* réchauffé *m*, ripopée *f* (de vieux contes, *etc.*).

hash up [ˈhæʃˈʌp] (**to**), *F:* = **hash**[3] (**to**).

hassle[1] [ˈhæsl] (*noun*) (*U.S.*), *F:* querelle*, bagarre*, barabille *f.*

hassle[2] [ˈhæsl] (**to**) (*U.S.*), *F:* **1.** se quereller, se battre*, se bagarrer. **2.** se tracasser*, se faire de la bile.

hat [hæt] (*noun*), *F:* **1. old h.,** vieux jeu; **that's old h.,** c'est du déjà vu, c'est vieux comme le monde. **2. to talk through one's h.,** parler* à tort et à travers, radoter. **3. to keep it under one's h.,** tenir qch. en secret (*ou* sous cape), garder qch. pour soi. **4. to pass the h. round,** faire la quête. **5. my h.!** mince alors! mes aïeux! **6. hard h.,** turbineur *m* de la brique, boulot *m* de la duraille; **the hard hats,** les gens du bâtiment. *Voir aussi* **bowler-hat**[1]**; brass-hat; cocked; drop**[1]**, 2.**

hatch [hætʃ] (*noun*), *F:* **down the h.!** à la vôtre!; **to put one down the h.,** en mettre un à l'abri de la pluie. *Voir aussi* **booby-hatch.**

hatchet [ˈhætʃit] (*noun*), *F:* **1. to bury the h.,** se réconcilier, se rabibocher. **2. h. man,** (*a*) bandit *m*, gangster *m*; (*b*) militant *m*, dur *m* (*politique*).

haul [hɔːl] (**to**), *F:* **to h. s.o. over the coals,** réprimander* qn; **to get hauled over the coals,** prendre qch. pour son rhume. *Voir aussi* **ashes, 2.**

haul-ass [ˈhɔːlæs] (**to**) (*U.S.*), *P:* partir* en vitesse, se tailler.

hauler [ˈhɔːlər] (*noun*), *F:* auto *f* très rapide, bolide *m.*

haul in [ˈhɔːlˈin] (**to**), *F:* arrêter*, agrafer, épingler.

have [hæv] (**to**). **1.** *P:* **to h. it,** coïter*, faire l'amour; **to h. s.o., to h. it away** (*or* **off**) **with s.o.,** coïter* avec qn. **2.** *F:* **to h. it away with sth.,** voler* qch., chiper qch. **3.** *F:* **to h. it away,** s'échapper; **he's had it away over the wall,** il a fait le mur (de la prison). *Voir aussi* **1, 2** *ci-dessus.* **4.** *F:* **to h. had it,** (*a*) rater sa chance, rater le coup; (*b*) mourir*, claquer; (*c*) être fatigué* (*ou* crevé); (*d*) être ruiné* (*ou* à plat); **you've had it, chum!** (*a*) tu es fait, mon vieux!; (*b*) tu es foutu, mon vieux! **5.** *F:* **to let s.o. h. it,** (*a*) battre* qn, frapper qn, flanquer un coup* à qn; (*b*) critiquer* qn; (*c*) réprimander* qn, éreinter qn; (*d*) dire son fait à qn; (*e*) régler son compte à qn. **6.** *F:* duper*, avoir (qn). **7.** *F:* vaincre, défaire (qn). **8.** *F:* **to h. it out with s.o.,** vider une querelle* avec qn, s'expliquer avec qn. **9.** *F:* **to h. it in for s.o.,** en vouloir à qn, avoir une dent contre qn. *Voir aussi* **any**[2]**, 1.**

have in [ˈhævˈin] (**to**), *F:* inviter (qn), donner l'hospitalité à (qn). *Voir aussi* **have (to), 9.**

have-nots [ˈhævˈnɔts] (*pl. noun*), *F:* les dépourvus *m.pl.*, les miséreux *m.pl.*, les déshérités *m.pl.*; **the haves and the h.-n.,** les riches* et les pauvres*, les rupins *m.pl.* et les purotins *m.pl.*

have on [ˈhævˈɔn] (**to**), *F:* **1.** duper*, faire marcher (qn); **he's having you on,** il te fait marcher. **2. to h. sth. o.,** être occupé, être pris.

have up [ˈhævˈʌp] (**to**), *F:* traduire (qn) en justice.

hawk[1] [hɔːk] (*noun*), *F:* qn qui pousse à la guerre et au chauvinisme; un faucon; *cf.* **dove.** *Voir aussi* **fairy, 1; news-hawk.**

hawk[2] [hɔːk] (**to**), *F:* graillonner.

hay [hei] (*noun*). **1.** *F:* **to hit the h.,** se coucher*, se pieuter. **2.** *P:* **to get in the h. with s.o.,** coïter* avec qn; *voir aussi* **roll**[1]**, 2. 3.** *P:* **(Indian) h.,** marijuana *f* (*drogues**), chanvre (indien). **4.** *F:* peu d'argent*, gnognot(t)e *f.* **5.** *F:* **to make h. (while the sun shines),** battre le fer pendant qu'il est chaud. **6.** *F:* **to make h. of sth.,** chambarder, bouleverser qch.

haybag [ˈheibæg] (*noun*), *P:* (*a*) femme* (*péj.*), tarderie *f*, vieille moukère; (*b*) prostituée* de basse classe, pute *f.*

hayhead [ˈheihed] (*noun*), *P:* (*a*) usager *m* de la marijuana; (*b*) habitué(e) de la marijuana; *cf.* **hay, 3.**

haymaker [ˈhei-meikər] (*noun*), *F:* coup*

* An asterisk indicates that the word so marked is included as a head-word in the Appendix.

puissant (mettant l'adversaire hors de combat).

hayseed [ˈheisi:d] (*noun*) (*U.S.*), *F:* paysan*, cul-terreux *m*.

haywire [ˈheiwaiər] (*adj.*), *F:* **1.** confus, embrouillé, vasouillard. **2.** emballé, excité, cinglé. **3. to go h.,** (*a*) (*d'une personne*) ne pas tourner rond; (*b*) (*d'un projet, etc.*) être loupé, finir en queue de poisson.

haze [heiz] (**to**) (*U.S.*), *F:* brimer (à l'école), faire des brimades *f.pl.* à (un nouvel élève).

head [hed] (*noun*). **1.** *F:* mal *m* de tête; **to have a (bad) h., to have a h. on one,** (*a*) avoir mal à la tête; (*b*) avoir la gueule de bois. **2.** *F:* **to yell one's h. off,** gueuler. **3.** *F:* **to be h. over heels in love,** aimer* qn, être toqué de qn, être éperdument amoureux de qn. **4.** *P:* usager *m* de drogues; drogué(e)*, camé(e); *voir aussi* **acid, 2; cokehead; cubehead; dopehead; hayhead; hophead; juicehead; methhead; pillhead; pothead; teahead; weedhead. 5.** *F:* **to go off one's h.,** devenir fou*, perdre la boule. **6.** *P:* W.C.*, chiottes *f.pl.* **7.** *F:* **I need it like a hole in the h.,** j'ai pas besoin de ça, c'est aussi souhaitable qu'une jambe cassée. **8.** *F:* **not to (be able to) make h. or tail of sth.,** ne comprendre goutte à qch., n'y comprendre que couic. **9.** *F:* **I could do it (standing) on my h.,** c'est simple comme bonjour. **10.** *F:* **to talk s.o.'s h. off,** étourdir qn; rompre les oreilles* à qn. **11.** *P:* la guêpe, la guenon. **12.** *P:* fana *mf.* **13.** *V:* **h. job,** coït* buccal, prise *f* de pipe; **h. chick,** femme qui pratique le coït* buccal, rogneuse *f* d'os. *Voir aussi* **balloon-head; big-head; blubberhead; bonehead; boofhead; bunhead; cabbagehead; chew off (to); chowderhead; chucklehead; cloghead; clothhead; clunkhead; deadhead; dumbhead; eat (to), 6; egghead; fathead; flathead; jughead; knock**[2] **(to); knothead; knucklehead; lughead; lunkhead; meathead; muscle-head; muttonhead; nail**[1], **2; pea-head; pinhead; puddinghead; pumpkinhead; redhead; rockhead; sap(head); screw**[2] **(to), 6; shithead; skinhead; sleepyhead; snap off (to); sore, 2; sorehead; squarehead; thickhead; turniphead; water, 2; wet-head.**

headache [ˈhedeik] (*noun*), *F:* ennui *m*, embêtement *m*, casse-tête *m*. *Voir aussi* **Dutchman, 2.**

header [ˈhedər] (*noun*), *F:* **to take a h.,** tomber* par terre, ramasser une bûche.

heading [ˈhediŋ] (*noun*), *F:* coup *m* de tête (sur la figure).

headlights [ˈhedlaits] (*pl. noun*), *P:* **1.** seins*, amortisseurs *m.pl.*, pare-chocs *m.pl.* **2.** gros diamants*, bouchons *m.pl.* de carafe.

headlines [ˈhedlainz] (*pl. noun*), *F:* **to hit the h.,** devenir fameux, faire la une.

head-merchant [ˈhedmə:tʃ(ə)nt] (*noun*), *F:* = **head-shrinker.**

head-piece [ˈhedpi:s] (*noun*), *F:* tête*, cerveau *m*, ciboulot *m*.

head-shrinker [ˈhedʃriŋkər] (*noun*), *F:* psychiatre *mf*, psychanalyste *mf*; *cf.* **shrink.**

health [helθ] (*noun*), *F:* **I don't do that for my h.,** je ne fais pas cela pour mon bon plaisir.

heap [hi:p] (*noun*), *F:* **1. to be (struck) all of a h.,** rester comme deux ronds de flan. **2.** (*a*) **to come out at the top of** (*or* **on top of**) **the h.,** être au premier rang, tenir le haut du pavé; (*b*) **to stay at the bottom of the h.,** être le dernier des derniers, être au fin fond. **3. a h. of nonsense,** un tissu d'âneries. **4.** nouille *f*, andouille *f*, nullité *f*. **5.** vieille voiture*, bagnole *f*. **6. heaps of . . .,** une abondance* de..., un tas de..., une tripotée de..., une flopée de... *Voir aussi* **scrap-heap.**

heart [hɑ:t] (*noun*), *F:* **have a h.!** (ne) parle pas de malheur! *Voir aussi* **purple.**

heart-throb [ˈhɑ:tθrɔb] (*noun*), *F:* objet *m* de l'amour, béguin *m*.

hearty [ˈhɑ:ti] (*noun*), *F:* **1.** un athlète (opposé à un esthète). **2.** (*pl.*) camarades *m.pl.*, copains *m.pl.*

heat [hi:t] (*noun*). **1.** *F:* pression *f*, feu *m*; **to turn on the h.,** (*a*) s'enflammer, s'échauffer; (*b*) faire pression sur qn, lui mettre le feu au derrière. **2.** *F:* interrogatoire* poussé, saignement *m* de nez. **3.** (*U.S.*) *P:* fonctionnaire *m* de l'ordre judiciaire. **4.** (*U.S.*) *P:* = **heater.**

heater [ˈhi:tər] (*noun*), *P:* revolver*, calibre *m*.

heave-ho [ˈhi:vˈhou] (*noun*), *P:* renvoi *m*, expulsion *f*; **to get the h.-h.,** être

* L'astérisque indique que le mot marqué de ce signe figure comme entrée dans le Répertoire.

congédié*, être flanqué à la porte; **to give s.o. the h.-h.,** se débarrasser* de qn, larguer, sacquer, virer qn.

heaven ['hevn] (*noun*), *F:* **1.** grand plaisir, ravissement *m*; **it's h. to relax,** c'est divin de pouvoir se reposer. **2. good heavens!** juste ciel! bonté du ciel! bonté divine!; **heavens above!** nom d'une pipe!; **for h.'s sake!** pour l'amour de Dieu! *Voir aussi* **dust**[1], **2** (*a*), (*b*).

heavenly ['hevnli] (*adj.*), *F:* divin, ravissant, délectable. *Voir aussi* **blue**[2], **1.**

heaves [hi:vz] (*pl. noun*), *F:* **to have the h.,** avoir des nausées *f.pl.*

heavy[1] ['hevi] (*adj.*). **1.** *F:* passionné, sexy; impudique, vicieux; **h. necking,** pelotage *m*, tripotage *m*. **2.** *F:* **h. date,** rendez-vous* sentimental important. **3.** *F:* **to make h. weather of sth.,** faire toute une affaire de qch. **4.** *P:* (butin) de valeur; **the h. mob,** bande* de voleurs* de grande envergure. **5.** *F:* **h. stuff,** renforts motorisés dans une descente de police. **6.** *P:* en grande quantité; **h. dough,** des tas de fric. **7.** *P:* malhonnête, louche. **8.** *F:* (*th.*) **h. rôle,** rôle *m* du vilain de la pièce; rôle pompeux. **9.** *P:* sale*, dégueulbif. **10.** *P:* super-beat, maxi-beat. **11.** *P:* excellent*, très agréable. **12.** *P:* enceinte*.

heavy[2] ['hevi] (*noun*). **1.** *F:* (*boxe*) (= *heavyweight*) poids lourd. **2.** *P:* (*a*) apache *m*, bandit *m*; (*b*) assassin*; **on the h.,** sur le chemin du crime, goupinant à la dure. **3.** *F:* le vilain dans une pièce *ou* un film. **4.** *P:* **to be in the h.,** avoir beaucoup d'argent*, être riche*, rouler dans le fric. **5.** *F:* **the Hollywood heavies,** les durs *m.pl.* de Hollywood.

hebe ['hi:bi] (*noun*). **1.** *P:* = **heeb. 2.** *F:* serveuse *f*, loufiate *f*.

heck [hek] (*noun & excl.*) (*euph. pour* **hell**), *F:* **1. h.!** sapristi! la barbe! morbleu!; **what the h....!** que diable...! **2. a h. of a lot,** une abondance*, une grande quantité, une foultitude, une bardée.

hedge [hedʒ] (**to**), *F:* **1. to h. one's bets,** étaler *ou* protéger ses paris. **2.** chercher des échappatoires *f.pl.* (*ou* des faux-fuyants *m.pl.*), s'échapper par la tangente.

hedge-hop ['hedʒhɔp] (**to**), *F:* (*av.*) faire du rase-mottes *m.pl.*

hedge-hopping ['hedʒhɔpiŋ] (*noun*), *F:* (*av.*) vol *m* en rase-mottes.

heeb [hi:b] (*noun*), *P:* Juif *m*, Youpe *m*, Youpin *m*.

heebie-jeebies ['hi:bi'dʒi:biz] (*pl. noun*), *F:* **1.** delirium *m* tremens, les rats bleus. **2.** angoisse *f*, nervosité *f* extrême, peur bleue; **to give s.o. the h.-j.,** donner un choc nerveux à qn.

heebies ['hi:biz] (*pl. noun*), *F:* (**leaping**) **h.** = **heebie-jeebies, 1, 2.**

heel [hi:l] (*noun*). **1.** *F:* individu* méprisable, gouape *f*; **to feel a** (**bit of a**) **h.,** friser la canaille. **2.** *P:* **to have round heels,** avoir la cuisse hospitalière; *cf.* **roundheel**(s). **3.** *F:* **to cool** (*or* **kick**) **one's heels,** se morfondre, croquer le marmot, faire le pied de grue, poireauter. *Voir aussi* **head, 3; kick up** (**to**), **4; shitheel.**

heeled [hi:ld] (*adj.*) (*U.S.*), *P:* **1.** = **well-heeled. 2.** armé d'un revolver*, flingué.

heesh [hi:ʃ] (*noun*), *P:* = **hash**[2], **3.**

heft [heft] (**to**), *F:* soulever, soupeser (qch.).

hefty ['hefti] (*adj.*), *F:* **1.** fort*, costaud, malabar. **2.** gros, important; **a h. bill,** une note de taille (*ou* d'un montant élevé); **a h. chunk,** un morceau imposant.

heifer ['hefər] (*noun*), *F:* jeune fille*.

he-ing and she-ing ['hi:iŋn'ʃi:iŋ] (*noun*), *P:* coït*, baisage *m*.

Heinie, heinie ['haini] (*noun*), *P:* (*a*) Allemand*, boche *m*; (*b*) soldat allemand, hun *m*.

Heinz 57 ['hainz'fifti'sevn] (*noun*), *F:* chien* bâtard. *Voir aussi* **bingo** (**57**).

heist[1] [haist] (*noun*) (*mainly U.S.*), *F:* **1.** cambriolage *m*, casse *m*, fric-frac *m* (par professionnels). **2.** = **heister. 3.** amélioration *f*, augmentation *f*.

heist[2] [haist] (**to**) (*mainly U.S.*), *F:* **1.** cambrioler*, faire un casse. **2.** arrêter (un camion, *etc.*) pour le voler, pirater. **3.** améliorer, augmenter, renforcer. **4.** se débarrasser* de (qch.), se défarguer de (qch.).

heister ['haistər] (*noun*) (*mainly U.S.*), *F:* cambrioleur*, bandit *m*, casseur *m*.

hell [hel] (*noun*). **1.** *P:* (*a*) **go to h.!** va au diable!; **to h. with it!** au diable que tout cela!; **get the** (*or* **to**) **h. out of here!** nom de Dieu débarrasse le

* An asterisk indicates that the word so marked is included as a head-word in the Appendix.

plancher!; **oh h.!** merde alors!; **h.'s bells (and buckets of blood)!** sacré nom de nom!; **would he go? would he h.!** partir? le bougre ne bougeait pas!; **h., I don't know,** diable, je n'en sais rien; (*b*) **what the h. does it matter?** qu'est-ce que ça peut bien faire?; **who the h. are you?** mais diable qui êtes-vous?; **who the h. do you think you are (anyway)?** tu te prends pour qui, que diable!; **what the h. do you think you're doing** (*or* **playing at**)? que diable es-tu en train de fabriquer?; **what in h.** (*or* **h.'s name**) **is that?** qu'est-ce que c'est que ce satané truc?; **why the h. doesn't he belt up?** pourquoi diable ne la ferme-t-il pas? **2.** *F:* **to give s.o. h.,** faire passer un mauvais quart d'heure à qn, en faire voir (de toutes les couleurs) à qn; **to get h., to have h. to pay,** être réprimandé* *ou* puni, être engueulé (*ou* incendié), prendre qch. pour son rhume. **3.** *F:* **like (all) h. let loose,** comme les damnés en enfer; **to create** (*or* **raise**) **(merry) h.,** (*a*) faire du boucan, faire un chambard du diable; (*b*) rouscailler, râler (comme un enragé). **4.** *P:* **in a** (*or* **one**) **h. of a mess** (*or* **state**), dans une pagaille infernale (*ou* du tonnerre); **a h. of a nice fellow,** un bien brave type; **you've got a h. of a nerve** (*or* **cheek**)**!** tu as un culot du diable!; **it's a h. of a bore** (*or* **bind**), c'est diablement embêtant; **a h. of a row,** (*a*) un bruit* d'enfer, un vacarme infernal; (*b*) une engueulade maison. **5.** *F:* **to do sth. for the h. of it,** faire qch. histoire de rire (*ou* pour s'en payer une tranche). **6.** *F:* **to play h. with s.o., sth.,** en faire voir à qn, cabosser qch. **7.** *F:* **to feel like h.,** se sentir au cent mille dessous. **8.** *P:* **sure as h.,** sûr et certain, dans la fouille. **9.** *P:* **to knock h. out of s.o.,** battre* qn comme plâtre, bourrer qn de coups. **10.** *P:* **all to h.,** démoli, gâché, coulé. **11.** *F:* **to go h. for leather,** galoper ventre à terre, courir avec le feu au derrière. **12.** *F:* **till h. freezes over,** jusqu'à la Saint-Glinglin. **13.** (*U.S.*) *F:* **from h. to breakfast,** entièrement, totalement, de A à Z. **14.** (*U.S.*) *F:* **to h. and gone,** (*a*) disparu, passé à l'as, évanoui; (*b*) aux antipodes, chez les damnés. **15.** *F:* **h.'s angels,** jeunes voyous *m.pl.* en moto. **16.** *F:* tripot *m*, boui-boui *m*. **17.** *F:* **come h. or high water,** advienne que pourra. *Voir aussi* **Chinaman, 2; kick up (to), 3; snowball[1], 2; stink[1], 1.**

hell-bender [ˈhel-bendər] (*noun*), *P:* **1.** bamboche infernale; *cf.* **bender, 1.** **2.** débauché *m*, noceur *m*.

hell-cat [ˈhel-kæt] (*noun*), *F:* **1.** jeune fille* pleine d'entrain et de témérité. **2.** vieille sorcière, carabosse *f*.

hell-hole [ˈhelhoul] (*noun*), *F:* endroit mal famé, coupe-gorge *m*.

hellion [ˈheljən] (*noun*) (*U.S.*), *F:* **1.** vaurien*, sale type *m*, fripouille *f*. **2.** enfant* terrible, petit diable.

hellishly [ˈheliʃli] (*adv.*), *F:* diablement, diaboliquement.

hello-dearie [ˈhəlouˈdiəri] (*noun*), *P:* prostituée*, frangipane *f*.

hell-raiser [ˈhelreizər] (*noun*), *P:* **1.** individu* déchaîné, téméraire *mf*. **2.** débauché *m*, noceur *m*.

helluva [ˈheləvə] (=*hell of a*), *P:* *voir* **hell, 4.**

he-man [ˈhiːmæn] (*noun*) (*pl.* **he-men**), *F:* (*a*) homme fort* et viril, malabar *m*; (*b*) un beau mâle.

hemp [hemp] (*noun*), *F:* **(Indian) h.,** cannabis *m* (*drogues**), chanvre (indien).

hen [hen] (*noun*), *F:* (*a*) femme* (*péj.*), mégère *f*, rombière *f*, vieille dinde; (*b*) jeune femme*, une petite poule; **h. party,** réunion *f* de femmes seules, volière *f*; *cf.* **stag[1], 1.**

Henry, henry [ˈhenri] (*noun*), *F:* héroïne *f* (*drogues**).

hep [hep] (*adj.*), *F:* (*a*) qui apprécie la musique swing; (*b*) qui est au courant (*ou* à la coule *ou* dans le vent); **a h. guy,** un affranchi; **to put s.o. h.,** mettre qn à la page, affranchir qn.

hep-cat [ˈhepkæt] (*noun*), *F:* **1.** (*a*) musicien *m* faisant partie d'un orchestre swing; (*b*) fanatique *mf* de la musique swing; (*c*) danseur *m* swing. **2.** individu* nouvelle vague (*ou* dans le vent).

hepped up [ˈheptˈʌp] (*adj.*), *F:* **1.** en colère*, à cran. **2.** très enthousiasmé, emballé.

herb [həːb] (*noun*), *F:* **(the) h.,** cannabis *m* (*drogues**), herbe *f*.

here [ˈhiər] (*adv.*), *F:* **1. that's neither h. nor there,** cela ne fait ni chaud ni froid, cela n'a aucune importance. **2. h. goes!** ça démarre! ça va barder!

* L'astérisque indique que le mot marqué de ce signe figure comme entrée dans le Répertoire.

3. **h. you are,** tenez, prenez-le, et voilà. 4. **from h. on in,** à partir de ce moment.

heron [ˈherən] (*noun*), *P:* héroïne *f* (*drogues**).

herring [ˈheriŋ] (*noun*), *F:* 1. **red h.,** procédé servant à détourner l'attention. 2. **the H. Pond,** l'océan *m* Atlantique, la Grande Tasse.

he-she [ˈhi:ʃi:] (*noun*), *P:* prostituée*, catin *f*.

het up [ˈhetˈʌp] (*adj.*), *F:* 1. énervé, agité, tracassé. 2. en colère*, en rogne.

hex[1] [heks] (*noun*), *F:* (*a*) malchance*; (*b*) porte-guigne *m*.

hex[2] [heks] (**to**), *F:* porter la guigne (*ou* la poisse) à (qn).

hi! [hai] (*excl.*), *F:* (*a*) salut! bonjour!; (*b*) **h.! you there!** eh! dites donc, là-bas!

hick[1] [hik] (*adj.*) (*U.S.*), *P:* 1. rustique, campagnard; **a h. town,** un patelin. 2. ignorant, rustaud.

hick[2] [hik] (*noun*) (*U.S.*), *P:* 1. paysan*, péquenaud *m*. 2. innocent *m*, couillon *m*, niguedouille *m*. 3. cadavre*, croni *m*.

hickey [ˈhiki] (*noun*) (*U.S.*), *F:* marque sur la peau faite par un baiser ardent; suçon *m*.

hide [haid] (*noun*), *F:* 1. peau *f* (de l'homme), cuir *m*; **to tan the h. off s.o.,** battre* qn, carder le cuir à qn. 2. **to have a thick h.,** avoir la peau dure; *cf.* **thick-skinned.**

hiding [ˈhaidiŋ] (*noun*), *F:* 1. **(good) h.,** volée *f* de coups*, dérouillée *f*, passage *m* à tabac. 2. **to be on a h. to nothing,** avoir tout à perdre sans rien à gagner.

hi-fi [ˈhaiˈfai] (=*high fidelity*), *F:* de haute fidélité.

high[1] [hai] (*adj.*), *F:* 1. **to be for the h. jump,** en être pour de la casse, être dans de mauvais draps; **he's for the h. jump,** qu'est-ce qu'il va prendre!; son affaire est bonne. 2. **to leave s.o. h. and dry,** laisser qn en plan. 3. **h. and mighty,** prétentieux*, poseur, bêcheur. 4. **to be h.,** (*a*) être ivre* (*ou* parti *ou* rétamé); (*b*) avoir un sentiment de bien-être; être dans un état d'euphorie dû aux drogues*; high; *voir aussi* **fly**[3] **(to)**, 2 (*b*); **kite,** 4. 5. (*U.S.*) **h. on sth., s.o.,** qui a une haute opinion de qch., de qn. 6. **to have a h. old time,** faire la fête* (*ou* la noce *ou* la ribouldingue). *Voir aussi* **horse**[1], 5; **jinks; knee-high.**

high[2] [hai] (*noun*), *F:* **to have a h.** = **to be high (high**[1], 4 (*b*)).

highbinder [ˈhai-baindər] (*noun*) (*U.S.*), *F:* 1. gangster *m*, assassin*, bandit *m*. 2. escroc*, filou *m*, empileur *m*. 3. politicien corrompu.

highbrow[1] [ˈhai-brau] (*adj.*), *F:* intellectuel, calé.

highbrow[2] [ˈhai-brau] (*noun*), *F:* intellectuel *m*, mandarin *m*, ponte *m*, grosse tête.

highfalutin [ˈhaifəˈlu:tin] (*adj.*), *F:* prétentieux*, déclamatoire, ronflant.

high-flier [ˈhaiˈflaiər] (*noun*), *F:* ambitieux *m*, qn qui va aux extrêmes; *cf.* **fly**[3] **(to)**, 2 (*a*).

high-muck-a-muck [ˈhaiˈmʌkəmʌk] (*noun*), *F:* personnage important, grosse légume.

highspots [ˈhai-spɔts] (*pl. noun*), *F:* **to hit the h.,** exceller, toucher les hauteurs *f.pl.*

hightail [ˈhai-teil] (**to**), *F:* **to h. it,** se dépêcher*, se magner le train.

high-ups [ˈhaiʌps] (*pl. noun*), *F:* hauts fonctionnaires, gros bonnets.

highway [ˈhaiwei] (*attrib. adj.*), *F:* **it's h. robbery!** c'est du vol manifeste!

hijack [ˈhaidʒæk] (**to**), *F:* détourner; **to h. a vehicle,** s'emparer de force d'un véhicule et de son contenu; **to h. a plane,** pirater un avion.

hijacker [ˈhaidʒækər] (*noun*), *F:* détourneur *m*; pirate *m* (de l'air), voleur* de voiture*.

hike[1] [haik] (*noun*), *P:* augmentation *f*, hausse *f*.

hike[2] [haik] (**to**), *F:* **to h. a cheque,** falsifier un chèque.

hike up [ˈhaikˈʌp] (**to**), *F:* augmenter, hausser (le prix), allonger le tir.

hillbilly [ˈhilˈbili] (*noun*) (*U.S.*), *F:* 1. petit fermier de montagne. 2. rustre *m*, rustaud *m*. 3. chanson montagnarde et rustique.

hinge [hindʒ] (*noun*), *P:* **to get** (*or* **take**) **a h.,** jeter un coup d'œil*, lancer un coup de châsse.

hip[1] [hip] (*adj.*). 1. *F:* = **hep,** (*a*), (*b*). 2. *F:* = **cool**[1], 1. 3. *P:* qui a été initié(e) à la drogue. *Cf.* **hipster.**

hip[2] [hip] (**to**), *F:* rendre morose et cafardeux.

* An asterisk indicates that the word so marked is included as a head-word in the Appendix.

hipped [hipt] (*adj.*), *P:* 1. **to be h. on sth.,** (*a*) être obsédé (*ou* hypnotisé) par qch.; (*b*) être au courant, être bien renseigné sur qch. 2. crevé d'ennui.

hippie, hippy [ˈhipi] (*noun*), *F:* hippie *mf*, hippy *mf*, yippie *mf*.

hipster [ˈhipstər] (*noun*). 1. *F:* = **hep-cat,** 2. 2. *F:* membre d'un groupe de cools. 3. *F:* membre de la génération beat (*ou* sacrifiée). 4. *P:* initié(e) à la drogue. *Cf.* **hip[1].**

hister [ˈhaistər] (*noun*) (*U.S.*), *F:* = **heister.**

hit[1] [hit] (*noun*). 1. *F:* pièce *f*, chanson *f*, *etc.*, à succès. 2. *F:* succès *m* populaire; **to make a h.,** faire un boum. 3. *F:* acteur *m*, chanteur *m*, *etc.*, en vogue. 4. *P:* réussite sexuelle, partie *f* de piquet. 5. *P:* rendez-vous* de contrebande; moyens *m.pl.* de contrebande. 6. *P:* plaquette *f* de drogues. 7. *P:* injection *f* de drogues, piquouse *f*. 8. *P:* meurtre prémédité. *Voir aussi* **smash-hit.**

hit[2] [hit] (**to**). 1. *F:* **to h. the hundred mark,** (*auto*) taper le 160. 2. *P:* provoquer une forte réaction (*drogues*); **to h. s.o.,** pourvoir un usager avec de la drogue. *Voir aussi* **bottle[1], 1; ceiling; deck, 1; feather[1], 6; hay, 1; highspots; jackpot; pad[1], 4; pipe[1], 2; road, 2; sack[1], 3; sauce[1], 2; track[1], 4; trail.**

hitch[1] [hitʃ] (*noun*), *F:* promenade *f* en voiture (*souvent* auto-stop).

hitch[2] [hitʃ] (**to**), *F:* 1. **to h. one's wag(g)on to a star,** être dévoré d'ambition, viser très haut. 2. **to get hitched,** se marier, se maquer; *cf.* **unhitched.** 3. **to h. a ride,** se faire conduire en voiture.

hit off [ˈhitˈɔf] (**to**), *F:* **to h. it o. with s.o.,** bien s'entendre avec qn; **they don't h. it o.,** il y a du tirage entre eux.

hit-parade [ˈhitpəreid] (*noun*), *F:* hit-parade *m*.

hit up [ˈhitˈʌp] (**to**), *F:* **to h. it u.,** avoir une conduite déchaînée, faire la vie.

hive off [ˈhaivˈɔf] (**to**), *F:* 1. mettre de côté, mettre à l'écart. 2. s'enfuir*, se cavaler.

hiya! [ˈhaijə] (*excl.*), *F:* salut!; *cf.* **hi!** (*a*).

hock[1] [hɔk] (*noun*). 1. *F:* **in h.,** (*a*) en gage, chez ma tante; (*b*) en prison*, en taule. 2. (*Austr.*) *P:* pédéraste*, lope *f*.

hock[2] [hɔk] (**to**), *F:* mettre en gage, mettre au clou.

hocker [ˈhɔkər] (*noun*) (*U.S.*), *P:* crachat*, graillon *m*.

hockshop [ˈhɔkʃɔp] (*noun*), *F:* mont-de-piété *m*, chez ma tante, le clou.

hocky [ˈhɔki] (*noun*) (*U.S.*), *P:* 1. mensonges*, exagération *f*, blagues *f.pl.* 2. merde *f*, caca *m*. 3. sperme*, blanc *m*. 4. nourriture* peu appétissante, boustifaille *f*, graille *f*.

ho-dad(dy) [ˈhouˈdæd(i)] (*noun*) (*U.S.*), *F:* 1. individu* farfelu, m'as-tu-vu *m*. 2. individu* qui aime fréquenter les sportifs sans en être un lui-même. 3. pète-sec *m*, collet monté, constipé *m*.

hoedown [ˈhoudaun] (*noun*) (*U.S.*), *F:* 1. danse *f* rustique; bal animé, guinche boumée. 2. querelle*, engueulade *f*. 3. bagarre*, rixe *f*, rififi *m*.

hog[1] [hɔg] (*noun*), *F:* 1. goinfre*, porc *m*. 2. **to go the whole h.,** aller jusqu'au bout, tout risquer, mettre le paquet; *cf.* **whole-hogger; whole-hoggism.** *Voir aussi* **road-hog; speed-hog.**

hog[2] [hɔg] (**to**), *F:* 1. goinfrer. 2. **to h. the limelight,** accaparer la vedette. 3. **to h. the road,** conduire au milieu de la route; *cf.* **road-hog.** 4. **to h. it,** vivre comme un cochon.

hog-tie [ˈhɔgtai] (**to**), *F:* réduire à l'impuissance.

hogwash [ˈhɔgwɔʃ] (*noun*), *F:* 1. bibine *f*, rinçure *f*, lavasse *f*. 2. bêtise*, sottise *f*, absurdité *f*. 3. boniments *m.pl.*, baratinage *m*.

hoist[1] [hɔist] (*noun*), *P:* 1. vol *m*, chouravage *m*, attaque *f* à main armée, hold-up *m*. 2. enquilleuse *f*. 3. vol *m* à l'étalage.

hoist[2] [hɔist] (**to**), *P:* 1. cambrioler*, voler*, caroubler; *cf.* **heist[2] (to), 1, 2.** 2. voler* à l'étalage, acheter à la foire d'empoigne. 3. (*Austr.*) procéder à une arrestation, coffrer.

hokey-pokey [ˈhoukiˈpouki] (*noun*), *F:* 1. = **hokum, 1.** 2. (*U.S.*) glace *f* *ou* bonbon *m* de mauvaise qualité.

hokum [ˈhoukəm] (*noun*), *F:* 1. bêtises*, blagues *f.pl.* 2. sensiblerie *f*, mélo(drame) *m*.

hokus [ˈhoukəs] (*noun*), *P:* drogues*, came *f*, narcs *m.pl.*

hold [hould] (**to**). 1. *F:* **h. everything!** arrêtez! attendez! 2. *P:* (*a*) fourguer

* L'astérisque indique que le mot marqué de ce signe figure comme entrée dans le Répertoire.

des drogues; (*b*) posséder des drogues. 3. *P:* se masturber*, se branler.

hold out on [ˈhouldˈautɔn] (**to**), *F:* faire des cachotteries *f.pl.* à (qn).

hold-up [ˈhouldʌp] (*noun*), *F:* 1. arrêt *m*, embarras *m* de voitures, embouteillage *m.* 2. vol *m* à main armée, braquage *m*, hold-up *m.*

hold up [ˈhouldˈʌp] (**to**), *F:* 1. voler* à main armée, braquer. 2. entraver, gêner, embarrasser, immobiliser. *Voir aussi* **wash**[1], 1.

hole [houl] (*noun*). 1. *F:* bouge *m*, bastringue *m*, caboulot *m.* 2. *F:* taudis *m*, gourbi *m*, piaule *f*; *cf.* **dog-hole.** 3. *F:* embarras *m*, pétrin *m*, impasse *f*; **to be in a h.,** être dans une situation difficile, être en rade. 4. *F:* **to make a h. in one's capital,** écorner (*ou* ébrécher) son capital. 5. *F:* **to pick holes in sth.,** trouver à redire à qch. 6. *V:* vagin*, fente *f*; *cf.* **manhole.** 7. *V:* anus*, trou *m* (de balle); *cf.* **arsehole; bumhole; bung-hole, 1; cornhole**[1]**; fart-hole; shit-hole.** 8. (*U.S.*) *P:* **the h.,** cachot *m* (disciplinaire), mitard *m.* 9. *F:* **h. in the wall,** petite maison *ou* lieu *m* de commerce, trou *m.* 10. *F:* **to burn a h. in one's stomach,** manger* *ou* boire* qch. de très fort, se brûler l'estomac *m.* 11. (*U.S.*) *P:* **to go in the h.,** s'endetter, s'encroumer. 12. *F:* **to put a h. through s.o., to drill a h.** (*or* **holes**) **in s.o.,** assassiner* qn, butter, démolir, fusiller, flinguer qn, transformer qn en passoire. 13. *F:* **h. in the heart,** (*a*) communication *f* inter-ventriculaire; (*b*) communication *f* inter-auriculaire. *Voir aussi* **cakehole; dog-hole; earhole; glory-hole; head, 7; hell-hole; keyhole; lugholes; nineteenth; square**[1]**, 7; top-hole.**

hole-and-corner [ˈhoulən(d)ˈkɔːnər] (*adj.*), *F:* fait en sous-main (*ou* sous la table); **h.-a.-c. work,** manigances *f.pl.*

hole away [ˈhouləˈwei] (**to**), *F:* cacher*, mettre à gauche.

hole up [ˈhoulˈʌp] (**to**), *F:* 1. s'installer, faire son nid (d'un soir). 2. se cacher*, se terrer, se planquer.

holier-than-thou [houliəðænðau] (*noun*), *F:* personne *f* hypocrite qui donne l'apparence de dévotion; Sainte-Nitouche *f.*

holler [ˈhɔlər] (**to**), *P:* 1. crier*, gueuler, beugler. 2. moucharder, cafarder.

holler-wag(g)on [ˈhɔləwægən] (*noun*), *P:* voiture-radio *f* de la police.

hollow [ˈhɔlou, ˈhɔlə] (*adv.*), *F:* **to beat s.o. h.,** battre qn à plate(s) couture(s).

holly-golly [ˈhɔliˈgɔli] (*noun*) (*U.S.*), *F:* 1. bêtises*, sornettes *f.pl.* 2. tintamarre *m*, vacarme *m*, remue-ménage *m.*

Hollywood [ˈhɔliwud] (*adj.*), *F:* 1. (*articles, vêtements*) clinquant, criard. 2. (*personnes*) artificiel, maniéré, affecté.

hols [hɔlz] (*pl. noun*) (*abbr.* = *holidays*), *F:* vacances *f.pl.* (scolaires), vacs *f.pl.*

holy [ˈhouli] (*adj.*). 1. *F:* **h. cow!** (*or* **cats!** *or* **mackerel!** *or* **Moses!** *or* **smoke!**), sapristi! saperlotte! saperlipopette! crénom de nom! 2. *P:* (*péj.*) **h. Joe,** (*a*) prêtre*, pasteur *m*; étudiant *m* en théologie, ratichon *m*; (*b*) personne dévote, grenouille *f* de bénitier. 3. *F:* **h. terror,** (*a*) enfant* malicieux, petit diable; (*b*) individu* canulant; colique *f*; (*c*) individu* qui fait peur, épouvantail *m. Voir aussi* **friar.**

home [houm] (*adv.*), *F:* 1. **h. and dry,** à bon port, sain et sauf. 2. **my suit is going h.,** mon costume est usé. 3. **nothing to write h. about,** rien qui vaille la peine, rien d'époustouflant.

home-bird [ˈhoumbəːd] (*noun*), *F:* casanier *m*, casanière *f.*

homestretch [ˈhoumˈstretʃ] (*noun*), *F:* dernière étape, dernier échelon.

homework [ˈhoumwəːk] (*noun*). 1. **to do one's h.,** (*a*) *F:* faire une préparation attentive; (*b*) *P:* remplir ses obligations conjugales (*rapports sexuels*). 2. *P:* (*a*) pelotage *m*, baisage *m*; (*b*) **a nice bit of h.,** une fille* à la cuisse hospitalière.

homie [ˈhoumi] (*noun*), *P:* = **homo**[2].

homo[1] [ˈhoumou] (*adj.*), *P:* homo(sexuel).

homo[2] [ˈhoumou] (*noun*), *P:* pédéraste*, homosexuel *m*, pédé *m.*

honest-to-goodness [ˈɔnist(t)əˈgudnis] (*adj.*), *F:* vrai, réel, authentique.

honey [ˈhʌni] (*noun*), *F:* 1. petit(e) ami(e), chéri(e), bien-aimé(e). 2. as *m*, crack *m*; **a h. of an acrobat,** un as d'acrobate. 3. qch. d'excellent* (*ou* de bath *ou* de chouette). 4. un vrai chou, un amour, un trognon. *Voir aussi* **bee, 2.**

* An asterisk indicates that the word so marked is included as a head-word in the Appendix.

honeybunch [ˈhʌnibʌntʃ] (*noun*), *F:* = **honey, 1, 4.**

honey-fuck [ˈhʌnifʌk] (**to**), *VV:* **1.** coïter* d'une manière romantique (*ou* à la douce). **2.** coïter* avec une fille très jeune, baiser la petite fleur.

honey-fuck(ing) [ˈhʌnifʌk(iŋ)] (*noun*), *VV:* **1.** coït* (*ou* crampette *f*) à la douce. **2.** coït* lent et agréable, soupe délayée à la quéquette. **3.** coït* avec une fille très jeune, baisage *m* de petite fleur.

honk [hɔŋk] (**to**). **1.** *P:* **to h.** (**one's chuff**), vomir*, dégobiller. **2.** *P:* **to get honked,** s'enivrer, se paffer. **3.** (*Austr.*) *F:* = **hoot**[2] (**to**), **2.**

honkers [ˈhɔŋkəz] (*adj.*), *P:* (**Harry**) **h.,** ivre*, rétamé, saoul.

honky-tonk [ˈhɔŋkiˈtɔŋk] (*noun*) (*U.S.*), *F:* **1.** cabaret *m* de basse classe, caboulot *m*, boui-boui *m*. **2.** petit théâtre de province. **3.** bordel*, bobinard *m*.

hooch [huːtʃ] (*noun*) (*U.S.*), *F:* (*a*) alcool*, gnôle *f* (de contrebande); (*b*) alcool* très fort, casse-gueule *m*; whisky *m*.

hood [hud] (*noun*), *P:* **1.** = **hoodlum. 2.** religieuse *f*, bonne sœur, bibine *f*.

hoodlum [ˈhuːdləm] (*noun*), *F:* vaurien*, chenapan *m*, jeune apache *m*.

hooey [ˈhuːiː] (*noun*), *P:* = **balon(e)y.**

hoof[1] [huːf] (*noun*). **1.** *F:* pied*, ripaton *m*; **to pad the h.,** aller à pied, aller à patte; *voir aussi* **pad**[2] (**to**). **2.** *P:* **iron h.** (*R.S.* = **poof**), pédéraste*; *cf.* **half-iron.**

hoof[2] [huːf] (**to**), *F:* **to h. it** = **to pad it** (**pad**[2] (**to**)).

hoof out [ˈhuːfˈaut] (**to**), *F:* **1.** sortir (qn) à coups de pied, expulser. **2.** congédier*, mettre à la porte, envoyer dinguer (qn).

hoo-ha(a) [ˈhuːhɑː] (*noun*), *F:* **1.** bruit*, boucan *m*. **2.** querelle*, barabille *f*. **3.** embarras *m.pl.*, chichis *m.pl.*

hook[1] [huk] (*noun*). **1.** *F:* **on the h.,** dans une mauvaise passe, dans le pétrin. **2.** *F:* **to get off the h.,** se débrouiller*, se tirer d'embarras (*ou* d'affaire); **that lets me off the h.,** cela m'a tiré d'affaire; **to get s.o. off the h.,** tirer qn d'affaire, sortir qn de mauvais draps. **3.** *P:* **to go off the hooks,** (*a*) devenir fou*, dérailler, partir du ciboulot; (*b*) mourir*. **4.** *F:* **on one's own h.,** sans appui, à son propre compte. **5.** *P:* **to sling one's h.,** partir*, s'enfuir, décamper, mettre les bouts. **6.** (*pl.*) *F:* mains*, croches *f.pl.*; **to get one's hooks on s.o., sth.,** mettre le grappin sur qn, qch.; *cf.* **grappling, 2; meat-hooks. 7.** *P:* drogue narcotique (héroïne *f*). **8.** (*U.S.*) *V:* **to put the hooks to s.o.,** coïter* avec qn, fourailler qn. **9.** *P:* voleur*, leveur *m*.

hook[2] [huk] (**to**). **1.** *P:* voler*, grappiner, enquiller. **2.** *P:* arrêter*, agrafer. **3.** *P:* **to get hooked for X pounds,** être estampé de X livres (au jeu). **4.** *F:* **to be hooked on drugs,** se droguer*, se camer, se (s)chnouffer. **5.** *F:* **to be hooked on s.o.,** être épris de qn, avoir le béguin pour qn. **6.** *F:* **to h. a husband,** crocheter (*ou* agrafer) un mari. **7.** *F:* agripper, empoigner. **8.** *F:* trouver*, dégot(t)er. **9.** *P:* **to h. it,** s'enfuir*, décamper.

hooker [ˈhukər] (*noun*), *P:* **1.** prostituée*, poule *f*, raccrocheuse *f*. **2.** dupeur *m*, entôleur *m*, roustisseur *m*; fourgueur *m* de drogues, joueur professionnel, *etc.* **3.** (*U.S.*) verre *m* d'alcool* *ou* de whisky.

hookey [ˈhuki] (*noun*) (*U.S.*), *F:* **to play h.,** faire l'école buissonnière.

hook-shop [ˈhukʃɔp] (*noun*), *P:* bordel*, clandé *m*, maison bancale.

hook up [ˈhukˈʌp] (**to**), *F:* **to be hooked up with s.o.,** être le complice* de qn, être de mèche (*ou* de cheville) avec qn.

hoop [huːp] (*noun*), *F:* **to go through the h.,** (*a*) passer un mauvais moment (*ou* quart d'heure); (*b*) être puni, en prendre pour son grade.

hooper-dooper [ˈhuːpəˈduːpər] (*adj.*), *F:* = **super-duper.**

hoop-la [ˈhuːplɑː] (*noun*), *F:* **1.** tapage *m*, chahut *m*, boucan *m*. **2.** publicité exagérée.

hoosegow [ˈhuːsgau] (*noun*) (*U.S.*), *F:* **1.** commissariat *m* de police, burlingue *m* de quart. **2.** prison*, bloc *m*, taule *f*.

hoot[1] [huːt] (*noun*), *F:* **1.** rigolade *f*, blague *f*. **2. I don't care** (*or* **give**) **a h.,** je m'en moque, je m'en balance. **3. it's not worth a h.,** ça ne vaut rien*, ça ne vaut pas chipette.

hoot[2] [huːt] (**to**), *F:* **1.** rire* aux éclats,

* L'astérisque indique que le mot marqué de ce signe figure comme entrée dans le Répertoire.

se bidonner. **2.** (*Austr.*) sentir* mauvais, puer.

hootch [hu:tʃ] (*noun*) (*U.S.*), *F:* = **hooch.**

hooter [ˈhu:tər] (*noun*), *P:* grand nez*, trompette *f.*

hop[1] [hɔp] (*noun*). **1.** *F:* danse *f,* sauterie *f,* surboum *f.* **2.** *F:* **a short h.,** une courte distance, un pas, un saut; **it's only a h., skip and a jump away,** c'est à deux pas d'ici, ce n'est qu'à trois enjambées d'ici. **3.** *F:* **to catch s.o. on the h.,** surprendre qn, prendre qn au pied levé. **4.** *F:* **to be full of hops,** (*a*) raisonner comme une grosse caisse, sortir des sornettes *f.pl.*; (*b*) avoir sa cuite de bière. **5.** *F:* **to be on the h.,** être toujours en mouvement, être toujours affairé, avoir la bougeotte. **6.** *P:* opium *m* (*drogues**); **h. fiend** = **hophead.** *Voir aussi* **bell-hop.**

hop[2] [hɔp] (**to**). **1.** *F:* **h. in!** allez hop! saute dedans! **2.** *F:* **h. it!** file! fiche le camp! **3.** *F:* **to h. on a bus,** sauter dans un autobus; **to h. off a bus,** sauter d'un autobus. **4.** *F:* **hopping mad,** très en colère*, en rogne. **5.** *P:* **to h. into bed with s.o.,** se foutre au lit avec qn. **6.** *P:* **to h. the twig,** (*a*) mourir*, sauter le pas; (*b*) s'esquiver, échapper à ses créanciers. *Voir aussi* **hedge-hop (to); lorry-hop (to); wag**[1]**.**

hophead [ˈhɔphed] (*noun*), *P:* morphinomane *mf.*

hop-joint [ˈhɔpdʒɔint] (*noun*), *P:* **1.** gargote *f,* boui-boui *m.* **2.** fumoir *m* d'opium, touffianerie *f.*

hopped up [ˈhɔptˈʌp] (*adj.*), *P:* **1.** stimulé par la drogue, dopé, chargé. **2.** = **souped up. 3.** surexcité, survolté.

hoppite [ˈhɔpait] (*noun*), *P:* fou*, aliéné (de l'asile de Broadmoor).

horn [hɔ:n] (*noun*). **1.** *V:* érection *f*; **to have the h.,** être en érection*, bander. **2.** (*U.S.*) *F:* (*jazz*) trompette *f.* *Voir aussi* **blow (to), 5.**

horn in [ˈhɔ:nˈin] (**to**), *F:* s'immiscer; **to h. i. on s.o.'s conversation,** fourrer le nez dans la conversation.

hornswoggle [ˈhɔ:nswɔgl] (**to**) (*U.S.*), *F:* = **hose (to), 2.**

horny [ˈhɔ:ni] (*adj.*), *V:* **to be h.,** (*a*) être en érection*, avoir le bambou (*ou* la canne *ou* le gourdin); (*b*) être lascif (*ou* libidineux *ou* allumé).

horror [ˈhɔrər] (*noun*), *F:* **1.** qch. de laid* et ridicule, horreur *f,* monstruosité *f.* **2.** individu* abominable, une horreur. **3.** (*a*) **h. film,** film *m* d'épouvante; (*b*) **h. comic,** bandes dessinées à thème d'épouvante. **4. to have the horrors,** (*a*) grelotter de peur*; être en proie au delirium tremens; (*b*) avoir des troubles mentaux dus aux amphétamines; (*c*) faire une dépression due au manque de drogues; (*d*) avoir des symptômes dus au sevrage d'héroïne. *Voir aussi* **chuck**[1]**, 3.**

horse[1] [hɔ:s] (*noun*). **1.** *F:* **he's a dark h.,** il cache son jeu, il n'a pas l'air d'y toucher. **2.** *F:* **it's straight from the h.'s mouth,** (*a*) ça vient de la source, tu l'as de première main; (*b*) c'est un tuyau increvable; **to have it straight from the h.'s mouth,** ne pas l'envoyer dire. **3.** *F:* **a h. of another colour,** une autre paire de manches. **4.** *F:* **to flog a dead h.,** faire des pas *m.pl.* inutiles, se dépenser en pure perte, enfoncer des portes ouvertes. **5.** *F:* **to get on one's high h.,** monter sur ses grands chevaux, le prendre de haut. **6.** *F:* **a willing h.,** un bûcheur, un turbineur. **7.** *F:* **hold your horses!** (*a*) ne t'emballe pas! du calme!; (*b*) attendez! arrêtez! **8.** (*U.S.*) *F:* **h. opera,** film *m* western. **9.** *P:* héroïne *f* (*drogues**), cheval *m*; *cf.* **Charl(e)y, 6. 10.** *P:* **to water the horses,** uriner*, changer son poisson d'eau. *Voir aussi* **clothes-horse; one-horse; switch**[2] **(to); war-horse.**

horse[2] [hɔ:s] (**to**) (*U.S.*). **1.** *F:* = **horse about (to). 2.** *P:* coïter* en adultère, biquer.

horse about [ˈhɔ:səˈbaut] (**to**), **horse around** [ˈhɔ:səˈraund] (**to**), *F:* faire le plaisant, batifoler, faire le zouave.

horse-doctor [ˈhɔ:sdɔktər] (*noun*), *F:* **1.** vétérinaire *mf.* **2.** médecin peu compétent, toubib *m* marron.

horseplay [ˈhɔ:s-plei] (*noun*), *F:* jeu brutal, jeu de mains, badinerie grossière.

horse-shit [ˈhɔ:sʃit] (*noun*) (*mainly U.S.*), *V:* **1.** mensonges*. **2.** conneries *f.pl.,* battages *m.pl.*

horse-trading [ˈhɔ:s-treidiŋ] (*noun*), *F:* manigance *f.*

hose [houz] (**to**). **1.** *V:* coïter* avec (qn), fourailler (qn). **2.** *P:* duper*, frauder, monter le coup à (qn).

* An asterisk indicates that the word so marked is included as a head-word in the Appendix.

hoss [hɔs] (*noun*) (*U.S.*) (=*horse*), *F:* cheval *m.*

hot [hɔt] (*adj.*). **1.** *P:* chaud(e) de la pince (*ou* de la pointe); **to have h. pants,** (*a*) avoir le feu aux fesses*; (*b*) avoir le feu au pantalon; **to be a h. skirt,** avoir le feu au jupon; **to be h. for s.o.,** bander pour qn; **h. mama,** femme* passionnée; *cf.* **red-hot, 2;** *voir aussi* **baby[2], 2; cookie, 6; number, 3; patootie. 2.** *F:* **h. pants,** les shorts *m.pl.* **3. h. stuff,** (*a*) *P:* un(e) chaud(e) lapin(e); (*b*) *P:* jeux provocants; (*c*) *F:* butin* facilement identifiable; (*d*) *F:* **he's h. stuff at tennis,** c'est un as du tennis. **4.** *F:* expert, as, crack. **5.** *F:* **to be h. under the collar,** être en colère*, fulminer, être en rogne. **6.** *F:* (*a*) énervé, excité, qui a les nerfs en pelote; (*b*) agité, effaré, en émoi; **to get all h. and bothered,** s'échauffer, se faire du mauvais sang. **7.** *F:* (*jazz*) improvisé avec passion, joué avec chaleur, hot; *cf.* **cool[1], 7; h. music,** le jazz, le swing; **h. cat,** fana(tique) *mf* du jazz *ou* du swing. **8.** *F:* très récent, sensationnel; **h. tip,** renseignement* sûr, tuyau *m* increvable; **h. from the press,** dernier cri. **9.** *P:* (*a*) (*objets volés*) recherché par la police, difficile à écouler; **h. drag,** auto volée; **h. money,** argent* volé; **h. rock,** bijou fauché; (*b*) criminel recherché par la police pour crime. **10.** *P:* dangereux, scandaleux, chiant. **11.** (*a*) (*U.S.*) *F:* **h. seat,** *P:* **h. squat,** chaise *f* électrique; (*b*) *F:* **to be in the h. seat,** être dans le fauteuil directorial. **12.** *F:* **to make it h. for s.o.,** faire des difficultés *f.pl.* à qn, être vache avec qn. **13.** *F:* **to give it to s.o.** (*or* **to let s.o. have it**) **h. (and strong),** passer un bon savon à qn, donner une belle engueulade à qn. **14.** *F:* **to be in h. water,** être dans de mauvais draps (*ou* dans la mélasse); **to get into h. water,** se mettre dans de vilains draps. **15.** *F:* **that's not so h.,** c'est pas formidable. **16.** *F:* **h. on the scent** (*or* **track**) **of . . .,** aux trousses *f.pl.* de... **17.** *F:* (*jeux*) **you're getting h.,** tu brûles. **18.** *F:* **to sell like h. cakes,** se vendre comme des petits pains. **19.** *F:* **to hold a h. hand,** avoir en main des cartes* maîtresses (au jeu); **to have a h. streak,** avoir une chance* persistante (au jeu). **20.** *F:* **a h. one,** (*a*) qch. *ou* qn de renversant; (*b*) une bonne blague. **21.** *F:* **h. war,** la guerre sanglante (*contraire de* la guerre froide). **22.** *F:* **h. rod,** bolide *m* (de course) (*automobile*). **23.** *F:* **h. spot,** (*a*) cabaret *m*, boîte *f* de nuit; (*b*) mauvaise passe, pétrin *m.* **24. h. shot,** (*a*) *F:* = **big shot** (**big[1], 1**); (*b*) *P:* injection *f* de drogues qui devient fatale. **25.** *F:* radio-actif; **h. laboratory,** laboratoire *m* traitant des matières radio-actives. **26.** (*U.S.*) *F:* **h. (diggety) dog!** hourra! vivat! bravo! *Voir aussi* **air[1], 8; blow (to), 14; dog[1], 15; drop[2] (to), 1; gospeller; potato, 3; red-hot.**

hotfoot [ˈhɔtˈfut] (**to**), *F:* **to h. it,** se dépêcher*, mettre les bouts.

hothouse [ˈhɔthaus] (*attrib. adj.*), *F:* **h. plant,** personne délicate.

hot-rod [ˈhɔtrɔd] (**to**) (*U.S.*), *V:* se masturber*, faire cinq contre un; *cf.* **rod, 1.** *Voir aussi* **hot, 22.**

hots [hɔts] (*pl. noun*) (*U.S.*), *P:* **the h.,** (*a*) amour *m*; (*b*) désir sexuel.

hotsie-totsie, hotsy-totsy [ˈhɔtsiˈtɔtsi] (*adj.*) (*U.S.*), *F:* = **hunky-dory.**

hotted up [ˈhɔtidˈʌp] (*adj.*), *F:* **1. h. u. food,** du réchauffé. **2. h. u. car,** voiture* au moteur poussé (*ou* gonflé).

hottie, hotty [ˈhɔti] (*noun*) (=*hot-water bottle*), *F:* bouillotte *f.*

hound-dog [ˈhaunddɔg, *U.S.* ˈhaunddɔːg] (*noun*), *F:* **1.** homme à femmes, cavaleur *m*, juponneur *m.* **2.** = **tripehound.**

house [haus] (*noun*), *F:* **1.** (*a*) **like a h. on fire,** vite*, à toute pompe, à pleins gaz; (*b*) **to get on like a h. on fire,** sympathiser, s'entendre comme des larrons en foire. **2. on the h.,** gratuit*, à l'œil, aux frais *m.pl.* de la princesse. **3. to bring the h. down,** faire crouler la salle (sous les applaudissements), casser la baraque. *Voir aussi* **barrelhouse; big[1], 15; bug-house[1, 2]; cathouse; chophouse; craphouse; crazyhouse; dog-house; doss-house; dress-house; flea-house; flop-house; glasshouse; hash-house; hot-house; jag-house; joy-house; kip-house; madhouse; meat-house; nut-house; pisshouse; power-house; rough-house; shit-house; whore-house.**

how[1] [hau] (*adv.*), *F:* **1. any old h.,** n'importe comment, à la va-comme-je-te-pousse. **2. h. come?** comment

* L'astérisque indique que le mot marqué de ce signe figure comme entrée dans le Répertoire.

est-ce possible? pourquoi? pour quelle raison? 3. **and h.!** et comment! 4. **all you know h.**, aussi bien que possible. *Voir aussi* **nohow.**

how![2] [hau] (*excl.*), *F:* comment va? ça va?

how-do-you-do [ˈhaudjuːduː,ˈhaudjəduː] (*noun*), *F:* = **how-d'ye-do.**

howdy! [ˈhaudi] (*excl.*) (*U.S.*), *F:* = **how!**[2].

how-d'ye-do [ˈhaudjəduː] (*noun*), *F:* **it's a fine** (**old**) (*or* **a right old**) **h.**, (*a*) c'est une mauvaise passe, c'est une sale affaire; (*b*) c'est une drôle d'histoire; nous voilà bien! en voilà du joli!

howl [haul] (*noun*), *F:* = **scream**[1], **1**, (*a*), (*b*).

how's-your-father [ˈhauzjəˈfɑːðər] (*noun*), *F:* = **how-d'ye-do.**

hubba-hubba [ˈhʌbəˈhʌbə] (*adv. & excl.*), *F:* vite*, à toute barde.

hubby [ˈhʌbi] (*noun*) (=*husband*), *F:* mari *m*, le légitime.

huddle [ˈhʌdl] (*noun*), *F:* 1. séance secrète; **to go into a h.**, tenir une séance secrète. 2. période *f* de réflexion personnelle.

hugsome [ˈhʌgsəm] (*adj.*), *F:* = **cuddlesome.**

hully-gully [ˈhʌliˈgʌli] (*noun*) (*U.S.*), *F:* = **holly-golly, 1, 2.**

hum [hʌm] (**to**), *F:* 1. **to be humming,** être en pleine activité, boumer. 2. sentir* mauvais, schlinguer.

humdinger [ˈhʌmˈdiŋər] (*noun*), *F:* qn *ou* qch. d'excellent*, du tonnerre.

hummy [ˈhʌmi] (*adj.*), *F:* 1. excellent*, admirable, épatant. 2. heureux, content, insouciant. 3. puant, cocotant.

hump[1] [hʌmp] (*noun*). 1. *F:* **to get over the h.**, surmonter le plus dur (d'un problème, *etc.*). 2. *F:* **to have the h.**, être de mauvaise humeur, broyer du noir; **to give s.o. the h.**, donner le cafard à qn. 3. *V:* (*a*) coït*; **to like one's h.**, aimer la crampette; (*b*) femme*, femelle *f*, garce *f*, gonzesse *f*; **she's good h.**, c'est une rude baiseuse, c'est une Marie-jambe(s)-en-l'air. 4. (*U.S.*) *F:* **to get a h. on,** se dépêcher*, se dégrouiller. 5. *P:* vaurien*, rien-du-tout *m*.

hump[2] [hʌmp] (**to**). 1. *V:* coïter* avec (qn), pinocher (qn). 2. *F:* porter sur le dos (avec difficulté), trimbal(l)er. 3. *F:* = **to get a hump on** (**hump**[1], **4**).

humpity [ˈhʌmpiti] (*adj.*), *F:* = **humpy.**

humpty-dumpty [ˈhʌm(p)tiˈdʌm(p)ti] (*noun*), *P:* **to do a h.-d.**, se casser la figure, être capout.

humpy [ˈhʌmpi] (*adj.*), *F:* = **umpit(t)y.**

Hun, hun[1] [hʌn] (*adj.*), *F:* allemand*, boche.

Hun, hun[2] [hʌn] (*noun*), *F:* (*a*) Allemand*, boche *m.*; (*b*) soldat* allemand, hun *m*, doryphore *m*.

hunch [hʌntʃ] (*noun*), *F:* intuition *f*, pressentiment *m*; **to have a h. that . . .,** soupçonner que...; **to play a h.**, agir par intuition.

hundred [ˈhʌndrəd] (*numeral noun*), *F:* 1. **a h.**, cent livres sterling; **half a h.**, cinquante livres sterling; *cf.* **century.** 2. **a h. proof,** le meilleur, vrai, authentique, cent pour cent.

hundred-percenter [ˈhʌndrədpəˈsentər] (*noun*), *F:* = **whole-hogger.**

hung [hʌŋ] (*adj.*), *P:* 1. fâché, irrité, embêté. 2. fatigué*, vanné. *Voir aussi* **well-hung.**

hunger [ˈhʌŋgər] (*noun*) (*U.S.*), *F:* **to be from h.**, être miteux (*ou* pouilleux *ou* toc).

hung up [ˈhʌŋˈʌp] (*adj.*), *F:* 1. collet monté, vieux jeu. 2. retardé, retenu. 3. trouvant des obstacles, tombant sur un accroc (*ou* un os). 4. en manque de drogues*. 5. obsédé, frustré, agité. *Voir aussi* **hang up** (**to**).

hunkers [ˈhʌŋkəz] (*pl. noun*), *F:* **on one's h.**, accroupi, à croupeton.

hunks [hʌŋks] (*noun*), *F:* 1. vieux birbe. 2. avare *m*, vieux grigou.

hunky[1] [ˈhʌŋki] (*adj.*) (*U.S.*), *F:* 1. = **chunky, 1.** 2. = **hunky-dory.**

hunky[2] [ˈhʌŋki] (*noun*) (*U.S.*), *P:* immigrant *m* de l'Europe centrale; *cf.* **bohunk, 1.**

hunky-dory [ˈhʌŋkiˈdɔːri] (*adj.*), *F:* parfait, ronflant, satisfaisant.

hurry-up[1] [ˈhʌriˈʌp] (*attrib. adj.*), *F:* **h.-u. wag(g)on** = **Black Maria.**

hurry-up[2] [ˈhʌriˈʌp] (*noun*), *P:* **to have it away for the h.-u.**, partir* en hâte, décamper.

hush [hʌʃ] (*noun*), *F:* **let's have some** (*or* **a little bit of**) **h.**, un peu de silence, s'il vous plaît.

hush-hush [ˈhʌʃˈhʌʃ] (*adj.*), *F:* très secret, confidentiel.

* An asterisk indicates that the word so marked is included as a head-word in the Appendix.

hush up [ˈhʌʃˈʌp] (**to**), *F:* étouffer, supprimer (par la censure).

hustle[1] [ˈhʌsl] (*noun*), *F:* **1.** tromperie *f*, arnaquage *m*, faisage *m* de graisse. **2.** bousculade *f*, grouillement *m*; **to get a h. on,** se dépêcher*, se grouiller. **3.** investigation *f*, recherche *f*.

hustle[2] [ˈhʌsl] (**to**), *P:* **1.** mendier*, mangaver. **2.** racoler*, faire le trottoir, faire le business. **3.** vendre (qch.), bazarder. **4.** gagner sa vie par des méthodes louches, fourguer, lessiver de la marchandise.

hustler [ˈhʌslər] (*noun*), *P:* **1.** qn qui gagne sa vie par des moyens louches, débrouillard *m*, brasseur *m* d'affaires. **2.** prostituée*, bisenesseuse *f*. **3.** souteneur*, marlou(pin) *m*.

hyp(e) [haip] (*noun*), *P:* **1.** (=*hypodermic needle*) aiguille *f* hypodermique. **2.** piqûre *f* de drogues*, piquouse *f*. **3.** fourgueur *m* de drogues*.

hype-stick [ˈhaip-stik] (*noun*), *P:* = **hyp(e), 1.**

hypo [ˈhaipou] (*noun*), *P:* **1.** (*a*) (=*hypochondria*) hypocondrie *f*; (*b*) (=*hypochondriac*) hypocondriaque *mf*. **2.** = **hyp(e), 1,2.** **3.** drogué*, camé *m*, usager *m* de la drogue.

* L'astérisque indique que le mot marqué de ce signe figure comme entrée dans le Répertoire.

I

I-am [aiˈ(j)æm] (*noun*), *F:* **he thinks he's the big I-am,** il se croit le bon Dieu en personne; il se prend pour Dieu le Père.

ice[1] [ais] (*noun*). **1.** *P:* diamant(s)*, diam *m*; **green i.,** émeraude(s) *f.* (*pl.*); **i. palace,** bijouterie *f*, brocaillerie *f.* **2.** *F:* **to break the i.,** rompre la glace. **3.** *F:* **to cut no i. with s.o.,** ne pas impressionner qn, ne pas faire d'effet sur qn. **4.** *F:* **to put on i.,** mettre au frigidaire (*ou* sur la planche). **5.** *F:* **to skate on thin i.,** marcher sur des œufs. **6.** *P:* **to be on i.,** (*a*) être assuré d'avance, être du tout cuit, être affiché; (*b*) = **to be iced** (**ice**[2] (**to**), **4**). **7.** *P:* **to have i. in one's shoes,** avoir peur de se donner à la drogue, avoir la hantise des drogues.

ice[2] [ais] (**to**), *P:* **1.** tuer*, refroidir (qn). **2.** feindre d'ignorer qn, ne pas s'occuper de qn, négliger qn. **3.** se taire*, la boucler. **4. to be iced,** être emprisonné* au secret, être quasi-mort.

iceberg [ˈaisbəːg] (*noun*), *F:* (*d'une personne*) glaçon *m*, bloc *m* de glace.

ice-cream [ˈaisˈkriːm] (*noun*), *P:* opium *m* (*drogues**), boue *f.*

iceman [ˈaismæn, ˈaismən] (*noun*), *P:* voleur* de bijoux, chopeur *m* de joncaille; *cf.* **ice**[1], **1.**

icky [ˈiki] (*adj.*), *P:* **1.** vieux jeu, rococo. **2.** poisseux, visqueux.

idiot-board [ˈidiətbɔːd] (*noun*), *F:* (*T.V.*) pancarte cachée des cameras qui «souffle» aux acteurs, pense-bête *m.*

idiot-box [ˈidiətbɔks] (*noun*), *F:* = **goggle-box;** *cf.* **box**[1], **2; idiot's lantern** (*voir* **lantern**).

iffy [ˈifi] (*adj.*), *F:* douteux, plein de «si», avec des «si» et des «mais».

Ikey (Mo) [ˈaiki(ˈmou)] (*pr. noun*), *P:* (*péj.*) Juif *m*, Youpin *m*, Youpe *m.*

imp [imp] (*noun*), *F:* petit diable, polisson *m.*

in[1] [in] (*attrib. adj.*), *F:* **i. joke,** plaisanterie *f* de coterie.

in[2] [in] (*adv.*). **1.** *P:* **to get (it) i.,** coïter*, mettre la cheville dans le trou. **2.** *F:* **to be (well) i. with s.o.,** être bien avec qn, être dans les petits papiers de qn. **3.** *F:* **to be i.,** (*a*) être dans le vent (*ou* à la page), être la rage du moment; (*b*) être accepté dans la bonne société, savoir nager, faire partie du Gotha. **4.** *F:* **to have it i. for s.o.,** (*a*) en vouloir à qn, avoir une dent contre qn; (*b*) détester* qn, avoir qn dans le nez. **5.** *F:* **to be i. on sth.,** être dans le bain (*ou* dans le coup). **6.** *F:* **he's i. for it!** son affaire est bonne! le voilà dans de beaux draps! il va écoper! **7.** *F:* **to be all i.,** être fatigué* (*ou* claqué *ou* vidé).

in[3] [in] (*noun*), *F:* **1. to have an i.,** avoir de l'influence, avoir le bras long; *cf.* **out**[2]. **2. the ins and outs,** les coins et recoins (d'une affaire), les tenants et les aboutissants.

include out [inˈkluːdˈaut] (**to**), *F:* exclure, mettre de côté; **you can i. me o.** tu peux compter que je n'y serai pas, compte sur tout sauf moi.

incy(-wincy) [ˈinsi(ˈwinsi)] (*adj.*), *F:* **an i. bit of...,** un petit peu* de... un chouia de...

India, india [ˈindiə] (*noun*), *P:* cannabis *m* (*drogues**), chanvre indien.

Indian [ˈindiən] (*adj.*), *P:* **1. I. gift** cadeau-hameçon *m*, cadeau-bidon *m*; **I. giver,** donneur *m* de cadeaux-hameçons. **2. I. hay** (*or* **hemp**) = **India.**

indigo [ˈindigou] (*adj.*), *F:* **i. mood** idées noires, cafard *m*, bourdon *m.*

influence [ˈinfluəns] (*noun*), *F:* **under the i.,** sous l'empire de la boisson, dans les vignes (du Seigneur).

info [ˈinfou] (*abbr.* = *information*), *F:* renseignement*, tuyau *m.*

infra dig [ˈinfrəˈdig] (*adv. phrase*), *F:* indigne, au-dessous de soi.

ink-slinger [ˈiŋk-sliŋər] (*noun*), *F:* gratte-papier *m*, rond-de-cuir *m.*

in-laws [ˈinlɔːz] (*pl. noun*), *F:* belle-

* An asterisk indicates that the word so marked is included as a head-word in the Appendix.

famille *f*; les beaux-parents *m.pl.*, les beaux-dabs *m.pl.*

innards [ˈinədz] (*pl. noun*), *F:* ventre*, boyaux *m.pl.*, tripes *f.pl.*

inner [ˈinər] (*adj.*), *F:* **the i. man,** appétit *m*, ventre*; **to look after the i. man,** se remplir le buffet.

innings [ˈiniŋz] (*noun*), *F:* 1. **to have (had) a good i.,** vivre vieux*, avoir couvert pas mal de chemin. 2. **your i.!** à vous de jouer! à vous le tour!

inside[1] [ˈinsaid] (*adj.*), *F:* 1. **i. information (*or* dope),** tuyaux confidentiels. 2. **the i. story,** l'histoire *f* authentique (*ou* véridique). 3. **an i. job,** un crime attribué à une personne de l'entourage de la victime, un coup fourré (*ou* monté).

inside[2] [inˈsaid, ˈinsaid] (*adv.*), *F:* 1. en prison*, à l'ombre. 2. **i. out,** (*a*) à fond; **to know sth. i. out,** connaître qch. comme sa poche (*ou* sur le bout du doigt); **to know Paris i. out,** connaître Paris dans ses tours et ses détours; (*b*) **to turn everything i. out,** mettre tout sens dessus dessous. 3. **to be i. on sth.,** connaître les dessous d'une affaire, être bien tuyauté.

inside[3] [ˈinˈsaid] (*noun*), *F:* 1. =**innards; I laughed so much my insides were all sore,** j'ai ri jusqu'à en avoir mal aux côtes. 2. **to be on the i.,** être dans le coup, être du bâtiment.

inside[4] [ˈinsaid] (*prep.*), *F:* **to do sth. i. (of) an hour,** faire qch. en moins d'une heure.

instrument [ˈinstru:mənt] (*noun*), *P:* pénis*, instrument *m*.

intended [inˈtendid] (*noun*), *F:* un(e) futur(e).

into [ˈintu:] (*prep.*), *F:* absorbé par (qch.), en proie à (qch.); **I'm i. Russian novels this week,** je suis plongé dans les romans russes cette semaine.

invite [ˈinvait] (*noun*), *F:* invitation *f*, invite *f*, appât *m*.

Irish[1] [ˈairiʃ] (*adj.*), *F:* 1. biscornu; **the whole sentence sounds a bit I.,** toute la phrase ne tient pas debout. 2. **I. coffee,** café* noir au whisky (couronné de crème Chantilly). 3. **I. confetti,** briques *f.pl.* 4. **I. banjo,** pelle *f.* 5. **I. grape,** pomme *f* de terre, patate *f*. 6. **I. wedding,** soûlerie générale.

Irish[2] [ˈairiʃ] (*noun*), *F:* **to get one's I. up,** se mettre en colère* (*ou* en rogne), voir rouge.

iron [ˈaiən] (*noun*). 1. *P:* **to carry i.,** être armé (*ou* enfouraillé); *voir aussi* **shooting-iron.** 2. *F:* **(eating) irons,** couteau *m*, fourchette *f* et cuiller *f*; les couverts *m.pl. Voir aussi* **cast-iron; half-iron; hoof**[1], **2.**

issue [ˈisju:, ˈiʃu:] (*noun*), *P:* **the whole (bloody) i.,** tout le bataclan, toute la sacrée bande.

it [it] (*pron.*). 1. *F:* du sex-appeal, du chien. 2. *F:* vermouth (italien). 3. *F:* **you've had i.!** t'as ton compte! tu l'as voulu! tu es fichu! 4. **to give i. to s.o.,** (*a*) *P:* coïter* avec qn, baiser (*ou* ramoner) qn; (*b*) *F:* battre* qn; (*c*) *F:* réprimander* qn. 5. *P:* **to make i. with s.o.,** (*a*) coïter* avec qn, faire l'amour avec qn; (*b*) plaire à qn, faire une touche, avoir un ticket. 6. *F:* **to step on i.** = **to step on the gas (gas**[2], **2).**

itch[1] [itʃ] (*noun*), *F:* 1. **the seven-year i.,** l'écueil *m* des sept ans* de mariage, la démangeaison de la septième année*; le démon de midi. 2. **to have an i. to do sth.,** mourir (*ou* crever) d'envie de faire qch.

itch[2] [itʃ] **(to),** *F:* **to i. to do sth.** = **to have an itch to do sth. (itch**[1], **2); he's itching for trouble,** la peau lui démange, ça le démange.

itchy [ˈitʃi] (*adj.*), *F:* qui brûle de faire qch. *Voir aussi* **palm, 2.**

itsy-bitsy [ˈitsiˈbitsi] (*adj.*), *F:* = **bitty.**

ivories [ˈaivəriz] (*pl. noun*), *F:* 1. dents*, clavier *m*; *voir aussi* **sluice**[2] **(to).** 2. boules *f.pl.* de billard. 3. dés*, doches *m.pl.*, bobs *m.pl.* 4. touches *f.pl.* d'un piano, clavier *m*; **to tickle the i.,** jouer du piano, taquiner les touches.

ivory [ˈaivəri] (*adj.*), *F:* **i. dome,** intellectuel *m*, grosse tête.

* L'astérisque indique que le mot marqué de ce signe figure comme entrée dans le Répertoire.

J

J [dʒei] = **jay, 1.**

jab[1] [dʒæb] (*noun*), *F:* (*a*) inoculation *f*, vaccin *m*, piqûre *f*; **have you had your jabs?** tu les a eues, tes piqûres?; (*b*) piqûre *f* de drogues, piquouse *f*, shoot *m*.

jab[2] [dʒæb] **(to),** *F:* (*a*) inoculer, faire une piqûre à (qn); (*b*) piquer, piquouser, shooter.

jabber [ˈdʒæbər] (*noun*), *F:* aiguille *f* hypodermique, poussette *f*, shooteuse *f*.

jab-off [ˈdʒæbɔf] (*noun*), *P:* (*a*) piqûre *f*, piquouse *f* (de narcotique); (*b*) effet *m* de la piqûre, le bang, le flash.

jack[1], **Jack** [dʒæk] (*noun*). **1.** *P:* **on one's j.,** tout seul, seulabre, esseulé. **2.** *F:* **every man j.,** tout un chacun. **3.** *VV:* **fuck you** (*or F:* **pull the ladder up**), **J., I'm all right,** ça tourne rond pour bibi, bibi lui il s'en tire; *cf.* **ladder. 4.** *V:* **to get the j.,** être en érection*, avoir le bambou (*ou* la canne). **5.** *P:* cachet *m* d'héroïne (*drogues**), cheval *m*. **6.** (*U.S.*) *F:* **to ball the j.,** (*a*) se dépêcher*, s'activer, se magner; (*b*) jouer son va-tout (*ou* le tout pour le tout), mettre le paquet. **7.** *F:* **j., J. Tar,** marin*, matelot *m*, mathurin *m*. **8.** *F:* **before you can** (*or* **could**) **say J.** (**Robinson**), en un clin d'œil, avant de pouvoir dire ouf, en moins de deux (*ou* de rien). **9.** (U.S.) *P:* argent*, galette *f*; **a nice piece of j.,** une somme rondelette. **10.** *P:* **J. the Ripper** (*R.S.* = *kipper*), hareng saur, kipper *m*. **11.** *P:* policier*, condé *m*. **12.** *P:* **J.'s alive,** (*a*) (billet* de) cinq livres sterling; (*b*) *voir* **bingo** (**5**). **13.** *F:* **yellow j.,** fièvre *f* jaune, godiche *f* jaune.

jack[2] [dʒæk] **(to),** *P:* **1.** = **jack in (to), 1. 2.** = **jack up (to), 3.**

jackaroo [ˈdʒækəˈruː] (*noun*), *P:* **1.** (*Austr.*) colon immigrant sans expérience. **2.** (*U.S.*) cowboy *m*.

jack around [ˈdʒækəˈraund] **(to),** *P:* **1.** traîner, lambiner, flemmarder. **2.** faire le zouave (*ou* le con), couillonner.

jacked up [ˈdʒæktˈʌp] (*adj.*), *P:* **1.** sous l'influence d'un stimulant. **2.** excité, tendu, énervé. *Voir aussi* **jack up (to), 1.**

jackeroo [ˈdʒækəˈruː] (*noun*), *P:* = **jackaroo.**

jacket [ˈdʒækit] **(to),** *P:* battre*, sauter sur le paletot à; *cf.* **dust**[2] **(to).**

jack in [ˈdʒækˈin] **(to),** *P:* **1.** abandonner*, lâcher, balancer, plaquer. **2. to j. it i.,** se taire*, la boucler, la fermer.

jack-in-office (*noun*), *F:* fonctionnaire plein de son importance, Monsieur Lebureau.

jack-in-the-box [ˈdʒækinðəbɔks] (*noun*), *F:* **1.** diablotin *m*, qn qui a un ressort au derrière. **2.** fantoche *m*.

jack-knife [ˈdʒæknaif] **(to)** (*U.S.*), *F:* suriner (qn).

jack off [ˈdʒækˈɔf] **(to),** *V:* se masturber*, s'astiquer le manche, se taper la colonne, se tirer son coup.

jackpot [ˈdʒækpɔt] (*noun*), *F:* **to hit the j.,** gagner le gros lot, décrocher la timbale, taper dans le mille.

jack-priest [ˈdʒækˈpriːst] (*noun*), *P:* prêtre*, ratichon *m*.

jacksie [ˈdʒæksi] (*noun*), *P:* **1.** fesses*, postérieur *m*; **you can stick it up your j.!** tu peux te le mettre quelque part!; *cf.* **stick**[2] **(to), 3; to boot s.o. up the j.,** donner un coup de pied dans le derrière de qn. **2.** (*Austr.*) bordel*, tringlodrome *m*.

jack up [ˈdʒækˈʌp] **(to). 1.** *P:* se faire piquouser, se faire shooter; *voir aussi* **jacked up, 1. 2.** *P:* = **jack in (to), 1. 3.** *P:* **to j. u. the price,** corser (*ou* fader) le prix, saler la note. **4.** *F:* **to j. s.o. u.,** encourager qn, donner du cœur au ventre à qn. **5.** (*Austr.*) *F:* protester, se regimber, piaffer. **6.** (*Austr.*) *P:* plaider innocent, se dire blanc, se blanchir.

jacky [ˈdʒæki] (*noun*) (*Austr.*), *P:* arrangement *m* louche.

* An asterisk indicates that the word so marked is included as a head-word in the Appendix.

jacob [ˈdʒeikəb] (*noun*), *P:* échelle *f*, montante *f*, lève-pieds *m*.

jade [dʒeid] (*noun*), *F:* **she's a real** (*or* **right**) **j.**, c'est une vraie rosse (*ou* carne).

jag[1] [dʒæg] (*noun*), *P:* **1.** piqûre *f*, piquouse *f*. **2.** état prolongé d'intoxication par une drogue. **3. to have a j. on,** (*a*) être drogué* (*ou* camé); (*b*) être ivre* (*ou* rond *ou* noir *ou* rétamé). **4. to go on a j.**, (*a*) se camer à bloc; (*b*) faire la noce (*ou* la bombe), se saouler, prendre une cuite; (*c*) faire une orgie de...; **to go on a culture j.**, se lancer dans une débauche culturelle, prendre une indigestion de culture. **5.** coup *m* de chance*, du pot.

Jag[2] [dʒæg] (*noun*), *F:* Jag(uar) *f* (*automobile; marque déposée*).

jagged [dʒægd] (*adj.*), *P:* **1.** ivre*, rond, noir, rétamé. **2.** drogué*, camé, (s)chnouffé.

jag-house [ˈdʒæghaus] (*noun*), *P:* bordel* de pédérastes*, musée *m* à jocondes.

jag off [ˈdʒægˈɔf] (**to**), *V:* = **jack off (to)**.

jail-bait [ˈdʒeilbeit] (*noun*), *P:* fille* de moins de seize ans, faux-poids *m*.

jailbird [ˈdʒeilbəːd] (*noun*), *F:* individu* qui est souvent en prison*, cheval *m* de retour, bois dur.

jake[1] [dʒeik] (*adv.*) (*U.S.*), *P:* **1.** d'accord*, dac, O.K.; **things are** (*or* **everything is**) **j.**, ça marche bien, ça biche, ça roule. **2.** excellent*, impec, de première.

jake[2] [dʒeik] (*noun*), *F:* **1.** (*U.S.*) valet *m*, valdingue *m* (*cartes*); *cf.* **jock, 4. 2.** (*pl.*) W.C.*, goguenots *m.pl*.

jalop(p)y [dʒəˈlɔpi] (*noun*), *F:* **1.** voiture*, bagnole *f*, tacot *m*. **2.** avion *m* de transport, coucou *m*.

jam[1] [dʒæm] (*adj.*), *P:* hétérosexuel, sexuellement normal.

jam[2] [dʒæm] (*noun*), *F:* **1. it's money for j.**, c'est de l'argent* facile, c'est donné. **2. to be in a j.**, être dans le pétrin (*ou* dans la mélasse). **3. a bit of j.**, un coup de chance*, du pot, du bol. **4.** pacotille *f*, bibelots *m.pl.* **5. do you want j. on it?** et quoi encore? tu le veux doré sur tranches? **6. that's real j.!** c'est du nanan! *Voir aussi* **jim-jams; session, 1.**

jam[3] [dʒæm] (**to**), *F:* (*jazz*) improviser.

jamboree [dʒæmbəˈriː] (*noun*), *F:* réjouissances*, bamboche *f*, foire *f*.

jam-jar [ˈdʒæmdʒɑːr] (*noun*), *P:* **1.** (*R.S. = car*) auto *f*. **2.** œillet *m* (des fleuristes).

jammed up [ˈdʒæmdˈʌp] (*adj.*), *P:* ayant dépassé une dose normale de drogue.

jammy [ˈdʒæmi] (*adj.*), *P:* **1.** facile comme bonjour. **2.** qui a de la chance*, veinard, bidard. **3.** de premier ordre, de prem(ière).

jam-packed [ˈdʒæmˈpækt] (*adj.*), *F:* au grand complet, bourré à craquer.

jam-pot [ˈdʒæm-pɔt] (*noun*), *F:* col romain, col à manger de la tarte.

jam-sheet [ˈdʒæmʃiːt] (*noun*), *P:* = **shit-list.**

jam up [ˈdʒæmˈʌp] (**to**), *F:* **to j. u. the works = to gum up the works.** *Voir aussi* **jammed up.**

jane, Jane [dʒein] (*noun*). **1.** *F:* fille* *ou* femme*, nénette *f*, nana *f*; **a plain J.**, une laidasse, une pas-jolie. **2.** *P:* la petite amie, la nénette. **3.** *P:* W.C.* pour femmes, chiottes *f.pl.* à poules; *cf.* **john, 1. 4. Calamity J.**, Cassandre *f*, rabat-joie *m*. *Voir aussi* **lady.**

jankers [ˈdʒæŋkəz] (*pl. noun*) (*mil.*), *F:* punitions *f.pl.*, la pelote, le bal; **to be on j.**, être au piquet des punis.

Jap[1] [dʒæp] (*adj.*), *F:* japonais, nippon.

Jap[2] [dʒæp] (*noun*), *F:* Japonais *m*, Nippon *m*.

jar [dʒɑːr] (*noun*). **1.** *F:* **to have** (*or* **down**) **a few jars,** boire*, s'envoyer quelques verres, se jeter des jattes. **2.** *P:* faux diamant*, faux diam(e), caillou *m*. *Voir aussi* **jam-jar.**

jarred [dʒɑːd] (*adj.*), *P:* **1.** ivre*, rétamé. **2.** = **jarred off.**

jarred off [ˈdʒɑːdˈɔf] (*adj.*), *P:* cafardeux; **to be j. o.**, avoir le cafard, en avoir ras le bol.

jasper [ˈdʒæspər] (*noun*), *P:* **1.** lesbienne*, gavousse *f*. **2.** puce *f*.

java [ˈdʒɑːvə] (*noun*) (*U.S.*), *P:* café*, caoua *m*, jus *m*.

jaw[1] [dʒɔː] (*noun*). **1.** *P:* bavardage *m*; **to have a good j.**, tailler une bonne bavette; **hold your j.! not so much of your j.!** tais-toi! ta gueule! la ferme!; **to be full of j.**, être fort en gueule; *cf.* **flapjaw. 2.** *P:* **pi j.**, bondieuseries *f.pl.*, sermon *m*, prêche *m*, paroles *f.pl.* de

* L'astérisque indique que le mot marqué de ce signe figure comme entrée dans le Répertoire.

curé. 3. *F:* **his j. dropped,** il fit une sale (*ou* une drôle de) tête. *Voir aussi* **stickjaw.**

jaw[2] [dʒɔː] (**to**), *P:* (*a*) bavarder*, jaspiner; (*b*) engueuler (qn).

jaw-breaker [ˈdʒɔː-breikər], **jaw-buster** [ˈdʒɔː-bʌstər] (*noun*), *F:* 1. nom *m ou* mot *m* à coucher dehors (*ou* à vous décrocher la mâchoire). 2. bonbon dur.

jawing [ˈdʒɔːiŋ] (*noun*), *P:* 1. bavardage *m*. 2. **to give s.o. a j.,** réprimander* qn, passer un savon à qn, sonner les cloches à qn.

jaw out [ˈdʒɔːˈaut] (**to**) (*U.S.*), *P:* **to j. s.o. o.** = **to give s.o. a jawing (jawing, 2).**

jaw-twister [ˈdʒɔː-twistər] (*noun*), *F:* = **jaw-breaker.**

jay [dʒei] (*noun*). 1. *P:* cigarette* de marijuana (*drogues**), joint *m*, stick *m*. 2. (*U.S.*) *F:* individu bête*, nouille *f*.

jaybird [ˈdʒeibəːd] (*noun*) (*U.S.*). 1. *F:* paysan*, plouc *m*, péquenot *m*. 2. *F:* = **jailbird.** 3. *P:* Juif *m*, Youpin *m*.

jayboy [ˈdʒeibɔi] (*noun*) (*U.S.*), *F:* = **jake**[2], 1.

jaywalk [ˈdʒeiwɔːk] (**to**), *F:* traverser en dehors des clous.

jaywalker [ˈdʒeiwɔːkər] (*noun*), *F:* piéton imprudent.

jazz[1] [dʒæz] (*noun*). 1. *F:* (*a*) garniture *f*, fioritures *f.pl.*, tape-à-l'œil *m*, fanfreluches *f.pl.*; (*b*) **. . . and all that j.,** et tout et tout, et tout ce qui s'ensuit. 2. (*U.S.*) *V:* (*a*) coït*; (*b*) vagin*, grippette *f*, chatte *f*. 3. (*U.S.*) *P:* emballement *m*, entrain *m*.

jazz[2] [dʒæz] (**to**). 1. (*U.S.*) *V:* coïter*, tirer un coup, godiller. 2. (*U.S.*) *P:* mettre en train, donner le branle à (qch.), aiguillonner. 3. *P:* (*a*) mentir*, bourrer le crâne; (*b*) exagérer*, en rajouter.

jazzed up [ˈdʒæzdˈʌp] (*adj.*). 1. *F:* élégant*, endimanché. 2. *P:* animé, survolté. 3. *P:* drogué*, camé, chargé, bourré.

jazz up [ˈdʒæzˈʌp] (**to**), *F:* émoustiller, échauffer, ravigoter, requinquer. *Voir aussi* **jazzed up.**

jazzy [ˈdʒæzi] (*adj.*). 1. *F:* tape-à-l'œil; psychédélique. 2. *P:* vieux-jeu, périmé.

J-boy [ˈdʒeibɔi] (*noun*) (*U.S.*), *F:* = **jake**[2], **1**; *cf.* **jayboy.**

jeepers (creepers)! [ˈdʒiːpəz(ˈkriːpəz)] (*excl.*) (*U.S.*), *F:* mon Dieu! sapristi!

jeez(e)! Jeez(e)! [dʒiːz] (*excl.*) (*euph. pour* **Jesus!**), *P:* mazette! (tonnerre de) Dieu!

jeff [dʒef] (*noun*), *P:* corde *f*, fil *m*.

jell [dʒel] (**to**), *F:* 1. (*d'idées, etc.*) (se) cristalliser. 2. bien s'entendre, sympathiser, être sur la même longueur d'ondes.

jelly [ˈdʒeli] (*noun*), *F:* 1. gélignite *f*, gelée *f*. 2. **to pound s.o. into a j.,** battre* qn comme plâtre, mettre qn en capilotade.

jelly-baby [ˈdʒeli-beibi] (*noun*), *P:* amphétamine *f* (*drogues**).

jellyfish [ˈdʒeli-fiʃ] (*noun*), *F:* larve *f*, mollasson *m*.

jelly-roll [ˈdʒeli-roul] (*noun*) (*U.S.*). 1. *V:* vagin*, baveux *m*, millefeuille *m*. 2. *P:* homme *m* à femmes, conassier *m*, queutard *m*. 3. *P:* amant *m*. 4. *P:* collage *m*, baisage *m*, conasserie *f*.

jemima [dʒəˈmaimə] (*noun*), *F:* pot *m* de chambre, Jules *m*, Thomas *m*.

jerk[1] [dʒəːk] (*noun*). 1. *P:* individu bête*, petit con, enflé *m*, emplâtré *m*, déplombé *m*; *voir aussi* **dumb,** 1 (*b*). 2. *P:* novice *m*, bleu *m*. 3. *F:* **put a j. in(to) it!** et que ça saute! 4. *F:* **physical jerks,** mouvements *m.pl.* de gymnastique.

jerk[2] [dʒəːk] (**to**), *V:* coïter* avec (qn), bourrer, bourriquer (qn). *Voir aussi* **gherkin.**

jerk off [ˈdʒəːkˈɔf] (**to**), *V:* = **jack off (to).**

jerkwater [ˈdʒəːkwɔːtər] (*noun*) (*U.S.*), *P:* = **one-horse town** (*voir* **one-horse**).

jerky [ˈdʒəːki] (*adj.*) (*U.S.*), *F:* bête*, cavé.

jerry[1] [ˈdʒeri] (*adj.*), *F:* inférieur, à la manque, à la noix, de carton, en papier mâché.

jerry,[2] **Jerry** [ˈdʒeri] (*noun*), *F:* 1. pot *m* de chambre, Thomas *m*, Jules *m*. 2. soldat* allemand*, Fritz, fridolin *m*, frizou *m*. 3. les Allemands*, les boches *m.pl.* 4. avion (char, *etc.*) allemand.

jerry-go-nimble [ˈdʒerigouˈnimbl] (*noun*), *P:* diarrhée*, courante *f*.

Jesus (Christ)! [ˈdʒiːzəs(ˈkraist)] (*excl.*), *P:* nom de Dieu! grands dieux!; *cf.* **Jeez(e)!; Christ.**

jet [dʒet] (*attrib. adj.*), *F:* 1. **the j. set,** les bringueurs *m.pl.* cosmopolites, le jet-set. 2. **j. job,** bolide *m*.

* An asterisk indicates that the word so marked is included as a head-word in the Appendix.

Jew[1] [dʒuː] (*noun*), *P:* **dirty old J.**: *voir* **bingo** (2).
jew[2] [dʒuː] (**to**), *P:* duper* (qn), mettre (qn) dedans.
jewboy, Jewboy [ˈdʒuːbɔi] (*noun*) (*péj.*), *P:* Juif *m*, Youpin *m*.
jew down [ˈdʒuːˈdaun] (**to**), *P:* marchander, chipoter, regratter (qn).
jew's-harp [ˈdʒuːzˈhɑːp] (*noun*), *F:* peigne recouvert de papier de soie qui sert d'harmonica; guimbarde *f*.
jiff [dʒif], **jiffy** [ˈdʒifi] (*noun*), *F:* **in (half) a j.**, dans un instant, en un clin d'œil, en moins de deux; *cf.* **mo; sec; shake**[1], 1, 2; **tick**[1], 3.
jig [dʒig] (*noun*). 1. *P:* gigolo *m*, lustucru *m*, frère mironton. 2. (*U.S.*) *P:* (*a*) nègre*, bougnoule *m*, bamboula *m*; (*b*) moricaud *m*, café *m* au lait. 3. *F:* **the j. is up**, c'est fichu, c'est dans le lac. 4. *F:* bal public, guinche *f*, pince-cul *m*.
jigamaree [dʒigəməˈriː] (*noun*), *F:* = **thingamy.**
jigger [ˈdʒigər] (*noun*). 1. *F:* truc *m*, machin *m*. 2. (*mil.*) *P:* prison*, bloc *m*. 3. *P:* pénis*, queue *f*.
jigger (up) [ˈdʒigər(ˈʌp)] (**to**), *F:* abîmer*, bousiller.
jiggered [ˈdʒigəd] (*adj.*), *F:* étonné*, estomaqué; **well I'm j.!** j'en suis comme deux ronds de flan!
jiggered up [ˈdʒigədˈʌp] (*adj.*), *F:* fatigué*, à bout, claqué.
jiggery-pokery [ˈdʒigəriˈpoukəri] (*noun*), *F:* manigance *f*, attrape *f*, tour *m* de passe-passe.
jiggumbob [ˈdʒigəmbɔb] (*noun*), *F:* = **thingamy.**
jig-jig [ˈdʒigˈdʒig] (*noun*), *P:* coït*, criquon-criquette *m*.
Jim Crow [ˈdʒimˈkrou] (*noun*) (*U.S.*), *F:* (*a*) nègre*, bamboula *m*; (*b*) la ségrégation raciale et tout ce qui s'y rapporte.
jiminy! [ˈdʒimini] (*excl.*), *F:* **(by) j.!** mince! pitchoun!
jim-jams [ˈdʒimdʒæmz] (*pl. noun*), *P:* (*a*) les nerfs *m.pl.* en boule, la chair de poule; (*b*) delirium tremens *m*, les rats bleus.
Jimmy [ˈdʒimi] (*pr. noun*), *P:* 1. **J. Riddle** (*R.S.* = **piddle**), pipi *m*; **to have a J. Riddle**, uriner*, faire pipi. 2. **J. Rix** (*or* **Hix**) (*R.S.* = *fix*) = **fix**[1], 1. 3. **J. Prescott** (*R.S.* = *waistcoat*), gilet *m*. 4. **Little J.**: *voir* **bingo** (1). 5. (*Marine*) **J. (the one)**, officier *m* qui commande en second à bord d'un navire (de guerre). *Voir aussi* **flash**[1], 1.
jingbang [ˈdʒiŋbæŋ] (*noun*), *F:* **the whole j.** = **the whole shooting-match.**
jing-jang [ˈdʒiŋdʒæŋ] (*noun*) (*U.S.*), *V:* 1. pénis*, zizi *m*. 2. vagin*, didi *m*. 3. coït*, zizi-panpan *m*.
jinks [dʒiŋks] (*pl. noun*), *F:* **high j.**, réjouissances*, noce *f*, bamboche *f*.
jinx[1] [dʒiŋks] (*noun*), *F:* 1. malchance*, guigne *f*, poisse *f*. 2. porte-poisse *m*, porte-guigne *m*.
jinx[2] [dʒiŋks] (**to**), *F:* porter malchance* (*ou* la guigne *ou* la poisse) à (qn).
jism [ˈdʒizm], **jissom** [ˈdʒis(ə)m] (*noun*) (*mainly U.S.*). 1. *V:* sperme*, jus *m*, came *f*. 2. *P:* dynamisme *m*, tonus *m*.
jitney[1] [ˈdʒitni] (*adj.*) (*U.S.*), *P:* camelote, piètre, piteux.
jitney[2] [ˈdʒitni] (*noun*) (*U.S.*), *F:* 1. pièce *f* de cinq cents. 2. microbus *m*. 3. **j. bag**, porte-monnaie*, artiche *m*, morlingue *m*.
jitter [ˈdʒitər] (**to**), *F:* (*a*) **to j. s.o.** = **to give s.o. the jitters**; (*b*) se trémousser, s'exciter, se démener.
jitterbug [ˈdʒitəbʌg] (*noun*), *F:* défaitiste *mf*, paniquard *m*.
jitters [ˈdʒitəz] (*pl. noun*), *F:* **to have the j.**, avoir les nerfs à fleur de peau, avoir la tremblote; **to give s.o. the j.**, flanquer la trouille à qn.
jittery [ˈdʒitəri] (*adj.*), *F:* crispé, à cran; **to feel j.**, avoir les nerfs en pelote, avoir la venette, serrer les fesses.
jive[1] [dʒaiv] (*noun*). 1. *F:* = **jazz**[1], 1 (*a*), (*b*); 2. (*a*); 3. 2. *P:* marijuana *f* (*drogues**).
jive[2] [dʒaiv] (**to**) (*U.S.*), *P:* 1. trouver les maillons de la chaîne, éclairer la lanterne. 2. bavarder*, bavasser, jacter, dévider le jars.
jizz [dʒiz] (*noun*) (*mainly U.S.*), *V:* = **jism**, 1.
joanna [dʒouˈænə] (*noun*) (*R.S.* = *piano*), *P:* (vieux) piano, chaudron *m*.
job [dʒɔb] (*noun*). 1. *F:* tout article façonné, manufacturé ou fabriqué; *cf.* **jet**, 2. 2. *P:* (*a*) réparation *f*; (*b*) boulot *m*. 3. *P:* vol *m*, coup *m*, fric-

* L'astérisque indique que le mot marqué de ce signe figure comme entrée dans le Répertoire.

frac *m.* 4. *P:* crime *m,* méfait *m,* coup *m,* combine *f.* 5. **to be on the j.,** (*a*) *F:* être sur le boulot; (*b*) *P:* être en train de coïter* (*ou* de besogner). 6. *F:* **it's a good j. that...,** heureusement que... 7. *F:* **... and a good j. too!** c'est pas malheureux! 8. *F:* **just the j.!** juste ce qu'il faut! c'est au poil! 9. *F:* défécation *f,* la grande commission; (*langage enfantin*) **to do small jobs,** faire sa petite commission; **to do big jobs,** faire sa grosse commission; *cf.* **number, 7.** 10. *P:* colis *m* de drogues*, la charge. 11. *F:* **to lie** (*or* **lay** *or* **fall**) **down on the j.,** paresser*, tirer au flanc, s'endormir sur le mastic. 12. *F:* **the blonde j. sitting over there,** la petite blonde assise là-bas. 13. *P:* (*taxi*) client *m,* griot *m.* 14. *F:* **to make a clean j. of sth.,** faire qch. à fond (*ou* de fond en comble). 15. *F:* **jobs for the boys,** l'assiette *f* au beurre, distribution *f* des planques, partage *m* du même gâteau. 16. *F:* **to have a j. to do sth.,** avoir du mal à faire qch. *Voir aussi* **bad[1], 6; blow-job; finger-job; frail[1]; hand-job; head, 13; pipe-job; put-up; shack-up; skull-job; snow-job; soup up (to),** (*a*).

jock [dʒɔk] (*noun*), *P:* 1. pédéraste*, emmanché *m.* 2. (*pl.*) testicules*, roustons *m.pl.* 3. *F:* = **jock-strap.** 4. *F:* valet (*cartes*); *cf.* **jake[2], 1.** 5. *F:* Écossais *m.*

jocker [ˈdʒɔkər], **jockey** [ˈdʒɔki] (*noun*), *P:* = **jock, 1.**

jock-strap [ˈdʒɔk-stræp] (*noun*), *F:* suspensoir *m,* soutien-couilles *m.*

joe, Joe [dʒou] (*noun*), *P:* 1. (*U.S.*) café*, cao *m,* jus *m.* 2. (*U.S.*) homme*, un Julot, un bon zigue. 3. (*U.S.*) soldat*, pioupiou; *cf.* **G.I. Joe.** 4. (*a*) prêtre*, cureton *m*; *cf.* **holy, 2;** (*b*) aumônier *m* militaire. 5. **J. Soap,** Père Tartempion. 6. **J. Blake** (*R.S.* = *cake*), gâteau *m.* 7. **J. Gurr** (*R.S.* = *stir* = *prison*), prison*, bloc *m.* 8. *F:* **not for j.,** pour rien au monde, dans aucun cas. *Voir aussi* **sloppy, 2.**

joey [ˈdʒoui] (*noun*). 1. *F:* clown *m,* gugusse *m,* pierrot *m.* 2. *P:* paquet passé en fraude. 3. (*Austr.*) *P:* fraude *f,* tartignole *f,* carotte *f.* 4. *P:* menstrues*, les anglais *m.pl.* 5. (*Austr.*) *F:* jeune kangourou *m.*

john, John [dʒɔn] (*noun*). 1. *F:* **the j.,** W.C.* pour hommes, azor *m,* gogues *m.pl.*; *cf.* **jane, 3.** 2. *P:* **J. Thomas,** pénis*, Popaul, Charles-le-Chauve. 3. *F:* **J. Barleycorn,** le whisky. 4. *P:* **the johns,** la police*, les flics *m.pl.* 5. (*U.S.*) *F:* **J. Doe,** l'Américain moyen (= Monsieur Blot, Monsieur Dupont-Durand). 6. *F:* **long Johns,** caleçon long, caneçon *m.* 7. *P:* client d'une prostituée*, miché *m,* michet *m,* micheton *m. Voir aussi* **amy-john.**

johnnie, Johnnie, johnny, Johnny [ˈdʒɔni] (*noun*). 1. *P:* jeune homme*, zigoto *m,* zigue *m,* loulou *m.* 2. *P:* homme élégant*, miche(ton) *m,* minet *m.* 3. *P:* capote (anglaise). 4. *P:* **J. Horner** (*R.S.* = *corner*), coin *m* (*surtout* un coin de rue *et souvent* le bistrot du coin). 5. *F:* **J. Raw,** bleu *m,* morveux *m.* 6. *F:* = **john, 1.**

Johnny-come-lately [ˈdʒɔnikʌmˈleitli] (*noun*), *F:* blanc-bec *m,* bleu *m,* serin *m.*

Johnny-on-the-spot [ˈdʒɔniɔnðəˈspɔt] (*noun*) (*U.S.*), *F:* 1. qn qui tombe à pic. 2. qn qui arrive au poil.

joint [dʒɔint] (*noun*), *P:* 1. logement*, cambuse *f,* piaule *f*; **a nice j.,** un beau petit coin; *voir aussi* **barber (to); case[2] (to), 2.** 2. bouge *m,* foutoir *m*; **gambling j.,** tripot *m.* 3. cigarette* de marijuana *f* (*drogues**), joint *m,* stick *m.* 4. attirail *m* pour s'injecter des drogues, la popote. 5. pénis*, queue *f,* gourdin *m. Voir aussi* **clip-joint; eats; hop-joint.**

joke[1] [dʒouk] (*noun*), *F:* 1. **it was no j. (I can tell you),** c'était pas rigolo (je t'assure). 2. **he must have his little j.,** il aime à plaisanter.

joke[2] [dʒouk] (**to**), *F:* **you must be** (*or* **you've got to be**) **joking!** c'est pas sérieux! c'est pas vrai! tu veux rire!

joker [ˈdʒoukər] (*noun*), *F:* 1. homme*, type *m,* client *m.* 2. malin *m,* loustic *m,* lascar *m.*

jollies [ˈdʒɔliz] (*pl. noun*), *F:* tout ce qui emballe et passionne.

jolly[1] [ˈdʒɔli] (*adj.*), *F:* 1. agréable, drôle, bath, rigolo. 2. légèrement ivre*, gris, éméché. 3. **J. Roger,** drapeau *m* des pirates, le pavillon noir. *Voir aussi* **bean, 9.**

jolly[2] [ˈdʒɔli] (*adv.*), *F:* 1. **it's a j. good**

* **An asterisk indicates that the word so marked is included as a head-word in the Appendix.**

job that..., bien heureusement que... 2. **it serves him j. well right!** c'est rudement bien fait pour lui! c'est pain bénit! 3. **she's j. nice,** elle est joliment bien. 4. **I should j. well think so!** c'est bien ce qui me semble! à qui le dis-tu?

jolly along [ˈdʒɔliəˈlɔŋ] (**to**), *F:* (*a*) dérider, ragaillardir (qn); (*b*) faire marcher (qn) (pour en obtenir qch.).

jolt[1] [dʒoult] (*noun*), *P:* 1. cigarette* de marijuana (*drogues**), stick *m.* 2. effets *m.pl.* primaires d'une drogue *ou* d'une cigarette* de marijuana. 3. (*a*) piqûre *f* d'un narcotique; (*b*) piqûre *f* d'héroïne. 4. un petit coup d'alcool*, une lampée. *Voir aussi* **overjolt.**

jolt[2] [dʒoult] (**to**), *P:* se faire une piqûre d'héroïne dans le bras.

jonah [ˈdʒounə] (*noun*), *F:* porte-guigne *m*, porte-poisse *m*, bonnet *m* de nuit.

Joneses [ˈdʒounziz] (*pl. pr. noun*), *F:* **to keep up with the J.,** imiter ses voisins, vivre au-dessus de ses moyens pour donner l'illusion d'un standing élevé.

jordan [ˈdʒɔːdn] (*noun*), *P:* pot *m* de chambre, Jules *m*, Thomas *m*.

josh[1] [dʒɔʃ] (*noun*), *F:* plaisanterie *f*, blague *f*.

josh[2] [dʒɔʃ] (**to**), *F:* taquiner, chiner, blaguer, mettre (qn) en boîte.

josher [ˈdʒɔʃər] (*noun*), *F:* blagueur *m*, chineur *m*.

joskin [ˈdʒɔskin] (*noun*) (*U.S.*), *F:* = **rube, 1, 2.**

josser [ˈdʒɔsər] (*noun*), *P:* individu*, type *m*, mec *m*.

Jove [dʒouv] (*noun*), *F:* **by J!** bon sang! sacrebleu!; **by J. it's cold!** bigre, qu'il fait froid!

joy [dʒɔi] (*noun*), *F:* chance*, veine *f*, pot *m*; **any j.?** ça a marché?; **no j.!** pas de chance*! tant pis!

joy-girl [ˈdʒɔi-gəːl] (*noun*), *P:* prostituée*, fille *f* de joie.

joy-house [ˈdʒɔihaus] (*noun*), *P:* bordel*, maison *f* de passe, maison bancale.

joy-pop [ˈdʒɔi-pɔp] (*noun*), *P:* emploi intermittent (*ou* pour le plaisir) d'une drogue par un non-initié; piqûre *f* de remonte-pente; *cf.* **pop**[1], **5.**

joy-popper [ˈdʒɔi-pɔpər] (*noun*), *P:* 1. qn qui se drogue* (*surtout* marijuana) pour la première fois; un neuf. 2. qn qui ne se drogue* pas régulièrement; un saccadeur.

joy-powder [ˈdʒɔi-paudər] (*noun*), *P:* morphine *f* (*drogues**).

joy-ride [ˈdʒɔi-raid] (*noun*). 1. *F:* (*a*) promenade *f* en voiture sans la permission du propriétaire; balade *f* à la sauvette; (*b*) promenade *f* à toute vitesse; (*c*) partie *f* de plaisir. 2. *P:* expérience de drogues faite par un non-initié; une saccade.

joy-rider [ˈdʒɔi-raidər] (*noun*), 1. *F:* qn qui se promène en voiture (*a*) sans la permission du propriétaire, (*b*) en allant à toute vitesse, (*c*) pour son plaisir. 2. *P:* = **joy-popper, 1, 2.**

joy-smoke [ˈdʒɔi-smouk] (*noun*), *P:* (*a*) marijuana *f* (*drogues**); (*b*) hachisch *m* (*drogues**).

joystick [ˈdʒɔi-stik] (*noun*), *P:* 1. pénis*, cigare *m* à moustache, l'instrument *m*. 2. (*a*) pipe *f* à opium, bambou *m*; (*b*) = **joint, 3.**

juana [dʒuːˈɑːnə, ˈhwɑːnə], **juane** [dʒuːˈɑːn, hwɑːn], **juanita** [djuəˈniːtə, hwɑːˈniːtə] (*noun*), *P: abréviations pour «marijuana»* (*drogues**), *surtout la cigarette;* juana *f*; *cf.* **marjie.**

judy [ˈdʒuːdi] (*noun*), *P:* 1. fille*, femme*, nénette *f*, nana *f*. 2. **to make a j. of oneself,** faire le guignol (*ou* le polichinelle).

jug[1] [dʒʌg] (*noun*), *P:* 1. prison*, tôle *f*, coffre *m*; **to go to j.,** aller en tôle (*ou* au coffre). 2. (*pl.*) seins*, boîtes *f.pl.* à lait. 3. récipient *m* contenant une drogue liquide, flacon *m*, fiole *f*. 4. banque *f*.

jug[2] [dʒʌg] (**to**), *P:* emprisonner*, coffrer, mettre en tôle, boucler.

jugful [ˈdʒʌgful] (*noun*), *F:* **not by a j.!** tant s'en faut! il s'en faut de beaucoup!

juggins [ˈdʒʌginz] (*noun*), *F:* = **muggins.**

jughead [ˈdʒʌghed] (*noun*), *F:* individu bête*, cruche *f*, cruchon *m*.

juice [dʒuːs] (*noun*). 1. *F:* courant *m* électrique, jus *m*. 2. *F:* essence *f*, coco *m*; **to step on the j.,** mettre les gaz *m.pl.;* 3. *P:* sperme*, jus *m*; *cf.* **baby-juice.** 4. *F:* **the J.,** la mer du Nord, le Bouillon. 5. *P:* alcool*,

***** L'astérisque indique que le mot marqué de ce signe figure comme entrée dans le Répertoire.

surtout whisky *m*; gnôle *f*. **6.** *P:* tonus *m*, force *f*, vigueur *f*. *Voir aussi* **cow-juice; stew**[2] **(to)**.

juiced (up) [ˈdʒuːstˈʌp] (*adj.*). **1.** *P:* (*a*) ivre*, chargé, fadé; (*b*) aiguillonné, survolté. **2.** *F:* (*auto*) = **hotted up, 2.**

juicehead [ˈdʒuːshed] (*noun*) (*U.S.*), *P:* ivrogne*, soûlard *m*, poivrot *m*.

juicer [ˈdʒuːsər] (*noun*) (*U.S.*), *F:* (*th.*) électricien *m*, projectionniste *m*, électro *m*.

juicy [ˈdʒuːsi] (*adj.*), *F:* **1.** juteux, savoureux, risqué. **2.** lucratif, qui rapporte, bien beurré.

juju, ju-ju [ˈdʒuːdʒuː] (*noun*), *P:* cigarette* de marijuana (*drogues**), juju *f*.

jumbo[1] [ˈdʒʌmbou] (*adj.*), *F:* de grande taille, maouss(e), mastodonte; **j. screen,** écran géant; **j. jet** (avion), gros porteur.

Jumbo, jumbo[2] [ˈdʒʌmbou] (*noun*), *F:* nom donné à un éléphant, Babar.

jumbuck [ˈdʒʌmbʌk] (*noun*) (*Austr.*), *F:* mouton *m*.

jump[1] [dʒʌmp] (*noun*). **1.** *P:* coït*, partie *f* de jambes en l'air; **to have a j., to give a woman a j.** = **jump**[2] **(to), 1** (*a*). **2.** *P:* **go (and) take a running j. (at yourself)!** va te faire voir! va te faire foutre!; *cf.* **jump**[2] **(to), 6. 3.** *F:* **to have the jumps,** ne pas rester en place, avoir la bougeotte, être sur une pile électrique. **4.** *P:* **on the j.,** en plein coup de feu. *Voir aussi* **ahead, 2; high**[1]**, 1.**

jump[2] [dʒʌmp] **(to)**. **1.** *P:* (*a*) coïter*, faire une partie de jambes en l'air; (*b*) coïter* avec (qn), sauter, enjamber (qn). **2.** *P:* voler*, faire sauter, faucher, gauler; **to j. a drag,** voler* une voiture*, faucher une tire. **3.** *F:* **to j. bail,** se dérober à la justice. **4.** *F:* **to j. ship,** tirer une bordée. **5.** *F:* **to j. the queue,** passer avant son tour; *cf.* **queue-jumper. 6.** *F:* **go (and) j. in the lake!** va te coucher! va te faire voir!; *cf.* **jump**[1]**, 2. 7.** *F:* **j. to it!** et que ça saute! **8.** *F:* **to j. on s.o.,** réprimander* qn, passer un savon à qn. **9.** *P:* attaquer*, sauter sur le paletot à (qn), agrafer. **10.** *F:* boumer, être en plein boum, ronfler, gazer. **11.** *F:* **to j. down s.o.'s throat, to j. all over s.o.,** tirer dans les pattes à qn, bouffer le nez à qn, rabrouer qn. **12.** *F:* **to j. off the deep end,** y aller d'autor, foncer. **13.** *F:* **to j. the hurdle,** se marier, sauter le pas, se passer la corde au cou. *Voir aussi* **bandwagon; gun**[1]**, 2.**

jumped up [ˈdʒʌmptˈʌp] (*adj.*), *F:* **1.** prétentieux*, crâneur, esbrouffeur. **2.** parvenu, nouveau-riche. **3.** bâclé, fait à la six-quatre-deux.

jumper [ˈdʒʌmpər] (*noun*). **1.** *P:* **(you can) stick it up your j.!** colle (*ou* fous) ça dans ta poche (et ton mouchoir par-dessus)!; *cf.* **stick**[2] **(to), 3. 2.** *P:* receveur *m*, -euse *f* (*autobus ou métro*). **3.** *F:* **counter j.,** vendeur *m*, -euse *f*, camelotier *m*. *Voir aussi* **queue-jumper.**

jungle [ˈdʒʌŋgl] (*noun*). **1.** *F:* la jungle, endroit *m* de mauvaises mœurs. **2.** *P:* lieu *m* de refuge des vagabonds, la zone, la cloche. **3.** *P:* **j. bunny** (*péj.*), nègre*, bougnoul(e) *m*.

junk[1] [dʒʌŋk] (*noun*). **1.** *F:* articles variés sans grande valeur, pacotille *f*, camelote *f*, gnognote *f*. **2.** *P:* (*a*) drogues*, stupéfiants *m.pl.*, stups *m.pl.*; **to be on the j.,** se droguer*, se camer; (*b*) héroïne *f* (*drogues**). **3.** *F:* bêtises*, balivernes *f.pl.* **4.** *F:* ferraille *f*; **heap of j.,** vieille voiture*, tacot *m*. **5.** *P:* ordures *f.pl.*, de la cochonnerie. **6.** *P:* bijoux *m.pl.* (comme butin*), joncaille *f*, broquille *f*.

junk[2] [dʒʌŋk] **(to)**, *P:* mettre au rebut (*ou* au rencart *ou* à la casse).

junked up [ˈdʒʌŋktˈʌp] (*adj.*), *P:* drogué*, camé, junké, junkie; *cf.* **junk**[1]**, 2.**

junker [ˈdʒʌŋkər] (*noun*), *P:* **1.** = **junkie. 2.** trafiquant *m* de drogues*, fourgueur *m*, agent *m* de voyage.

junkie, junky[1] [ˈdʒʌŋki] (*noun*), *P:* toxico(mane) *mf*, junkie *mf*, camé(e).

junky[2] [ˈdʒʌŋki] (*adj.*), *F:* qui n'a pas de valeur, bon à foutre en l'air, camelote, toc.

* An asterisk indicates that the word so marked is included as a head-word in the Appendix.

K

kale [keil] (*noun*) (*U.S.*), *P:* = **cabbage.**

kangaroo [ˈkæŋgəruː] (*noun*), *F:* **1. k. court,** tribunal illégal, guignol *m* à l'estoc. **2.** (*pl.*) titres *m.pl.* de bourse australiens, des mous *m.pl.*

kaput(t) [kæˈput] (*adj.*), *F:* cassé, fichu, flingué; **to be k.,** être à plat (*ou* rousti).

karzy [ˈkɑːzi] (*noun*), *P:* W.C.*, le petit coin; **k. paper,** papier *m* hygiénique, torche-cul *m.*

kayo[1] [ˈkeiˈjou] (*noun*), *F:* = **k.o.**[1].

kayo[2] [ˈkeiˈjou] (**to**), *F:* = **k.o.**[2] (**to**).

kazoo [kəˈzuː] (*noun*), *P:* mirliton *m* de jazz.

K-boy [ˈkeibɔi] (*noun*) (*U.S.*), *P:* roi *m* (*cartes*), le papa.

keef [kiːf] (*noun*), *P:* marijuana *f* (*drogues**), kif *m.*

keel over [ˈkiːlˈouvər] (**to**), *F:* s'évanouir*, tourner de l'œil, tomber dans le cirage.

keep [kiːp] (**to**), *F:* **1. to k. the party clean,** ne pas dire de bêtises* et ne pas faire de bêtises. **2. to k. oneself to oneself,** faire bande à part. **3. to k. at it,** persévérer, s'accrocher à qch., en vouloir; **to k. s.o. at it,** serrer les côtes (*ou* la vis) à qn. *Voir aussi* **hat, 3.**

keep in [ˈkiːpˈin] (**to**), *F:* **to k. i. with s.o.,** rester bien avec qn, cultiver qn, peaufiner (une relation); **to k. i. with both sides,** ménager la chèvre et le chou, nager entre deux eaux.

keep on [ˈkiːpˈɔn] (**to**), *F:* **to k. o. at s.o.,** seriner qn, être sur le dos de qn.

keep out [ˈkiːpˈaut] (**to**), *F:* **you k. o. of this!** mêle-toi de ce qui te regarde! occupe-toi de tes oignons!

keeps [kiːps] (*pl. noun*), *F:* **for k.,** pour de bon, pas pour la frime, à perpète, jusqu'à plus soif.

keep up [ˈkiːpˈʌp] (**to**), *F:* **k. it u.!** vas-y! continue! tu l'auras! *Voir aussi* **end, 6; Joneses.**

keester [ˈkiːstər] (*noun*) (*U.S.*), *P:* **1.** fesses*, postérieur *m,* derche *m.* **2.** poche* arrière de pantalon, fouille(tte) *f,* profonde *f.* **3.** valise *f* de camelot, valdingue *f,* valoche *f.* **4.** coffre-fort *m,* coffiot *m.*

kef [keif, kef] (*noun*), *P:* = **keef.**

kefuffle [kəˈfʌfl] (*noun*), *F:* = **kerfuffle.**

keister [ˈkiːstər] (*noun*) (*U.S.*), *P:* = **keester.**

Kelly, kelly [ˈkeli] (*noun*). **1.** *P:* chapeau*, galurin *m,* bada *m,* doulos *m.* **2.** *F:* **K.'s eye:** *voir* **bingo** (**1**). *Voir aussi* **Derby Kelly.**

kerdoying! [kəˈdɔiŋ] (*excl.*), *F:* = **gerdoing!**

kerflooie [kəːˈfluːi] (*adv.*) (*U.S.*), *F:* **to go k.,** échouer*, foirer, finir en queue de poisson.

kerfuffle [kəˈfʌfl] (*noun*), *F:* commotion *f,* agitation *f,* perturbation *f.*

kerplunk [kəˈplʌŋk] (*adv.*), *F:* **to go k.,** tomber*, partir à dame, ramasser un gadin.

kettle [ˈketl] (*noun*). **1.** *P:* montre* (en or*); **k. and piece,** montre et chaîne, toccante et pendante. **2.** *F:* **here's a nice** (*or* **fine** *or* **pretty**) **k. of fish!** (*a*) en voilà une affaire! en voilà des histoires!; (*b*) nous voilà dans de beaux draps (*ou* dans un beau gâchis *ou* dans un bel embrouillamini)!

key [kiː] (*noun*), *F:* **k. of the door:** *voir* **bingo** (**21**).

keyed up [ˈkiːdˈʌp] (*p.p. & adj.*), *F:* gonflé à bloc.

keyhole [ˈkiːhoul] (*noun*), *P:* **to play K. Kate,** faire le voyeur, fouiner à la serrure.

keyster [ˈkiːstər] (*noun*) (*U.S.*), *P:* = **keester.**

khazi [ˈkɑːzi] (*noun*), *P:* = **karzy.**

Khyber [ˈkaibər] (*noun*) (*R.S.* = *Khyber Pass* = **arse**), *P:* **he can stick it up his K.,** il peut se le mettre (*ou* se le fourrer) quelque part; *cf.* **stick**[2] (**to**), **3.**

ki [kai] (*noun*), *P:* cacao *m ou* chocolat *m* de prison.

kibitz [ˈkibits] (**to**), *F:* **1.** suivre une

* L'astérisque indique que le mot marqué de ce signe figure comme entrée dans le Répertoire.

partie de cartes en donnant son avis. **2.** se mêler de ce qui ne regarde pas, mettre son grain de sel, canuler, ramener sa fraise.

kibitzer ['kibitsər] (*noun*), *F:* individu qui donne des conseils non sollicités, qui se mêle de tout; canule *f*, canulard *m*.

kibosh ['kaibɔʃ] (*noun*), *F:* **1.** = **bosh.** **2. to put the k. on sth.**, mettre fin (*ou* son veto *ou* le holà) à qch., étouffer qch.

kick[1] [kik] (*noun*). **1.** *F:* frisson *m* (de plaisir), piquant *m* (d'une chose); le fade; **to get a k. out of sth.**, prendre (*ou* éprouver du) plaisir à qch.; **to do sth. for kicks,** faire ce qui botte (*ou* ce qui chante). **2.** *F:* (*d'une boisson*) du goût, une certaine force alcoolique; **it's got a k. in it,** c'est une boisson qui remonte. **3.** *F:* (*d'une drogue*) le pied, le râle, la renaude, l'extase *f*; **to go on a k.,** se lancer dans la drogue*, prendre le pied, aller à la défonce; **bum kicks,** mauvaise expérience d'un drogué*, flippage *m*, mauvais voyage. **4.** *F:* **he's got no k. left in him,** il est à plat, il est vide (*ou* pompé). **5.** (*a*) *F:* **that's better than a k. in the pants,** ça vaut mieux qu'un coup de pied au derrière, ça vaut mieux que de se casser la jambe, ça vaut mieux qu'une jambe cassée; (*b*) *P:* **he's had a k. in the arse** (*U.S.* **ass**) (*or* **pants**), il s'est fait botter le cul, il s'est fait asseoir; *voir aussi* **pants, 3. 6.** *F:* **the k.,** sacquage *m*; **to get the k.,** recevoir son paquet, être boulé. **7.** *P:* poche* (*surtout* de pantalon), fouille *f*. **8.** *P:* grogne *f*, rouspétance *f*, rouscaille *f*. *Voir aussi* **sidekick.**

kick[2] [kik] (**to**). **1.** *P:* grogner*, bougonner, rouspéter, ronchonner, râler. **2.** *F:* résister, ruer dans les brancards. *Voir aussi* **alive, 1; bucket, 1; habit, 1; heel, 3.**

kick along ['kikə'lɔŋ] (**to**), *F:* se maintenir, se défendre.

kick around ['kikə'raund] (**to**), *F:* **1.** retourner, ruminer, ergoter sur (une idée, *etc.*). **2. to k. s.o. a.,** mener qn à la trique, être chien (*ou* vache) avec qn. **3.** rouler sa bosse, bourlinguer. **4. there are lots of people like that kicking around,** des gens comme ça, ce n'est pas ce qui manque. **5. I've lost my gloves, but they must be kicking around somewhere,** j'ai perdu mes gants, mais ils doivent traîner quelque part. *Voir aussi* **gong, 2.**

kickback ['kikbæk] (*noun*). **1.** *F:* réaction violente, coup *m* de boomerang, retour *m* de manivelle. **2.** *P:* ristourne *f*, dessous-de-table *m*. **3.** *P:* récidive *f* dans la drogue, rebranchage *m*.

kicker ['kikər] (*noun*) (*U.S.*), *P:* piège *m*, hic *m*, os *m*, cactus *m*. *Voir aussi* **shitkicker.**

kick in ['kik'in] (**to**), *F:* payer sa part, payer son écot.

kickman ['kikmæn] (*noun*), *P:* approvisionneur *m* (*ou* fourgueur *m*) de drogues.

kick-off ['kikɔf] (*noun*), *F:* coup *m* d'envoi, démarrage *m*.

kick off ['kik'ɔf] (**to**). **1.** *F:* donner le départ (*ou* le coup d'envoi), démarrer. **2.** *P:* partir*, lever l'ancre, se tirer, se tailler. **3.** *P:* mourir*, claquer, clamser.

kick out ['kik'aut] (**to**), *F:* (*a*) flanquer (qn) à la porte, balancer, larguer (qn); (*b*) congédier* (qn), sacquer (qn).

kick-stick ['kik-stik] (*noun*), *P:* = **joint, 3.**

kick-up ['kikʌp] (*noun*), *F:* **1.** chahut *m*, tapage *m*, chambard *m*. **2.** réjouissances*, bamboche *f*, bamboula *f*, ribouldingue *f*.

kick up ['kik'ʌp] (**to**). **1.** *F:* **to k. u. a fuss,** faire des chichis *m.pl.* (*ou* des embarras *m.pl.*). **2.** *F:* (*a*) **to k. u. a row** (*or* **a racket** *or* **a shindig** *or* **a shindy** *or* **a hullabaloo**), faire beaucoup de bruit*, faire du boucan (*ou* du chambard); (*b*) **to k. u. a dust,** mener grand bruit*, faire de la musique, faire une scène; *voir aussi* **rumpus. 3.** *P:* **to k. u. hell,** faire un scandale du diable. **4.** *F:* **to k. u. one's heels,** sauter de joie. *Voir aussi* **stink**[1]**, 1.**

kick upstairs ['kikʌp'stɛəz] (**to**), *F:* **to k. s.o. u.,** donner de l'avancement à qn pour s'en débarrasser*, *souvent* donner un titre de noblesse, faire un limogeage doré.

kid[1] [kid] (*adj.*), *F:* **1.** jeunet, cadet; **a k. sister,** une sœur cadette. **2.** enfantin, puéril; **k. stuff,** enfantillage *m*, gaminerie *f*; **it's k. stuff,** c'est du

* An asterisk indicates that the word so marked is included as a head-word in the Appendix.

primaire, c'est une amusette. 3. **to handle** (*or* **treat**) **s.o. with k. gloves,** (*a*) ménager qn, traiter qn avec ménagement, manier qn comme du verre cassé; (*b*) dorloter, chouchouter qn.

kid² [kid] (*noun*), *F:* 1. enfant*, gosse *mf*, môme *mf*. 2. farce *f*, blague *f*; **no k.?** = **are you kidding?** (**kid³** (**to**), 2); **no k.!** = **no kidding!** *Voir aussi* **whiz(z)¹**, 2.

kid³ [kid] (**to**), *F:* 1. en conter à (qn), faire marcher (qn); **don't k. yourself!** ne te fais pas d'illusion!; **who are you trying to k.?** tu te fiches de moi? 2. plaisanter; **are you kidding?** tu me fais marcher? tu veux me mener en bateau?; **stop kidding!** arrête ton char!; *cf.* **kidding.**

kid along ['kidə'lɔŋ] (**to**), *F:* bourrer le crâne à (qn), emberlificoter (qn).

kidder ['kidər] (*noun*), *F:* farceur *m*, blagueur *m*, loustic *m*.

kiddie ['kidi] (*noun*), *F:* = **kiddy.**

kidding ['kidiŋ] (*noun*), *F:* blague *f*, mise *f* en boîte, charriage *m*; **no k?** = **are you kidding?** (**kid³** (**to**), 2); **no k.!** sans blague! blague à part! sans char!; *cf.* **kid³** (**to**), 2.

kiddy ['kidi], **kiddywink(y)** ['kidiwiŋk(i)] (*noun*), *F:* petit enfant*, mioche *mf*; *cf.* **kid²**, 1.

kidology [ki'dɔlədʒi] (*noun*), *F:* l'art *m* de faire gober les gens.

kief [ki:f], **kif** [kif] (*noun*), *P:* = **keef.**

kike [kaik] (*noun*), *P:* (*péj.*) Juif *m*, Youpe *m*, Youpin *m*.

kill¹ [kil] (*noun*), *F:* 1. assassinat *m*, butage *m*, saignage *m*. 2. (*a*) descente *f* (d'avion ennemi), inscription *f* au tableau de chasse; (*b*) coulée *f* (d'un navire ennemi). 3. **a k. or cure,** un remède de cheval. *Voir aussi* **set up** (**to**), 2.

kill² [kil] (**to**), *F:* 1. **to k. a bottle,** sécher une bouteille, faire cul sec, tout avaler. 2. ruiner, enfoncer, couler (qn *ou* qch.). 3. (*th.*) **to k. an audience,** brûler les planches, casser la baraque, faire un emportage. 4. éteindre, écraser (une cigarette, *etc.*). 5. **to k. time,** paresser*, flemmarder. *Voir aussi* **dressed.**

killer ['kilər] (*noun*), *P:* 1. flambard *m*, enjôleur *m*. 2. tombeur *m* (de femmes), dénicheur *m* de fauvettes; *cf.* **lady-killer.** 3. = **lulu.** 4. qch. qui émoustille *ou* transporte *ou* ragaillardit. 5. cigarette* de marijuana (*drogues**), stick *m*.

killing¹ ['kiliŋ] (*adj.*), *F:* 1. très amusant*, tordant, crevant; **it's too k. for words,** c'est à mourir de rire. 2. emballant, fascinant. 3. fatigant, tuant, crevant.

killing² ['kiliŋ] (*noun*), *F:* **to make a k.,** faire de gros profits, affurer.

kind [kaind] (*noun*), *F:* 1. **I don't have that k. of money,** je n'ai pas des sommes pareilles. 2. **these k. of things annoy me,** ce genre de choses m'agace. *Voir aussi* **kind of.**

kinda ['kaində] (*adv.*) *F:* = **kind of.**

kind of ['kaindəv] (*adv.*), *F:* 1. **he's k. o. careful with money,** il est radin sur les bords. 2. **I k. o. expected it,** je m'en doutais presque. 3. **it's k. o. chilly,** il fait passablement froid (*ou* frisquet).

kingdom-come ['kiŋdəm'kʌm] (*noun*). 1. *F:* le paradis, le paradouze. 2. *P:* **to knock s.o. to k.-c.,** battre* qn, foutre une trempe à qn. 3. *P:* (*R.S.* = *rum*) rhum *m*; *cf.* **Tom,** 4; **touch-your-bum.**

king-pin ['kiŋpin] (*noun*), *F:* personne (la plus) importante, caïd *m*, magnat *m*, grand manitou.

king-size(d) ['kiŋsaiz(d)] (*adj.*), *F:* (*a*) = **jumbo¹**; (*b*) gros* et long; **k.-s. cigarettes,** cigarettes* grand format.

kink [kiŋk] (*noun*), *F:* 1. truc *m*, lubie *f*, manie *f*, dada *m*; **he's got a k.,** il est un peu timbré. 2. **to be in kinks,** se tordre de rire.

kinky¹ ['kiŋki] (*adj.*). 1. *F:* fantasque, excentrique, fada. 2. *F:* bizarre, équivoque. 3. *P:* inverti. 4. *P:* louche, injuste, inique. 5. *P:* volé*, chipé, chopé, barboté.

kinky² ['kiŋki] (*noun*), *P:* 1. pédéraste*, fagot *m*, empapaouté *m*. 2. lesbienne*, goudou *f*, gouchotte *f*.

kip¹ [kip] (*noun*), *P:* 1. lit*, pieu *m*, plumard *m*. 2. pension *f* de famille, chambre meublée, garno *m*, crèche *f*. 3. sommeil *m*; **to have a k.,** dormir*, piquer un roupillon.

kip² [kip] (**to**), *P:* 1. se coucher*, se pieuter. 2. dormir*, pioncer, roupiller. 3. coucher sur la dure.

kip down [ˈkipˈdaun] (**to**), *P:* = **kip**[2] (**to**), **1**.

kipe [kaip] (**to**), *P:* = **kype** (**to**).

kip-house [ˈkiphaus] (*noun*), *P:* = **doss-house.**

kipper [ˈkipər] (*noun*), *P:* individu*, type *m*, client *m*.

kip-shop [ˈkipʃɔp] (*noun*), *P:* bordel*, bocard *m*, boxon *m*.

kiss[1] [kis] (*noun*), *F:* **the k. of death,** le coup de grâce. *Voir aussi* **French**[1], **1; tongue-kiss.**

kiss[2] [kis] (**to**), *F:* **1. to k. sth. goodbye,** faire ses adieux à qch., tirer un trait sur qch., en faire son deuil. **2. never been kissed:** *voir* **bingo** (**16**). **3. to k. and be friends,** se réconcilier, se rebonneter, faire ami-ami. *Voir aussi* **arse, 6; dust**[1], **4**.

kiss-ass [ˈkisæs] (*noun*) (*U.S.*), *V:* = **arse-kisser.**

kisser [ˈkisər] (*noun*), *P:* **1.** bouche*, museau *m*, margoulette *f*. **2.** lèvres*, baiseuses *f.pl.*, babines *f.pl.* **3.** visage*, binette *f*, fiole *f*; **one right in the k.,** une pêche en pleine poire. *Voir aussi* **arse-kisser; baby-kisser.**

kiss-off [ˈkisɔf] (*noun*) (*U.S.*), *P:* **1.** mort *f*, crève *f*, crevaison *f*. **2.** sacquage *m*, limogeage *m*.

kiss off [ˈkisˈɔf] (**to**) (*U.S.*), *P:* **1.** tuer*, effacer (qn). **2.** se débarrasser* de (qn), sacquer, balancer, débarquer.

kissy [ˈkisi] (*adj.*), *P:* servile, flagorneur.

kit [kit] (*noun*), *F:* (*a*) barda *m*, bataclan *m*, Saint-Frusquin *m*; *voir aussi* **caboodle;** (*b*) effets *m.pl.* (de voyageur). *Voir aussi* **shelf-kit.**

kitchen-sink[1] [ˈkitʃinˈsiŋk] (*attrib. adj.*), *F:* **k.-s. novel,** *etc.*, roman *m*, *etc.*, boîte à ordures.

kitchen-sink[2] [ˈkitʃinˈsiŋk] (*noun*), *F:* **everything but the k.-s.,** tout sans exception, y compris la cage aux serins.

kite [kait] (*noun*). **1.** *F:* avion *m*, coucou *m*. **2.** *F:* **to fly a k.,** (*a*) mettre une fausse traite en circulation; (*b*) tâter le terrain, lancer un ballon d'essai; (*c*) (*finances*) tirer en l'air, tirer en blanc. **3.** *P:* chèque *m*; **k. man,** faussaire *m*, mornifleur *m*. **4.** *F:* **high as a k.,** (*a*) ivre*, parti, rétamé; (*b*) drogué*, chargé, bourré à zéro, défoncé. **5.** *P:* prostituée*, roulure *f*, radeuse *f*.

kitsch [kitʃ] (*noun*), *F:* bêtises* prétentieuses, sornettes *f.pl.*, esbrouf(f)e *f*.

kittens [ˈkitnz] (*pl. noun*), *F:* **to (nearly) have k.,** (*a*) être très en colère*, piquer une crise, avoir le coup de sang; (*b*) avoir peur*, avoir les foies *m.pl.*, avoir chaud aux fesses *f.pl.* *Voir aussi* **sex-kitten.**

kitty [ˈkiti] (*noun*). **1.** *F:* chaton *m*, petit(e) chat(te). **2.** *F:* (*a*) cagnotte *f*; (*b*) magot *m*. **3.** *P:* prison*, trou *m*, tôle *f*.

Kiwi, kiwi [ˈkiːwiː] (*noun*), *F:* **1.** Néo-Zélandais *m*, Kiwi *m*. **2.** employé d'un aéroport affecté à terre; rampant *m*.

klink [kliŋk] (*noun*), *P:* = **clink.**

k-man [ˈkeimæn] (*abbr.*), *P:* = **kick-man.**

knacker [ˈnækər] (**to**), *P:* **1.** châtrer, abélarder. **2.** réduire à quia, démonter. *Voir aussi* **knackered.**

knackered [ˈnækəd] (*p.p. & adj.*), *P:* **to be k.,** (*a*) être fatigué*, être éreinté (*ou* vanné); (*b*) se trouver en mauvaise posture, être emmerdé, ne pas savoir sur quel pied danser.

knackers [ˈnækəz] (*pl. noun*), *P:* testicules*, balloches *f.pl.*

knap [næp] (**to**), *P:* voler*, barboter.

knee [niː] (*noun*), *F:* **1. housemaid's k.,** épanchement *m* de synovie, genou *m* en compote. **2. gone at the knees,** décrépit, décati, avachi, vachement amorti. *Voir aussi* **bee, 1.**

knee-high [ˈniːˈhai] (*adj.*), *F:* **to be k.-h. to a bumble-bee** (*or* **a daisy** *or* **a duck** *or* **a frog** *or* **a grasshopper** *or* **a mosquito** *or* **a sparrow**), être une courte-botte (*ou* un petit poucet) (*petit* individu*).

kneesies [ˈniːziz] (*pl. noun*), *F:* **to play k. (under the table),** faire du genou; *cf.* **footsy.**

knees-up [ˈniːzʌp] (*noun*), *F:* gambade *f*, cabriole *f*, trémoussements *m.pl.*

knee-trembler [ˈniː-tremblər] (*noun*), *V:* **to do a k.-t.,** coïter* debout, sabrer à la verticale.

knickers [ˈnikəz] (*pl. noun*), *P:* **don't get your k. in a twist,** ne te mets pas dans tous tes états.

knicks [niks] (*pl. noun*), *F:* (=*knickers*) culotte *f* (de femme).

knife [naif] (*noun*), *F:* **1. to get one's k. into s.o., to have one's k. in s.o.,** avoir

* An asterisk indicates that the word so marked is included as a head-word in the Appendix.

une dent contre qn, s'acharner sur qn. 2. **to put the k. in,** entamer le morceau.

knob [nɔb] (*noun*). 1. *V:* pénis*, (gros) bout, polard *m*, zob *m*. 2. *P:* = **nob**[1], 1. 3. *P:* **with knobs on,** et le pouce, et mèche, et le rab.

knob-gobbler [ˈnɔbgɔblər] (*noun*), *V:* = **cock-sucker,** 1.

knobstick [ˈnɔb-stik] (*noun*), *P:* ouvrier non-syndiqué, jaune *m*.

knock[1] [nɔk] (*noun*). 1. *F:* critique *f*, éreintement *m*, abattage *m*. 2. *P:* ennui *m*, pépin *m*, os *m*, cactus *m*. 3. *P:* coït*, bourre *f*, carambolage *m*. 4. *F:* **to take a k.,** essuyer un échec* (*ou* une déception), recevoir un coup dans les gencives. 5. *F:* **it's your k.,** c'est ton tour, c'est ta passe.

knock[2] [nɔk] (**to**). 1. *F:* critiquer*, trouver à redire à (qn, qch.), éreinter, débiner. 2. *F:* **to k. sth. on the head,** battre qch. en brèche, mettre le holà, arrêter les frais. 3. *F:* **to be knocking 60,** friser la soixantaine. 4. *P:* escroquer*, refaire, carotter; **to k. s.o. for sth.,** écorcher qn de qch. 5. *P:* **to k. 'em,** épater la galerie, époustoufler; **that'll k. 'em cold,** cela va leur en boucher un coin; *cf.* **aisle,** 2. 6. (*Austr.*) *P:* violer, riper. 7. *P:* coïter* avec (une femme), bourrer, caramboler. 8. *F:* **to k. s.o. silly** (*or* **for six**), battre qn à plate(s) couture(s), donner une tabassée à qn, démolir qn, ébouzer qn. 9. *F:* **k. at the door:** *voir* **bingo** (4). *Voir aussi* **sideways; week.**

knock about *or* **around** [ˈnɔkəˈbaut, ˈnɔkəˈraund] (**to**), *F:* 1. = **kick around (to),** 3. 2. **to k. a. with s.o.,** s'acoquiner avec qn, sortir avec qn, fréquenter qn.

knock back [ˈnɔkˈbæk] (**to**), *F:* 1. **to k. b. a drink,** boire*, lamper un verre, s'en jeter un derrière la cravate; **k. it b.!** cul sec!. 2. coûter, peser; **it knocked him back a packet,** ça lui a pesé un sac. 3. renvoyer, faire rebondir; **he knocked it back at me,** il me l'a balanstiqué.

knocked out [ˈnɔktˈaut] (*p.p. & adj.*), *P:* 1. = **knocked up,** 2. 2. épaté, estomaqué, médusé. 3. = **jagged,** 2. *Voir aussi* **knock out (to).**

knocked up [ˈnɔktˈʌp] (*p.p. & adj.*), *P:* 1. malade*, patraque. 2. très fatigué*, éreinté, claqué. 3. enceinte*, engrossée, en cloque. *Voir aussi* **knock up (to).**

knocker [ˈnɔkər] (*noun*). 1. *F:* critique *m* sévère, éreinteur *m*, esquinteur *m*, abatteur *m*. 2. *P:* personne importante (ou qui se croit telle), gros bonnet, grosse légume. 3. (*pl.*) *P:* seins*, nichons *m.pl.*, rondins *m.pl.* 4. *P:* **on the k.,** à crédit, à tempérament, au croum(e), au crayon. *Voir aussi* **dress up (to),** 2.

knock in [ˈnɔkˈin] (**to**), *F:* (*football*) **to k. it i.,** marquer un but, envoyer dans le filet. *Voir aussi* **tooth,** 5.

knocking [ˈnɔkiŋ] (*adj.*), *P:* 1. **k. company,** maison *f* de ventes à crédit, croumiers *m.pl.* 2. **k. shop,** bordel*, maison *f* d'abattage.

knockings [ˈnɔkiŋz] (*pl. noun*), *P:* **to be on the last k.,** être à la dernière étape (*ou* au dernier échelon).

knock-kneed [ˈnɔkˈni:d] (*adj.*), *F:* poltron*, froussard, péteux.

knock-off [ˈnɔkɔf] (*noun*), *P:* **to have a k.-o.,** coïter*, avoir un carambolage.

knock off [ˈnɔkˈɔf] (**to**). 1. *P:* **to k. it o. with a woman,** coïter*, caramboler. 2. *P:* **k. it o. (will you)!** basta! écrase! passe la main! 3. *F:* **to k. o. a pint,** étouffer (*ou* étrangler) un demi, s'envoyer un coup. 4. *P:* voler*, faucher. 5. *F:* finir de travailler, débrayer, boucler, dételer. 6. *F:* finir vite, exécuter avec rapidité, liquider, expédier. 7. *P:* arrêter*, agrafer. 8. *P:* tuer*, démolir, dessouder. 9. *F:* faire un rabais (*ou* un avantage *ou* une ristourne) de... *Voir aussi* **block,** 1.

knockout[1] [ˈnɔkaut] (*adj.*), *F:* 1. **k. drops,** stupéfiant *m* qu'on met dans la boisson de la victime pour lui faire perdre connaissance (dans le but de la dépouiller), coup *m* d'assommoir. 2. mirobolant, transcendant.

knockout[2] [ˈnɔkaut] (*noun*), *F:* 1. une merveille, un phénomène, qch. *ou* qn de mirifique. 2. (*d'une femme*) prix *m* de Diane. *Voir aussi* **k.o.**[1]

knock out [ˈnɔkˈaut] (**to**), *F:* 1. **to k. oneself o.,** travailler* dur, s'éreinter, s'esquinter. 2. époustoufler, éblouir, fasciner, épater. *Voir aussi* **knocked out; k.o.**[2] **(to).**

knock-over [ˈnɔkouvər] (*noun*), *P:*

* L'astérisque indique que le mot marqué de ce signe figure comme entrée dans le Répertoire.

cambriolage *m*, caroublage *m*, mise *f* en l'air.

knock over [ˈnɔkˈouvər] (**to**), *P:* **1.** cambrioler*, caroubler, mettre en l'air. **2.** faire une descente (de police) dans..., rafler.

knock together [ˈnɔktəˈgeðər] (**to**), *F:* = **knock up (to), 1.**

knock up [ˈnɔkˈʌp] (**to**). **1.** *F:* préparer, concocter, combiner. **2.** *F:* (*a*) réveiller, secouer; (*b*) tambouriner à une porte à une heure tardive. **3.** *P:* rendre enceinte*, engrosser, mettre en cloque. **4.** *P:* abîmer*, amocher, saboter. **5.** *F:* **to k. u. £100 a week,** se faire cent livres par semaine.

knot [nɔt] (*noun*), *F:* **1. to tie the k.,** se marier, se mettre la corde au cou. **2. to get tied (up) in knots,** s'embrouiller, s'emberlificoter, ne pas s'en sortir. *Voir aussi* **top-knot.**

knothead [ˈnɔthed] (*noun*), *F:* = **knucklehead.**

knotted [ˈnɔtid] (*p.p. & adj.*), *P:* **get k.!** va te faire voir!

know[1] [nou] (*noun*), *F:* **to be in the k.,** être affranchi, être au parfum, être dans le coup.

know[2] [nou] (**to**), *F:* **1. I don't want to k.,** rien à faire, je ne marche pas. **2. not that I k. of,** pas que je sache. **3. for all I k.,** autant que je sache. **4.** (*a*) **what do you k.?** quoi de neuf?; (*b*) **well, what do you k.!** sans blague! sans char! **5. don't I k. it!** à qui le dites-vous! **6. not if I k. (anything about) it!** pour rien au monde! **7. I wouldn't k.,** je ne saurais dire. **8. he knows a good thing when he sees one** (*or* **it**), c'est un connaisseur, il sait ce qui est bon. **9. you k. what you can do with that, you k. where you can put** (*or* **stick** *or* **shove**) **that,** tu peux te le mettre quelque part. **10. to k. a thing or two, to k. what's what,** être malin*, être à la coule.

know-all [ˈnouwɔːl] (*noun*), *F:* je-sais-tout *m*; **Mr K.,** Monsieur Je-sais-tout.

know-how [ˈnouhau] (*noun*), *F:* (*a*) savoir-faire *m*, habileté *f*; (*b*) savoir-faire (technique), connaissances *f.pl.* techniques, mise *f* en pratique.

knuckle [ˈnʌkl] (*noun*), *F:* **near the k.,** scabreux, grivois.

knuckle down [ˈnʌklˈdaun] (**to**), *F:* se ranger des voitures, s'y mettre, avoir du plomb dans la tête.

knucklehead [ˈnʌklhed] (*noun*), *F:* individu bête*, niguedouille *m*, empoté *m*.

knuckle under [ˈnʌklˈʌndər] (**to**), *F:* se soumettre, filer doux, baisser pavillon.

k.o., K.O.[1] [ˈkeiˈjou] (*abbr.* = *knockout*), *F:* (*boxe, lutte*) K.O. *m*, knock-out *m*.

k.o., K.O.[2] [ˈkeiˈjou] (**to**) (*abbr.* = *knock out*), *F:* **1.** (*boxe, lutte*) mettre K.O., knockouter. **2.** = **to knock on the head (knock**[2] **(to), 2).**

kokomo [kouˈkoumou] (*noun*), *P:* = **cokomo.**

kook [kuːk] (*noun*), *P:* excentrique *m*, braque *m*, branquignol(le) *m*, louftingue *m*.

kooky [ˈkuːki] (*adj.*), *F:* **1.** un peu fou*, braque, louftingue. **2.** (*vêtements*) sophistiqué, raffiné.

kosher [ˈkouʃər] (*adj.*), *F:* au poil, impec, réglo.

kowtow [ˈkautau] (**to**), *F:* **to k. to s.o.,** s'aplatir (*ou* se mettre à genoux) devant qn.

kraut, Kraut [kraut], **krauthead** [ˈkrauthed] (*noun*), *P:* (*péj.*) Allemand*, fridolin *m*, frizou *m*.

kudos [ˈkjuːdɔs] (*noun*), *F:* panache *m*, gloriole *f*.

kybo [ˈkaibou] (*noun*), *P:* W.C.*, goguenots *m.pl.*

kype [kaip] (**to**), *P:* voler* (de petites choses), chiper, chaparder.

* An asterisk indicates that the word so marked is included as a head-word in the Appendix.

L

lab [læb] (*abbr.* = *laboratory*), *F:* labo *m.*

lace [leis] (**to**), *F:* alcooliser, corser, arroser; **laced coffee,** café* au rhum.

lace around [ˈleisəˈraund] (**to**), *F:* foncer, se précipiter.

lace into [ˈleisˈintuː] (**to**), *F:* **1. to l. i. s.o.,** (*a*) battre*, rosser qn; (*b*) critiquer*, éreinter, dégrainer qn. **2. to l. i. sth.,** y aller de tout son cœur (*ou* avec ardeur), y mettre toute la sauce.

lacy [ˈleisi] (*adj.*), *P:* efféminé, homosexuel sur les bords.

lad [læd] (*noun*), *F:* **1. he's a bit of a l. (with the women),** c'est un tombeur de filles, c'est un chaud lapin. **2. one of the lads,** un gai luron, un joyeux compère.

ladder [ˈlædər] (*noun*), *F:* **pull the l. up (, Jack), take the l. away (, Jack),** *c.p.*, après nous le déluge (*ou* la fin du monde); *cf.* **Jack, 3.**

laddie [ˈlædi] (*noun*), *F:* (petit) gars, gamin *m.*

la-de-da, la-di-da, ladidah [ˈlɑːdiˈdɑː] (*adj.*), *F:* **1.** élégant*, (super-)chic, à grand tralala; **it was a very l. gathering,** tout le gratin se trouvait là. **2.** (*péj.*) **she's so l.!** elle fait la prétentieuse*, elle jette du jus; **she's got such a l. accent,** elle parle avec affectation, elle veut mousser du claque-merde.

lady [ˈleidi] (*noun*), *P:* **L. Jane,** vagin*, mimi *m*, pâquerette *f. Voir aussi* **fat[1], 6; lollipop-lady; old, 4.**

lady-killer [ˈleidi-kilər] (*noun*), *F:* bourreau *m* des cœurs, tombeur *m* de filles; *cf.* **killer, 2.**

lag[1] [læg] (*noun*), *F:* (*a*) forçat *m*, bagnard *m*, fague *m*; (*b*) forçat libéré, fagot affranchi; **old l.,** cheval *m* de retour, forçat chevronné.

lag[2] [læg] (**to**), *F:* (*a*) arrêter*, épingler; (*b*) emprisonner*, bloquer, boucler.

lah-de-dah [ˈlɑːdiˈdɑː] (*adj.*), *F:* = **la-de-da.**

laid up [ˈleidˈʌp] (*p.p. & adj.*), *F:* malade*, alité, mal fichu.

lair [ˈlɛər] (*noun*) (*Austr.*), *F:* élégant *m*, tape-à-l'œil *m.*

lairy [ˈlɛəri] (*adj.*) (*Austr.*), *F:* voyant, tapageur.

lake [leik] (*noun*), *F:* **go (and) jump in the l.!** va te faire pendre! va te faire voir!

lam[1] [læm] (*noun*) (*U.S.*), *P:* **on the l.,** (*a*) en fuite, en cavale; (*b*) en déplacement, en voyage, par monts et par vaux.

lam[2] [læm] (**to**), *P:* **1.** battre*, rosser, étriller. **2.** (*U.S.*) partir* précipitamment, mettre les bouts, décambuter.

lamb [læm] (*noun*). **1.** *P:* **l. (chop),** piqûre *f* de narcotique, piquouse *f*, fixe *m*. **2.** *F:* (*a*) (*d'un enfant*) lapin *m*, agneau *m*; (*b*) (*terme d'affection*) poulet *m*, coco *m*. **3.** (*U.S.*) *F:* individu* crédule, gobeur *m*, cave *m*, pigeon *m*. **4.** *F:* **he took it like a l.,** il s'est laissé faire, il n'a pas rouspété.

lambaste [ˈlæmˈbeist] (**to**), *F:* (*a*) battre*, dérouiller; (*b*) critiquer*, éreinter.

lambasting [ˈlæmˈbeistiŋ] (*noun*), *F:* (*a*) raclée *f*, frottée *f*; (*b*) critique *f*, éreintage *m*, abattage *m.*

lame [leim] (*adj.*), *P:* = **square[1], 4** (*a*). *Voir aussi* **duck[1], 6.**

lame-brain [ˈleimˈbrein] (*noun*) (*U.S.*), *F:* individu bête*, imbécile *m*, sot *m.*

lam into [ˈlæmˈintuː] (**to**), *P:* = **lam[2] (to), 1.**

lamming [ˈlæmiŋ] (*noun*), *P:* = **lambasting.**

lam out [ˈlæmˈaut] (**to**) (*U.S.*), *P:* = **lam[2] (to), 2.**

lamp [læmp] (**to**), *P:* regarder*, zyeuter, reluquer, mater.

lamp-post [ˈlæmppoust] (*noun*), *F:* **between you and me and the l.-p.,** tout à fait entre nous, entre quat'zyeux; *cf.* **gate-post.**

lamps [læmps] (*pl. noun*), *P:* (*a*) yeux*, quinquets *m.pl.*, lanternes *f.pl.*, lampions *m.pl.*; (*b*) yeux* pochés, coquards *m.pl.*

***** L'astérisque indique que le mot marqué de ce signe figure comme entrée dans le Répertoire.

land [lænd] (**to**), *F:* **1.** gagner, obtenir, dénicher, dégot(t)er. **2.** arriver*, débarquer, s'abouler. **3.** **to l. s.o. a blow,** filer (*ou* flanquer) à qn un coup* (*ou* une taloche *ou* une baffe). **4.** **that will l. you in prison,** cela vous vaudra de la prison*, ça va vous faire entôler. *Voir aussi* **mire; muck, 3; shit**³, **2.**

landed [ˈlændid] (*p.p. & adj.*), *F:* dans le pétrin; **to be l. with s.o.,** avoir qn sur les bras, être empêtré de qn.

land up [ˈlændˈʌp] (**to**), *F:* (*a*) **to l. u. with nothing,** n'aboutir à rien, finir en queue de poisson; (*b*) **to l. u. somewhere,** aboutir quelque part; aboutir à qch.; (*c*) **to l. u. in a bar,** atterrir finalement dans un bar.

language [ˈlæŋgwidʒ] (*noun*), *F:* **to speak s.o.'s l.,** parler la même langue, être sur la même longueur d'ondes.

lantern [ˈlæntən] (*noun*), *F:* **idiot's l.** = **goggle-box;** *cf.* **box**¹, **2; idiot-box.**

lap [læp] (*noun*), *F:* **1.** **to lay sth. in s.o.'s l.,** coller qch. sur le dos de qn; **it fell right into his l.,** ça lui est tombé tout rôti. **2.** **in the l. of luxury,** en plein luxe, au sein de l'abondance. *Voir aussi* **cat-lap.**

lap it up [ˈlæpitˈʌp] (**to**), *F:* **1.** gober, avaler qch., boire du petit lait. **2.** boire* beaucoup, picoler, biberonner.

lark [lɑːk] (*noun*), *F:* **1.** **talk about a l.!** quelle rigolade! quelle bonne blague! **2.** **he did it for a l.,** il l'a fait pour rigoler (*ou* histoire de rigoler); *cf.* **skylark (to).**

lark about [ˈlɑːkəˈbaut] (**to**), *F:* folichonner, rigoler, faire le pitre.

larrikin [ˈlærikin] (*noun*) (*Austr.*), *F:* gavroche *m*, gamin *m* des rues; petit voyou.

larrup [ˈlærəp] (**to**), *F:* **1.** battre*, frapper, rosser. **2.** battre (un adversaire) à plate(s) couture(s).

larruping [ˈlærəpiŋ] (*noun*), *F:* (*a*) volée *f* de coups*, rossée *f*, raclée *f*, roulée *f*; (*b*) victoire *f* facile (*ou* les doigts dans le nez).

larry up [ˈlæriˈʌp] (**to**), *P:* blesser*, amocher, abîmer* (qch.).

lash [læʃ] (*noun*) (*Austr.*), *F:* **to have a l. at sth.,** tenter sa chance, tenter le coup.

lashings [ˈlæʃiŋz] (*pl. noun*), *F:* une abondance* de..., des tas *m.pl.* de...; **l. of sauce,** une tapée de sauce.

lash out [ˈlæʃˈaut] (**to**), *F:* **1.** lâcher un coup*, décocher des coups*. **2.** dépenser, larguer son fric; **I lashed out on a new coat,** je me suis lancée dans la dépense: j'ai acheté un manteau neuf. **3.** invectiver, se déchaîner.

lash-up [ˈlæʃʌp] (*noun*), *P:* (*a*) expédient *m*, échappatoire *f*, moyen *m* de fortune; (*b*) réunion *f* intime (*ou* à la bonne franquette).

last [lɑːst] (*adj.*), *F:* **the l. word,** le dernier cri; **the l. word in socks,** des chaussettes dernier cri. *Voir aussi* **leg**¹, **9; straw, 1, 2.**

last-ditch [ˈlɑːstˈditʃ] (*adj.*), *F:* **a l.-d. effort,** un dernier effort, un baroud d'honneur.

latch on [ˈlætʃˈɔn] (**to**), *F:* comprendre, piger, entraver.

latch onto (*or* **on to**) [ˈlætʃˈɔntuː] (**to**), *F:* obtenir, agrafer, mettre le grappin sur (qch.).

latest [ˈleitist] (*noun*), *F:* **to be up on the l.,** être à la page, être au courant, être dans le vent.

lather¹ [ˈlɑːðər] (*noun*), *F:* **to work oneself (up) into a l.,** (*a*) se mettre en colère*, fulminer, sortir de ses gonds; (*b*) s'inquiéter, se faire du mauvais sang.

lather² [ˈlɑːðər] (**to**), *F:* battre*, rosser, tabasser.

laugh¹ [lɑːf] (*noun*), *F:* **1.** **that's a l.!** quelle blague! c'est marrant! **2.** **to do sth. for laughs,** faire qch. pour rigoler (*ou* à la rigolade). *Voir aussi* **belly-laugh**¹.

laugh² [lɑːf] (**to**), *F:* **1.** **don't make me l.!** ne me fais pas rire* (*ou* marrer)! **2.** **to l. on the other side of one's face,** rire jaune; **I soon made him l. on the other side of his face,** je lui ai bientôt fait passer son envie de rire*. **3.** **to be laughing,** se la couler douce, vivre pépère; **if you win the pools you'll be laughing,** si vous gagnez à la loterie vous aurez le filon (*ou* les poches bien garnies). **4.** **to l. to oneself,** rire* aux anges. *Voir aussi* **belly-laugh**² **(to); drain**¹, **2.**

launching-pad [ˈlɔːntʃiŋpæd] (*noun*), *P:* = **shooting-gallery.**

lav [læv] (*noun*) (*abbr.* = *lavatory*), *F:*

* An asterisk indicates that the word so marked is included as a head-word in the Appendix.

W.C.*, cabinets *m.pl.*, cabinces *f.pl.*; **to go to the l.**, aller aux vécés *m.pl.*

lavatorial [ˈlævəˈtɔːriəl] (*adj.*), *F:* ordurier, cochon.

law, Law [lɔː] (*noun*), *F:* **the l.**, (*a*) la police*, la rousse; (*b*) policier*, flic *m*; **I'll have the l. on you,** je vais vous poursuivre en justice.

lay[1] [lei] (*noun*). **1.** *P:* **to have a l.**, coïter*, coucher avec une femme, fourailler. **2.** *P:* femelle *f*, fendue *f*; **an easy l.**, une môme facile, une cavaleuse, une tombeuse, une baiseuse. **3.** *P:* projet *m*, ligne *f* de conduite, résolution *f*. **4.** *P:* besogne délictueuse, bis(e)ness *m*, turbin *m*. **5.** *F:* pari *m*, mise *f*. **6.** *F:* **to get the l. of the land,** tâter le terrain, se rencarder sur qch.

lay[2] [lei] (**to**), *P:* **1. to l. a woman,** coïter* avec une femme, coucher avec une femme, sch(e)nailler une femme. **2. to l. one on s.o.**, battre* qn, flanquer une taloche à qn. **3. to l. for s.o.**, attendre qn au tournant.

lay down [ˈleiˈdaʊn] (**to**), *P:* **1.** (=*lie down*) se coucher*, s'étendre. **2.** renvoyer (qn) avec détention provisoire.

lay-in [ˈleiˈin] (*noun*), *F:* = **lie-in.**

lay into [ˈleiˈintuː] (**to**), *F:* (*a*) attaquer*, agrafer, serrer (qn); (*b*) critiquer*, éreinter (qn).

lay off [ˈleiˈɔf] (**to**). **1.** *P:* lâcher, larguer, plaquer (qn). **2.** *P:* **l. o., will you?** laisse tomber! c'est marre! écrase! **3.** *F:* **to l. a ball o. to s.o.**, (*football*) faire une passe à qn. **4.** *P:* **to l. o. s.o.**, (*a*) ficher (*ou* foutre) la paix à qn; (*b*) congédier*, bouler, virer qn. **5.** (*Austr.*) *P:* **to l. o. with a woman** = **to lay a woman (lay[2] (to), 1).**

lay on [ˈleiˈɔn] (**to**), *F:* **1. to l. it o. thick** (*or* **with a shovel** *or* **with a trowel**), (*a*) flatter*, passer la pommade, casser le nez à coups d'encensoir; (*b*) exagérer*, y aller fort, charrier, broder, forcer la dose. **2.** arranger, préparer, amarrer, arnaquer; **it's all laid on,** tout est bien branché.

layout [ˈleiaʊt] (*noun*), *P:* **1. to be sick of the whole l.**, en avoir assez* (de tout le fourbi), en avoir ras le bol. **2.** = **fit[2], 5.**

lay out [ˈleiˈaʊt] (**to**), *F:* **1.** assommer, étendre (qn) sur le carreau. **2. to l. oneself o. (to do sth.)**, se mettre en quatre, se démener, se décarcasser (pour faire qch.).

lay up [ˈleiˈʌp] (**to**), *F:* se la couler douce, se prélasser. *Voir aussi* **laid up.**

lazybones [ˈleizibounz] (*noun*), *F:* paresseux*, cossard *m*.

lead[1] [led] (*noun*). **1.** *F:* **to fill s.o. with l., to pump s.o. full of l.**, fusiller, flinguer, truffer qn, transformer qn en passoire; *cf.* **lead-poisoning. 2.** *F:* **to swing the l.**, tirer au flanc (*ou* au cul); *cf.* **lead-swinger. 3. to have l. in one's pencil,** (*a*) *P:* être en érection*, avoir la canne (*ou* le bambou); (*b*) *P:* être prêt à ouvrir l'allumage (*coïter**); (*c*) *F:* avoir de l'allant, péter le feu. **4.** *P:* (*a*) **to get the l. out of one's arse** (*U.S.:* **ass**) (*or* **pants**), se dépêcher*, se magner (le derrière), se démerder; (*b*) **to have l. in one's arse** (*U.S.:* **ass**) (*or* **pants**), paresser*, tirer au cul.

lead[2] [liːd] (*noun*), *F:* (*a*) **to have a l. on sth.**, avoir des renseignements* sur qch., avoir un tuyau (*ou* un rencart); (*b*) **to have a l. on s.o.**, avoir barre (*ou* le pas) sur qn.

lead-off [ˈliːdɔf] (*noun*), *F:* démarrage *m*, point *m* de départ.

lead off [ˈliːdˈɔf] (**to**), *F:* **to l. o. at s.o.**, passer un abattage à qn, redresser qn.

lead-poisoning [ˈled-pɔizniŋ] (*noun*), *F:* **to have l.-p.**, être fusillé, être farci (*ou* bourré) de plomb; *cf.* **lead[1], 1.**

lead-swinger [ˈled-swiŋər] (*noun*), *F:* paresseux*, tire-au-flanc *m*; *cf.* **lead[1], 2.**

league [liːg] (*noun*), *F:* **not to be in the same l. as s.o.**, ne pas être dans la même catégorie, ne pas arriver à la cheville de qn.

leak[1] [liːk] (*noun*). **1.** *P:* **to go for a l.**, (*U.S.*) **to spring a l.**, uriner*, lansquiner, égoutter son cyclope (*ou* sa sardine). **2.** (*a*) *P:* donneur *m*, macaron *m*, passoire *f*; (*b*) *F:* fuite *f* (de secrets, nouvelles, *etc.*), divulgation *f*, macaronage *m*.

leak[2] [liːk] (**to**), *F:* divulguer, laisser filtrer (nouvelles, *etc.*); cabasser, faire du ragoût.

lean and lurch [ˈliːnənˈləːtʃ] (*noun*) (*R.S.* = *church*), *P:* église *f*.

lean on [ˈliːnɔn] (**to**), *F:* faire pression sur (qn), serrer la vis à (qn), passer (qn) à la casserole.

leap [liːp] (*noun*), *F:* **to take the big l.,**

* L'astérisque indique que le mot marqué de ce signe figure comme entrée dans le Répertoire.

se marier, se maquer, se mettre la corde au cou.

leaper [ˈliːpər] (*noun*), *P:* amphétamine *f* (*drogues**).

learn [ləːn] (**to**), *P:* **I'll l. you!** je t'apprendrai!

leary [ˈliəri] (*adj.*), *F:* = **leery.**

leather[1] [ˈleðər] (*noun*), *P:* **1. to put the l. in,** flanquer un coup de pied (à qn). **2.** voleur* à la tire (*ou* à la fourche); **to snatch l.,** voler* (*ou* piquer) un portefeuille à la tire. *Voir aussi* **hell, 11.**

leather[2] [ˈleðər] (**to**), *F:* battre*, carder le cuir à (qn), étriller.

leather-man [ˈleðəmæn] (*noun*), *P:* = **leather**[1]**, 2.**

leatherneck [ˈleðənek] (*noun*) (*U.S.*), *F:* fusilier marin, marsouin *m.*

lech[1] [letʃ] (*noun*), *P:* **1.** (=*lecher*) débauché *m*, paillard *m*, noceur *m.* **2.** (*a*) (=*lechery*) paillardise *f*, lubricité *f*; (*b*) = **yen**[1]**, 1.**

lech[2] [letʃ] (**to**), *P:* **to l. for s.o.,** en pincer pour qn, en mouiller pour qn.

leery [ˈliəri] (*adj.*), *F:* méfiant; **to be l. of s.o.,** se méfier de qn.

leftfooter [ˈleftˈfutər] (*noun*), *P:* catholique *mf.*

left-handed [ˈleftˈhændid] (*adj.*), *P:* homosexuel, emmanché.

leftover [ˈleftouvər] (*noun*), *F:* **1.** laissé(e) pour compte. **2.** (*pl.*) restes *m.pl.*, arlequins *m.pl.*, rogatons *m.pl.*

lefty [ˈlefti] (*noun*), *F:* gaucher *m.*

leg[1] [leg] (*noun*). **1.** *F:* **to show a l.,** se lever, sortir du lit. **2.** *F:* **l. show,** spectacle *m* avec de la fesse. **3.** *F:* **to shake a l.,** (*a*) danser*, gambiller; (*b*) se dépêcher*, se grouiller; (*c*) jouer des guibolles *f.pl.* **4.** *F:* **he hasn't a l. to stand on,** on lui a rivé son clou. **5.** *F:* **to pull s.o.'s l.,** faire marcher qn, mettre qn en boîte, monter un bateau à qn; *cf.* **leg-pull. 6.** *F:* **to have l. room,** être au large. **7.** *F:* **to give s.o. a l. up,** (*a*) faire la courte échelle à qn; (*b*) dépanner qn, donner un coup de main à qn. **8.** *F:* **to get (up) on one's hind legs,** se mettre debout. **9.** *F:* **to be on one's last legs,** (*a*) être très malade*, filer un mauvais coton, avoir un pied dans la tombe, battre de l'aile; (*b*) être très fatigué*, être à bout de course (*ou* au bout de son rouleau), tirer à sa fin, être crevé. **10.** *F:* **to have a l. up on s.o.,** avoir barre (*ou* le pas) sur qn. **11.** *F:* **to stretch one's legs,** se dérouiller (*ou* se dégourdir) les jambes. **12.** *P:* **middle** (*or* **third**) **l.,** pénis*, jambe *f* du milieu. **13.** *P:* **to get one's l. over,** (*pour un homme*) coïter*, enjamber. **14.** *F:* **legs eleven:** *voir* **bingo (11).** *Voir aussi* **donkey, 1; open**[2] **(to), 1; peg-leg; show**[1]**, 1.**

leg[2] [leg] (**to**), *F:* **1.** faire trébucher (qn). **2. to l. it,** marcher*, courir*, s'enfuir*, se cavaler, jouer des flûtes *f.pl.*

leggo! [ˈleˈgou] (*excl.*) (=*let go!*), *F:* lâche (tout)!

legit [leˈdʒit] (*adj.*) (=*legitimate*), *F:* vrai, authentique; **on the l.,** officiel, légal.

legman [ˈlegmæn] (*noun*), *F:* **1.** reporter *m*, envoyé spécial. **2.** celui qui travaille activement, turbineur *m*; *cf.* **legwork.**

leg-pull [ˈlegpul] (*noun*), *F:* blague *f*, mise *f* en boîte; *cf.* **leg**[1]**, 5.**

legwork [ˈlegwəːk] (*noun*), *F:* travail* actif, turbin *m*; *cf.* **legman, 2.**

lemon [ˈlemən] (*noun*). **1.** *F:* **the answer's a l.,** rien à faire! des clous! bernique! **2.** *F:* **to feel a (right) l.,** se sentir un peu bête*, être comme deux ronds de flan. **3.** *P:* femme* laide, tartignole *f*, mocheté *f*, remède *m* d'amour. **4.** *P:* coup monté, doublage *m*, fumisterie *f.* **5.** *P:* **to squeeze the l.,** uriner*, ouvrir les écluses *f.pl.*

length [leŋ(k)θ] (*noun*), *P:* **1. to go one's l.,** chercher des embêtements *m.pl.*; **you're going your l.!** tu le cherches! **2. to give** (*or* **slip**) **(a woman) a l.,** coïter* avec une femme, filer un coup (d'arbalète *ou* de patte) (à une femme). *Voir aussi* **wavelength.**

lergi [ˈləːdʒi] (*noun*) (=*allergy*), *P:* allergie *f.*

les[1] [lez] (*adj.*) (=*lesbian*), *P:* lesbienne, qui aime (*ou* tape) l'ail.

les[2] [lez] (*noun*) (=*lesbian*), *P:* lesbienne*, gougnote *f*, goudou *f.*

lesbie [ˈlezbi], **lesbo** [ˈlezbou] (*noun*), *P:* = **les**[2]**; they're a couple of lesbies, lesbos,** c'est deux marchandes d'ail.

let [let] (**to**), *P:* **to l. one** = **let (one) off (to).**

letch [letʃ] (*noun & verb*), *P:* = **lech.**

let-down [ˈletdaun] (*noun*), *F:* déception *f*, déboire *m.*

let down [ˈletˈdaun] (**to**), *F:* **1.** décevoir (qn), laisser (qn) en panne, faire faux

* An asterisk indicates that the word so marked is included as a head-word in the Appendix.

bond à (qn). **2. to l. s.o. d. gently** (*or* **lightly**), contrecarrer qn avec ménagement.

let in on [ˈletˈinɔn] (**to**), *F:* **to l. s.o. i. o. sth.**, mettre qn dans le coup (*ou* au parfum).

let off [ˈletˈɔf] (**to**), *P:* **to l. (one) o.**, péter*, en lâcher un, en écraser un. *Voir aussi* **steam, 1.**

let on [ˈletˈɔn] (**to**), *F:* **1. to l. o. (about sth.) to s.o.**, mettre qn au courant (*ou* à la page); **don't l. o.!** bouche cousue! **2.** prétendre, frimer, chiquer.

let-out [ˈletaut] (*noun*), *F:* (*a*) porte *f* de sortie; (*b*) alibi *m*, parapluie *m*.

lettuce [ˈletis] (*noun*), *P:* argent*, galette *f*; billets*, faf(f)iots *m.pl.*; *cf.* **cabbage; kale.**

letty [ˈleti] (*noun*), *P:* lit*, plumard *m*.

let-up [ˈletʌp] (*noun*), *F:* **with no l.-u.**, sans cesse (*ou* pause *ou* relâche), sans débrider.

let up [ˈletˈʌp] (**to**). **1.** *F:* cesser, diminuer, relâcher, ralentir. **2.** *P:* **to l. u. on s.o.**, ficher (*ou* foutre) la paix à qn.

level¹ [ˈlevəl] (*adj.*), *F:* **to do one's l. best**, faire de son mieux, en mettre un bon coup, mettre le paquet. *Voir aussi* **pegging.**

level² [ˈlevəl] (*noun*), *F:* **on the l.**, honnête, régulier, réglo.

level³ [ˈlevəl] (**to**), *F:* **to l. with s.o.**, (*a*) parler franchement, vider son sac; (*b*) rendre la pareille, garder un chien de sa chienne.

lez [lez], **lezo** [ˈlezou] (*noun*), *P:* = **les².**

lick¹ [lik] (*noun*). **1.** *F:* démarrage *m*, coup *m* de vitesse (*ou* de collier). **2.** *P:* coup*, torgnole *f*, raclée *f*. **3.** *F:* **a l. and a promise**, un bout (*ou* brin) de toilette, une toilette de chat; *cf.* **cat-lick. 4.** *F:* **to get a l. at sth.**, tenter de faire qch., tâter de qch., se faire la main à qch. *Voir aussi* **dumb-lick.**

lick² [lik] (**to**), *F:* **1.** (*a*) venir à bout de (qch.), vaincre, enfoncer, maîtriser, écraser (un problème, une difficulté, *etc.*); (*b*) **to l. s.o. = to give s.o. a licking**, (*a*), (*b*); (*c*) **if you can't l. them** (*or* **'em**) **join them** (*or* **'em**), *c.p.*, si tu ne peux pas les mettre pattes en l'air, serre-leur la pince. **2. to l. sth. into shape**, finir un travail, boucler une affaire; **to l. s.o. into shape**, former qn, dégrossir qn. **3. to l. one's chops**, (*a*) faire des gorges chaudes de qn; (*b*) s'en lécher (*ou* pourlécher) les babouines *f.pl.* *Voir aussi* **arse-lick (to); boot, 10; dust¹, 5; pants, 6.**

licketysplit [ˈlikətiˈsplit] (*adv.*) (*U.S.*), *F:* très vite*, à plein gaz, à fond de train.

licking [ˈlikiŋ] (*noun*), *F:* **to give s.o. a l.**, (*a*) donner une volée de coups* (*ou* une rossée *ou* une raclée) à qn; (*b*) vaincre, écraser, griller qn. *Voir aussi* **arse-licking.**

lid [lid] (*noun*). **1.** *F:* chapeau*, galurin *m*, casquette*, bâche *f*; **to dip one's l.**, soulever son bibi. **2.** *F:* **to take** (*or* **blow**) **the l. off sth.**, faire éclater (*ou* exposer) un scandale. **3.** *F:* **to put the l. on sth.**, interdire qch., mettre le holà à qch.; **that puts the l. on it!** c'est le comble! **4.** *P:* deux grammes de marijuana. **5.** *F:* capote *f* (d'une voiture). *Voir aussi* **dustbin; flip³ (to), 2; skid-lid; tin¹, 1, 2.**

lid-popper [ˈlidpɔpər] (*noun*), *P:* amphétamine *f* (*drogues**).

lie-in [ˈlaiˈin] (*noun*), *F:* **to have a l.-i.**, faire la grasse matinée.

life [laif] (*noun*), *F:* **1. for the l. of me I can't remember**, j'ai beau chercher à me souvenir, je n'y arrive pas. **2. to worry the l. out of s.o.**, tourmenter, asticoter qn. **3. he turned up the next day as large as l.**, il reparut le lendemain comme si de rien n'était; **as large as l. and twice as natural**, dans toute sa beauté, grandeur nature. **4. to see l.**, rouler sa bosse, en voir des vertes et des pas mûres. **5. not on your l.!** pas de danger! rien à faire! **6. to get l.**, être condamné* à perpétuité, être gerbé à perpète. **7. to get another l.**, repartir à zéro, avoir une autre possibilité. **8.** (*a*) **l. begins:** *voir* **bingo (40)**; (*b*) **l.'s begun:** *voir* **bingo (41)**. *Voir aussi* **dog¹, 25; Riley; sweet¹, 2.**

lifemanship [ˈlaifmənʃip] (*noun*), *F:* l'art *m* de se montrer supérieur aux autres, l'art de se faire mousser.

lifer [ˈlaifər] (*noun*), *F:* (*a*) prisonnier *m* à perpétuité, enchetibé *m* à perpète (*ou* à perte de vue); (*b*) gerbement *m* à perpète.

lifesaver [ˈlaif-seivər] (*noun*), *F:* planche *f* de salut.

*** L'astérisque indique que le mot marqué de ce signe figure comme entrée dans le Répertoire.**

lift[1] [lift] (*noun*), *F:* **to give s.o. a l.,** (*a*) faire monter qn (en voiture) avec soi, épargner à qn une partie de la route; (*b*) remonter le moral à qn; **l. pill,** amphétamine *f* (*drogues**). *Voir aussi* **face-lift.**

lift[2] [lift] (**to**), *F:* **1.** voler*, chiper, faucher. **2.** plagier, démarquer. **3.** augmenter, hausser. *Voir aussi* **elbow, 6.**

lifter [ˈliftər] (*noun*), *F:* voleur*, faucheur *m. Voir aussi* **shirt-lifter.**

light[1] [lait] (*adj.*), *F:* **to be sth. l.,** (*a*) avoir qch. qui manque; (*b*) être à court d'argent*.

light[2] [lait] (*noun*). **1.** *F:* (*a*) **to be out like a l.,** (i) être ivre*, être éteint (*ou* cuit); (ii) dormir*, en écraser, être occis; (*b*) **to go out like a l.,** s'évanouir*, tomber dans les pommes (*ou* dans le cirage); **... and then the lights went out,** ...et puis je me suis évanoui* (*ou* j'ai tourné de l'œil). **2.** (*pl.*) *P:* yeux (*œil**), lanternes *f.pl.*, quinquets *m.pl.* **3.** *F:* **the l.,** compréhension *f*, comprenette *f*; **to see the l.,** comprendre, entraver, piger. **4.** *F:* **to see the red l. (flashing),** flairer le danger. *Voir aussi* **green**[1], **3; headlights; red-light; strike (to), 1; tosh-light.**

light-footed [ˈlaitˈfutid] (*adj.*), *P:* homosexuel, chochotte, chouquette.

light into [ˈlaitˈintuː] (**to**), *F:* **to l. i. s.o.,** (*a*) attaquer* qn, tomber (à bras raccourcis) sur qn, agrafer qn; (*b*) réprimander* qn sévèrement, enguirlander, engueuler qn.

lightweight [ˈlait-weit] (*noun*), *F:* individu* qui ne fait pas le poids, un minus.

like[1] [laik] (*adv.*), *F:* **1.** comme qui dirait; **you're one of the family, l.,** vous êtes comme qui dirait de la famille. **2. very l., (as) l. as not, l. enough,** probablement, vraisemblablement.

like[2] [laik] (*conj.*), *F:* **1.** (=*as if*) **he treated me l. I was dirt,** il m'a traité comme si j'étais de la crotte; **seems l. it works,** on dirait que ça marche. **2.** (=*as*) **l. I said,** comme je l'ai (si bien) dit; **I can't knit l. mother does,** je ne sais pas tricoter comme le fait maman.

like[3] [laik] (*noun*), *F:* **the likes of us,** des gens comme nous, nos semblables.

like[4] [laik] (**to**), *F:* **(well,) I l. that!** elle est bien bonne, celle-là! en voilà une bonne! par exemple!

likely [ˈlaikli] (*adj.*), *F:* **1. a l. lad,** un joyeux gaillard, un gars qui promet. **2. as l. as not,** vraisemblablement, il y a beaucoup de chance (que...). **3. not l.!** pas de danger! jamais de la vie!; *voir aussi* **bloody**[2].

lily [ˈlili] (*noun*) (*U.S.*), *P:* pédéraste*, tapette *f*.

lily-livered [ˈlililivəd] (*adj.*), *F:* = **yellow-bellied.**

lily-white [ˈliliwait] (*adj.*), *F:* = **snow-white; she's not so l.-w.!** ce n'est pas un prix de vertu!

limb [lim] (*noun*), *F:* **out on a l.,** en plan, sur la corde raide, le bec dans l'eau.

limey [ˈlaimi] (*noun*), *P:* **1.** Anglais *m*, Angliche *m*. **2.** matelot *m* britannique (*ou* engliche).

limit [ˈlimit] (*noun*). **1.** *F:* **that's the l.!** c'est le comble! c'est le bouquet!; **she's the l.!** elle est marrante (*ou* impayable)! **2. to go the l.,** (*a*) *F:* y aller à fond, mettre le paquet; (*b*) *P:* (*d'une femme*) coïter*, lever la jambe. **3.** *F:* **the sky's the l.,** vers monts et merveilles!

limy [ˈlaimi] (*noun*), *P:* = **limey, 1, 2.**

line [lain] (*noun*), *F:* **1. what's your l. (of business)?** quel est votre genre d'affaires? quelle est votre partie?; **that's not in my l., that's not my l. (of country),** ce n'est pas mon rayon (*ou* mon blot); **that's more in his l.,** c'est plus dans son genre (*ou* dans ses cordes); **a rice pudding or something in that l.,** du riz au lait ou quelque chose dans ce genre-là. **2.** (*a*) **to get a l. on sth.,** reconnaître*, retapisser, reconnobler qch.; (*b*) **to get a l. on s.o.,** se renseigner* sur qn, se rencarder sur qn. **3. to win all along the l.,** gagner sur toute la ligne. **4. to toe the l.,** rentrer dans les rangs, marcher au pas. **5. to read between the lines,** lire entre les lignes. **6. to put it on the l.,** dire en toutes lettres, ne pas mâcher les mots. **7. to be in l.,** se conformer (aux idées, *etc.*); **to be out of l.,** être rebelle. **8. to come to the end of the l.,** mourir*, lâcher la rampe. *Voir aussi* **drop**[2] **(to), 8; hard**[1], **3; headlines; main-line**[1];

* An asterisk indicates that the word so marked is included as a head-word in the Appendix.

pipeline; punch-line; shoot[2] (to), 5; sweet[1], 3; top-line.

linen [ˈlinin] (*noun*). **1.** *F:* **to wash one's dirty l. in public,** laver son linge sale en public. **2.** *P:* **l. draper** (*R.S.* = *newspaper*), journal*.

line-shooter [ˈlainʃuːtər] (*noun*), *F:* vantard*, esbrouf(f)eur *m*, baratineur *m*, rambineur *m*; *cf.* **shoot[2] (to), 5.**

line-shooting [ˈlainʃuːtiŋ] (*noun*), *F:* rambin *m*, esbrouf(f)e *f*, baratin *m*; *cf.* **shoot[2] (to), 5.**

lingo [ˈliŋgou] (*noun*). **1.** *F:* langue étrangère, baragouin *m*. **2.** *P:* argot*; **to shoot** (*or* **sling**) **the l.,** parler l'argot*, dévider (*ou* bagouler *ou* rouler) le jars.

lip [lip] (*noun*). **1.** *P:* effronterie *f*; **don't give me** (*or* **I don't want**) **any of your l.!** ne te fiche pas de moi! ne te paye pas ma tête! ne la ramène pas! **2.** *F:* **to keep a stiff upper l.,** ne pas broncher, garder son courage et faire contre mauvaise fortune bon cœur, serrer les dents. *Voir aussi* **flip[3] (to), 6.**

lippy [ˈlipi] (*adj.*), *P:* **1.** effronté, culotté. **2.** bavard*, bavasseur, jacasseur.

liquidate [ˈlikwideit] (**to**), *F:* tuer*, liquider, effacer.

liquored up [ˈlikədˈʌp] (*p.p.* & *adj.*), *F:* ivre*, qui a pris une bit(t)ure (*ou* une cuite).

listed [ˈlistid] (*adj.*), *P:* aliéné.

lit [lit] (*p.p.* & *adj.*), *F:* = **lit up.**

literally [ˈlitərəli] (*adv.*), *F:* absolument; **l. speaking,** à proprement parler.

litter-bug [ˈlitəbʌg], **litter-lout** [ˈlitəlaut] (*noun*), *F:* qn qui fait des ordures *f.pl.*, ordurier *m*.

little [ˈlitl] (*adj.*), *F:* **1. l. go,** (*a*) examen *m* propédeutique à l'Université de Cambridge; (*b*) (*U.S.*) banalité *f*, trivialité *f*. **2. the l. woman,** mon épouse*, ma moitié.

lit up [ˈlitˈʌp] (*p.p.* & *adj.*), *F:* (*a*) légèrement ivre*, éméché; **well l. u.,** ivre*, noir; (*b*) drogué*, camé, bourré.

live it up [ˈlivitˈʌp] (**to**), *F:* faire la noce, faire bombance.

lively [ˈlaivli] (*adj.*), *F:* **look l. (about it)!** et que ça saute!

liver [ˈlivər] (*noun*), *F:* **to have a l.,** (*a*) être malade* du foie; (*b*) être de mauvaise humeur (*ou* d'humeur massacrante), être en rogne.

liverish [ˈlivəriʃ] (*adj.*), *F:* qui a le foie dérangé; **to feel l.,** se sentir mal en train (*ou* détraqué).

livid [ˈlivid] (*adj.*), *F:* blême de colère*, à cran.

lizard [ˈlizəd] (*noun*) (*U.S.*), *P:* pénis*, frétillard *m*; **to stroke the l.,** se masturber*, s'astiquer.

lizzie [ˈlizi] (*noun*). *F:* **1.** (**tin**) **l.,** vieille voiture*, tinette *f*. **2.** *P:* pédéraste*, tantouse *f*.

load [loud] (*noun*). **1.** *P:* **get a l. of that!** écoutez ça! regardez* ça! vise! **2.** *P:* **a l. of baloney** (*or* **balls** *or* **cobblers** *or* **cock** *or* **codswallop** *or* **crap**), un tissu d'âneries *f.pl.*, un tas de foutaises *f.pl.*; *cf.* **muck, 2; swill[1], 3. 3.** *P:* **to drop one's l.,** déféquer*, lâcher un colombin. **4.** *P:* stock illégal de drogues, charge *f*. **5.** *F:* **loads of...,** une abondance* de..., une bardée (*ou* une flopée) de... **6.** *F:* **take the l. off your feet!** asseyez-vous! pose tes fesses! **7.** *F:* **he's a l. of wind,** il parle pour ne rien dire. **8.** *P:* sperme*, jus *m*; **to shoot one's l.,** éjaculer*, lancer son jus. *Voir aussi* **cartload; tie on (to).**

loaded [ˈloudid] (*adj.*). **1.** *P:* riche*, plein aux as; **to be l.,** être à l'as, avoir du foin dans ses bottes. **2.** *P:* ivre* *ou* drogué, chargé, bourré. **3.** *F:* (*d'un discours, d'une entreprise*) explosif.

loaf [louf] (*noun*) (*R.S.* = *loaf of bread* = *head*), *F:* tête*, caboche *f*; **use your l.!** fais travailler tes méninges!

lob[1] [lɔb] (*noun*), *P:* **1.** pénis*, zob *m*. **2.** oreille*, pavillon *m*. **3.** paye *f*, gages *m.pl.*; **gash l.,** économies *f.pl.*, care *f*, bas *m* de laine. **4.** (*U.S.*) gourde *f*, andouille *f*. **5.** tiroir-caisse *m*.

lob[2] [lɔb] (**to**), *P:* **1.** jeter, envoyer dinguer; **l. it over!** balance-moi ça! **2.** (*Austr.*) **to l. somewhere,** arriver*, s'abouler quelque part; **to l. back,** revenir, rabouler, radiner.

local [ˈloukəl] (*noun*), *F:* café* de quartier, bistrot *m* du coin.

lock-up [ˈlɔkʌp] (*noun*), *F:* prison*, violon *m*, taule *f*.

lock up [ˈlɔkˈʌp] (**to**), *F:* emprisonner*, mettre au violon.

loco [ˈloukou] (*adj.*), *F:* fou*, maboul, dingo.

lofty [ˈlɔfti] (*noun*), *F:* **1.** individu* grand, une grande perche. **2.** (*iron.*) petit* individu, un astèque.

* L'astérisque indique que le mot marqué de ce signe figure comme entrée dans le Répertoire.

lollie [ˈlɔli] (*noun*), *F:* = **lolly, 5.**

lollipop-man, -lady [ˈlɔlipɔpˈmæn, -ˈleidi] (*nouns*), *F:* contractuel(le) qui fait traverser la rue aux enfants.

lollop [ˈlɔləp] (**to**), *F:* **1.** marcher* lourdement, se traîner. **2.** sauter, rebondir, faire des sauts de carpe. **3.** paresser*, flânocher.

lolly [ˈlɔli] (*noun*). **1.** *F:* argent*, flouze *m*; **lay off the l.!** (ne) touchez pas au grisbi! **2.** *P:* agent* de police, flic *m*, cogne *m*. **3.** (*Austr.*) *P:* un timide, un tiède, un frileux. **4.** (*Austr.*) *P:* = **alec, 2. 5.** *F:* (=*lollipop*) sucette *f*; **ice(d) l.,** sucette glacée.

loner [ˈlounər] (*noun*), *F:* homme qui fait bande à part (*ou* qui fait cavalier seul).

lonesome [ˈlounsəm] (*noun*), *F:* **(all) on one's l.,** tout seulabre; *cf.* **ownsome.**

long¹ [lɔŋ] (*adj.*), *F:* **to be l. on sth.,** avoir des masses *f.pl.* de qch., déborder de qch. *Voir aussi* **draw² (to), 5; shot², 5; tooth, 2; vac.**

long² [lɔŋ] (*noun*), *F:* **1. the l. and short of it is . . .,** le fin mot de l'histoire c'est que... **2. the L.,** (*écoles*) les grandes vacances.

long-hair¹ [ˈlɔŋhεər] (*adj.*), *F:* = **long-haired.**

long-hair² [ˈlɔŋhεər] (*noun*), *F:* intellectuel *m*, grosse tête, ponte *m*.

long-haired [ˈlɔŋhεəd] (*adj.*), *F:* intellectuel, calé.

long-tailed [ˈlɔŋteild] (*adj.*), *P:* **l.-t. 'uns,** billets* de banque.

loo [luː] (*noun*), *F:* W.C.*, ouatères *m.pl.*; **l. paper = bumf, 1.**

look¹ [luk] (*noun*), *F:* **to take a long, hard l. at sth.,** examiner qch. sur toutes les coutures.

look² [luk] (**to**), *F:* **1. to l. like a million dollars,** être très élégant*, être très chic. **2. here's looking at you!** à la tienne! à la bonne vôtre! **3. l. here!** dis donc! *Voir aussi* **nose, 7.**

looker [ˈlukər] (*noun*), *F:* **a (good) l.,** une beauté, un prix de Diane, un joli lot.

look-in [ˈlukˈin] (*noun*), *F:* **1.** belle occasion, beau jeu. **2.** chances *f.pl.* de succès; **he won't get a l.-i.,** il n'a pas la moindre chance. **3.** coup *m* d'œil rapide. **4.** visite-éclair *f*.

look-out [ˈlukaut] (*noun*), *F:* **1.** guetteur *m*, vigie *f*, gaffe *m*, gaffeur *m*. **2. that's your l.-o.!** c'est ton affaire! c'est tes oignons!

look-see [ˈlukˈsiː] (*noun*), *F:* coup *m* d'œil*, coup de sabord.

look up [ˈlukˈʌp] (**to**), *F:* **business is looking up,** les affaires reprennent; **things are looking up with him,** ses affaires s'améliorent.

looloo [ˈluːluː] (*noun*), *F:* = **lulu.**

loony [ˈluːni] (*noun & adj.*), *F:* fou*, tapé (*m*), cinglé (*m*), dingue (*m*).

loony-bin [ˈluːnibin] (*noun*), *P:* maison *f* de fous, cabanon *m*, asile *m* de dingues; **to be fit for the l.-b.,** être bon (*ou* mûr) pour Sainte-Anne.

looped [luːpt] (*adj.*), *P:* ivre*, plein, rond; **l. to the eyeballs,** plein comme une bourrique.

loop-the-loop [ˈluːpðəˈluːp] (*noun*) (*R.S.* = *soup*), *P:* soupe *f*, rata *m*.

loopy [ˈluːpi] (*adj.*), *F:* fou*, dingo, tapé, cinglé, maboul.

loose [luːs] (*noun*), *F:* **to be (out) on the l.,** (*a*) être déchaîné, faire les quatre cents coups; (*b*) être en bordée, mener une vie de bâtons de chaise.

loosen up [ˈluːsənˈʌp] (**to**), *F:* se détendre, se relaxer.

loot [luːt] (*noun*), *P:* (*a*) argent*, artiche *m*, flouse *m*; (*b*) bénéfice* financier, gratte *f*, gratouille *f*.

lorry-hop [ˈlɔrihɔp] (**to**), *F:* faire de l'auto-stop *m* (dans les camions).

lose [luːz] (**to**). **1.** *P:* **get lost!** va te faire fiche (*ou* foutre)! va te faire voir! au bout du quai les ballots! **2.** *F:* **you've lost me!** je n'y suis plus, j'ai perdu le fil.

lose out [ˈluːzˈaut] (**to**), *F:* perdre, paumer.

lotties [ˈlɔtiz] (*pl. noun*), *P:* seins*, boîtes *f.pl.* à lolo, nénés *m.pl.*

loud [laud] (*adv.*), *F:* **for crying out l.!** (sacré) nom d'un chien! nom de nom!

loudmouth [ˈlaudmauθ] (*noun*), *F:* gueulard *m*, va-de-la-gueule *m*.

loudmouthed [ˈlaudmauðd] (*adj.*), *F:* gueulard, fort en gueule.

louse [laus] (*noun*), *F:* vaurien*, saligaud *m*, salope *f*.

louse around [ˈlausəˈraund] (**to**), *P:* traîner, traînasser, lambiner.

louse up [ˈlausˈʌp] (**to**), *P:* bousiller, gâcher, saloper, louper.

lousy [ˈlauzi] (*adj.*). **1.** *F:* mauvais*,

* An asterisk indicates that the word so marked is included as a head-word in the Appendix.

moche; miteux, pouilleux; **a l. trick,** un tour de cochon, une vacherie. **2.** *P:* **l. with . . .,** plein de...; **the place was l. with cops,** ça grouillait de flics.

love [lʌv] (*noun*), *F:* **hello, l.!** salut!; **thanks, l.!** merci mon pote! *Voir aussi* **bug[1], 9; puppy, 2; smother-love.**

lovebird [ˈlʌvbəːd] (*noun*), *F:* amoureux *m*, amoureuse *f*, soupirant(e) *m(f)*.

love-in [ˈlʌvin] (*noun*), *F:* festival *m* hippie.

lovely[1] [ˈlʌvli] (*adj.*), *F:* **1. it's been (just) l. seeing you again,** ça a été charmant de vous revoir. **2. she's l.:** *voir* **bingo (16).**

lovely[2] [ˈlʌvli] (*noun*), *F:* belle* fille*, une vénus.

lover-boy [ˈlʌvəbɔi] (*noun*), *F:* **1.** beau* gars, un Adonis, un Apollon, un jeune premier. **2.** un don Juan, coureur *m* de jupons, cavaleur *m*.

love-up [ˈlʌvʌp] (*noun*), *P:* caresses *f.pl.* intimes, papouilles *f.pl.*

love up [ˈlʌvˈʌp] (**to**), *P:* caresser (qn) en palpant, peloter (qn).

love-weed [ˈlʌvwiːd] (*noun*), *P:* marijuana *f* (*drogues**), herbe douce.

lovey [ˈlʌvi] (*noun*), *F:* chéri(e), petit chou.

lovey-dovey [ˈlʌviˈdʌvi] (*adj.*), *F:* **1.** affectueux, amoureux, sentimental. **2.** à la guimauve, à l'eau de rose.

lowbrow[1] [ˈlou-brau] (*adj.*), *F:* (*a*) sans prétentions intellectuelles, terre à terre; (*b*) faubourien, populo.

lowbrow[2] [ˈlou-brau] (*noun*), *F:* (*a*) prolétaire *m*, prolo *m*, inculte *mf*, simplet *m*; (*b*) qn qui ne s'intéresse pas aux choses intellectuelles, individu* peu relevé.

lowdown[1] [ˈlouˈdaun] (*adj.*), *F:* méprisable, moche, dégueulasse.

lowdown[2] [ˈloudaun] (*noun*). **1.** *F:* (*a*) renseignements* privés; tuyau *m*, rencart *m*; (*b*) renseignements* généraux, pleins tubes. **2.** *P:* tour *m* de cochon, coup fourré, sale coup.

lube [luːb] (*noun*), *P:* huile *f* de graissage.

lubricate [ˈluːbrikeit] (**to**), *F:* **1.** graisser la patte à (qn). **2.** enivrer, soûler (qn).

luck [lʌk] (*noun*), *F:* **you never know your l.,** on ne sait jamais ce qui vous pend au nez. *Voir aussi* **push[2] (to), 2; pot-luck.**

lucre [ˈluːkər] (*noun*), *F:* argent*, lucre *m*; bénéfice*, bénef *m*; **filthy l.,** (*a*) gain *m*, gratte *f*; (*b*) argent*, carbure *m*; **to do sth. for filthy l.,** faire qch. par amour du lucre.

lucy [ˈluːsi] (*noun*), *P:* **sweet l.,** marijuana *f* (*drogues**), herbe *f*, kif *m*.

lug[1] [lʌg] (*noun*), *P:* **1.** (*a*) oreille*, esgourde *f*; *cf.* **lugholes;** (*b*) visage*; menton *m*; gueule *f*; (*c*) (*pl.*) (*U.S.*) mains*, paluches *f.pl.* **2.** (*a*) homme*, mec *m*; (*b*) ballot *m*, baluchard *m*. **3.** (*U.S.*) (*a*) demande *f* d'argent*, botte *f*; (*b*) dessous-de-table *m*, gratte *f*, tour *m* de bâton.

lug[2] [lʌg] (**to**) (*Austr.*), *P:* **to l. s.o. for money,** emprunter* de l'argent à qn, taper qn, bottiner qn.

lughead [ˈlʌghed] (*noun*), *P:* individu bête*, ballot *m*, cruche *f*.

lugholes [ˈlʌg(h)oulz] (*pl. noun*), *P:* oreilles*; **pin back your l.!** dessable tes portugaises! écarquille tes esgourdes!; *cf.* **lug[1], 1** (*a*).

lulu [ˈluːluː] (*noun*), *F:* (*a*) as *m*, vedette *f*; (*b*) fille* bath, môme formid(able); (*c*) qch. de sensas(s) (*ou* de super).

lumber [ˈlʌmbər] (**to**). **1.** *P:* arrêter*, agrafer, épingler; **to get lumbered,** se faire agrafer (*ou* épingler). **2.** *F:* **to get lumbered with s.o., sth.,** être chargé (*ou* encombré) de qn, de qch.

lumme! [ˈlʌmi] (*excl.*), *F:* mon Dieu! mince alors!

lummox [ˈlʌməks] (*noun*) (*U.S.*), *P:* individu bête*, cornichon *m*, niguedouille *m*.

lummy! [ˈlʌmi] (*excl.*), *F:* = **lumme!**

lump[1] [lʌmp] (*noun*), *F:* **1.** personne bête*, crétin *m*, cruche *f*. **2. a big l. of a girl,** une grosse dondon, une godiche.

lump[2] [lʌmp] (**to**), *F:* **1.** porter, trimbal(l)er. **2. like it or l. it,** que ça plaise ou non, c'est le même prix; **you'll have to l. it,** il faudra l'avaler, il faut passer par là.

lunch [lʌntʃ] (*noun*), *P:* **to be out to l.,** se mettre le doigt dans l'œil. *Voir aussi* **box[1], 1.**

lunkhead [ˈlʌŋkhed] (*noun*), *P:* = **lughead.**

lush[1] [lʌʃ] (*adj.*), *F:* chouette, badour; **she's a l. piece,** elle est bath (*ou* juteuse).

lush[2] [lʌʃ] (*noun*) (*U.S.*), *F:* **1.** ivrogne*, poivrot *m*, soûlard *m*. **2.** soûlerie *f*, bringue *f*. **3.** alcool*, gnôle *f*.

* L'astérisque indique que le mot marqué de ce signe figure comme entrée dans le Répertoire.

lush[3] [lʌʃ] (**to**) (*U.S.*), *F:* boire* de l'alcool*, biberonner, siffler.
lush-hound [ˈlʌʃhaʊnd] (*noun*) (*U.S.*), *F:* = **lush**[2], **1.**
lush-roller [ˈlʌʃroulər] (*noun*) (*U.S.*), *P:* voleur* d'ivrognes, poivrier *m.*
lush-rolling [ˈlʌʃrouliŋ] (*noun*) (*U.S.*), *P:* vol *m* au poivrier.
lush up [ˈlʌʃˈʌp] (**to**) (*U.S.*), *F:* soûler, charger, bourrer.
luv [lʌv] (*noun*), *F:* = **love.**

* An asterisk indicates that the word so marked is included as a head-word in the Appendix.

M

M [em] (*abbr.*), *P:* (*a*) morphine *f* (*drogues**), morph *f*; (*b*) marijuana *f* (*drogues**), Maria *f*, Marie *f*.

ma [mɑː] (*noun*), *F:* mère*, maman.

Mac[1] [mæk] (*noun*). **1.** *F:* Écossais *m*. **2.** *P:* = **mack**[1], **3**.

mac[2] [mæk] (*noun*) (*abbr.* = *mackintosh*), *F:* imper(méable) *m*; **the dirty m. brigade,** individus qui vont voir des films, *etc.*, orduriers; pornos *m.pl.*

macaroni [mækəˈrouni] (*noun*), *P:* Italien *m*, macaroni *m*, Rital *m*.

mace [meis] (**to**), *P:* obtenir qch. pour rien, faire de la resquille.

machine [məˈʃiːn] (*noun*), *P:* seringue *f* hypodermique, poussette *f*, shooteuse *f*.

machinery [məˈʃiːnəri] (*noun*), *P:* attirail *m* de camé.

mack[1] [mæk] (*noun*). **1.** *F:* = **mac**[2]. **2.** *P:* souteneur*, maquereau *m*, mac *m*. **3.** *P:* mec *m*, zigoto *m*.

mack[2] [mæk] (**to**), *P:* rabattre le client (pour une prostituée*), maquereauter.

Mackay [məˈkai] (*noun*), *F:* **the real M.,** (*a*) boisson *f* de bonne qualité; de la vraie (de vraie); (*b*) tout à fait ce qui convient; de l'authentique; (*c*) marchandise *f* irréprochable.

mackerel [ˈmækərəl] (*noun*), *P:* = **mack**[1], **2.** *Voir aussi* **holy, 1.**

macking [ˈmækiŋ] (*noun*), *P:* maquereautage *m*.

mackman [ˈmækmən] (*noun*), *P:* = **mack**[1], **2.**

mad[1] [mæd] (*adj.*), *F:* **1.** en colère*; **to be m. at s.o.,** être à cran contre qn. **2. to be m. about s.o., sth.,** raffoler de qn, de qch. **3. like m.,** (*a*) comme un enragé, comme un perdu; (*b*) très vite*; **to run like m.,** foncer, gazer. *Voir aussi* **man-mad; sex-mad; woman-mad.**

mad[2] [mæd] (*adv.*), *F:* **m. keen on sth., s.o.,** emballé par (*ou* entiché de) qch., qn.

madam[1] [ˈmædəm] (*noun*). **1.** *P:* **it's a load of old m.,** c'est de la foutaise; *cf.* **load, 2. 2.** *P:* **don't come the old m. with me!** ne monte pas sur tes grands chevaux! ne la ramène pas! **3.** *F:* patronne* (de maison de tolérance), madame, taulière *f*, maquerelle *f*.

madam[2] [ˈmædəm] (**to**), *P:* **1.** mentir*, bourrer le crâne. **2.** = **to tell the tale** (**tale, 1**).

madame [mæˈdɑːm] (*noun*) (*pl.* **madames** [mæˈdɑːmz]), *F:* = **madam**[1], **3.**

made [meid] (*p.p.*): *voir* **make** (**to**).

madhouse [ˈmædhaus] (*noun*), *F:* maison *f* de fous, Charenton; **this place is like a m.,** on se croirait à Charenton, chez les fous.

mag [mæg] (*abbr.*), *F:* **1.** (=*magazine*) magazine *m*, revue *f*. **2.** (=*magneto*) magnéto *f*.

main-line[1] [ˈmeinˈlain] (*noun*), *P:* veine apparente (pour piqûre intraveineuse).

main-line[2] [ˈmeinˈlain] (**to**), *P:* se piquer, se piquouser.

main-liner [ˈmeinˈlainər] (*noun*), *P:* drogué* qui se fait des piqûres intraveineuses, piquouseur *m*.

make[1] [meik] (*noun*). **1.** *P:* **easy m.,** femme* facile (*ou* à la cuisse hospitalière); *cf.* **lay**[1], **2. 2. on the m.,** (*a*) *F:* âpre au gain, chercheur d'affure; (*b*) *P:* en quête d'aventures amoureuses, dragueur. **3.** *P:* **to get a m. on** (**a criminal,** *etc.*), identifier, détrancher, tapisser (un criminel, *etc.*). **4.** *P:* fade *m*, bouquet *m*, taf *m*.

make[2] [meik] (**to**). **1.** (*a*) *F:* **to m. it,** réussir, gagner le cocotier, l'avoir belle; (*b*) *P:* **to m. (it with) a woman,** avoir les faveurs *f.pl.* d'une femme*, lever une fille*. **2.** *F:* **he's as sharp as they m. 'em,** c'est un malin s'il en est. **3.** *F:* gagner*; **how much do you m.?** qu'est-ce que tu gagnes comme pèze? **4.** *P:* voler*, faire, fabriquer (qch.). **5.** *P:* = **to get a m. on** (**make**[1], **3**). **6.** *P:* comprendre, piger, entraver (qn, qch.). **7.** *F:* arriver* à, débarquer à (un endroit). **8.** *F:* **do you**

* L'astérisque indique que le mot marqué de ce signe figure comme entrée dans le Répertoire.

want to m. sth. (out) of it? veux-tu chercher noise (*ou* du grabuge)? veux-tu en faire toute une histoire? **9.** *F:* **to have it made,** se la couler douce, avoir le filon. **10.** *F:* **I just made my train,** j'ai eu mon train mais au poil. *Voir aussi* **daft**[1], **1; side, 1.**

make out [ˈmeikˈaut] (**to**). **1.** *F:* prospérer, faire des progrès; aller, marcher (bien *ou* mal); **how do your children m.o. at school?** comment vos enfants se débrouillent-ils à l'école? **2.** *F:* subsister; **I can m. o. on bread and water,** je peux vivre de pain et d'eau. **3.** *F:* faire semblant. **4.** *P:* s'étreindre, s'enlacer passionnément.

make up [ˈmeikˈʌp] (**to**), *F:* **1.** inventer (une histoire, *etc.*). **2. to m. it u.,** se rabibocher.

malark(e)y [məˈlɑːki] (*noun*), *F:* **1.** flatteries *f.pl.*, boniment *m.* **2.** balivernes *f.pl.*

mammie, mammy [ˈmæmi] (*noun*) (*U.S.*), *F:* **1.** mère*, maman. **2.** nourrice *f*, nounou noire. **3. m. boy,** homme faible, femmelette *f*, chiffe molle.

man [mæn] (*noun*). **1.** *F:* **why, m., you're crazy!** mais mon pauvre vieux, tu es fou*! **2.** *F:* **come here, young m.!** viens ici, mon petit bonhomme!; **good m.!** bravo! **3.** *F:* **he's a big m.,** c'est quelqu'un; *cf.* **big**[1], **1. 4.** *F:* **her m.,** son mari, son homme. **5.** *F:* **my young m.,** (*a*) mon bon ami; (*b*) mon futur, mon promis, mon fiancé. **6.** *P:* **the m., the M.,** (*a*) la police*, ces Messieurs *m.pl.*; (*b*) fourgueur *m* (de drogues); **to make the m.,** acheter des drogues, brancher; (*c*) patron*, dab *m*, chef *m*. *Voir aussi* **ad-man; arse-man; boss-man; busman; cave-man; chive-man; dead**[1], **2, 9; dog**[1], **20; dustman; G-man; he-man; ice-man; kickman; k-man; leather-man; legman; lollipop-man; mackman; media-man; middleman; muscle-man; old, 1; one-man; penman; peterman; prop-man; rod-man; sandman; screws-man; showman; sideman; snowman; spiderman; swagman; swordsman; tail-man; trigger-man; yes-man.**

manage [ˈmænidʒ] (**to**), *F:* **can you m. a few more cherries?** peux-tu manger encore quelques cerises?

man-crazy [ˈmænˈkreizi] (*adj.*), *F:* nymphomane; *cf.* **woman-crazy.**

manhole [ˈmænhoul] (*noun*), *V:* vulve*, fente *f*, con(n)asse *f*.

man-mad [ˈmænˈmæd] (*adj.*), *F:* = **man-crazy;** *cf.* **woman-mad.**

manor [ˈmænər] (*noun*), *P:* (*a*) territoire *m*, champ *m* d'action (d'un criminel); (*b*) secteur couvert par un commissariat de police; *cf.* **patch, 2; morguey m.,** quartier farci (*ou* pourri) de flics. *Voir aussi* **mystery.**

man-size(d) [ˈmænsaiz(d)] (*adj.*), *F:* (*a*) gros*, de taille; (*b*) costaud, maousse; **a m.-s. meal,** un repas copieux (*ou* abondant *ou* solide).

map [mæp] (*noun*). **1.** *F:* **to put on the m.,** populariser, mettre en vedette. **2.** *F:* **off the m.,** inaccessible, au diable vauvert. **3.** (*Austr.*) *P:* **to throw a m.,** vomir*, aller au refil(e). **4.** *P:* visage*, boule *f*, bobine *f*. **5.** (*U.S.*) *P:* chèque *m*.

maracas [məˈrækəz] (*pl. noun*), *P:* seins*, ropoplots *m.pl.*, rotoplots *m.pl.*

marbles [ˈmɑːblz] (*pl. noun*), *P:* **1. to pass in one's m.,** mourir*, passer l'arme à gauche. **2. go and play m.!** va te faire cuire un œuf! **3. to lose one's m.,** devenir fou*, perdre le nord, perdre la boule, déménager. **4.** testicules*, billes *f.pl.*

marching [ˈmɑːtʃiŋ] (*noun*), *F:* **to give s.o. his m. orders,** se débarrasser* de qn, flanquer qn à la porte.

mare [mɛər] (*noun*), *P:* femme* méprisable, carne *f*, vache *f*.

marge [mɑːdʒ] (*noun*). **1.** *F:* (=*margarine*) margarine *f*. **2.** *P:* lesbienne*, goudou *f*.

Marine [məˈriːn] (*noun*), *F:* **tell that to the Marines!** à d'autres! allez conter ça ailleurs! *Voir aussi* **dead**[1], **2.**

marjie [ˈmɑːdʒi], **marjorie** [ˈmɑːdʒəri] (*noun*), *P:* marijuana *f* (*drogues**), kif *m*, Marie-Jeanne *f*; *cf.* **juana.**

mark[1] [mɑːk] (*noun*), *F:* **to feel up to the m.,** être en train, être en pleine forme; **I don't feel up to the m.,** je ne suis pas dans mon assiette. *Voir aussi* **easy**[1], **3; tide-mark.**

mark[2] [mɑːk] (**to**), *P:* **1. to m. s.o.'s card,** mettre qn sur ses gardes, faire ouvrir l'œil à qn. **2.** chercher *ou* trouver un cave (*ou* un bon casse).

marker [ˈmɑːkər] (*noun*), *P:* reconnaissance *f* de dette.

mark up [ˈmɑːkˈʌp] (**to**), *F:* donner un

* An asterisk indicates that the word so marked is included as a head-word in the Appendix.

bon point pour (qch.); **to m. it u. to s.o.,** mettre (qch.) au crédit de qn.

marm [mɑːm] (*noun*), *F:* madame; *cf.* **schoolmarm.**

marriage [ˈmæridʒ] (*attrib. adj.*), *P:* **m. gear** (*or* **prospects**), testicules*, bijoux *m.pl.* de famille.

marrow-bones [ˈmæroubounz, ˈmærəbounz] (*pl. noun*), *P:* genoux *m.pl.*, coussinets *m.pl.*

marshmallows [ˈmɑːʃˈmælouz] (*pl. noun*), *P:* **1.** seins*. **2.** testicules*.

marvellous [ˈmɑːv(ə)ləs] (*adj.*), *F:* excellent*, super; **isn't it m.!** (*iron.*), voilà bien le bouquet!

Mary, mary [ˈmɛəri] (*noun*). **1.** *P:* pédéraste* (qui joue le rôle de femme), persilleuse *f.* **2.** *P:* lesbienne*, gouine *f.* **3.** *P:* = **Mary-Ann(e).** **4.** *F:* **bloody M.,** cocktail *m* de vodka et jus de tomate.

Mary Ann(e) [ˈmɛəriˈæn], **Mary-Jane** [ˈmɛəriˈdʒein], **Mary Warner** [ˈmɛəriˈwɔːnər] (*pr. nouns*), *P:* (*a*) marijuana *f* (*drogues**), Marie-Jeanne; (*b*) cigarette* de marijuana, juju *f*, joint *m.*

masher [ˈmæʃər] (*noun*), *F:* **1.** gigolo *m*, gommeux *m*, coco-bel-œil *m.* **2.** (*pl.*) dents*, croquantes *f.pl.*

mat [mæt] (*noun*), *F:* **on the m.** = **on the carpet** (**carpet**[1], **2**). *Voir aussi* **doormat; welcome-mat.**

mate [meit] (*noun*), *F:* **1.** ami*, copain *m*, pote *m.* **2.** mec *m*, zigoto *m*; **that's too bad, m.!** tant pis pour toi, vieux frère!

matey[1] [ˈmeiti] (*adj.*), *F:* **to be m.,** être à tu et à toi, copiner.

matey[2] [ˈmeiti] (*noun*), *F:* = **mate, 1, 2.**

mateyness [ˈmeitinis] (*noun*), *F:* copinage *m.*

matlo(w) [ˈmætlou] (*noun*), *F:* marin*, matelot *m.*

maverick[1] [ˈmævərik] (*adj.*) (*U.S.*), *F:* indépendant, n'appartenant à aucun parti, réfractaire, hors série.

maverick[2] [ˈmævərik] (*noun*) (*U.S.*), *F:* homme politique indépendant, franc-tireur *m.*

maxi [ˈmæksi] (*adj. & noun*), *F:* (manteau, jupe, *etc.*) maxi (*m*); lèche-trottoir *m*; *cf.* **midi; mini.**

maybe [ˈmeibiː] (*adv.*), *F:* **... and I don't mean m.!** ...et je ne plaisante (*ou* rigole) pas!

mazuma [məˈzuːmə] (*noun*), *P:* argent*, pognon *m*, fric *m.*

McCoy [məˈkɔi] (*pr. noun*), *F:* = **Mackay.**

meal-ticket [ˈmiːl-tikit] (*noun*), *F:* gagne-pain *m*, vache *f* à lait.

mealy-mouthed [ˈmiːliˈmauðd] (*adj.*), *F:* mielleux, benoît.

mean [miːn] (*adj.*). **1.** *F:* **m. weather,** mauvais (*ou* sale) temps; **m. job,** travail* désagréable, fichu boulot. **2.** *P:* formid(able), du tonnerre.

meanie, meany [ˈmiːniː] (*noun*), *F:* grigou *m*, rapiat *m*, minable *m.*

measly [ˈmiːzli] (*adj.*), *F:* **1.** misérable, insignifiant. **2.** avare*, constipé du crapaud, radin, pingre.

meat [miːt] (*noun*). **1.** *F:* fond *m*, moelle *f*, substance *f.* **2.** *P:* **to love one's m.,** être porté sur l'article *m* (*ou* sur la chose). **3.** *V:* pénis*; **small m.,** un petit pénis*, petit bout; **to beat the m.** = **to beat the dummy** (**dummy, 5**). **4.** *P:* (*a*) mâle (considéré sexuellement); (*b*) jouissance *f* (d'un pédéraste*), nanan *m.* **5.** *F:* **to make cold m. of s.o.,** tuer* qn, refroidir qn. *Voir aussi* **easy**[1], **5; mincemeat; pig-meat; plate**[1], **2.**

meathead [ˈmiːthed] (*noun*), *P:* individu bête*, saucisse *f*, gourde *f.*

meat-hooks [ˈmiːthuks] (*pl. noun*), *P:* grandes mains*, battoirs *m.pl.*, croches *f.pl.*; *cf.* **hook**[1], **6.**

meat-house [ˈmiːthaus] (*noun*), *P:* bordel*, maison *f* d'abattage.

meat-show [ˈmiːtʃou] (*noun*), *P:* spectacle *m* du nu, parade *f* de fesses.

meat-wag(g)on [ˈmiːt-wægən] (*noun*), *P:* **1.** ambulance *f.* **2.** corbillard*, roulotte *f* à refroidis, trottinette *f* à macchabs. **3.** car* de police, panier *m* à salade.

mebbe [ˈmebi] (*adv.*), *P:* (=*maybe*) ça se peut, des fois.

medals [ˈmed(ə)lz] (*pl. noun*), *F:* **your m. are showing,** ta braguette est ouverte; n'expose pas tes bijoux.

media-man [ˈmiːdiəmæn] (*noun*), *F:* agent *m* publicitaire.

medic(o) [ˈmedik(ou)] (*noun*), *F:* **1.** médecin *m*, toubib *m.* **2.** étudiant *m* en médecine, carabin *m.*

meemies [ˈmiːmiz] (*pl. noun*) (*U.S.*), *P:* **the screaming m.** = **the screaming abdabs** (*voir* **abdabs**).

meet [miːt] (*noun*), *P:* **1.** = **gig**[1], **5.** **2.** rendez-vous*, rancart *m.* **3. to make**

* L'astérisque indique que le mot marqué de ce signe figure comme entrée dans le Répertoire.

a m. = to make the man (**man, 6** (*b*)).

mental ['ment(ə)l] (*adj.*), *F:* **to go m.,** devenir fou*; **you must be m.!** t'es pas fou* (*ou* dingue *ou* maboul)?

merchant ['mə:tʃənt] (*noun*), *F:* individu*, type *m*, mec *m*. *Voir aussi* **chive-merchant; speed-merchant.**

merry ['meri] (*adj.*), *F:* légèrement ivre*, pompette, éméché. *Voir aussi* **hell, 3.**

mess [mes] (*noun*). **1.** *P:* andouille *f*, gourdichon *m*, tourte *f*. **2.** *F:* **isn't she a m.!** ce qu'elle est tarte! **3.** *F:* **what a m.!** quel gâchis! quelle pagaille! **4.** *F:* **to be in a** (**bit of a**) **m.,** être dans le pétrin (*ou* dans de mauvais draps); **to help s.o. out of a m.,** repêcher qn. **5.** *P:* **to make a m. of s.o.,** battre* qn, tabasser, amocher qn. **6.** *F:* **to make a m. of things** (**or it**), tout gâcher; **he always makes a m. of things,** il n'en rate pas une. *Voir aussi* **right, 1.**

mess about (*or* **around**) ['mesə'baut, 'mesə'raund] (**to**). **1.** *F:* patauger (dans la boue). **2.** *F:* traîner, bricoler, lambiner. **3.** *F:* **to m. s.o. a.,** tourmenter, turlupiner qn. **4.** *P:* **to m. a. with s.o.,** (*a*) peloter, pelotailler qn; (*b*) s'acoquiner avec qn.

message ['mesidʒ] (*noun*), *F:* **to get the m.,** comprendre, piger, entraver.

mess-up ['mesʌp] (*noun*), *F:* **1.** gâchis *m*, méli-mélo *m*, pagaille *f*. **2.** malentendu *m*, embrouillamini *m*, cafouillage *m*.

mess up ['mes'ʌp] (**to**), *F:* **1.** salir, bousiller, saloper. **2.** abîmer*, amocher, saboter; **he's messed his face up,** il s'est abîmé le portrait.

metal-spiv ['met(ə)l-spiv] (*noun*), *P:* marchand *m* (*ou* trafiquant *m*) en ferraille; *cf.* **spiv.**

meth [meθ] (*noun*) (*abbr.*). **1.** *P:* (=*methedrine*) méthédrine *f* (*drogues*), meth *f*. **2.** (*pl.*) *F:* (=*methylated spirits*) alcool *m* à brûler.

methhead ['meθhed] (*noun*), *P:* habitué *m* de la méthédrine.

mezz [mez] (*noun*) (*mainly U.S.*), *P:* cigarette* de marijuana (*drogues**), stick *m*.

miaow! [mi:'au, mjau] (*excl.*), *F:* oh (que) t'es rosse!

mick, Mick [mik] (*noun*), *P:* **1.** (*a*) Irlandais *m*; (*b*) qn d'origine irlandaise. **2. to take the m. = to take the mick(e)y** (**mick(e)y, 2**).

mick(e)y, Mick(e)y ['miki] (*noun*). **1.** *P:* = **mick, Mick, 1.** **2.** *F:* **to take the m. out of s.o.,** faire marcher qn, se payer la tête de qn; **stop taking the m.!** ne charrie pas! n'attige pas!; *cf.* **mick(e)y-taker.** **3.** *P:* pomme *f* de terre, patate *f*. **4.** *F:* **M.** (**Finn**), (*a*) boisson droguée; (*b*) casse-pattes *m*. **5.** *P:* **to do a m. = slope off** (**to**). *Voir aussi* **Mickey Mouse[2].**

Mickey Mouse[1] ['miki'maus] (*adj.*), *P:* **1.** camelote, inférieur. **2.** simple, facile, pas dif. **3.** routinier, train-train. **4.** louche, toc.

Mickey Mouse[2] ['miki'maus] (*noun*) (*R.S.* = *house*), *P:* maison *f*.

mick(e)y-taker ['miki-teikər] (*noun*), *F:* moqueur *m*, railleur *m*, lardeur *m*, gouailleur *m*; *cf.* **mick(e)y, 2.**

middleman ['midlmæn] (*noun*), *F:* = **carrier.**

middle-of-the-road ['midl-əvðəroud] (*adj.*), *F:* modéré; **the Party has a m.-o.-t.-r. policy,** le parti poursuit une politique modérée *ou* centriste.

middling ['midliŋ] (*adv.*), *F:* **fair to m.,** pas mal, couci-couça, entre les deux.

midi ['midi] (*adj. & noun*), *F:* (vêtement *m*, *etc.*) de longueur moyenne, midi (*m*); *cf.* **maxi; mini.**

miff[1] [mif] (*noun*), *F:* (*a*) mauvaise humeur, cran *m*, rogne *f*; (*b*) pique *f*, brouille *f*.

miff[2] [mif] (**to**), *F:* **1.** (*a*) offenser, vexer; (*b*) se draper dans sa dignité. **2.** rater, louper.

mighty ['maiti] (*adv.*), *F:* bigrement, bougrement, fichtrement, vachement; **it's m. cold,** il fait bougrement froid; **I'm m. glad to see you,** je suis vachement content de te voir. *Voir aussi* **high[1], 3.**

mike[1] [maik] (*noun*). **1.** *P:* = **mick, 1.** **2.** *F:* **to take the m. = to take the mick(e)y** (**mick(e)y, 2**). **3.** *F:* (=*microphone*) micro(phone) *m*. **4.** *P:* **to take a m. at sth.,** regarder* qch., lorgner qch. **5.** *P:* **to do a m. = slope off** (**to**). **6.** *P:* **to have a m. = mike[2]** (**to**). **7.** *P:* **M. Malone** (*R.S.* = *telephone*), téléphone*.

mike[2] [maik] (**to**), *P:* paresser*, se tourner les pouces, tirer sa cosse.

mile [mail] (*noun*), *F:* **1. you're a m.** (*or* **miles**) **out,** tu en es à mille lieues, tu n'y

* An asterisk indicates that the word so marked is included as a head-word in the Appendix.

es pas du tout; **you're miles too slow,** tu es mille fois trop lent. **2. I'd go a m.** (*or* **miles) for that,** je ferais des kilomètres pour cela. **3. a miss is as good as a m.,** but manqué, fût-ce de peu, n'est pas atteint. **4. to be miles away,** être ailleurs, rêvasser, décoller. **5. it sticks out a m.** = **it sticks out like a sore thumb (thumb, 4).**

milk [milk] **(to).** **1.** *F:* traire (qn, qch.). **2.** *V:* masturber*, allonger (qn).

milk-bottles [ˈmilkbɔtlz] (*pl. noun*), **milk-shop** [ˈmilkʃɔp] (*noun*), *P:* seins*, boîtes *f.pl.* à lolo.

milk-train [ˈmilk-trein] (*noun*), *F:* **to catch the m.-t.,** rentrer au petit matin.

milk-wag(g)on [ˈmilk-wægən] (*noun*), *P:* car* de police, panier *m* à salade.

milky [ˈmilki] (*adj.*), *F:* **to turn m.,** avoir peur*, avoir le trac (*ou* la trouille).

mill[1] [mil] (*noun*), *F:* **1.** bagarre*, empoignade *f*, rixe *f*. **2. to go through the m.,** en voir de toutes les couleurs, en baver; **to put s.o. through the m.,** faire passer qn par la filière. *Voir aussi* **run-of-the-mill.**

mill[2] [mil] **(to),** *F:* bourrer de coups*, tabasser.

milling [ˈmiliŋ] (*noun*), *F:* **to give s.o. a m.,** donner une raclée (*ou* une rossée) à qn.

million [ˈmiljən] (*numeral adj. & noun*), *F:* **1. thanks a m.!** merci mille fois! **2. to feel like a m. (dollars),** être au septième ciel, être aux nues.

miln [miln] **(to),** *P:* = **chubb in (to);** *cf.* **unchubb (to); unmiln (to).**

min [min] (*noun*), *P:* agent* de police, flic *m*.

mince (*noun*), *F:* **at a fast m.,** vite*, à toute barde.

mincemeat [ˈmins-miːt] (*noun*), *F:* **to make m. (out) of s.o.,** mettre qn en bouillie, mettre qn dans sa poche.

mince on [ˈminsˈɔn] **(to),** *P:* **to m. o., to go mincing on,** radoter, rabâcher.

mince-pies [ˈminsˈpaiz] (*pl. noun*) (*R.S. = eyes*), *P:* yeux (*œil**), mirettes *f.pl.*

mincers [ˈminsəz] (*pl. noun*), *P:* = **mince-pies.**

mind-bender [ˈmaindbendər] (*noun*), *P:* **1.** drogue *f* qui affine l'intelligence; euphorisant *m*. **2.** qn ou qch. qui élargit l'esprit et l'approfondit.

mind-blower [ˈmaindblouər] (*noun*), *P:* (*a*) expérience inaccoutumée; (*b*) choc soudain, coup *m* de massue; (*c*) drogue *f* hallucinogène extatique, bonbon *m* à kick.

minge [mindʒ] (*noun*), *V:* vulve*, barbu *m*; **m. fringe,** (*d'une femme*) poils *m.pl.* du pubis, paquet *m* de tabac.

mingy [ˈmindʒi] (*adj.*), *F:* = **measly, 1, 2.**

mini [ˈmini] (*adj. & noun*), *F:* (vêtement, *etc.*) très court, mini (*m*); rase-pet *m*; *cf.* **maxi, midi.**

minstrel [ˈminstrəl] (*noun*), *P:* **black and white** (*or* **nigger) m.,** amphétamine *f* (*drogues**), capsule *f* «Durophet», speed *m*.

mint [mint] (*noun*), *F:* **to cost a m. (of money),** coûter les yeux de la tête.

mintie, minty[1] [ˈminti] (*adj.*), *P:* homosexuel, tata, chochotte.

mintie, minty[2] [ˈminti] (*noun*), *P:* lesbienne* masculine et agressive.

mire [ˈmaiər] (*noun*), *F:* **to land** (*or* **drop) s.o. in the m.,** mettre qn dans la mouscaille (*ou* dans le pétrin).

mischief [ˈmis-tʃif] (*noun*), *F:* enfant* espiègle, petit diable.

mish-mash [ˈmiʃmæʃ] (*noun*), *F:* méli-mélo *m*.

miss [mis] (*noun*), *F:* **to give sth. a m.,** laisser passer qch., laisser courir qch.; sécher (un cours). *Voir aussi* **mile, 3.**

missis [ˈmisiz] (*noun*), *F:* **the** (*or* **my) m.,** mon épouse*, la bourgeoise; **I'll have to ask the m.,** faut demander à mon gouvernement.

miss out on [ˈmisˈautɔn] **(to),** *F:* manquer, louper, rater (qch.); **I missed out on my best chance,** j'ai raté ma meilleure occasion.

missus [ˈmisiz] (*noun*), *F:* = **missis.**

missy [ˈmisi] (*noun*), *F:* mademoiselle.

mistake [misˈteik] (*noun*), *F:* **. . . and no m.!** ...et tu peux en être sûr!, ...je t'en réponds.

mitt [mit] (*noun*), *P:* **1.** main*, patte *f*; **keep your mitts off!** (à) bas les pattes! **2.** gant *m* de boxe, mitaine bourrée. **3.** (*pl.*) menottes*, pinces *f.pl.* **4. to put one's mitts on sth.,** voler* qch., faire main basse sur qch.

mitten [ˈmitn] (*noun*), *F:* **to give s.o. the m.** = **to walk out on s.o. (walk out (to), 2).**

mitt-reader [ˈmit-riːdər] (*noun*), *P:* diseur *m* (diseuse *f*) de bonne aventure (*ou* de bonne ferte), chiromancien *m*, chiromancienne *f*.

* L'astérisque indique que le mot marqué de ce signe figure comme entrée dans le Répertoire.

mix [miks] (**to**), *F:* **to m. it with s.o.,** se battre* avec qn, se bagarrer, se tabasser.

mixer [ˈmiksər] (*noun*), *F:* **he's a good m.,** il est sociable, il se lie facilement, il a de l'entregent; **he's a bad m.,** c'est un ours, il est sauvage.

mix-up [ˈmiksʌp] (*noun*), *F:* **1.** confusion *f*, pagaille *f*. **2.** (*U.S.*) bagarre*, mêlée *f*.

miz(z) [miz] (*adj.*), *P:* malheureux, tout chose, cafardeux.

mizzers [ˈmizəz] (*pl. noun*), *P:* **to have the m.,** avoir le cafard (*ou* le bourdon), être dans le 36ème dessous.

mizzle [ˈmizl] (**to**), *P:* **1.** s'enfuir*, se cavaler, mettre les bouts. **2.** rouspéter, râler.

mizzler [ˈmizlər] (*noun*), *P:* geignard *m*, pleurnicheur *m*.

mo [mou] (*noun*) (=*moment*), *F:* **half a m.!** une seconde!; *cf.* **jiff(y); sec; shake**[1], **1, 2; tick**[1], **3.**

moan[1] [moun] (*noun*), *F:* **to have a (good) m. = moan**[2] **(to).**

moan[2] [moun] (**to**), *F:* grogner*, ronchonner, rouscailler.

moaner [ˈmounər] (*noun*), *F:* ronchonneur *m*, rouscailleur *m*, râleur *m*.

moaning [ˈmouniŋ] (*adj.*), *F:* **a m. Minnie,** une geignarde, une rouspéteuse.

mob [mɔb] (*noun*), *F:* bande* de criminels, flèche *f*, gang *m*, soce *f*; *voir aussi* **heavy**[1], **4; swell**[1], **3.**

mobile [ˈmoubail] (*adj.*), *F:* **to get m.,** (*a*) travailler* plus vite, se décarcasser, se démancher; (*b*) se dépêcher*, se magner, se grouiller.

mobster [ˈmɔbstər] (*noun*) (*U.S.*), *F:* homme* du milieu, dur *m*, truand *m*.

mockers [ˈmɔkəz] (*pl. noun*), *F:* **to put the m. on s.o., sth.,** jeter un sort sur qn, qch., enguignonner qn, qch.

mockie, mocky [ˈmɔki] (*noun*), *P:* (*péj.*) Juif *m*, Youpin *m*.

mod[1] [mɔd] (*adj.*), *F:* moderne.

mod[2] [mɔd] (*noun*), *F:* scootériste *m*, blouson noir; *cf.* **rocker, 1.**

mog [mɔg], **moggie, moggy** [ˈmɔgi] (*noun*), *F:* chat *m*, matou *m*, griffard *m*.

mojo [ˈmoudʒou] (*noun*), *P:* stupéfiant(s) *m* (*pl.*) (en poudre), stups *m.pl.* (*drogues**).

moke [mouk] (*noun*), *F:* âne *m*, bourricot *m*, martin *m*.

mola [ˈmoulə] (*noun*) (*U.S.*), *P:* pédéraste*, pédé *m*.

moll [mɔl] (*noun*). **1.** *P:* jeune femme*, gonzesse *f*, mousmé(e) *f*. **2.** *P:* prostituée*, catin *f*. **3.** *F:* la poule (*ou* la môme) d'un gangster.

molly-shop [ˈmɔli-ʃɔp] (*noun*), *P:* = **meat-house.**

Molotov cocktail [ˈmɔlɔtɔvˈkɔkteil] (*noun*), *F:* bouteille remplie d'essence servant de bombe, cocktail *m* molotov.

mom [mɔm] (*noun*) (*U.S.*), *F:* mère*, mam(an).

moments [ˈmouməntz] (*pl. noun*), *F:* **I've had my m.,** j'ai eu mes bons moments; j'ai fait mes entourloupettes *f.pl.*

Monday [ˈmʌndi] (*noun*), *F:* **that M. morning feeling = that Mondayish feeling.**

Mondayish[1] [ˈmʌndiiʃ] (*adj.*), *F:* **that M. feeling,** l'humeur *f* du lundi, l'après-week-end *m*.

Mondayish[2] [ˈmʌndiiʃ] (*adv.*), *F:* **to feel M.,** être dans les vapes du lundi, avoir le cafard du lundi.

money [ˈmʌni] (*noun*), *F:* **1. to be in the m.,** être riche*, rouler sur l'or, avoir le sac. **2. he's the man for my m.,** c'est juste l'homme qu'il me faut; il a tous mes suffrages. **3. to throw good m. after bad,** (*a*) jouer à quitte ou double; (*b*) remplir le tonneau des Danaïdes, lancer l'argent* par les fenêtres. **4. I'm not made of m.,** je ne suis pas cousu d'or, je ne roule pas sur l'or.

moneybags [ˈmʌnibægz] (*noun*), *F:* individu très riche*, rupin *m*, richard *m*.

moniker [ˈmɔnikər] (*noun*), *P:* nom*, blaze *m*, centre *m*.

monkey [ˈmʌŋki] (*noun*). **1.** *F:* **to get one's m. up,** se mettre en colère, prendre la mouche; **to get s.o.'s m. up,** mettre qn en colère (*ou* en rogne). **2.** *P:* billet (*ou* faf(f)iot *m*) de cinq cents livres, un gros talbin. **3.** *P:* **I don't give a m.'s!** je m'en fous et contrefous! **4.** *F:* **to make a m. (out) of s.o.,** se payer la tête de qn. **5.** *F:* **m. business,** (*a*) affaire peu sérieuse (*ou* peu loyale), fricotage *m*; (*b*) conduite *f* malhonnête, procédé irrégulier; (*c*) coup fourré, goupinage *m*; (*d*) fumisterie *f*. **6.** *F:* **to stand there like a stuffed m.,** rester là comme une souche. **7.** *F:* **right m.!** à bon entendeur

* An asterisk indicates that the word so marked is included as a head-word in the Appendix.

salut! 8. *P:* habitude *f* de la drogue, la guêpe, la guenon; **to get the m. off,** se désintoxiquer, chasser la guenon; **to have a m. on one's back,** (*a*) être drogué* (*ou* camé); (*b*) avoir une dent contre qn. 9. *F:* **m. jacket,** veste courte, spencer *m.* 10. *F:* **m. suit,** uniforme *m* de gala. *Voir aussi* **balls, 8; grease**[1], 2.

monkey about (*or* **around**) [ˈmʌŋkiəˈbaut, ˈmʌŋkiəˈraund] (**to**), *F:* **to m. a. with s.o., sth.,** tripoter, tripatouiller qn, qch.

monniker [ˈmɔnikər] (*noun*), *P:* = **moniker.**

monthlies [ˈmʌnθliz] (*pl. noun*), *F:* **the m.,** menstrues*, histoires (mensuelles).

moo [mu:] (*noun*), *P:* 1. **she's a (right old) m.,** c'est une belle vache; **silly (old) m.!** espèce de vieille bique! 2. = **moola(h).**

moocah [ˈmu:kɑ:, ˈmu:kə] (*noun*), *P:* marijuana *f* (*drogues**), Marie-Jeanne *f.*

mooch [mu:tʃ] (**to**), *P:* 1. mendier*, mendigoter. 2. voler*, chaparder. 3. flâner, traîner ses lattes *f.pl.* (*ou* ses patins *m.pl.*), baguenauder. 4. emprunter*, taper, sonner.

moocher [ˈmu:tʃər] (*noun*), *P:* 1. mendiant*, mendigot *m.* 2. voleur*, chapardeur *m.* 3. baguenaudeur *m,* traîne-patins *m.* 4. tapeur *m,* torpilleur *m.*

mooching [ˈmu:tʃiŋ] (*noun*), *P:* 1. mendicité*, mendiche *f.* 2. vol *m,* chaparderie *f.* 3. baguenaudage *m.* 4. tapage *m,* sonnage *m.*

moo-cow [ˈmu:-kau] (*noun*). 1. *F:* (*langage enfantin*) vache *f,* meu-meu *f.* 2. *P:* = **cow, 1.**

moody [ˈmu:di] (*noun*), *P:* flatterie *f,* boniment *m;* **cut out the m.!** assez de baratin! suffit les boniments!

moola(h) [ˈmu:lɑ:, ˈmu:lə] (*noun*), *P:* argent*, pognon *m,* fric *m.*

moon [mu:n] (*noun*). 1. *P:* **a m.,** un mois de prison, un marqué. 2. *F:* **over the m.,** au septième ciel, aux nues. *Voir aussi* **blue**[1], **3; shoot**[2] **(to), 9.**

moon about (*or* **around**) [ˈmu:nəˈbaut, ˈmu:nəˈraund] (**to**), *F:* lambiner, musarder, cueillir les pâquerettes.

moonlight [ˈmu:nlait] (**to**), *F:* faire le travail noir, cumuler.

moonlighter [ˈmu:nlaitər] (*noun*), *F:* cumulard *m;* **he's a m.,** il cumule.

moonshine [ˈmu:nʃain] (*noun*), *F:* 1. alcool* illicitement distillé (*ou* en contrebande), gnôle *f* sous les fagots. 2. bêtises*, fariboles *f.pl.*, balivernes *f.pl.*

moony [ˈmu:ni] (*adj.*), *P:* un peu fou*, toqué.

moosh [muʃ] (*noun*), *P:* = **mush**[2], **1, 2.**

mooters [ˈmu:təz] (*pl. noun*), *P:* = **muggles, 3.**

mop [mɔp] (*noun*), *F:* 1. **that's the way the m. flops,** c'est comme ça que tombent les dés (*ou* les bobs); c'est ainsi que la roue tourne; c'est comme ça et pas autrement; *cf.* **cookie, 1; onion, 1.** 2. tignasse *f,* tête *f* de loup.

moppy [ˈmɔpi] (*adj.*), *P:* ivre*, paf, dans le cirage.

mop up [ˈmɔpˈʌp] (**to**). 1. *F:* exterminer, nettoyer, liquider. 2. *P:* aplatir, rouler (qn).

more-ish [ˈmɔ:riʃ] (*adj.*), *F:* **these sweets are m.,** ces bonbons ont un goût de revenez-y.

morguey [ˈmɔ:gi] (*adj.*), *P: voir* **manor.**

mosey along [ˈmouziəˈlɔŋ] (**to**), *F:* aller son petit bonhomme de chemin, aller mollo.

mosey off [ˈmouziˈɔf] (**to**), *F:* s'enfuir*, décamper, les mettre, se barrer.

moss [mɔs] (*noun*), *P:* cheveux*, crins *m.pl.*, cresson *m.*

mostest [ˈmoustist] (*noun*), *F:* **the m.,** le super, l'archi(bien).

mota [ˈmoutɑ:, ˈmoutə] (*noun*), *P:* marijuana *f* (*drogues**) de haute qualité.

mote [mout] (**to**) (*Austr.*), *F:* filer à toute allure, brûler le pavé.

mother [ˈmʌðər] (*noun*). 1. *F:* **to be m.,** servir le thé. 2. *P:* **m.'s ruin** (*R.S.* = *gin*), genièvre *m,* gin *m.*

motherfucker [ˈmʌðəfʌkər] (*noun*) (*U.S.*), *VV:* 1. (belle) saloperie, (espèce de) con *m,* empaffé *m,* (tas de) fumier *m.* 2. (*terme vulgaire et familier employé entre hommes*) cucul *m* (la praline), connard *m* (à la crème).

motherfucking [ˈmʌðəfʌkiŋ] (*adj.*) (*U.S.*), *VV:* 1. charognard, pourri, saligaud, chiasseux. 2. emmerdant, canulant.

mother-in-law [ˈmʌðərinlɔ:] (*noun*), *F:* mélange *m* de *stout* (bière brune forte) et de *bitter* (bière amère); panaché *m* nègre.

motor-bike (*attrib. adj.*), *F:* **m.-b. boys** = **rockers (rocker, 1).**

moula [ˈmu:lɑ:, ˈmu:lə] (*noun*), *P:* = **moola(h).**

* L'astérisque indique que le mot marqué de ce signe figure comme entrée dans le Répertoire.

mouldy [ˈmouldi] (*adj.*), *F:* moche(ton), toc(ard), tarte, tartignol(l)e.

mount[1] [maʊnt] (*noun*), *P:* **to do a m.,** coïter*, grimper, bourrer une femme; *cf.* **mounties.**

mount[2] [maʊnt] (**to**), *P:* = **to do a mount.**

mountain [ˈmaʊntin] (*noun*), *F:* **1. to make a m. out of a molehill,** faire d'un œuf un bœuf, se noyer dans un verre d'eau. **2. a m. of a man,** un homme* fort (*ou* bien baraqué), une armoire à glace. **3. a m. of work,** un tas de travail*, un boulot du diable.

mounties [ˈmaʊntiz] (*pl. noun*), *P:* **to join the m.,** coïter*, pousser sa pointe; *cf.* **mount**[1,2].

mourning [ˈmɔːniŋ] (*noun*), *F:* **to have one's (finger-)nails in m.,** avoir les ongles sales (*ou* en deuil).

mouse [maʊs] (*noun*) (*pl.* **mice**), *F:* **1. are you a man or a m.?** *c.p.*, t'es un homme ou une bûche? t'en as ou t'en as pas? **2.** fille* *ou* jeune femme* piquante, gisquette *f*, gosseline *f*. *Voir aussi* **cat, 10; Mickey Mouse**[1,2]; **rat**[1], **11.**

mouth [maʊθ] (*noun*), *F:* **1. to have a big m.,** être une grande gueule; *cf.* **big**[1], **8; blow off (to), 2; loudmouth; shoot off (to), 2. 2. to be down in the m.,** avoir le cafard, être abattu (*ou* défrisé), être au 36ème dessous. *Voir aussi* **foul-mouth; horse**[1], **2.**

mouthful [ˈmaʊθful] (*noun*), *F:* **you've said a m.!** tu as parlé d'or! tu l'as dit bouffi!

mouth on [ˈmaʊðˈɔn] (**to**), *F:* discutailler, pinailler, titiller.

mouthpiece [ˈmaʊθpiːs] (*noun*). **1.** *F:* porte-parole *m*. **2.** *P:* avocat*, débarbot *m*, débarbotteur *m*.

move[1] [muːv] (*noun*), *F:* **1. to get a m. on,** se dépêcher*, se magner. **2. to be up to every m.,** la connaître dans les coins.

move[2] [muːv] (**to**), *P:* voler*, lever, piquer.

movie [ˈmuːvi] (*noun*) (*mainly U.S.*), *F:* film *m*; **the movies,** le cinéma; **to go to the movies,** aller au cinoche.

much [mʌtʃ] (*adv.*), *F:* **1. that's a bit m.!** (*a*) c'est un peu beaucoup*; (*b*) c'est le comble! c'est le bouquet! **2. m. of a muchness,** kif-kif, bonnet blanc et blanc bonnet, jus vert et verjus, du pareil au même.

muchly [ˈmʌtʃli] (*adv.*) (*emploi humoristique de* **much**), *F:* beaucoup*, bézef.

muck [mʌk] (*noun*), *P:* **1. to make a m. of sth.,** abîmer*, gâcher, bousiller qch.; *voir aussi* **right, 1. 2. it's a load of m.,** (*a*) c'est un tas de conneries; (*b*) c'est de la saleté* (*ou* de la cochonnerie). **3. to land (or drop) s.o. in the m.** = **to land s.o. in the mire** (*voir* **mire**). **4. common as m.** = **common as mud** (**mud 6** (*b*)). **5. dog m.,** crotte *f* de chien. **6.** confusion *f*, pagaille *f*. **7. Lord M.,** Monsieur J'en-fous-plein-la-vue. *Voir aussi* **high-muck-a-muck.**

muck about (*or* **around**) [ˈmʌkəˈbaʊt, ˈmʌkəˈraʊnd] (**to**). **1.** *F:* traîner, lambiner, bricoler. **2.** *F:* flâner, flânocher, traîner ses lattes. **3.** *F:* **to m. s.o. a.,** faire tourner qn en bourrique. **4.** *P:* **to m. a. with s.o.** = **to mess about with s.o.** (**mess about (to), 4** (*a*)).

mucker [ˈmʌkər] (*noun*), *P:* **1.** qn qui est sale* (*ou* crasseux). **2.** ami*, copain *m*, pote *m*, aminche *m*. **3.** (*U.S.*) rustre *m*, grossier personnage. **4.** chute *f*, culbute *f*, bûche *f*; **to come a m.,** tomber*, ramasser un billet de parterre.

muck in [ˈmʌkˈin] (**to**), *F:* **1. to m. i. with s.o.,** chambrer avec qn, faire gourbi ensemble. **2. to m. i. together,** (*a*) partager, fader, décarpiller; (*b*) s'actionner (*ou* s'escrimer *ou* se dépatouiller) ensemble.

muck-raker [ˈmʌk-reikər] (*noun*), *F:* (*journalisme*) fouille-merde *m*.

muck up [ˈmʌkˈʌp] (**to**), *F:* **1.** emberlificoter. **2.** abîmer*, gâcher, bousiller, cochonner.

mucky [ˈmʌki] (*adj.*), *F:* **1. a m. eater,** qn qui mange comme un cochon. **2. a m. pup,** un enfant qui fait des saletés *ou* qui se tient mal; un petit goret.

mud [mʌd] (*noun*). **1.** *F:* **here's m. in your eye!** à votre santé! à la bonne vôtre! **2.** *P:* (*drogues**) (*a*) opium brut; (*b*) opium, dross *m*, boue *f*; *voir aussi* **green**[1], **1. 3.** (*U.S.*) *P:* café* (*boisson*), jus *m* (de chaussette). **4.** (*U.S.*) *P:* pudding *m* au chocolat. **5.** (*U.S.*) *P:* signes télégraphiques brouillés, brouillage *m*. **6.** *F:* **common as m.,** (*a*) du tout-venant, chemin battu; (*b*) qui traîne partout (*ou* dans les ornières), qui sent le pavé. **7.** *F:* cancan *m*, déblatérage *m*, débinage *m*; **to throw**

* An asterisk indicates that the word so marked is included as a head-word in the Appendix.

(*or* **sling**) **m. at s.o.**, éclabousser qn, traîner qn dans la boue (*ou* dans la fange). **8.** *F:* **his name is m.**, sa réputation est moins que rien. *Voir aussi* **clear**[1]; **stick-in-the-mud**[1,2].

muddler [ˈmʌdlər] (*noun*), *F:* brouillon *m*, pagailleur *m*.

mudslinger [ˈmʌd-sliŋər] (*noun*), *F:* calomniateur *m*, médisant *m*, débineur *m*, casseur *m* de sucre.

mudslinging [ˈmʌd-sliŋiŋ] (*noun*), *F:* attaque calomnieuse, médisance *f*, bêche *f*.

muff[1] [mʌf] (*noun*). **1.** *F:* échec*, loupage *m*, coup raté. **2.** *V:* vulve*, barbu *m*, chatte *f*, chagatte *f*.

muff[2] [mʌf] (**to**). **1.** *F:* faire une erreur, commettre une faute, louper. **2.** *F:* bousiller, bâcler, rater, gâcher. **3.** *V:* exécuter un cunnilingus, faire minette; *cf.* **pearl-dive (to)**.

muff-diver [ˈmʌfdaivər] (*noun*), *V:* cunnilinguiste *mf*, buveur *m* de bénitier, lécheur *m* de minette; *cf.* **pearl-diver.**

mug[1] [mʌg] (*noun*). **1.** *P:* visage*, fiole *f*; **ugly m.**, gueule *f* d'empeigne; **m. and dabs**, photo et empreintes digitales; **to have one's m. and dabs taken**, passer au pied et au sommier. **2.** *F:* dupe *f*, cavé *m*, bonnard *m*; **mugs wanted**, on cherche des poires *f.pl.*; **to be a m.**, être poire; **to be the m.**, être le dindon de la farce; **mugs' tax**, impôt *m* sur le revenu, l'impôt des poires. *Voir aussi* **fly-mug; thunder-mug.**

mug[2] [mʌg] (**to**), *F:* attaquer* (les passants) à main armée, tabasser, voler*.

mugger [ˈmʌgər] (*noun*), *F:* **1.** voleur* à main armée, cogneur *m*. **2.** (*U.S.*) acteur *m* qui grimace pour faire rire; farineux *m*.

mugging [ˈmʌgiŋ] (*noun*), *F:* attaque *f* (de passants) à main armée.

muggins [ˈmʌginz] (*noun*), *P:* individu bête*, gourde *f*, cruche *f*.

muggles [ˈmʌglz] (*noun*), *P:* **1.** (*drogues**) (*a*) marijuana *f*; (*b*) cigarette* de marijuana, kif *m*. **2.** habitué(e) de la marijuana. **3.** hachisch *m* (*drogues**), merde *f*.

mug up [ˈmʌgˈʌp] (**to**), *F:* bûcher, piocher, potasser.

mularky [məˈlɑːki] (*noun*), *F:* = **malark(e)y.**

mulberry-bush [ˈmʌlbəribuʃ] (*noun*), *F:* **to go (all) round the m.-b.**, tourner en rond, tourner autour du pot.

muldoon [ˈmʌlˈduːn] (*noun*), *P:* goinfre*, bâfreur *m*, gueulard *m*.

mule [mjuːl] (*noun*), *P:* passeur *m* (de drogues), mule *f* (à came).

mullarky [məˈlɑːki] (*noun*), *F:* = **malark(e)y.**

mulligans [ˈmʌligənz] (*pl. noun*) (*Austr.*), *P:* cartes* à jouer, brèmes *f.pl.*, cartons *m.pl.*

mull over [ˈmʌlˈouvər] (**to**), *F:* ruminer, ressasser, gamberger.

mum [mʌm] (*adj.*), *F:* **to keep m.**, se taire*, ne pas moufter; **m.'s the word!** motus et bouche cousue!

murder[1] [ˈməːdər] (*noun*), *F:* **1. it's (sheer) m. in the rush-hour,** c'est (absolument) épouvantable (*ou* monstrueux) aux heures de pointe. **2. to get away with m.**, s'en tirer à bon compte, tirer les marrons du feu. *Voir aussi* **blue**[1], **2.**

murder[2] [ˈməːdər] (**to**). **1.** *P:* battre* (qn) comme plâtre, tabasser (qn). **2.** *F:* massacrer, écorcher, estropier (un morceau de musique, *etc.*).

Murphy [ˈməːfi] (*noun*), *P:* = **spud (Murphy).**

muscle-head [ˈmʌslhed] (*noun*), *F:* individu bête*, bûche *f*, truffe *f*.

muscle in [ˈmʌslˈin] (**to**), *F:* **1.** se pousser, jouer des coudes. **2. he muscled his way in,** il s'introduisit de force, il força la porte. **3. to m. i. on a conversation,** s'injecter dans une conversation.

muscle-man [ˈmʌslmæn] (*noun*), *F:* homme fort*, malabar *m*, costaud *m*, homme à pogne.

mush[1] [mʌʃ] (*noun*), *F:* **1.** propos *m.pl.* bêtes*, niaiseries *f.pl.* **2.** flatterie *f*. **3.** cafouillage *m*. **4.** amourette *f*.

mush[2] [muʃ] (*noun*), *P:* **1.** (*a*) visage*, frime *f*; (*b*) bouche*, goule *f*. **2.** (*a*) individu*, type *m*, mec *m*; (*b*) corniaud *m*, cornichon *m*, con *m*.

mushy [ˈmʌʃi] (*adj.*), *F:* à l'eau de rose, à la guimauve.

music [ˈmjuːzik] (*noun*), *F:* **to face the m.**, (*a*) tenir le coup, payer d'audace; (*b*) braver l'orage, payer les pots cassés, avaler la pilule. *Voir aussi* **chin-music.**

mutt [mʌt] (*noun*), *P:* **1. poor m.!** le

* L'astérisque indique que le mot marqué de ce signe figure comme entrée dans le Répertoire.

pauvre (*ou* pauv') mec! **2.** chien* (bâtard), clebs *m*, cabot *m*.

mutton [ˈmʌtn] (*noun*), *F:* **m. dressed up as lamb,** vieux tableau, vieille poupée.

mutton-fancier [ˈmʌtnfænsiər] (*noun*), *P:* pédéraste*, enviandé *m*.

muttonhead [ˈmʌtnhed] (*noun*), *F:* individu bête*, andouille *f*, saucisse *f*.

muzzle [ˈmʌzl] (*noun*), *P:* **1.** chance*, veine *f*, pot *m*. **2.** visage*, museau *m*, frimousse *f*.

muzzy [ˈmʌzi] (*adj.*), *F:* légèrement ivre*, paf, éméché.

mystery [ˈmist(ə)ri] (*noun*), *P:* femme* inconnue dans le pays; **a m. in the manor,** une nouvelle venue dans le coin. *Voir aussi* **bag**¹, **9.**

* An asterisk indicates that the word so marked is included as a head-word in the Appendix.

N

nab[1] [næb] (*noun*), *P:* agent* de police, flic *m*.

nab[2] [næb] (**to**), *P:* **1.** (*a*) arrêter*, pincer, agrafer, cueillir (qn); **the police nabbed the lot,** la police les a tous ratissés (*ou* cueillis *ou* embarqués); **to get nabbed,** se faire pincer (*ou* piger), se faire faire; (*b*) prendre (qn) sur le fait (*ou* la main dans le sac); *cf.* **nip**[3] **(to), 4. 2.** (*a*) voler*, chiper, chaparder (qch.); (*b*) saisir, escamoter (qch.).

nadgers [ˈnædʒəz] (*pl. noun*), *P:* **to put the n. on s.o.,** donner la malchance* à qn, foutre la poisse à qn.

nadget [ˈnædʒit] (*noun*) (*Austr.*), *P:* tête*, caboche *f*, gadin *m*.

nag [næg] (*noun*), *F:* cheval*, bidet *m*, canasson *m*; **to follow the nags** = **to follow the gee-gees.**

nagsbody [ˈnægzbɔdi] (*noun*), *P:* rouspéteur *m*, rouscailleur *m*.

nail[1] [neil] (*noun*), *F:* **1. to pay (cash) on the n.,** payer cash (*ou* recta *ou* rubis sur l'ongle). **2. to hit the n. on the head,** mettre le doigt dessus. *Voir aussi* **coffin, 2; doornail; tooth, 6.**

nail[2] [neil] (**to**), *P:* **1.** filer un coup* à (qn), frapper. **2.** (*a*) intercepter (qn); (*b*) arrêter*, coincer (qn). **3.** demander un prix exorbitant à (qn), fusiller (qn), extorquer de l'argent* à (qn). **4.** coïter* avec (qn), aiguiller (qn). *Voir aussi* **hammer (to), 3.**

nailer [ˈneilər] (*noun*), *F:* as *m*, épée *f*, crack *m*.

name [neim] (*noun*), *F:* **to call s.o. names,** injurier* qn. *Voir aussi* **pack-drill; what's-(h)er-name; what's-(h)is-name.**

name-dropper [ˈneimdrɔpər] (*noun*), *F:* qn qui a la langue trop longue, boîte *f* à cancans.

nana [ˈnɑːnə] (*noun*), *P:* **he's a right n.!** c'est un vrai gugusse!; **to feel a right n.,** se sentir tout bête* (*ou* ballot *ou* gourdiflot); **you silly great n.!** espèce de grande gourde!

nance [næns], **nancy(-boy)** [ˈnænsi(bɔi)] (*noun*), *P:* **1.** pédéraste* (qui tient le rôle de la femme), persilleuse *f*, joconde *f*, chouquette *f*. **2.** homme* efféminé, femmelette *f*, mauviette *f*.

nanna [ˈnænə] (*noun*), *F:* grand-mère, mémé *f*.

nap[1] [næp] (*noun*), *F:* **to go n. on sth.,** être sûr et certain de qch., en mettre sa main au feu, foutre son billet.

nap[2] [næp] (**to**), *F:* **to be caught napping,** (*a*) être pris au dépourvu; (*b*) être pris en faute.

napoo[1] [næˈpuː] (*adj.*), *P:* fini, fichu, foutu, rétamé.

napoo[2] [næˈpuː] (*noun*), *P:* (*a*) la fin, le bout du rouleau; **to n.,** jusqu'à la gauche, jusqu'à plus soif; (*b*) la mort, la canne, la crève.

napper [ˈnæpər] (*noun*), *P:* tête*, caboche *f*.

nappy [ˈnæpi] (*noun*) (=(*baby's*) *napkin*), *F:* couche *f*.

narc(o) [ˈnɑːk(ou)] (*noun*), *P:* agent *m* de la Brigadeféd érale des Stupéfiants.

nark[1] [nɑːk] (*noun*), *P:* **1.** qn qui sert de piège, coqueur *m*. **2.** indicateur* de police, mouton *m*, bordille *m*, mouchard *m*. **3.** = **narc(o).**

nark[2] [nɑːk] (**to**), *P:* **1.** mettre en colère, braquer, mettre en rogne, prendre à rebrousse-poil. **2. to get narked,** (*a*) être en colère*, fulminer; (*b*) se faire arrêter* (*ou* agrafer *ou* pincer). **3.** moucharder, bourriquer, en croquer, en manger. **4. n. it!** écrase! la ferme! fous-moi la paix!

narky [ˈnɑːki] (*adj.*), *P:* **1.** en colère*, en rogne, de mauvais poil. **2.** = **sarky.**

natch! [nætʃ] (*excl.*), *P:* naturellement! naturliche!

natter[1] [ˈnætər] (*noun*), *F:* baratinage *m*, jactage *m*, tapette *f*; **to have a n.** = **natter**[2] **(to), 1.**

natter[2] [ˈnætər] (**to**), *F:* **1.** bavarder*, baver, jacter. **2.** gronder, criailler.

* L'astérisque indique que le mot marqué de ce signe figure comme entrée dans le Répertoire.

natural [ˈnætʃrəl] (*noun*), *F:* **1. never** (*or* **not**) **in all my n.**, jamais de la vie. **2. a n.**, qui est né pour ça, tout trouvé pour..., qui va comme un gant.

naughty [ˈnɔːti] (**to**) (*Austr.*), *P:* coïter* avec (qn), godiller avec (qn).

n.b.g., N.B.G. [ˈenˈbiːˈdʒiː] (*abbr.* = *no bloody good*), *P:* bon à rien*, bon à nib.

nearly [ˈniəli] (*adv.*), *F:* **n. there:** *voir* **bingo (89).**

necessary [ˈnesəsəri] (*noun*), *F:* **the n.**, argent*, galette *f*, beurre *m*, blé *m*, carbure *m*; **to do the n.**, payer* la note, casquer.

neck[1] [nek] (*noun*), *F:* **1. to get it in the n.**, écoper, en avoir pour son compte (*ou* son grade), trinquer. **2. you've got a n.!** quel toupet! quel culot! **3. to stick one's n. out,** prendre des risques, se mouiller. **4. it's n. or nothing,** il faut risquer (*ou* jouer) le tout pour le tout. **5. to be up to one's n. in work,** être débordé de travail*, en avoir jusque-là. **6. to be in sth. up to one's n.**, être submergé, y être jusqu'au cou. **7. to have a n. (with s.o.)** = **neck**[2] **(to), 1. 8. to be thrown out on one's n.** (*or* **n. and crop**), être flanqué dehors avec perte(s) et fracas. **9. to break** (*or* **be breaking**) **one's n. (to spend a penny)**, mourir d'envie d'aller au petit coin. *Voir aussi* **deadneck; leatherneck; pain; roughneck; rubberneck**[1]**; stiffneck; wood, 3.**

neck[2] [nek] (**to**), *F:* **1.** s'embrasser, se bécoter, se peloter; rouler une pelle. **2.** boire*, pinter, picoler. *Voir aussi* **rubberneck**[2] **(to).**

necking [ˈnekiŋ] (*noun*), *F:* = **petting.**

necktie [ˈnektai] (*noun*) (*U.S.*), *F:* corde *f* du gibet, cravate *f*; **to throw a n. party,** lyncher, pendre*, béquiller.

needful [ˈniːdful] (*noun*), *F:* **the n.** = **the necessary.**

needle[1] [ˈniːdl] (*noun*), *P:* **1.** (*a*) **to give s.o. the n.** = **to needle s.o. (needle**[2] **(to), 1–5)**; (*b*) **to have the (dead) n. for s.o.**, avoir une (sacrée) dent contre qn; (*c*) **to get** (*or* **cop**) **the n.**, se mettre en colère*, piquer une crise. **2. to be on the n.**, (*a*) être de la piquouse, tenir à la poussette; (*b*) être drogué* (*ou* camé *ou* toxico). **3. n. and pin** (*R.S.* = *gin*), gin *m*. *Voir aussi* **pins, 2; piss**[2] **(to), 2.**

needle[2] [ˈniːdl] (**to**). **1.** *F:* agacer, asticoter, enquiquiner (qn); **to be needled,** être de mauvais poil. **2.** *F:* aiguillonner, inciter, tanner. **3.** *F:* harceler, bassiner. **4.** *F:* taquiner, canuler, chiner. **5.** *P:* inoculer, vacciner. **6.** *P:* extirper des renseignements* de (qn), pomper (qn).

needle-candy [ˈniːdl-kændi] (*noun*), *P:* (*a*) stupéfiant pris par injection, liqueur *f* de shooteuse; (*b*) héroïne *f* (*drogues**), cheval *m*, jus *m*.

nellie, Nellie, nelly, Nelly [ˈneli] (*noun*). **1.** *P:* pédéraste*, persilleuse *f*. **2.** *F:* **not on your n.!** jamais de la vie! rien à faire! tu peux courir!

Nelson [ˈnelsən] (*pr. noun*), *F:* **N.'s blood,** rhum *m*. *Voir aussi* **tear**[1]**, 2.**

nerve [nəːv] (*noun*), *F:* **1. to get on s.o.'s nerves,** courir (*ou* taper) sur les nerfs *m.pl.* (*ou* le système) à qn. **2. you've got a n.!** quel culot! quel toupet!; **what a n. you've got!** t'as un rude toupet!; **I like your n.!** t'es culotté! **3. to have the n. to do sth.**, avoir de l'audace (*ou* du ventre *ou* du poil au cul) pour faire qch. *Voir aussi* **bundle, 6.**

nest-egg [ˈnesteg] (*noun*), *F:* économies *f.pl.*, argent* mis de côté; **to have a nice little n.-e. (tucked away)**, avoir un bas de laine bien garni.

never [ˈnevər] (*adv.*), *F:* **1. well I n.!** pas possible! ça par exemple! je n'en reviens pas! **2. n. been kissed:** *voir* **bingo (16). 3. n. fear** (*R.S.* = *beer*), bière *f*.

never-never [ˈnevərˈnevər] (*noun*), *F:* **to buy sth. on the n.-n.**, acheter qch. à crédit (*ou* à croume).

Newfie [ˈnjuːfi] (*pr. noun*) (*U.S.*), *F:* Terre-neuvien *m*.

news-hawk [ˈnjuːzhɔːk], **news-hound** [ˈnjuːzhaund] (*noun*), *F:* journaliste *mf*, reporter *m*, chasseur *m* de copie.

newt [njuːt] (*noun*), *F:* **tight as a n.**, ivre* mort.

newy [ˈnjuːi] (*noun*) (*Austr.*), *F:* **1.** novice *m*, bleu *m*. **2.** qch. de nouveau, nouveauté *f*.

next [nekst] (*adv.*), *P:* **1. to get n. to s.o.**, se mettre bien avec qn, se mettre dans les petits papiers de qn. **2. n. off,** puis, après, alors.

nibble [ˈnibl] (*noun*), *P:* **to have a n.**, coïter*, faire un carton.

nibs, Nibs [nibz] (*noun*), *F:* **his n.**,

* An asterisk indicates that the word so marked is included as a head-word in the Appendix.

(*a*) gros bonnet, grosse légume, milord; (*b*) individu élégant*, type bien sapé (*ou* bien frusqué); (*c*) cézig(ue) *m*.

nice and... [ˈnaisənd] (*adv.*), *F:* fort bien...; **n. a. handy,** bien commode; **n. a. comfy,** bien à l'aise, tout bien.

nick¹ [nik] (*noun*). **1.** *P:* (*a*) prison*, bloc *m*, taule *f*; (*b*) commissariat *m* de police, le quart. **2.** *P:* **in good n.,** (*a*) en bon état; (*b*) en forme, d'attaque. **3.** *F:* **Old N.,** le diable, le Malin, le barbet.

nick² [nik] (**to**), *P:* **1.** voler*, faucher, chiper. **2.** arrêter*, agrafer, cravater, épingler; **to get nicked,** se faire pincer (*ou* pingler). **3.** faire payer*, extorquer, étriller.

nickel [ˈnikl] (*noun*) (*U.S.*), *F:* pièce *f* de 5 cents.

nicker [ˈnikər] (*noun*), *P:* **1.** billet* d'une livre sterling **2.** mégot*, clope *m*.

niff¹ [nif] (*noun*), *P:* **1.** (*a*) puanteur *f*, (s)chlingage *m*; (*b*) odeur *f*, effluve *m*; **to catch a n. of perfume,** prendre une bouffée de parfum. **2.** reniflette *f*; **take a n. at that,** renifle-moi ça.

niff² [nif] (**to**), *P:* puer, (s)chlinguer, cocoter.

niffy [ˈnifi] (*adj.*), *P:* = **nifty, 3.**

nifty [ˈnifti] (*adj.*). **1.** *F:* beau*, pimpant, bath, choucard. **2.** *P:* malin*, débrouillard. **3.** *P:* qui sent* mauvais, puant.

nig [nig] (*abbr.*), *P:* (*péj.*) = **nigger, 1.**

nigger [ˈnigər] (*noun*), *P:* (*péj.*) **1.** nègre*, bougnoul(e) *m*, bamboula *m*. **2. there's a n. in the woodpile,** il y a anguille sous roche; **that's the n. in the woodpile,** voilà le fin mot de l'histoire. **3. to work like a n.,** travailler* comme un nègre (*ou* comme une brute *ou* comme quatre), trimer comme un forçat. *Voir aussi* **minstrel.**

nigger-driver [ˈnigə-draivər] (*noun*), *P:* négrier *m*, garde-chiourme *m*.

nigger-lover [ˈnigə-lʌvər] (*noun*) (*U.S.*), *P:* (*péj.*) anti-ségrégationiste *mf*, protecteur *m* du noir.

niggly [ˈnigli] (*adj.*), *F:* de mauvaise humeur, ronchonnard.

night-bird [ˈnaitbəːd] (*noun*), *F:* = **fly-by-night, 3.**

nightie [ˈnaiti] (*noun*), *F:* = **nighty.**

nightspot [ˈnait-spɔt] (*noun*), *F:* night-club *m*, boîte *f* (de nuit).

nighty [ˈnaiti] (*noun*) (=*night-dress*), *F:* chemise *f* (*ou* liquette *f*) de nuit.

nighty-night! [ˈnaitiˈnait] (*excl.*), *F:* bonne nuit!

nignog [ˈnignɔg] (*noun*), *P:* **1.** individu bête*, niguedouille *mf*. **2.** (*péj.*) nègre*, bougnoul(e) *m*.

nineteen [ˈnaintiːn] (*numeral adj. & noun*), *F:* **to talk n. to the dozen,** (*a*) parler* vite, faire couler le crachoir; (*b*) bavarder* (*ou* bavasser *ou* jaser) comme une pie borgne.

nineteenth [ˈnaintiːnθ] (*numeral adj.*), *F:* **the n. hole,** le bar d'un club de golf.

ninnies [ˈniniz] (*pl. noun*), *P:* seins*, nénés *m.pl.*, tétons *m.pl.*

nip¹ [nip] (*noun*), *F:* **1. there's a n. in the air,** ça pince; le fond de l'air est froid. **2. a n. of gin,** une rincette de gin. **3. to make a n. for it,** se trotter, décaniller, prendre la poudre d'escampette. **4.** =**nipper, 1.**

Nip² [nip] (*noun*), *P:* Jap(onais) *m*.

nip³ [nip] (**to**), **1.** *F:* **to n. round** (*or* **along** *or* **over**) **to s.o.'s house,** faire un saut chez qn. **2.** *P:* **to n. s.o. for money,** emprunter* de l'argent à qn, taper qn. **3.** *P:* voler*, barboter, faucher. **4.** *P:* prendre (qn) la main dans le sac, prendre (qn) en flag, faire marron sur le tas.

nip along [ˈnipəˈlɔŋ] (**to**), *F:* se dépêcher*, se décarcasser; *voir aussi* **nip³ (to), 1.**

nip in [ˈnipˈin] (**to**), *F:* **1.** entrer (lestement). **2. to n. i. (smartly),** tirer avantage d'une situation.

nip off [ˈnipˈɔf] (**to**), *F:* partir*, jouer des flûtes, prendre le large.

nipper [ˈnipər] (*noun*). **1.** *F:* (*a*) gamin *m*, gavroche *m*, loupiot *m*; (*b*) **I've got two nippers,** j'ai deux enfants*. **2.** (*pl.*) *P:* menottes*, bracelets *m.pl.*

nippy¹ [ˈnipi] (*adj.*), *F:* **1.** froid, frisquet, frisco. **2.** rapide, alerte, vif; **to be n.,** se dépêcher*, se grouiller.

nippy² [ˈnipi] (*noun*), *P:* serveuse *f*, loufiate *f*.

nishte [ˈniʃtə] (*noun*), *P:* rien*, nib.

nit [nit] (*noun*), *F:* **1.** individu bête*, crétin *m*; **a steaming n.,** un couillon fini, un duschnock achevé, un triple crétin. **2.** (*Austr.*) **to keep n.,** monter la garde, faire le pet; *cf.* **cockatoo(er)**; *voir aussi* **nit-nit!**

nitery [ˈnaitəri] (*noun*) (*U.S.*), *F:* = **nightspot.**

* L'astérisque indique que le mot marqué de ce signe figure comme entrée dans le Répertoire.

nit-nit! ['nit'nit] (*excl.*), *P:* tais-toi! (*se taire**), boucle-la! gare! vingt-deux! acré!
nitty ['niti] (*adj.*), *F:* bête*, baluchard.
nitty-gritty ['niti'griti] (*noun*), *F:* **the n.-g.,** le (fin) fond, le tréfonds (d'une affaire), le substratum.
nix![1] [niks] (*excl.*), *P:* pas mèche! rien à faire!
nix[2] [niks] (*noun*), *P:* rien*, nib, nix.
no[1] [nou] (*adj.*), *F:* **long time n. see!** une éternité qu'on s'est vu! *Voir aussi* **fear; go**[2], **1.**
no[2] [nou] (*adv.*), *F:* **n. can do,** compte pas sur bibi.
nob[1] [nɔb] (*noun*). **1.** *P:* tête*, coco *m*, caboche *f*, nénette *f*; **so much a n.,** tant par tête de pipe; *cf.* **copper-nob. 2.** *P:* aristo(crate) *m*, gommeux *m*; **the nobs,** les rupins *m.pl.* **3.** *V:* = **knob, 1.**
nob[2] [nɔb] (**to**), *P:* assommer, étourdir (qn).
nobble ['nɔbl] (**to**). **1.** *F:* doper, écloper (un cheval); acheter (un jockey, *etc.*). **2.** *P:* affurer, faucher, rafler. **3.** *P:* duper*, entôler. **4.** *P:* enlever, kidnapper.
nobby ['nɔbi] (*adj.*), *P:* élégant*, chic, flambard.
nobody ['noubɔdi] (*noun*), *F:* **a n.,** une nullité, un zéro, un rien-du-tout.
nod [nɔd] (*noun*), *P:* **1. on the n.,** (*a*) ahuri par la drogue, envapé; (*b*) (*U.S.*) à crédit, à crôme, à la gagne. **2. to get the n.,** être choisi (*ou* élu). **3. to give the n.,** donner le feu vert.
noddle ['nɔdl] (*noun*), *F:* tête*, ciboulot *m*, caboche *f*; **use your n.!** = **use your loaf!**
nod off ['nɔd'ɔf] (**to**), *F:* s'endormir, piquer un roupillon.
nog [nɔg] (*noun*), *F:* = **noggin, 2.**
noggin ['nɔgin] (*noun*), *F:* **1.** = **noddle. 2.** verre *m* de bière, pot *m*, demi *m*.
no-good ['nou'gud] (*adj.*), *F:* bon à rien.
no-gooder ['nou'gudər], **nogoodnik** ['nou'gudnik] (*noun*), *F:* vaurien*, bon-à-rien *m*, loquedu *m*.
nohow ['nouhau] (*adv.*), *P:* en aucune façon.
noise [nɔiz] (*noun*), *F:* **to make the right noises,** savoir se tirer d'affaire. *Voir aussi* **big**[1], **1.**
non-com ['nɔn'kɔm] (*abbr.* = *non-commissioned officer*) (*mil.*), *F:* sous-off *m*, sous-officier *m*.
non-starter ['nɔn'stɑːtər] (*noun*), *F:* (*a*) non-partant *m*; (*b*) projet, *etc.*, fichu d'avance.
noodle ['nuːdl] (*noun*), *F:* **1.** individu bête*, nouille *f*, andouille *f*. **2.** (*U.S.*) tête*, tronche *f*; *voir aussi* **flip**[3] (**to**), **2.**
nookie, nooky ['nuki] (*noun*), *P:* coït*, crampe *f*, crampette *f*.
nope [noup] (*adv.*) (=*no*), *P:* non*.
norgies ['nɔːgiz], **norgs** [nɔːgz], **norkers** ['nɔːkəz], **norks** [nɔːks] (*pl. noun*) (*Austr.*), *P:* seins*, rotoplots *m.pl.*
north and south ['nɔːθən(d)'sauθ, 'nɔːfən'sauf] (*R.S.* = *mouth*), *P:* bouche*, goule *f*.
nose [nouz] (*noun*). **1.** *F:* **to poke one's n. in (where it's not wanted),** fourrer son nez*, mettre son grain de sel. **2.** *F:* **to pay through the n. for sth.,** payer* les yeux de la tête pour qch., acheter qch. au poids de l'or. **3.** *P:* **to keep one's n. clean,** se tenir à carreau, ne pas se mouiller. **4.** *P:* indicateur* de police, mouton *m*. **5.** *F:* **to put s.o.'s n. out of joint,** faire une contrecarre à qn, contrer qn. **6.** *F:* **to turn one's n. up (at sth.),** faire le dégoûté, faire la petite bouche. **7.** *F:* **to look down one's n. at s.o., sth.,** toiser qn, qch., regarder* qn, qch., de haut (en bas). **8.** *F:* **to have a n. (for sth.),** avoir le nez creux, avoir du pif. **9.** *F:* **he gets up my n.,** il me fait monter la moutarde au nez. **10.** *F:* **the parson's n.,** le croupion (d'une volaille), as *m* de pique. *Voir aussi* **bottle-nose; dog**[1], **6; skin**[1], **2, 3; toffee-nose.**
nose about (*or* **around**) ['nouzə'baut, 'nouzə'raund] (**to**), *F:* fureter, fouiner.
nosebag ['nouzbæg] (*noun*), *P:* **to put** (*or* **tie**) **on the n.,** manger*, casser la croûte, se remplir le bocal.
nose-candy ['nouzkændi] (*noun*), *P:* cocaïne *f* (*drogues**), neige *f*.
nosedive[1] ['nouzdaiv] (*noun*), *F:* baisse *f* (de prix, *etc.*), plongeon *m*.
nosedive[2] ['nouzdaiv] (**to**), *F:* (*prix, etc.*) tomber à pic, dégringoler, s'effondrer.
nose on ['nouzɔn] (**to**), *P:* dénoncer*, moutonner, bourdiller (qn).
nose-rag ['nouzræg], **nose-wipe** ['nouz-

* An asterisk indicates that the word so marked is included as a head-word in the Appendix.

waip], **nose-wiper** ['nouz-waipər] (*noun*), *P:* mouchoir*, tire-jus *m*.

nosey ['nouzi] (*adj.*), *F:* = **nosy.**

nosh[1] [nɔʃ] (*noun*), *P:* **1.** nourriture*, boustifaille *f*. **2.** repas *m*, boulottage *m*; *voir aussi* **chinky.**

nosh[2] [nɔʃ] (**to**), *P:* **1.** manger*, boulotter, croûter. **2.** mettre la main sur (qch.).

nosh-bar ['nɔʃbɑːr] (*noun*), *P:* snack (-bar) *m*.

nosher ['nɔʃər] (*noun*), *P:* mangeur *m*, bouffeur *m*.

nosh-up ['nɔʃʌp] (*noun*), *P:* bon repas, noce *f*, bombe *f*.

nostrils ['nɔstrilz] (*pl. noun*), *F:* **he gets up my n.** = **he gets up my nose** (**nose, 9**).

nosy ['nouzi] (*adj.*), *F:* fureteur, fouinard; **n. parker,** fouine *f*, fouille-merde *mf*.

nothing ['nʌθiŋ] (*noun*). **1.** *F:* **n. doing!** rien à faire! macache! **2.** *F:* **to do sth. in n. flat,** faire qch. très vite* (*ou* illico *ou* en cinq secs). **3.** *P:* **you don't know** (**from**) **n.,** tu es ignorant*, tu n'y piges que dalle, tu es en retard d'une rame. *Voir aussi* **sweet**[1], **5; write** (**to**).

nowt [naut] (*noun*), *F:* rien*, nib, que dalle; *cf.* **owt.**

nubbies ['nʌbiz] (*pl. noun*) (*Austr.*), *P:* = **bubbies.**

number ['nʌmbər] (*noun*), *F:* **1. your n.'s up,** ton compte est bon. **2. to look after n. one,** penser à mézigue, soigner bibi, tirer la couverture à soi. **3. a hot n.,** (*a*) une chaude lapine, une chaude de la pince; (*b*) morceau de musique enlevé avec fougue; (*c*) article *m* qui se vend bien, article-réclame *m*. **4. to have s.o.'s n.,** en savoir long sur qn, être rencardé sur qn. **5. to have the wrong n.,** être sur la mauvaise piste, se gour(r)er. **6.** (*langage enfantin*) **to do n. one** = **to do small jobs** (**job, 9**); **to do n. two** = **to do big jobs** (**job, 9**). **7.** (*Marine*) **n. one,** officier *m* qui commande en second à bord d'un navire (de guerre). *Voir aussi* **back-number; cushy.**

nunky ['nʌŋki] (*noun*), *F:* **1.** (*langage enfantin*) oncle *m*, tonton *m*. **2.** = **uncle, 5.**

nurd [nəːd] (*noun*) (*U.S.*), *P:* = **jerk**[1], **1.**

nut[1] [nʌt] (*noun*). **1.** *P:* tête*, caboche *f*, ciboulot *m*; **use your n.!** = **use your loaf!;** (*Austr.*) **to nod the n.** = **to bow the crumpet** (**crumpet, 3**); **off one's n.,** fou*, dingue, dingo; **to go off one's n.,** devenir fou*, perdre la boule; *cf.* **nuts**[1]. **2.** *P:* = **nut-case. 3.** *P:* **to do one's n.,** se mettre en colère*, sortir de ses gonds. **4.** *F:* **he's a hard n.** (**to crack**), c'est un têtu (*ou* un cabochard *ou* une bourrique *ou* une tête de mule); *cf.* **tough**[1], **1. 5.** *F:* **she can't play** (**sing,** *etc.*) **for nuts,** elle joue (chante, *etc.*) comme un pied; **he can't drive for nuts,** il conduit comme un manche; *cf.* **toffee. 6.** (*pl.*) *V:* testicules*, noix *f.pl.*; **to get hot nuts,** être en érection*, bander; **to get one's nuts off,** éjaculer*, vider ses burettes; **to have one's nuts cracked,** coïter*, tirer sa chique. **7.** *P:* **to talk nuts,** dire des bêtises* (*ou* des conneries *f.pl.*). *Voir aussi* **peanut.**

nut[2] [nʌt] (**to**). **1.** *P:* donner un coup de tête* (*ou* de caboche *ou* de ciboulot) à (qn). **2.** (*U.S.*) *V:* coïter* avec (qn), buriner (qn).

nut-case ['nʌtkeis] (*noun*), *P:* **he's a n.-c.,** c'est un cas.

nut-house ['nʌthaus] (*noun*), *P:* maison *f* de fous, asile *m* de dingues, cabanon *m*, Charenton.

nuts[1] [nʌts] (*adj.*), *P:* **1.** = **off one's nut** (**nut**[1], **1**). **2. to be n. about** (*or* **on**) **s.o., sth.,** être toqué (*ou* fana) de qn, de qch.; être mordu pour qn, qch.; **he's n. about basket-ball,** il raffole (*ou* c'est un mordu) du basket; *cf.* **nutty, 2.**

nuts![2] [nʌts] (*excl.*), *P:* **n.** (**to you**)! zut! merde!

nutter ['nʌtər] (*noun*), *P:* = **nut-case.**

nutters ['nʌtəz] (*adj.*), *P:* = **off one's nut** (**nut**[1], **1**).

nuttiness ['nʌtinis] (*noun*), *P:* folie *f*, loufoquerie *f*, maboulisme *m*.

nutting ['nʌtiŋ] (*noun*), *P:* = **heading.**

nutty ['nʌti] (*adj.*), *P:* **1.** loufoque, maboul(e). **2.** fou* (à lier), cinglé; *voir aussi* **fruit-cake, 2. 3. to be n. about s.o., sth.** = **to be nuts about s.o., sth.** (**nuts**[1], **2**).

nymphet [nim'fet] (*noun*), *F:* petite poule, nénette *f*.

nympho ['nimfou] (*noun*), *F:* (=*nymphomaniac*) nymphomane *f*, femme* à passions.

* L'astérisque indique que le mot marqué de ce signe figure comme entrée dans le Répertoire.

O

O [ou] (*abbr.* = *opium*), *P:* op(ium) *m* (*drogues**), boue *f.*

oats [outs] (*pl. noun*). **1.** *P:* **to get one's o.,** être satisfait sexuellement, ne pas mettre ses chaussettes à la fenêtre. **2.** *F:* **to feel one's o.,** (*a*) se sentir important, se monter du collet; (*b*) avoir de l'entrain (*ou* de l'allant). **3.** *F:* **to be off one's o.,** se sentir patraque (*ou* tout chose *ou* pas dans son assiette).

obstropolous [ɔbˈstrɔpələs] (*adj.*), *F:* bruyant, tapageur.

ochre [ˈoukər] (*noun*) (*mainly U.S.*), *P:* argent*, osier *m*, blanc *m*.

O.D. [ˈouˈdiː] (*abbr.* = *overdose*), *F:* dose trop forte (de narcotiques), (*a*) dose nuisible; (*b*) dose mortelle.

oddball[1] [ˈɔdbɔːl] (*adj.*), *P:* **1.** excentrique, loufoque, farfelu. **2.** gaffeur.

oddball[2] [ˈɔdbɔːl] (*noun*), *P:* **1.** excentrique *mf*, drôle *m* de zigoto, farfelu *m*. **2.** flagorneur *m*. **3.** dissident(e) *m(f)*. **4.** pédéraste*.

odds [ɔdz] (*pl. noun*). **1.** *P:* **o. and sods,** petits bouts, bibelots *m.pl.*, bribes et morceaux. **2.** *F:* **over the o.,** beaucoup trop, bien plus. **3.** *F:* **what o. does it make? what's the o.?** qu'est-ce que ça fait? **4.** *P:* **to shout the o.,** se vanter, faire de la gloriole. **5.** *F:* **to be within the o.,** être bien possible. **6.** *F:* volumes dépareillés; livres *m.pl.* supplémentaires.

odds-on [ˈɔdzɔn] (*adj.*), *F:* **to have an o.-o. chance,** jouer gagnant; **it's an o.-o. chance he'll get arrested,** il y a bien des chances qu'il se fasse arrêter*.

off[1] [ɔf] (*adj.*), *F:* **to have an o. day,** se sentir un peu malade*, ne pas être en train.

off[2] [ɔf] (*adv.*), *F:* **that's a bit o.,** (*a*) c'est un peu de travers, ce n'est pas tout à fait ça; (*b*) ça dépasse les bornes; (*c*) ça commence à être mauvais.

off[3] [ɔf] (*noun*), *F:* **ready for the o.,** prêt à partir*, sur le départ.

off[4] [ɔf] (*prep.*). **1.** *F:* **o. colour,** (*a*) un peu malade*, patraque, mal fichu; (*b*) (*U.S.*) scabreux, osé, salé, pimenté. **2.** *P:* **o. (of) . . .,** de...; **I got it o. (of) my brother,** je le tiens de mon frère. *Voir aussi* **go off (to), 2.**

off-beat [ˈɔfˈbiːt] (*adj.*), *F:* original, qui sort de l'ordinaire.

office [ˈɔfis] (*noun*), *P:* signal particulier, œillade *f*. *Voir aussi* **jack-in-office.**

offish [ˈɔfiʃ] (*adj.*), *F:* (*a*) distant, hautain; (*b*) mal en train.

off-putting [ˈɔfputiŋ, ˈɔfˈputiŋ] (*adj.*), *F:* déconcertant, déroutant.

offy [ˈɔfi] (*noun*) (=*off-licence*), *F:* débit *m* (où on vend des boissons à emporter).

oh-be-joyful [ˈoubiːˈdʒɔifəl] (*noun*), *F:* bouteille *f* de rhum.

oil [ɔil] (*noun*), *F:* **1.** flatterie *f*, boniment *m*, pommade *f*; *cf.* **palm-oil. 2.** pot-de-vin *m*, dessous-de-table *m*. **3.** **to strike o.,** gagner* beaucoup d'argent, trouver un bon filon.

oil-can [ˈɔil-kæn] (*noun*) (*U.S.*), *P:* échec*, four *m*, fiasco *m*.

oiled [ɔild] (*adj.*), *F:* **(well) o.,** ivre*, fadé, bituré, cuit, dans le cirage.

oil-painting [ˈɔil-peintiŋ] (*noun*), *F:* **she's no o.-p.,** elle est laide*, c'est un vieux tableau.

oily [ˈɔili] (*adj.*), *F:* (*péj.*) onctueux. *Voir aussi* **rag**[1], **10.**

oink [ɔiŋk] (*noun*) (*U.S.*), *P:* policier*, condé *m*.

O.K.[1], **o.k., okay** [ˈouˈkei] (*adj.*), *F:* O.K., impec, au poil; **an O.K. guy,** un type bien. *Voir aussi* **scene, 3** (*a*).

O.K.[2], **o.k., okay** [ˈouˈkei], **oke** [ouk], **okey-doke** [ˈoukiˈdouk], **okey-dokey** [ˈoukiˈdouki] (*adv.*), *F:* d'accord*, dac, O.K., banco; **it's O.K. by me,** quant à moi c'est d'accord.

O.K.[3], **o.k., okay** [ˈouˈkei] (*noun*), *F:* accord *m*, conciliation *f*, approbation *f*, O.K. *m*; **to give s.o. the O.K.,** donner le feu vert à qn.

O.K.[4], **o.k., okay** [ˈouˈkei] **(to),** *F:* être

* An asterisk indicates that the word so marked is included as a head-word in the Appendix.

d'accord avec, approuver; opiner du bonnet.

old [ould] (*adj.*), **1. the o. man,** (*a*) *F:* mari *m*, l'homme *m*, le vieux; (*b*) *F:* le père*, papa; **my o. man,** mon homme, mon vieux; (*c*) *F:* le patron*, le singe; (*d*) (*majuscules initiales*) *F:* le capitaine d'un navire; (*e*) *P:* pénis*, le petit frère. **2.** *F:* **hello, o. man!** salut, vieille branche (*ou* vieux pote)!; *cf.* **thing, 8. 3.** *F:* **o. woman,** (*a*) épouse*, la moitié; (*b*) mère*, la vieille; (*c*) individu* qui fait des manières, chichiteux *m*. **4.** *F:* **o. lady = old woman** (*voir* **old,** 3 (*a*) *ci-dessus*); *voir aussi* **white**[2], **4. 5.** *F:* **the same o. story** (*or* **tune**), la même rengaine. **6.** *F:* **I met o. Smith the other day,** j'ai rencontré l'ami Smith l'autre jour. **7.** *F:* **it's a funny o. world** (**we live in**), *c.p.*, tout est bizarre autant qu'étrange. **8.** *F:* **put them down any o. where,** pose-les n'importe où. *Voir aussi* **army, 2; bean, 2; boot, 9; boy**[2]; **chap; crock**[1], **2; fruit, 3; Harry, 1, 2; hat, 1; high**[1], **6; how**[1], **1; how-d'ye-do; nick**[1], **3; rare; soldier**[1], **3; stick**[1], **9** (*b*); **thing, 8.**

old-boy [ˈouldˈbɔi] (*attrib. adj.*), *F:* **the o.-b. network,** la franc-maçonnerie des anciens (d'une école, *etc.*).

oldie [ˈouldi] (*noun*), *F:* **1.** vieux*, viocard *m*, vioque *m*. **2.** vieillerie *f*, antiquaille *f*.

old-timer [ouldˈtaimər] (*noun*), *F:* un vieux de la vieille.

oldy [ˈouldi] (*noun*) = **oldie.**

Oliver (Twist) [ˈɔlivə(ˈtwist)] (*noun*) (*R.S.* = *fist*), *P:* poing*.

on[1] [ɔn] (*adj.*). **1.** *V:* (pénis) en érection*, en l'air. **2.** *P:* (*a*) euphorisé par la drogue, high; (*b*) habitué des drogues, branché; *cf.* **switched on, 2.**

on[2] [ɔn] (*adv.*), *F:* **1. it's o.,** ça marche, ça va; **it's not o.,** rien à faire, pas mèche. **2. I'm o.,** j'en suis. **3. to be always o. at s.o.,** être toujours sur le dos de qn.

on[3] [ɔn] (*prep.*), *F:* **the drinks are o. me, this one's o. me,** j'offre la tournée, c'est moi qui régale.

once [wʌns] (*adv.*), *P:* **o. a week** (*R.S.* = *cheek*) = **cheek**[1,2].

once-over [ˈwʌnsouvər] (*noun*), *F:* **to give sth., s.o., the o.-o.,** regarder*, reluquer, mirer qch., qn.

oncer [ˈwʌnsər] (*noun*), *P:* billet* d'une livre, faf(f)iot *m*.

one [wʌn] (*pron.*). **1.** *F:* un verre, un coup; **to have (had) o. too many,** avoir (pris) un coup de trop; **o. for the road** (*or* **for the swing of the gate**), le coup du départ (*ou* de l'étrier); *voir aussi* **eight, 1; quick, 1. 2.** *F:* (=*plaisanterie*) **that's a good o.!** elle est bien bonne celle-là! **3.** *F:* (=*coup**) **he landed** (*or* **fetched**) **him o. on the nose,** il lui a donné un ramponneau sur le nez*; *voir aussi* **fourpenny. 4.** *F:* **he pulled a fast o. on me,** il m'a eu (*ou* fait *ou* refait), il m'a joué un tour (de cochon). **5.** *F:* **you are a o.!** tu me la copieras! **6.** *F:* **to be a o. for sth.,** être un fana (*ou* un mordu) de qch. **7.** *F:* (= *nigaud*) **there's o. born every minute,** *c.p.*, on pend les andouilles sans les compter; *cf.* **sucker**[2], **1. 8.** *F:* **my o. and only,** mon cher et tendre, ma chère et tendre. **9.** *F:* **it's** (*or* **that's**) **a new o. on me!** ça m'en bouche un coin! **10.** *P:* **ones and twos** (*R.S.* = *shoes*), chaussures*, croquenots *m.pl. Voir aussi* **eye, 23; number, 7; stick**[2] **(to), 11.**

one-eyed [ˈwʌnaid] (*adj.*), *P:* insignifiant, de rien du tout, pitoyable, piètre; **a o.-e. town,** un patelin insignifiant, un bled. *Voir aussi* **trouser-snake.**

one-horse [ˈwʌnhɔːs] (*adj.*), *F:* **a o.-h. town,** une petite ville de province, un trou (perdu).

one-man [ˈwʌnˈmæn] (*adj.*), *F:* **o.-m. band,** homme-orchestre *m* (=*amant parfait* ou *qn qui fait tout lui-même*).

one-nighter [ˈwʌnˈnaitər] (*noun*), *P:* = **one-night stand (stand**[1], **1).**

one-off [ˈwʌnɔf] (*adj.*), *F:* (*a*) (*T.V.*) **o.-o. film,** film *m* en exclusivité; (*b*) **o.-o. book,** livre *m* à tirage limité.

oner [ˈwʌnər] (*noun*), *F:* **1.** sommité *f*, ongle *m*, as *m*, crack *m*. **2.** un expert, un calé. **3.** coup* de la fin, assommoir *m*.

one-two [ˈwʌnˈtuː] (*noun*), *F:* coup* sec de gauche suivi d'un direct de droite.

one-upmanship [ˈwʌnˈʌpmənʃip] (*noun*), *F:* refus *m* de se laisser jeter la poudre aux yeux, l'escalade *f*, l'art *m* des raménoïdes; **to practise o.-u.,** renchérir, avoir la dragée haute.

onion [ˈʌnjən] (*noun*). **1.** *F:* **that's the way the o. peels = that's the way the mop flops** (*voir* **mop, 1**); *cf.* **cookie, 1. 2.** *F:* **to know one's onions,** connaître son

* L'astérisque indique que le mot marqué de ce signe figure comme entrée dans le Répertoire.

sujet à fond, être à la coule (*ou* à la hauteur). 3. *P:* tête*, poire *f*; **off one's o.**, fou*, maboul(e).

oodles [ˈuːdlz] (*pl. noun*), *F:* **o. of...**, beaucoup de..., une abondance* de..., des tas de...

oof [uːf] (*noun*), *P:* argent*, fric *m*.

oojamaflip [ˈuːdʒəməflip], **oojie** [ˈuːdʒi] (*noun*), *F:* machin *m*, chose *mf*, machin-chose *m*.

oo-la-la! [ˈuːlɑːˈlɑː] (*excl.*), *F:* ho-la-la!

oomph [umf] (*noun*), *F:* charme *m*, personnalité *f*, sex-appeal *m*, chien *m*, allant *m*.

oops-a-daisy! [ˈupsəˈdeizi] (*excl.*), *F:* hop-là! youp-là (boum)!

oozer [ˈuːzər] (*noun*), *P:* = **boozer, 2.**

open[1] [ˈoup(ə)n] (*adj.*), *F:* **it's an o. and shut case,** c'est sûr et certain, c'est du tout cuit, c'est couru, c'est dans le sac.

open[2] [ˈoup(ə)n] (**to**). 1. *P:* **to o. one's legs (for s.o.)**, (*d'une femme*) coïter*, faire une partie de jambes en l'air. 2. *F:* **o. the door:** *voir* **bingo (44).**

openers [ˈoup(ə)nəz] (*pl. noun*), *F:* **for o.**, pour commencer, comme hors-d'œuvre.

open up [ˈoup(ə)nˈʌp] (**to**), *F:* 1. (*a*) avouer*, dégorger, manger le morceau; (*b*) parler franchement, vider son sac. 2. se déchaîner, y aller de tout son saoul. 3. (*fusil, revolver*) tirer*, flinguer.

operator [ˈɔpəreitər] (*noun*), *P:* 1. voleur* (à la tire), escroc*, filou *m*, empileur *m*. 2. fourgueur *m* (*ou* pourvoyeur *m*) de drogues. *Voir aussi* **smooth, 2.**

organize [ˈɔːgənaiz] (**to**), *P:* = **wangle (to).**

ornery [ˈɔːnəri] (*adj.*) (*U.S.*), *P:* d'humeur maussade, de mauvais poil.

Oscar [ˈɔskər] (**to**), *V:* pratiquer le coït* anal sur (qn), emproser (qn).

other [ˈʌðər] (*noun*), *P:* **to have a bit of the o.**, coïter*, faire un peu de truc. *Voir aussi* **tother.**

out[1] [aut] (*adv.*). 1. *F:* **o. on one's feet,** fatigué*, flapi, flagada. 2. *F:* (*a*) **to be o. of it,** (i) ne pas être de connivence; (ii) être laissé à l'écart; (*b*) **to feel o. of it,** (i) se sentir dépaysé; (ii) se sentir de trop. 3. *P:* **o. of sight,** bœuf, du tonnerre. *Voir aussi* **light, 1.**

out[2] [aut] (*noun*), *F:* **to find an o.**, se tirer d'affaire, se débrouiller*, se dépatouiller, trouver une porte de sortie; *cf.* **get out (to); in**[3], **1.** *Voir aussi* **in**[3], **2.**

out-and-abouter [ˈautəndəˈbautər] (*noun*), *F:* vadrouilleur *m*.

outfit [ˈautfit] (*noun*), *F:* 1. équipe *f*, groupement *m*. 2. firme *f*, (maison *f* de) travail *m*.

outside[1] [ˈautˈsaid] (*noun*), *F:* **to be on the o. looking in,** ne pas faire partie d'une société *ou* d'un groupe; être un outsider.

outside[2] [ˈautˈsaid] (*prep.*), *F:* **get o. that!** enfile-toi ça!

overcoat [ˈouvəkout] (*noun*), *F:* **wooden** (*or* **pine**) **o.**, cercueil*, paletot *m* (*ou* redingote *f*) de sapin, pardessus *m* sans manches.

overjolt [ˈouvə-dʒoult] (*noun*), *F:* dose trop forte (d'une drogue).

overspill [ˈouvə-spil] (*noun*), *F:* ville *f* satellite.

ownsome [ˈounsəm], **owny-o** [ˈouniou] (*noun*), *F:* **on one's o.**, tout seul, seulabre; *cf.* **lonesome.**

owt [aut] (*noun*), *F:* quelque chose; **I don't do o. for nowt,** je ne fais rien pour rien; *cf.* **nowt.**

oyster [ˈɔistər] (*noun*), *P:* 1. crachat*, glaviot *m*. 2. bouche*, boîte *f*.

ozzy [ˈɔzi] (*noun*), *P:* hôpital*, host(e)au *m*, hosto *m*.

* An asterisk indicates that the word so marked is included as a head-word in the Appendix.

P

p [piː], *F:* **1. to mind** (*or* **watch**) **one's p's and q's,** (*a*) bien se tenir, se tenir convenablement; (*b*) s'occuper de ses affaires (*ou* de ses oignons) **2. to know one's p's and q's,** être débrouillard (*ou* démerdeur).

pa [pɑː] (*noun*), *F:* perè*, papa *m.*

pace [peis] (*noun*), *F:* **to go the p.,** mener la vie à grandes guides; mener un train d'enfer.

pack[1] [pæk] (*noun*). **1.** *P:* pochette *f* d'héroïne (*drogues*). **2.** *F:* **p. of lies,** tissu *m* (*ou* tas *m*) de mensonges*.

pack[2] [pæk] (**to**), *F:* **1. to p. a gun,** être armé (*ou* chargé). **2. to p. a punch,** (*a*) boxer dur, perloter; (*b*) (*boisson*) être corsé. **3. to send s.o. packing,** envoyer dinguer qn, envoyer promener qn, envoyer qn sur les roses.

pack-drill [ˈpækdril] (*noun*), *F:* **no names, no p.-d.,** *c.p.*, pas de nom, pas de démon.

packet [ˈpækit] (*noun*). **1.** *P:* **to catch** (*or* **cop**) **a p.,** (*a*) écoper, en prendre pour son grade; (*b*) être bouclé, être envoyé en villégiature; (*c*) = **to get a dose** (**dose, 1**). **2.** *F:* **to cost a p.,** coûter cher*, être salé (*ou* lerche). **3.** *F:* (*a*) **to make a p.,** gagner* beaucoup d'argent, prendre le paquet, en ramasser, se sucrer, faire son beurre; (*b*) **to lose a p.,** perdre beaucoup d'argent*, ramasser une culotte, être paumard. **4.** *F:* un sale coup, une bonne dose. *Voir aussi* **buy**[2] (**to**), **2.**

pack in [ˈpækˈin] (**to**). **1.** *P:* **to p. s.o. i.,** cesser de voir qn, débarquer, plaquer, envoyer bouler qn. **2.** (*a*) *F:* **to p. sth. i.,** cesser de faire qch., larguer, laisser choir qch.; (*b*) *P:* **p. it i.!** (i) arrête!; (ii) ta gueule! la ferme! **3.** *F:* **to p. them** (*or* **'em**) **i.,** faire salle comble (*théâtre, cinéma, etc.*).

pack up [ˈpækˈʌp] (**to**). **1.** *P:* **to p. s.o. u.** = **to pack s.o. in** (**pack in** (**to**), **1**). **2.** *F:* **to p. sth. u.** = **to pack sth. in** (**pack in** (**to**), **2** (*a*), (*b*)). **3.** *F:* arrêter le travail, débrayer. **4.** *F:* se détraquer, sombrer, s'effondrer. **5.** (*a*) *F:* partir*, plier bagage, prendre ses cliques et ses claques; (*b*) *P:* mourir*, lâcher la rampe, se laisser glisser.

pad[1] [pæd] (*noun*). **1.** *F:* logement*, piaule *f*, case *f*, pied-à-terre *m*; *cf.* **crash-pad; pill-pad; tea-pad. 2.** *P:* **the pads** = **paddy, 2. 3.** *P:* route*, tire *f*; **to be on the p.,** être sur le trimard. **4.** *P:* lit*, pieu *m*; **to hit the p.,** se coucher*, se pieuter. *Voir aussi* **launching-pad.**

pad[2] [pæd] (**to**), *F:* marcher* (péniblement), trimarder; **to p. it,** aller à pied, affûter des pinceaux, prendre le train onze; *voir aussi* **hoof**[1], **1; hoof**[2] (**to**).

paddler [ˈpædlər] (*noun*) (*Austr.*), *P:* agent* de police, tige *f.*

paddles [ˈpædlz] (*pl. noun*) (*Austr.*), *F:* pieds*, péniches *f.pl.*, ripatons *m.pl.*

pad down [ˈpædˈdaʊn] (**to**), *F:* dormir*, roupiller.

paddy [ˈpædi] (*noun*). **1.** *F:* (*a*) mauvaise humeur; (*b*) éclat *m* de colère, coup *m* de sang. **2.** *P:* cellule matelassée, cabanon *m*. **3.** Irlandais *m.*

paddy-wag(g)on [ˈpædiwægən] (*noun*) (*U.S.*), *F:* = **Black Maria** (**black**[1], **6**).

paddywhack [ˈpædi(h)wæk] (*noun*), *F:* **1.** = **paddy, 1. 2.** (*langage enfantin*) fessée *f.*

pain [pein] (*noun*), (*a*) *F:* **a p. in the neck,** individu ennuyeux* *ou* antipathique, raseur *m*, casse-pieds *m*; (*b*) *F:* **he gives me a p. in the neck,** il me tape sur le système; (*c*) *P:* **a p. in the arse,** un emmerdeur.

paint [peint] (**to**), *F:* **to p. a picture,** faire le point. *Voir aussi* **red**[1], **3.**

painter [ˈpeintər] (*noun*). **1.** *F:* **to slip the p.,** mourir*, lâcher la rampe. **2.** *P:* **to have the painters in,** avoir ses menstrues*, repeindre sa grille en rouge; *cf.* **decorators.**

pak(k)i-basher [ˈpæki-bæʃər] (*noun*), *P:* chasseur *m* de Pakistanais.

* L'astérisque indique que le mot marqué de ce signe figure comme entrée dans le Répertoire.

pak(k)i-bashing [ˈpæki-bæʃiŋ] (*noun*), *P:* chasse *f* aux Pakistanais.

pal [pæl] (*noun*), *F:* ami*, copain *m*, pote *m*; *cf.* **pal up (to)**.

palaver[1] [pəˈlɑːvər] (*noun*), *F:* **1.** bavardages *m.pl.*, palabres *f. pl.* **2.** embarras *m.pl.*, chichis *m.pl.* **3.** flagornerie *f*, baratin *m*.

palaver[2] [pəˈlɑːvər] (**to**), *F:* **1.** parler*, palabrer. **2.** flagorner, baratiner.

pally [ˈpæli] (*adj.*), *F:* (*a*) liant; (*b*) **to be p. with s.o.**, être copain (*ou* lié) avec qn.

palm [pɑːm] (*noun*), *F:* **1. to grease** (*or* **oil**) **s.o.'s p.**, graisser la patte à qn. **2. to have an itchy** (*or* **itching**) **p.**, être grippe-sou (*ou* grigou), les avoir crochues.

palm-grease [ˈpɑːmgriːs] (*noun*), *P:* graissage *m* de patte.

palm off [ˈpɑːmˈɔf] (**to**), *F:* **to p. sth. o. on to s.o.**, colloquer, refiler, pastiquer, coller qch. à qn.

palm-oil [ˈpɑːmɔil] (*noun*), *P:* = **palm-grease.**

palm-tree [ˈpɑːmtriː] (*noun*), *P:* voiture *f* difficile à vendre, un rossignol; *cf.* **bottler; square-wheeler.**

palooka [pəˈluːkə] (*noun*), *P:* **1.** joueur peu compétent, nullité *f*, nouille *f*. **2.** un gros plein de soupe.

palsy-walsy [ˈpælziˈwælzi] (*adj.*), *F:* **to be (all) p.-w. (with s.o.)**, être bons amis*, être à tu et à toi, être comme cul et chemise.

pal up [ˈpælˈʌp] (**to**), *F:* **to p. u. with s.o.**, copiner, se lier avec qn.

pan[1] [pæn] (*noun*). **1.** *P:* **to go down the p.** = **to go down the drain** (**drain**[1], **1**). **2.** *P:* visage*, burette *f*, fiole *f*. **3.** *F:* compte-rendu *m* défavorable, éreintage *m*, abattage *m*. *Voir aussi* **flash**[2], **2.**

pan[2] [pæn] (**to**), *F:* **1.** critiquer*, éreinter (qn, qch.). **2.** panoramiquer (une vue).

pancake [ˈpænkeik] (**to**), *F:* (*av.*) atterrir en crash (*ou* sur le gésier).

pancakes [ˈpænkeiks] (*pl. noun*), *P:* seins* aplatis, blagues *f.pl.* à tabac, tétasses *f.pl.*

panhandle [ˈpænhændl] (**to**) (*U.S.*), *F:* mendier*, pilonner, torpiller.

panhandler [ˈpænhændlər] (*noun*) (*U.S.*), *F:* mendiant*, mendigot *m*, torpilleur *m*.

panic [ˈpænik] (*noun*). **1.** *F:* **p. stations,** (*fig.*) postes *m.pl.* de combat, garde-à-vous *m*. **2.** *F:* **to push** (*or* **hit**) **the p. button,** (*a*) appuyer sur l'accélérateur, mettre les gaz; (*b*) être pris de panique, paniquer, avoir les foies. **3.** *P:* manque *m* (de drogues).

panicky [ˈpæniki] (*adj.*), *F:* (*a*) paniqué, paniquard; **don't get p.**, ne t'affole pas!; (*b*) (*d'un journal, etc.*) alarmiste.

panning [ˈpæniŋ] (*noun*), *F:* = **pan**[1], **3.**

pan out [ˈpænˈaut] (**to**). **1.** *F:* finir, se terminer, aboutir. **2.** *P:* rapporter (de l'argent), donner. **3.** *P:* **to p. o. about sth.**, s'étendre sur un sujet.

pansified [ˈpænzifaid], **pansy**[1] [ˈpænzi] (*adj.*), *F:* **1.** homosexuel, pédé. **2.** efféminé.

pansy[2] [ˈpænzi] (*noun*), *F:* **1.** pédéraste*, lopette *f*. **2.** homme efféminé, chochotte *f*, femmelette *f*, mauviette *f*.

pansyland [ˈpænzilænd] (*noun*), *F:* **1.** le monde des pédérastes*, la pédale, les tuyaux *m.pl.* de poêle; *cf.* **fairyland. 2. in p.**, au pays des contes de fées.

panties [ˈpæntiz] (*pl. noun*), *F:* culotte *f* de femme, culbute *f*.

pants [pænts] (*pl. noun*). **1.** *F:* (*a*) pantalon*, falzar *m*; (*b*) caleçon *m*, slip *m*; (*c*) = **panties. 2.** *P:* **to be caught with one's p. down,** être pris au dépourvu (*ou* la main dans le sac *ou* sur le tas), se trouver en mauvaise posture. **3.** *F:* **to get a kick in the p.,** être réprimandé* sévèrement, recevoir un coup de pied aux fesses* (*ou* quelque part); *voir aussi* **kick**[1],**5. 4.** *P:* **to scare the p. off s.o.,** faire peur* à qn, donner (*ou* foutre) la pétoche à qn, les mouiller. **5.** *P:* **to tear the p. off s.o.,** prendre qn à partie, habiller qn, secouer les puces à qn. **6.** *P:* **to beat** (*or* **lick**) **the p. off s.o.,** battre qn à plate(s) couture(s), écraser qn. **7.** (*U.S.*) *F:* **to wear the p.** = **to wear the trousers** (*voir* **trousers**). *Voir aussi* **ants; fancy**[1], **3; hot, 1, 2; lead**[1], **4; smarty(-pants).**

paper[1] [ˈpeipər] (*noun*), *P:* (*th.*) billets *m.pl.* de faveur, bif(fe)tons *m.pl.*

paper[2] [ˈpeipər] (**to**). **1.** *P:* (*th.*) **to p. the house,** jouer à la bif(fe)tonnade. **2.** *F:* **to p. over the cracks,** essayer de rafistoler les choses.

paper-hanger [ˈpeipehæŋər], **paper-pusher** [ˈpeipə-puʃər] (*noun*), *P:* faux-monnayeur *m*, faux-mornifleur *m*.

* An asterisk indicates that the word so marked is included as a head-word in the Appendix.

paralytic [ˈpærəˈlitik] (*adj.*), *F:* ivre* mort, bituré.

pard [pɑːd], **pardner** [ˈpɑːdnər] (*noun*) (*U.S.*), *F:* (*a*) associé *m*, assoce *m*, baron *m*; (*b*) ami*, pote *m*.

park [pɑːk] (**to**), *F:* **to p. oneself somewhere,** se mettre (*ou* s'installer) quelque part; **p. it over there!** mets-le (*ou* colle le) là! *Voir aussi* **ticket, 2.**

parky [ˈpɑːki] (*adj.*), *F:* (*du temps*) frais, frisco, frisquet.

parney [ˈpɑːni] (*noun*), *P:* pluie*, flotte *f*, saucée *f*.

party [ˈpɑːti] (*noun*), *F:* **a certain p.,** un certain individu*, un loustic, un numéro. *Voir aussi* **hen; keep** (**to**), **1; stag**[1]**; tea-party.**

pash [pæʃ] (*noun*), *F:* **to have a p. on s.o.,** aimer* qn, avoir le béguin pour qn, en pincer pour qn, être mordu pour qn.

pass [pɑːs] (*noun*), *F:* **to make a p. at s.o.,** essayer de séduire qn, flirter, faire du boniment à qn.

passenger [ˈpæsindʒər] (*noun*), *F:* un poids mort.

pass up [ˈpɑːsˈʌp] (**to**), *F:* se passer de (qch.), sauter, supprimer (qch.).

past [pɑːst] (*prep.*), *F:* **I wouldn't put it p. him,** il en est bien capable.

paste [peist] (**to**), *F:* battre*, rosser, dérouiller, étriller.

pasting [ˈpeistiŋ] (*noun*), *F:* **to give s.o. a p.,** (*a*) coller une raclée à qn, passer une peignée à qn; (*b*) (*sports, etc.*) battre qn à plate(s) couture(s).

pasture [ˈpɑːstjər] (*noun*), *F:* **to be put out to p.,** être mis à la retraite (*ou* au vert).

pat-ball [ˈpætbɔːl] (*noun*), *F:* tennis mal joué, jeu *m* à la raquette.

patch [pætʃ] (*noun*). **1.** *F:* **she's not a p. on him,** elle n'est pas de taille, elle ne lui arrive pas à la cheville. **2.** *P:* (*argot du milieu*) territoire *m*, champ *m* d'action, chasse gardée; *cf.* **manor.** **3.** *F:* **bad p.,** malchance*, guigne *f*, pétrin *m*. **4.** *P:* devise inscrite sur le dos des blousons de cuir des «Hell's Angels».

patch up [ˈpætʃˈʌp] (**to**), *F:* **to p. u. a quarrel,** rabibocher (*ou* replâtrer) une querelle*.

pathetic [pəˈθetik] (*adj.*), *F:* **it's p.!** c'est de la gnognot(t)e! c'est lamentable!

patootie [pəˈtuːti] (*noun*) (*U.S.*), *P:* **hot p.,** petite amie; blonde incendiaire.

patsy [ˈpætsi] (*noun*) (*U.S.*), *P:* **1.** dupe *f*, victime *f*, gogo *m*, jobard *m*. **2.** pleutre *m*, poule mouillée.

patter [ˈpætər] (*noun*), *F:* bavardage *m*, causette *f*, jaserie *m*, baratinage *m*.

patteran [ˈpætəræn] (*noun*), *P:* langage *m* par signes des bohémiens, manouche muet.

paw[1] [pɔː] (*noun*), *P:* main*, patte *f*, paluche *f*; **paws off! keep your paws to yourself!** (à) bas les pattes! pas touche! *Voir aussi* **southpaw.**

paw[2] [pɔː] (**to**), *F:* peloter, tripoter (une femme); patouiller (qn, qch.).

pax! [pæks] (*excl.*), *F:* (*langage enfantin*) pouce!; **end of p.,** pouce cassé.

pay [pei] (**to**), *P:* battre*, rosser, tabasser, étriller. *Voir aussi* **call, 1; visit.**

pay-off [ˈpei-ɔf] (*noun*), *F:* **1.** règlement *m* de comptes. **2.** le bouquet, le comble (qch. de tout à fait inattendu). **3.** pot-de-vin *m*, dessous-de-table *m*. **4.** (*a*) facteur décisif; (*b*) le fin mot (de l'histoire).

pay off [ˈpeiˈɔf] (**to**), *F:* avoir du succès, être rentable, faire un boum, boumer.

payola [peiˈjoulə] (*noun*), *F:* ristourne *f*, gratte *f*, gant *m*.

payroll [ˈpeiroul] (*noun*), *F:* **to be on the p.,** faire partie de la bande*, être du même bâtiment.

p.d.q. [ˈpiːˈdiːˈkjuː] (*abbr.* = *pretty damn quick*), *P:* très vite*, en cinq secs.

peach[1] [piːtʃ] (*noun*). **1.** *F:* belle* fille, jolie pépée, bath petit lot; **she's a p. of a girl,** c'est un beau brin de fille, c'est une belle petite caille. **2.** *F:* qch. de super (*ou* de sensass), un délice; **it's a p. of a party,** c'est une super boum, c'est une bath surboum. **3.** *P:* amphétamine *f* (*drogues**).

peach[2] [piːtʃ] (**to**), *P:* dénoncer*, moucharder, cafarder, bourdiller; **to p. on s.o.,** trahir, vendre, moutonner qn.

peachy [ˈpiːtʃi] (*adj.*), *F:* agréable, jojo, juteux.

pea-head [ˈpiːhed] (*noun*), *P:* individu bête*, tête *f* de linotte.

peanut [ˈpiːnʌt] (*noun*). **1.** *P:* barbiturique *m* (*drogues**). **2.** (*pl.*) *F:* presque rien*, de la gnognot(t)e, des clous, des prunes. **3.** (*U.S.*) *F:* (*th.*) **p. gallery** = **chicken-roost.**

* L'astérisque indique que le mot marqué de ce signe figure comme entrée dans le Répertoire.

pearl-dive [ˈpəːl-daiv] (**to**), *V:* = **muff**[2] (**to**), 3.

pearl-diver [ˈpəːl-daivər] (*noun*), *V:* = **muff-diver.**

pearlies [ˈpəːliz] (*pl. noun*), *F:* dents*, dominos *m.pl.*

pearls [pəːlz] (*pl. noun*), *P:* = **amy.**

pearly [ˈpəːli] (*adj.*), *P:* **p. gates,** graines *f.pl.* de volubilis (drogue hallucinogène); *cf.* **heavenly blues** (**blue**[2], 1).

pea-shooter [ˈpiː-ʃuːtər] (*noun*), *P:* revolver*, rigolo *m*; *cf.* **shooter.**

pea-souper [ˈpiːˈsuːpər] (*noun*), *F:* brouillard *m* (à couper au couteau), purée *f* de pois.

peck [pek] (**to**), *F:* manger* du bout des dents; **to p. at one's food,** pignocher, mangeotter son repas.

pecker [ˈpekər] (*noun*). 1. *P:* pénis*, goupillon *m*, chibre *m*. 2. *F:* courage *m*, cran *m*; **to keep one's p. up,** ne pas se laisser abattre, tenir bon, tenir le coup.

peckish [ˈpekiʃ] (*adj.*), *F:* **to be** (*or* **feel**) **p.,** avoir faim*, claquer du bec.

pedigree [ˈpedigriː] (*noun*), *P:* casier *m* judiciaire d'un criminel, faffes *m.pl.*, blase *m*.

pee[1] [piː] (*noun*), *P:* urine *f*, pipi *m*; **to have a p.,** uriner*; **to go for a p.,** aller faire pipi.

pee[2] [piː] (**to**), *P:* 1. uriner*, pisser. 2. pleuvoir à torrent, flotter, pisser.

peed off [ˈpiːdˈɔf] (*adj.*), *P:* = **pissed off.**

pee down [ˈpiːˈdaun] (**to**), *P:* = **pee**[2] (**to**), 2.

peek [piːk] (*noun*), *P:* **the p.** = **the peep.**

peeker [ˈpiːkər] (*noun*), *P:* curieux *m*, indiscret *m*, voyeur *m*.

peel (off) [ˈpiːl(ˈɔf)] (**to**), *F:* se déshabiller*, se décarpiller, se dénipper. *Voir aussi* **banana, 1; onion, 1.**

peeler [ˈpiːlər] (*noun*), *P:* strip-teaseuse *f*, effeuilleuse *f*.

peenie [ˈpiːni] (*noun*), *P:* pénis*, pine *f*.

pee off [ˈpiːˈɔf] (**to**), *P:* = **piss off** (**to**).

peep [piːp] (*noun*). 1. *P:* **the p.,** cellule *f* (*ou* cellot(t)e *f*) de remouchage, cage *f* à poules. 2. *F:* **I don't want to hear another p. out of you,** tâche de ne pas piper.

peepers [ˈpiːpəz] (*pl. noun*), *F:* yeux *m.pl.* (*œil**), mirettes *f.pl.*, châsses *m.pl.*

pee-slit [ˈpiː-slit] (*noun*), *V:* vagin*, fente *f*.

peeve[1] [piːv] (*noun*), *F:* ennui *m*, barbe *f*, crampon *m*, emmerdement *m*; **pet p.,** barbe *f* de premier ordre, poison violent.

peeve[2] [piːv] (**to**), *F:* ennuyer*, barber, canuler, empoisonner.

peeved [piːvd] (*adj.*), *F:* fâché, irrité, ennuyé.

peg[1] [peg] (*noun*), *F:* 1. **off the p.,** prêt à porter, confection. 2. (*a*) **to take s.o. down a p.,** rabattre le caquet à qn, rogner les ailes à qn, faire déchanter qn; (*b*) **to come down a p.,** en rabattre, baisser le ton, baisser d'un cran, déchanter. 3. doigt *m* (de whisky, *etc.*). 4. (*pl.*) jambes*, bâtons *m.pl.*, cannes *f.pl.* *Voir aussi* **square**[1], 7.

peg[2] [peg] (**to**), *F:* **to have s.o., sth., pegged** = **to have s.o., sth., taped** (**tape**[2] (**to**)).

peg away [ˈpegəˈwei] (**to**), *F:* travailler* dur, turbiner, piocher.

peg back [ˈpegˈbæk] (**to**), *F:* stabiliser, maintenir (le prix, *etc.*, de qch.).

peg-leg [ˈpegleg] (*noun*), *F:* (*a*) jambe *f* de bois, pilon *m*; (*b*) pilonneur *m*.

peg out [ˈpegˈaut] (**to**), *F:* 1. mourir*, lâcher la rampe, casser sa pipe. 2. **to be pegged out,** être très fatigué* (*ou* éreinté *ou* fourbu).

pen [pen] (*noun*), *F:* (=*penitentiary*) prison*, taule *f*, ballon *m*.

pen and ink [ˈpenəndˈiŋk] (**to**), *P:* 1. (*R.S.* = *to stink*) puer, schlinguer. 2. (*R.S.* = *to drink*) boire*.

pencil [ˈpensl] (*noun*), *P:* pénis*, le bout, la pointe; *cf.* **lead**[1], 3.

penguin [ˈpeŋgwin] (*noun*), *F:* 1. (*av.*) = **ground walla**(**h**) (**walla**(**h**), 2). 2. **p. suit,** habit *m* (de soirée), queue *f* de pie.

penman [ˈpenmən] (*noun*), *P:* faussaire *m*, homme *m* de lettres, maquilleur *m*.

penny [ˈpeni] (*noun*), *F:* 1. **then the p. dropped,** alors on a compris (*ou* pigé). 2. **to spend a p.,** aller aux W.C.*, aller au petit coin. 3. **a p. for your thoughts,** *c.p.*, à quoi penses-tu? 4. **she cost me a pretty p.,** elle m'en a fait écosser. *Voir aussi* **bad**[1], 3.

penny-pincher [ˈpeni-pintʃər] (*noun*), *F:* avare *m*, radin *m*, rapiat *m*.

penny-pinching[1] [ˈpeni-pintʃiŋ] (*adj.*), *F:* avare*, constipé du morlingue, grippe-sou.

* An asterisk indicates that the word so marked is included as a head-word in the Appendix.

penny-pinching[2] [ˈpeni-pintʃiŋ] (*noun*), *F:* avarice *f*, radinerie *f*.

pen-pusher [ˈpenpuʃər] (*noun*), *F:* gratte-papier *m*, rond-de-cuir *m*.

pension [ˈpenʃ(ə)n] (*noun*), *F:* **old-age p.**: *voir* **bingo (65)**.

pen-yen [ˈpenˈjen] (*noun*) (*U.S.*), *P:* opium *m* (*drogues**), op *m*, touffiane *f*.

people [ˈpi:pl] (*pl. noun*), *F:* **1. the income-tax p.**, les gens du fisc, les dégraisseurs *m.pl.* **2. to know the right p.**, avoir des relations *f.pl.* (utiles), avoir le bras long. **3.** famille *f*, parents*, smala *f*.

pep [pep] (*noun*), *F:* **1. to be full of p.**, être plein d'entrain, péter le feu. **2. p. pill**, stimulant *m*, topette *f*, remontant *m*, excitant *m*. **3. p. talk**, paroles encourageantes qui remontent le moral et émoustillent, petit discours* d'encouragement.

pepper-upper [ˈpepəˈrʌpər] (*noun*), *F:* apéritif *m*, remontant *m*, coup *m* de fouet, stimulant *m*; *cf.* **pep up (to)**.

peppy [ˈpepi] (*adj.*), *F:* plein d'allant et de vitalité.

pep up [ˈpepˈʌp] (**to**), *F:* **1.** émoustiller, ravigoter (qch.). **2.** remonter, ragaillardir (qn).

Perce [pə:s], **Percy** [ˈpə:si] (*noun*), *P:* pénis*, cyclope *m*, Popaul; **to point P. at the porcelain**, uriner*, égoutter son cyclope.

perch [pə:tʃ] (*noun*), *F:* **to knock s.o. off his p., to make s.o. come down from his p.**, faire descendre qn de son perchoir, déboulonner qn; **to come off one's p.**, jeter du lest.

perfect [ˈpə:fikt] (*adj.*), *F:* vrai, absolu; **he's a p. idiot**, c'est un idiot fini; **he's a p. menace**, c'est une vraie menace.

perform [pəˈfɔ:m] (**to**), *P:* **1.** déféquer*, déballer. **2.** coïter*, niquer.

period [ˈpiəriəd] (*noun*), *F:* **He's no good at maths. – He's no good, period,** Il est nul en math. – Il est nul, tout court.

perished [ˈperiʃt] (*adj.*), *F:* exténué de froid *ou* de faim, rétamé, plombé.

perisher [ˈperiʃər] (*noun*), *F:* sale type *m*, chameau *m*, saligaud *m*.

perishing [ˈperiʃiŋ] (*adj.*), *F:* **1. it's p.**, il fait un froid de loup; **I'm p.**, je suis transi de froid. **2.** sacré, satané, maudit.

perks [pə:ks] (*pl. noun* = *perquisites*), *F:* gratte *f*, affure *f*, grinche *f*, tour *m* de bâton; les petits à-côtés, les petits bénefs.

perk up [ˈpə:kˈʌp] (**to**), *F:* (*a*) ravigoter, requinquer (qn); (*b*) se ravigoter, se requinquer.

perm[1] [pə:m] (*noun*), *F:* **1.** (=*permanent wave*) indéfrisable *f*, permanente *f*, modelling *m*. **2.** (=*permutation*) permutation *f* (au tiercé du football).

perm[2] [pə:m] (**to**), *F:* **1. to have one's hair permed,** se faire faire une indéfrisable. **2.** (*tiercé du football*) faire une permutation; permuter.

pernickety [pəˈnikəti] (*adj.*), *F:* vétilleux, pointilleux; **to be p. about one's food,** être difficile (*ou* délicat) sur la nourriture*.

persuader [pəˈsweidər] (*noun*), *P:* **1.** pénis*, baïonnette *f*. **2.** arme *f*, flingue *m*.

perve[1] [pə:v] (*noun*), *P:* perverti *m*; inverti *m*.

perve[2] [pə:v] (**to**) (*Austr.*), *P:* **to p. on s.o.**, se rincer l'œil (en regardant qn).

pesky [ˈpeski] (*adj.*) (*U.S.*), *F:* ennuyeux*, scie, rasoir.

pest [pest] (*noun*), *F:* enquiquineur *m*, poison *mf*, plaie *f*.

pet [pet] (**to**), *F:* se caresser, se peloter; *cf.* **petting.**

Pete [pi:t] (*pr. noun*), *F:* **for P.'s sake!** au nom des Saints! pour l'amour de Dieu!

peter [ˈpi:tər] (*noun*), *P:* **1.** coffre-fort *m*, coffiot *m*. **2. P.** (*or* **P. Bell**) (*R.S.* = (*prison*) *cell*), cellule *f* de prison, cellot(t)e *f*; *cf.* **flowery (dell)**. **3.** pénis*, Charles-le-Chauve, Popaul.

peterman [ˈpi:təmən] (*noun*), *P:* casseur *m* de coffre-fort (*ou* de coffiot).

petticoat-chaser [ˈpetikout-tʃeisər] (*noun*), *F:* coureur *m* de jupons.

petting [ˈpetiŋ] (*noun*), *F:* badinage amoureux, pelotage *m*; **p. party**, party *f* de pelote maison; **p. session,** séance *f* de bécotage *m* (*ou* de pelotage *m*); *cf.* **pet (to)**.

pew [pju:] (*noun*), *F:* **to take a p.**, s'asseoir, poser ses fesses.

pewter [ˈpju:tər] (*noun*), *P:* argent *m* (*métal*).

phenie [ˈfi:ni] (*noun*), *F:* phénobarbital *m*; barbiturique *m* (*drogues**).

phiz [fiz], **phizog** [ˈfizɔg] (*noun*), *P:* visage*, frime *f*, frimousse *f*.

* An asterisk indicates that the word so marked is included as a head-word in the Appendix.

phon(e)y[1] [ˈfouni] (*adj.*). **1.** *F:* faux*, chinetoque, bidon, toc(ard). **2.** (*a*) *F:* contrefait, falsifié; (*b*) *P:* **p. white,** fausses pièces d'argent*, mornifle truquée.
phon(e)y[2] [ˈfouni] (*noun*). **1.** *F:* charlatan *m*, bluffeur *m*, chiqueur *m*. **2.** *P:* qn qui fait des appels téléphoniques obscènes.
phooey! [ˈfuːi] (*excl.*), *F:* fi! fi donc! flûte!
phut [fʌt] (*adv.*), *F:* **to go p.,** échouer*, rater, louper, s'en aller en eau de boudin, claquer.
phy [fai] (*abbr.* = *physeptone*), *P:* physeptone *f* (*drogues*).
pi [pai] (*adj.*), *P:* papelard, cagot, bondieusard. *Voir aussi* **jaw**[1], **2.**
Piccadilly Circus [ˈpikədiliˈsəːkəs] (*pr. noun*), *F:* **it's like P. C.!** quel embouteillage!
pick [pik] (*noun*), *F:* **the p. of the bunch,** le dessus du panier, la fleur des petits pois.
picker [ˈpikər] (*noun*) (*U.S.*), *P:* = **peeker.** *Voir aussi* **winkle-pickers.**
pickle [ˈpikl] (*noun*), *F:* **1. to be in a p.,** être dans le pétrin (*ou* dans de mauvais draps). **2.** petit diable, diablotin *m*.
pickled [ˈpikld] (*adj.*), *F:* ivre*, rétamé.
pick-me-up [ˈpikmi(ː)ʌp] (*noun*), *F:* cordial *m*, remontant *m*, stimulant *m*, coup *m* de fouet.
pick on [ˈpikɔn] (**to**), *F:* chercher noise à (qn).
pick-up [ˈpikʌp] (*noun*). **1.** *F:* rencontre *f* de fortune, femme dont on fait connaissance dans la rue. **2.** *F:* **to have a p.-u.,** être conduit quelque part en voiture. **3.** *F:* redressement *m*, relèvement *m*, reprise *f*. **4.** *P:* drogues* obtenues d'un pourvoyeur.
pick up [ˈpikˈʌp] (**to**). **1.** *F:* arrêter*, agrafer, pincer. **2.** *F:* (*d'une prostituée*) ramasser (un client), faire (un levage). **3.** *F:* ramasser, récolter (microbes, *etc.*). **4.** *F:* **to p. u. the pieces,** repartir à zéro, recoller les restes. **5.** *F:* reprendre, corriger (qn). **6.** *F:* **to p. u. with s.o.,** faire la connaissance de qn. **7.** *P:* obtenir des drogues* d'un pourvoyeur. **8.** *F:* **to p. u. on sth.,** assimiler, digérer qch. **9.** *F:* (*physiquement, financièrement*) se rebecter, se rebecqueter, se remplumer.
picky [ˈpiki] (*adj.*), *F:* méticuleux, chichiteux; **to be p.,** chercher la petite bête.
picnic [ˈpiknik] (*noun*), *P:* **1.** occupation *f* agréable et facile, partie *f* de plaisir. **2.** rigolade *f*, un vrai cirque.
picture [ˈpiktʃər] (*noun*), *F:* **1. to put s.o. in the p.,** mettre qn au courant (*ou* à la page). **2. she's a real p.!** c'est une beauté! elle est ravissante! **3.** (*a*) **to step into the p.,** se montrer, se manifester; (*b*) **to step out of the p.,** s'effacer, se retirer. **4. get the p.?** tu comprends? tu piges? *Voir aussi* **paint (to).**
piddle[1] [ˈpidl] (*noun*), *F:* urine *f*, pipi *m*.
piddle[2] [ˈpidl] (**to**). *F:* uriner*, faire pipi. **2.** *P:* pleuvoter, pleuvasser.
piddle about (*or* **around**) [ˈpidl-əˈbaut, ˈpidl-əˈraund] (**to**), *P:* paresser*, flânocher, galvauder.
piddling [ˈpidliŋ] (*adj.*), *F:* bête*, niais, futile.
pidgin [ˈpidʒin] (*noun*), *F:* **1.** = **pigeon, 2. 2. to talk p.,** parler petit nègre.
pie [pai] (*noun*), *F:* **p. in the sky,** le miel de l'autre monde. *Voir aussi* **apple-pie**[1,2]; **easy**[1], **6**; **finger**[1], **5**; **fruity-pie**[1,2]; **hairpie**; **mince-pies**; **resurrection pie**; **sweetie-pie**; **tongue-pie**; **tweety(-pie).**
piece [piːs] (*noun*). **1.** *P:* fille*, femme*, un (beau) petit lot; *voir aussi* **lush**[1]. **2.** *F:* **to go to pieces,** (*d'un individu*) s'effondrer, se catastropher, s'écrouler. **3.** *P:* deux grammes d'héroïne *ou* de stupéfiant. **4.** *F:* **to pull s.o. to pieces,** déchirer qn à belles dents, mettre qn en capilotade, éreinter qn. **5.** (*U.S.*) *F:* arme *f*. *Voir aussi* **ass**[1], **2**; **cake, 1, 3**; **head-piece**; **kettle, 1**; **mouth-piece**; **pick up (to), 4**; **ring-piece**; **sky-piece**; **tail**[1], **4**; **think-piece**; **two-piece**; **work**[1].
pie-eyed [ˈpai-aid] (*adj.*), *F:* ivre*, gris, éméché.
piffle [ˈpifl] (*noun*), *F:* bêtises*, futilités *f.pl.*, balivernes *f.pl.*
piffling [ˈpifliŋ] (*adj.*), *F:* = **piddling.**
pig[1] [pig] (*noun*). **1.** *F:* goinfre*, gueulard *m*, morfalou *m*. **2.** *F:* salaud *m*, saligaud *m*, vache *f*. **3.** *P:* agent* de police, perdreau *m*. **4.** *P:* **p.'s ear** (*R.S.* = *beer*), bière *f*. **5.** *P:* **in p.,** enceinte*, en cloque. **6.** *F:* **to buy a p. in a poke,** acheter chat en poche.

* L'astérisque indique que le mot marqué de ce signe figure comme entrée dans le Répertoire.

pig² [pig] (**to**), *P:* **1.** se goinfrer, s'empiffrer, bâfrer, manger comme un goret. **2. to p. it,** vivre comme un cochon, vivre dans une écurie. **3. to p. together,** partager la même chambre.

pig-boat [ˈpigbout] (*noun*), *P:* sous-marin *m*, plongeant *m*.

pigeon [ˈpidʒin] (*noun*), *F:* **1.** dupe *f*, dindon *m*, poire *f*, poireau *m*. **2. it's not my p.,** ça ne me regarde pas, c'est pas mes oignons; **that's your p.,** ça te regarde, c'est ton rayon (*ou* ton affaire). **3.** jeune fille*. *Voir aussi* **stool-pigeon.**

pigeon-roost [ˈpidʒinru:st] (*noun*), *F:* (*th.*) le poulailler, le paradis; *cf.* **chicken-roost.**

piggy¹ [ˈpigi] (*adj.*), *F:* goinfre*, goulu.

piggy² [ˈpigi] (*noun*), *F:* **1.** cochonnet *m*, cochon *m* de lait, porcelet *m*. **2.** petit goret, petit goulu.

piggyback [ˈpigibæk] (*noun*), *F:* **to give s.o. a p.,** porter qn sur le dos *ou* sur les épaules.

piggy-bank [ˈpigibæŋk] (*noun*), *F:* tire-lire *f*, boîte *f* à sous (en forme de cochon).

pig-meat [ˈpigmi:t] (*noun*), *P:* **1.** prostituée*, bourrin *m*. **2.** la Veuve Montretout, une vieille paillasse. **3.** fille bête*, andouille *f*.

pigwash [ˈpig-wɔʃ] (*noun*), *F:* = **hogwash, 1.**

pike¹ [paik] (*noun*), *P:* route*, trime *f*.

pike² [paik] (**to**), *P:* marcher*, trimarder, aller à pattes.

piker [ˈpaikər] (*noun*), *P:* avare *m*, grigou *m*.

pile [pail] (*noun*), *F:* **1.** (*a*) **to make a p. (of money),** gagner* beaucoup d'argent, en amasser, faire sa pelote; (*b*) **to make one's p.,** devenir riche*, faire son beurre. **2. a p. of work,** un tas (*ou* un monceau *ou* une pile) de travail* (*ou* de boulot).

pile-driver [ˈpail-draivər] (*noun*), *F:* coup* d'assommoir, direct *m*, marron *m*.

pile in [ˈpailˈin] (**to**), *F:* s'empiler dans un véhicule.

pile into [ˈpailˈintu:] (**to**), *F:* **to p. i. s.o.,** attaquer* qn, rentrer dedans, agrafer qn.

pile on [ˈpailˈɔn] (**to**), *F:* **to p. it o.,** exagérer*, y aller fort, charrier. *Voir aussi* **agony, 2.**

pile-up [ˈpailʌp] (*noun*), *F:* **1.** embouteillage *m*, bouchon *m*. **2.** carambolage *m*, emboutissage *m*.

pill [pil] (*noun*). **1.** *F:* balle *f*, ballon *m*. **2.** (*pl.*) *P:* testicules*, billes *f.pl.*, roupettes *f.pl.* **3.** *F:* (**bitter**) **p.,** personne *f ou* chose *f* désagréable, pilule *f*, poison *mf*, colique *f*. **4.** capsule *f* de Nembutal (*drogues*). **5.** *P:* boulette *f* d'opium (*drogues**); *cf.* **pill-pad. 6.** *F:* **to be on the p.,** prendre la pilule.

pillhead [ˈpilhed] (*noun*), *P:* habitué(e) des opiacés, opiomane *mf*.

pillow-talk [ˈpilou-tɔ:k] (*noun*), *F:* semonce conjugale, discours *m* sur l'oreiller, engueulade *f* entre deux draps.

pill-pad [ˈpil-pæd] (*noun*), *P:* fumerie *f* d'opium, repaire *m* (*ou* turne *f*) de drogués*.

pimple [ˈpimpl] (*noun*), *P:* **p. and blotch** (*R.S.* = *Scotch* (*whisky*)), whisky *m*.

pin [pin] (**to**), *F:* **to p. sth. on s.o.,** rendre qn responsable, mettre qch. sur le dos de qn.

pinball [ˈpinbɔ:l] (*noun*), *F:* flipper *m*.

pinch¹ [pintʃ] (*noun*), *F:* **1. to feel the p.,** tirer le diable par la queue. **2. at a p.,** au besoin.

pinch² [pintʃ] (**to**), *F:* **1.** voler*, chiper, chaparder. **2.** arrêter*, agrafer; **to get pinched,** se faire épingler. **3. to be pinched for time (money,** *etc.*), être à court de temps (d'argent, *etc.*).

pinchers [ˈpintʃəz] (*pl. noun*), *P:* menottes*, pinces *f.pl.*

pinching [ˈpintʃiŋ] (*noun*), *F:* vol *m*, chapardage *m*. *Voir aussi* **penny-pinching².**

pine [pain] (*noun*), *F:* **p. overcoat** = **wooden overcoat** (*voir* **overcoat**).

pineapple [ˈpainæpl] (*noun*), *F:* grenade *f* à main, poire *f*.

ping [piŋ] (*noun*), *P:* piqûre *f* de drogue; **p. in the wing,** piquouse *f* dans l'aile.

pinhead [ˈpinhed] (*noun*), *P:* **1.** petite tête*, tête d'épingle. **2.** qn d'ignorant*, tête *f* de linotte.

pink¹ [piŋk] (*adj.*), *F:* à tendances socialistes, rose (*ou* rouge) sur les bords. *Voir aussi* **elephant, 2; strike (to), 1; tickle² (to), 2.**

pink² [piŋk] (*noun*), *F:* **to be in the p.,** se porter à merveille (*ou* comme un charme).

* L'astérisque indique que le mot marqué de ce signe figure comme entrée dans le Répertoire.

pinkie, pinky [ˈpiŋki] (*noun*). **1.** *F:* le petit doigt, le riquiqui. **2.** *P:* un (homme) blanc; *cf.* **whitie.**

pinny [ˈpini] (*noun*) (=*pinafore*), *F:* tablier *m*, bavette *f*.

pin-pricks [ˈpinpriks] (*pl. noun*), *F:* tracasseries *f.pl.*, asticotages *m.pl.*

pins [pinz] (*pl. noun*), *F:* **1.** jambes*, fusains *m.pl.*, quilles *f.pl.* **2. to be on p. and needles,** être sur des charbons ardents. *Voir aussi* **piss**[2] **(to), 2.**

pinta [ˈpaintə] (*noun*), *F:* bouteille *f* de lait; demi-litre *m* (de lait, *etc.*).

pint-size(d) [ˈpaint-saiz(d)] (*adj.*), *F:* **a p.-s. person,** individu *m* de petite* taille, courte-botte *f*, demi-portion *f*.

pin-up [ˈpinʌp] (*noun*), *F:* **1.** belle fille*, pin-up *f*, prix *m* de Diane; **p.-u. mag(azine),** magazine *m* de pin-up.

pip[1] [pip] (*noun*), *F:* **1. to give s.o. the p.,** déprimer qn, flanquer le cafard à qn. **2.** (*mil.*) galon *m*, ficelle *f*; **to get one's p.,** recevoir ses galons, arborer la ficelle; **he's just got his third p.,** il vient d'avoir sa troisième ficelle. **3.** jeune personne alléchante, charmeuse *f*.

pip[2] [pip] **(to). 1.** *P:* blackbouler (qn). **2.** *F:* **the horse was pipped on the post,** le cheval a été battu au poteau d'arrivée. **3.** *F:* **to p. an exam,** être recalé à un examen.

pipe[1] [paip] (*noun*). **1.** *F:* **put that in your p. and smoke it!** mets ça dans ta poche et ton mouchoir par-dessus! **2.** *P:* **to hit the p.,** fumer de l'opium, y aller du chilom. **3.** *P:* = **gonga.** *Voir aussi* **drainpipe; stove-pipe.**

pipe[2] [paip] **(to),** *P:* laisser savoir, laisser transpirer, mettre au parfum.

pipe down [ˈpaipˈdaun] **(to),** *P:* (*a*) faire moins de bruit*, mettre un bémol (*ou* une sourdine) (à la clef); **p. d., will you!** baisse un peu ta musique!; (*b*) se taire*, la boucler.

pipe-job [ˈpaipdʒɔb] (*noun*), *V:* coït* buccal, prise *f* de pipe; *cf.* **blow-job.**

pipeline [ˈpaip-lain] (*noun*), *F:* **1. to be in the p.,** être en cours (*ou* en voie *ou* en train). **2. to have a p.,** avoir une filière.

pipe up [ˈpaipˈʌp] **(to),** *F:* se faire entendre, l'ouvrir tout d'un coup.

pip out [ˈpipˈaut] **(to),** *P:* mourir*, faire couic.

pippins [ˈpipinz] (*pl. noun*), *P:* seins*, nénés *m.pl.*

pipsqueak[1] [ˈpip-skwiːk] (*adj.*), *F:* petit, minuscule, insignifiant.

pipsqueak[2] [ˈpip-skwiːk] (*noun*), *F:* **1.** gringalet *m*, minus *m*, minable *m*. **2.** mobylette *f*, pétrolette *f*.

piss[1] [pis] (*noun*), *P:* **1.** urine *f*, pipi *m*, pisse *f*. **2. to take the p. (out of s.o.),** faire marcher qn, se payer la tête de qn; *cf.* **piss-taker. 3. a long streak of p.,** (*a*) une perche, un échalas, un individu long comme un jour sans pain; (*b*) un gros plein de soupe. **4.** bêtises*, foutaises *f.pl.*, conneries *f.pl.* **5. cat's** (*or* **gnat's**) **p.,** pipi *m* de chat. **6. to be full of p. and wind,** être comme une bulle de savon. **7. to be full of p. and vinegar,** être plein d'entrain, péter le feu. **8. to beat the p. out of s.o.,** battre* qn comme plâtre, tabasser qn.

piss[2] [pis] **(to),** *P:* uriner*, pisser, lansquiner. **2. to p. pins and needles,** être atteint de gonorrhée* (*ou* de chaude-pisse), pisser des lames de rasoir (en travers). **3. to p. oneself laughing,** se tordre les côtes de rire, rire* à s'en mouiller. **4. to p. blood,** suer sang et eau, s'échiner. **5.** = **piss down (to).**

piss-artist [ˈpis-ɑːtist] (*noun*) (*Austr.*), *P:* ivrogne*, poivrier *m*.

piss away [ˈpisəˈwei] **(to),** *P:* dépenser* sans compter, bouffer, claquer (de l'argent*).

piss down [ˈpisˈdaun] **(to),** *P:* = **pee**[2] **(to), 2.**

pissed [pist] (*adj.*), *P:* ivre*; **to get p.,** s'enivrer, prendre une cuite (*ou* une bit(t)ure); *voir aussi* **arsehole, 2.**

pissed off [ˈpistˈɔf] (*adj.*), *P:* **1. to be p. o.,** en avoir assez* (*ou* ras le bol *ou* plus que marre). **2.** (*U.S.*) très en colère*, en rage.

pisser [ˈpisər] (*noun*), *P:* **to pull s.o.'s p.,** faire marcher qn, monter un bateau à qn, faire monter qn à l'échelle.

pisshouse [ˈpishaus] (*noun*), *P:* W.C.*, pissotière *f*.

piss off [ˈpisˈɔf] **(to),** *P:* s'enfuir*, se tirer, se trisser; **p. o.!** fous le camp! *Voir aussi* **pissed off.**

piss on [ˈpisɔn] **(to),** *P:* dénigrer, débiner (qn), traiter (qn) comme du poisson pourri.

* An asterisk indicates that the word so marked is included as a head-word in the Appendix.

piss-poor [ˈpisˈpɔːr] (*adj.*), *P:* 1. très pauvre*, purotin, déchard, dans la purée noire. 2. de mauvaise qualité, tocard, camelote.

pisspot [ˈpispɔt] (*noun*), *P:* 1. pot *m* de chambre, Jules, Thomas. 2. saligaud *m*, salaud *m*. 3. ivrogne*, sac *m* à vin.

piss-taker [ˈpis-teikər] (*noun*), *P:* blagueur *m*, persifleur *m*; *cf.* **mick(e)y-taker; piss**[1], 2.

piss-tank [ˈpis-tæŋk] (*noun*), *P:* = **piss-pot, 3.**

pit [pit] (*noun*), *P:* 1. lit*, pageot *m*. 2. poche* intérieure d'un vêtement, profonde *f*. *Voir aussi* **fleapit.**

pitch[1] [pitʃ] (*noun*), *P:* 1. «paroisse» *f* d'une prostituée*, chasse gardée. 2. le «mâle» dans un couple homosexuel, chauffeur *m*. 3. discours*, boniment *m*, speech *m*; laïus *m*; **to make a p.**, bonimenter, pleurer misère. *Voir aussi* **queer**[3] **(to), 1.**

pitch[2] [pitʃ] (**to**), *F:* **to be in there pitching,** y aller de tout son saoul, se décarcasser. *Voir aussi* **fly-pitch (to); yarn**[1].

pitcher [ˈpitʃər] (*noun*) (*Austr.*), *F:* = **bugler, 1.** *Voir aussi* **fly-pitcher.**

pitch in [ˈpitʃˈin] (**to**), *F:* 1. s'empiffrer, s'en mettre plein la lampe. 2. se mettre au travail*, embrayer, rentrer dans le mastic, s'y mettre. 3. donner de l'argent*, les abouler, filer à la manche.

pitch into [ˈpitʃˈintuː] (**to**), *F:* 1. attaquer*, tomber sur le poil de (qn), rentrer dans le lard à (qn). 2. réprimander*, attraper, secouer les puces à (qn).

pix[1] [piks] (*noun*) (*U.S.*), *P:* pédéraste*, lope *f*.

pix[2] [piks] (*pl. noun*) (*=pictures*) (*U.S.*), *F:* (*a*) film *m*; cinéma *m*, cinoche *m*; (*b*) images *f.pl.*, illustrations *f.pl.*

pixil(l)ated [ˈpiksileitid] (*adj.*), *F:* 1. un peu fou*, cinglé. 2. (*U.S.*) ivre*, bit(t)uré, rétamé.

place[1] [pleis] (*noun*), *F:* 1. **to go places,** (*a*) voir du pays et du monde; (*b*) réussir dans la vie, monter les échelons, faire un boum. 2. **come and lunch at our p.,** venez déjeuner chez nous.

place[2] [pleis] (**to**), *F:* **I can't p. him,** je ne le remets pas.

plain [plein] (*adv.*), *F:* **p. daft** (*or* **dumb**), bête* comme chou, complètement borné.

plank [plæŋk] (**to**), *F:* = **plonk**[2] **(to).**

plant[1] [plɑːnt] (*noun*), *P:* 1. faux-frère *m*, pisteur *m*, chevilleur *m*. 2. piège *m*, amarre *f*, duperie *f*, roustissure *f*. 3. fabrication *f* de faux témoignage, boucanade *f*. 4. planque (voulue *ou* délibérée). 5. cachette*, lieu sûr, planque *f*, planquouse *f*.

plant[2] [plɑːnt] (**to**). 1. *F:* **to p. s.o.,** planter qn, laisser qn en plan. 2. *F:* **to p. sth.,** cacher* qch., mettre qch. en planque. 3. *P:* enterrer, mettre dans le royaume des taupes, faire manger les pissenlits par la racine. 4. *P:* donner, flanquer, foutre (un coup* à qn). 5. *F:* **to p. oneself in front of s.o.,** se planter devant qn; **to p. oneself on s.o.,** s'implanter chez qn.

plaster [ˈplɑːstər] (**to**), *P:* 1. battre*, rosser, rouer de coups*, filer une pâtée à (qn). 2. battre (un adversaire) à plate(s) couture(s). 3. bombarder, tabasser.

plastered [ˈplɑːstəd] (*adj.*), *P:* ivre*, rétamé, blindé, fadé.

plastering [ˈplɑːstəriŋ] (*noun*), *F:* 1. volée *f* de coups*, pâtée *f*, raclée *f*. 2. défaite *f*, raclée *f*. 3. (*mil.*) bombardement *m* d'artillerie lourde, artiflottage *m*. 4. (*mil.*) bombardement *m* de saturation.

plate[1] [pleit] (*noun*). 1. *F:* **to have plenty** (*or* **a lot**) **on one's p.,** avoir du pain sur la planche, avoir de quoi faire. 2. *P:* **plates** (**of meat**) (*R.S. = feet*), pieds*. 3. *F:* **to give** (*or* **hand**) **s.o. sth. on a p.,** le servir sur un plateau, l'offrir tout rôti.

plate[2] [pleit] (**to**), *V:* manger, sucer (*coït buccal**).

play[1] [plei] (*noun*), *F:* **to make a p. for s.o., sth.,** user de tout son talent (*ou* de tout son charme) pour obtenir qch. ou pour séduire qn, faire du gringue (*ou* du palass), faire du charme. *Voir aussi* **horseplay.**

play[2] [plei] (**to**), *F:* 1. **to p. with oneself,** se masturber*, jouer de la mandoline, faire cinq contre un. 2. **don't p. games with me!** ne te paye pas ma tête! ne me fais pas marcher! ne me fais pas tourner en bourrique! n'essaie pas de me rouler! *Voir aussi* **ball**[1], **3; cool**[2]; **fool**[2]; **Harry, 2; safe**[2]; **sucker**[2], **1.**

play about (*or* **around**) [ˈpleiəˈbaut,

* L'astérisque indique que le mot marqué de ce signe figure comme entrée dans le Répertoire.

ˈpleiəˈraund] (**to**), *F:* **1. to p. a. with women,** courir le jupon, juponner. **2. don't p. a. with me! = don't play games with me! (play[2] (to), 2).**

play-act [ˈplei-ækt] (**to**), *F:* faire du théâtre, jouer la comédie (*fig.*).

play along [ˈpleiəlɔŋ] (**to**), *F:* **to p. a. with s.o.,** être de mèche (*ou* en cheville) avec qn, aller de barre avec qn.

playboy [ˈpleibɔi] (*noun*), *F:* homme riche* qui aime s'amuser, grand viveur, noceur *m*, playboy *m*.

played out [ˈpleidˈaut] (*adj.*). **1.** *F:* très fatigué*, vanné, éreinté. **2.** *F:* vieux jeu, démodé. **3.** *F:* banal, usé, rebattu. **4.** *P:* très pauvre*, sans le sou, dans la purée, décavé, à sec.

playgirl [ˈpleigəːl] (*noun*), *F:* femme* qui aime s'amuser, bambocheuse *f*, noceuse *f*.

play up [ˈpleiˈʌp] (**to**), *F:* **1. my rheumatism is playing me up,** mes douleurs me font mal. **2.** ennuyer*, asticoter, enquiquiner. **3. to p. sth. u.,** monter qch. en épingle, faire ressortir qch. **4. to p. u. to s.o.,** (*a*) flatter* qn, lécher les bottes à qn, pommader qn; (*b*) collaborer avec qn, baronner qn.

pleb[1] [pleb], **plebby** [ˈplebi] (*adj.*), *P:* vulgaire, populo, populmiche.

pleb[2] [pleb] (*noun*), *P:* faubourien *m*, prolo *m*.

plenty [ˈplenti] (*adv.*), *F:* **it's p. good enough,** ça suffit grandement; **it's p. big enough,** c'est bien assez gros.

plonk[1] [plɔŋk] (*noun*), *F:* vin* ordinaire, gros rouge, vinasse *f*, décapant *m*.

plonk[2] [plɔŋk] (**to**), *F:* (*a*) mettre, flanquer, coller, ficher; **to p. money on a horse,** miser sur un cheval*; (*b*) laisser tomber lourdement.

plonker [ˈplɔŋkər] (*noun*), *P:* pénis*, défonceuse *f*, dardillon *m*; **to pull one's p.,** se masturber*, s'astiquer (la colonne).

plonko [ˈplɔŋkou] (*noun*), *P:* ivrogne*, sac *m* à vin; *cf.* **wino.**

plonk out [ˈplɔŋkˈaut] (**to**), *P:* (*a*) payer*, les allonger, les abouler; (*b*) placer de l'argent*.

plough[1] [plau] (*noun*), *F:* échec *m* (à un examen), recalade *f*, recalage *m*.

plough[2] [plau] (**to**), *F:* **to p. an exam(ination),** échouer*, être recalé (*ou* collé) à un examen. *Voir aussi* **deep[2].**

ploughed (*U.S.:* **plowed**) [plaud] (*adj.*), *P:* ivre*, blindé, bourré (à zéro).

plough (*U.S.:* **plow**) **into** [ˈplauˈintuː] (**to**), *F:* **to p. i. s.o. = to pitch into s.o.**

ploy [plɔi] (*noun*), *F:* stratagème *m*, roublardise *f*.

plug[1] [plʌg] (*noun*). **1.** *F:* publicité *f*, battage *m*, postiche *f*, coup *m* de pouce. **2.** *P:* **to give s.o. a p. (in the earhole),** donner* (*ou* foutre) une beigne (*ou* une baffe) à qn. **3.** *P:* balle* (*arme à feu*), bastos *f*, pastille *f*. **4.** (*U.S.*) *F:* cheval* médiocre, canasson *m*, bourrin *m*. **5.** *F:* **to pull the p. on sth.,** faire échouer* qch.; **to pull the p. on s.o.,** couler qn (à fond).

plug[2] [plʌg] (**to**). **1.** *F:* (*a*) faire de la réclame (*ou* du battage); (*b*) promouvoir (qch.). **2.** *P:* coïter* avec (une femme), fourrer, égoïner. **3.** *P:* battre*, frapper, rosser (qn). **4.** *F:* = **plug away (to), 1, 2. 5.** *P:* fusiller, flinguer, flingoter (qn).

plug away [ˈplʌgəˈwei] (**to**), *F:* **1.** travailler* dur, turbiner, bûcher. **2.** s'acharner, s'obstiner.

plugger [ˈplʌgər] (*noun*), *F:* **1.** agent *m* de publicité, posticheur *m*, promoteur *m* de vente. **2.** trimeur *m*, turbineur *m*, bûcheur *m*, coltineur *m*.

plug-ugly [ˈplʌgʌgli] (*noun*) (*U.S.*), *F:* vaurien*, affreux *m*, charogne *f*, dur *m*.

plum [plʌm] (*noun*), *F:* **1.** travail* facile et bien rétribué, boulot *m* en or (*ou* aux petits oignons), filon *m*. **2.** assiette *f* au beurre, vache *f* à lait.

plumb [plʌm] (*adv.*), *F:* **p. crazy,** fou* à lier.

plumbing [ˈplʌmiŋ] (*noun*), *F:* **to have a look at the p.,** aller aux W.C.*, faire pipi.

plummy [ˈplʌmi] (*adj.*), *F:* **1.** (travail, *etc.*) agréable, bien payé, bath, en or. **2.** (voix) profonde, caverneuse.

plunge[1] [plʌndʒ] (*noun*), *F:* **to take the p.,** prendre le taureau par les cornes, plonger au large.

plunge[2] [plʌndʒ] (**to**), *F:* jouer gros jeu, se mouiller.

plunger [ˈplʌndʒər] (*noun*), *F:* joueur *m* de grosse mise, ponte *m*.

plunk[1] [plʌŋk] (*noun*) (*U.S.*), *P:* **1.** dollar *m*. **2.** coup* bien asséné, une bonne beigne.

plunk[2] [plʌŋk] (**to**) (*U.S.*), *P:* = **plug[2] (to), 5.**

* An asterisk indicates that the word so marked is included as a head-word in the Appendix.

plushy ['plʌʃi] (*adj.*), *F:* riche*, rupin, époustouflant.

plute [pluːt] (*abbr.* = *plutocrat*), *F:* plutocrate *m*, rupin(os) *m*.

po [pou] (*noun*), *F:* pot *m* de chambre, Jules; *cf.* **po-faced.**

pock [pɔk] (*noun*), *P:* **the p.** = **(the) pox.**

pod [pɔd] (*noun*), *P:* 1. (*a*) marijuana *f* (*drogues**), thé vert; (*b*) cigarette* de marijuana, stick *m*. 2. **to be in p.,** être enceinte*, être en cloque; *cf.* **pod up (to).** 3. ventre*, bidon *m*, bide *m*; *cf.* **podge,** 2 (*b*).

podge [pɔdʒ] (*noun*), *F:* 1. individu gros*, bouboule *m*, patapouf *m*. 2. (*a*) graisse *f*, gras-double *m*, pneu *m* Michelin; (*b*) bedaine *f*, panse *f*.

pod up ['pɔd'ʌp] (**to**), *P:* cloquer (*femme enceinte*); *cf.* **pod,** 2.

po-faced ['pou-feist] (*adj.*), *P:* avec une figure* d'enterrement (*ou* de bedeau).

point [pɔint] (*noun*), *P:* shooteuse *f* (*piqûre de drogues*).

poison ['pɔizn] (*noun*), *F:* 1. **name your p.!** qu'est-ce que tu veux boire? 2. **to put the p. in,** empoisonner l'esprit de qn (contre qn), semer le venin. *Voir aussi* **rat**[1], 5.

poke[1] [pouk] (*noun*), *P:* 1. coït*, bourre *f*, coup *m* d'arbalète. 2. **to take a p. at s.o.,** donner (*ou* filer *ou* foutre) une taloche à qn. 3. portefeuille*, lazingue *m*. *Voir aussi* **cow-poke; pig**[1], **6; slow-poke.**

poke[2] [pouk] (**to**), *P:* 1. coïter* avec (une femme), bourrer, filer un coup d'arbalète à (une femme). 2. **to p. s.o.** = **to take a poke at s.o. (poke**[1], 2). *Voir aussi* **nose,** 1.

poke about (*or* **around**) ['poukə'baut, 'poukə'raund] (**to**), *F:* fouiller, farfouiller.

poker ['poukər] (*noun*), *P:* (*université*) (*a*) masse *f* universitaire; (*b*) massier *m*, appariteur *m*. *Voir aussi* **strip**[1], 2.

pokey ['pouki] (*noun*) (*U.S.*), *F:* prison*, trou *m*, boîte *f*, coffre *m*. *Voir aussi* **hokey-pokey.**

pole [poul] (*noun*), *F:* 1. **to go up the p.,** devenir fou*, partir du ciboulot, perdre la boule (*ou* la boussole). 2. **to drive s.o. up the p.,** rendre qn fou*, lui faire perdre la boule (*ou* le ciboulot *ou* le nord). 3. **I wouldn't touch it with a ten-foot p.** = **I wouldn't touch it with a barge-pole,** *q.v.* *Voir aussi* **bean-pole; flag-pole.**

polisher ['pɔliʃər] (*noun*) (*Austr.*), *P:* échappé *m* de prison*, gibier *m* de potence. *Voir aussi* **apple-polisher.**

polish off ['pɔliʃ'ɔf] (**to**), *F:* 1. tuer*, dégommer, démolir, liquider. 2. terminer, liquider, boucler. 3. achever (un plat, une bouteille), solder, nettoyer.

pom [pɔm] (*noun*). 1. *F:* (*abbr.* = *Pomeranian*) loulou *m* (de Poméranie). 2. (*Austr.*) *P:* (*péj.*) = **pommy**[2].

pommy[1] ['pɔmi] (*adj.*) (*Austr.*), *F:* anglais, engliche.

pommy[2], **Pommy** ['pɔmi] (*noun*) (*Austr.*), *F:* Anglais *m*, Engliche *m*.

ponce[1] [pɔns] (*noun*), *P:* souteneur*, marle *m*, marlou *m*, marloupin *m*.

ponce[2] [pɔns] (**to**), *P:* 1. se conduire comme un souteneur*. 2. mendier*, taper, torpiller, pilonner; **to p. a smoke from s.o.,** taper qn d'une cigarette*.

ponce off ['pɔns'ɔf] (**to**), *P:* partir*, plaquouser, se trotter; **p. o.!** fous le camp! décampe! file!

ponce up ['pɔns'ʌp] (**to**), *P:* **to get ponced up, to p. oneself u.,** se mettre sur son trente et un.

poncy ['pɔnsi] (*adj.*), *P:* **a p. individual,** un individu* qui semble se faire entretenir par les femmes, maquereau *m* sur les bords.

pond, Pond [pɔnd] (*noun*), *F:* 1. **the P.** = **the Herring Pond (herring,** 2). 2. **the frog p.,** caste enrichie de la société, les B.O.F.'s, les deux cents familles. *Voir aussi* **fish-pond.**

pong[1] [pɔŋ] (*noun*), *P:* ce qui sent* mauvais; puanteur *f*, (s)chlingage *m*.

pong[2] [pɔŋ] (**to**), *P:* sentir* mauvais; puer, (s)chlinguer, cocoter.

pongo ['pɔŋgou] (*noun*), *P:* (*argot de la Marine*) soldat*, bidasse *m*; fusilier marin, chie-dans-l'eau *m*.

ponk[1] [pɔŋk] (*noun*), *P:* = **pong**[1].

ponk[2] [pɔŋk] (**to**), *P:* = **pong**[2] **(to).**

pontoon [pɔn'tuːn] (*noun*), *P:* 21 mois de prison.

pony ['pouni] (*noun*), *P:* 1. 25 livres sterling. 2. petit verre de liqueur, bourgeron *m*.

poo[1] [puː] (*noun*), *F:* excrément *m*, caca *m*.

* L'astérisque indique que le mot marqué de ce signe figure comme entrée dans le Répertoire.

poo² [puː] (**to**), *F:* déféquer*, faire caca.

pooch [puːtʃ], **poochy** [ˈpuːtʃi] (*noun*), *P:* (*a*) chien* (bâtard), cabot *m*; (*b*) chien* favori, toutou *m*.

poodle on [ˈpuːdlˈɔn] (**to**), *F:* bavasser, jacasser, jaspiner.

poof [puf, puːf] (*pl.* **poofs** *or* **pooves** [pufs, puːfs, puːvz]), **poofdah** [ˈpufdɑː], **poofter** [ˈpuftər], **poofty** [ˈpufti] (*noun*), *P:* pédéraste*, empaffé *m*, empapaouté *m*.

poofy [ˈpufi, ˈpuːfi] (*adj.*), *P:* à tendance homosexuelle, pédé sur les bords.

pooh! [puː] (*excl.*), *F:* **1.** ça pue! **2.** (*expression de dédain*) quelle affaire! la belle affaire!

poop [pup, puːp] (*noun*). **1.** *P:* individu bête*, ballot *m*, baluchard *m*. **2.** *P:* excrément *m*, merde *f*. **3.** (*U.S.*) *F:* renseignement*, rencard *m*; **to know the (latest) p.**, être dans le vent (*ou* à la coule); **p. sheet**, formulaire *m* de renseignements, rencardage *m*.

pooped (out) [ˈpuːpt(ˈaut)] (*adj.*), *P:* très fatigué*, éreinté, épuisé, exténué.

poor [puər, pɔər, pɔːr] (*adj.*), *F:* **to take a p. view (of sth.)** = **to take a dim view (of sth.)** (**dim, 1**). *Voir aussi* **piss-poor.**

poorly [ˈpuəli, ˈpɔəli, ˈpɔːli] (*adj.*), *F:* malade*, patraque, pas dans son assiette; *voir aussi* **proper.**

poove [puːv] (*noun*), *P:* = **poof.**

poovy [ˈpuːvi] (*adj.*), *P:* = **poofy.**

pop¹ [pɔp] (*noun*). **1.** *F:* (*a*) **p.** (**music**), musique *f* pop, yé-yé *m*; **p. singer,** chanteur *m* de pop; **p. song,** chanson *f* en vogue (*ou* du moment); **top of the pops,** palmarès *m* de la chanson, hit-parade *m*; **p. art,** le pop'art. **2.** *F:* père*, papa; vieux *m*, croulant *m*. **3.** *F:* boisson pétillante. **4.** *P:* = **poppy.** **5.** *P:* piqûre (de drogue) intermittente *ou* pour le plaisir; *cf.* **joy-pop; joy-popper.** **6.** (*Austr.*) *F:* **to give sth. a p.,** s'attaquer à qch., faire un essai. **7.** *F:* **to be in p.,** être chez ma tante (*ou* au clou).

pop² [pɔp] (**to**). **1.** *P:* injecter (une drogue), shooter; *cf.* **joy-pop; skin-pop (to).** **2.** *F:* **to p. the question,** proposer le mariage* (à une femme). **3.** *P:* avoir un orgasme*, décharger, dégorger. **4.** *F:* mettre en gage (*ou* chez ma tante *ou* au clou).

pop along [ˈpɔpəˈlɔŋ] (**to**), *F:* **1.** aller voir qn, faire un saut (chez qn). **2.** = **pop off (to), 1.**

popcorn [ˈpɔpkɔːn] (*noun*), *F:* = **corn, 1, 2, 3.**

pop-eyed [ˈpɔpaid] (*adj.*), *F:* (*a*) aux yeux protubérants (*ou* saillants); (*b*) aux yeux en boules de loto.

pop in [ˈpɔpˈin] (**to**), *F:* (*a*) entrer en passant; (*b*) entrer à l'improviste.

pop off [ˈpɔpˈɔf] (**to**), *F:* **1.** partir*, filer, déguerpir. **2.** mourir* (subitement); **he just popped off,** il n'a pas fait couic. **3.** tuer*, but(t)er, estourbir; **to get popped off,** se faire tuer*. **4.** **to p. o. a gun,** lâcher un coup de fusil.

pop out [ˈpɔpˈaut] (**to**), *F:* sortir (de la maison, *etc.*) pour peu de temps, faire un saut dehors; **I saw him p. o. of the house,** je l'ai vu sortir.

pop outside [ˈpɔpautˈsaid] (**to**), *F:* aller faire pipi.

pop over [ˈpɔpˈouvər] (**to**), *F:* = **pop along (to), 1.**

poppa [ˈpɔpə] (*noun*) (*U.S.*), *F:* = **pop¹, 2.**

popper [ˈpɔpər] (*noun*). **1.** *P:* = **amy.** **2.** *F:* bouton *m* (à) pression. *Voir aussi* **joy-popper; lid-popper; skin-popper.**

poppet [ˈpɔpit] (*noun*), *F:* (*a*) petit(e) chéri(e), petit chou; (*b*) enfant* adorable, chérubin *m*.

popping [ˈpɔpiŋ] (*noun*), *P:* (**skin**) **p.,** piqûre subcutanée de drogue.

poppy [ˈpɔpi] (*noun*), *P:* opium *m* (*drogues**), pavot *m*, fée brune.

poppycock [ˈpɔpikɔk] (*noun*), *F:* bêtises*, idioties *f.pl.*, fadaises *f.pl.*

pop round [ˈpɔpˈraund] (**to**), *F:* faire une petite visite à qn.

popsy [ˈpɔpsi] (*noun*). **1.** *F:* petite amie, petite chérie. **2.** *P:* = **amy.**

pop up [ˈpɔpˈʌp] (**to**), *F:* apparaître, surgir, émerger.

porky [ˈpɔːki] (*adj.*), *F:* **1.** gros* et gras, gravos. **2.** (*U.S.*) très mauvais*, blèche, loquedu. **3.** (*U.S.*) en colère*, ronchonnant.

porn [pɔːn], **porno** [ˈpɔːnou] (*noun*), *F:* porno(graphie) *f*.

porn-shop [ˈpɔːn-ʃɔp] (*noun*), *F:* boutique* érotique, sex(e)-shop *f*.

porridge [ˈpɔridʒ] (*noun*), *P:* **to dish out the p.,** ne pas y aller avec le dos de la cuiller, y aller carrément; (*d'un juge*) condamner au maximum; **to eat** (*or* **do**)

* An asterisk indicates that the word so marked is included as a head-word in the Appendix.

p., purger sa peine en prison*, être mis au frais.

port [pɔːt] (*noun*) (*Austr.*), *F:* valise *f*, valoche *f*.

posh [pɔʃ] (*adj.*), *F:* élégant*, chic.

posh up [ˈpɔʃˈʌp] (**to**), *F:* **to p. oneself u.**, se pomponner, se bichonner; **all poshed up,** sur son trente et un.

possum [ˈpɔsəm] (*noun*) (=*opossum*), *F:* **to play p.**, (*a*) faire le mort; (*b*) se tenir coi.

posted [ˈpoustid] (*p.p.*), *F:* **to keep s.o. p.**, tenir qn au courant (*ou* au parfum).

pot[1] [pɔt] (*noun*), *F:* **1.** (*a*) marijuana *f* (*drogues**), pot *m*; (*b*) cigarette* de marijuana, joint *m*, kif *m*; (*c*) hachisch *m* (*drogues**); **p. party,** séance collective au hachisch *ou* à la marijuana. **2. a big p.**, (*a*) (=*pot-belly*) ventre*, bide *m*, bedaine *f*, brioche *f*; (*b*) = **big noise** (**big**[1], **1**). **3. to go to p.**, tomber en décrépitude, aller à la ruine, aller à la dérive; **he's gone to p.**, il est fichu; **his plans went** (**all**) **to p.**, ses projets sont tombés à l'eau. **4. pots of money,** une abondance* (*ou* une tapée) d'argent*; **to make pots of money,** gagner gros, gagner des mille et des cents. **5.** trophée *m*, coupe *f*. **6.** (*pl.*) (=*potatoes*) pommes *f.pl.* de terre, patates *f.pl.* **7.** = **kitty, 2** (*a*). *Voir aussi* **fusspot; glue-pot; jackpot; pisspot; sexpot; shitpot; stinkpot; swillpot; tinpot; toss-pot.**

pot[2] [pɔt] (**to**), *F:* **1. to p. a child,** asseoir un enfant sur le pot de chambre. **2. to p. at sth.**, tirer sur une cible peu éloignée.

potato [pəˈteitou, pəˈteitə] (*noun*). **1.** *P:* trou *m* dans une chaussette, patate *f*. **2.** *F:* **small potatoes,** (*a*) de la petite bière; (*b*) personnes *ou* choses insignifiantes, racaille *f*, gnognot(t)e *f*. **3.** (*U.S.*) **hot p.**, (*a*) *F:* casse-tête (chinois); (*b*) *F:* affaire épineuse; (*c*) *P:* = **hot patootie** (*voir* **patootie**). *Voir aussi* **cold**[1], **6; drop**[2] (**to**), **1; sack**[1], **2.**

pot-boiler [ˈpɔtbɔilər] (*noun*), *F:* abattage *m*, ticket *m* de pain.

pothead [ˈpɔthed] (*noun*), *P:* habitué(e) de la marijuana; amateur *m* de hachisch; *cf.* **pot**[1], **1.**

pot-luck [ˈpɔtˈlʌk] (*noun*), *F:* **to take p.-l.**, choisir au hasard (*ou* à l'aventure), y aller au petit bonheur.

pot-shot [ˈpɔtʃɔt] (*noun*), *F:* (*a*) **to take a p.-s. at sth.**, faire qch. au petit bonheur; (*b*) **to take a p.-s. at sth., s.o.**, lâcher à l'aveuglette un coup de fusil à qch., qn.

potted[1] [ˈpɔtid] (*adj.*), *F:* abrégé, épitomé.

potted[2] **(up)** [ˈpɔtid(ˈʌp)] (*adj.*) (*U.S.*), *P:* **1.** ivre*, rond, rondibé, rétamé. **2.** drogué*, camé, chargé.

pottie [ˈpɔti] (*noun*), *F:* = **potty**[2].

potty[1] [ˈpɔti] (*adj.*), *F:* **1. to go p.**, devenir fou* (*ou* maboul(e)). **2. to be p. about** (*or* **on**) **s.o., sth.**, être mordu pour (*ou* toqué de) qn, qch., en pincer pour qn, qch. **3.** minable, insignifiant.

potty[2] [ˈpɔti] (*noun*), *F:* pot *m* de chambre (d'enfant).

poufdah [ˈpufdɑː], **pouff** [puf] (*noun*), *P:* = **poof.**

pound [paund] (**to**), *P:* (*a*) coïter*, aller à la bourre, bourriquer; (*b*) coïter* avec (une femme), bourrer, dérouiller.

powder [ˈpaudər] (*noun*), *P:* **1. to do** (*or* **take**) **a p.**, (*a*) déserter (de l'armée), faire chibis; (*b*) s'enfuir*, prendre la poudre d'escampette. **2.** cocaïne *f* (*drogues**), poudrette *f*. *Voir aussi* **birdie-powder; joy-powder.**

powder-room [ˈpaudəˈruːm] (*noun*), *F:* W.C.*, toilette *f*.

power-house [ˈpauəhaus] (*noun*), *F:* individu* dynamique.

pow-wow [ˈpauwau] (*noun*), *F:* = **palaver**[1], **1.**

pox [pɔks] (*noun*), *P:* (**the**) **p.**, syphilis*, (s)chtouille *f*, lazziloffe *f*.

poxed (up) [ˈpɔkst(ˈʌp)] (*adj.*), *P:* **p. (u.) (to the eyebrows),** naze(broque) poivré, plombé.

prance about (*or* **around**) [ˈprɑːnsəˈbaut, ˈprɑːnsəˈraund] (**to**), *F:* **1.** caracoler, trépigner de colère*, piaffer. **2.** se pavaner, poser.

prang[1] [præŋ] (*noun*), *F:* **1.** exploit *m*, coup fumant. **2.** raid *m* de bombardement. **3.** collision *f*, crash *m*, emboutissage *m*.

prang[2] [præŋ] (**to**), *F:* **1.** bombarder, tabasser. **2.** emboutir, bousiller (un avion, une auto, *etc.*).

prat [præt] (*noun*), *P:* **1.** fesses*, derche *m*, popotin *m*. **2.** vagin*, con *m*, conasse *f*, cramouille *f*. **3.** individu bête*, couillon *m*.

* L'astérisque indique que le mot marqué de ce signe figure comme entrée dans le Répertoire.

preachify [ˈpriːtʃifai] (**to**), *F:* sermonner.

preachy [ˈpriːtʃi] (*adj.*), *F:* sermonneur, tartuffeur.

preggers [ˈpregəz] (*adj.*), *P:* (**Harry**) **p.**, enceinte*, en cloque.

pretty-pretty [ˈpriti-priti] (*adj.*), *F:* tout plein coquet, fanfreluché, affété.

previous [ˈpriːvjəs] (*adv.*), *F:* trop tôt, trop vite*; **you're a bit p., aren't you?** tu y vas un peu fort?

priceless [ˈpraislis] (*adj.*), *F:* **1.** très amusant*, impayable. **2.** très bête*, unique.

pricey [ˈpraisi] (*adj.*), *F:* cher*, chérot, coûteux, salé.

prick [prik] (*noun*), *V:* **1.** pénis*, pine *f.* **2.** vaurien*, sale coco *m*, couillon *m.* **3. a spare p.**, un pas grand-chose, un bon à rien, un cautère sur une jambe de bois; **to feel like a spare p. at a wedding,** *c.p.*, être un onguent miton mitaine. *Voir aussi* **pin-pricks.**

prick-tease [ˈprik-tiːz], **prick-teaser** [ˈprik-tiːzər] (*noun*), *V:* allumeuse *f*, bandeuse *f*, aguicheuse *f*; *cf.* **cock-teaser; tease; teaser, 2.**

printed [ˈprintid] (*p.p.*), *P:* **to get p.**, se faire prendre les empreintes digitales, jouer du piano, passer au piano.

printers [ˈprintəz] (*pl. noun*), *P:* **to have the p. in** = **to have the painters in** (**painter, 2**).

prissy [ˈprisi] (*adj.*), *F:* bégueule, collet monté, guindé, chochotte.

prize [praiz] (*adj.*), *F:* **a p. idiot,** un ballot de premier ordre, une andouille enracinée. *Voir aussi* **swill**[1], **3.**

pro [prou] (*noun*). **1.** *P:* (=*prostitute*) prostituée*, catin *f*, pute *f.* **2.** *F:* (=*professional*) professionnel *m*; **he's a real p.,** il n'a rien d'un amateur. **3.** *F:* **the pros and cons,** le pour et le contre.

pronto [ˈprɔntou] (*adv.*), *F:* vite*, illico, presto.

prop [prɔp] (*noun*), *P:* épingle *f* de cravate. *Voir aussi* **props.**

proper [ˈprɔpər] (*adv.*), *F:* vraiment, extrêmement; **p. poorly,** vraiment malade*. *Voir aussi* **champion, 1.**

prop-man [ˈprɔpmæn] (*noun*), *F:* = **props, 2.**

proposition [ˈprɔpəˈziʃ(ə)n] (**to**), *F:* **1.** proposer un plan ou un projet à (qn). **2. to p. a woman,** faire des propositions indécentes à une femme, proposer la botte à une femme.

props [prɔps] (*noun*), *F:* **1.** (*pl.*) (*th.*) accessoires *m.pl.*, bouts *m.pl.* de bois. **2.** (*sing.*) accessoiriste *mf.* *Voir aussi* **prop.**

prop up [ˈprɔpˈʌp] (**to**), *F:* **to p. u. the bar,** boire dans un bar, être accoudé au zinc.

pross [prɔs], **prossie, prossy** [ˈprɔsi], **prostie, prosty** [ˈprɔsti] (*noun*), *P:* prostituée*, pute *f*, putain *f.*

proud [praud] (*adv.*), *F:* **1. to do s.o. p.,** (*a*) recevoir qn comme un roi, traiter qn à la hauteur; (*b*) se mettre en frais pour qn. **2. to do oneself p.,** (*a*) faire un bon travail*, se montrer à la hauteur; (*b*) se bien soigner, ne se priver de rien.

prowl [praul] (*noun*), *F:* **to be on the p.,** chercher les aventures (amoureuses), chercher les bonnes fortunes.

prowl-car [ˈpraul-kɑːr] (*noun*), *F:* voiture *f* de police, voiture-pie *f.*

pseudo [ˈsjuːdou] (*adj.*), *F:* pseudo, insincère, faux.

psycho[1] [ˈsaikou] (*adj.*), *P:* fou*, dérangé, détraqué, dévissé.

psycho[2] [ˈsaikou] (*noun*), *F:* **1.** psycho(pathe) *mf.* **2.** (*a*) psychanalyste *mf*; (*b*) psychiatre *mf.*

p.t., P.T. [ˈpiːˈtiː] (*abbr.*), *P:* = **prick-tease(r)**; *cf.* **C.T.**

pub [pʌb] (*noun*), *F:* bistro(t) *m*, pub *m.*

pubbing [ˈpʌbiŋ] (*verbal noun*), *F:* **to go p.,** faire la tournée des bistro(t)s, godailler.

pub-crawl[1] [ˈpʌbkrɔːl] (*noun*), *F:* tournée *f* des bistro(t)s.

pub-crawl[2] [ˈpʌbkrɔːl] (**to**), *F:* = **to go pubbing.**

pub-crawler [ˈpʌbkrɔːlər] (*noun*), *F:* coureur *m* de bistro(t)s, vadrouilleur *m.*

pud [pud] (*noun*) (*abbr.* = *pudding*), *F:* **1.** pudding *m.* **2.** dessert *m.*

pudding [ˈpudiŋ, ˈpudn] (*noun*), *P:* **to pull one's p.,** se masturber*, se l'allonger, s'astiquer (la colonne). *Voir aussi* **club, 2.**

pudding-face [ˈpudiŋfeis, ˈpudnfeis] (*noun*), *F:* visage* empâté, pleine lune.

puddinghead [ˈpudiŋhed, ˈpudnhed] (*noun*), *F:* individu bête*, gourde *f*, empoté *m.*

* An asterisk indicates that the word so marked is included as a head-word in the Appendix.

puff[1] [pʌf] (*noun*), *F:* **1. to be out of p.,** être hors d'haleine, être essoufflé. **2. never in all my p.!** jamais de la vie! **3.** critique *f* favorable, battage *m*, puffisme *m*. *Voir aussi* **creampuff.**

puff[2] [pʌf] (**to**), *F:* prôner, vanter.

puffer(-train) [ˈpʌfər(trein)], **puff-puff** [ˈpʌfpʌf] (*noun*), *F:* (*langage enfantin*) teuf-teuf *m*.

pug [pʌg] (*noun*), *P:* pugiliste *m*, boxeur *m*.

puka [ˈpuːkə] (*noun*) (*U.S.*), *P:* vulve*, fente *f*, crac *m*.

puke [pjuːk] (*noun*), *P:* vomissement *m*, dégobillade *f*, fusée *f*, dégueulis *m*.

pukka [ˈpʌkə] (*adj.*), *F:* **p. sahib** [sɑːb], un vrai monsieur, un vrai gentleman. *Voir aussi* **gen.**

pull[1] [pul] (*noun*). **1.** *P:* coït*, carambolage *m*. **2.** *F:* influence *f*, piston *m*, bras long. *Voir aussi* **leg-pull.**

pull[2] [pul] (**to**). **1.** *P:* coïter* avec (une femme), caramboler; *voir aussi* **train. 2.** *F:* **to p. a gun,** sortir un revolver*. *Voir aussi* **bell, 2; leg**[1]**, 5; one, 4; plonker; pudding; rank; wire, 2, 8; yarn**[1]**.**

pull-in [ˈpulin] (*noun*), *F:* café* des routiers.

pull in [ˈpulˈin] (**to**), *F:* **1.** arrêter*, embarquer, choper. **2.** exécuter, réaliser. **3.** s'arrêter, faire une étape.

pull off [ˈpulˈɔf] (**to**). **1.** *F:* **to p. o. a deal,** réussir une opération, boucler une affaire. **2.** *P:* se masturber*, s'astiquer (la colonne).

pull out [ˈpulˈaut] (**to**), *F:* **1.** partir*, se (re)tirer. **2.** (*U.S.*) se dérober, tirer son épingle du jeu. **3. to p. o. all the stops,** donner un coup de collier, donner le maximum, mettre le paquet. *Voir aussi* **finger**[1]**, 2.**

pump [pʌmp] (**to**), *F:* **to p. s.o.,** pomper qn (pour avoir des renseignements*). *Voir aussi* **lead**[1]**, 1.**

pumpkinhead [ˈpʌmpkinhed] (*noun*) (*U.S.*), *F:* individu bête*, nouille *f*, andouille *f*.

punch[1] [pʌntʃ] (*noun*), *F:* **1.** allant *m*, énergie *f*, dynamisme *m*. **2. he didn't pull his punches,** il n'a pas ménagé son adversaire, il n'a pas pris de gants. *Voir aussi* **pack**[2] **(to), 2.**

Punch[2] [pʌntʃ] (*pr. noun*), *F:* (*a*) **(as) proud as P.,** fier comme Artaban; (*b*) **(as) pleased as P.,** heureux comme un roi, aux anges.

punch-drunk [ˈpʌntʃˈdrʌŋk] (*adj.*), *F:* ivre de coups, ahuri, hébété (par des coups reçus), groggy.

punch-line [ˈpʌntʃ-lain] (*noun*), *F:* phrase-clef *f* (dans une histoire), astuce *f*, mot *m* de la fin.

punch-up [ˈpʌntʃʌp] (*noun*), *F:* échange *f* de coups de poing, raclée *f*, tabassée *f*.

pundit [ˈpʌndit] (*noun*), *F:* ponte *m*.

punk[1] [pʌŋk] (*adj.*), *P:* de basse qualité, moche, tocard, tarte.

punk[2] [pʌŋk] (*noun*), *P:* **1.** tordu *m*, tête *f* de lard, face *f* de rat, bille *f* de clown. **2.** débutant *m*, novice *m*, bleu *m*, blanc-bec *m*. **3.** pédéraste*, fiotte *f*, tapette *f*. **4.** jeune vaurien*, bizet *m*, fias *m*. **5.** jeune animal *m*, jeune bestiole *f*. **6.** qch. de toc(ard) (*ou* de moche), pacotille *f*, camelote *f*.

punk out [ˈpʌŋkˈaut] (**to**), *P:* se dégonfler, caner.

pup [pʌp] (*noun*), *F:* **to sell s.o. a p.,** escroquer*, faisander, rouler qn. *Voir aussi* **mucky, 2.**

puppy [ˈpʌpi] (*attrib. adj.*), *F:* **1. p. fat,** grassouille *f* du bébé. **2. p. love,** premier amour, amour juvénile.

purler [ˈpəːlər] (*noun*), *F:* **to come a p.,** tomber*, ramasser une bûche, prendre un gadin.

purple [ˈpəːpl] (*adj.*), *P:* **p. hearts,** barbituriques *f.pl.* (*drogues**), mélange barbituré.

purty [ˈpəːrti] (*adj.*) (*mainly U.S.*), *F:* joli, mignon.

push[1] [puʃ] (*noun*). **1.** *P:* bande*, gang *m*, flèche *f*. **2.** *F:* **to give s.o. the p.,** flanquer qn à la porte, sacquer qn; *cf.* **sack**[1]**, 1. 3.** *F:* **at a p.,** au moment critique, en cas de besoin; **when it comes to the p.,** quand il est question d'agir, au moment de l'exécution.

push[2] [puʃ] (**to**), *F:* **1. to p. drugs,** fourguer des drogues. **2. to p. one's luck,** pousser, aller trop loin, attiger, aller un peu fort. *Voir aussi* **queer**[3]**, 4.**

push around [ˈpuʃəˈraund] (**to**), *F:* **to p. s.o. a.,** malmener, maltraiter qn, être vache (*ou* chien) avec qn.

push-bike [ˈpuʃbaik] (*noun*), *F:* = **bike, 1.**

* L'astérisque indique que le mot marqué de ce signe figure comme entrée dans le Répertoire.

pusher [ˈpuʃər] (*noun*), *F:* **1.** fourgueur *m* (*ou* pourvoyeur *m*) (de drogues); *cf.* **push**[2] **(to)**, **1.** **2.** ambitieux *m*, arriviste *m*, joueur *m* de coudes. *Voir aussi* **cock-pusher; paper-pusher; pen-pusher.**

pushface [ˈpuʃfeis] (*noun*), *P:* gueule *f* en coin (de rue), gueule de raie, tête *f* de pipe.

push off [ˈpuʃˈɔf] (**to**), *P:* partir*, déguerpir, décamper; **p. o.!** file! débarrasse (le plancher)! fous le camp!

push on [ˈpuʃˈɔn] (**to**), *F:* **1.** pousser en avant, activer, faire avancer. **2.** pousser, exciter (qn). **3.** **to p. o. with sth.**, chauffer une affaire.

pushover [ˈpuʃouvər] (*noun*), (*a*) *F:* qch. de facile, du tout cuit, du tout rôti, du gâteau; (*b*) *P:* femme* facile (*ou* à la cuisse hospitalière *ou* qui donne dans le panneau).

pushy [ˈpuʃi] (*adj.*), *F:* arriviste, plastronneur, poseur.

puss [pus] (*noun*). **1.** *F:* chat *m*, minou *m*, minet *m*. **2.** *P:* visage*, frime *f*, frimousse *f*. **3.** *P:* bouche*, gueule *f*, goule *f*, margoulette *f*. **4.** *P:* = **pussy, 2.** *Voir aussi* **angel-puss; drizzle-puss; glamour-puss; sourpuss.**

pussy [ˈpusi] (*noun*). **1.** *F:* = **puss, 1.** **2.** *P:* vulve*, chat *m*, chatte *f*. **3.** *F:* (=*cat-o'-nine-tails*) fouet *m* (à neuf cordes), garcette *f*.

pussyfoot[1] [ˈpusifut] (*noun*) (*U.S.*), *F:* prohibitionniste *m*, partisan *m* du sec.

pussyfoot[2] [ˈpusifut] (**to**) (*U.S.*), *F:* **1.** marcher* à pas étouffés (*ou* sur la pointe des pieds). **2.** faire patte de velours. **3.** ne pas se mouiller, ménager la chèvre et le chou, nager entre deux eaux, zigzaguer.

pussyfooter [ˈpusifutər] (*noun*) (*U.S.*), *F:* qn qui ne veut pas se compromettre (*ou* qui tourne autour du pot), ennemi *m* du oui et du non.

pussyfooting [ˈpusifutiŋ] (*noun*) (*U.S.*) *F:* l'art *m* de ne pas se mouiller.

puta [ˈpuːtə] (*noun*) (*U.S.*), *P:* prostituée*, pute *f*.

put across [ˈputəˈkrɔs] (**to**), *F:* **1.** **to p. it a. s.o.**, tromper*, refaire, rouler qn. **2.** **to p. it a. to s.o.**, faire comprendre (*ou* piger) à qn, éclairer la lanterne à qn.

put away [ˈputəˈwei] (**to**). **1.** *P:* (*boxe*) mettre (qn) knock-out. **2.** *F:* **to p. it a.** = **to tuck it away (tuck away (to), 2)**. **3.** *F:* emprisonner*, faire enfermer, boucler, bloquer. **4.** *P:* tuer*, descendre, dessouder, dézinguer. **5.** *F:* mettre à côté; *cf.* **rainy.**

put-down [ˈputdaun] (*noun*), *F:* jugement *m* défavorable, éreintage *m*, sabrage *m*.

put-on [ˈputɔn] (*noun*), *F:* bateau *m*, boniment *m*, pilule *f*.

put on [ˈputˈɔn] (**to**), *F:* **1.** **to p. it o.**, (*a*) prétendre, en installer, faire de la graisse, faire sa poire; (*b*) exagérer*, charrier, y aller fort; **he puts it on a bit,** il est un peu crâneur. **2.** interloquer (qn), brouiller les idées à (qn). **3.** **who p. you o. to it?** qui vous a donné **le** tuyau? *Voir aussi* **ritz.**

put out [ˈputˈaut] (**to**). **1.** *F:* déconcerter, décontenancer, embarrasser (qn). **2.** (*U.S.*) *P:* (*d'une femme*) avoir la cuisse hospitalière, être tombeuse (*ou* paumée).

putrid [ˈpjuːtrid] (*adj.*), *F:* dégueulasse, dégueulbif, débectant.

put-up [ˈputʌp] (*adj.*), *F:* **a p. u. job,** un coup monté, une affaire bricolée, un micmac.

putz [puts] (*noun*) (*U.S.*), *P:* pénis*, pine *f*, paf *m*.

pyjies [ˈpidʒiz] (*pl. noun*), *F:* pyjama *m*, pyj *m*.

python [ˈpaiθ(ə)n] (*noun*), *P:* **to siphon the p.,** uriner*, égoutter son cyclope.

* An asterisk indicates that the word so marked is included as a head-word in the Appendix.

Q

q.t., Q.T. ['kju:'ti:] (*abbr.*), *F:* **1.** (= *quiet time*) petite prière, méditation *f.* **2. on the (strict) q.t.** (=*quiet*), en douce, discrètement, en sourdine, en confidence; **to do sth. on the q.t.,** faire qch. en cachette (*ou* à la dérobée); **I am telling you on the q.t.,** je vous dis ça entre nous (*ou* entre quat'zyeux).

quack [kwæk] (*noun*), *P:* **the q.,** le médecin, le toubib, le charlatan.

quack-quack ['kwæk'kwæk] (*noun*), *F:* (*langage enfantin*) canard *m*, coin-coin *m.*

quad [kwɔd] (*noun*). **1.** *F:* (=*quadrangle*) cour carrée (d'une école, université, *etc.*). **2.** *P:* prison*, boîte *f*, bloc *m*, taule *f*; **in q.,** au bloc, à l'ombre. **3.** *F:* (=*quadruplet*) quadruplé(e). **4.** (*U.S.*) *P:* auto *f* à quatre phares *m.pl.*; (*pl.*) les quatre phares d'une auto.

quail [kweil] (*noun*), *P:* **1.** femme*, fille*, fumelle *f*, souris *f.* **2.** (*U.S.*) élève (fille) d'une école mixte.

quarter ['kwɔ:tər] (*noun*) (*U.S.*), *F:* pièce *f* de 25 cents.

quean [kwi:n] (*noun*) *P:* = **queen, 1, 2.**

queen [kwi:n] (*noun*). **1.** *F:* fille* *ou* femme* séduisante, une beauté, une (petite) reine. **2.** *P:* pédéraste* qui joue le rôle de femme, persilleuse *f*; **an old q.,** une vieille pédale; **dinge q.,** pédéraste* blanc qui s'accouple de préférence avec des nègres. **3.** *F:* **q. bee,** femme* active, maîtresse-femme. **4.** *F:* **Q. Mary,** long véhicule.

queenie ['kwi:ni] (*noun*), *P:* = **queen, 2.**

queer[1] [kwiər] (*adj.*). **1.** *F:* homosexuel, pédé. **2.** *F:* **to be in q. street,** être dans la mélasse, tirer le diable par la queue. **3.** *F:* un peu fou*; **q. in the head,** maboul(e), loufoque; *voir aussi* **attic; fish[1], 1. 4.** *P:* criminel, suspect, louche. **5.** *P:* faux, contrefait. **6.** *F:* **to feel q.,** se sentir tout chose (*ou* patraque *ou* pas dans son assiette).

queer[2] [kwiər] (*noun*). **1.** *F:* (*a*) pédéraste*, tante *f*; (*b*) lesbienne*, gouine *f*; *voir aussi* **quim. 2.** *P:* **in q.,** dans le pétrin, dans la mélasse. **3.** *P:* **on the q.,** par des moyens louches (*ou* peu honnêtes). **4.** (*U.S.*) *P:* monnaie contrefaite, fausse mornifle; **to push the q.,** passer de la fausse monnaie, faire la fournaise.

queer[3] [kwiər] (**to**), *P:* **1.** déranger, détraquer; **to q. the pitch,** mettre des bâtons dans les roues, mettre des chaînes dans les engrenages; **to q. s.o.'s pitch,** contrecarrer qn. **2. to q. oneself with s.o.,** perdre l'estime de qn, se brouiller avec qn, ne plus être dans les petits papiers de qn. **3. to q. for sth.,** aimer* qch., en mordre pour qch.

queer-basher ['kwiə-bæʃər] (*noun*), *P:* chasseur *m* de pédés.

queer-bashing ['kwiə-bæʃiŋ] (*noun*), *P:* chasse *f* aux pédés.

quencher ['kwentʃər] (*noun*), *F:* boisson *f*, consommation *f*; **let's have a q.,** on va boire*, on va se rincer la dalle (*ou* se mouiller la meule).

queue-jumper ['kju:-dʒʌmpər] (*noun*), *F:* qn qui passe avant son tour, resquilleur *m.*

quick [kwik] (*adj.*), *F:* **1. a q. one** = **quickie, 1, 2. 2. to do sth. in q. order,** faire qch. vite* (*ou* à la hâte *ou* en cinq secs). *Voir aussi* **double-quick; draw[1], 1; p.d.q.; uptake** (*a*).

quickie, quicky ['kwiki] (*noun*). **1.** *F:* un (petit) verre (*ou* un (petit) coup) bu en vitesse; **to have a q.,** s'en envoyer un; **have a q.?** tu prendras vite qch.? **2.** *P:* coït* hâtif; **to have a q.,** s'en envoyer un petit coup. **3.** *P:* prostituée* rapide, pute *f* à la grouille. **4.** *F:* qch. fait rapidement (*ou* à la six-quatre-deux); du vite-fait. **5.** *F:* question-éclair *f* (dans un jeu de devinette). **6.** (*U.S.*) *F:* grève soudaine et irrationnelle.

quid [kwid] (*noun*), *F:* **1.** une livre sterling. **2. to be quids in,** avoir de la marge, marcher comme sur des roulettes; **he's quids in,** il a de la chance* (*ou* du pot).

* L'astérisque indique que le mot marqué de ce signe figure comme entrée dans le Répertoire.

quiet[1] [ˈkwaiət] (*adj.*), *F:* **anything for a q. life!** tout ce que tu voudras, mais fiche-moi (*ou* fous-moi) la paix!

quiet[2] [ˈkwaiət] (*noun*), *F:* **on the q.** = **on the q.t.** (**q.t.**, 2).

quiff [kwif] (*noun*). **1.** *P:* argent*, pèze *m.* **2.** *P:* prostituée* bon marché, pute *f* de la basse. **3.** *P:* bon tour, tour de passe-passe. **4.** *V:* vulve*, baba *m*, didi *m.* **5.** *P:* conseil *m*, avis *m*, tuyau *m.*

quill [kwil] (**to**), *P:* s'efforcer de gagner les bonnes grâces de (qn), lécher les bottes à (qn).

quim [kwim] (*noun*), *VV:* vagin*, grippette *f*, millefeuille *m*; **q. queer,** lesbienne*, goudou *f.*

quin [kwin] (*noun*), *F:* (=*quintuplet*) quintuplé(e).

quince [kwins] (*noun*), *P:* pédéraste*, fiotte *f.*

quit [kwit] (**to**). **1.** *F:* abandonner*, lâcher, débarquer, déposer. **2.** *P:* **to q. it,** mourir*, se laisser glisser. **3.** *P:* **to q. the scene,** (*a*) mourir*, lâcher la rampe; (*b*) partir*, lever l'ancre.

quitter [ˈkwitər] (*noun*), *P:* lâcheur *m*, tire-au-flanc *m.*

quod [kwɔd] (*noun*), *P:* = **quad, 2.**

quote [kwout] (*noun*), *F:* **1.** citation *f* (*d'un auteur, etc.*). **2.** (*pl.*) guillemets *m.pl.* qui indiquent la citation.

* An asterisk indicates that the word so marked is included as a head-word in the Appendix.

R

rab [ræb] (*noun*), *P:* tiroir-caisse *m.*

rabbit[1] [ˈræbit] (*noun*), **1.** *P:* salade *f*, crudités *f.pl.* **2.** *P:* bavardage *m*, jactance *f*; **I never heard anyone with so much r.,** je n'ai jamais entendu une telle tapette. **3.** *F:* **r. punch,** le coup du lapin.

rabbit[2] **(on)** [ˈræbit(ˈɔn)] (**to**), *P:* avoir la langue bien pendue, jacter.

rabbity [ˈræbiti] (*adj.*), *P:* insignifiant, toc, tocard, camelote.

racket[1] [ˈrækit] (*noun*), *F:* **1. to make a r.,** faire du bruit* (*ou* du tapage *ou* du vacarme *ou* du tintamarre); *voir aussi* **kick up (to). 2.** coup fourré, combine *f*, trafic *m* louche. **3. to stand the r.,** (*a*) payer* les frais *m.pl.*, casquer, essuyer le coup de fusil, payer les pots cassés; (*b*) tenir le coup. **4.** escroquerie*, arnaque *f.* **5. to go on the r.** = **to go on the razzle.**

racket[2] **(about)** [ˈrækit(əˈbaut)] (**to**) *F:* = **to make a racket (racket**[1]**, 1).**

rag[1] [ræg] (*noun*). **1.** *F:* vêtement*; **I haven't a r. to wear,** je n'ai rien à me mettre; **the r. trade,** l'industrie *f* de l'habillement; *voir aussi* **glad. 2.** *P:* serviette *f* hygiénique, tampon *m*; **to be on the r., to have the r.** (*or* **rags**) **on, to have the r. out,** avoir ses menstrues*, avoir la rue barrée. **3.** *F:* journal*, canard *m*, torchon *m*; **local r.,** la feuille de chou du pays. **4.** *F:* **like a red r. to a bull,** comme le rouge pour les taureaux. **5.** *P:* **to lose one's r., to get one's r. out,** se mettre en colère*, voir rouge. **6.** *P:* langue*, chiffe *f*, chiffon *m* rouge. **7.** *F:* **r., tag and bobtail,** la canaille, la merdaille, la chienlit. **8.** *F:* **to be in rags and tatters,** (*fig.*) être raté, être dans la mouscaille. **9.** *F:* carnaval *m*, monôme *m* d'étudiants, canular *m*. **10.** *P:* **oily r.** (*R.S.* = *fag* = *cigarette*), cigarette*, cibiche *f*. **11.** *F:* **to feel like a wet r.,** se sentir mou comme une chiffe, être une vraie loque. *Voir aussi* **chew (to); dishrag; nose-rag; snitch-rag; snot-rag.**

rag[2] [ræg] (**to**), *F:* **1.** brimer (un camarade). **2.** chahuter (un professeur). **3.** faire du chahut, railler, persifler.

ragbag [ˈrægbæg] (*noun*), *F:* individu mal vêtu (*ou* mal ficelé *ou* mal fagoté), souillon *mf*, loqueteux *m*.

raggle [ˈrægl] (*noun*) (*U.S.*), *P:* pin-up *f*, allumeuse *f*.

rag-top [ˈrægtɔp] (*noun*), *F:* voiture *f* décapotable.

railroad [ˈreilroud] (**to**) (*U.S.*), *F:* **1.** bousculer, tarabuster (qn). **2.** se débarrasser* de (qn), faire dinguer (qn) à la boucanade. **3.** pousser, bouler (qch.).

rails [reilz] (*pl. noun*), *F:* **to go off the r.,** dérailler, être détraqué.

rain [rein] (**to**), *F:* **it never rains but it pours,** *c.p.*, un malheur n'arrive jamais seul.

rainbows [ˈreinbouz] (*pl. noun*), *P:* tuinal *m* (*drogues*) barbiturique, tricolore *m*.

raincheck [ˈrein-tʃek] (*noun*) (*U.S.*), *F:* invitation remise, partie remise.

rainy [ˈreini] (*adj.*), *F:* **to put sth. away** (*or* **by**) **for a r. day,** garder une poire pour la soif.

rainy-day [ˈreinidei] (*attrib. adj.*), *P:* **r.-d. woman,** cigarette* de marijuana (*drogues**), joint *m*, stick *m*.

rake in [ˈreikˈin] (**to**), *F:* **to r. it i.,** gagner* beaucoup d'argent, (le) ramasser à la pelle, faire du pèze.

rake-off [ˈreikɔf] (*noun*), *F:* commission *f*, ristourne *f*, pot-de-vin *m*.

raker [ˈreikər] (*noun*) (*Austr.*), *F:* **to go a r.,** tomber*, ramasser une bûche (*ou* un gadin), se casser la figure.

ram[1] [ræm] (*noun*), *P:* **1.** (*Austr.*) = **shill(aber). 2.** individu porté sur le sexe, chaud lapin.

ram[2] [ræm] (**to**), *V:* **1.** coïter* avec (une femme), égoïner, bourrer. **2.** avoir un coït* anal avec (qn), empaffer, enculer (qn). *Voir aussi* **throat, 1.**

rambunctious [ræmˈbʌŋkʃəs] (*adj.*), *F:* tapageur, chahuteur.

* L'astérisque indique que le mot marqué de ce signe figure comme entrée dans le Répertoire.

ramp [ræmp] (*noun*), *F:* = **racket**[1], **2.**

randy [ˈrændi] (*adj.*), *P:* = **horny** (*b*).

rangoon [ræŋˈguːn] (*noun*), *P:* cannabis naturel (*drogues**).

rank [ræŋk] (*noun*), *F:* **to pull r. (on s.o.)**, user et abuser de son rang *ou* de sa position.

rap[1] [ræp] (*noun*), *F:* **1.** réprimande *f*, punition *f*, attrapage *m*, engueulade *f*; **to take the r.**, payer les pots cassés. **2.** condamnation*, gerbage *m*, sape(ment) *m*, sucrage *m*; **murder r.**, accusation *f* de meurtre, dévidage *m* de but(t)e; **to beat the r.**, se faire acquitter (en justice), se soustraire à une amende, déjouer la loi, faire un coup de nib; **to square a r.**, faire enlever une punition *ou* une amende, défarguer. **3. not to care a r.**, s'en ficher éperdument. **4. not to be worth a r.**, ne rien* valoir, ne pas valoir tripette. **5.** (*U.S.*) conversation *f*, bavardage *m*.

rap[2] [ræp] (**to**). **1.** *F:* critiquer*, tancer, bêcher. **2.** *P:* arrêter*, choper, épingler; gerber, sucrer. **3.** *P:* tuer*, but(t)er, bousiller.

rare [rɛər] (*adj.*), *F:* **we had a r. old time,** on s'en est payé, on s'en est donné à cœur joie.

rarin' [ˈrɛərin], **raring** [ˈrɛəriŋ] (*adj.*), *F:* **to be r. to go,** piaffer d'impatience *ou* d'anticipation, être prêt à ruer, attendre le gong.

raspberry [ˈrɑːzb(ə)ri] (*noun*), *P:* **1.** (*a*) pet*, pastille *f*, perlouse *f*; (*b*) bruit *m* avec les lèvres qui imite un pet. **2.** désapprobation *f*, engueulade *f*. **3.** rebuffade *f*, défargage *m*, vidage *m*. **4.** (*a*) **to give s.o. a** (*or* **the**) **r.**, dire zut à qn, faire nargue à qn, envoyer chier qn; (*b*) **to get a r.** (**from s.o.**), se faire rabrouer. *Voir aussi* **flip**[3] (**to**), **2.**

rat[1] [ræt] (*noun*). **1.** *F:* sale type *m*, salopard *m*, peau *f* de vache; *cf.* **dirty**[1], **2. 2.** *F:* indicateur*, chacal *m*, chevreuil *m*. **3.** *F:* briseur *m* de grève, jaune *m*, faux frère, gâte-métier *m*. **4.** *F:* **to smell a r.**, sentir qch. de louche, soupçonner anguille sous roche, avoir la puce à l'oreille. **5.** *F:* **r. poison,** alcool* de mauvaise qualité, casse-gueule *m*, camphre *m*, mort-aux-rats *f*. **6.** *F:* **the r. race,** la course au bifteck. **7.** *F:* **to have the rats,** (*a*) être en colère* (*ou* en rogne); (*b*) être en proie au delirium tremens, voir les rats bleus. **8.** *F:* **rats to you!** zut! va-t'en voir! va donc! sans blague! **9.** *F:* (*mil.*, *W.W.II*) **the Desert Rats,** les Rats du Désert (7e division blindée en Afrique du Nord). **10.** *P:* logement*, piaule *f*, niche *f*. **11.** *P:* **r. and mouse** (*R.S.* = *house*), maison *f*.

rat[2] [ræt] (**to**), *F:* **1. to r. on s.o.**, (*a*) revenir sur un marché; (*b*) dénoncer*, cafarder, bourdiller qn. **2.** abandonner* ses complices, les lâcher (*ou* plaquer), les laisser en carafe; judasser, renarder.

ratbag [ˈrætbæg] (*noun*), *P:* **1.** vaurien*, sale coco *m*, salaud *m*. **2.** (*Austr.*) excentrique *mf*, original *m*.

rate [reit] (**to**), *F:* **1.** avoir un dû, recevoir son dû, empocher la monnaie de sa pièce. **2.** être coté (*ou* estimé *ou* considéré).

ratfink [ˈrætfiŋk] (*noun*), *P:* sale mouchard *m*, vieille gamelle; *cf.* **fink**[1], **3.**

rat out [ˈrætˈaut] (**to**), *P:* partir*, déguerpir.

ratter [ˈrætər] (*noun*), *F:* = **rat**[1], **2, 3.**

rattle [ˈrætl] (**to**), *F:* consterner, bouleverser, retourner (qn); **he never gets rattled,** il ne se laisse pas démonter, il ne s'épate jamais.

rattle on [ˈrætlˈɔn] (**to**), *F:* **she does r. o.!** c'est un moulin à paroles, elle a la langue bien pendue.

rattler [ˈrætlər] (*noun*), *F:* **1.** (*chemin de fer*) train *m*, dur *m*. **2.** (=*rattlesnake*) serpent *m* à sonnettes. **3.** personne *ou* chose excellente* (*ou* épatante *ou* super *ou* foutrale). *Voir aussi* **bone-rattler.**

rattling [ˈrætliŋ] (*adj.*), *F:* **1.** vif, déluré, d'attaque. **2.** excellent*, du tonnerre. **3. at a r. pace,** au grand trot.

rat-trap [ˈrættræp] (*noun*), *P:* bouche*, trappe *f*; *cf.* **trap, 1.**

ratty [ˈræti] (*adj.*). **1.** *F:* méchant*, chameau, teigne. **2.** *F:* râleur, ronchonneur, rouscailleur. **3.** (*U.S.*) *P:* (*a*) moche; (*b*) mal soigné; (*c*) délabré.

raunchy [ˈrɔːntʃi] (*adj.*) (*U.S.*), *F:* **1.** vieux*, croulant, bon pour la casse, esquinté. **2.** moche, toc, tocard. **3.** salingue, cracra. **4.** criard. **5.** ivre*, rondibé. *Cf.* **ronchie, ronchy.**

rave[1] [reiv] (*noun*), *F:* **1.** louange *f* enthousiaste, concert *m* de louanges, coup *m* d'encensoir; **r. review,** compte-

* An asterisk indicates that the word so marked is included as a head-word in the Appendix.

rendu élogieux. 2. amoureux *m*. 3. béguin *m*, tocade *f*.

rave[2] [reiv] **(to)**, *F:* 1. être dans le vent (*ou* dans le mouvement). 2. s'extasier.

raver [ˈreivər] (*noun*), *F:* 1. **a (little) r.**, une beauté, un prix de Diane. 2. individu* à la mode (*ou* dans le vent).

rave-up [ˈreivʌp] (*noun*), *F:* **to have a r.-u.**, se déchaîner, sortir de ses gonds.

raw[1] [rɔː] (*adj.*), *F:* 1. **it's a r. deal,** il y a de l'abus, c'est dur à avaler; **to give s.o. a r. deal,** en faire voir de dures à qn. 2. nu*, à poil. 3. risqué, scabreux, cru. 4. **a r. hand,** un novice, un bleu, un mal dégrossi.

raw[2] [rɔː] (*noun*), *F:* 1. **to catch s.o. on the r.**, piquer qn au vif, toucher le point sensible de qn. 2. **in the r.**, (*a*) = **raw**[1]**, 2**; (*b*) fruste, brut.

ray [rei] (*noun*), *F:* **to be s.o.'s little r. of sunshine,** être le rayon de soleil de qn.

razz[1] [ræz] (*noun*) (*U.S.*), *F:* dérision *f*, ridicule *f*; huées *f.pl.*

razz[2] [ræz] **(to)** (*U.S.*), *F:* taquiner, narguer, railler, se moquer* de (qn), se payer la tête de (qn).

razzle [ˈræzl] (*noun*), *F:* **on the r.**, en réjouissances*; **to go on the r.**, faire la bringue (*ou* la ribouldingue *ou* la noce).

razzle-dazzle[1] [ˈræzldæzl] (*noun*) (*U.S.*), *F:* 1. bouleversement *m*, chambardement *m*, remue-ménage *m*. 2. brouillamini (*ou* micmac) voulu. 3. fraude *f*, supercherie *f*, filouterie *f*, roustissure *f*. 4. agitation *f*, éclat *m*, clinquant *m*, tape-à-l'œil *m*. 5. réjouissances*, bombe *f*, nouba *f*.

razzle-dazzle[2] [ˈræzldæzl] **(to)** (*U.S.*), *F:* éblouir, en mettre plein la vue.

razzmatazz[1] [ˈræzməˈtæz] (*adj.*), *F:* vieux jeu, usé, rococo, à l'eau de rose.

razzmatazz[2] [ˈræzməˈtæz] (*noun*), *F:* brouillamini *m*, tape-à-l'œil *m*, clinquant *m*.

reach-me-downs [ˈriːtʃmidaunz] (*pl. noun*), *F:* prêt-à-porter *m*, décrochez-moi-ça *m*; *cf.* **hand-me-downs.**

read [riːd] **(to)**, *F:* 1. **I can r. him like a book,** je le connais comme (le fond de) ma poche, je le lis comme un livre. 2. comprendre, piger.

reader [ˈriːdər] (*noun*), *P:* 1. (*argot des prisons*) livre *m*, revue *f*, journal *m*, de la lecture. 2. (*argot des drogués*) ordonnance *f* pour des drogues. *Voir aussi* **mitt-reader.**

ready [ˈredi] (*noun*), *F:* **the r.**, argent*, pèze *m*, fric *m*.

real [riəl] (*adv.*), *F:* 1. **for r.**, (*a*) réel, vraisemblable, authentique; (*b*) trop beau pour y croire, incroyable. 2. réellement, véritablement, vraisemblablement, effectivement; **that's r. nice of you,** c'est très gentil de votre part.

ream [riːm] **(to)**, *P:* **to r. s.o.**, (*a*) rentrer qch. dans le rectum de qn; (*b*) = **ram**[2] **(to), 2.**

ream out [ˈriːmˈaut] **(to)** (*U.S.*), *P:* **to r. s.o. o., to r. s.o.'s ass o.**, réprimander* qn sévèrement, enguirlander, engueuler qn.

rear (-end) [ˈriər(end)] (*noun*), *F:* fesses*, postérieur *m*, popotin *m*; *cf.* **end, 1.**

recap[1] [ˈriːkæp] (*noun*), *F:* (=*recapitulation*) résumé *m*, récapitulation *f*.

recap[2] [ˈriːˈkæp] **(to)**, *F:* (=*recapitulate*) récapituler, faire un résumé (de qch.).

recce[1] [ˈreki] (*noun*), *F:* (=*reconnaissance*) exploration *f*, investigation *f*.

recce[2] [ˈreki] **(to)**, *F:* (=*reconnoitre*) faire une reconnaissance, éclairer le terrain.

red[1] [red] (*adj.*). 1. *F:* communiste, communo, rouge. 2. *F:* **to roll out the r. carpet for s.o.,** faire les honneurs à qn, mettre les petits plats dans les grands. 3. *F:* **to paint the town r.**, être en réjouissances*, faire les quatre cents coups, faire la noce (*ou* la ribouldingue). 4. *P:* **r. birds** (*or* **devils** *or* **jackets**) = **reds (red**[2]**, 5)**. *Voir aussi* **herring, 1; light**[2]**, 4; rag**[1]**, 4; tape**[1]**.**

red[2] [red] (*noun*). 1. *F:* communiste *mf*, communo *m*, rouge *mf*. 2. *P:* or*, joncaille *f*, dorure *f*. 3. *F:* **in the r.**, déficitaire, dans le rouge. 4. *F:* **to see r.**, voir rouge, piquer une colère*. 5. (*pl.*) *P:* diables *m.pl.* rouges (barbituriques) (*drogues**); *voir aussi* **red**[1]**, 4. 6.** *P:* **to have the reds,** avoir ses menstrues*, repeindre sa grille en rouge.

red-cap [ˈredkæp] (*noun*), *F:* 1. (*mil.*) soldat *m* de la police militaire. 2. (*U.S.*) porteur *m* (dans une gare).

reddite [ˈredait] (*noun*), *P:* 1. bijoutier *m*, brocandier *m*. 2. qn qui s'occupe d'or*, marchand *m* de jonc; *cf.* **red**[2]**, 2.**

red-eye [ˈredai] (*noun*) (*U.S.*), *P:* 1.

*** L'astérisque indique que le mot marqué de ce signe figure comme entrée dans le Répertoire.**

whisky *m* de contrebande, casse-pattes *m*. 2. alcool*, tord-boyau(x) *m*, gnôle *f*.

redhead ['redhed] (*noun*), *F:* rouquin(e), poil *m* de carotte, poil *m* de brique.

red-hot ['red'hɔt] (*adj.*), *F:* 1. plein de nouvelles scandaleuses et de cancans; **a r.-h. magazine,** un journal* à sensations. 2. (*a*) plein de sève (*ou* d'allant), qui pète le feu; (*b*) avec du sex-appeal; (*U.S.*) **a r.-h. mam(m)a,** (i) une petite amie pétillante; (ii) vocaliste plantureuse, chanteuse de jazz. 3. **a r.-h. communist,** un communiste à tous crins. 4. très récent, tout chaud, tout brûlant, dernière heure; **a r.-h. tip,** un tuyau récent et sensationnel.

red-lamp ['red'læmp] (*attrib. adj.*), *F:* **a r.-l. district,** un quartier à prostituées*.

red-letter ['red'letər] (*attrib. adj.*), *F:* **r.-l. day,** jour *m* de fête, jour mémorable.

red-light ['red'lait] (*attrib. adj.*), *F:* = **red-lamp.**

redneck ['rednek] (*noun*) (*U.S.*), *F:* paysan*, plouc *m*, cul-terreux *m*.

reef[1] [ri:f] (*noun*), *F:* **to let out a r.,** se desserrer, lâcher d'un cran.

reef[2] [ri:f] (**to**) (*Austr.*), *P:* prendre; chaparder, faucher, ratiboiser.

reefer ['ri:fər] (*noun*). 1. *F:* cigarette* de marijuana (*drogues**), reefer *m*. 2. *P:* fumeur *m* de marijuana. 3. (*Austr.*) *P:* complice *m* (d'un pickpocket), baron *m*.

re-entry [ri:'entri] (*noun*), *P:* fin *f* de voyage d'un drogué.

ref[1] [ref] (*noun*), *F:* (*sports*) (=*referee*) arbitre *m*.

ref[2] [ref] (**to**), *F:* (*sports*) (=*referee*) arbitrer (un match).

reign [rein] (**to**) (*Austr.*), *P:* être en liberté, profiter de la fraîche.

rent [rent] (*noun*), *P:* prostitué mâle.

rep [rep] (*abbr.*), *F:* 1. (=*representative*) commis voyageur *m*, gaudissart *m*. 2. (=*reputation*) réputation *f*. 3. (=*repertory* (*theatre*)) théâtre *m* de province, théâtre municipal; **to be in r.,** être acteur/actrice au théâtre municipal.

repeaters [ri'pi:təz] (*pl. noun*), *P:* dés* truqués, balourds *m.pl.*, matuches *m.pl.*

resurrection pie [rezə'rekʃ(ə)n'pai] (*noun*), *F:* nourriture* réchauffée, arlequin *m*.

retread ['ri:tred] (*noun*) (*U.S.*), *F:* rappelé *m* au service militaire; naphtalinard *m*.

revamp [ri:'væmp] (**to**), *F:* renouveler, remettre à neuf, retaper.

reviver [ri'vaivər] (*noun*), *F:* remontant *m*, apéritif *m*.

rhino ['rainou] (*noun*). 1. *F:* (=*rhinoceros*) rhino(céros) *m*. 2. *P:* argent*, galette *f*; paie *f*, salaire *m*, sonnettes *f.pl.*

rhubarb ['ru:bɑ:b] (*noun*), *P:* 1. bêtises*, balivernes *f.pl.*, sornettes *f.pl.* 2. cacophonie *f*, tumulte *m*, chambard *m*. 3. querelle*, chahut *m*, grabuge *m*.

rheumaticky [ru:'mætiki] (*adj.*), *F:* rhumatisant.

rib[1] [rib] (*noun*), *P:* **on the ribs,** pauvre*, fauché, dans la dèche.

rib[2] [rib] (**to**), *F:* taquiner, mettre en boîte, chiner (qn).

ribbing ['ribiŋ] (*noun*), *F:* **to give s.o. a r.,** taquiner qn.

rib-tickler ['ribtiklər] (*noun*), *F:* plaisanterie *f*, rigolade *f*.

rich[1] [ritʃ] (*adj.*), *F:* 1. (*d'un incident*) très divertissant, rigolo; épatant, impayable. 2. scabreux, osé, cochon. *Voir aussi* **filthy, 2.**

rich[2] [ritʃ] (*adv.*), *F:* **to strike it r.,** décrocher le gros lot.

Richard, richard ['ritʃəd] (*noun*), *P:* 1. (*R.S.* = *Richard the Third* =) (*a*) (*word*) mot *m*; *cf.* **dicky-bird;** (*b*) (*bird*) oiseau *m*; (*c*) (*turd*) étron*, colombin *m*. 2. fille*, nénette *f*, pépée *f*. 3. (*U.S.*) = **dick, 2.**

ride[1] [raid] (*noun*). 1. *P:* coït*, dérouillage *m*, grimpage *m*. 2. *F:* **to take s.o. for a r.,** (*a*) entraîner et tuer qn, aller dézinguer qn; (*b*) tromper* qn, jouer un sale tour à qn, mener qn en bateau. 3. *F:* **to go along (just) for the r.,** suivre le gros de la troupe, y aller pour y aller. *Voir aussi* **joy-ride.**

ride[2] [raid] (**to**). 1. *P:* coïter* avec (une femme), dérouiller, grimper. 2. (*U.S.*) *F:* asticoter, canuler, enquiquiner. 3. *F:* **to let sth. r.,** laisser courir qch.

riff [rif] (*noun*), *P:* 1. court motif mélodique de jazz. 2. chicane *f*, chamaillerie *f*.

rig[1] [rig] (*noun*), *P:* pénis*, colonne *f*.

rig[2] [rig] (**to**), *F:* arranger (*ou* manigancer) à son avantage.

right [rait] (*adj.*). 1. *P:* **to make a r. mess** (*or* **muck**) **of it,** tout gâcher, tout bousiller, foutre une vraie pagaille; *cf.* **balls-up;** *voir aussi* **nana; so-and-so, 2;**

* An asterisk indicates that the word so marked is included as a head-word in the Appendix.

sucker[2], 1. 2. *F:* **as r. as rain,** en parfait état, comme un charme. 3. (*U.S.*) *F:* **a r. guy,** (*a*) un chic type, un mec bien; (*b*) un vrai de vrai, un régulo, un correct. 4. *F:* **to get on the r. side of s.o.,** être bien vu de qn, se mettre dans les petits papiers de qn. *Voir aussi* **noise; people, 2.**

righteous ['raitʃəs] (*adj.*), *P:* 1. ivre*, raide. 2. tapageur, chahuteur.

right-ho! ['rait'hou], **right-o(h)!** ['rait'ou] (*excl.*), *F:* oui*, d'ac(cord)! O.K., entendu.

right on ['rait'ɔn] (*adv.*), *F:* au poil, impec.

righty-(h)o! ['raiti'(h)ou] (*excl.*), *F:* = **right-ho!**

rigid ['ridʒid] (*adj.*), *P:* 1. **to bore s.o. r.,** ennuyer* qn au plus haut point, emmerder qn jusqu'à la moelle. 2. (*U.S.*) ivre* mort, bituré.

rig-out ['rigaut] (*noun*), *F:* toilette *f*, tenue *f*, accoutrement *m*, attifage *m*.

rig out ['rig'aut] (**to**), *F:* habiller*, accoutrer, attifer, fringuer, harnacher.

rig-up ['rigʌp] (*noun*), *F:* appareil improvisé, installation *f* de fortune.

rig up ['rig'ʌp] (**to**), *F:* 1. apprêter, préparer, concocter (un repas, une excuse, *etc.*). 2. = **rig out (to).**

Riley ['raili] (*noun*), *F:* **to live the life of R.,** se la couler douce, se la faire belle, vivre comme un coq en pâte.

rim [rim] (**to**), *P:* = **ream (to),** (*a*).

ring[1] [riŋ] (*noun*). 1. *P:* anus*, anneau *m*, bague *f*. 2. *F:* **to run** (*or* **make**) **rings round s.o.,** l'emporter sur qn, surpasser qn, remporter la palme, tenir la corde.

ring[2] [riŋ] (**to**). 1. *F:* **it rings a bell,** cela me dit quelque chose. 2. *F:* **to r. the changes,** (*a*) escroquer*, arnaquer, empiler; (*b*) écouler de la fausse monnaie, faire la fournaise; (*c*) ressasser (un sujet, *etc.*). 3. *F:* substituer un cheval pour un autre dans une course, aller de cheval à canasson. 4. *P:* maquiller des objets volés.

ringer ['riŋər] (*noun*), *F:* 1. **to be a (dead) r. for s.o.,** être qn tout craché, être le portrait (tout) craché de qn. 2. qn qui substitue un cheval pour un autre dans une course.

ring-piece ['riŋpi:s] (*noun*), *P:* = **ring**[1], 1.

ringtail ['riŋteil] (*noun*) (*Austr.*), *F:* (*a*) lâche *m*, caneur *m*, frileux *m*; (*b*) faux frère, macaron *m*, mouton *m*.

rinky-dink ['riŋki'diŋk] (*noun*) (*U.S.*), *F:* 1. camelote *f*, pacotille *f*, saloperie *f*. 2. guinche *f*, boui-boui *m*.

riot ['raiət] (*noun*), *F:* 1. grand succès, boum *m* (du tonnerre), fureur *f*. 2. boute-en-train *m*, rigolo *m*, rigolboche *m*. 3. déchaînement *m*, tapage *m*, débauche *f*. 4. **to read the R. Act to s.o.,** (*a*) avertir, menacer qn; (*b*) réprimander* qn, passer un savon à qn.

rip [rip] (**to**), *F:* **to let r.,** exploser, vider son sac; **let it r.!** fonce! appuie sur le champignon!

ripe [raip] (*adj.*), *F:* 1. indécent, scabreux, osé. 2. ivre*, mûr, rétamé. 3. amusant*, gondolant, crevant.

rip into ['rip'intu:] (**to**), *F:* attaquer* (qn), rentrer dans le lard à (qn).

rip off ['rip'ɔf] (**to**), *P:* 1. voler*, faucher; **to get ripped off,** être ratiboisé. 2. exploiter, arnaquer. 3. coïter* avec (une femme), égoïner. 4. tuer*, zigouiller.

ripped [ript] (*adj.*), *P:* 1. malheureux, piteux. 2. (*a*) (*drogues*) défoncé, très high; (*b*) très ivre*, rétamé.

ripping ['ripiŋ] (*adj.*), *F:* excellent*, formid(able), super.

rip-roaring ['rip-rɔ:riŋ] (*adj.*), *F:* (*a*) endiablé, piaffant, pétardant; (*b*) **a r.-r. success,** une réussite du tonnerre, une fureur de tous les diables, un succès fulgurant.

ripsnorter ['rip-snɔ:tər] (*noun*), *F:* personne *ou* chose remarquable, crack *m*, as *m*.

ripsnorting ['rip-snɔ:tiŋ] (*adj.*), *F:* excellent*, bœuf, du tonnerre.

rise[1] [raiz] (*noun*), *F:* **to take a** (*or* **the**) **r. out of s.o.,** faire monter (*ou* mousser) qn.

rise[2] [raiz] (**to**), *F:* **r. and shine!** *c.p.*, debout les morts!

ritz [rits] (*noun*), *F:* **to put on the r.,** être prétentieux*, se donner des airs, crâner, plastronner, faire du vent.

ritzy ['ritsi] (*adj.*), *F:* 1. bariolé, tape-à-l'œil, voyant, clinquant; **a r. tart,** une pépée qui en jette, une minette. 2. élégant*, fastueux, ultra-chic. 3. crâneur, esbrouf(f)eur, plastronneur.

river ['rivər] (*noun*), *F:* 1. **to sell s.o. down the r.,** trahir, vendre, moutonner qn. 2. **to send s.o. up the r. = to send s.o. up (send up (to), 2).**

* L'astérisque indique que le mot marqué de ce signe figure comme entrée dans le Répertoire.

roach [routʃ] (*noun*), *P:* mégot* de cigarette de marijuana.

road [roud] (*noun*), *F:* **1. to be on the r.**, vivre sur les grands chemins, vagabonder. **2. to hit the r.**, partir*, se mettre en route, prendre le large. *Voir aussi* **middle-of-the-road; one, 1.**

road-hog [ˈroudhɔg] (*noun*), *F:* chauffeur *m* qui conduit au milieu de la chaussée, chauffard *m*, écraseur *m*.

roast[1] [roust] (*noun*), *F:* (*a*) critique *f* défavorable, éreintage *m*, bêchage *m*; (*b*) calomnie *f*, débinage *m*, cassage *m* de sucre.

roast[2] [roust] (**to**), *F:* critiquer*, éreinter, bêcher, jardiner.

roasting [ˈroustiŋ] (*noun*), *F:* **to give (s.o.) a r.** = **roast**[2] **(to)**.

rock[1] [rɔk] (*noun*). **1.** *F:* (*jazz*) rock *m*; *cf.* **rock-'n-roll. 2.** *F:* **on the rocks,** (*a*) (boisson) servie avec de la glace; (*b*) ruiné*, fauché, nettoyé, passé; (*c*) (mariage) en échec*, à (vau-)l'eau; (*d*) (*commerce*) en faillite, dans le bouillon. **3.** (*pl.*) *P:* diamants*, diames *m.pl.*, pierres *f.pl.*, cailloux *m.pl.*; *voir aussi* **hot, 9. 4.** *F:* **to touch r. bottom,** être arrivé au fin fond, être tout à fait à plat.

rock[2] [rɔk] (**to**). **1.** *F:* secouer, ébranler, alarmer. **2.** *F:* **to r. the boat,** secouer la barque (*ou* la baraque), secouer les puces, faire du grabuge. **3.** *P:* coïter* avec (une femme), biquer.

rock-candy [ˈrɔkˈkændi] (*noun*), *P:* = **rocks (rock**[1]**, 3)**.

rocker [ˈrɔkər] (*noun*), *F:* **1.** blouson noir sur grosse moto (*ou* trail bike); *cf.* **mod**[2]. **2. off one's r.,** fou*, timbré, loufoque, maboul(e), échappé de Charenton. **3.** rocking-chair *f*.

rocket [ˈrɔkit] (*noun*), *F:* **to give s.o. a r.,** réprimander* qn, passer un savon à qn. *Voir aussi* **sky-rocket.**

rockhead [ˈrɔkhed] (*noun*), *P:* individu bête*, buse *f*, bas-de-plafond *m*, ballot *m*.

rock-'n-roll[1] [ˈrɔkənroul] (*noun*), *F:* rock-and-roll *m*; *cf.* **rock**[1]**, 1.**

rock-'n-roll[2] [ˈrɔkənroul] (**to**), *F:* faire le rock-and-roll.

rocky [ˈrɔki] (*adj.*), *F:* (*a*) vacillant, flageolant; **a r. marriage,** un mariage branlant; (*b*) chancelant, titubant (de boisson *ou* de fatigue).

rod [rɔd] (*noun*), *P:* **1.** pénis*, canne *f*, gourdin *m*; *cf.* **hot-rod (to)**. **2.** revolver*, calibre *m*, flingue *m*. **3.** pardessus*, lardosse *m*. *Voir aussi* **hot, 22.**

rod-man [ˈrɔdmæn] (*noun*) (*U.S.*), *P:* gangster *m*, bandit *m*, voleur* armé.

Roger! roger![1] [ˈrɔdʒər] (*excl.*), *F:* oui*, d'ac! O.K.!

roger[2] [ˈrɔdʒər] (**to**), *P:* coïter* avec (une femme), égoïner.

roll[1] [roul] (*noun*). **1.** *F:* liasse *f* de billets* (de banque), matelas *m* (de faf(f)iots). **2.** *P:* (*a*) coït*, giclée *f* du mâle; (*b*) **a r. in the hay,** coït*, couchage *m*, baisage *m*, une partie de jambes en l'air; *voir aussi* **hay, 2; jelly-roll; payroll; rock-'n-roll**[1].

roll[2] [roul] (**to**). **1.** *P:* voler*, rouler, roustir, ratiboiser. **2.** *F:* **to be rolling in it,** être très riche*, être plein aux as, rouler sur l'or. **3.** *F:* **to get rolling,** partir*, se déhotter, démarrer. **4.** *P:* coïter* avec (une femme), envoyer (une femme) en l'air. *Voir aussi* **aisle, 2; rock-'n-roll**[2] **(to)**.

roll along [ˈrouləˈlɔŋ] (**to**), *F:* avancer tranquillement, suivre son petit bonhomme de chemin.

rollicking [ˈrɔlikiŋ] (*noun*), *P:* engueulade *f*, savon *m*.

roll on [ˈroulˈɔn] (**to**), *F:* **r. o., Christmas!** vite Noël!

roll-ons [ˈroulɔnz] (*pl. noun*), *F:* gaine *f* (élastique).

roll out [ˈroulˈaut] (**to**), *F:* **they rolled out of the pub at closing time,** à la fermeture ils sortirent du café en titubant. *Voir aussi* **red**[1]**, 2.**

roll-up [ˈroulʌp] (*noun*), *P:* cigarette* roulée (main), cibiche *f* maison; *cf.* **roll up (to), 2.**

roll up [ˈroulˈʌp] (**to**). **1.** *F:* arriver*, s'abouler, débouler. **2.** *P:* faire une cigarette* de marijuana, rouler un reefer; *cf.* **roll-up.**

roll-your-own [ˈrouljəˈroun] (*noun*), *F:* (*a*) machine *f* à rouler les cigarettes*; (*b*) = **roll-up.**

roly-poly [ˈrouliˈpouli] (*noun*), *F:* individu* rondouillard, patapouf *m*, bouboule *m*, dondon *m*.

Roman [ˈroumən] (*adj.*), *P:* **1. R. candle,** catholique *mf*. **2.** (=*roaming*) (*a*) **R. hands,** mains caressantes (*ou* baladeuses); (*b*) **R. eyes,** yeux farfouilleurs.

* An asterisk indicates that the word so marked is included as a head-word in the Appendix.

romp[1] [rɔmp] (*noun*), *F:* **1. to have a r. on the sofa,** prendre ses ébats sur le canapé. **2.** chose facile à réaliser, du nanan, du beurre, du nougat.

romp[2] [rɔmp] (**to**), *F:* **to r. home,** (*d'un cheval*) gagner facilement, arriver dans un fauteuil.

ronchie, ronchy [ˈrɔntʃi] (*adj.*) (*U.S.*), *F:* = **raunchy.**

roof [ruːf] (*noun*). **1.** *F:* **to go through** (*or* **hit**) **the r.,** piquer une colère, monter sur ses grands chevaux, sortir de ses gonds. **2.** *F:* **to raise the r.,** faire du chahut (*ou* du chambard *ou* du grabuge). **3.** *P:* **to fall off the r.,** avoir ses menstrues*, repeindre sa grille (en rouge).

rook [rʊk] (**to**), *F:* escroquer*, faisander, pigeonner.

rookie [ˈrʊki] (*noun*), *F:* recrue *f*, débutant *m*, blanc-bec *m*.

rooking [ˈrʊkiŋ] (*noun*), *F:* **to get a r.,** payer* trop cher, se faire empiler, être faisandé.

rooky [ˈrʊki] (*noun*), *F:* = **rookie.**

room [ruːm] (*noun*), *F:* **the smallest r.,** W.C.*, le petit endroit, le petit coin; *cf.* **throne-room.** *Voir aussi* **barrack-room.**

roost [ruːst] (*noun*), *F:* **1.** logement*, niche *f*, guitoune *f*. **2. to hit the r.,** se coucher*, se zoner, aller au paddock. *Voir aussi* **chicken-roost; pigeon-roost.**

root[1] [ruːt] (*noun*), *P:* **1.** cigarette*, cibiche *f*. **2.** amphétamine *f* (*drogues**). **3.** pénis*, bout *m*, queue *f*.

root[2] [ruːt] (**to**). **1.** (*Austr.*) *P:* coïter* avec (une femme), fourrer, tringler. **2.** (*Austr.*) *P:* **get rooted!** = **get knotted! 3.** *F:* **to r. for s.o.,** applaudir, encourager qn.

rooted [ˈruːtid] (*adj.*) (*Austr.*), *P:* très fatigué*, vanné.

rooter [ˈruːtər] (*noun*), *F:* partisan *m*, fana(tique) *mf* (d'une équipe, *etc.*).

rootie [ˈruːti] (*noun*), *P:* nourriture*, repas *m*, bectance *f*, fricot *m*.

rootin'-tootin' [ˈruːtinˈtuːtin] (*adj.*) (*U.S.*), *F:* bruyant, chahuteur, pétardier.

rooty [ˈruːti] (*adj.*), *P:* = **horny.**

rope [roup] (*noun*). **1.** *F:* **it's money for old r.,** c'est donné pour une bouchée de pain. **2.** *P:* tabac* fort, perlot *m*, trèfle *m*. **3.** *P:* (*a*) marijuana *f* (*drogues**), chanvre *m*; (*b*) cigarette* de marijuana (*drogues**), stick *m*. **4.** *F:* **to know the ropes,** être au courant (*ou* à la roue *ou* à la coule), savoir nager, connaître la combine (*ou* les tenants et les aboutissants). **5.** *F:* **to give s.o. plenty of r.,** lâcher la bride (*ou* la jambe) à qn. *Voir aussi* **bell-rope.**

rope in [ˈroupˈin] (**to**), *F:* **to r. s.o. i.,** s'assurer le concours de qn.

rop(e)y [ˈroupi] (*adj.*), *F:* camelote, toc, tocard, ordurier.

rort [rɔːt] (*noun*) (*Austr.*), *F:* **1.** coup monté (*ou* fourré), combine bien cuisinée. **2.** boniment *m*, baratin *m*.

rorty [ˈrɔːti] (*adj.*), *P:* **1.** réjoui, de bonne humeur, guilleret, folichon. **2.** = **horny** (*b*).

Rory (O'Moore) [ˈrɔːri(ouˈmɔər)] (*pr. noun*), *P:* **1.** (*R.S.* = *door*) porte *f*, lourde *f*. **2. on the R.,** pauvre*, fauché, sans le sou.

Roscoe, roscoe [ˈrɔskou] (*noun*), *P:* revolver*, pétoire *m*, rigolo *m*.

rosy [ˈrouzi] (*noun*), *P:* **1.** = **claret. 2.** vin* rouge, pinard *m*, rouquin *m*. **3. ring around the r.** = **daisy chain** (**daisy**[2], **6**). **4. R. Lee** (*R.S.* = *tea*), thé *m*.

rot [rɔt] (*noun*), *F:* bêtises*, sottises *f.pl.*, âneries *f.pl.*; (**what**) **r.!** allons donc! quelle blague!; **to talk** (**utter**) **r.,** dire des imbécillités *f.pl.*; *cf.* **tommy-rot.**

rot-gut [ˈrɔtgʌt] (*noun*), *F:* alcool* de mauvaise qualité, tord-boyau(x) *m*.

rotten [ˈrɔtn] (*adj.*), *F:* **1.** désagréable, dégueulasse, débectant, moche, lamentable; **r. weather,** temps *m* de chien; **r. luck!** quelle guigne! pas de veine! **2.** toc, tocard, camelote, ordurier. **3.** malade*, patraque. **4.** ennuyeux*, barbant, emmerdant. *Voir aussi* **sod**[1], **2.**

rotter [ˈrɔtər] (*noun*), *F:* vaurien*, fripouille *f*, charogne *f*.

rough[1] [rʌf] (*adj.*), *F:* **1. r. diamond,** personne aux dehors grossiers mais bon enfant, un diamant dans sa gangue. **2. that's r.!** c'est vache! c'est dur à avaler! **3. he's had a r. deal,** il en a bavé, il a mangé de la vache enragée, il en a vu (des vertes et des pas mûres). **4. they're a r. lot,** c'est une bande* de sales types; **a r. customer,** un mauvais coucheur, un dur à cuire. **5. r. and ready,** (*a*) **a r. and ready person,** une personne nature (pas très fine ni distinguée), un pecnaud sur

* L'astérisque indique que le mot marqué de ce signe figure comme entrée dans le Répertoire.

les bords; (*b*) **a r. and ready method,** une méthode peu précise mais pratique; (*c*) **a r. and ready piece of work,** un ouvrage grossièrement fait. **6. r. stuff,** brutalités *f.pl.*, vacheries *f.pl.* **7. to give s.o. a r. time,** maltraiter qn, être chien (*ou* vache) avec qn.

rough² [rʌf] (*adv.*), *F:* **1. to sleep r.,** coucher* sur la dure. **2. to feel r.,** (*a*) se sentir malade* (*ou* patraque); (*b*) se sentir moulu; (*c*) avoir la gueule de bois. *Voir aussi* **cut up (to), 3.**

rough³ [rʌf] (*noun*). **1.** *F:* **to take the r. with the smooth,** prendre le bien avec le mal; à la guerre comme à la guerre. **2.** *P:* = **roughneck. 3.** *P:* **to have a bit of r.** = **to have a bit on the side (side, 2).**

rough-house [ˈrʌfhaus] (*noun*), *F:* (*a*) conduite *f* de vaurien*, voyouterie *f*; (*b*) bagarre* générale, badaboum *m*, barouf(fe) *m*, ramdam(e) *m*.

rough it [ˈrʌfit] **(to),** *F:* vivre à la dure.

roughneck [ˈrʌfnek] (*noun*), *F:* vaurien*, canaille *f*, voyou *m*; un dur.

rough-up [ˈrʌfʌp] (*noun*), *P:* violente querelle*, cognage *m*, tabassage *m*, dérouillée *f*.

rough up [ˈrʌfˈʌp] **(to),** *P:* battre*, tabasser, bourrer (qn) de coups.

roundabouts [ˈraundəbauts] (*pl. noun*), *F:* **what you lose on the r. you gain on the swings,** *c.p.*, à tout prendre on ne gagne ni ne perd.

roundheel(s) [ˈraundhiːl(z)] (*noun*) (*U.S.*), *P:* **to be a r.,** être une femme facile, avoir les talons courts; *cf.* **heel, 2.**

round-up [ˈraundʌp] (*noun*), *F:* **1.** rassemblement *m*, compilation *f*, résumé *m* (des dernières nouvelles, *etc.*). **2. to be heading for the last r.-u.,** être près de mourir*, sentir le sapin, graisser ses bottes.

rouser [ˈrauzər] (*noun*), *P:* **1.** qch. de sensationnel (*ou* de saisissant), un boum. **2.** gros mensonge*, bobard *m* maouss, bourrage *m* de crâne.

roust out [ˈraustˈaut] **(to),** *F:* **to r. s.o. o.,** se débarrasser* de qn, flanquer qn à la porte, balancer qn, envoyer balader qn.

roust up [ˈraustˈʌp] **(to),** *F:* aller chercher, dégot(t)er, repérer.

row¹ [rau] (*noun*). **1.** *F:* querelle*, rififi *m*, badaboum *m*. **2.** (*a*) *F:* chahut *m*, charivari *m* (du diable); (*b*) *P:* **hold** (*or* **shut**) **your r.!** tais-toi! (*se taire**), la ferme! la boucle!

row² [rau] **(to),** *F:* se quereller, s'attraper, pétarder, s'engueuler.

rozzer [ˈrɔzər] (*noun*), *P:* agent* de police, flic *m*, poulet *m*.

rubadub [ˈrʌbəˈdʌb] (*noun*) (*R.S.* = *club*), *P:* club *m*.

rub along [ˈrʌbəˈlɔŋ] **(to),** *F:* se tirer d'affaire, se débrouiller.

rubber [ˈrʌbər] (*noun*). **1.** *P:* capote anglaise, imper *m* à Popaul. **2.** (*pl.*) *F:* galoches *f.pl.*, caoutchoucs *m.pl. Voir aussi* **bum-rubber.**

rubberneck¹ [ˈrʌbənek] (*noun*) (*U.S.*), *F:* touriste *mf*, badaud *m*, glaude *f*.

rubberneck² [ˈrʌbənek] **(to)** (*U.S.*), *F:* excursionner, visiter (monuments, *etc.*).

rubber-stamp [ˈrʌbəˈstæmp] (*noun*), *F:* (*a*) fonctionnaire *m* qui exécute aveuglément les ordres de ses supérieurs, rond-de-cuir *m*; (*b*) béni-oui-oui *m*.

rube [ruːb] (*noun*) (*U.S.*), *P:* **1.** fermier *m*, cul-terreux *m*. **2.** paysan*, pétrousquin *m*, plouc *m*.

rub in [ˈrʌbˈin] **(to),** *F:* **to r. it i.,** insister, remuer le couteau dans la plaie.

rub off [ˈrʌbˈɔf] **(to),** *P:* **1.** coïter*, caramboler. **2.** se masturber*, s'astiquer. **3. to r. o. on s.o.,** tomber dessus, s'abouler, débouler (*l'argent, la chance, etc.*).

rub-out [ˈrʌbaut] (*noun*), *P:* **1.** assassinat *m*, tuerie *f*, but(t)age *m*, dessoudage *m*. **2.** coït*, baisage *m*, frottage *m*, carambolage *m*.

rub out [ˈrʌbˈaut] **(to),** *P:* **1.** tuer*, but(t)er, dessouder, démolir. **2.** battre*, bourrer de coups*, dérouiller.

rub-up [ˈrʌbʌp] (*noun*), *P:* acte *m* de masturbation, moussage *m*; *cf.* **rub up (to), 2.**

rub up [ˈrʌbˈʌp] **(to). 1.** *F:* **to r. s.o. u. the wrong way,** prendre qn du mauvais côté (*ou* à rebrousse-poil). **2.** *P:* se masturber*, s'astiquer. **3.** *P:* caresser activement (qn), faire mousser (qn); allumer les gaz.

ruck¹ [rʌk] (*noun*), *P:* querelle*, prise *f* de bec (*ou* de gueule).

ruck² [rʌk] **(to),** *P:* **1.** agacer, énerver, ronchonner. **2.** faire beaucoup de bruit*, faire du chahut (*ou* du chambard *ou* du grabuge).

ruckus [ˈrʌkəs] (*noun*), *P:* = **ruck**[1].
ructions [ˈrʌkʃənz] (*pl. noun*), *F:* bagarre*, tapage *m*, vacarme *m*; désordre *m*; scène *f*; **if you come home late there'll be r.,** si tu rentres tard, tu te feras incendier (*ou* engueuler).
ruddy [ˈrʌdi] (*adj. & adv.*), *P:* (*euph. pour* **bloody**) **a r. liar,** un sacré menteur; **he's a r. nuisance,** il est vachement enquiquinant; **ain't it grand to be r. well dead,** *c.p.*, on s'en fout quand on est mort et enterré.
rug [rʌg] (*noun*). **1.** *F:* **to cut a r.,** danser*, guincher, gambiller. **2.** *P:* perruque *f*, moumoute *f*. **3.** *F:* **to pull the r. from under s.o.** (*or* **from under s.o.'s feet**), couper l'herbe sous les pieds de qn. *Voir aussi* **dirt**[1], **4.**
rugger [ˈrʌgər] (*noun*), *F:* le rugby.
rum [rʌm] (*adj.*), *F:* bizarre; **a r. one,** un drôle de type (*ou* de zèbre), un drôle d'oiseau.
rumble[1] [ˈrʌmbl] (*noun*), *P:* bagarre*; bataille arrangée entre bandes* de voyous.
rumble[2] [ˈrʌmbl] (**to**), *F:* flairer, se douter de (qch.), voir venir (qn).
rumbustical [rʌmˈbʌstikl], **rumbustious** [rʌmˈbʌstiəs] (*adj.*), *F:* tapageur, chachuteur.
rumdum [ˈrʌmdʌm], **rumhound** [ˈrʌmhaund] (*noun*), *P:* ivrogne*, poivrot *m*, saoulot *m*, saoulard *m*.
rummy[1] [ˈrʌmi] (*adj.*), *F:* = **rum.**
rummy[2] [ˈrʌmi] (*noun*), *P:* = **rumdum.**
rump [rʌmp] (**to**), *P:* se droguer à l'héroïne.
rumpot [ˈrʌmpɔt] (*noun*), *P:* = **rumdum.**
rumpus [ˈrʌmpəs] (*noun*), *F:* querelle*, chahut *m*, vacarme *m*; **to kick up a r.,** faire une scène.
run [rʌn] (*noun*), *F:* **1. to have a r. for one's money,** en avoir pour son argent*. **2. the runs,** diarrhée*, courante *f*, chiasse *f*. **3. to be on the r.,** être recherché par la police, être en cavale. **4. dry r.,** essai *m*, répétition *f*.
run-around [ˈrʌnəraund] (*noun*), *F:* **to give s.o. the r.-a.,** donner le change à qn, faire marcher qn.
run-down [ˈrʌndaun] (*noun*), *F:* résumé *m*, récapitulation *f*, topo *m*.
run down[1] [ˈrʌnˈdaun] (*adj.*), *F:* anémié, débile.
run down[2] [ˈrʌnˈdaun] (**to**), *F:* critiquer*, éreinter, débiner.
run-in [ˈrʌnin] (*noun*), *F:* **1.** rôdage *m*. **2.** voie *f* d'accès, abords *m.pl.*
run in [ˈrʌnˈin] (**to**), *F:* arrêter*, embarquer, ramasser.
run-of-the-mill [ˈrʌnəvðəmil] (*adj.*), *F:* ordinaire, quelconque.
run-out [ˈrʌnaut] (*noun*), *P:* **1.** simulacre *m*, de vente aux enchères, lavage truqué. **2. to have a r.-o.,** uriner*, se l'égoutter.
run out [ˈrʌnˈaut] (**to**), *F:* **to r. o. on s.o.,** se défiler, prendre la poudre d'escampette.
runt [rʌnt] (*noun*), *F:* (*a*) nain *m*, nabot *m*; (*b*) avorton *m*, crapoussin *m*, crapaud *m*.
run-through [ˈrʌn-θruː] (*noun*), *F:* (*th., etc.*) lecture *f* rapide, répétition *f*.
runty [ˈrʌnti] (*adj.*), *F:* rabougri, riquiqui.
rush[1] [rʌʃ] (*noun*), *P:* impression *f* de plénitude physique et psychique avec une drogue; flash *m*.
rush[2] [rʌʃ] (**to**), *F:* **to r. s.o. for sth.,** pratiquer le coup de fusil sur qn, écorcher qn.
rush-hour [ˈrʌʃauər] (*noun*), *F:* heure *f* de pointe.
Russky [ˈruski, ˈrʌski] (*noun*), *F:* Russe *m*, Rusco *m*.
rustle up [ˈrʌslˈʌp] (**to**), *F:* dénicher, concocter; **she can always r. u. a meal,** elle sait toujours se débrouiller pour faire de quoi manger.
rusty[1] [ˈrʌsti] (*adj.*), *F:* **to cut up r. = to cut up nasty** (**cut up** (**to**), 3).
rusty[2] [ˈrʌsti] (*noun*), *F:* = **redhead.**

* L'astérisque indique que le mot marqué de ce signe figure comme entrée dans le Répertoire.

S

sack[1] [sæk] (*noun*). **1.** *F:* **to get the s.,** être congédié* (*ou* renvoyé *ou* sacqué *ou* flanqué à la porte); **to give s.o. the s.,** se débarrasser* de qn, sacquer, virer, balancer qn. **2.** *F:* **to look like a s. of potatoes,** avoir l'air de l'as de pique. **3.** *F:* **to hit the s.,** se coucher*, dormir*, pioncer, se pieuter; **s. time,** (*a*) temps passé au lit*, temps de pieutage; (*b*) heure *f* du coucher (*ou* du plumard). **4.** *P:* **s. game,** cour amoureuse, jeux amoureux, fleurette *f*; *voir aussi* **tiger.**

sack[2] [sæk] (**to**), *F:* **to s. s.o. = to give s.o. the sack (sack**[1], **1).**

sack out (*or* **up**) [ˈsækˈaut, ˈsækˈʌp] (**to**), *P:* se coucher*, se pieuter.

saddle [ˈsædl] (**to**), *F:* **to be saddled with s.o., sth.,** avoir qn, qch., sur le dos.

safe[1] [seif] (*adj.*), *F:* **to be s., to be on the s. side,** (*a*) être du bon côté; (*b*) agir pour plus de sûreté; **I'll take an extra £1 (just) to be on the s. side,** je prendrai une livre en supplément pour plus de sûreté.

safe[2] [seif] (*adv.*), *F:* **to play (it) s.,** agir à coup sûr, jouer serré.

safety [ˈseifti] (*noun*), *P:* capote anglaise, doigt *m* de sécurité.

sail [seil] (*noun*), *F:* **to take the wind out of s.o.'s sails,** couper l'herbe sous les pieds de qn.

sailing [ˈseiliŋ] (*noun*), *F:* **to be (all) plain s.,** aller tout seul, ne pas faire un pli.

sail into [ˈseilˈintuː] (**to**), *F:* (*a*) attaquer*, assaillir, agrafer (qn); (*b*) entamer (un travail) avec élan.

sail through [ˈseilˈθruː] (**to**), *F:* terminer (un travail, *etc.*) en moins de deux, faire (qch.) presto, liquider (qch.) comme sur des roulettes; **to s. t. an exam,** passer un examen haut la main.

sale [seil] (*noun*), *P:* **no s.!** pas mèche! rien à faire!

salt[1] [sɔːlt] (*noun*), *F:* **(old) s.,** marin*, vieux loup de mer. *Voir aussi* **dose, 2.**

salt[2] [sɔːlt] (**to**), *F:* **1. to s. a mine,** saler une mine (d'or, *etc.*), tapisser le front d'une mine. **2.** truquer, cuisiner (les bénéfices, les comptes, *etc.*). **3. to s. the bill,** saler l'addition.

salt-cellars [ˈsɔːlt-seləz] (*pl. noun*), *F:* salières *f.pl.* (derrière les clavicules).

salty [ˈsɔːlti] (*adj.*), *F:* **1.** hardi, audacieux, casse-cou, intrépide. **2.** un peu fort, difficile à digérer. **3.** obscène, scabreux, osé, salé, épicé. **4.** désagréable, horrible, difficile à avaler. **5.** fringant, pimpant.

sam, Sam [sæm] (*noun*), *P:* **1. to stand s.,** payer la tournée, liquider l'ardoise. **2.** (*U.S.*) agent *m* de la Brigade fédérale des Stupéfiants. *Voir aussi* **Uncle, 6.**

sambo, Sambo [ˈsæmbou] (*noun*), *P:* (*péj.*) nègre*, bamboula *m*.

sample [ˈsɑːmpl] (**to**), *F:* **to s. the goods,** mettre la main au panier (avec une fille).

sand [sænd] (*noun*) (*U.S.*), *F:* courage *m*, cran *m*, estome *m*, vigueur *f*; *cf.* **grit.**

sandboy [ˈsæn(d)bɔi] (*noun*), *F:* **(as) happy as a s.,** gai comme un pinson, heureux comme un poisson dans l'eau.

sandman [ˈsæn(d)mæn, ˈsæn(d)mən] (*noun*), *F:* **the s. is coming,** le marchand de sable passe; *cf.* **dustman.**

sap(head) [ˈsæp(hed)] (*noun*), *P:* individu bête*, niguedouille *mf*.

sappiness [ˈsæpinis] (*noun*), *F:* inexpérience *f*, nigauderie *f*.

sappy [ˈsæpi] (*adj.*), *F:* **1.** bête*, ballot, baluchard. **2.** sans expérience, nigaud.

sarge [sɑːdʒ] (*noun*), *F:* (*=sergeant*) (*mil.*) sergent *m*, serpied *m*, sergot *m*.

sarky [ˈsɑːki] (*adj.*), *F:* sarcastique, mordant, ironique, caustique, persifleur.

sass[1] [sæs] (*noun*) (*U.S.*), *F:* = **sauce**[1], **1.**

sass[2] [sæs] (**to**) (*U.S.*), *F:* = **sauce**[2] **(to).**

sassy [ˈsæsi] (*adj.*) (*U.S.*), *F:* = **saucy, 1.**

* An asterisk indicates that the word so marked is included as a head-word in the Appendix.

satch [sætʃ], **satchelmouth** [ˈsætʃəl-mauθ] (*noun*), *F:* qn qui a une grande bouche*, grande gueule.

sauce[1] [sɔːs] (*noun*), *F:* **1.** effronterie *f*, toupet *m*, culot *m*. **2.** (*U.S.*) alcool*, goutte *f*; **to hit the s.**, boire* beaucoup, tomber sur la bouteille; **to be off the s.**, ne plus prendre d'alcool*, suivre la croix bleue, être au régime sec. *Voir aussi* **apple-sauce.**

sauce[2] [sɔːs] (**to**), *F:* = **cheek**[2] (**to**).

saucebox [ˈsɔːsbɔks] (*noun*), *F:* effronté(e) *m(f)*, mufle *m*, butor *m*, malotru *m*.

saucy [ˈsɔːsi] (*adj.*), *F:* **1.** impertinent, audacieux, gonflé, affronté, culotté. **2.** aguichant, coquet, chic. **3.** (livre, pièce de théâtre, *etc.*) scabreux, osé, risqué, épicé.

sausage [ˈsɔsidʒ] (*noun*). **1.** *F:* **not a s.**, rien* du tout, que dalle. **2.** *F:* **(you) silly s.!** gros bête! gros ballot! **3.** *F:* **s. dog,** chien *m* dachshund. **4.** *P:* cigarette* de marijuana, stick *m* (*drogues**). **5.** *P:* **s. and mash** (*R.S.* = *cash*), argent*, fric *m*, pognon *m*.

savage [ˈsævidʒ] (*adj.*), *P:* excellent*, sensas(s), du tonnerre. *Voir aussi* **cut up (to), 3.**

saver [ˈseivər] (*noun*), *F:* (*turf*) pari *m* de protection. *Voir aussi* **lifesaver.**

savvy[1] [ˈsævi] (*noun*), *F:* bon sens, jugeot(t)e *f*.

savvy[2] [ˈsævi] (**to**), *F:* savoir, connaître, piger, con(n)obler.

sawbones [ˈsɔː-bounz] (*noun*) (*now mainly U.S.*), *F:* chirurgien *m*, charcuteur *m*, coupe-toujours *m*.

sawder [ˈsɔːdər] (*noun*) (*U.S.*), *F:* **soft s.** = **soft soap (soap**[1]**, 1).**

sawney [ˈsɔːni] (*noun*). **1.** *F:* Écossais *m*, kiltie *m*. **2.** *P:* individu bête*, baluchard *m*.

sawn-off [ˈsɔːnɔf] (*adj.*), *F:* petit* (individu), demi-portion, inachevé.

sax [sæks] (*noun*) (*abbr.* = *saxophone*), *F:* saxo(phone) *m*.

say [sei] (**to**). **1.** *F:* **I'll s.!** vous avez raison! et comment donc! **2.** *F:* **you don't s.!** ça par exemple! **3.** *P:* **says you!** que tu dis!; *cf.* **sez you! 4.** *P:* **says who?** chiche?

say-so [ˈseisou] (*noun*), *F:* **1. to have the s.-s.**, avoir voix au chapitre. **2.** parole *f*, mot *m*, dire *m*.

scab[1] [skæb] (*noun*), *F:* briseur *m* de grève, jaune *m*.

scab[2] [skæb] (**to**), *F:* briser la grève.

scabby [ˈskæbi] (*adj.*), *P:* minable, mesquin.

scalper [ˈskælpər] (*noun*), *F:* qn qui pratique le coup de fusil, empileur *m*.

scamp[1] [skæmp] (*noun*), *F:* **you young** (*or* **little**) **s.!** petit galopin! petit polisson!

scamp[2] [skæmp] (**to**), *F:* **1.** = **skive (to). 2.** bâcler, saboter (un travail); faire (un travail) au galop.

scamper [ˈskæmpər] (*noun*), *F:* bâcleur *m* (de travail).

scamping [ˈskæmpiŋ] (*noun*), *F:* **1.** oisiveté *f*, flânerie *f*, traînaillerie *f*. **2.** bâclage *m*, sabotage *m* (d'un travail).

scanties [ˈskæntiz], **scants** [skænts] (*pl. noun*), *F:* cache-truc *m*, vignette *f*, minislip *m*.

scarce [skεəs] (*adj.*), *F:* **to make oneself s.**, partir*, prendre le large (*ou* la tangente).

scare-baby [ˈskεə-beibi], **scaredy-cat** [ˈskεədi-kæt] (*noun*), *F:* poltron*, lâche *m*, couard *m*, poule mouillée, vessard *m*.

scare up [ˈskεərˈʌp] (**to**), *F:* chercher et trouver (qch.).

scarper [ˈskɑːpər] (**to**), *P:* s'enfuir*, déguerpir.

scary [ˈskεəri] (*adj.*), *F:* qui fait peur*, effroyable, redoutable.

scat![1] [skæt] (*excl.*), *P:* décampe! détale! file! barre-toi!

scat[2] [skæt] (*noun*), *P:* **1.** (*a*) chantonnement *m*, fredonnage *m*; (*b*) baragouin *m*, charabia *m*. **2.** héroïne *f* (*drogues**), jus *m*.

scatterbrain [ˈskætə-brein] (*noun*), *F:* Jean-de-la-lune *m*, étourdi *m*, écervelé *m*.

scatterbrained [ˈskætə-breind] (*adj.*), *F:* étourdi, écervelé, évaporé, à tête de linotte.

scatty [ˈskæti] (*adj.*), *F:* **1.** un peu fou*, toqué, maboul(e). **2.** farfelu.

scene [siːn] (*noun*). **1.** *F:* **behind the scenes,** dans la coulisse, dessous les cartes. **2.** *F:* action *f*, pratique *f*; **it's all part of today's s.**, cela fait partie des activités du jour. **3.** *P:* (*a*) endroit *m* où les drogués se réunissent, le lieu; **okay s.**, partouze réussie (de drogués); (*b*) groupement *m* de drogués. **4.** *F:* **to make a s.**, faire une scène, faire de

* L'astérisque indique que le mot marqué de ce signe figure comme entrée dans le Répertoire.

l'esclandre *m*. 5. *F:* **to make the s.,** (*a*) arriver*, s'abouler, se pointer; faire acte de présence; (*b*) réussir, arriver, y avoir la main (*ou* l'oignon *ou* l'os). 6. *F:* **bad s.,** mauvaise posture. 7. *F:* **it's not my s.,** ce n'est pas mon genre, ce n'est pas mon train-train.

schiz(o) [ˈskits(oʊ)] (*adj. & noun*), *F:* schizo(phrène) (*mf*).

schlemiel, schlemihl [ʃləˈmiːl, ʃleˈmiːl] (*noun*), *P:* nullité *f*, zéro *m*; ballot *m*, gourde *f*.

schlenter [ˈʃlentər] (*adj.*), *P:* toc, camelote.

schlep [ʃlep] (**to**), *P:* tirer, hâler, remorquer.

schlimazel [ʃliˈmɑːzl] (*noun*) (*U.S.*), *P:* qn qui a de la malchance*, poissard *m*.

schliver [ˈʃlivər] (*noun*), *P:* = **chiv**[1], **1.**

schlong [ʃlɔŋ] (*noun*) (*U.S.*), *P:* pénis*, trique *f*.

schmal(t)z [ʃmælts, ʃmɔːlts, ʃmɔlts] (*noun*), *F:* (*a*) (musique, *etc.*) très sentimental(e); (*b*) sensiblerie *f*.

schmal(t)zy [ˈʃmæltsi, ˈʃmɔːltsi, ˈʃmɔltsi] (*adj.*), *F:* à l'eau de rose.

schmeck [ʃmek], **schmee** [ʃmiː] (*noun*), *P:* = **shmeck.**

schmeer [ˈʃmiər] (*noun*), *P:* 1. = **dope**[1], **1.** 2. pot-de-vin *m*. 3. calomnie *f*, bêche *f*.

schmier [ʃmiər] (*noun*), *P:* ristourne *f*, commission *f*, dessous-de-table *m*.

schmo [ʃmoʊ], **schmock** [ʃmɔk], **schmoe** [ʃmoʊ] (*noun*), *P:* 1. individu bête*, nigaud *m*, baluchard *m*. 2. individu ennuyeux*, raseur *m*, casse-pieds *m*.

schmoose, schmooze [ʃmuːz] (**to**), *P:* bavarder*, papoter, ragoter.

schmuck [ʃmʊk] (*noun*), *P:* = **prick, 1, 2.**

schnide [ʃnaid] (*noun*), *P:* = **snide**[2], **1, 2.**

schnook [ʃnʊk, ʃnuːk] (*noun*), *P:* = **schmo, 1, 2.**

schnorrer [ˈʃnɔːrər] (*noun*) (*U.S.*), *P:* mendiant*, mangav(eur) *m*.

schnozz [ʃnɔz], **schnozzle** [ˈʃnɔzl], **schnozzola** [ʃnɔˈzoulə] (*noun*), *P:* nez*, pif *m*.

schnuk [ʃnʊk] (*noun*), *P:* = **schnook.**

school [skuːl] (*noun*), *F:* personnes réunies pour jouer de l'argent*.

schoolmarm [ˈskuːl-mɑːm] (*noun*), *F:* (*a*) maîtresse *f* d'école, pionne *f*; (*b*) **she's a real s.,** (i) c'est une pédante; (ii) c'est une vraie prude.

schoolmarmish [ˈskuːl-mɑːmiʃ] (*adj.*), *F:* pédantique, cuistre.

schooner [ˈskuːnər] (*noun*), *F:* grand verre* (d'apéritif, *etc.*).

schpieler [ˈʃpiːlər] (*noun*), *P:* = **spieler.**

schwar(t)z [ʃwɔːts] (*noun*) (*U.S.*), *P:* (*péj.*) nègre*, bamboula *m*, bougnoul(e) *m*.

scoff[1] [skɔf] (*noun*), *P:* nourriture*, boustifaille *f*.

scoff[2] [skɔf] (**to**), *P:* (*a*) se goinfrer, s'en foutre plein la lampe; (*b*) manger*, bouffer, boulotter.

scone [skoun] (*noun*) (*Austr.*), *P:* tête*, cassis *m*; **to duck the s.** = **to bow the crumpet (crumpet, 3).**

scoop[1] [skuːp] (*noun*), *F:* 1. coup *m* de chance*. 2. (*journal*) nouvelle sensationnelle (que l'on est seul à publier), rafle *f*, scoop *m*.

scoop[2] [skuːp] (**to**), *F:* 1. avoir un droit exclusif de publication, faire un scoop. 2. rafler, ratiboiser (qn). 3. déjouer les intentions de (qn), dépasser (qn) en finesse.

scoot [skuːt] (**to**), *F:* 1. s'enfuir*, déguerpir (en quatrième vitesse); **s.!** détale! file! 2. filer à toute vitesse.

scorch[1] [skɔːtʃ] (*noun*), *F:* allure effrénée, bride abattue.

scorch[2] **(along)** [ˈskɔːtʃ(əˈlɔŋ)] (**to**), *F:* conduire comme un fou, aller à un train d'enfer, aller à fond de train.

scorcher [ˈskɔːtʃər] (*noun*), *F:* 1. journée *f* torride; vague *f* de chaleur; **it's a s.,** on se croirait dans un four. 2. amateur *m* de vitesse, avaleur *m* de kilomètres. 3. remarque (*ou* réplique) coupante (*ou* sarcastique), riposte cinglante.

score[1] [skɔːr, skɔər] (*noun*). 1. *F:* **to know the s.,** être au courant (*ou* à la page *ou* dans le coup). 2. *P:* vingt livres sterling. 3. *P:* **to make a s.** = **score**[2] **(to), 1, 2.** 4. *P:* butin*, affure *f*, 5. *P:* affaire réussie (*ou* bien enlevée).

score[2] [skɔːr, skɔər] (**to**), *P:* 1. obtenir de la drogue. 2. faire une touche; (*prostituée*) faire un levage. 3. être au mieux avec qn, être dans les petits papiers de qn. 4. réussir, se tailler un succès, épater la galerie.

* An asterisk indicates that the word so marked is included as a head-word in the Appendix.

Scotch [skɔtʃ] (*adj.*), *F:* **to see through S. mist,** avoir des visions.

Scouse [skaʊs] (*noun*), *F:* **1.** habitant *m* de Liverpool. **2.** patois *m* de Liverpool.

scout [skaʊt] (*noun*), *F:* un brave homme*, un chic type.

scrag[1] [skræg] (*noun*). **1.** *F:* cou décharné, cou de grue, mince collier. **2.** *P:* femme* efflanquée (*ou* décharnée).

scrag[2] [skræg] (**to**). **1.** *P:* pendre*, garrotter (qn). **2.** *F:* (*a*) tuer*, tordre le cou à (qn); (*b*) saisir (un adversaire) au collet.

scram [skræm] (**to**), *P:* partir*, ficher le camp, détaler; **s.!** fous le camp!

scramble! [ˈskræmbl] (*excl.*), *F:* (*R.A.F.*) décollage! (pour intercepter l'ennemi).

scran [skræn] (*noun*), *F:* restes *m.pl.* (de nourriture*), rogatons *m.pl.*

scrap[1] [skræp] (*noun*), *F:* (*a*) querelle*, rixe *f*; (*b*) bagarre*, batterie *f*; (*c*) (*boxe*) match *m*; **to have a s.** = **scrap**[2] **(to), 2** (*a*), (*b*).

scrap[2] [skræp] (**to**), *F:* **1.** mettre (qch.) au rancart. **2.** (*a*) se quereller*; (*b*) se battre*, se bagarrer.

scrape[1] [skreip] (*noun*). **1.** *F:* **to get into a s.,** se mettre dans un mauvais pas (*ou* dans le pétrin); **to get out of a s.,** se tirer d'affaire. **2.** *F:* mince couche *f* de beurre sur une tartine, raclage *m*. **3.** *P:* **to have a s.,** se raser*, se racler, se gratter la couenne.

scrape[2] [skreip] (**to**), *F:* **1. to s. the (bottom of the) barrel,** gratter le fond du panier. **2. to s. a car,** érafler une voiture. **3. to s. clear of prison,** friser la prison*.

scrape along [ˈskreipəˈlɔŋ] (**to**), *F:* s'en tirer péniblement, vivoter, à peine joindre les deux bouts.

scrap-heap [ˈskræphiːp] (*noun*), *F:* **to be thrown on the s.-h.,** (*d'une personne*) être mis au rebut; *cf.* **wind up (to).**

scratch[1] [skrætʃ] (*noun*). **1.** *P:* argent*, pognon *m*, fric *m*. **2.** *F:* **to come up to s.,** être à la hauteur. **3.** *V:* vagin*, craque(tte) *f*, cicatrice *f*.

scratch[2] [skrætʃ] (**to**), *P:* chasser la drogue. *Voir aussi* **back**[2]**, 4.**

scratcher [ˈskrætʃər] (*noun*), *P:* **1.** faussaire *m*, «homme de lettres». **2.** allumette *f*, bûche *f*, soufrante *f*. *Voir aussi* **backscratcher.**

scream[1] [skriːm] (*noun*). **1.** *F:* (*a*) **she's a s.,** elle est rigolotte, elle est désopilante; (*b*) **it's a s.,** c'est à se tordre, c'est à mourir de rire. **2.** *P:* **to put in a s.,** loger un appel en cours de justice.

scream[2] [skriːm] (**to**). **1.** *F:* rire* aux éclats (*ou* à ventre déboutonné *ou* à gorge déployée); **he made us s.,** il nous a fait tordre. **2.** *P:* = **to put in a scream (scream**[1]**, 2).**

screamer [ˈskriːmər] (*noun*), *P:* **1.** client jamais satisfait, rouspéteur *m*. **2.** grosse en-tête, grande manchette.

screaming [ˈskriːmiŋ] (*adj.*) (*Austr.*), *F:* **s. on s.o., sth.,** monté contre qn, qch. *Voir aussi* **abdabs; meemies.**

screamingly [ˈskriːmiŋli] (*adv.*), *F:* **s. funny,** tordant, crevant.

screaming-match [ˈskriːmiŋmætʃ] (*noun*), *F:* coups *m.pl.* de gueule, engueulade *f* maison.

screw[1] [skruː] (*noun*). **1.** *P:* gardien* de prison, gaffe *m*, gâfe *m*, matuche *m*. **2.** *V:* (*a*) coït*, baisage *m*; (*b*) femme*, fendue *f*; **a good s.,** une rude baiseuse. **3.** *P:* gages *m.pl.*, salaire *m*; **to get a good s.,** être bien payé. **4.** *F:* **to have a s. loose,** être un peu fou*, être déboulonné. **5.** *F:* **to put the s.** (*or* **screws**) **on s.o.,** forcer (*ou* pressurer) qn, serrer la vis à qn. **6.** *F:* cheval*, bidet *m*, canasson *m*. **7.** *P:* (*a*) clef*; (*b*) passe-partout *m*, carouble *f*. **8.** *P:* coup *m* d'œil*, coup *m* de sabord; **take a s. at this!** zyeute ça!

screw[2] [skruː] (**to**). **1.** *V:* coïter* avec (une femme), baiser. **2.** *V:* enculer, encaldosser. **3.** *P:* **to s. a gaff** (*or* **a drum**), casser une crèche, caroubler une baraque; **to go screwing,** cambrioler*, faire un casse; **to do a screwing job,** faire un fric-frac, caroubler; *cf.* **screwing, 3. 4.** *F:* **to s. money out of s.o.,** extorquer (*ou* soutirer) de l'argent* à qn, taper qn. **5.** (*Austr.*) *P:* regarder*, lorgner, gaffer. **6.** *F:* **to have one's head (well) screwed on** (*or* **screwed on the right way**), avoir la tête* solide (*ou* sur les épaules). **7.** (*U.S.*) *P:* s'enfuir*, décamper, se barrer, se débiner. **8.** *P:* duper*, tromper, empiler. **9.** *V:* **s. you! get screwed!** va te faire foutre! **10.** *P:* gâcher, cafouiller.

screwball[1] [ˈskruːbɔːl] (*adj.*) (*U.S.*), *F:* fou*, tapé, dingue.

screwball[2] [ˈskruːbɔːl] (*noun*) (*U.S.*),

* L'astérisque indique que le mot marqué de ce signe figure comme entrée dans le Répertoire.

F: personne étrange, bizarre, excentrique, cinglée; personne excessivement capricieuse.

screwed [skru:d] (*adj.*), *P:* ivre*, rétamé, rondibé; *cf.* **half-screwed.**

screwing [ˈskru:iŋ] (*noun*). **1.** *V:* coït*, carambolage *m*, dérouillage *m*. **2.** *V:* enculage *m*, encaldossage *m*. **3.** *P:* cambriolage *m*, cambriole *f*, fric-frac *m*; *cf.* **screw² (to), 3.**

screw off [ˈskru:ˈɔf] (**to**), *V:* se masturber*, se branler, s'astiquer.

screwsman [ˈskru:zmən] (*noun*), *P:* cambrioleur*, casseur *m*, fracasseur *m*.

screw up [ˈskru:ˈʌp] (**to**). **1.** *P:* fermer, boucler, brider. **2.** *P:* bousiller, rater (qch.). **3.** *F:* **to be all screwed up,** (*a*) se tromper, se ficher dedans, se mettre le doigt dans l'œil; (*b*) avoir des idées confuses, être embarbouillé, être dans le brouillard.

screwy [ˈskru:i] (*adj.*). **1.** *F:* fou*, cinglé, dingue. **2.** *P:* louche, suspect.

scrip(t) [skrip(t)] (*noun*), *P:* ordonnance *f* (de docteur) pour obtenir des drogues.

scrounge¹ [skraundʒ] (*noun*), *F:* **1.** = **scrounger, 1, 2. 2. he's always on the s.,** c'est un vrai pique-assiette; il ne cherche qu'à vivre aux crochets des autres.

scrounge² [skraundʒ] (**to**), *F:* **1.** écornifler. **2.** voler*, chiper, chaparder, barboter.

scrounge around [ˈskraundʒəˈraund] (**to**), *F:* (*a*) rabioter à la ronde; (*b*) **to s. a. for sth.,** aller à la recherche de qch, fouiner.

scrounger [ˈskraundʒər] (*noun*), *F:* **1.** pique-assiette *m*, écornifleur *m*. **2.** voleur*, chapardeur *m*, barboteur *m*.

scrub [skrʌb] (**to**), *F:* (*a*) passer l'éponge sur (qch.); **let's s. it,** passons l'éponge là-dessus; (*b*) effacer, démagnétiser (une bande).

scrubber [ˈskrʌbər] (*noun*), *P:* (*péj.*) femme* *ou* fille* laide* *ou* peu appétissante, mocheté *f*.

scrub round [ˈskrʌbˈraund] (**to**), *F:* = **scrub (to)** (*a*).

scruff [skrʌf] (*noun*), *F:* (*a*) individu* mal soigné (*ou* mal fichu), débraillé *m*.; (*b*) clodo(t) *m*.

scrum [skrʌm] (*noun*), *F:* mêlée *f*, bousculade *f*.

scrumptious [ˈskrʌmpʃəs] (*adj.*), *F:* (*a*) excellent*, épatant, fameux, remarquable; (*b*) délicieux.

scrumpy [ˈskrʌmpi] (*noun*), *F:* cidre *m*, gaulé *m*.

scuffer [ˈskʌfər] (*noun*), *P:* prostituée*, greluche *f*.

scumbag [skʌmbæg] (*noun*), *P:* = **ratbag.**

scummy [ˈskʌmi] (*adj.*), *P:* méprisable, sans valeur.

scunner [ˈskʌnər] (*noun*), *F:* **to take a s. to s.o.,** prendre qn en grippe, avoir qn dans le nez.

scupper [ˈskʌpər] (**to**), *F:* couler, abîmer, massacrer.

sea [si:] (*noun*), *F:* **to be all at s.,** être dérouté (*ou* désorienté); perdre le nord. *Voir aussi* **half-seas-over.**

search [sə:tʃ] (**to**), *F:* **s. me!** je n'en ai pas la moindre idée; je n'en ai pas la queue d'une; mystère et boule de gomme!

sec [sek] (*noun*) (*abbr.* = *second*), *F:* **just a s.! half a s.!** un moment!; *cf.* **jiff(y); mo; shake¹, 1, 2; tick¹, 3.**

secko [ˈsekou] (*adj.*) (*Austr.*), *P:* perverti.

seconds [ˈsekəndz] (*pl. noun*), *F:* **1.** articles défectueux (*ou* démarqués). **2.** portion *f* (de nourriture*) supplémentaire; rab(iot) *m*.

see [si:] (**to**), *F:* **s. you!** au revoir! ciao! *Voir aussi* **dog¹, 20; thing, 7.**

seed [si:d] (*noun*). **1.** *F:* **to go to s.,** (*d'une personne*) se décatir, s'avachir. **2.** *P:* = **roach.** *Voir aussi* **hayseed.**

seedy [ˈsi:di] (*adj.*), *F:* **1.** pauvre*, minable, râpé, usé, élimé. **2.** malade*, patraque, pas dans son assiette.

see off [ˈsi:ˈɔf] (**to**), *F:* (*a*) **to s. s.o. o.,** régler le compte à qn; (*b*) **to s. sth. o.,** régler, liquider, conclure qch.

see out [ˈsi:ˈaut] (**to**), *F:* survivre à (qn).

see-through [ˈsi-θru:] (*adj.*), *F:* transparent.

sell¹ [sel] (*noun*), *F:* **1.** attrape *f*, carotte *f*, blague *f*, fumisterie *f*. **2.** déception *f*, désappointement *m*. *Voir aussi* **hard¹, 5; soft¹, 5.**

sell² [sel] (**to**), *F:* **1.** duper* (qn), amener (qn) à la balançoire, monter le cou à (qn). **2. to s. s.o. short,** sous-estimer qn. **3. to be sold on s.o., sth.,** être amené vers qn, qch. **4. to s. oneself,** se faire accepter, se faire valoir. **5.** convaincre, persuader. *Voir aussi* **river, 1.**

* An asterisk indicates that the word so marked is included as a head-word in the Appendix.

sell-out [ˈselaut] (*noun*), *F:* **1.** trahison *f*, judasserie *f*, macaronage *m.* **2.** vente *f* de tous les billets pour un spectacle; séance *f* à guichet fermé. **3.** vente *f* de liquidation.

sell out [ˈselˈaut] (**to**), *F:* **1.** (*a*) dénoncer*, vendre (qn); (*b*) trahir, judasser, lessiver, macaroner (qn). **2.** (*d'une personne*) se vendre. *Voir aussi* **sold out.**

semi [ˈsemi] (*noun*) (=*semi-detached house*), *F:* maison jumelée.

send [send] (**to**), *F:* **1. she sends me!** elle me transporte! **2.** (*drogues*) faire partir, faire voyager (qn).

send-off [ˈsendɔf] (*noun*), *F:* **1.** fête *f* d'adieu, souhaits *m.pl.* de bon voyage. **2.** inauguration réussie. **3.** enterrement *m.*

send-up [ˈsendʌp] (*noun*), *F:* satire *f*, parodie *f*, éreintage *m*, éreintement *m.*

send up [ˈsendˈʌp] (**to**). **1.** *F:* satiriser, parodier, se moquer de, ridiculiser, éreinter. **2.** *P:* **to s. s.o. u.**, emprisonner*, boucler, coffrer qn, mettre qn en taule (*ou* au bloc).

septic [ˈseptik] (*adj.*), *P:* **1.** désagréable, puant. **2. s. tank** (*R.S.* = *Yank*), Américain *m*, Amerlo *m*, Yankee *m.*

serve [səːv] (**to**), *F:* **(it) serves you right!** c'est bien fait!

session [ˈseʃ(ə)n] (*noun*), *F:* **1. jam s.**, réunion *f* de musiciens qui improvisent collectivement; concert *m* de jazz, jam session *f.* **2.** longue séance. *Voir aussi* **petting.**

set[1] [set] (*adj.* & *p.p.*), *F:* **to be all s.**, être fin prêt.

set[2] [set] (*noun*), *F:* **to make a dead s. at s.o.**, (*a*) attaquer furieusement qn (à la tribune); (*b*) se jeter à la tête de qn, relancer qn, poursuivre qn de ses avances.

set about [ˈsetəˈbaut] (**to**), *F:* **1. to s. a. s.o.**, attaquer* qn, tomber sur qn. **2. to s. a. (doing) sth.**, entreprendre qch., se mettre à qch.

set back [ˈsetˈbæk] (**to**), *F:* coûter, peser; **the round of drinks s. him b. a pound,** la tournée lui a pesé un faf(f)iot.

set-to [ˈsetˈtuː] (*noun*), *F:* bagarre*, lutte *f*, torchage *m.*

set-up [ˈsetʌp] (*noun*). **1.** *F:* structure *f*, organisation *f*, fonctionnement *m.* **2.** *F:* édifice *m*, installation *f*; **a nice s.-u. you have here,** vous êtes bien installé ici. **3.** *P:* = **frame-up.**

set up [ˈsetˈʌp] (**to**), *F:* **1. to s. 'em u. again,** remplir les verres de nouveau, remettre ça, faire une autre tournée. **2. to s. s.o. u. for the kill,** conditionner qn pour le coup de massue.

sew up [ˈsouˈʌp] (**to**), *F:* **it's all sewn up,** c'est tout fixé, c'est tout arrangé.

sex [seks] (*noun*), *F:* **1. to have s. with s.o.**, coïter* avec qn, faire l'amour avec qn. **2. the third s.**, homosexuels *m.pl.*, le troisième sexe.

sex-bomb [ˈseksbɔm] (*noun*), *F:* allumeuse *f*, blonde incendiaire.

sexcited [ˈsekˈsaitid] (*adj.*), *F:* = **sexed up.**

sex-crazy [ˈseksˈkreizi] (*adj.*), *F:* = **sex-mad.**

sexed up [ˈsekstˈʌp] (*adj.*), *F:* excité, allumé, aguiché.

sex-kitten [ˈseks-kitn] (*noun*), *F:* fille* aguichante, jeune pin-up alléchante, nénette ronronnante.

sex-mad [ˈseksˈmæd] (*adj.*), *F:* **he's s.-m.**, c'est un obsédé sexuel.

sexo [ˈseksou] (*adj.*) (*Austr.*), *P:* = **secko.**

sex-pot [ˈseks-pɔt] (*noun*), *P:* femme* qui a du sex-appeal, aguicheuse *f*, allumeuse *f.*

sex-ridden [ˈseksridn] (*adj.*), *F:* porté sur la bagatelle, farci de sexe.

sex-starved [ˈsekstɑːvd] (*adj.*), *F:* souffrant du manque d'activité sexuelle, victime de diète sexuelle.

sexy [ˈseksi] (*adj.*), *F:* sensuel, chaud, sexy.

sez you! [ˈsezˈjuː] (*excl.*), *P:* = **says you!** (**say** (**to**), **3**).

shack [ʃæk] (*noun*), *F:* (*a*) taudis *m*, cambuse *f*, bouge *m*; (*b*) guitoune *f*, cabane *f.*

shack-up [ˈʃækʌp] (*attrib. adj.*), *P:* **a s.-u. job,** (*a*) nuit passée avec n'importe quelle femme*; (*b*) femme* d'un soir.

shack up [ˈʃækˈʌp] (**to**), *P:* **to s. u. with s.o.**, vivre ensemble, se coller avec qn, s'antifler.

shade [ʃeid] (*noun*). **1.** *F:* **to put s.o. in the s.**, laisser qn dans l'ombre, éclipser qn. **2.** (*pl.*) *P:* lunettes* de soleil, vitraux *m.pl.*

shadow[1] [ˈʃædou] (*noun*), *F:* **1. to put a s. on s.o.** = **to put a tail on s.o.** (**tail**[1], **5**). **2. five-o'clock s.**, la barbe du soir, le foin de la journée.

* L'astérisque indique que le mot marqué de ce signe figure comme entrée dans le Répertoire.

shadow[2] [ˈʃædoʊ] (**to**), *F:* = **tail**[2] (**to**).

shady [ˈʃeidi] (*adj.*), *F:* louche, équivoque, trouble, véreux.

shaft[1] [ʃɑːft] (*noun*), *V:* pénis*, colonne *f.*

shaft[2] [ʃɑːft] (**to**). **1.** *V:* coïter* avec (une femme), pinocher. **2.** (*U.S.*) *P:* escroquer*, carotter (qn). **3.** (*U.S.*) *P:* congédier*, sacquer, dégommer (qn).

shag[1] [ʃæg] (*noun*). **1.** *V:* coït*, dérouillage *m.* **2.** *V:* **she's a good s.**, c'est une rude baiseuse, c'est une Marie-jambe(s)-en-l'air. **3.** *P:* **it's a (bit of a) s.**, c'est ennuyeux*, c'est pénible (*ou* lassant).

shag[2] [ʃæg] (**to**). **1.** *V:* (*a*) coïter* avec (une femme), dérouiller, égoïner; (*b*) coïter*, se dérouiller; *cf.* **arse, 9.** **2.** *P:* fatiguer*, vider, pomper; **to feel shagged,** être vanné.

shag-ass [ˈʃægæs] (**to**) (*U.S.*), *V:* s'enfuir*, se carapater, prendre ses cliques et ses claques.

shagbag [ˈʃægbæg] (*noun*), *V:* vieille rombière-patte-en-l'air.

shaggable [ˈʃægəbl] (*adj.*), *V:* = **fuckable.**

shagged (out) [ˈʃægd(ˈaʊt)] (*adj.*), *P:* très fatigué*, éreinté.

shagger [ˈʃægər] (*noun*), *V:* habitué(e) du baisage (*coït**).

shaggy-dog [ˈʃægiˈdɔg] (*attrib. adj.*), *F:* **s.-d. story,** histoire *f* de fous, histoire farfelue (*ou* loufoque), loufoquerie *f.*

shag-happy [ˈʃægˈhæpi] (*adj.*), *V:* qui pratique avec entrain le baisage (*coït**).

shag-nasty [ˈʃægˈnɑːsti] (*adj.*), *P:* très désagréable, emmerdant.

shag off [ˈʃægˈɔf] (**to**), *V:* partir*, décamper; **s. o.!** déguerpis! file!

shake[1] [ʃeik] (*noun*). **1.** *F:* **half a s.!** un moment! une seconde! **2.** *F:* **in two shakes (of a cat's** (*or* **lamb's) tail,)** en moins de deux, en deux temps trois mouvements. **3.** *F:* **to give s.o. a fair s.,** agir loyalement envers qn, être régulier avec qn; **to get a fair s.,** être traité comme il faut, être traité régulier (*ou* réglo). **4.** *F:* **to have the shakes,** (*a*) avoir peur*, avoir les foies; (*b*) avoir le delirium tremens. **5.** *F:* **no great shakes,** médiocre, rien d'extraordinaire, quelconque. **6.** *P:* **to put the s. on s.o.** = **to shake s.o. down (shake down (to), 4).** *Voir aussi* **handshake.**

shake[2] [ʃeik] (**to**), *F:* **1. that'll s. him!** cela le fera tiquer! **2. s. on it!** tope là! **3.** (*Austr.*) **shook on s.o.,** entiché de qn. *Voir aussi* **leg**[1], **3.**

shakedown [ˈʃeikdaʊn] (*noun*). **1.** *F:* lit* de fortune; hébergement *m* d'une nuit. **2.** *P:* chantage *m*, rançon *f.*

shake down [ˈʃeikˈdaʊn] (**to**). **1.** *P:* = **strong-arm**[2] **(to). 2.** *P:* fouiller (un prisonnier), fourober. **3.** *F:* se coucher*, se pieuter. **4.** *P:* faire casquer (qn), faire cracher (qn).

shakers [ˈʃeikəz] (*pl. noun*), *P:* seins*, flotteurs *m.pl.*

shake-up [ˈʃeikʌp] (*noun*), *F:* **1.** remaniement *m* (du personnel). **2.** commotion *f*, bouleversement *m*. **3.** mélange *m* d'alcool* et de whisky.

shaky [ˈʃeiki] (*adj.*), *F:* **a s. do,** une affaire mal menée (*ou* branlante).

shamateur [ˈʃæməˈtəːr] (*noun*), *F:* (athlète) professionnel qui prétend être amateur.

shambles [ˈʃæmblz] (*noun*), *F:* **a s.,** une pagaille.

shambolic [ʃæmˈbɔlik] (*adj.*), *P:* en pleine pagaille.

shammy [ˈʃæmi] (*noun*), *F:* peau *f* (de chamois).

shampers [ˈʃæmpəz] (*noun*), *F:* = **champers.**

shanghai [ʃæŋˈhai] (**to**), *F:* forcer (qn) à un travail désagréable; **I was shanghaied into doing it,** on m'a forcé à le faire.

shanks [ʃæŋks] (*pl. noun*), *F:* **1.** jambes*, gambilles *f.pl.* **2. to ride S.'s pony** (*or* **mare** *or* **nag**), voyager à pied, prendre le train onze, prendre la voiture de Saint-Crépin.

shapes [ʃeips] (*pl. noun*) (*U.S.*), *P:* dés* truqués, balourds *m.pl.*

shark [ʃɑːk] (*noun*), *F:* **1.** escroc*, arnaqueur *m*, dragueur *m*, requin *m*. **2.** (*U.S.*) as *m*, champion *m*, crack *m*.

sharp[1] [ʃɑːp] (*adj.*) (*U.S.*), *F:* élégant*, coquet, chic, jojo.

sharp[2] [ʃɑːp] (*noun*), *F:* = **shark, 1.**

sharp[3] [ʃɑːp] (**to**), *P:* escroquer*, arnaquer, roustir.

sharper [ˈʃɑːpər] (*noun*), *F:* tricheur* (aux cartes), entôleur *m*.

sharpie [ˈʃɑːpi] (*noun*), *P:* **1.** = **shark, 1.** **2.** (*U.S.*) gandin *m*, minet *m*. **3.** malin *m*, dégourdi *m*, débrouillard *m*.

sharpish [ˈʃɑːpiʃ] (*adv.*), *F:* **(a bit) s.,** vite*, presto, rapidos.

* An asterisk indicates that the word so marked is included as a head-word in the Appendix.

shave [ʃeiv] (*noun*), *F*: **to have a close** (*or* **narrow**) **s.**, l'échapper belle, échapper à un cheveu près; **it was a close** (*or* **narrow**) **s.**, il était moins une.

shaved [ʃeivd] (*adj.*) (*U.S.*), *F*: ivre*, bourré, rétamé; *cf.* **half-shaved.**

shaver [ˈʃeivər] (*noun*), *F*: gamin *m*, gosse *m*, môme *m*.

shebang [ʃiˈbæŋ] (*noun*). **1.** *F*: **the whole s.**, tout le bataclan, tout le tremblement; *cf.* **boiling; caboodle; shoot**[1], **1; shooting-match. 2.** *P*: cabane *f*, cambuse *f*; boutanche *f*. **3.** *P*: bordel*, clandé *m*, volière *f*.

she-cat [ˈʃiːˈkæt] (*noun*), *F*: chipie *f*, souris *f*, bique *f*.

shee [ʃiː] (*noun*), *P*: = **yen-shee.**

sheenie, sheeny [ˈʃiːni] (*noun*), *P*: (*péj.*) Juif *m*, Youpin *m*.

sheepdog [ˈʃiːpdɔg] (*noun*), *F*: chaperon *m*, chien *m* de garde.

sheer off [ˈʃiərˈɔf] (**to**), *F*: s'écarter; partir*, prendre le large.

sheet [ʃiːt] (*noun*). **1.** *F*: **to be three** (*or* **four**) **sheets in** (*or* **to**) **the wind,** être ivre*, avoir du vent dans les voiles, en rouler une. **2.** *P*: une livre sterling; **half a s.**, 50 pence. **3.** *P*: journal*, feuille *f* (de chou). **4.** *P*: casier *m* judiciaire (d'un criminel), faffes *m.pl.* *Voir aussi* **swindle-sheet.**

sheila [ˈʃiːlə] (*noun*) (*Austr.*), *F*: jeune fille*, jeune femme*, nénette *f*.

shekels [ˈʃekəlz] (*pl. noun*), *P*: argent*, fric *m*, pognon *m*.

shelf [ʃelf] (*noun*), *F*: **on the s.**, (*a*) célibataire, laissé(e) pour compte; (*b*) mis(e) de côté, resté(e) dans les cartons.

shelf-kit [ˈʃelfkit] (*noun*), *P*: seins*, avant-scène *f*.

shellac(k) [ʃeˈlæk] (**to**), *F*: **1.** battre*, rosser (qn), passer (qn) à tabac. **2.** vaincre, écraser, griller (qn).

shellacked [ʃeˈlækt] (*adj.*) (*U.S.*), *P*: ivre*, rétamé, culbuté.

shellacking [ʃeˈlækiŋ] (*noun*), *P*: **1.** rossée *f*, flo(p)pée *f*. **2.** (*sports*) défaite *f*, raclée *f*.

shellback [ʃel-bæk] (*noun*), *F*: vieux marin*, vieux loup de mer.

shell out [ˈʃelˈaut] (**to**), *P*: payer*, (les) abouler, casquer.

shemozzle[1] [ʃiˈmɔzl] (*noun*), *P*: (*a*) bruit*, boucan *m*, chahut *m*, chambard *m*; (*b*) difficultés *f.pl.*, ennuis *m.pl.*, emmerdement *m*.

shemozzle[2] [ʃiˈmɔzl] (**to**), *P*: = **skedaddle (to).**

shenanagin(s) [ʃəˈnænəgin(z)] ((*pl.*) *noun*), *F*: fumisterie *f*, truquage *m*, mystification *f*.

shice [ʃais] (**to**), *P*: **1.** trahir, plaquer, planter. **2.** = **welsh (to).**

shickered [ˈʃikəd] (*adj.*), *P*: ivre*, paf, éméché.

shift[1] [ʃift] (*noun*), *F*: **1.** échappatoire *f*, faux-fuyant *m*, biaisement *m*. **2. to get a s. on,** se dépêcher*, se magner le train.

shift[2] [ʃift] (**to**). **1.** *P*: **s.!** file! bouge-toi!; **he didn't half s.!** il s'est calté en moins de deux! **2.** *F*: **to s. a pint,** écluser un verre, en étrangler un, s'en jeter un derrière la cravate. **3.** *F*: **to s. for oneself,** se débrouiller, se dépatouiller.

shiksa [ˈʃiksə] (*noun*), *P*: (*péj.*) fille* non-juive, goyette *f*.

shill(aber) [ˈʃil(əbər)] (*noun*), *P*: compère *m* dans un tripot de jeux, jockey *m*; compère d'un camelot qui simule un achat pour encourager les clients, baron *m*, appeau *m*.

shimmy[1] [ˈʃimi] (*noun*), *F*: chemise *f*, liquette *f*.

shimmy[2] [ˈʃimi] (**to**), *F*: osciller, vaciller, brimbaler.

shindig [ˈʃindig] (*noun*), *F*: **1.** querelle*, chambard *m*, raffut *m*, ramdam *m*; *voir aussi* **kick up (to), 2. 2.** réunion bruyante, boum *f*, partouze *f*.

shindy [ˈʃindi] (*noun*), *F*: = **shindig, 1.**

shine [ʃain] (*noun*). **1.** *F*: **to take a s. to s.o.**, s'éprendre de qn, s'amouracher de qn, prendre qn en affection, s'enticher de qn. **2.** (*U.S.*) *P*: (*péj.*) nègre*, bougnoul(l)e *m*, cireur *m*. **3.** (*U.S.*) *P*: pièce *f* d'or. **4.** (*U.S.*) *P*: = **moonshine, 1. 5.** *P*: = **shindig, 1, 2. 6.** *F*: **to take the s. out of s.o.**, éclipser, dépasser qn. *Voir aussi* **bullshine.**

shiner [ˈʃainər] (*noun*). **1.** *F*: œil* poché (*ou* au beurre noir), coquard *m*. **2.** (*U.S.*) *P*: (*péj.*) = **shine, 2. 3.** *F*: voiture neuve. **4.** *F*: diamant*, brillant *m*. **5.** *F*: pièce (d'argent*) neuve.

shine up to [ˈʃainˈʌptuː] (**to**), *F*: **to s. u. t. s.o.**, chercher à se faire bien voir de qn, faire de la lèche auprès de qn.

*** L'astérisque indique que le mot marqué de ce signe figure comme entrée dans le Répertoire.**

shin(ny) up [ˈʃin(i)ˈʌp] (**to**), *F:* grimper, escalader.

ship [ʃip] (*noun*), *F:* **when my s. comes home,** quand il m'arrivera de l'argent*, quand mes galions seront arrivés, quand j'aurai décroché le gros lot.

ship out [ˈʃipˈaut] (**to**), *P:* s'enfuir*, se calter, décamper.

shirash [ʃiˈræʃ] (*noun*), *P:* = **charas(h).**

shirt [ʃəːt] (*noun*), *F:* **1. to put one's s. on sth.,** miser le tout pour le tout, parier sa chemise. **2. to lose one's s.,** (*a*) tout perdre, être lessivé; (*b*) (*U.S.*) s'emporter, prendre la chèvre. **3. keep your s. on!** ne t'énerve pas! ne t'emballe pas! **4. to have one's s. out,** être de mauvais poil, être à rebrousse-poil. **5. stuffed** (*or* **boiled**) **s.,** crâneur *m*, plastronneur *m*, collet monté.

shirt-lifter [ˈʃəːtliftər] (*noun*), *P:* pédéraste*, enculé *m.*

shirty [ˈʃəːti] (*adj.*), *F:* **to be s.,** être de mauvaise humeur, faire la gueule; **to get s.,** se mettre en colère* (*ou* en rogne).

shit[1] [ʃit] (*adv.*), *VV:* extrêmement, complètement, tout à fait; **to be s. poor,** être vachement pauvre*; **to be s. out of luck,** avoir une poisse noire, être dans la merde; **to be s. hot at sth.,** être vachement calé sur qch.

shit![2] [ʃit] (*excl.*), *VV:* merde alors!

shit[3] [ʃit] (*noun*), *VV:* **1.** merde*, caca *m*, chiasse *f.* **2. to land** (*or* **drop**) **s.o. in the s.,** mettre (*ou* foutre) qn dans la merde. **3. to be** (**right**) **in the s.,** être emmerdé jusqu'au cou. **4. to scare the s. out of s.o.,** rendre qn foireux, donner la chiasse (*ou* les chocottes *f.pl.*) à qn; *cf.* **shit-scared. 5. to eat s.,** traîner dans la merde. **6. don't talk s.!** ne dis pas de conneries! **7. I don't give a s.,** je m'en fous et contrefous. **8. full of s.,** mal renseigné, chiasseux. **9.** (**it's**) **no s.,** c'est la vérité, c'est pas de la merde. **10.** =**shitbag. 11.** emmerdeur *m.* **12.** camelote *f*, de la merde. **13.** (*a*) (*a*) héroïne *f* (*drogues**), shit *m*; (*b*) hachisch *m* (*drogues**), merde *f*; (*c*) drogues* en général, came *f.* **14. the shits,** diarrhée*, chiasse *f. Voir aussi* **bullshit**[1]; **creek; crock**[1], **5; horseshit; s.o.b.**

shit[4] [ʃit] (**to**), *VV:* **1.** déféquer*, chier. **2.** exagérer*, chier dans la colle; **don't s. me!** ne me bourre pas le crâne! **3. s. or bust,** tout ou rien, marche ou crève, pisse ou fais-toi éclater la vessie. *Voir aussi* **bullshit**[2] (**to**).

shit-ass [ˈʃitæs] (*noun*) (*U.S.*), *VV:* = **shitbag.**

shitbag [ˈʃitbæg] (*noun*), *VV:* merdaillon *m*, merdeux *m.*

shitcan [ˈʃitkæn] (**to**), *V:* **1.** (*Austr.*) casser, enfoncer (qn). **2.** (*U.S.*) se défaire de (qch.), balancer, larguer (qch.).

shite[1] [ʃait] (*noun*), *VV:* = **shit**[3], **1.**

shite[2] [ʃait] (**to**), *VV:* = **shit**[4] (**to**), **1.**

shithead [ˈʃithed], **shitheel** [ˈʃithiːl] (*noun*), *VV:* = **shitbag.**

shit-hole [ˈʃithoul] (*noun*), *VV:* anus*, trou *m* du cul, rondibé *m.*

shit-house [ˈʃithaus] (*noun*), *VV:* W.C.*, chiottes *f.pl.*, débourre *f.*

shitkicker [ˈʃitkikər] (*noun*) (*U.S.*), *VV:* **1.** traîne-la-merde *m.* **2.** paysan*, rustaud *m.* **3.** but(t)eur *m*, katangais *m.*

shitless [ˈʃitlis] (*adj.*), *VV:* **to be scared s.** = **to be shit-scared.**

shit-list [ˈʃitlist] (*noun*), *V:* tableau *m* des mal-vus, liste *f* des hors-petits-papiers, groupe *m* des abominations; *cf.* **stink-list.**

shit off [ˈʃitˈɔf] (**to**), *VV:* s'enfuir*, mettre les bouts; **s. o.!** calte-toi!

shitpot [ˈʃitpɔt] (*noun*), *VV:* = **shitbag.**

shit-scared [ˈʃitˈskɛəd] (*adj.*), *VV:* chiasseux, foireux; *cf.* **shit**[3], **4.**

shitstick [ˈʃit-stik] (*noun*) (*U.S.*), *VV:* = **shitbag.**

shitters [ˈʃitəz] (*pl. noun*), *V:* **the s.,** diarrhée*, la chiasse.

shitty [ˈʃiti] (*adj.*), *VV:* **1.** méprisable, débectant, dégueulasse. **2.** (*U.S.*) douteux, plein de gourance.

shiv [ʃiv] (*noun*), *P:* = **chiv**[1], **1, 2.**

shive [ʃaiv] (**to**), *P:* = **chiv**[2] (**to**), **1, 2.**

shivers [ˈʃivəz] (*pl. noun*), *F:* **to give s.o. the s.,** donner la tremblote (*ou* le frisson) à qn.

shivoo [ˈʃaiˈvuː] (*noun*) (*Austr.*), *F:* réjouissances*, bamboula *f*, raout *m.*

shliver [ˈʃlivər] (*noun*), *P:* = **chiv**[1], **1, 2.**

shlonger [ˈʃlɔŋər] (*noun*) (*U.S.*), *P:* = **schlong.**

shmeck [ʃmek], **shmee** [ʃmiː] (*noun*), *P:* héroïne *f* (*drogues**), schmeck *m.*

shmo(e) [ʃmou] (*noun*), *P:* = **schmo, 1, 2.**

shnockered [ˈʃnɔkəd] (*adj.*), *P:* hébété par un narcotique, bourré à bloc.

* An asterisk indicates that the word so marked is included as a head-word in the Appendix.

shocker [ˈʃɔkər] (*noun*), *F:* horreur *f*, affreux *m* (*personne ou chose*); **you're a s.!** tu es impossible!

shoes [ʃuːz] (*pl. noun*), *F:* **that's another pair of s.**, c'est une autre paire de manches. *Voir aussi* **dead**[1], 9; **ice**[1], 7.

shoestring [ˈʃuː-striŋ] (*noun*), *F:* **to do business on a s.**, faire des affaires avec des moyens financiers très limités; tirer sur la corde.

shonk [ʃɔŋk] (*noun*), *P:* (*péj.*) Juif *m*, Youpin *m*.

shook [ʃuk] (*p.p.*): *voir* **shake**[2] **(to)**, 3.

shook up [ˈʃukˈʌp] (*adj.*), *P:* **(all) s. u.**, secoué, émotionné, remué.

shoot[1] [ʃuːt] (*noun*). 1. *F:* **the whole (bang) s.**, tout le bataclan, tout le tremblement; *cf.* **boiling; caboodle; shebang**[1], 1; **shooting-match.** 2. *P:* piqûre *f*, piquouse *f* (*drogues*).

shoot[2] [ʃuːt] **(to)**. 1. *P:* **s.!** vas-y! rentre dedans! 2. *P:* éjaculer*, arroser; *voir aussi* **load**, 8. 3. *F:* filmer, photographier. 4. *F:* **to get shot of s.o., sth.**, se débarrasser* de qn, de qch., défarguer, larguer qn, qch. 5. *F:* **to s. a line**, exagérer*, blouser, se vanter, en installer, esbrouf(f)er; **to s. s.o. a line**, lancer de la poudre aux yeux de qn; *cf.* **line-shooter; line-shooting.** 6. *P:* **to s. the cat**, vomir*, évacuer le couloir. 7. (*U.S.*) *P:* **to s. the bull** (*or* **the crap** *or* **the breeze**), bavarder*, dire des banalités *f.pl.*, tailler une bavette. 8. *F:* **to s. the works**, (*a*) dilapider son argent*, lessiver son pognon; (*b*) avouer*, manger le morceau, faire des aveux *m.pl.*; (*c*) jouer (*ou* miser *ou* risquer) le tout pour le tout, jouer sa chemise; (*d*) y aller de tout son saoul, donner un coup de collier. 9. *P:* **to s. the moon**, déménager à la cloche de bois. 10. *F:* **he has shot his bolt**, il a vidé son carquois, il a jeté tout son feu. 11. *P:* (*à table*) passer (la nourriture); **s. the gravy!** passe la sauce! 12. *P:* se shooter (*drogues*). *Voir aussi* **lingo**, 2; **wad**, 4.

shoot down [ˈʃuːtˈdaun] **(to)**, *F:* **to s. s.o. d. (in flames)**, rabattre le caquet à qn, torcher le bec à qn, ramener qn à ses justes proportions; **to get shot down in flames**, l'avoir dans l'os.

shooter [ˈʃuːtər] (*noun*), *P:* arme *f* à feu, flingue *m*. *Voir aussi* **line-shooter; pea-shooter; six-shooter.**

shooting-gallery [ˈʃuːtiŋgæləri] (*noun*), *P:* endroit où on se pique à la drogue, shooterie *f*.

shooting-iron [ˈʃuːtiŋaiən] (*noun*), *F:* revolver*, flingot *m*, pétard *m*.

shooting-match [ˈʃuːtiŋmætʃ] (*noun*), *F:* **the whole s.-m.** = **the whole (bang) shoot (shoot**[1], 1).

shoot off [ˈʃuːtˈɔf] **(to)**. *P:* 1. = **shoot**[2] **(to)**, 2. 2. **to s. one's mouth** (*or* **face**) **o.**, (*a*) révéler un secret, vendre la mèche; (*b*) bavasser, être atteint de diarrhée verbale.

shoot up [ˈʃuːtˈʌp] **(to)**. 1. *P:* se piquer, se shooter, avoir la piquouse. 2. *F:* terroriser (une ville, *etc.*).

shop[1] [ʃɔp] (*noun*). 1. *F:* **all over the s.**, (*a*) en vrac, comme dans un bordel; (*b*) partout, dans tous les coins. 2. *P:* **you've come to the wrong s.**, vous n'êtes pas au bon guichet, il y a erreur d'aiguillage. 3. *F:* **to talk s.**, parler affaires, parler boutique; *cf.* **shop-talk.** 4. *F:* **to shut up s.**, (*sports*) fermer le jeu. 5. *P:* prison*, boîte *f*. 6. *F:* **top of the s.**: *voir* **bingo** (90). *Voir aussi* **cop-shop; dolly-shop; fish-shop; hock-shop; hook-shop; kip-shop; milk-shop; molly-shop; porn-shop; slopshop; sweat-shop; whore-shop.**

shop[2] [ʃɔp] **(to)**, *P:* 1. dénoncer*, trahir, moutonner. 2. traduire (qn) en justice. 3. emprisonner*, mettre en boîte.

shop-talk [ˈʃɔp-tɔːk] (*noun*), *F:* jargon *m* de métier, d'un groupe professionnel, d'une (soi-disant) science, *etc.*; *cf.* **shop**[1], 3.

short[1] [ʃɔːt] (*adj.*), 1. *F:* **to be a bit s.**, être à court (d'argent*). 2. *P:* **s. time**, courte séance (*prostituée*). 3. *P:* **s. arm**, pénis*, la troisième jambe. *Voir aussi* **curly**, 2; **hair**, 6.

short[2] [ʃɔːt] (*adv.*), *F:* **to be caught s.**, (*a*) être pris d'un besoin pressant; (*b*) être pris de court. *Voir aussi* **sell**[2] **(to)**, 2.

short[3] [ʃɔːt] (*noun*), *F:* 1. un petit verre d'alcool* (*ou* de goutte *f*). 2. (*U.S.*) petite voiture de sport, petit bolide.

short-arse [ˈʃɔːtɑːs] (*noun*), *V:* bas-du-cul *m*, basduc *m*; *cf.* **shorty.**

shortchange[1] [ˈʃɔːt-tʃeindʒ] (*attrib. adj.*), *F:* **s. artist**, escroc*, filou *m*, estampeur *m*.

* L'astérisque indique que le mot marqué de ce signe figure comme entrée dans le Répertoire.

shortchange[2] [ˈʃɔːtˈtʃeindʒ] **(to),** *F:* **to s. s.o.,** voler* qn en lui rendant la monnaie (lui rendre moins qu'il ne lui revient).

short-sheet [ˈʃɔːtˈʃiːt] **(to),** *F:* **to s.-s. a bed,** mettre un lit en portefeuille.

shortweight [ˈʃɔːtˈweit] **(to),** *F:* estamper sur le poids de qch.

shorty [ˈʃɔːti] (*noun*), *F:* homme de petite* taille, courte-botte *m*.

shot[1] [ʃɔt] (*adj.*), *F:* **1.** ivre*, bituré, rétamé, rond; *cf.* **half-shot. 2.** très fatigué*, vanné.

shot[2] [ʃɔt] (*noun*), *F:* **1.** piqûre *f*, piquouse *f* (*drogues*); *voir aussi* **hot, 24** (*b*). **2.** une mesure d'alcool*, un dé, une rincette. **3. a s. in the arm,** un remontant, un stimulant, un coup de fouet. **4. to have a s. at sth.,** essayer qch., tenter le coup. **5.** (*a*) **a long s.,** (i) un gros risque; (ii) un gros risque (*cheval de course, etc.*); une chance sur mille; (iii) (*cinéma*) une scène filmée à distance; (*b*) **not by a long s. = not by a long chalk (chalk, 1). 6. like a s.,** (*a*) très vite* comme l'éclair; (*b*) volontiers, de bon cœur. **7. to make a s, in the dark,** deviner au hasard. **8.** dada *m*, habitude *f*, manie *f*. *Voir aussi* **big**[1]**, 1; pot-shot.**

shotgun [ˈʃɔtgʌn] (*attrib. adj.*), *F:* **1. s. agreement,** convention signée sous la contrainte. **2. s. wedding,** mariage forcé, régularisation *f*.

shoulder [ˈʃouldər] (*noun*), *F:* **1. to rub shoulders with s.o.,** frayer avec qn, se frotter à qn. **2. straight from the s.,** carrément, sans mettre de gants; **he let me have it straight from the s.,** il ne me l'a pas envoyé dire. *Voir aussi* **cold**[1]**, 3; cold-shoulder (to).**

shout [ʃaut] (*noun*), *F:* **1. it's my s.,** c'est ma tournée. **2. give me a s. when you're ready,** fais signe quand tu es prêt.

shouting [ˈʃautiŋ] (*noun*), *F:* **it's all over bar the s.,** c'est dans le sac, les applaudissements suivront.

shove [ʃʌv] **(to),** (*a*) *P:* **you know where you can s. that!** tu sais où tu peux te le mettre!; (*b*) *V:* **you can s. that (right) up your arse!** tu peux te le mettre au cul!

shove around [ˈʃʌvəˈraund] **(to),** *F:* bousculer, ballotter (qn), faire marcher (qn).

shove off [ˈʃʌvˈɔf] **(to),** (*a*) *F:* partir*, décamper; (*b*) *P:* **s. o.!** fiche le camp!

shovel it down [ˈʃʌvəlitˈdaun] **(to),** *F:* se goinfrer, se gaver.

show[1] [ʃou] (*noun*), *F:* **1. a s. of leg,** un étalage de cuisses; **free s.,** strip-tease *m* à l'œil; **it's a free s.,** elle a soulevé son capot, on voit le moteur. **2. good s.!** bravo! c'est au poil! c'est épatant! **3. to give the s. away,** vendre (*ou* éventer) la mèche, débiner le truc. **4. to stop the s.,** (*th.*) être applaudi avec enthousiasme par les spectateurs, casser la baraque. **5. to steal the s.,** capter l'attention, magnétiser l'assemblée, tirer à soi la couverture. *Voir aussi* **boss**[3] **(to), 1; leg**[1]**, 2; meat-show.**

show[2] [ʃou] **(to),** *F:* = **show up (to), 1.** *Voir aussi* **leg**[1]**, 1.**

showbiz [ˈʃoubiz] (*noun*). **1.** *F:* l'industrie *f* du spectacle. **2.** *P:* demi-monde *m*, entourage *m* de demi-mondains, le monde où l'on s'amuse.

showdown [ˈʃoudaun] (*noun*), *F:* **1.** confrontation *f*, déballage *m* (de ses intentions). **2.** révélation *f* d'adversité, mise *f* au point; mise *f* à jour.

shower [ˈʃauər] (*noun*), *P:* (*a*) nullité *f*, nouille *f*; **he's a right s.!** quelle andouille! (*b*) **what a s.!** quelle bande* (*ou* quel tas) de crétins!

showman [ˈʃoumən] (*noun*), *F:* (*jazz*) musicien *m* spectaculaire, showman *m*.

show-off [ˈʃouɔf] (*noun*), *F:* individu qui fait du flafla (*ou* de l'épate *f*), esbrouf(f)eur *m*, poseur *m*, m'as-tu-vu *m*, plastronneur *m*.

show off [ˈʃouˈɔf] **(to),** *F:* parader, plastronner, se donner des airs, chercher à épater.

show up [ˈʃouˈʌp] **(to),** *F:* **1.** faire une apparition, faire acte de présence, se pointer. **2.** (*a*) révéler, dévoiler, démasquer; (*b*) attirer l'attention sur (qn); **he's been shown up,** il est grillé.

shrimp [ʃrimp] (*noun*), *F:* individu de petite* taille, crapoussin *m*.

shrink [ʃriŋk] (*noun*), *P:* = **head-shrinker.**

shtup [ʃtʌp] **(to)** (*U.S.*), *P:* = **tup (to).**

shuck[1] [ʃʌk] (*noun*), *F:* **1.** (*U.S.*) mystification *f*, supercherie *f*. **2. it's not worth shucks,** ça ne vaut pas chipette.

shuck[2] [ʃʌk] **(to)** (*U.S.*), *F:* **1.** faire

* An asterisk indicates that the word so marked is included as a head-word in the Appendix.

marcher (qn), mystifier (qn). **2.** dire des bêtises*, déconner.

shucks! [ʃʌks] (*excl.*), *F:* mince! zut alors!

shudders [ˈʃʌdəz] (*pl. noun*), *F:* **to give s.o. the s.** = **to give s.o. the shivers.**

shuffles [ˈʃʌflz] (*pl. noun*), *P:* cartes* à jouer, brèmes *f.pl.*

shufty [ˈʃufti] (*noun*), *F:* regard *m*, coup *m* de châsse, clinc *m*.

shush [ʃuʃ] (**to**), *F:* faire taire* (qn), river le clou à (qn); **s.!** tais-toi! un peu de silence!

shut [ʃʌt] (**to**), *P:* **to s. it,** se taire*, fermer sa boîte (*ou* son clapet), la fermer; *voir aussi* **face[1], 1; gob[1], 1; trap, 1.**

shuteye [ˈʃʌtai] (*noun*), *F:* sommeil *m*, somme *m*; **to get** (*or* **grab**) **some s.,** dormir*, piquer un roupillon, roupillonner.

shutters [ˈʃʌtəz] (*pl. noun*), *F:* **to put the s. up,** se retirer en soi-même, baisser la vitrine, faire le hibou.

shut up [ˈʃʌtˈʌp] (**to**), (*a*) *F:* faire taire* (qn), clouer le bec à (qn); (*b*) *P:* **s. u.!** la ferme! ferme ça!

shy[1] [ʃai] (*noun*), *F:* **1.** jet *m*, lancement *m*. **2.** tentative *f*, essai *m*.

shy[2] [ʃai] (**to**), *F:* jeter*, lancer, balancer.

shyster [ˈʃaistər] (*noun*), *F:* homme d'affaires, *etc.* véreux; marron *m*.

sick [sik] (*adj.*). **1.** *F:* furieux, furibard. **2.** *F:* déçu, chocolat. **3.** *F:* **s. joke,** plaisanterie *f* macabre. **4.** *F:* **I'm s.** (**and tired**) **of it,** j'en ai plein le dos, j'en ai marre. **5.** *P:* en manque de drogues.

sickener [ˈsikənər] (*noun*), *F:* **1.** aventure écœurante. **2.** spectacle écœurant.

sick-making [ˈsikmeikiŋ] (*adj.*), *F:* écœurant, navrant.

sick up [ˈsikˈʌp] (**to**), *F:* vomir* (qch.), dégobiller.

side [said] (*noun*). **1.** *F:* **to make sth.** (*or* **a bit**) **on the s.,** se faire des petits à-côtés. **2.** *P:* **to have a bit on the s.,** dérouiller sa crampette hors du ménage, prendre un petit à-côté. **3.** *F:* **to split one's sides** (**with**) **laughing,** se tordre de rire*; *cf.* **side-splitting. 4.** *F:* crânerie *f*, esbrouf(f)e *f*; **to put on s.,** faire sa poire (anglaise). *Voir aussi* **bed[1], 2; right, 4; safe[1].**

sideboards [ˈsaidbɔːdz], **sideburns** [ˈsaidbəːnz] (*pl. noun*), *F:* favoris *m.pl.*, pattes *f.pl.* de lapin.

sidekick [ˈsaidkik] (*noun*), *F:* **1.** ami*, copain *m*. **2.** associé *m*, assistant *m*, sous-fifre *m*.

sideman [ˈsaidmæn] (*noun*), *P:* (*jazz*) musicien *m* de pupitre.

side-splitting [ˈsaid-splitiŋ] (*adj.*), *F:* tordant, désopilant, marrant, crevant; *cf.* **side, 3.**

sideways [ˈsaid-weiz] (*adv.*), *F:* **to knock s.o. s.,** époustoufler, ébahir, ébaubir qn.

siff [sif] (*noun*), *P:* = **syph.**

sight [sait] (*noun*), *F:* **1. I can't bear** (*or* **stand**) **the s. of him,** je ne peux pas le voir en peinture. **2.** (*a*) **you do look a s.!** te voilà bien arrangé! tu es fichu comme l'as de pique!; (*b*) **his face was a s.,** si vous aviez vu son visage*! **3. a s. of...,** énormément de...; **he's a (damn(ed)) s. too clever for you,** il est beaucoup trop malin* pour vous. *Voir aussi* **damned[1], 5.**

sign off [ˈsainˈɔf] (**to**), *F:* conclure, terminer, finocher.

silly [ˈsili] (*noun*), *F:* individu bête*, ballot *m*, baluchard *m*.

sim [sim] (*noun*) (*Austr.*), *P:* = **alec, 2.**

simmer down [ˈsiməˈdaun] (**to**), *F:* se calmer, ne pas s'emballer.

simp [simp] (*noun*), *P:* nigaud *m*, niguedouille *mf*.

simply [ˈsimpli] (*adv.*), *F:* absolument, complètement; **you look s. lovely!** vous êtes absolument ravissante!; **it's s. ghastly weather,** il fait un temps de chien.

sing [siŋ] (**to**). **1.** *P:* = **squeal[2] (to), 1, 2. 2.** *P:* payer du chantage. **3.** *F:* **to s. small,** se conduire avec humilité, baisser pavillon.

sing out [ˈsiŋˈaut] (**to**), *F:* **s. o. if you need me,** appelez si vous avez besoin de moi.

sink [siŋk] (**to**), *F:* **1. s. or swim!** au petit bonheur! **2. to s. a pint,** s'envoyer un demi.

sinker [ˈsiŋkər] (*noun*) (*U.S.*), *F:* mauvaise pièce (d'argent).

sink in [ˈsiŋkˈin] (**to**), *F:* se l'enfoncer dans la tête, pénétrer la comprenette.

sin-shifter [ˈsin-ʃiftər] (*noun*) (*Austr.*), *P:* aumônier *m* militaire, radis-noir *m*.

sirree [ˈsəːˈriː] (*noun*), *F:* **no s.!** (*négation facétieuse mais catégorique*) non, monsieur! non, mon cher!

sissy [ˈsisi] (*noun*), *F:* = **cissy.**

*** L'astérisque indique que le mot marqué de ce signe figure comme entrée dans le Répertoire.**

sit [sit] (**to**), *F:* **to be sitting pretty,** (*a*) tenir le bon bout (*ou* le filon), avoir la vie belle, être bidard, être dans les eaux grasses, se la couler douce; (*b*) rouler sur l'or. *Voir aussi* **behind; duck[1], 3; fence[1], 2; tight[2].**

sit-in [ˈsitin] (*noun*), *F:* occupation *f* (des locaux), sit-in *m.*

sit-me-down [ˈsitmi-daʊn] (*noun*), *F:* fesses*, arrière-train *m.*

sit on [ˈsitɔn] (**to**), *F:* **1. to s. o. sth.,** ne pas s'occuper de qch., laisser dormir qch., faire des conserves avec qch. **2. to get sat on,** être réprimandé*, recevoir un abattage. **3. to s. o. s.o.,** rabrouer qn, rabaisser le caquet à qn; **he won't be sat on,** il ne se laisse pas marcher sur les pieds.

sitter [ˈsitər] (*noun*), *F:* **1** = **sitting duck** (**duck[1], 3**). **2.** une certitude, du tout cuit, la loi et les prophètes.

sit up [ˈsitˈʌp] (**to**), *F:* **to s. u. and take notice,** se réveiller, se secouer; **I'll make you s. u.!** tu auras de mes nouvelles!

sit-upon [ˈsitəpɔn] (*noun*), *F:* = **sit-me-down.**

six [siks] (*numeral adj. & noun*), *F:* **1. to be s. feet** (*or* **foot**) **under,** être enterré, être dans le royaume des taupes. **2. at sixes and sevens,** sens dessus dessous, en pagaille. **3. it's s. of one and half a dozen of the other,** c'est bonnet blanc et blanc bonnet, c'est kif-kif. *Voir aussi* **knock[2] (to), 8.**

six-footer [ˈsiksˈfʊtər] (*noun*), *F:* homme* (haut) de six pieds, homme très grand, double-mètre *m.*

six-shooter [ˈsiksˈʃuːtər] (*noun*), *F:* revolver* (à six coups), flingue *m,* pétard *m.*

sixty-four [ˈsikstiˈfɔːr] (*numeral adj. & noun*), *F:* **the s.-f.** (**thousand**) **dollar question,** (*a*) la question du gros lot, la question super-banco; (*b*) la question vitale (*ou* cruciale *ou* qui compte le plus).

sixty-nine [ˈsikstiˈnain] (*numeral adj. & noun*), *P:* six-à-neuf *m* (coït* buccal respectif et simultané).

size [saiz] (*noun*), *F:* **1. to cut s.o. down to s.,** rabaisser qn, rabattre le caquet à qn, rogner les ailes à qn. **2. that's about the s. of it,** (*a*) c'est à peu près cela; (*b*) c'est ainsi (et pas autrement). *Voir aussi* **king-size(d); man-size(d); pint-size(d).**

size up [ˈsaizˈʌp] (**to**), *F:* évaluer, classer, juger.

sizzler [ˈsizlər] (*noun*), *F:* = **scorcher, 1.**

skag [skæg] (*noun*), *P:* héroïne *f* (*drogues**), shmeck *m.*

skate [skeit] (*noun*). **1.** (*U.S.*) *P:* = **cheapskate, 2. 2.** (*U.S.*) *P:* canasson *m,* bidet *m.* **3.** *F:* **to put** (*or* **get**) **one's skates on,** se dépêcher*, se grouiller, se magner le train.

skating-rink [ˈskeitiŋriŋk] (*noun*), *F:* tête chauve*, mouchodrome *m,* boule *f* de billard.

skedaddle [skiˈdædl] (**to**), *F:* s'enfuir*, ficher le camp, filer, s'esquiver.

skelp [skelp] (**to**), *F:* battre* (qn), talocher.

skerrick [ˈskerik] (*noun*) (*Austr.*), *F:* un peu* (de...), un chouia.

skewer [ˈskjuːər] (*noun*), *F:* (*a*) épée *f;* (*b*) baïonnette *f.*

skew-eyed [ˈskjuːaid] (*adj.*), *F:* **to be s.-e.,** loucher*, avoir un œil qui dit merde (*ou* zut) à l'autre.

skew-whiff[1] [ˈskjuːˈwif] (*adj.*), *F:* tordu, biscornu.

skew-whiff[2] [ˈskjuːˈwif] (*adv.*), *F:* en biais, de traviole.

skid-lid [ˈskid-lid] (*noun*), *F:* casque *m* de moto.

skid-row [ˈskidˈroʊ] (*noun*) (*mainly U.S.*), *F:* quartier mal famé; bas-fonds *m.pl.,* zone *f;* **a s.-r. joint,** un boui-boui de la plus basse catégorie.

skids [skidz] (*pl. noun*), *F:* **1.** (*U.S.*) **on the s.,** sur la pente savonneuse, en train de perdre prestige, richesse, *etc.*; en perte de vitesse. **2.** (*a*) **to put the s. under s.o., sth.,** faire échouer* qn, qch., huiler la pente; (*b*) **to put the s. under s.o.,** congédier* qn, flanquer qn à la porte.

skin[1] [skin] (*noun*). **1.** *F:* **to get under s.o.'s s.,** ennuyer*, barber, raser qn. **2.** *F:* **it's no s. off my nose,** ce n'est pas mon affaire, ça ne me touche pas, c'est pas mes oignons. **3.** *F:* **s. off your nose!** (*toast*) à la bonne vôtre! **4.** *F:* **to have s.o. under one's s.,** être entiché de qn, avoir qn dans la peau. **5.** *P:* (*a*) **s. game,** escroquerie*, arnaquage *m;* (*b*) **s. artist,** escroc*, arnaqueur *m.* **6.** (*U.S.*) *P:* billet *m* de un dollar. **7.** *P:* capote anglaise. **8.** (*pl.*) *P:* (*jazz*) ensemble *m* de tambours, batterie *f.*

* An asterisk indicates that the word so marked is included as a head-word in the Appendix.

9. *P:* pneu *m* de voiture (usé), boudin *m.* 10. *P:* **gimme some s.!** touche là! tope là! 11. *P:* **s. and blister** (*R.S.* = *sister*), sœur *f.* *Voir aussi* **popping; thick**[1], 4.

skin[2] [skin] (**to**), *F:* 1. carotter (de l'argent), dépouiller, écorcher, plumer (qn). 2. anéantir, écraser. *Voir aussi* **eye, 8.**

skin-flick [ˈskinflik] (*noun*), *F:* film *m* porno(graphique).

skinful [ˈskinful] (*noun*), *P:* 1. **to have (had) a s.,** être ivre*, avoir une cuite. 2. = **bellyful.**

skinhead [ˈskinhed] (*noun*), *F:* 1. homme chauve* (*ou* à la tête rasée), individu qui a une perruque en peau de fesses. 2. jeune voyou *m*, skinhead *m.*

skin-pop [ˈskinpɔp] (**to**), *P:* (*drogues*) se faire une injection intramusculaire; *voir aussi* **popping.**

skin-popper [ˈskinpɔpər] (*noun*), *P:* qn qui se fait lui-même des piqûres *f.pl.* de drogues, piquouseur *m* maison.

skint [skint] (*adj.*), *P:* très pauvre*, fauché, raide.

skip [skip] (**to**). 1. *P:* coïter* avec (une femme), envoyer en l'air. 2. *F:* **to s. the country,** fuir le pays; **to s. school,** faire l'école buissonnière. 3. **s. it!** (*a*) *F:* laisse courir!; (*b*) *P:* file! décampe!

skipper [ˈskipər] (*noun*), *F:* (*sports*) chef *m* d'équipe.

skip off [ˈskipˈɔf] (**to**), *F:* s'enfuir*, décamper, filer.

skippy [ˈskipi] (*noun*), *P:* (*a*) pédéraste*, lopette *f*; (*b*) homme efféminé.

skirt [skəːt] (*noun*), *P:* femme*, jeune fille*, poupée *f*; **a nice bit of s.,** une jolie pépée; **to go out looking for s.,** courir les femmes, cavaler; *cf.* **stuff**[1], 3. *Voir aussi* **hot, 1.**

skirt-chaser, skirt-hunter [ˈskəːt-tʃeisər, ˈskəːthʌntər] (*noun*), *P:* cavaleur *m*, coureur *m* de jupons.

skite[1] [skait] (*noun*) (*Austr.*), *F:* vantard*, bluffeur *m.*

skite[2] [skait] (**to**) (*Austr.*), *F:* se vanter, esbrouf(f)er.

skive [skaiv] (**to**), *F:* s'esquiver, tirer au flanc.

skiver [ˈskaivər] (*noun*), *F:* tire-au-flanc *m.*

skiving [ˈskaiviŋ] (*noun*), *F:* tirage-au-flanc *m.*

skivvy [ˈskivi] (*noun*), *F:* 1. bonne *f* à tout faire, bonniche *f.* 2. (*U.S.*) (*a*) sous-vêtement *m* d'homme, sweat-shirt *f*, tee-shirt *f*; (*b*) caleçon *m*, calcif *m*, short *m* (en coton).

skivy [ˈskaivi] (*adj.*), *P:* (*a*) malhonnête, filou; (*b*) renâcleur, tire-au-flanc.

skull [skʌl] (*noun*), *P:* = **egghead.**

skull-job [ˈskʌl-dʒɔb] (*noun*), *V:* = **blow-job.**

skunk [skʌŋk] (*noun*), *F:* chameau *m*, mufle *m*, rossard *m.*

sky [skai] (*noun*), *P:* **to see the s. through the trees,** (*d'une femme*) coïter*, voir les feuilles (*ou* la feuille) à l'envers. *Voir aussi* **limit, 3.**

skyjack [ˈskai-dʒæk] (**to**), *F:* pirater (un avion).

skyjacker [ˈskai-dʒækər] (*noun*), *F:* pirate *m* de l'air.

skylark [ˈskai-lɑːk] (**to**), *P:* batifoler, chahuter, plaisanter.

sky-piece [ˈskai-piːs] (*noun*), *P:* chapeau*, capet *m.*

sky-pilot [ˈskai-pailət] (*noun*), *P:* prêtre*, pasteur *m*, chapelain *m.*

sky-rocket [ˈskai-rɔkit] (*noun*) (*R.S.* = *pocket*), *P:* poche*, fouille *f.*

slab [slæb] (*noun*), *F:* 1. table *f* d'opération, billard *m.* 2. dalle *f* funéraire, pierre *f* de macchab(e).

slag [slæg] (*noun*), *P:* vieille prostituée*, tarderie *f.*

slam [slæm] (**to**), *F:* 1. battre avec conviction. 2. frapper avec violence, flanquer par terre. 3. critiquer* sévèrement, éreinter, débiner.

slams [slæmz] (*pl. noun*) (*U.S.*), *P:* **the s.,** prison*, taule *f.*

slanging-match [ˈslæŋiŋmætʃ] (*noun*), *F:* prise *f* de bec, engueulade *f* maison.

slanguage [ˈslæŋgwidʒ] (*noun*), *F:* argot*, jar(s) *m.*

slant[1] [slɑːnt] (*noun*). 1. *F:* (*a*) point *m* de vue, manière *f* de voir; (*b*) préjugé *m*, biais *m*, point de vue détourné. 2. *P:* coup d'œil*; **take a s. at that!** jette un coup de châsse!

slant[2] [slɑːnt] (**to**), *F:* donner un biais (*ou* un tournant) à (une question, *etc.*).

slanter [ˈslɑːntər] (*noun*) (*Austr.*), *P:* tour *m*, ruse *f*, astuce *f.*

slap[1] [slæp] (*adv.*), *F:* (*a*) directement, tout droit; **s. in the middle,** en plein (dans le) milieu, en plein mitan; (*b*)

* L'astérisque indique que le mot marqué de ce signe figure comme entrée dans le Répertoire.

brusquement, brutalement, rudement; **she put it s. on the table,** elle l'a flanqué sur la table; *cf.* **slap-bang(-wallop); smack**[1]; **wallop**[1].

slap[2] [slæp] (*noun*), *F:* **1. s. in the eye** (*or* **face**), affront *m*, camouflet *m*, rebuffade *f*; *cf.* **eye, 23. 2. s. and tickle,** partie *f* de pelotage *m*; **we were having a bit of (the old) s. and tickle,** on était en train de se peloter (*ou* de se faire des mamours).

slap[3] [slæp] (**to**), *F:* **s. it on the bill!** flanque-le sur l'addition!

slap-bang(-wallop) [ˈslæpˈbæŋ-(ˈwɔləp)] (*adv.*), *F:* (*a*) tout à coup, de but en blanc, hâtivement; (*b*) brusquement. *Voir aussi* **wallop**[1], **3.**

slap down [ˈslæpˈdaun] (**to**), *F:* réprimander*, rabrouer rudement.

slap-happy [ˈslæpˈhæpi] (*adj.*), *F:* **1.** plein d'entrain (*ou* d'allant), d'humeur joyeuse. **2.** farfelu, téméraire, insouciant. **3.** (*boxe*) ivre de coups.

slap together [ˈslæp-təˈgeðər] (**to**), *F:* préparer hâtivement, bâcler.

slap-up [ˈslæpʌp] (*adj.*), *F:* chic, dernier cri, prodigue; *cf.* **bang-up.**

slash [slæʃ] (*noun*), *P:* **to have a s.,** uriner*, jeter de la lance; **to go for a s.,** aller aux W.C.*

slashing [ˈslæʃiŋ] (*adj.*), *F:* excellent*, terrible, du tonnerre.

slate[1] [sleit] (*noun*), *F:* **1. on the s.,** sur la note, sur le compte. **2. to have a s. loose,** être un peu fou*, onduler de la toiture.

slate[2] [sleit] (**to**), *F:* (*a*) réprimander* (qn) vertement, passer un savon à (qn); (*b*) critiquer*, éreinter (un livre, *etc.*).

slater [ˈsleitər] (*noun*), *F:* critique *m* sévère, abatteur *m*, éreinteur *m*.

slating [ˈsleitiŋ] (*noun*), *F:* (*a*) verte réprimande, savon *m*; (*b*) éreintement *m*.

slats [slæts] (*pl. noun*) (*U.S.*), *P:* côtes *f.pl.*, côtelettes *f.pl.*

slaughter[1] [ˈslɔːtər] (*noun*), *F:* victoire décisive, coup *m* de Trafalgar, hécatombe *f*.

slaughter[2] [ˈslɔːtər] (**to**), *F:* battre à plate(s) couture(s), mettre à bas.

slave (away) [ˈsleiv(əˈwei)] (**to**), *F:* travailler* dur, se crever, s'échiner.

slave-driver [ˈsleivdraivər] (*noun*), *F:* garde-chiourme *m*.

slavey [ˈsleivi] (*noun*), *F:* = **skivvy, 1.**

slay [slei] (**to**), *F:* **you s. me!** tu me fais rigoler! tu me fais tordre!

sleazy [ˈsliːzi] (*adj.*), *F:* sordide, répugnant, dégueulasse, débectant; mal soigné.

sleep [sliːp] (**to**), *F:* **this room sleeps four,** on peut coucher à quatre dans cette chambre.

sleep around [ˈsliːpəˈraund] (**to**), *F:* coucher avec n'importe qui; fréquenter les lits.

sleeper [ˈsliːpər] (*noun*), *F:* **1.** somnifère *m*, barbiturique *m* (*drogues**), barbitos *m.pl.* **2.** (*lutte, judo*) prise *f* qui abasourdit l'adversaire. **3.** film *m* qui rapporte beaucoup plus qu'on n'escomptait. **4.** livre *m* qui se vend couramment pendant une longue période sans publicité spéciale. **5.** (*commerce*) article auquel on découvre soudainement une plus-value jusque-là ignorée. **6.** wagon-lit *m*.

sleep off [ˈsliːpˈɔf] (**to**), *F:* **to s. it o.,** cuver son vin.

sleepy-byes [ˈsliːpibaiz] (*pl. noun*), *F:* = **bye-byes.**

sleepyhead [ˈsliːpihed] (*noun*), *F:* individu (*surtout* enfant) à moitié endormi, (bon) client du marchand de sable.

slewed [sluːd] (*adj.*), *P:* ivre*, blindé, bourré; *cf.* **half-slewed.**

slice [slais] (*noun*), *P:* **to knock a s. off (a woman),** coïter* avec une femme, filer un coup d'arbalète. *Voir aussi* **tongue-pie.**

slick [slik] (*adj.*), *F:* **1.** (*a*) malin*, rusé, marle, roublard; (*b*) habile, adroit. **2.** beau parleur. **3.** séduisant, aguichant, désirable.

slicker [ˈslikər] (*noun*), *F:* escroc* adroit, combinard *m*; **city s.,** roustisseur *m* de ville, affranchi *m*, mec *m* du milieu.

slide off [ˈslaidˈɔf] (**to**), *F:* partir* (sans bruit), se défiler, se débiner.

slim [slim] (*adj.*), *F:* = **slick 1** (*a*).

slime[1] [slaim] (*noun*), *P:* **1.** flatterie *f*, lèche *f*, pommade *f*. **2.** grossier personnage, rustaud *m*, valetaille *f*. **3.** calomnie *f*, diffamation *f*, débinage *m*, médisance *f*, bêche *f*.

slime[2] [slaim] (**to**), *P:* flatter*, cirer, pommader.

slim(e)y [ˈslaimi] (*noun*), *P:* lèche-cul *m*, lèche-bottes *m*.

* An asterisk indicates that the word so marked is included as a head-word in the Appendix.

slimy [ˈslaimi] (*adj.*), *F:* servile, obséquieux, mielleux, sirupeux.

sling [sliŋ] (**to**) (*U.S.*), *P:* **to s. it** (*or* **the bull**) = **to shoot the bull** (**shoot**[2] (**to**), 7). *Voir aussi* **hook**[1], 5; **lingo**, 2; **mud**, 7.

slinger [ˈsliŋər] (*noun*), *P:* individu* qui écoule la fausse monnaie, fournaise *f*. *Voir aussi* **gunslinger; hash-slinger; ink-slinger; mudslinger.**

sling in [ˈsliŋˈin] (**to**), *P:* **to s. i. one's job,** lâcher son travail, rendre son tablier.

sling off [ˈsliŋˈɔf] (**to**) (*Austr.*), *P:* = **smoke**[2] (**off**) (**to**).

sling out [ˈsliŋˈaut] (**to**), *P:* faire déguerpir, flanquer dehors.

slinky [ˈsliŋki] (*adj.*), *F:* 1. élégant*, mince. 2. qui se meut avec élégance, gandin. 3. (vêtement) collant, ajusté.

slinter [ˈslintər] (*noun*) (*Austr.*), *P:* = **slanter.**

slip[1] [slip] (*noun*), *F:* **to give s.o. the s.,** fausser compagnie à qn.

slip[2] [slip] (**to**), *F:* 1. glisser, faufiler (qch. à qn). 2. **you're slipping,** tu perds les pédales. 3. **to s. one over on s.o.,** duper* qn, tirer une carotte à qn. *Voir aussi* **cut**[2], 4.

slip-on [ˈslipɔn] (*noun*), *F:* vêtement *m* (*ou* gaine *f*) facilement enfilé(e).

slipover [ˈslipouvər] (*noun*), *F:* pull-over *m* sans manches, débardeur *m*.

slippy [ˈslipi] (*adj.*), *F:* (*a*) glissant; (*b*) rapide, presto.

slipslop [ˈslip-slɔp] (*noun*), *F:* 1. aliments *m.pl.* liquides, bouillie *f*, jaffe *f*. 2. sensiblerie *f*, fadeur sentimentale.

slip-up [ˈslipʌp] (*noun*), *F:* erreur *f*, gaffe *f*, accident *m*.

slip up [ˈslipˈʌp] (**to**), *F:* faire une erreur, gaffer.

slit [slit] (*noun*), *V:* vagin*, fente *f*; *cf.* **pee-slit.**

slob [slɔb] (*noun*), *P:* **1. a big** (**fat**) **s.,** un gros (sac à) lard, un gros patapouf. 2. = **slouch.**

slobber [ˈslɔbər] (**to**), *F:* 1. faire du sentimentalisme, larmoyer, s'attendrir. 2. baver, avoir la bouche* souillée de nourriture*.

slobberchops [ˈslɔbə-tʃɔps] (*noun*), *F:* individu *m* aux bajoues baveuses.

slobbery [ˈslɔbəri] (*adj.*), *F:* 1. sentimental, larmoyant. 2. baveux de nourriture.

slog[1] [slɔg] (*noun*), *F:* 1. coup* violent, ramponneau *m*, gnon *m*. 2. travail* dur, turbin *m*, boulot *m*. 3. marche *f* pénible.

slog[2] [slɔg] (**to**), *F:* 1. battre* violemment, tabasser (qn). 2. (*au jeu de cricket*) marquer des points en frappant fort sur la balle. 3. travailler* dur, turbiner, bosser. 4. = **foot-slog** (**to**).

slogger [ˈslɔgər] (*noun*), *F:* 1. (*boxe*) cogneur *m*. 2. travailleur* acharné, turbineur *m*, bosseur *m*, bûcheur *m*. *Voir aussi* **foot-slogger.**

slop [slɔp] (*noun*), *P:* 1. agent* de police, flic *m*. 2. sensiblerie *f*. *Voir aussi* **slipslop; slops.**

slop about (*or* **around**) [ˈslɔpəˈbaut, ˈslɔpəˈraund] (**to**), *F:* patauger, barboter.

slope [sloup] (*noun*), *P:* **to do a s.** = **slope off** (**to**).

slope off [ˈsloupˈɔf] (**to**), *P:* s'enfuir*, se barrer, déguerpir.

sloppy [ˈslɔpi] (*adj.*). 1. *F:* sale*, souillon, désordonné, cradingue. 2. *F:* **s. joe,** paletot *m* de laine vague. 3. (*U.S.*) *P:* ivre*, éméché. 4. *F:* mièvre, sirupeux; **s. sentimentality,** sensiblerie *f*. 5. *F:* avec du laisser-aller, sans soin; **s. English,** anglais mal parlé, anglais débraillé.

slops [slɔps] (*pl. noun*), *F:* (*argot de la Marine*) vêtements*, uniforme *m*, harnais *m*. *Voir aussi* **slop.**

slopshop [ˈslɔpʃɔp] (*noun*), *P:* 1. braderie *f*, décrochez-moi-ça *m*. 2. (*argot de la Marine*) boutique *f* à bord d'un bateau de guerre, bouterne *f*, cambuse *f*.

slosh[1] [slɔʃ] (*noun*), *P:* 1. sensiblerie *f*, sentimentalité *f* fadasse. 2. coup*, gnon *m*, marron *m*. 3. (*a*) (le) boire; (*b*) boisson *f*, pictance *f*.

slosh[2] [slɔʃ] (**to**). 1. *P:* flanquer un coup* à (qn), tabasser. 2. *F:* **to s. paint on,** flanquer de la peinture partout.

sloshed [slɔʃt] (*adj.*), *P:* ivre*, gris, pompette.

slot [slɔt] (*noun*). 1. *P:* (*a*) emploi *m*, situation *f*, job *m*; (*b*) place *f*; **to finish in third s.,** finir en troisième place. 2. (*Austr.*) *P:* cellule *f* de prison*, cellotte *f*. 3. *V:* = **slit.**

slouch [slautʃ] (*noun*), *F:* bousilleur *m*, gâte-métier *m*; **he's no s.,** il est malin*, il n'est pos empoté.

slow [slou] (*adv.*), *F:* 1. **to go s.,** marcher

* L'astérisque indique que le mot marqué de ce signe figure comme entrée dans le Répertoire.

(*ou* fonctionner) au ralenti; *cf.* **go-slow.** 2. **to take it s.,** aller doucement, y aller mollo, ne pas agir à la hâte.

slowcoach [ˈslou-koutʃ] (*noun*), *F:* flâneur *m*, traînard *m*, lambin *m*.

slowpoke [ˈsloupouk] (*noun*) (*U.S.*), *F:* = **slowcoach.**

slug[1] [slʌg] (*noun*), *P:* 1. balle* de revolver, pastille *f*. 2. pièce fausse, mornifle *f*. 3. coup*, triquée *f*, taloche *f*. 4. **to have a s.,** boire* un coup. 5. (*U.S.*) un dollar.

slug[2] [slʌg] (**to**), *P:* 1. battre*, frapper, tabasser. 2. boire*, avaler, ingurgiter. 3. tirer un coup de fusil (*ou* de revolver*) à qn, fusiller qn.

slugfest [ˈslʌgfest] (*noun*), *P:* match *m* de boxe (entre boxeurs qui frappent dur).

slugger [ˈslʌgər] (*noun*), *F:* boxeur *m* (qui frappe dur), cogneur *m*.

slug it out [ˈslʌgitˈaut] (**to**), *F:* se battre* en frappant de grands coups*, se rentrer dedans.

slug-up [ˈslʌgʌp] (*noun*) (*Austr.*), *P:* = **frame-up.**

sluice[1] [slu:s] (*noun*), *P:* trempette *f*, débarbouillage *m*.

sluice[2] [slu:s] (**to**), *P:* **to s. one's ivories** = **to w(h)et one's whistle** (**whistle**[1], 1).

slum [slʌm] (**to**). 1. *F:* **to go slumming,** fréquenter les bars des bas quartiers, faire la zone. 2. *P:* **to s. it** = **to pig it** (**pig**[2], 2).

slurp [slə:p] (**to**), *F:* boire* *ou* siroter bruyamment, laper.

slush [slʌʃ] (*noun*). 1. *F:* sensiblerie *f*. 2. *P:* fausse monnaie, mornifle *f*.

slushy [ˈslʌʃi] (*adj.*), *F:* sentimental, fadasse.

sly [slai] (*noun*), *F:* **on the s.,** à la dérobée, en cachette, en sourdine.

slyboots [ˈslaibu:ts] (*noun*), *F:* 1. cachotteur *m*, sournois *m*. 2. malin *m*, finaud *m*. 3. vaurien*, coquin *m*.

smack[1] [smæk] (*adv.*), *F:* 1. **to hit s.o. s. between the eyes,** frapper qn en plein entre les deux yeux. 2. **s. in the middle,** au beau milieu; *cf.* **slap**[1].

smack[2] [smæk] (*noun*). 1. *F:* **s. in the eye** (*or* **face**) = **slap in the eye** (*or* **face**) (**slap**[2], 1). 2. *F:* **to have a s. at sth.,** essayer de faire qch., tenter le coup. 3. *F:* **to have a s. at s.o.,** donner un coup de patte à qn. 4. *F:* = **smacker,** 1. 5. *P:* = **schmeck.**

smack[3] [smæk] (**to**), *P:* donner un coup de poing (*ou* des coups de poing) à (qn), cogner.

smack-bang(-wallop) [ˈsmækˈbæŋ-(ˈwɔləp)] (*adv.*), *F:* = **slap-bang(-wallop).**

smack-botty [ˈsmækˈbɔti] (*noun*), *F:* tutu-panpan *m*; **to give a child a s.-b.,** administrer une fessée à un enfant; *cf.* **bottom**[2], 1; **botty.**

smack down [ˈsmækˈdaun] (**to**), *F:* = **slap down (to).**

smacker [ˈsmækər] (*noun*). 1. *F:* gros baiser, bizou(t) *m*. 2. *P:* (*a*) une livre sterling; (*b*) (*U.S.*) un dollar. 3. *P:* **to rub smackers,** se sucer le caillou. 4. *P:* = **kisser,** 1,2. 5. *P:* coup* retentissant.

small [smɔ:l] (*adj.*), *F:* **the s. print,** les petits caractères, l'important du bas de la page. *Voir aussi* **potato,** 2; **room.**

smalls [smɔ:lz] (*pl. noun*), *F:* sous-vêtements *m.pl.*, lingerie *f*.

small-time [ˈsmɔ:l-taim] (*adj.*), *F:* insignifiant, médiocre, tocard; **a s.-t. crook,** un petit escroc*; *cf.* **big-time.**

small-timer [ˈsmɔ:l-taimər] (*noun*), *F:* individu* insignifiant, minus *m*; *cf.* **big-timer.**

smarm [smɑ:m] (**to**), *F:* 1. **to s. (all) over s.o.,** flatter* qn, passer la main dans le dos de qn. 2. **to s. one's hair down,** s'aplatir (*ou* se pommader) les cheveux*.

smarmer [ˈsmɑ:mər] (*noun*), *F:* flagorneur *m*, lèche-bottes *m*.

smarmy [ˈsmɑ:mi] (*adj.*), *F:* patelin, mielleux, flagorneur.

smart [smɑ:t] (*adj.*), *F:* 1. **don't get s. with me!** ne fais pas le malin avec moi! ne la raméne pas! 2. **s. guy,** malin *m*, fortiche *m*, roublard *m*. *Voir aussi* **Alec,** 1.

smart-arsed [ˈsmɑ:t-ɑ:st] (*adj.*), *P:* malin*, fortiche, démerdard.

smarty(-pants) [ˈsmɑ:ti(pænts)] (*noun*), *F:* cuistre *m*, savantas(se) *m*, Je-sais-tout *m*.

smash[1] [smæʃ] (*adv.*), *F:* **to go s.,** (*a*) se briser; (*b*) faire faillite, mettre la clef sous la porte.

smash[2] [smæʃ] (*noun*). 1. *F:* = **smash-hit.** 2. *P:* petite monnaie*, ferraille *f*, mitraille *f*.

* An asterisk indicates that the word so marked is included as a head-word in the Appendix.

smashed [smæʃt] (*adj.*), *P:* (*a*) ivre*, bit(t)uré, blindé; (*b*) défoncé par la drogue*.

smasher [ˈsmæʃər] (*noun*), *F:* **1. she's a s.**, c'est une jolie pépée; **what a s.!** ce qu'elle est belle* (*ou* bath *ou* bien roulée)! **2.** qch. d'excellent* (*ou* d'époustouflant *ou* de foutral). **3.** coup* violent, châtaigne *f*, marron *m*. **4. to come a s.**, tomber*, ramasser un gadin, prendre une pelle.

smash-hit [ˈsmæʃˈhit] (*noun*), *F:* réussite *f*, grand boum.

smash in [ˈsmæʃˈin] (**to**), *P:* **to s. s.o.'s face i.**, casser la gueule à qn.

smashing [ˈsmæʃiŋ] (*adj.*), *F:* excellent*, formid(able), du tonnerre.

smash up [ˈsmæʃˈʌp] (**to**), *P:* **1.** = **bash up (to)**. **2. to be all smashed up**, être écrasé (*ou* assommé *ou* fracassé).

smell [smel] (**to**), *F:* sembler louche, ne pas avoir l'air catholique. *Voir aussi* **rat**[1], **4**.

smelly [ˈsmeli] (*adj.*), *F:* suspect, louche.

smice [smais] (**to**) (*Austr.*), *P:* partir*, déguerpir, lever le pied.

smidgen [ˈsmidʒən] (*noun*) (*U.S.*), *F:* un peu*, un chouia, une miette.

smithereens [ˈsmiðəˈri:nz] (*pl. noun*), *F:* morceaux *m.pl.*, miettes *f.pl.*; **to smash sth. to s.**, briser qch. en mille morceaux, mettre qch. en capilotade.

smizz [smiz] (*noun*) (*U.S.*), *P:* = **shmeck.**

smoke[1] [smouk] (*noun*). **1.** *F:* **to go up in s.**, ne servir à rien, partir en fumée. **2.** *F:* **the S.**, une grande métropole; **the (Big) S.**, Londres. **3.** *F:* **a s.**, (*a*) cigarette*, cibiche *f*; (*b*) cigarette* de marijuana (*drogues**), stick *m*; *voir aussi* **giggle, 4**. **4.** (*Austr.*) *P:* **in s.**, en cachette, planqué. **5.** (*U.S.*) *P:* (*péj.*) nègre*, noyama *m*. *Voir aussi* **holy, 1; joy-smoke.**

smoke[2] **(off)** [ˈsmouk(ˈɔf)] (**to**) (*Austr.*), *P:* = **smice (to)**.

smoke-o(h) [ˈsmoukou] (*noun*) (*Austr.*), *F:* pause-café *f*, pause-thé *f*.

smoker [ˈsmoukər] (*noun*). **1.** *F:* compartiment *m* de fumeur. **2.** *P:* voiture *f* à haut kilométrage. **3.** *P:* pot *m* de chambre.

smoky [ˈsmouki] (*adj.*), *P:* en colère*, en rogne, à cran.

smooch [smu:tʃ] (**to**). **1.** *F:* s'embrasser*, se bécoter, se baisoter, se faire des mamours *m.pl.* **2.** *P:* voler*, chiper, garder ce qu'on a emprunté.

smoocher [ˈsmu:tʃər] (*noun*). **1.** *F:* embrasseur *m*, peloteur *m*. **2.** *P:* voleur*, chipeur *m*, chapardeur *m*.

smooching [ˈsmu:tʃiŋ] (*noun*). **1.** *F:* caressage *m*, pelotage *m*, fricassée *f* de museaux. **2.** *P:* vol *m*, chapardage *m*.

smoodge [smu:dʒ] (**to**), **smoodger** [ˈsmu:dʒər] (*noun*), **smoodging** [ˈsmu:dʒiŋ] (*noun*) (*Austr.*), *F:* = **smooch (to), 1, smoocher 1, smooching 1.**

smooth [smu:ð] (*adj.*), *F:* **1.** (*a*) agréable, chouette, badour; (*b*) doucereux. **2. s. operator**, individu malin*, démerdard *m*.

smoothie, smoothy [ˈsmu:ði] (*noun*), *F:* **1.** homme* doucereux (*ou* papelard). **2.** homme* qui se prend pour un don Juan.

smother [ˈsmʌðər] (*noun*), *P:* (*a*) pardessus*; (*b*) imperméable *m*, imper *m*.

smother-love [ˈsmʌðəlʌv] (*noun*), *F:* amour étouffant (*ou* accaparant) (d'une mère).

snaffle [ˈsnæfl] (**to**), *P:* voler*, barbot(t)er, chiper.

snafu, S.N.A.F.U. [ˈsnæˈfu:] (*adj.*) (*abbr.* = *situation normal, all fucked* (or *fouled*) *up*), *P:* en désordre, en pagaille, confus; amoché, bousillé.

snags [snægz] (*pl. noun*) (*Austr.*), *F:* saucisses *f.pl.*, bifteck *m* de pan(n)é.

snake-eyes [ˈsneik-aiz] (*pl. noun*), *F:* double un (*jeu de dés*).

snake-hips [ˈsneikhips] (*noun*), *F:* qn de souple et flexible, danseur *m* (-euse *f*) de corde.

snake off [ˈsneikˈɔf] (**to**), *F:* s'esquiver, jouer rip.

snap[1] [snæp] (*noun*), *F:* **1.** vigueur *f*, entrain *m*, allant *m*, dynamisme *m*. **2.** = **cinch.**

snap[2] [snæp] (**to**), *F:* **1.** s'exprimer avec aigreur, parler* d'un ton sec. **2.** (*d'une personne*) avoir une maladie mentale, perdre la raison. **3. to s. into it**, agir avec énergie et rapidité. **4. to s. out of it**, se secouer, se remettre d'aplomb, reprendre du poil de la bête.

snaped [sneipt] (*adj.*) (*mainly U.S.*), *F:* ivre*, bourré, saoul; *cf.* **half-snaped.**

snap off [ˈsnæpˈɔf] (**to**), *F:* **to s. s.o.'s head o.**, manger le nez à qn, avaler qn.

* L'astérisque indique que le mot marqué de ce signe figure comme entrée dans le Répertoire.

snapper [ˈsnæpər] (*noun*). **1.** *V:* vagin*, étau *m.* **2.** *P:* = **amy.** **3.** *P:* contrôleur *m* d'autobus. **4.** (*pl.*) *P:* (*a*) = **falsies, 1;** (*b*) dents*, croquantes *f.pl.* *Voir aussi* **whipper-snapper.**

snappy [ˈsnæpi] (*adj.*), *F:* **1.** acariâtre, hargneux, bourru. **2. look s.! make it s.!** dépêchez*-vous! remuez-vous! grouille-toi! **3.** élégant*, flambard, badour. **4.** sarcastique, mordant, spirituel. *Voir aussi* **catch**[1], **2.**

snap up [ˈsnæpˈʌp] (**to**), *F:* **1. to s. u. a bargain,** enlever une affaire, saisir une occasion. **2. to s. it u.,** activer le mouvement; **s. it u.!** grouille-toi!

snarky [ˈsnɑːki] (*adj.*), *F:* désagréable, de mauvais poil, râleur.

snarl [snɑːl] (*noun*), *F:* = **snarl-up.**

snarled up [ˈsnɑːldˈʌp] (*adj.*), *F:* embouteillé, encombré, coincé.

snarl-up [ˈsnɑːlʌp] (*noun*), *F:* embouteillage *m*, embarras *m* de voitures.

snarly [ˈsnɑːli] (*adj.*), *F:* = **snarky.**

snatch[1] [snætʃ] (*noun*). **1.** *V:* (*a*) vagin*, cramouille *f*; (*b*) coït*. **2.** *P:* (*a*) arrestation, accrochage *m*, agrafage *m*; (*b*) enlèvement *m*; **to put the s. on s.o.,** (*a*) arrêter* qn; (*b*) enlever qn. **3.** *F:* vol *m*, cambriolage *m*, casse *m*; **wages s.,** ratissage *m* de la paye.

snatch[2] [snætʃ] (**to**). **1.** *P:* arrêter*, accrocher, agrafer. **2.** *P:* enlever, kidnapper. **3.** *P:* voler*, barbot(t)er. **4. to s. a quick one,** (*a*) *F:* boire *un coup; (*b*) *P:* coïter*, s'envoyer un petit coup.

snazzy [ˈsnæzi] (*adj.*), *F:* (*a*) élégant*, chic; (*b*) criard, voyant, clinquant.

sneak[1] [sniːk] (*adj.*), *F:* **s. attack,** attaque sournoise (*ou* en dessous); **s. preview,** banc *m* d'essai (*film, pièce de théâtre, etc.*); **s. thief,** chapardeur *m*, chipeur *m*, barbot(t)eur *m*.

sneak[2] [sniːk] (*noun*), *F:* indicateur*, mouchard *m*, rapporteur *m*.

sneak[3] [sniːk] (**to**), *F:* **1.** voler* furtivement, barbot(t)er, chaparder. **2.** dénoncer*, moucharder, cafarder. **3.** se conduire en pleutre, caner.

sneakers [ˈsniːkəz] (*pl. noun*), *F:* chaussures* souples à semelle en caoutchouc, sneakers *m.pl.*

sneak in [ˈsniːkˈin] (**to**), *F:* **1.** inclure (*ou* glisser) furtivement. **2.** se glisser furtivement, se faufiler, entrer à la dérobée.

sneak on [ˈsniːk-ɔn] (**to**), *F:* dénoncer*, cafarder, moutonner.

sneak out [ˈsniːkˈaut] (**to**), *F:* partir* furtivement, s'éclipser, se défiler.

sneaky [ˈsniːki] (*adj.*), *F:* **1.** sournois, dissimulé. **2.** rampant, servile.

sneeze at [ˈsniːzˈæt] (**to**), *F:* **it's not to be sneezed at,** ce n'est pas de la petite bière, ce n'est pas à cracher dessus.

sneezer [ˈsniːzər] (*noun*), *P:* **1.** nez*, tarin *m*. **2.** prison*, bloc *m*.

snide[1] [snaid] (*adj.*), *F:* **1.** faux, tocard, à la manque. **2.** roublard, ficelle. **3.** sarcastique, persifleur.

snide[2] [snaid] (*noun*), *P:* **1.** voleur*, filou *m*, truqueur *m*. **2.** fausse monnaie, bijouterie *f* factice, toc *m*.

snidy [ˈsnaidi] (*adj.*), *P:* malin*, astucieux.

sniff [snif] (**to**). **1.** *P:* inhaler une poudre narcotique, prendre une reniflette. **2.** *F:* **it's not to be sniffed at = it's not to be sneezed at.**

sniffer [ˈsnifər] (*noun*), *P:* **1.** nez*, reniflant *m*. **2.** mouchoir*, blave *m*.

sniffles [ˈsniflz] (*pl. noun*), *F:* **to have the s.,** être enchifrené.

sniffy [ˈsnifi] (*adj.*). **1.** *F:* arrogant, hautain, pimbêche. **2.** *P:* = **niffy.**

snifter [ˈsniftər] (*noun*). *P:* **1.** vent carabiné. **2.** petit verre d'alcool*, goutte *f*.

snip [snip] (*noun*), *F:* **1.** affaire* avantageuse, trouvaille *f*, occasion *f*. **2.** certitude *f*, affaire* certaine; (*courses aux chevaux*) gagnant sûr., une grosse cote. **3.** tailleur *m*, fringueur *m*. **4.** gamin *m*, gavroche *m*.

snipe[1] [snaip] (*noun*), *P:* (*a*) mégot*, clope *m*; (*b*) mégot* de cigarette de marijuana.

snipe[2] [snaip] (**to**), *P:* voler*, faucher.

sniper [ˈsnaipər] (*noun*), *P:* mégot(t)ier *m*, mégot(t)eur *m*; *cf.* **snipe**[1].

snippy [ˈsnipi] (*adj.*), *P:* insolent, impudent, effronté, culotté.

snitch[1] [snitʃ] (*noun*), *P:* **1.** vol *m*, filouterie *f*. **2.** indicateur* de police, mouchard *m*. **3.** un tout petit peu* (de qch.), un chouia. **4.** nez*, tarin *m*, pif *m*. **5.** (*Austr.*) aversion *f*, dégoût *m*.

snitch[2] [snitʃ] (**to**), *P:* = **sneak**[3] **(to), 1, 2.**

snitcher [ˈsnitʃər] (*noun*), *P:* **1.** indicateur*, rapporteur *m*, cafeteur *m*. **2.** (*pl.*) menottes*, cadènes *f.pl.*

* **An asterisk indicates that the word so marked is included as a head-word in the Appendix.**

snitch-rag [ˈsnitʃræg] (*noun*), *P:* mouchoir*, tire-jus *m*, tire-moelle *m*.
snob [snɔb] (*noun*), *P:* cordonnier *m*, bouif *m*, ribouis *m*.
snoddy [ˈsnɔdi] (*noun*), *P:* soldat*, bidasse *m*.
snodger [ˈsnɔdʒər] (*noun*) (*Austr.*), *P:* délectation *f*, agrément *m*.
snog[1] [snɔg] (*noun*), *P:* = **petting session** (*voir* **petting**).
snog[2] [snɔg] (**to**), *P:* = **pet (to)**.
snogger [ˈsnɔgər] (*noun*), *P:* peloteur *m*; flirteur *m*, juponneur *m*.
snook [snuːk] (*noun*), *F:* **to cock a s. at s.o.,** faire un pied de nez à qn.
snooker [ˈsnuːkər] (**to**), *F:* **to s. s.o.,** mettre qn dans une impasse; **to be snookered,** se trouver en mauvaise posture, être réduit à l'impuissance.
snooks [snuːks], **snookums** [ˈsnuːkəmz] (*noun*) (*U.S.*), *F:* chéri(e), cocotte *f*.
snoop[1] [snuːp] (*noun*), *F:* **1.** fureteur *m*, fouineur *m*. **2.** (*a*) investigateur *ou* inspecteur officiel; (*b*) détective privé, limier *m*.
snoop[2] [snuːp] (**to**), *F:* fureter, fouiner, fourrer le nez* partout.
snooper [ˈsnuːpər] (*noun*), *F:* = **snoop**[1], **1, 2.**
snoopy [ˈsnuːpi] (*adj.*), *F:* curieux, fouineur, fureteur.
snoot[1] [snuːt] (*noun*), *P:* **1.** nez*, pif *m*. **2.** grimace *f*, grigne *f*.
snoot[2] [snuːt] (**to**), *P:* dédaigner, mépriser, traiter de haut en bas.
snootful [ˈsnuːtful] (*noun*) (*U.S.*), *P:* **to have (had) a s.,** être ivre*, avoir une cuite.
snootiness [ˈsnuːtinis] (*noun*), *F:* morgue *f*, crânage *m*, pose *f*.
snooty [ˈsnuːti] (*adj.*), *F:* hautain, orgueilleux, dédaigneux; gommeux.
snooze[1] [snuːz] (*noun*), *F:* petit somme; **to have a s.,** piquer un roupillon.
snooze[2] [snuːz] (**to**), *F:* dormir*, roupiller, pioncer, dormasser.
snoozer [ˈsnuːzər] (*noun*), *F:* roupilleur *m*, pionceur *m*.
snort[1] [snɔːt] (*noun*), *P:* **1.** = **snorter, 1.** **2.** dose *f* d'une drogue.
snort[2] [snɔːt] (**to**), *P:* = **sniff (to), 1.**
snorter [ˈsnɔːtər] (*noun*). **1.** *P:* = **snifter, 2.** **2.** *F:* qch. qui donne du fil à retordre. **3.** *F:* réponse *f ou* lettre *f* qui assoit; lettre carabinée. *Voir aussi* **ripsnorter.**
snorty [ˈsnɔːti] (*adj.*), *F:* fâché, contrarié, ronchonneur.
snot [snɔt] (*noun*), *P:* **1.** morve *f*, chandelle *f*. **2.** morveux *m*, merdeux *m*.
snot-rag [ˈsnɔt-ræg] (*noun*), *P:* = **snitch-rag.**
snottie [ˈsnɔti] (*noun*), *F:* = **snotty**[2].
snotty[1] [ˈsnɔti] (*adj.*), *P:* **1.** qui a le nez* enchifrené. **2.** prétentieux*, culotté, gonflé. **3.** sale*, salingue. **4.** avare*, radin.
snotty[2] [ˈsnɔti] (*noun*), *F:* aspirant *m* de Marine, aspi *m*.
snotty-nosed [ˈsnɔti-nouzd] (*adj.*), *P:* **1.** morveux. **2.** = **snooty.**
snout [snaut] (*noun*), *P:* **1.** nez*, blaireau *m*. **2.** (*a*) tabac*, perlot *m*; (*b*) cigarette*, sèche *f*; **s. baron,** prisonnier *m* qui vend du tabac aux autres détenus.
snow[1] [snou] (*noun*). **1.** *P:* cocaïne *f* en poudre (*drogues**), neige *f*. **2.** *P:* (*quelquefois*) morphine *f* ou autre narcotique (*drogues**). **3.** *P:* pièce *f ou* article *m* en argent; blanc *m*, blanquette *f*. **4.** *F:* points blancs mobiles sur écran de télévision, neige *f*.
snow[2] [snou] (**to**). **1.** *P:* duper*, berner, mystifier. **2.** *F:* **it's snowing down south,** ta combinaison passe; tu cherches une belle-mère?; *cf.* **Charl(e)y**[2], **2.**
snowball[1] [ˈsnoubɔːl] (*noun*), *P:* **1.** (*U.S.*) (*péj.*) nègre*, bougnoul(l)e *m*. **2. he doesn't stand a s.'s chance in hell,** il n'a pas l'ombre d'une chance. **3.** = **snowbird.**
snowball[2] [ˈsnoubɔːl] (**to**), *F:* faire boule *f* de neige (*dettes, foule, etc.*).
snowbird [ˈsnoubəːd] (*noun*), *P:* drogué*, cocaïnomane *mf*.
snow-dropping [ˈsnou-drɔpiŋ] (*noun*), *P:* vol *m* de linge séchant dans les jardins.
snowed [snoud] (*adj.*). **1.** *P:* drogué* à la cocaïne, enneigé. **2.** *F:* **s. under,** accablé de travail*, abruti.
snow-job [ˈsnou-dʒɔb] (*noun*) (*U.S.*), *F:* flatterie intéressée, pommade *f*; **to give s.o. a s.-j.** = **to shoot s.o. a line (shoot**[2] **(to), 5).**
snowman [ˈsnoumən] (*noun*), *F:* **the Abominable S.,** grand animal inconnu de l'Himalaya, yéti *m*.
snow-white [ˈsnouˈwait] (*adj.*), *F:* innocent, blanc (comme la neige); *cf.* **lily-white.**

* L'astérisque indique que le mot marqué de ce signe figure comme entrée dans le Répertoire.

snuff [snʌf] (*noun*), *F:* **up to s.**, (*a*) à la hauteur, à la coule; (*b*) malin*, dessalé, dégourdi.

snuff it [ˈsnʌfit] (**to**), *P:* mourir*, éteindre sa lampe, avaler sa chique.

snuffles [ˈsnʌflz] (*pl. noun*), *F:* **to have the s.** = **to have the sniffles.**

snuff out [ˈsnʌfˈaut] (**to**), *P:* **1.** = **snuff it** (**to**). **2.** tuer*, zigouiller.

so [sou] (*adv. & conj.*), *F:* **1. s. long!** à bientôt! à tout à l'heure! **2. s. what?** et après?

soak[1] [souk] (*noun*), *P:* **1.** ivrogne*, pionnard *m*, poivrot *m*. **2.** ivrognerie *f*, saoulerie *f*, ribote *f*, cuite *f*.

soak[2] [souk] (**to**). **1.** *P:* boire* beaucoup, pomper, s'ivrogner; **to get soaked,** s'enivrer, avoir une cuite. **2.** *F:* (*a*) faire payer* trop cher, écorcher; (*b*) taxer à haute dose, assaisonner.

soaker [ˈsoukər] (*noun*), *F:* **1.** = **soak**[1], **1. 2.** pluie* forte, averse *f*, bouillon *m*.

so-and-so [ˈsouənsou] (*noun*), *F:* **1. Mr. S.-a.-s., Mrs. S.-a.-s.,** Monsieur un tel, Madame une telle; Monsieur (Madame) Machin(-truc). **2.** (*péj.*) sale mec *m*, peau *f* de vache; **she's a right old s.-a.-s.,** c'est une vraie salope.

soap[1] [soup] (*noun*). **1.** *F:* **(soft) s.,** flatterie *f*, eau bénite. **2.** *P:* argent* de subornation, fric *m* de chantage. **3.** *F:* **no s.!** = **no dice!** (**dice**[1], **1**). **4.** *F:* **s. opera,** feuilleton *m* (*radio ou T.V.*) à l'eau de rose.

soap[2] [soup] (**to**), *P:* = **soft-soap** (**to**).

soapbox [ˈsoupbɔks] (*noun*), *F:* estrade *f* (en plein air pour orateur); **s. orator,** orateur *m* s'adressant au public en plein air; orateur de carrefour.

soapy [ˈsoupi] (*adj.*), *F:* doucereux, mielleux, patelin.

s.o.b. [ˈesouˈbiː] (*abbr.*), *P:* **1.** = **shit or bust** (**shit**[4] (**to**), **3**). **2.**) = **son-of-a-bitch**

sob-act [ˈsɔbækt] (*noun*, *P:* **to put on a.** (*or* **the**) **s.-a.,** pleurer des larmes *f.pl.* de crocodile.

sobs [sɔbz] (*pl. noun*), *P:* livres *f.pl.* sterling.

sob-sister [ˈsɔb-sistər] (*noun*) (*mainly U.S.*), *F:* **1.** journaliste spécialisée dans le mélodrame. **2.** actrice *f* qui joue le mélo(drame), chialeuse *f*.

sob-story [ˈsɔb-stɔːri] (*noun*), *F:* histoire larmoyante. (*ou* au jus de mirettes).

sob-stuff [ˈsɔb-stʌf] (*noun*), *F:* sensiblerie *f*, eau *f* de guimauve.

soccer [ˈsɔkər] (*noun*), *F:* foot(ball) *m*.

sock[1] [sɔk] (*noun*). **1.** *P:* **put a s. in it!** passe la main! la ferme! **2.** *P:* coup* de poing, gifle *f*, taloche *f*. **3.** *F:* **to pull one's socks up,** se remuer, remonter la pente, faire mieux que ça. *Voir aussi* **bobbysock; wet**[1], **6.**

sock[2] [sɔk] (**to**), *P:* **1.** donner un coup* à (qn), flanquer une raclée à (qn). **2. s. it to me!** (*a*) passe-moi ça! flanque-moi ça!; (*b*) fais-moi la cour! fais-moi du plat!; (*c*) continue, tu te débrouilles bien!

sod[1] [sɔd] (*noun*), *V:* **1.** pédéraste*, pédé *m*. **2. poor s.!** pauvre con! pauvre enculé!; **silly s.!** espèce d'andouille!; **rotten s.!** peau *f* de vache! **3. I don't give** (*or* **care**) **a s.,** je m'en fous (comme de l'an quarante *ou* de ma première chemise). *Voir aussi* **odds, 1.**

sod[2] [sɔd] (**to**), *V:* **1.** enculer, empaffer (*coit* anal, 1*). **2. s. you!** va te faire foutre!; **s. it!** merde alors! bordel de Dieu!

sod about (*or* **around**) [ˈsɔdəˈbaut, ˈsɔdəˈraund] (**to**), *V:* = **bugger about** (**to**).

sod-all [ˈsɔdˈɔːl] (*noun*), *V:* = **bugger-all.**

sod off [ˈsɔdˈɔf] (**to**), *V:* = **bugger off** (**to**).

sod up [ˈsɔdˈʌp] (**to**), *V:* = **bugger up** (**to**).

soft[1] [sɔft] (*adj.*), *F:* **1.** (*a*) crédule, sentimental; (*b*) bête*, niais, nigaud; **s. in the head,** faible d'esprit; (*c*) poltron*, lâche, caneur. **2. a s. job,** un filon, un bon fromage, une planque; **to have a s. time** (**of it**), se la couler douce; *cf.* **berth, 2; cushy. 3. to be s. on s.o.,** être épris (*ou* entiché) de qn. **4. s. drugs,** drogues (toxiques) mineures; *cf.* **hard**[1], **2. 5. s. sell,** publicité discrète; *cf.* **hard**[1], **5.** *Voir aussi* **sawder; soap**[1], **1; spot, 4; touch**[1], **3.**

soft[2] [sɔft] (*adv.*), *F:* **1. don't talk s.!** ne dis pas de bêtises*! **2. to have it s.** = **to have a soft time** (**of it**) (**soft**[1], **2**).

soft-pedal [ˈsɔftˈpedl] (**to**), *F:* y aller doucement, ne pas trop insister, garder le secret, pédaler doux.

soft-soap [ˈsɔftˈsoup] (**to**), *F:* flatter*, passer de la pommade à (qn), pommader, flagorner.

softy [ˈsɔfti] (*noun*), *F:* (*a*) homme mou (*ou* efféminé), hommelette *f*; (*b*) couard

* An asterisk indicates that the word so marked is included as a head-word in the Appendix.

m, lavette *f*; (*c*) personne *f* frêle, mauviette *f*; (*d*) individu sentimental à l'excès.

sold [sould] (*p.p.*): *voir* **sell**[2] **(to)**; *voir aussi* **sold out.**

soldier[1] [ˈsouldʒər] (*noun*). **1.** *P:* = **Billingsgate pheasant (Billingsgate, 2). 2.** *F:* (*a*) cigare* entier (*ou* cigare qu'on fume); (*b*) bouteille *f* de bière *ou* de whisky; **dead s.,** (*a*) mégot* froid; (*b*) = **dead man (dead**[1]**, 2). 3.** *F:* **old s.,** soudard *m*, brisquard *m*; **to come the old s.,** la faire au vieux sergent, poser au vieux brisquard.

soldier[2] [ˈsouldʒər] **(to)**, *P:* **to s. on the job,** renâcler à la besogne, flémarder.

soldier on [ˈsouldʒəˈɔn] **(to)**, *F:* continuer à se maintenir (*ou* se défendre *ou* se débattre).

sold out [ˈsouldˈaut] (*adj.*), *P:* très fatigué*, vanné, crevé.

solid[1] [ˈsɔlid] (*adj.*). **1.** *F:* **five s. hours,** cinq heures pleines; **six s. weeks,** six bonnes semaines. **2.** *P:* (*a*) excellent*, foutral, épatant; (*b*) emballant, époustouflant.

solid[2] [ˈsɔlid] (*adv.*), *F:* **to be in s. with s.o.,** être dans les petits papiers de qn.

solitary [ˈsɔlitəri] (*noun*), *F:* **in s.,** en réclusion *f*, dans les bondes *f.pl.*

some[1] [sʌm] (*adj.*), *F:* **1.** excellent*, formid(able); **she's s. girl!** elle est sensas(s)!; c'est une fille* formidable! **2. s. hope!** quelle illusion!

some[2] [sʌm] (*adv.*), *F:* (*a*) dans une certaine mesure; (*b*) considérablement; **to go s.,** y aller en plein, gazer.

some[3] [sʌm] (*pron.*), *F:* **. . . and then s.,** . . .et le reste, . . .et encore plus.

somebody [ˈsʌmbɔdi, ˈsʌmbədi] (*noun*), *F:* **he's a s.,** c'est vraiment quelqu'un, c'est un personnage; *cf.* **nobody.**

something[1] [ˈsʌmθiŋ] (*adv.*), *P:* très, beaucoup*; **she went off at him s. awful,** elle lui a passé un bon savon; *voir aussi* **chronic**[2].

something[2] [ˈsʌmθiŋ] (*noun*), *F:* **1. that's s. like it!** voilà qui est bien! voilà qui est mieux! **2. isn't that s.! that really is s.!** n'est-ce pas super!

song [sɔŋ] (*noun*). **1.** *F:* **to make a s. (and dance) about sth.,** faire des histoires (*ou* des tas d'histoires) au sujet de qch. **2.** *F:* **to buy sth. for a s.,** acheter qch. pour un morceau (*ou* une bouchée) de pain. **3.** *P:* aveu *m*, déboutonnage *m*, accouchage *m*. *Voir aussi* **torch-song.**

sonk [sɔŋk] (*noun*) (*Austr.*), *P:* pédéraste*, lope *f*.

sonny (Jim) [ˈsʌni(ˈdʒim)] (*noun*), *F:* (mon) petit, (mon) fiston.

son-of-a-bitch [ˈsʌnəvəˈbitʃ] (*noun*), *P:* **1.** vaurien*, gredin *m*, fils *m* de pute. **2.** embêtation *f*, emmerdement *m*.

soppiness [ˈsɔpinis] (*noun*), *F:* mollesse *f*, fadasserie *f*.

soppy [ˈsɔpi] (*adj.*), *F:* (*a*) bête*, baluchard; **s. ha'porth!** gros bêta!; *cf.* **date**[1]**, 1**; (*b*) mou, fadasse.

sore [sɔːr] (*adj.*), *F:* **1.** en colère*, fâché, à cran; **to get s. with s.o.,** en vouloir à qn. **2. to be like a bear with a s. head,** être d'une humeur massacrante. *Voir aussi* **eye, 15; thumb, 4.**

sorehead [ˈsɔːhed] (*noun*), *P:* rancunier *m*, qn plein de ressentiment.

sort [sɔːt] (*noun*). **1.** *F:* **a good s.,** un brave homme*, un chic type. **2.** *F:* **out of sorts,** patraque, pas dans son assiette. **3.** *P:* (*a*) fille*, môme *f*; (*b*) petite amie, nénette *f*.

sort of [ˈsɔːtəv] (*adv.*), *F:* = **kind of.**

sort out [ˈsɔːtˈaut] **(to)**, *F:* **to s. s.o. o.,** remettre qn à sa place.

so-so [ˈsousou] (*adv.*), *F:* couci-couça, entre les deux.

soul [soul] (*noun*), *F:* **poor s.!** pauvre créature! pauvre bonhomme! pauvre bonne femme!; **she's a good s.,** c'est une bien brave femme, c'est une bonne pâte.

soul-brother [ˈsoul-brʌðər] (*noun*), *F:* nègre* (parlant d'un autre nègre).

soulful [ˈsoulful] (*adj.*), *F:* (*jazz*) = **funky, 3.**

sound off [ˈsaundˈɔf] **(to)**, *F:* **to s. o. at s.o.,** réprimander* qn, engueuler qn.

soup [suːp] (*noun*). **1.** *F:* **in the s.,** dans le pétrin (*ou* la panade). **2.** *P:* (*a*) nitroglycérine *f* (pour faire sauter les coffres-forts), jus *m*; (*b*) dynamite *f*. **3.** *F:* puissance *f* d'un moteur, jus *m*; *cf.* **soup up (to), (*a*).** *Voir aussi* **duck**[1]**, 13.**

soup up [ˈsuːpˈʌp] **(to)**, *F:* (*a*) augmenter considérablement la puissance du moteur d'une auto (en vue d'une course), gonfler; **a souped-up job,** une affaire survoltée; (*b*) exagérer*, épicer (une publicité, *etc.*).

* L'astérisque indique que le mot marqué de ce signe figure comme entrée dans le Répertoire.

soupy [ˈsuːpi] (*adj.*), *F:* (*a*) sentimental, à l'eau de rose; (*b*) (voix) larmoyante.
sourpuss [ˈsauəpus] (*noun*), *F:* individu* morose (*ou* revêche *ou* renfrogné), bonnet *m* de nuit.
souse[1] [saus] (*noun*), *P:* **1.** = **sozzler. 2.** ivresse*, cuite *f*, saoulerie *f*.
souse[2] [saus] (**to**), *P:* = **sozzle (to).**
soused [saust] (*adj.*), *P:* = **sozzled.**
southpaw [ˈsauθpɔː] (*noun*), *F:* gaucher *m*.
sozzle [ˈsɔzl] (**to**), *P:* **1.** boire* beaucoup, picoler. **2.** s'enivrer, se charger.
sozzled [ˈsɔzld] (*adj.*), *P:* ivre*, saoul.
sozzler [ˈsɔzlər] (*noun*), *P:* ivrogne*, pionnard *m*, saoulard *m*.
sozzling [ˈsɔzliŋ] (*noun*), *P:* ivresse*, poivrade *f*.
spade [speid] (*noun*). **1.** *P:* (*péj.*) nègre*, bougnoul(l)e *m*. **2.** *F:* **to call a s. a s.,** appeler les choses par leur nom, appeler un chat un chat.
spank along [ˈspæŋkəˈlɔŋ] (**to**), *F:* aller vite*, filer, foncer, gazer.
spanker [ˈspæŋkər] (*noun*), *F:* **1.** beau spécimen, qch. d'épatant (*ou* de super). **2.** cheval* rapide, crack *m*.
spanking[1] [ˈspæŋkiŋ] (*adj.*), *F:* **1.** rapide, à pleins tubes. **2.** grand, énorme, maousse. **3.** excellent*, épatant.
spanking[2] [ˈspæŋkiŋ] (*adv.*), *F:* **s. new,** flambant neuf.
spanner [ˈspænər] (*noun*), *F:* **to put** (*or* **throw**) **a s. in the works,** mettre des bâtons dans les roues.
spare[1] [ˈspɛər] (*adj.*), *F:* **1.** (*a*) **to go s.,** être furieux, fulminer, pétarder; (*b*) **to drive s.o. s.,** rendre qn furieux, faire marronner qn. **2. s. tyre** (*U.S.:* **tire**), bourrelet *m* de graisse, pneu *m* Michelin.
spare[2] [ˈspɛər] (*noun*), *P:* **to have a bit of s. = to have a bit on the side (side, 2).**
spare-part [ˈspɛəˈpɑːt] (*attrib. adj.*), *F:* **s.-p. surgery,** chirurgie *f* de greffage.
spark [spɑːk] (**to**) (*Austr.*), *P:* = **screw**[2] **(to), 5.**
sparkle plenty [ˈspɑːklˈplenti] (*noun*), *P:* amphétamine *f* (*drogues**).
sparklers [ˈspɑːkləz] (*pl. noun*), *F:* diamants*, diames *m.pl.*
sparks [spɑːks] (*noun*), *F:* opérateur *m* de TSF, radio *m* (*bateaux, avions*).
sparring-partner [ˈspɑːriŋpɑːtnər] (*noun*), *F:* épouse*, ma (chère) moitié.
sparrow-fart [ˈspærou-fɑːt] (*noun*), *P:* **at s.-f.,** aux aurores, dès potron-ja(c)quet, dès potron-minet.
spat [spæt] (*noun*), *F:* **1.** bout filtré (d'une cigarette). **2.** (*U.S.*) petite querelle*, bisbille *f*.
speakeasy [ˈspiːk-iːzi] (*noun*) (*U.S.*), *F:* bar clandestin.
spec [spek] (*noun*) (*abbr.* = *speculation*), *F:* **on s.,** à tout hasard. *Voir aussi* **specs.**
specimen [ˈspesimən, ˈspesimin] (*noun*), *F:* individu*, type *m*; **an odd** (*or* **a queer**) **s.,** un drôle de numéro (*ou* de client *ou* d'oiseau).
specs [speks] (*pl. noun*) (*abbr.* = *spectacles*), *F:* lunettes*, berniches *f.pl.*
speed [spiːd] (*noun*). **1.** *P:* amphétamine *f* (*drogues**), speed *m*. **2.** (*U.S.*) *P:* hédoniste *mf*. **3.** *F:* **it's not my s. = it's not my scene (scene, 7).**
speedball [ˈspiːdbɔːl] (*noun*), *P:* = **goofball, 3, 4, 5.**
speed-cop [ˈspiːdkɔp] (*noun*), *F:* motard *m*.
speed-hog [ˈspiːdhɔg] (*noun*), *F:* chauffard *m*.
speed-merchant [ˈspiːdməːtʃənt] (*noun*), *F:* passionné *m* de la vitesse, fou *m* du volant.
speed-up [ˈspiːdʌp] (*noun*), *F:* allure accélérée.
spellbinder [ˈspel-baindər] (*noun*), *F:* orateur entraînant (*ou* fascinant).
spell out [ˈspelˈaut] (**to**), *F:* expliquer dans le langage le plus simple, comme a, b, c.
spiderman [ˈspaidəmæn] (*noun*), *F:* ouvrier *m* qui travaille au sommet des édifices, homme-mouche *m*.
spiel[1] [spiːl, ʃpiːl] (*noun*), *F:* boniment *m*, baratin *m*.
spiel[2] [spiːl, ʃpiːl] (**to**), *F:* avoir du bagou(t); baratiner, pérorer.
spieler [ˈspiːlər, ˈʃpiːlər] (*noun*). **1.** *P:* tricheur* (aux cartes), bonneteur *m*. **2.** *P:* escroc*, arnaqueur *m*. **3.** *P:* tripot *m* de jeux. **4.** *P:* embobineur *m*. **5.** *F:* beau parleur, baratineur *m*, bonimenteur *m*.
spiel off [ˈspiːlˈɔf, ˈʃpiːlˈɔf] (**to**), *F:* **to s. o. a whole list of names,** débiter (*ou* dégoiser) toute une liste de noms.
spiffing [ˈspifiŋ] (*adj.*), *F:* ravissant, charmant, délicieux.

* An asterisk indicates that the word so marked is included as a head-word in the Appendix.

spifflicate [ˈspiflikeit] (**to**), *F:* écraser, aplatir, fracasser, démolir, écrabouiller (un adversaire).

spifflicated [ˈspiflikeitid] (*adj.*), *P:* ivre*, rétamé.

spike[1] [spaik] (*noun*), *P:* **1.** aiguille *f* hypodermique (pour piqûre de drogues). **2. to get** (*or* **cop**) **the s.**, se mettre en colère*, prendre la mouche.

spike[2] [spaik] (**to**). **1.** *P:* injecter (des drogues), piquouser, shooter. **2.** *F:* **to s. a drink,** ajouter de l'alcool* à une boisson non alcoolisée; **to s. coffee with cognac,** corser du café avec du cognac. **3.** *F:* **to s. s.o.'s guns,** contrarier, contrecarrer qn; **I spiked his guns for him,** je lui ai damé le pion.

spiked [spaikt] (*adj.*), *P:* drogué*, défoncé, high.

spiky [ˈspaiki] (*adj.*), *F:* susceptible, chatouilleux.

spin [spin] (*noun*), *F:* **1. to be in a flat s.,** être paniqué (*ou* affolé). **2. to go for a s.,** aller se balader (en auto), aller faire une randonnée. **3.** station *f* de taxis. **4. to give sth. a s.,** prendre qch. à l'essai. *Voir aussi* **tail-spin.**

spin-off [ˈspinɔf] (*noun*), *F:* produit(s) *m.*(*pl.*) secondaire(s); dérivé(s) *m.*(*pl.*).

spit [spit] (*noun*). **1.** *F:* **s. and polish,** astiquage *m*, fourbissage *m*; **to give sth. a s. and polish,** faire reluire qch., astiquer qch. **2.** *P:* **s. and drag** (*R.S.* = *fag*), cigarette*. *Voir aussi* **dead**[1]**, 6.**

spit-curl [ˈspitkəːl] (*noun*), *F:* accroche-cœur *m*.

spit out [ˈspitˈaut] (**to**), *F:* **to s. it o.,** dire, accoucher, vider son sac.

spiv [spiv] (*noun*), *F:* trafiquant *m*, chevalier *m* d'industrie. *Voir aussi* **metal-spiv.**

spivvy [ˈspivi] (*adj.*), *F:* louche, parasite.

splash[1] [splæʃ] (*noun*), *F:* **1. to make a (big) s.,** (*a*) faire sensation, jeter du jus; (*b*) = **splash out** (**to**). **2.** étalage *m*, déploiement *m*. **3.** jet *m* de siphon; **a whisky and s.,** un whisky-soda.

splash[2] [splæʃ] (**to**), *F:* **1.** annoncer en grande manchette. **2. to s. one's money about** = **splash out** (**to**). *Voir aussi* **boot, 7.**

splash out [ˈsplæʃˈaut] (**to**), *F:* dépenser* sans compter, claquer du fric.

splay [splei] (*noun*), *P:* marijuana *f* (*drogues**).

splendiferous [splenˈdifərəs] (*adj.*), *F:* splendide, rutilant.

spliced [splaist] (*p.p. & adj.*), *F:* **to get s.,** se marier, s'antifler.

spliff [splif] (*noun*), *P:* cigarette* de marijuana (*drogues**), stick *m*.

split[1] [split] (*noun*). **1.** *F:* = **splitter, 1. 2.** *P:* détective *m*, condé *m*. **3.** *P:* part *f* (de butin), gratte *f*. **4.** *P:* allumette *f*, bûche *f*. **5.** *F:* (*a*) demi-bouteille *f* d'eau gazeuse; (*b*) demi-verre *m* de liqueur.

split[2] [split] (**to**). **1.** *F:* (*a*) vendre la mèche; (*b*) **to s. on s.o.,** dénoncer*, cafarder, vendre, donner qn. **2.** *P:* partager (bénéfices, butin, *etc.*), faire le fade. **3.** *P:* = **split out** (**to**), (*a*), (*b*). **4.** *F:* **my head is splitting,** j'ai un mal de tête fou. *Voir aussi* **side, 3.**

split-arse [ˈsplitɑːs] (*adv.*), *P:* **to run s.-a.,** courir avec le feu au derrière.

split out [ˈsplitˈaut] (**to**), *P:* (*a*) partir*, ficher le camp; (*b*) s'enfuir*, se carapater, mettre les bouts.

splitter [ˈsplitər] (*noun*), *F:* **1.** dénonciateur*, cafard *m*, donneur *m*. **2.** mal *m* de tête fou.

split-up [ˈsplitʌp] (*noun*), *F:* **1.** querelle*, brisure *f*. **2.** divorce *m*, séparation légale.

split up [ˈsplitˈʌp] (**to**), *F:* **1.** rompre avec qn. **2.** divorcer, se démaquer.

splodge[1] [splɔdʒ] (*noun*), *F:* tache *f* (de couleur, *etc.*).

splodge[2] [splɔdʒ] (**to**), *F:* flanquer, asperger.

sploff [splɔf] (*noun*), *P:* = **spliff.**

sploshed [splɔʃt] (*adj.*), *P:* = **sloshed.**

splurge[1] [spləːdʒ] (*noun*), *F:* esbrouf(f)e *f*; démonstration bruyante; **to make a s.** = **splurge**[2] (**to**).

splurge[2] [spləːdʒ] (**to**), *F:* faire de l'esbrouf(f)e *f* (*ou* de l'épate *f ou* de la chique).

spon [spɔn] (*noun*), *P:* = **spondulic(k)s.**

spondulic(k)s [spɔnˈdjuːliks] (*pl. noun*), *P:* argent*, fric *m*, oseille *f*.

sponge[1] [spʌndʒ] (*noun*), *F:* = **sponger.** *Voir aussi* **throw in** (**to**).

sponge[2] [spʌndʒ] (**to**), *F:* (*a*) écornifler, écumer les marmites; (*b*) **to s. a drink,** se faire offrir une tournée; **to s. on s.o.,** vivre aux dépens de qn.

sponger [ˈspʌndʒər] (*noun*), *F:* écornifleur *m*, tapeur *m*, torpille *f*.

* L'astérisque indique que le mot marqué de ce signe figure comme entrée dans le Répertoire.

sponging [ˈspʌndʒiŋ] (*noun*), *F:* écornifiage *m*.

spoof[1] [spuːf] (*noun*), *F:* plaisanterie *f*, blague *f*.

spoof[2] [spuːf] (**to**). **1.** (*U.S.*) *F:* dire des bêtises*, sortir des sornettes *f.pl.* **2.** *P:* flatter*, pommader. **3.** *F:* tromper*, filouter, empiler; **you've been spoofed,** on vous a eu. **4.** *F:* duper*, faire marcher; mettre en boîte.

spook[1] [spuːk] (*noun*), *F:* fantôme *m*, revenant *m*, apparition *f*.

spook[2] [spuːk] (**to**), *F:* faire peur* à (qn), ficher la frousse à (qn).

spooky [ˈspuːki] (*adj.*), *F:* (*a*) hanté; (*b*) sinistre, étrange, surnaturel.

spoon [spuːn] (**to**), *F:* se faire des mamours *m.pl.* (*ou* des cajoleries *f.pl.*).

spooner [ˈspuːnər] (*noun*), *F:* = **spoon(e)y**[2].

spoon(e)y[1] [ˈspuːni] (*adj.*), *F:* qui fait des mamours *m.pl.*, cajoleur, caressant.

spoon(e)y[2] [ˈspuːni] (*noun*), *F:* cajoleur *m*, peloteur *m*.

sport [spɔːt] (*noun*). **1.** *F:* **a (good) s.,** individu* sympathique, bon type, bonne nature; **be a s.!** sois chic! **2.** *P:* fille*, petite amie. **3. hello, (old) s.!** salut, mon pote!

sporting [ˈspɔːtiŋ] (*adj.*). **1.** *F:* qui a bon caractère, d'un bon naturel. **2.** *P:* **s. woman,** femme facile, Marie-couche-toi-là.

sporty [ˈspɔːti] (*adj.*), *F:* **1.** sportif. **2. the s. set,** les (bons) viveurs. **3.** (vêtement, *etc.*) de couleurs criardes.

spot [spɔt] (*noun*). **1.** *F:* **to be in a (bit of a) s.,** être dans une situation difficile, être dans le pétrin. **2.** *F:* **to get into a s. of bother,** avoir des ennuis *m.pl.*, être dans de mauvais draps. **3.** *F:* **to knock spots off s.o.,** exceller sur qn, rendre des points à qn, battre qn à plate(s) couture(s). **4.** *F:* **to have a soft s. for s.o., sth.,** avoir un faible pour qn, qch. **5.** *F:* projecteur *m* (de lumière). **6.** *P:* cinq ans *f.pl.* de prison*, gerbement *m* de cinq longes *f.pl.* **7.** *F:* **a s.,** un (petit) peu*; **a s. of whisky,** un petit coup de whisky; **how about a s. of lunch?** si nous allions déjeuner? **8.** *F:* **on the s.,** (*a*) en danger, sur la corde raide; (*b*) mis à tâche; (*c*) alerte, vif, éveillé, actif; (*d*) immédiatement, sur-le-champ; **to put s.o. on the s.,** (*a*) *P:* assassiner* qn, descendre qn; (*b*) *F:* mettre qn dans une situation difficile, handicaper qn. **9.** *F:* (*T.V.*) message *m* publicitaire. **10.** *F:* **s. below:** *voir* **bingo** (**89**). *Voir aussi* **five-spot; highspots; hot, 23; Johnny-on-the-spot; night-spot; ten-spot.**

spotlight [ˈspɔtlait] (**to**), *F:* mettre en vedette (*ou* en relief), souligner.

spot-on [ˈspɔtˈɔn] (*adj.*), *F:* dans le mille, qui fait mouche.

spout[1] [spaut] (*noun*), *P:* **1. up the s.,** en gage, chez ma tante. **2. down the s.,** perdu, fichu, foutu. **3. to put a girl up the s.,** rendre une fille enceinte*, mettre une fille en cloque.

spout[2] [spaut] (**to**), *F:* dégoiser, déblatérer, débiter.

spread [spred] (*noun*), *F:* **1.** repas copieux, gueuleton *m*. **2. middle-age(d) s.,** l'embonpoint *m* de la maturité, pneu *m* Michelin de la quarantaine.

spring [spriŋ] (**to**). **1.** (*U.S.*) *P:* faire libérer (qn) de prison*, cautionner. **2.** *P:* faire échapper (qn) de prison*, faire larguer (qn). **3.** *F:* annoncer à l'improviste, révéler à brûle-pourpoint. **4.** *F:* **where did you s. from?** d'où sortez-vous? *Voir aussi* **leak**[1], **1.**

sprog [sprɔg] (*noun*), *P:* **1.** recrue *f*, conscrit *m*, bleu *m*. **2.** enfant*, mioche *mf*, moutard *m*.

sprout [spraut] (**to**), *F:* **to s. wings,** (*a*) faire une bonne action, se faire pousser des ailes; (*b*) mourir*, aller au paradis.

sprung [sprʌng] (*adj.*) (*mainly U.S.*), *F:* ivre*, raide, rondibé; *cf.* **half-sprung.**

spud [spʌd] (*noun*), *F:* **s. (Murphy),** pomme *f* de terre, patate *f*.

spud-basher [ˈspʌdbæʃər] (*noun*), *F:* (*mil.*) éplucheur *m* de pommes de terre.

spud-bashing [ˈspʌdbæʃiŋ] (*noun*), *F:* (*mil.*) corvée *f* de patates, pluches *f.pl.*

spug [spʌg], **spuggy** [ˈspʌgi] (*noun*), *F:* moineau *m*, piaf *m*.

spunk [spʌŋk] (*noun*). **1.** *V:* sperme*, jus *m*. **2.** *P:* courage *m*, cran *m*, estomac *m*. **3.** *P:* **to put fresh s. into sth.,** ravigoter qch. **4.** (*U.S.*) *P:* colère *f*, emportement *m*, soupe *f* au lait.

spunkless [ˈspʌŋklis] (*adj.*), *P:* **1.** amorphe, larveux. **2.** poltron, froussard.

* An asterisk indicates that the word so marked is included as a head-word in the Appendix.

spunky [ˈspʌŋki] (*adj.*), *F:* courageux*, qui en a dans le bide.

spur [spəːr] (**to**) (*Austr.*), *F:* contrecarrer, mettre des bâtons dans les roues de (qn).

spurge [spəːdʒ] (*noun*) (*Austr.*), *P:* pédéraste*, pédalo *m.*

squad-car [ˈskwɔdkɑːr] (*noun*), *F:* car* de police, porte-poulaille *m.*

squaddie, squaddy [ˈskwɔdi] (*noun*), *F:* (*mil.*) (*a*) recrue *f*, conscrit *m* de l'escouade, bleu *m*, blaireau *m*; (*b*) soldat*, bidasse *m.*

square[1] [skwɛər] (*adj.*). **1.** *F:* **a s. deal,** une affaire* honnête, un coup régulier. **2.** *F:* **a s. meal,** un bon repas. **3.** *F:* **to be all s.,** être quitte, être à égalité, être réglo. **4.** *F:* (*a*) vieux jeu, croulant, périmé; (*b*) honnête, régulier, réglo. **5.** *P:* sexuellement normal; *cf.* **straight**[1], **2. 6.** *F:* **to get s. with s.o.,** (*a*) se venger de qn; (*b*) être quitte envers qn. **7.** *F:* **to be a s. peg in a round hole,** être inapte à qch. *Voir aussi* **fair**[1], **2.**

square[2] [skwɛər] (*noun*), *F:* **1. to be back to s. one,** repartir à zéro. **2.** (*a*) bourgeois démodé croulant *m*; **he's a s.,** il est tout à fait vieux jeu; (*b*) individu* honnête (*ou* réglo). **3. on the s.,** droit, honnête, comme il faut.

square[3] [skwɛər] (**to**), *F:* (*a*) suborner, soudoyer, acheter; (*b*) obtenir la complicité de (qn). *Voir aussi* **rap**[1], **2.**

square-bash [ˈskwɛə-bæʃ] (**to**), *F:* faire l'exercice *m* (militaire).

square-basher [ˈskwɛə-bæʃər] (*noun*), *F:* soldat* à l'exercice.

square-bashing [ˈskwɛə-bæʃiŋ] (*noun*), *F:* exercices *m.pl.* (*ou* manœuvres *f.pl.*) militaires; l'exercice *m.*

squarehead [ˈskwɛəhed] (*noun*), *P:* **1.** Allemand*, boche *m.* **2.** (*Austr.*) criminel *m* en liberté.

square off [ˈskwɛərˈɔf] (**to**) (*Austr.*), *P:* se tirer d'un mauvais pas.

squaresville [ˈskwɛəzvil] (*noun*), *P:* société conformiste et bourgeoise.

square up [ˈskwɛərˈʌp] (**to**), *F:* **1.** être prêt à se battre, se mettre en quarante. **2. to s. u. to the facts,** faire face à la réalité. **3.** régler une affaire avec qn.

square-wheeler [ˈskwɛəˈ(h)wiːlər] (*noun*), *P:* = **palm-tree**; *cf.* **bottler.**

squarie [ˈskwɛəri] (*noun*) (*Austr.*), *P:* = **squarehead, 2.** *Voir aussi* **half-squarie.**

squash[1] [skwɔʃ] (*noun*), *F:* réunion pleine de monde, cohue *f.*

squash[2] [skwɔʃ] (**to**), *F:* **1.** faire taire*, la faire boucler, rembarrer. **2.** vaincre, battre à plate(s) couture(s), tailler en pièces.

squawk[1] [skwɔːk] (*noun*), *P:* **1.** pétition *f* (à un directeur de prison, *etc.*). **2.** appel *m* d'une condamnation, rappel *m.* **3.** plainte *f*, réclamation *f.*

squawk[2] [skwɔːk] (**to**), *P:* **1.** faire des aveux *m.pl.*, confesser (à la police). **2.** se plaindre, rouspéter, ronchonner, rouscailler.

squawker [ˈskwɔːkər] (*noun*), *P:* rouspéteur *m*, ronchonneur *m.*

squeak[1] [skwiːk] (*noun*). **1.** *P:* = **squeal**[1]. **2.** *P:* = **squealer, 1, 3. 3.** *F:* **to have a narrow s.,** l'échapper belle, revenir de loin. **4.** *F:* **I don't want to hear another s. out of you,** je ne veux pas entendre le moindre murmure. *Voir aussi* **bubble-and-squeak; pip-squeak**[2].

squeak[2] [skwiːk] (**to**), *P:* = **squeal**[2] (**to**), **1, 2.**

squeaker [ˈskwiːkər] (*noun*), *P:* **1.** = **grasser. 2.** résultat serré, aboutissement *m* à un fil.

squeal[1] [skwiːl] (*noun*), *P:* plainte *f* (à la police); **to put the s. in,** moutonner, cafarder.

squeal[2] [skwiːl] (**to**), *P:* **1.** avouer*, manger le morceau, accoucher, vider son sac. **2.** moucharder, vendre (*ou* éventer) la mèche; **to s. on s.o.,** dénoncer* qn, balancer, cafarder, donner qn.

squealer [ˈskwiːlər] (*noun*), *P:* **1.** = **grasser. 2.** = **holler-wag(g)on. 3.** rouspéteur *m*, ronchonneur *m.*

squeeze[1] [skwiːz] (*noun*). **1.** *F:* **to put the s. on s.o.,** forcer la main à qn. **2.** *F:* **a tight s.,** (*a*) presse *f*, cohue *f*; (*b*) **it was a tight s.,** on tenait tout juste. **3.** *P:* empreinte *f* d'une clef*, douce *f.* **4.** *P:* **main s.,** épouse*. **5.** *P:* soie *f.*

squeeze[2] [skwiːz] (**to**), *F:* **to s. s.o.** = **to put the squeeze on s.o.** (**squeeze**[1], **1**). *Voir aussi* **lemon, 5.**

squeezebox [ˈskwiːzbɔks] (*noun*), *F:* **1.** concertina *f.* **2.** accordéon *m.*

* L'astérisque indique que le mot marqué de ce signe figure comme entrée dans le Répertoire.

squelch[1] [skweltʃ] (*noun*), *F:* = **squelcher.**

squelch[2] [skweltʃ] (**to**), *F:* faire taire* (qn), river le clou à (qn).

squelcher [ˈskweltʃər] (*noun*), *F:* réplique cinglante, riposte *f* qui vous rive le clou.

squiffy [ˈskwifi] (*adj.*), *F:* **1.** légèrement ivre*, paf. **2.** de travers, biscornu, tordu. **3.** bête*, nigaud.

squint[1] [skwint] (*noun*), *P:* coup *m* d'œil*, coup de châsse; **let's have a s. at it!** fais voir!; **take a s. at that!** zyeute-moi ça!

squint[2] [skwint] (**to**), *P:* (*a*) regarder*, jeter un coup d'œil*, bigler; (*b*) **to s. at sth.,** regarder* qch. de côté (*ou* furtivement); bigler, zyeuter qch.

squirt [skwəːt] (*noun*), *P:* **1.** (*a*) freluquet *m*, merdaillon *m*; (*b*) rapiat *m*, rat *m*. **2.** rafale *f* de mitraillette. **3. to have a s.,** uriner*, jeter de la lance.

squish [skwiʃ] (*noun*). **1.** *F:* boue *f*, bouillabaisse *f*, pulpe *f*. **2.** *P:* marmelade *f* d'orange.

squishy [ˈskwiʃi] (*adj.*), *F:* détrempé, pulpeux, bourbeux.

squit [skwit] (*noun*), *P:* **1.** = **squirt, 1,** (*a*), (*b*). **2.** (*a*) camelote *f*, saleté *f*; (*b*) bêtises*, conneries *f.pl.*, balivernes *f.pl.* **3.** (*pl.*) diarrhée*, foirade *f*.

squitters [ˈskwitəz] (*pl. noun*), *P:* **1.** = **squit, 3. 2. to have the s.,** avoir peur*, avoir les foies *m.pl.*

squitty [skwiti] (*adj.*), *P:* connard, loquedu.

stab [stæb] (*noun*), *F:* **to have a s. (at sth.),** faire un essai, tenter le coup.

stable-companion [ˈsteiblkəmˈpænjən] (*noun*), *F:* membre *m* d'une même société, bande*, *etc.*

stack [stæk] (*noun*). **1.** *F:* (*a*) **to have a s.** (*or* **stacks**) **of money,** être très riche*, être cousu d'or, avoir le sac; (*b*) **to have a s.** (*or* **stacks**) **of work,** avoir beaucoup de travail*, avoir du pain sur la planche. **2.** *P:* **to blow one's s.** = **to blow one's top** (**top**[1], **2**). **3.** *F:* **twin stacks,** double tuyau *m* d'échappement (*auto*). **4.** *P:* quantité *f* de cigarettes de marijuana.

stacked [stækt] (*adj.*) = **well-stacked, 1, 2.**

stag[1] [stæg] (*noun*), *F:* **1.** célibataire *m*, vieux garçon; **s. party,** réunion *f ou* dîner *m* d'hommes seuls. **2.** (*Bourse*) loup *m*.

stag[2] [stæg] (**to**). **1.** *P:* coïter* avec (une femme), piner. **2.** *F:* **to s. it,** se rendre seul à une réunion d'hommes (sans être accompagné de sa femme), sortir en garçon.

stager [ˈsteidʒər] (*noun*), *F:* **an old s.,** un vieux routier, un vieux de la vieille.

staggers [ˈstægəz] (*pl. noun*), *F:* **to have the s.,** chanceler, tituber, être zigzag.

stalk [stɔːk] (*noun*), *P:* pénis*, queue *f*. *Voir aussi* **corn-stalk.**

stamping-ground [ˈstæmpiŋgraund] (*noun*), *F:* lieu *m* que l'on fréquente, coin favori.

stand[1] [stænd] (*noun*). **1.** *F:* **(one-night) s.,** représentation *f* d'un soir (*troupe théâtrale, jazz-band, etc.*). **2.** *P:* **to have a s.,** être en érection*, avoir le bambou; *cf.* **cock-stand. 3.** (*U.S.*) *F:* barre *f* (de témoins).

stand[2] [stænd] (**to**), *F:* **1. to s. s.o. a drink,** offrir un verre (*ou* une tournée) à qn; **I'm standing this one,** c'est ma tournée; *cf.* **sam, 1. 2.** = **stick**[2] **(to), 8.** *Voir aussi* **gaff, 4; racket**[1]**, 3.**

stand for [ˈstændfɔːr] (**to**), *F:* tolérer, supporter.

stand-in [ˈstændin] (*noun*), *F:* délégué *m*, remplaçant *m*.

stand in [ˈstændˈin] (**to**), *F:* **1. to s. i. for s.o.,** être délégué à la place de qn, remplacer qn. **2. to s. i. (well) with s.o.,** être dans les bonnes grâces (*ou* les petits papiers) de qn.

stand off [ˈstændˈɔf] (**to**), *F:* faire chômer (qn), licencier (qn).

stand-offish [ˈstændˈɔfiʃ] (*adj.*), *F:* distant, raide, réservé.

stand-offishness [ˈstændˈɔfiʃnis] (*noun*), *F:* raideur *f*, réserve *f*, morgue *f*.

stand-out [ˈstændaut] (*noun*), *F:* (*personnes*) éminence *f*, sommité *f*; (*choses*) hors-ligne *m*, perle *f*.

stand over [ˈstændˈouvər] (**to**) (*Austr.*), *F:* = **strong-arm**[2] **(to).**

stand up [ˈstændˈʌp] (**to**), *F:* **1.** faire attendre* (qn), faire poireauter (qn). **2.** lâcher (qn), planter là. **3.** tromper*, posséder, refaire (qn). **4. to take it standing up,** ne pas broncher, encaisser le coup.

* An asterisk indicates that the word so marked is included as a head-word in the Appendix.

star [stɑːr] (*noun*), *F:* **1.** **to see stars,** voir trente-six chandelles. **2.** **there's a s. in the east,** votre braguette est déboutonnée; on voit le moteur. *Voir aussi* **superstar.**

stardust [ˈstɑːdʌst] (*noun*). **1.** *F:* illusion *f*, vision *f*. **2.** *P:* = **snow[1], 1.**

stare [stɛər] (**to**), *F:* **it's staring you in the face,** ça vous saute aux yeux.

starkers [ˈstɑːkəz] (*adj.*), *P:* (**Harry**) **s.,** tout nu*, à poil.

starry-eyed [ˈstɑːriˈaid] (*adj.*), *F:* idéaliste, inexpérimenté, ingénu, songe-creux.

stash[1] [stæʃ] (*noun*), *P:* cachette *f*, lieu sûr; **s. man,** homme de carre, carreur *m* (pour des marchandises volées, drogues, *etc.*).

stash[2] [stæʃ] (**to**), *P:* **1.** cacher*, planquer, planquouser. **2.** arrêter, finir, finocher; **s. it!** arrête!

stashed [stæʃt] (*adj.*), *F:* (**well**) **s.,** riche*, plein aux as, galetteux, rupin.

stash away [ˈstæʃəˈwei] (**to**), *P:* **1.** = **stash[2] (to), 1.** **2.** accumuler, amasser, entasser (argent, *etc.*).

state [steit] (*noun*), *F:* **to be in a (bit of a) s.,** être dans tous ses états; **to get into a terrible s.,** (*a*) se mettre dans tous ses états; (*b*) se trouver dans un état lamentable.

statistics [stəˈtistiks] (*pl. noun*), *F:* **vital s.,** les trois mesures essentielles de la femme (poitrine, taille, hanches).

steady[1] [ˈstedi] (*adv.*), *F:* **to go s.,** se fréquenter, sortir ensemble (*fille et garçon*).

steady[2] [ˈstedi] (*noun*), *F:* petit(e) ami(e), l'attitré(e).

steam [stiːm] (*noun*), *F:* **1.** **to let** (*or* **blow**) **off s.,** (*a*) dépenser son superflu d'énergie; (*b*) épancher sa bile. **2.** **to get up s.,** (*a*) rassembler son énergie; se mettre sous pression; (*b*) s'exciter, s'emballer, péter le feu. **3.** **s. radio,** la TSF des familles, la vieille radio.

steamed up [ˈstiːmdˈʌp] (*p.p. & adj.*), *F:* **to get (all) s. u.,** (*a*) = **to get up steam (steam, 2** (*b*)); (*b*) se mettre en colère*, mousser.

steamer [ˈstiːmər] (*noun*), *P:* individu bête*, con *m*, couillon *m*; *cf.* **nit, 1.**

steep [stiːp] (*adj.*), *F:* **1.** trop cher*, exorbitant, excessif, salé. **2.** outrageux, abusif, incroyable; **that's a bit s.!** c'est un peu fort!

steer[1] [stiər] (*noun*) (*U.S.*). **1.** *F:* renseignement*, tuyau *m*; *voir aussi* **bum[1].** **2.** *P:* = **steerer.**

steer[2] [stiər] (**to**), *P:* amorcer les clients (pour tripot, casino, *etc.*).

steerer [ˈstiərər] (*noun*), *P:* rabatteur *m*, racoleur *m* de clients (*bordels, etc.*).

stem [stem] (*noun*), *P:* pipe *f* à opium, chilom *m*.

step[1] [step] (*noun*). **1.** *P:* **up the steps,** renvoyé aux Assises, devant le comptoir. **2.** *F:* **all the steps:** *voir* **bingo (39).** *Voir aussi* **doorstep.**

step[2] [step] (**to**), *F:* **to s. outside,** sortir pour se battre*. *Voir aussi* **gas[2], 2.**

step in [ˈstepˈin] (**to**), *F:* intervenir; s'interposer.

step-up [ˈstepʌp] (*noun*), *F:* promotion *f*, avancement *m*.

step up [ˈstepˈʌp] (**to**), *F:* **1.** **to s. u. the pace,** accélérer le pas, allonger la sauce. **2.** avoir une promotion, monter d'un échelon.

stern [stəːn] (*noun*), *F:* fesses*, postérieur *m*.

stew[1] [stjuː] (*noun*). **1.** *F:* **in a s.,** (*a*) sur des charbons ardents, sur le gril, dans tous ses états; (*b*) (*U.S.*) en colère*, à cran. **2.** *F:* **to work oneself (up) into a s.** = **to work oneself (up) into a lather (lather[1],** (*a*), (*b*)). **3.** (*Austr.*) *P:* = **jacky.**

stew[2] [stjuː] (**to**), *F:* **to s. in one's own juice,** cuire (*ou* mijoter) dans son jus.

stewed [stjuːd] (*adj.*), *P:* ivre*, rétamé; *voir aussi* **gills; half-stewed.**

stick[1] [stik] (*noun*). **1.** *F:* **to give s.o. s.,** réprimander* qn, engueuler qn; **to take a lot of s.,** être pilonné, recevoir une dégelée. **2.** *F:* **to wave the big s.,** faire les gros yeux. **3.** *F:* **over the sticks,** steeplechases *m.pl.*, course *f* d'obstacles. **4.** *F:* **the sticks,** (*a*) la campagne*, le bled, la cambrousse; (*b*) la banlieue. **5.** *P:* **s. (of tea),** cigarette* de marijuana (*drogues**), stick *m*; *cf.* **cancer-stick.** **6.** *P:* pince-monseigneur*, rossignol *m*. **7.** *V:* pénis* en érection*, canne *f*. **8.** (*Austr.*) *F:* = **stickybeak.** **9.** *F:* (*a*) **a queer s.,** un drôle de type, un drôle de zigoto; (*b*) **old s.,** père tartempion; **he's a good old s.,** c'est un brave zigue. *Voir aussi* **bean-stick; drumstick; end, 11; fiddlestick; hype-stick; joystick; kick-stick;**

* L'astérisque indique que le mot marqué de ce signe figure comme entrée dans le Répertoire.

knobstick; shitstick; up⁵ (to), 1; walking-sticks.

stick² [stik] (to). 1. *F:* mettre, placer, coller; **s. it in your pocket,** fourrez-le dans votre poche*. 2. *F:* **to s. at sth.,** persévérer (*ou* s'accrocher) à qch. 3. *P:* **you know where you can s. that,** tu sais où tu peux te le mettre!; *cf.* **arse, 6; flue, 2; gonga; jacksie, 1; jumper, 1; Khyber; shove (to).** 4. *F:* **to get stuck with s.o.,** avoir qn de coller à soi, avoir qn sur le dos. 5. *F:* **to be stuck on s.o.,** être amoureux de qn, être pincé (*ou* entiché) de qn. 6. *F:* **to s. with s.o.,** se cramponner à qn, soutenir qn. 7. *F:* **to make sth. s.,** faire obéir (un ordre, *etc.*). 8. *F:* supporter, endurer, tenir; **I can't s. him (at any price),** je ne peux pas le sentir (*ou* le blairer). 9. *F:* rester; **to s. to one's room,** ne pas sortir de sa chambre. 10. *F:* **to s. to sth.,** garder qch. pour soi. 11. *P:* **to s. one on s.o.,** battre* qn, rosser qn, passer une peignée à qn. *Voir aussi* **bill, 3; gun¹, 5.**

stick around [ˈstikəˈraund] (to), *F:* attendre* sur place, poireauter; **to s. a. the house all day,** traîner dans la maison toute la journée; **s. a.! I'll be back in five minutes,** bouge pas! je reviens dans cinq minutes.

stick down [ˈstikˈdaun] (to), *F:* 1. **s. it d. anywhere,** collez-le n'importe où; *cf.* **stick² (to), 1.** 2. **to s. sth. d. in a notebook,** inscrire qch. sur un carnet.

sticker [ˈstikər] (*noun*), *F:* 1. article *m* invendable, rossignol *m*. 2. travailleur* appliqué, bûcheur *m*. 3. problème *m* difficile, colle *f*, casse-tête *m*. 4. (*d'une personne*) crampon *m*.

stick in [ˈstikˈin] (to). 1. *F:* **to get stuck in,** se cramponner, se maintenir. 2. *V:* **to s. it i.,** coïter*, mettre la cheville dans le trou.

stick-in-the-mud¹ [ˈstikinðəmʌd] (*adj.*), *F:* conservateur, immobiliste, casanier.

stick-in-the-mud² [ˈstikinðəmʌd] (*noun*), *F:* vieux croûton, vieille perruque.

stickjaw [ˈstikdʒɔː] (*noun*), *F:* colle-mâchoires *m* (*caramel, chewing-gum, etc.*).

stick out [ˈstikˈaut] (to), *F:* 1. **to s.o. for higher wages,** demander avec insistance une augmentation de salaire. 2. **to s. it o.,** tenir jusqu'au bout. 3. **she sticks out in all the right places,** elle est bien carrossée. *Voir aussi* **neck¹, 3; thumb, 4.**

stick-up [ˈstikʌp] (*noun*), *F:* = **hold-up, 2.**

stick up [ˈstikˈʌp] (to), *F:* 1. attaquer* *ou* voler à main armée, braquer. 2. **s. 'em u.!** haut les mains! 3. **to s. u. for s.o.,** prendre la défense de qn.

sticky [ˈstiki] (*adj.*), *F:* 1. peu accommodant, difficile. 2. mauvais*, tocard, désagréable. 3. **to have s. fingers,** voler* avec facilité, chiper, avoir de la poix aux mains, ne rien laisser traîner; *cf.* **sticky-fingered.** 4. **to bat (*or* be) on a s. wicket,** agir lorsqu'il y a peu de chance de réussite, marcher sur un terrain glissant; être dans le pétrin, être dans de mauvais draps.

stickybeak [ˈstikibiːk] (*noun*) (*Austr.*), *F:* curieux *m*, fouinard *m*, fouineur *m*.

sticky-fingered [ˈstikiˈfiŋgəd] (*adj.*), *F:* qui a les doigts crochus; *cf.* **sticky, 3.**

stiff¹ [stif] (*adj.*). 1. *P:* mort, raide. 2. *P:* ivre*, raide. 3. *F:* **that's a bit s.!** c'est un peu raide! *Voir aussi* **bill, 2; lip, 2.**

stiff² [stif] (*adv.*), *F:* 1. **to bore s.o. s.,** scier (le dos à) qn. 2. **to be scared s.,** avoir une peur* bleue.

stiff³ [stif] (*noun*), *P:* 1. cadavre*, macchabé(e) *m*. 2. ivrogne*, poivrot *m*. 3. **working stiffs,** travailleurs*, ouvriers*, salariés *m.pl*. 4. lettre *f* de prisonnier passée en fraude. 5. cheval* certain de perdre, fer à repasser. 6. (*U.S.*) clochard*, clodot *m*. *Voir aussi* **big¹, 9; bindle, 3.**

stiff⁴ [stif] (to) (*U.S.*), *P:* voler*, barbot(t)er, carotter.

stiffener [ˈstif(ə)nər] (*noun*), *F:* boisson alcoolisée, apéritif *m*, remontant *m*.

stiffneck [ˈstifnek] (*noun*), *F:* pharisien *m*, individu entiché de sa personne.

sting [stiŋ] (to), *F:* **to s. s.o. for sth.,** faire payer qch. à qn à un prix exorbitant; **to be (*or* get) stung,** attraper (*ou* essuyer) le coup de fusil, se faire écorcher; **he stung me for a quid,** il m'a tapé d'une livre.

stinger [ˈstiŋər] (*noun*), *F:* 1. coup* cinglant, coup raide, torgnole *f*. 2. (*poisson*) (*a*) méduse *f*; (*b*) torpille *f*.

* An asterisk indicates that the word so marked is included as a head-word in the Appendix.

stink[1] [stiŋk] (*noun*). 1. *P:* **to raise** (*or* **kick up**) **a s.**, faire de l'esclandre *m*, rouspéter; **there's going to be a hell of a s.**, il va y avoir du grabuge; **a big s.**, (*a*) chahut *m*, ramdam *m*; (*b*) scandale *m*. 2. (*pl.*) *F:* la chimie. 3. *P:* **to work like s.**, travailler* dur, bûcher, se fouler la rate.
stink[2] [stiŋk] (**to**). 1. *P:* être un vrai salaud; **he** (**positively**) **stinks!** c'est un type infect! 2. *F:* être puant (*ou* infect). 3. *F:* = **smell** (**to**).
stinkador [ˈstiŋkədɔːr], **stinkaduro** [ˈstiŋkəˈd(j)uːrou] (*noun*), *P:* crapulos *m*.
stinkaroo [ˈstiŋkəˈruː] (*noun*), *P:* article *m* de mauvaise qualité, peau *f* de zèbre.
stink-bomb [ˈstiŋkbɔm] (*noun*), *F:* boule puante.
stinker [ˈstiŋkər] (*noun*), *F:* 1. individu* méprisable, sale type *m*. 2. individu* qui sent* mauvais (*ou* qui pue). 3. **to write s.o. a s.**, (*a*) écrire une verte réprimande à qn; (*b*) écrire une lettre carabinée à qn. 4. rhume carabiné. 5. **the algebra paper was a s.**, on a eu une sale (*ou* rosse) composition d'algèbre. 6. cigare* *ou* cigarette* bon marché. 7. **to play a s.**, (*sports*) jouer comme un pied. 8. camelote *f*, navet *m*, toc *m*.
stinking [ˈstiŋkiŋ] (*adj.*). 1. *F:* **s.** (**rich**), **s. with money**, très riche*, plein aux as. 2. *P:* ivre*, blindé. 3. *F:* puant, nauséabond, infect. 4. *F:* **s. weather**, temps *m* de cochon; **a s. cold**, un sale rhume. *Voir aussi* **fish**[1], 2.
stink-list [ˈstiŋk-list] (*noun*), *P:* **to have s.o. on one's s.-l.**, avoir qn dans le nez, ne pas pouvoir encadrer qn; *cf.* **shit-list.**
stinko [stiŋkou] (*adj.*), *P:* = **stinking, 2.**
stinkpot [ˈstiŋkpɔt] (*noun*), *P:* saligaud *m*, salopard *m*.
stir[1] [stəːr] (*noun*), *P:* prison*, bloc *m*, taule *f*; **in s.**, en prison, à l'ombre.
stir[2] [stəːr] (**to**), *F:* **to s. it** = **to stir it up.** *Voir aussi* **stumps.**
stirrer [ˈstəːrər] (*noun*), *F:* agitateur *m*, fomenteur *m* de difficultés.
stir up [ˈstəːˈrʌp] (**to**), *F:* **to s. it u.**, fomenter la dissension, remuer les eaux *f.pl.* troubles.
stodge[1] [stɔdʒ] (*noun*), *F:* 1. aliment bourratif, étouffe-chrétien *m*. 2. qch. de difficile à retenir (*ou* de dur à digérer).
stodge[2] [stɔdʒ] (**to**), *F:* se goinfrer, se caler les joues *f.pl.*, s'empiffrer.
stoke up [ˈstoukˈʌp] (**to**), *F:* manger* de bon cœur, bouffer.
stomach [ˈstʌmək] (**to**), *F:* endurer, supporter, tolérer, digérer.
stomp[1] [stɔmp] (*noun*), *F:* (*jazz*) tempo assez vif.
stomp[2] [stɔmp] (**to**). 1. *F:* (*jazz*) jouer d'un tempo assez vif. 2. *P:* battre*, passer une raclée à (qn).
stone-cold [ˈstounˈkould] (*adv.*), *F:* **I've got him s.-c.**, je le tiens (à ma merci). *Voir aussi* **cold**[1], 1.
stoned [stound] (*adj.*), *P:* (*a*) ivre*, raide; (*b*) drogué*, camé, chargé.
stone-ginger [ˈstounˈdʒindʒər] (*noun*), *P:* certitude *f*, du tout cuit.
stones [stounz] (*pl. noun*), *P:* testicules*, burettes *f.pl.*
stonewall [ˈstounˈwɔːl] (**to**), *F:* donner des réponses évasives; faire de l'obstruction *f*.
stonkered [ˈstɔŋkəd] (*adj.*), *P:* = **stinking, 2.**
stony [ˈstouni] (*adj.*), *F:* **s.** (**broke**), archi-pauvre*, à sec, dans la dèche.
stooge[1] [stuːdʒ] (*noun*) (*often péj.*). 1. *F:* délégué *m*, remplaçant *m*, nègre *m*. 2. *F:* individu* trop serviable, ramasse-boulot *m*. 3. *F:* (*th.*) comparse *m*, faire-valoir *m*. 4. *P:* indicateur*, bourdille *m*.
stooge[2] [stuːdʒ] (**to**), *F:* 1. faire le nègre. 2. servir de comparse *m* (*ou* de faire-valoir *m*) (à un acteur).
stooge about (*or* **around**) [ˈstuːdʒəˈbaut, ˈstuːdʒəˈraund] (**to**), *P:* 1. faire un tour, flâner. 2. bricoler.
stoolie [ˈstuːli], **stool-pigeon** [ˈstuːlpidʒin] (*noun*), *F:* (*a*) indicateur*, mouchard *m*; (*b*) compère *m* (d'un escroc).
stop [stɔp] (*noun*), *P:* receleur *m*, fargue *m*. *Voir aussi* **pull out** (**to**), 3.
stop by [ˈstɔpˈbai] (**to**), *F:* rendre visite (à qn), entrer en passant, passer chez qn.
stop-off [ˈstɔpɔf] (*noun*), *F:* étape *f*, (point *m* d')arrêt *m*, halte *f*.
stop off [ˈstɔpˈɔf] (**to**), *F:* faire une halte (*ou* un arrêt); **to s. o. in London**, faire étape à Londres.

* L'astérisque indique que le mot marqué de ce signe figure comme entrée dans le Répertoire.

stopover [ˈstɔpouvər] (*noun*), *F:* arrêt *m* (au cours d'un voyage).

stop over [ˈstɔpˈouvər] (**to**), *F:* interrompre son voyage, s'arrêter.

stopper [ˈstɔpər] (*noun*), *F:* **1. to put the s. on sth.,** mettre fin à qch. **2.** (*boxe*) coup* knock-out.

stork [stɔ:k] (*noun*), *F:* **a visit from the s.,** l'arrivée *f* d'un bébé.

story [ˈstɔ:ri] (*noun*), *F:* mensonge*, conte *m*; **to tell stories,** mentir*, raconter des blagues *f.pl.*; *voir aussi* **sob-story; tall**[1]**, 2.**

storyteller [ˈstɔ:ri-telər] (*noun*), *F:* menteur *m*, batteur *m*, chiqueur *m*.

stove [stouv] (*noun*), *P:* chauffage *m* (*auto*).

stove-pipe [ˈstouvpaip] (*noun*). **1.** *P:* crapouillot *m*. **2.** *F:* chapeau* haut de forme, tuyau *m* de poêle, huit-reflets *m*. **3.** (*U.S.*) *P:* avion *m* de chasse à réaction.

stow [stou] (**to**), *P:* **s. it!** c'est marre!; ferme ça!

strafe [strɑ:f] (**to**), *F:* réprimander*, passer un savon à (qn), engueuler (qn).

strafing [ˈstrɑ:fiŋ] (*noun*), *F:* réprimande *f*, verte semonce, engueulade *f*.

straight[1] [streit] (*adj.*). **1.** *F:* (*a*) (cigarettes, tabac) ordinaire (sans narcotiques); (*b*) (*d'une boisson*) sec. **2.** *P:* (sexuellement) normal. **3.** *P:* qui ne se drogue pas. **4.** *F:* **s. man = stooge**[1]**, 3.** *Voir aussi* **strait; ticket, 3.**

straight[2] [streit] (*adv.*): **to go s.,** (*a*) *F:* marcher droit, suivre le droit chemin; (*b*) *P:* se désintoxiquer (de drogues), se décamer; (*c*) *P:* abandonner la pédérastie. *Voir aussi* **horse**[1]**, 2; shoulder, 2; straight up.**

straight[3] [streit] (*noun*), *F:* **to act on the s.,** agir loyalement.

straighten out [ˈstreit(ə)nˈaut] (**to**). **1.** *P:* **to s. s.o. o. = to put s.o. wise (wise, 2). 2.** *F:* **I expect that things will s. o.,** je pense que ça s'arrangera.

straight up [ˈstreitˈʌp] (*adj.*), *F:* honnête, régulier, réglo; **s. u.!** c'est du vrai! sans blague!

strain [strein] (*noun*), *P:* **to have a s.,** uriner*, lancequiner; **to go for a s.,** aller aux W.C.*.

strait [streit] (*adj.*), *F:* **to follow the s.** (*faussement* **straight**) **and narrow,** se conduire honnêtement, cheminer (*ou* marcher) droit.

stranger [ˈstreindʒər] (*noun*), *F:* **1.** (*U.S.*) **say, s.!** pardon, monsieur! **2.** (*dans une tasse à thé*) chinois *m*.

strap[1] [stræp] (*noun*), *P:* **on the s. = on the drop (drop**[1]**, 8).** *Voir aussi* **jock-strap.**

strap[2] [stræp] (**to**), *P:* coïter* avec (une femme), calecer.

strap-hanger [ˈstræphæŋər] (*noun*), *F:* voyageur *m* debout (dans le métro, le train, *etc.*).

strapper [ˈstræpər] (*noun*), *F:* grand gaillard, escogriffe *m*.

straw [strɔ:] (*noun*), *F:* **1. that's the last s.,** c'est le coup de grâce! c'est le comble! c'est la fin des haricots! il ne manquait plus que cela! **2. it's the last s. that breaks the camel's back,** *c.p.*, c'est la dernière goutte (d'eau) qui fait déborder le vase.

stray [strei] (*noun*), *P:* **to have a bit** (*or* **piece**) **of s. = to have a bit on the side (side, 2).**

streak[1] [stri:k] (*noun*), *F:* **a losing s.,** une série de malchance* (série noire) aux jeux; **a winning s.,** une série de chance*. *Voir aussi* **piss**[1]**, 3; yellow, 1.**

streak[2] **(along)** [ˈstri:k(əˈlɔŋ)] (**to**), *F:* aller à toute vitesse, gazer.

streaker [ˈstri:kər] (*noun*), *F:* nudiste galopant(e).

street [stri:t] (*noun*), *F:* **1. to be streets ahead of s.o.,** dépasser qn par des mille et des cents. **2. it's right up your s.,** cela te connaît; *cf.* **alley, 1. 3. the horse won by a s.,** le cheval a gagné dans un fauteuil. **4. it's not in the same s.,** ce n'est pas du même acabit (*ou* de la même catégorie). **5. to be on the streets,** racoler*, faire le trottoir. *Voir aussi* **easy**[1]**, 1; sunny.**

stretch[1] [stretʃ] (*noun*), *P:* **to do a s.,** faire de la prison*, faire une longe; **he was given a s.,** on l'a mis au trou. *Voir aussi* **homestretch.**

stretch[2] [stretʃ] (**to**). **1.** *F:* **that's stretching it a bit,** c'est le tirer par les cheveux. **2.** *P:* être pendu* (*ou* béquillé *ou* gruppé).

strewth! [stru:θ] (*excl.*), *P:* sacrebleu! sapristi! mince (alors)!

strides [straidz] (*pl. noun*), *P:* pantalon*, falzar *m*.

* An asterisk indicates that the word so marked is included as a head-word in the Appendix.

strike [straik] (**to**), *F:* **1. s. a light!** morbleu! saperlipopette!; **s. me pink!** tu m'assois! bigre de bougre! scarabombe! **2. to get struck on s.o.,** s'enticher de qn. *Voir aussi* **cunt-struck; gobstruck; heap, 1; rich**[2].

Strine [strain] (*noun*), *F:* la langue australienne.

string [striŋ] (*noun*). *F:* **1. to have s.o. on a (piece of) s.,** mener qn par le bout du nez. **2. no strings attached,** sans obligations, sans à-côtés, sans os. **3. to pull (the) strings,** faire jouer le piston. *Voir aussi* **apron-strings; G-string; shoestring.**

string along [ˈstriŋəˈlɔŋ] (**to**), *F:* **1.** tenir (qn) en suspens, mener (qn) en bateau. **2. to s. a. (with s.o.),** filer le train à qn.

string-bean [ˈstriŋˈbiːn] (*noun*) (*U.S.*), *F:* = **bean-pole.**

string out [ˈstriŋˈaut] (**to**). **1.** *F:* faire durer (qch.). **2.** *P:* être drogué*, être camé (*ou* chargé); **to be strung out,** être défoncé.

string up [ˈstriŋˈʌp] (**to**), *F:* pendre* (un condamné). *Voir aussi* **strung up.**

strip[1] [strip] (*noun*), *F:* **1. to tear s.o. off a s.,** réprimander* qn, passer un rude savon à qn, sonner les cloches à qn. **2. s. show,** spectacle *m* de nus, striptease *m*; **s. poker,** poker *m* de déshabillage, striptease-poker *m*.

strip[2] [strip] (**to**), *F:* (*mil.*) faire perdre ses galons *m.pl.*, dégrader, faire passer chez le dernier tailleur.

strip off [ˈstripˈɔf] (**to**), *F:* se déshabiller*, se mettre à poil.

stripper [ˈstripər] (*noun*), *F:* stripteaseuse *f*, effeuilleuse *f*.

strong-arm[1] [ˈstrɔŋɑːm] (*attrib. adj.*), *F:* **s.-a. man,** (*a*) homme fort, fortiche *m*, balèze *m*; (*b*) battant *m*, un dur; **s.-a. tactics,** manœuvres *f.pl.* de poids (*ou* à la matraque).

strong-arm[2] [ˈstrɔŋɑːm] (**to**), *F:* manier rudement, mener à la baguette.

stroppy [ˈstrɔpi] (*adj.*), *P:* de mauvaise humeur, à cran, de mauvais poil.

struck [strʌk] (*p.p.*): *voir* **strike (to).**

strung up [ˈstrʌŋˈʌp] (*p.p. & adj.*). **1.** *F:* **to be s. u.,** être pendu* (*ou* béquillé); *cf.* **string up (to). 2.** *F:* **to be (all) s. u.,** être tendu (*ou* énervé). **3.** *P:* malade par le manque de drogues; en manque.

struth! [struːθ] (*excl.*), *P:* = **strewth!**

stuck[1] [stʌk] (*adj.*), *F:* en panne, en rade. *Voir aussi* **stick**[2] **(to), 4, 5; stick in (to), 1.**

stuck[2] [ʃtuk] (*noun*), *P:* **to be in s.,** être dans une mauvaise posture (*ou* dans de mauvais draps).

stuck-up [ˈstʌkˈʌp] (*adj.*), *F:* prétentieux*, crâneur, plastronneur.

stud [stʌd] (*noun*) (*U.S.*), *F:* **1.** un mâle. **2.** un malin, un roué. **3.** un homme dans le vent, un minet.

stuff[1] [stʌf] (*noun*). **1.** *F:* **to know one's s.,** être capable, s'y connaître, être à la hauteur. **2.** *F:* **that's the s. (to give the troops)!** voilà ce qu'il faut (pour remonter la République)! **3.** *P:* **a nice bit of s.,** une belle pépée, une môme bath; *cf.* **skirt. 4.** *P:* (*a*) héroïne *f* (*drogues**); (*b*) drogues*, stups *m.pl.* **5.** *P:* butin*, contrebande *f*, pluc *m*. **6.** *F:* **to do one's s.,** faire ce qu'on doit, faire son boulot. *Voir aussi* **heavy**[1]**, 5; rough**[1]**, 6; sob-stuff; white**[1]**, 1.**

stuff[2] [stʌf] (**to**). **1.** *V:* coïter* avec (une femme), bourrer, égoïner. **2.** *P:* **get stuffed!** va te faire voir! va te faire foutre! **3.** *F:* manger* abondamment, se goinfrer, s'empiffrer. *Voir aussi* **shirt, 5.**

stuffing [ˈstʌfiŋ] (*noun*), *F:* **to knock the s. out of s.o.,** (*a*) battre qn à plate(s) couture(s), flanquer une tripotée à qn, étriper qn; (*b*) désarçonner, démonter, dégonfler qn, mettre qn à plat.

stuffy [ˈstʌfi] (*adj.*), *F:* collet monté, constipé.

stum [stʌm] (*noun*), *P:* **1.** marijuana *f* (*drogues**), kif *m*. **2.** = **stumbler.**

stumbler [ˈstʌmblər] (*noun*), *P:* somnifère *m*, barbiturique *m*, barbitos *m.pl.*

stumer [ˈstuːmər] (*noun*), *P:* **1.** chose *f* qui ne vaut rien. **2.** chèque *m* sans provision, billet *m* à découvert. **3.** bévue*, boulette *f*, bourde *f*; **to drop a s.,** faire une gaffe. **4.** perdant *m*, paumé *m* (*cheval, etc.*). **5.** raté *m*, paumé *m*. **6.** faillite *f*, banqueroute *f*, binelle *f*.

stump [stʌmp] (**to**), *F:* coller (qn), réduire (qn) à quia; **to s. s.o. on a subject,** faire sécher qn sur un sujet; **this stumped me,** sur le coup je n'ai su que répondre, ça m'a cloué le bec.

stumps [stʌmps] (*pl. noun*), *F:* jambes*,

* L'astérisque indique que le mot marqué de ce signe figure comme entrée dans le Répertoire.

guibolles *f.pl.*; **to stir one's s.**, (*a*) se dépêcher*, se décarcasser; (*b*) se remuer.

stump up [ˈstʌmpˈʌp] (**to**), *F:* payer*, les abouler.

stun [stʌn] (**to**), *F:* **1.** emballer, combler. **2.** abasourdir, abrutir. *Voir aussi* **stunned.**

stung [stʌŋ] (*p.p.*): *voir* **sting (to).**

stunned [stʌnd] (*adj.*) (*U.S.*), *P:* ivre*, fadé. *Voir aussi* **stun (to).**

stunner [ˈstʌnər] (*noun*), *F:* (*a*) qn d'irrésistible *ou* de formidable, prix *m* de Diane, Apollon *m*; (*b*) chose épatante.

stunning [ˈstʌniŋ] (*adj.*), *F:* (*a*) excellent*, formid(able), épatant; (*b*) très beau*, ravissant, irrésistible.

stupe [stu:p] (*noun*) (*U.S.*), *P:* individu bête*, cruche *f*, cruchon *m*.

stymie [ˈstaimi] (**to**), *F:* entraver, gêner, contrecarrer; **I'm completely stymied,** je suis dans une impasse.

sub[1] [sʌb] (*noun abbr.*), *F:* **1.** (=*subscription*) abonnement *m*, cotisation *f*. **2.** (=*sub-editor*) secrétaire *mf.* de rédaction (*journal*). **3.** (=*subaltern*) subalterne *mf*. **4.** (=*substitute*) substitut *m*, remplaçant *m*. **5.** (=*submarine*) sous-marin *m*. **6. to get a s. from s.o.,** emprunter* à qn, faire un emprunt.

sub[2] [sʌb] (**to**) (*verb abbr.*), *F:* **1.** (=*sub-edit*) corriger, mettre au point (un article, *etc.*). **2.** (=*substitute*) **to s. for s.o.,** remplacer qn. **3. to s. s.o.,** preter de l'argent* a qn, financer qn.

suck [sʌk] (**to**). **1.** *F:* **s. it and see,** *c.p.*, essaie et tu verras; suce et tu goûteras. **2.** *F:* **to s. s.o. dry** = **to drain s.o. dry (drain**[2] **(to)).** **3.** *V:* **to s. s.o.** = **to go down on s.o. (go down (to), 5).** **4.** *F:* **to s. s.o.'s brains,** exploiter l'intelligence *f* de qn.

suck around [ˈsʌkəˈraund] (**to**) (*U.S.*), *P:* **to s. a. s.o.** = **to suck up to s.o.**

suckass [ˈsʌkæs] (*noun*) (*U.S.*), *P:* lèche-cul *m*, lèche-bottes *m*.

sucker[1] [ˈsʌkər] (*attrib. adj.*), *F:* **s. punch,** (*boxe*) coup* de pré-attaque.

sucker[2] [ˈsʌkər] (*noun*), *F:* **1.** dupe *f*, poire *f*, dindon *m*; **there's a s. born every minute,** *c.p.*, les poires se cueillent tous les jours; *cf.* **one, 7; to make a (right) s. out of s.o.,** faire tourner qn en bourrique; **to be played for a s.,** être escroqué* (*ou* entubé); **he made a right s. out of you!** il t'a eu jusqu'à la gauche! **2.** admirateur *m*, fana *m*, mordu *m*; **I'm a s. for a beautiful blonde,** je suis mordu pour une belle blonde, je suis porté vers les belles blondes. *Voir aussi* **bum-sucker; cock-sucker.**

suck in [ˈsʌkˈin] (**to**), *P:* escroquer*, carotter, empiler.

suck off [ˈsʌkˈɔf] (**to**), *V:* faire un coït* buccal à (qn), pomper (qn).

suck up [ˈsʌkˈʌp] (**to**), *F:* **to s. u. to s.o.,** flatter* qn, faire de la lèche à qn.

sudden [ˈsʌdn] (*adj.*), *F:* **s. death,** match (*golf, etc.*) terminé par élimination.

sugar[1] [ˈʃugər] (*noun*). **1.** *P:* (*a*) argent*, galette *f*; (*b*) bénéfices*, affure *f*, gâteau *m*. **2.** *F:* (*a*) une belle* fille*, une môme bath; (*b*) petite amie, fiancée. **3.** *P:* (*a*) héroïne *f*, cocaïne *f*, *ou* morphine *f* (*drogues**), came blanche, sucre *m*; (*b*) **s. (lump),** LSD 25, acide *m* lysergique; *cf.* **acid, 2.** **4.** *F:* flatterie *f*, pommade *f*. **5.** *P:* pot-de-vin *m*, dessous-de-table *m*.

sugar[2] [ˈʃugər] (**to**). **1.** *F:* flatter*, pommader. **2.** *P:* soudoyer, acheter.

sugar-daddy [ˈʃugə-dædi] (*noun*), *F:* vieux protecteur (envers une maîtresse), papa-gâteau *m*; **she's got a s.-d.,** elle s'est trouvé un vieux.

sugar-hill [ˈʃugəˈhil] (*noun*) (*U.S.*), *P:* quartier *m* des bordels* dans une région habitée par les noirs.

summat [ˈsʌmət, ˈsumət] (*adv. & noun*), *P:* = **something,** *q.v.*

Sunday [ˈsʌndi] (*attrib. adj.*), *F:* **1. S. driver,** chauffeur peu expérimenté, chauffard *m* du dimanche. **2. S. punch,** (*boxe*) coup* meurtrier.

sundowner [ˈsʌn-daunər] (*noun*), *F:* **1.** boisson alcoolisée (prise le soir). **2.** (*Austr.*) clochard*, cloche *m*. **3.** (*U.S.*) pète-sec *m*, garde-chiourme *m*, gendarme *m*.

sunk [ˈsʌŋk] (*adj.*), *F:* ruiné*, perdu, fichu.

sunny [ˈsʌni] (*adj.*), *F:* **1. the s. side of the street,** la vie en rose. **2. s. side up,** (un œuf) sur le plat.

sunset strip [ˈsʌnsetˈstrip] (*noun*), *F:* *voir* **bingo (77).**

super[1] [ˈs(j)u:pər] (*adj.*), *F:* excellent*, super, épatant.

super[2] [ˈs(j)u:pər] (*noun*) (*abbr.*), *F:* **1.** (=*Superintendent* (*of Police*)) commissaire *m* de police, quart (d'œil) *m*. **2.** (=*supernumerary*) (*th.*) doublure *f*.

* An asterisk indicates that the word so marked is included as a head-word in the Appendix.

super-duper [ˈs(j)uːpəˈd(j)uːpər] (*adj.*), *F:* excellent*, formid(able), bœuf.
superstar [ˈs(j)uːpə-stɑːr] (*noun*), *F:* superstar *m.*
supup [ˈsʌpˈʌp] (**to**), *F:* lamper son verre.
sure[1] [ʃuər, ʃɔər, ʃɔːr] (*adj.*), *F:* **(it's a) s. thing,** c'est une certitude, c'est sûr et certain; **s. thing!** = **sure!**[2]. *Voir aussi* **egg, 5.**
sure![2] [ʃuər, ʃɔər, ʃɔːr] (*excl.*), *F:* naturellement! bien sûr!
sure-fire [ˈʃuəˈfaiər, ˈʃɔəˈfaiər, ˈʃɔːˈfaiər] (*adj.*), *F:* sûr et certain.
surfie [ˈsəːfi] (*noun*) (*Austr.*), *F:* **1.** aquaplaniste *mf*, fana *mf* du surfing. **2.** habitué(e) de la plage.
suss [sʌs] (**to**), *P:* soupçonner, avoir à l'œil.
suss out [ˈsʌsˈaut] (**to**), *P:* (*a*) **to s. s.o. o.,** cataloguer qn, mettre qn en fiche; (*b*) **to s. sth. o.,** classifier qch., éclairer sa lanterne.
swab [swɔb] (*noun*), *P:* lourdaud *m*, andouille *f*, propre à rien *m.*
swacked [swækt] (*adj.*), *P:* ivre*, blindé.
swaddie, swaddy [ˈswɔdi] (*noun*), *F:* = **squaddie, squaddy.**
swag [swæg] (*noun*), *F:* butin*, fade *m*, taf *m.*
swagger [ˈswægər] (*adj.*), *F:* élégant*, chic, riflo.
swagman [ˈswægmæn] (*noun*) (*Austr.*), *F:* (*a*) clochard*, vagabond *m*; (*b*) excursionniste *m*, randonneur *m* (à pied).
swallow[1] [ˈswɔlou] (*noun*), *F:* **to have a big s.,** avoir un bon avaloir, avoir la dalle en pente.
swallow[2] [ˈswɔlou] (**to**), *F:* **1. I can't s. that,** je ne peux pas l'avaler, je ne peux pas le gober; **hard to s.,** difficile à avaler. **2. he won't s. that,** il ne le croira* pas, il ne donnera pas dans le panneau.
swank[1] [swæŋk] (*adj.*), *F:* = **swanky** (*b*).
swank[2] [swæŋk] (*noun*), *F:* **1.** élégance *f*, chic *m*, coquetterie *f*. **2. to put on (the) s.,** prendre des airs *m.pl.*, faire de l'esbrouf(f)e *f*. **3.** prétention *f*, gloriole *f*, épate *f*. **4.** épateur *m*, poseur *m*, crâneur *m.*
swank[3] [swæŋk] (**to**), *F:* se donner des airs *m.pl.*, crâner, faire de l'épate *f.*
swanker [ˈswæŋkər] (*noun*), *F:* = **swank**[2]**, 4.**
swanky [ˈswæŋki] (*adj.*), *F:* (*a*) prétentieux*, poseur; (*b*) élégant*, flambard, ridère.
Swan(n)ee [ˈswɔni] (*noun*), *P:* **up the S.** = **up the creek.**
swan off [ˈswɔnˈɔf] (**to**), *F:* faire l'école buissonnière, jouer rip.
swap[1] [swɔp] (*noun*), *F:* (*a*) échange *m*, troquage *m*; (*b*) article *m* que l'on échange, troc *m*; (*pl.*) doubles *m.pl.*
swap[2] [swɔp] (**to**), *F:* échanger, troquer.
swear [swɛər] (*noun*), *F:* **to have a good s.,** lâcher une bordée de jurons.
swear off [ˈswɛərˈɔf] (**to**), *F:* abandonner*, balanstiquer.
sweat[1] [swet] (*noun*), *F:* **1.** travail* pénible, corvée *f*, turbin *m*; **it's no s.,** c'est du tout cuit, c'est pas du durillon. **2.** (*mil.*) **an old s.,** un vieux troupier, un vétéran. **3. to work oneself (up) into a s.** = **to work oneself (up) into a lather** (**lather**[1]**,** (*a*), (*b*)). **4. to be in a cold s.,** s'inquiéter, avoir le trac.
sweat[2] [swet] (**to**), *F:* **to be sweating on the top line,** être agité (*ou* excité *ou* emballé), être sur des charbons ardents. *Voir aussi* **blood, 6.**
sweater-girl [ˈswetə-gəːl] (*noun*), *F:* fille* qui porte des vêtements collants, femme* bien roulée.
sweat out [ˈswetˈaut] (**to**), *F:* **to s. it o.,** attendre* patiemment, compter les pavés. *Voir aussi* **guts, 6.**
sweat-shop [ˈswetʃɔp] (*noun*), *F:* vieille usine où les ouvriers sont exploités, vrai bagne.
Sweeney [ˈswiːni] (*noun*), *P:* **1. S. Todd** (*R.S.* = *Flying Squad*), la brigade mobile (de la police). **2.** = **holler-wag(g)on.**
sweep[1] [swiːp] (*noun*), *F:* **1.** sweepstake *m*. **2.** vaurien*, voyou *m*, fripouille *f*. **3. to make a clean s.,** faire table rase, faire rafle, rafler le tout, tout ramasser.
sweep[2] [swiːp] (**to**), *F:* **1. to be swept off one's feet,** (*a*) être emballé, s'emballer pour qn; (*b*) être débordé de travail*. **2. to s. the board,** emporter tout, nettoyer le tapis. *Voir aussi* **dirt**[1]**, 4.**
sweeper [ˈswiːpər] (*noun*), *F:* **1.** (*football*) arrière *m* de défense. **2. leave it for the s.,** ne ramassez rien, laissez pousser.
sweep up [ˈswiːpˈʌp] (**to**), *F:* (*football*) jouer en arrière de défense.
sweet[1] [swiːt] (*adj.*). **1.** *F:* **to be s. on**

* L'astérisque indique que le mot marqué de ce signe figure comme entrée dans le Répertoire.

s.o., être amoureux de qn, avoir le béguin pour qn. **2.** *F:* **you can bet your s. life!** tu peux en mettre la main au feu. **3.** *F:* **to hand s.o. a s. line,** faire marcher qn, faire de la lèche à qn. **4.** *P:* **s. Fanny Adams** (*or P:* **s. F.A.** *or V:* **s. fuck-all**), rien*, moins que rien, peau de balle (et balai de crin), que dalle, des prunes. **5.** *F:* **to whisper s. nothings,** murmurer des mots d'amour, conter fleurette. **6.** *F:* **s. talk,** flatterie *f*, lèche *f*, pommade *f*. **7.** *F:* facile, lucratif; **a s. job,** une planque. **8.** *F:* aimable, accueillant, gentil. **9.** *P:* homosexuel, chouquette. *Voir aussi* **tooth, 1.**

sweet[2] [swi:t] (*noun*)**:** *voir* **sweets.**

sweeten [ˈswi:tn] (**to**), *F:* (*a*) soudoyer, acheter (qn), graisser la patte à (qn); (*b*) flatter*, cajoler, pommader (qn).

sweetener [ˈswi:tnər] (*noun*), *F:* (*a*) pot-de-vin, *m*; (*b*) pourboire*, pourliche *m*; **I had to give him a s.,** j'ai dû lui graisser la patte.

sweeten up [ˈswi:tnˈʌp] (**to**), *F:* = **sweeten (to).**

sweetie [ˈswi:ti] (*noun*). **1.** *F:* bonbon *m*. **2.** *F:* chéri(e) *m*(*f*), cocotte *f*. **3.** *P:* Préludine *f* (*marque déposée*) (*drogues*).

sweetie-pie [ˈswi:tipai] (*noun*), *F:* = **sweetie, 2.**

sweets [swi:ts] (*pl. noun*), *P:* amphétamines *f.pl.* (*drogues**), bonbons *m.pl.*

sweet-talk [ˈswi:ttɔ:k] (**to**), *F:* cajoler, enjôler (qn).

sweet-talker [ˈswi:ttɔ:kər] (*noun*), *F:* cajoleur *m*, enjôleur *m*.

sweety [ˈswi:ti], **sweety-pie** [ˈswi:tipai] (*noun*), *F:* = **sweetie, sweetie-pie.**

swell[1] [swel] (*adj.*). **1.** *F:* élégant*, flambard. **2.** excellent*, chouettos, épatant. **3.** *P:* **s. mob,** pickpockets bien fringués.

swell[2] [swel] (*noun*), *F:* **1.** élégant *m*, faraud *m*, suiffard *m*; **the swells,** les gens chics, le grand monde. **2.** grand personnage, grosse légume.

swellhead [ˈswelhed] (*noun*) (*U.S.*), *F:* prétentieux *m*, crâneur *m*, esbrouf(f)eur *m*.

swig[1] [swig] (*noun*), *F:* grand trait, lampée *f* (de bière, *etc.*); **to take a s. at** (*or* **from**) **the bottle,** boire à même la bouteille.

swig[2] [swig] (**to**), *F:* boire (un verre) à grands traits (*ou* à grands coups), lamper.

swill[1] [swil] (*noun*), *P:* **1.** nourriture*, bouftance *f*. **2.** (*a*) alcool* de mauvaise qualité, gn(i)ole *f*; (*b*) lampée *f*, rasade *f*. **3.** bêtises*, foutaises *f.pl.*; **a prize load of s.,** un vrai tissu d'âneries.

swill[2] [swil] (**to**). **1.** *P:* **to s. one's food,** s'empiffrer de la nourriture*. **2.** *F:* **to s. beer,** s'entonner de la bière.

swiller [ˈswilər], **swillpot** [ˈswilpɔt] (*noun*), *P:* ivrogne*, vide-bouteille *m*.

swim [swim] (*noun*), *F:* **in the s.,** dans le bain, dans le vent, à la coule; **to get back in the s.** (*or* **into the s. of things**), se remettre dans le bain; **out of the s.,** hors du coup, pas à la page.

swimmingly [ˈswimiŋli] (*adv.*), *F:* à merveille, comme sur des roulettes.

swindle-sheet [ˈswindlʃi:t] (*noun*), *P:* indemnité *f* pour frais professionnels, frais de la princesse.

swine [swain] (*noun*), *F:* salopard *m*, salaud *m*, saligaud *m*.

swing[1] [swiŋ] (*noun*), *F:* **1. to get into the s. of it** (*or* **of things**), se mettre dans le mouvement. **2. everything went with a s.,** tout a très bien marché. **3. in full s.,** en pleine activité, en plein boum. **4. to take a s. at s.o.,** lancer un coup de poing à qn. *Voir aussi* **one, 1; roundabouts.**

swing[2] [swiŋ] (**to**). **1.** *F:* bien marcher, gazer, ronfler. **2.** *P:* **to s. it** (*or* **a fast one**) **on s.o.,** duper* qn, (re)faire qn, tirer une carotte à qn, jouer un tour de cochon à qn. **3.** *F:* être pendu* (*ou* béquillé); **I'll s. for him,** je me vengerai quitte à y aller du caillou. **4.** *F:* prendre du plaisir à (qch.). **5.** *F:* faire balancer (qch.) en sa faveur. **6.** *P:* **to s. both ways,** être ambivalent, marcher à voiles et à vapeur. *Voir aussi* **lead**[1]**, 2.**

swinger [ˈswiŋər] (*noun*). **1.** *F:* qn *ou* qch. de formid(able) (*ou* d'épatant *ou* de super). **2.** (*pl.*) *P:* seins*, flotteurs *m.pl.* *Voir aussi* **lead-swinger.**

swinging [ˈswiŋiŋ] (*adj.*), *F:* (*a*) plein d'allant (*ou* de ressort); (*b*) dans le vent, avant-garde, flambard.

swipe[1] [swaip] (*noun*), *F:* **1.** (*a*) coup*, taloche *f*; **to take a s. at s.o.,** flanquer une raclée (*ou* une torgnole) à qn;

* An asterisk indicates that the word so marked is included as a head-word in the Appendix.

(*b*) **to have** (*or* **take**) **a s. at sth.**, se lancer à faire qch. **2.** (*pl.*) la petite bière.

swipe² [swaip] (**to**), *F:* **1.** = **to take a swipe at** (**swipe¹, 1**). **2.** voler*, chiper, chaparder (qch. à qn).

swish¹ [swiʃ] (*adj.*), *F:* élégant*, chic.

swish² [swiʃ] (*noun*), *P:* pédéraste*, lopaille *f*.

swish³ [swiʃ] (**to**), *P:* être efféminé, agir en pédé.

switch¹ [switʃ] (*noun*), *F:* **to do a s.**, échanger, troquer, chanstiquer.

switch² [switʃ] (**to**), *F:* **to s. horses (in midstream)**, changer son fusil d'épaule (au milieu du combat), changer de cheval de bataille.

switched on [ˈswitʃtˈɔn] (*p.p.* & *adj.*), *F:* **1.** faux*, forcé, artificiel. **2.** euphorique, chargé (par les drogues, *etc.*). **3.** à la mode, dernier cri, dans le vent. *Cf.* **switch on (to)**.

switcheroo [ˈswitʃəˈruː] (*noun*) (*U.S.*) *P:* = **switch¹**.

switch-hitter [ˈswitʃhitər] (*noun*), *P:* un ambivalent, qn qui marche à voiles et à vapeur.

switch off [ˈswitʃˈɔf] (**to**), *F:* se détacher (de qch.), couper l'allumage *m*.

switch on [ˈswitʃˈɔn] (**to**). **1.** *F:* **to s. s.o. o.**, (*a*) éveiller l'intérêt *m ou* la curiosité de qn; (*b*) exciter, émoustiller qn (sexuellement). **2.** *P:* fumer de la marijuana. **3.** *P:* initier (par une première piqûre) à la drogue. *Cf.* **switched on.**

swiz(z) [swiz] (*noun*), *F:* = **swizzle¹, 1, 2.**

swizzle¹ [ˈswizl] (*noun*), *F:* **1.** escroquerie*, filoutage *m*, doublage *m*. **2.** déception *f*, déboire *m*. **3.** (*U.S.*) cocktail *m*.

swizzle² [ˈswizl] (**to**), *F:* escroquer*, filouter, doubler.

swop [swɔp] (*noun* & *verb*), *F:* = **swap.**

swordsman [ˈsɔːdzmən] (*noun*), *P:* **1.** receleur*, fourgue *m*. **2.** (*U.S.*) libertin *m*, cavaleur *m*.

swot¹ [swɔt] (*noun*), *F:* (*a*) bûcheur *m*, potasseur *m*; (*b*) fort *m* en thème.

swot² [swɔt] (**to**), *F:* étudier, bûcher, potasser.

swot up [ˈswɔtˈʌp] (**to**), *F:* rabâcher par cœur, potasser.

syph [sif] (*noun*), *P:* (*a*) syphilis*, syphilo *f*, syphlotte *f*; (*b*) syphilitique *mf*, naze *mf*, nazebroque *mf*.

syrupy [ˈsirəpi] (*adj.*), *F:* sirupeux, sentimental.

system [ˈsistəm, ˈsistim] (*noun*), *F:* **1. the s.**, le Système, la République. **2. it's all systems go!** tout gaze: on démarre.

* L'astérisque indique que le mot marqué de ce signe figure comme entrée dans le Répertoire.

T

T [ti:]. **1.** *F:* **that suits me to a T,** cela me va parfaitement, cela me botte. **2.** *P:* = **tea.**

ta [tɑ:] (*excl.*), *F:* merci.

tab [tæb] (*noun*). **1.** *P:* cigarette*, cibiche *f.* **2.** *P:* oreille*, étiquette *f.* **3.** (*U.S.*) *F:* note *f,* facture *f,* addition *f.* **4.** *F:* **to keep tabs on s.o.,** surveiller qn, avoir l'œil sur qn. **5.** (*Austr.*) *F:* **to keep t.** = **to keep nit** (**nit, 2**). **6.** *P:* (*abbr.* = *tablet*) comprimé *m.*

tab-end [ˈtæbˈend] (*noun*), *F:* mégot*, clope *f.*

table [ˈteibl] (*noun*), *F:* **to be under the t.,** être ivre*, rouler sous la table.

tack [tæk] (*noun*), *F:* **1.** (*a*) **soft t.,** pain*, bricheton *m;* (*b*) **hard t.,** biscuits *m.pl.* de marin. **2.** nourriture*, fricot *m. Voir aussi* **brass[1].**

tacky [ˈtæki] (*adj.*), *F:* minable.

Taffy [ˈtæfi] (*noun*), *F:* habitant *m* du pays de Galles, Gallois *m.*

tag[1] [tæg] (*noun*), *F:* **1.** nom* *ou* surnom *m,* blaze *m.* **2.** (*automobile*) plaque *f* (d'immatriculation). **3.** = **ticket, 2. 4.** (*th.*) **t. line,** mot *m* de la fin. *Voir aussi* **dog-tag.**

tag[2] [tæg] (**to**). **1.** *P:* **to be tagged,** être coincé, être pris (dans une bande*, *etc.*). **2.** *F:* être sur les talons de (qn), filer le train à (qn). **3.** *P:* arrêter*, choper, ceinturer. **4.** *F:* (*boxe*) mettre knock-out, knockouter (qn).

tag along [ˈtægəˈlɔŋ] (**to**), *F:* suivre, être à la traîne de qn.

tag around [ˈtægəˈraund] (**to**), *F:* **to t. a. with s.o.,** être accroché à qn, rouler sa bosse avec qn.

tag on [ˈtægˈɔn] (**to**), *F:* **1.** se joindre à qn, s'accrocher à qn. **2.** apposer, fixer.

tail[1] [teil] (*noun*). **1.** *P:* fesses*, pont-arrière *m.* **2.** *P:* pénis*, queue *f.* **3.** *P:* vagin*, cramouille *f,* conasse *f.* **4.** *P:* **a piece of t.,** un bout de fesses (*ou* de cuisse), conasserie *f.* **5.** *F:* policier*, détective *m* (suivant, épiant qn), limier *m;* **to be on s.o.'s t.,** (*a*) filer le train à qn; (*b*) être sur le dos de qn; **to put a t. on s.o.,** faire suivre qn, faire filer qn, faire la filoche à qn. **6.** *F:* **to go top over t.,** faire une culbute. **7.** (*pl.*) *F:* habit *m* à queue, queue-de-pie *f;* **to wear tails,** porter l'habit. **8.** *F:* **to turn t.,** s'enfuir*, tourner le dos. **9.** *F:* **to have one's t. up,** (*a*) se sentir très heureux, se sentir pousser des ailes; (*b*) être très optimiste, être en pleine forme. **10.** *F:* **to keep one's t. up,** ne pas se laisser abattre. *Voir aussi* **ringtail.**

tail[2] [teil] (**to**), *F:* suivre, épier (qn). *Voir aussi* **hightail** (**to**).

tail-end [ˈteilˈend] (*noun*), *F:* **the t.-e.,** la fin, le bout.

tail-ender [ˈteilˈendər] (*noun*), *F:* dernier *m,* lanterne *f* rouge, der *m* (des ders).

tailgate [ˈteilgeit] (**to**) (*U.S.*), *F:* coller (une voiture, *etc.*).

tail-man [ˈteilmæn] (*noun*), *P:* coureur *m* (de jupons), cavaleur *m,* juponneur *m.*

tail-spin [ˈteil-spin] (*noun*), *F:* **to go into a t.-s.,** être saisi de panique, paniquer.

take[1] [teik] (*noun*), *F:* **the t.,** la recette, les revenus *m.pl.,* le beurre.

take[2] [teik] (**to**). **1.** *F:* **to have what it takes,** (*a*) avoir du courage* (*ou* du battant); (*b*) être capable, être à la hauteur. **2.** *F:* endurer, encaisser. **3.** *P:* tirer sur une cigarette de marijuana *ou* hachisch. **4.** *F:* **I'm not taking any of that!** je ne gobe rien de tout cela! *Voir aussi* **lamb, 4; plunge[1].**

take apart [ˈteikəˈpɑ:t] (**to**), *F:* réprimander* fortement, passer un bon savon à (qn).

take in [ˈteikˈin] (**to**), *F:* **1.** comprendre, piger. **2. he takes it all in,** il prend tout ça pour argent comptant. **3.** tromper*, ficher dedans.

take-off [ˈteikɔf] (*noun*), *F:* **1.** départ *m,* décollage *m.* **2.** imitation *f,* mimique *f,* pastiche *m.*

take off [ˈteikˈɔf] (**to**). **1.** *F:* s'enfuir*, s'en aller, se barrer; **t. o.!** fiche le camp! déguerpis! **2.** *F:* imiter, copier, singer,

* An asterisk indicates that the word so marked is included as a head-word in the Appendix.

mimer. 3. *F:* s'octroyer (une petite vacance, un congé, *etc.*). 4. *P:* (*a*) se faire une piqûre de drogues, se shooter; (*b*) être high, être défoncé par la drogue. 5. *P:* voler*, chiper; **to get taken off,** être empilé. 6. *P:* mourir*, lâcher la rampe.

take-on [ˈteikɔn] (*noun*), *F:* mystification *f*, farce *f*, canular(d) *m*.

take on [ˈteikˈɔn] (**to**), *F:* 1. s'émotionner, se retourner. 2. devenir populaire, prendre.

talc [tælk] (*noun*), *P:* cocaïne *f* (*drogues**), talc *m*.

tale [teil] (*noun*). 1. *F:* **to tell the t.,** raconter des boniments *m.pl.*, faire du baratin. 2. *F:* **to live to tell the t.,** survivre, être là pour en parler. 3. *P:* **T. of Two Cities** (*R.S.* = *titties*): *voir* **titty;** *cf.* **Bristols; fit**[2], 4; **threepenny-bits; trey-bits.** 4. *P:* **sorrowful t.** (*R.S.* = *jail*), prison*. *Voir aussi* **tall**[1], 2.

talent [ˈtælənt] (*noun*), *P:* les filles* (*sexuellement parlant*).

talk [tɔːk] (**to**), *F:* 1. **now you're talking!** maintenant tu y es (*ou* tu y viens)! 2. **money talks,** l'argent* veut tout dire. 3. **t. about luck!** tu parles d'une veine! *Voir aussi* **Dutch**[1], 5; **hat,** 2; **head,** 10; **sweet-talk** (**to**).

talkie [ˈtɔːki] (*noun*), *F:* (*cinéma*) film parlant, talkie *m*.

talking-to [ˈtɔːkiŋtuː] (*noun*), *F:* réprimande *f*, attrapade *f*, savon *m*.

tall[1] [tɔːl] (*adj.*), *F:* 1. **a t. order,** un travail* dur, un sacré boulot. 2. **a t. story** (*U.S.:* **tale**), un mensonge*, un bateau, un bidon.

tall[2] [tɔːl] (*adv.*), *F:* avec jactance *f*, avec fanfaronnade *f*.

tammy [ˈtæmi] (*noun*), *F:* (=*tam-o'-shanter*) béret écossais.

tampi [ˈtæmpi] (*noun*), *P:* marijuana *f* (*drogues**), tampi *m*.

tangle [ˈtæŋgl] (**to**), *F:* **to t. with s.o.,** (*a*) se brouiller avec qn; (*b*) embrasser* qn, étreindre qn, serrer qn dans ses bras.

tanglefoot [ˈtæŋglfut] (*noun*) (*U.S.*), *F:* whisky *m* (de mauvaise qualité), casse-pattes *m*.

tank [tæŋk] (*noun*), *P:* 1. coffre-fort *m*, coffio(t) *m*; **to blow a t.,** faire sauter un coffiot. 2. (*U.S.*) (*a*) prison*, coffre *m*; (*b*) cellule *f*, cage *f* à poules; *cf.* **fish-tank.** 3. ivrogne*, sac *m* à vin. 4. **to go in the t.** = **to throw a fight** (**throw** (**to**), 4). *Voir aussi* **piss-tank; septic,** 2; **think-tank.**

tanked up [ˈtæŋktˈʌp] (*adj.*), *P:* ivre*, bourré, chargé, blindé.

tank up [ˈtæŋkˈʌp] (**to**), *P:* boire* beaucoup d'alcool, picoler, pinter.

tanner [ˈtænər] (*noun*), *F:* pièce *f* de six pennies d'autrefois ou 2½ nouveaux pennies.

tanning [ˈtæniŋ] (*noun*), *F:* volée *f* de coups*, raclée *f*, peignée *f*; *cf.* **hide,** 1; **hiding.**

tap[1] [tæp] (*noun*), *F:* 1. **to be on t.,** être disponible, être à la disposition. 2. **to be on the t.,** quémander.

tap[2] [tæp] (**to**), *F:* demander de l'argent* à (qn), taper. *Voir aussi* **claret.**

tape[1] [teip] (*noun*), *F:* **red t.,** paperasserie *f*, chinoiseries administratives, bureaucratie *f*.

tape[2] [teip] (**to**), *F:* **to have s.o., sth., taped,** avoir qn, qch., bien catalogué (*ou* étiqueté *ou* pointé).

tapped out [ˈtæptˈaut] (*p.p. & adj.*) (*U.S.*), *P:* ruiné*, paumé.

tapper [ˈtæpər] (*noun*), *P:* mendiant*, frappeur *m*, tapeur *m*.

tar[1] [tɑːr] (*noun*), *P:* opium *m* (*drogues**), noir *m*. *Voir aussi* **Jack,** 7.

tar[2] [tɑːr] (**to**), *F:* **to be tarred with the same brush,** être du pareil au même, être dans le même panier, faire la paire.

tar-brush [ˈtɑː-brʌʃ] (*noun*), *F:* **to have a touch of the t.-b.,** avoir du négrillon dans les veines.

tarnation! [tɑːˈneiʃən] (*excl.*) (*U.S.*), *F:* *euph. pour* **damnation,** *q.v.*

tart [tɑːt] (*noun*), *P:* 1. prostituée*, fille *f*, cocotte *f*, grue *f*, poule *f*. 2. jeune fille* *ou* femme*, donzelle *f*, gonzesse *f*; *voir aussi* **ritzy,** 1.

tart up [ˈtɑːtˈʌp] (**to**), *P:* (*a*) décorer (qch.) avec du tape-à-l'œil; (*b*) **to t. oneself u.,** s'affubler, s'attifer de clinquant, faire le carnaval.

tarty [ˈtɑːti] (*adj.*), *P:* qui a l'air d'une prostituée*, à la pute.

tash [tæʃ] (*noun*), *F:* moustache*, bacchante *f*.

tassel [ˈtæs(ə)l] (*noun*), *P:* 1. pénis*, goupillon *m*. 2. **don't get your t. in a twist,** ne te mets pas dans tous tes états.

taste [teist] (*noun*). 1. *P:* bénéfice* *ou* partie *f* d'un bénéfice, rabe *m*. 2. *F:*

* L'astérisque indique que le mot marqué de ce signe figure comme entrée dans le Répertoire.

boisson *f* alcoolique; **would you like a t.?** tu veux boire* un coup? 3. *P:* **to have a t.,** coïter*, s'en payer un petit coup.

tasty [ˈteisti] (*adj.*), *P:* élégant*, chic.

ta-ta [ˈtæˈtɑː, tæˈtɑː] (*excl.*), *F:* au revoir, r'voir.

tater [ˈteitər], **tatie** [ˈteiti] (*noun*), *P:* pomme *f* de terre, patate *f.*

taters [ˈteitəz] (*adj.*), *P:* **to be t.,** avoir froid, être frisco, cailler.

Tattersalls [ˈtætəsɔːlz, ˈtætəsəlz] (*noun*), *F:* (*courses de chevaux*) la pelouse.

tatty-bye [ˈtætiˈbai] (*excl.*), *P:* = **ta-ta.**

tea [tiː] (*noun*), *P:* marijuana *f* (*drogues**), thé *m*; **bush t.,** concoction *f* d'herbes et de marijuana. *Voir aussi* **cup, 1, 2; stick[1], 5; weed-tea.**

teach [tiːtʃ] (**to**), *F:* **that'll t. you!** ça t'apprendra!; **that'll t. him a thing or two!** ça va (bigrement) le dégourdir; *cf.* **learn (to).**

teach-in [ˈtiːtʃin] (*noun*), *F:* colloque *m*, teach-in *m*, table ronde.

tead-up [ˈtiːdˈʌp] (*p.p. & adj.*), *P:* drogué* à la marijuana.

teahead [ˈtiːhed] (*noun*), *P:* habitué(e) de la marijuana.

tea-leaf [ˈtiːliːf] (*noun*), *P:* (*R.S.* = *thief*) voleur*; *cf.* **corned beef.**

team-up [ˈtiːmʌp] (*noun*), *F:* (*vêtements*) coordonnés *m.pl.*

team up [ˈtiːmˈʌp] (**to**), *F:* **to t. u. with s.o.,** collaborer (*ou* coéquiper) avec qn.

tea-pad [ˈtiː-pæd] (*noun*), *P:* fumerie *f* de marijuana.

tea-party [ˈtiː-pɑːti] (*noun*), *P:* réunion *f* pour fumer la marijuana.

tear[1] [tiər] (*noun*). 1. *P:* perle *f*, perlouse *f.* 2. *F:* **to shed a t. for Nelson,** uriner*, changer son poisson d'eau.

tear[2] [tɛər] (**to**), *F:* **that's torn it!** ça a tout gâché, ça a tout bousillé. *Voir aussi* **pants, 5; tearing.**

tear along [ˈtɛərəˈlɔŋ] (**to**), *F:* aller très vite*, foncer, brûler le pavé.

tear apart [ˈtɛərəˈpɑːt] (**to**), *F:* **to t. s.o. a.,** écharper qn, engueuler qn.

tear-arse [ˈtɛərɑːs], **tearaway** [ˈtɛərəwei] (*noun*), *P:* braillard *m*, grande-gueule *f.*

tearing [ˈtɛəriŋ] (*pres. part. & adj.*), *F:* **to be in a t. hurry,** avoir le feu au derrière, filer dare-dare.

tear-jerker [ˈtiədʒəːkər] (*noun*), *F:* mélo-(drame) *m*, (histoire, *etc.*) larmoyant(e).

tear off [ˈtɛərˈɔf] (**to**). 1. *F:* s'enfuir*, se carapater, se cavaler. 2. *P:* **to t. it o. (together),** coïter*, arracher un copeau (*ou* un pavé). *Voir aussi* **strip[1], 1.**

tease [tiːz] (*noun*), *P:* = **prick-tease.**

teaser [ˈtiːzər] (*noun*). 1. *F:* casse-tête (chinois). 2. *P:* = **prick-teaser.**

tea-stick [ˈtiː-stik] (*noun*), *P:* = **stick of tea (stick[1], 5).**

tec [tek] (*noun*) (*abbr.* = *detective*), *F:* détective *m*, condé *m.*

tech [tek] (*noun*) (*abbr.* = *technical college*), *F:* collège *m* technique.

Ted, ted [ted], **Teddy-boy, teddy-boy** [ˈtedibɔi] (*noun*), *F:* zazou *m*, zaz *m.*

teed off [ˈtiːdˈɔf] (*p.p. & adj.*), *P:* **to be t. o.,** en avoir par-dessus la tête, en avoir ras le bol.

teed up [ˈtiːdˈʌp] (*p.p. & adj.*), *P:* ivre*, rétamé.

teeny [ˈtiːni] (*adj.*), *F:* = **teeny-weeny.**

teeny-bopper [ˈtiːnibɔpər] (*noun*), *F:* jeune yé-yé *mf* (*ou* hippie *mf*) en bordée.

teeny-weeny [ˈtiːniˈwiːni] (*adj.*), *F:* minuscule, archi-petit, rikiki.

teeth [tiːθ] (*pl. noun*); *voir* **tooth.**

telegraph [ˈteligrɑːf] (**to**), *F:* **to t. a punch,** (*boxe*) annoncer un direct.

tell [tel] (**to**), *F:* **you're telling me!** tu l'as dit bouffi! et comment! *Voir aussi* **another; marine; tale, 1, 2.**

telling-off [ˈteliŋˈɔf] (*noun*), *F:* réprimande *f*, engueulade *f.*

tell off [ˈtelˈɔf] (**to**), *F:* réprimander*, enguirlander.

tell on [ˈtelɔn] (**to**), *F:* dénoncer*, cafarder, bourdiller; **I'll t. Mum o. you!** je (m'en) vais le dire à maman!

telly [ˈteli] (*noun*), *F:* (*a*) la télé(vision); (*b*) poste *m* de télé; *cf.* **box[1], 2.**

ten [ten] (*numeral noun*), *F:* 1. **the upper t.,** l'aristocratie *f*, les aristos *m.pl.*, les cent familles. 2. **the top t.,** palmarès *m* des dix; **in the top t.,** (disque, livre, *etc.*) sélectionné parmi les dix meilleurs.

tenderloin [ˈtendəlɔin] (*noun*) (*U.S.*), *F:* quartier *m* louche, bas-fonds *m.pl.*

tenner [ˈtenər] (*noun*), *F:* 1. dix livres *f.pl.* sterling. 2. billet* de dix livres *ou* de dix dollars.

ten-spot [ˈten-spɔt] (*noun*) (*U.S.*), *F:* 1. billet* de dix dollars. 2. emprisonnement *m* de dix années, dix longes *f.pl.* (*ou* berges *f.pl.*).

* An asterisk indicates that the word so marked is included as a head-word in the Appendix.

terrible [ˈteribl] (*adj.*), *F:* excessif, formidable; **t. prices,** des prix exorbitants (*ou* formidables); **a t. talker,** un bavard du diable.

terribly [ˈteribli, ˈterəbli] (*adv.*), *F:* extrêmement, vachement; **t. rich,** excessivement riche.

terrific [təˈrifik] (*adj.*), *F:* **1.** excellent*, sensas(s), du tonnerre. **2. a t. bore,** un sacré casse-pieds.

terrifically [təˈrifik(ə)li] (*adv.*), *F:* terriblement, énormément; **I'm t. impressed,** cela m'a fait une énorme impression; **it's t. nice of you,** c'est extrêmement gentil de votre part.

terror [ˈterər] (*noun*), *F:* fléau *m*, cauchemar *m*, peste *f*. *Voir aussi* **holy,** 3.

test-tube [ˈtesttjuːb] (*attrib. adj.*), *F:* **t.-t. baby,** bébé-éprouvette *m*.

Thames [temz] (*pr. noun*), *F:* **he'll never set the T. on fire,** il n'a pas inventé la poudre (*ou* le fil à couper le beurre); on ne lui élèvera pas une statue; il est passé à côté de la distribution; il n'a jamais cassé trois pattes à un canard.

that[1] [ðæt] (*adv.*), *F:* jusque-là, si; **he's not t. clever** [ˈðætklevər], il n'est pas si malin*.

that[2] [ðæt] (*pron.*), *F:* **... and t.'s t.!** un point, c'est tout!; et voilà!; **and t. was t.,** plus rien à dire; **Will you help me? – T. I will!** Allez-vous m'aider? – Mais bien sûr!

thatch [θætʃ] (*noun*), *F:* **to lose one's t.,** devenir chauve*, être dégazonné, perdre ses plumes.

them[1] [ðem] (*used as adj.* = *those*), *P:* **get up t. stairs!** grimpe cet escalier!; **give me t. pencils!** donne-moi ces crayons!; **I know t. people,** je connais ces gens-là. *Voir aussi* **there, 5.**

them[2] [ðem] (*used as pron.* = *those*), *P:* **t.'s my sentiments,** voilà ce que je pense, moi.

there [ˈðɛər] (*adv.*), *F:* **1. ... so t.!** ...et voilà! **2. all t.,** malin*, débrouillard; **not all t.,** bête*, un peu fou*, loufoque, demeuré; *voir aussi* **all**[1], **5. 3. t. you are!** je te l'avais bien dit! **4. t. you go (again)!** te voilà reparti! tu recommences! tu remets ça! **5. them t. sheep,** ces moutons-là. **6. t. you have me,** ça me dépasse. **7. his name was – let me think – t., I've forgotten!** il s'appelait – voyons – allons, bon! j'ai oublié! **8. nearly t.:** *voir* **bingo (89).**

thick[1] [θik] (*adj.*), *F:* **1.** bête*, ballot, gourde; **he's as t. as a plank,** il est bête* comme ses pieds; **to have a t. head,** (*a*) être bête*, être bouché à l'émeri; (*b*) avoir la gueule de bois. **2. that's a bit t.,** (*a*) cela coûte les yeux de la tête; (*b*) cela dépasse les bornes; c'est un peu raide. **3.** amical, bon copain; **they're as t. as thieves,** ils s'entendent comme des larrons en foire. **4. to have a t. skin,** avoir une peau d'hippopotame (*ou* de rhinocéros). *Voir aussi* **ear, 5.**

thick[2] [θik] (*noun*), *F:* **through t. and thin,** contre vents et marées.

thickhead [ˈθikhed] (*noun*), *F:* individu bête*, andouille *f*, bas-de-plafond *m*; *cf.* **thick**[1]

thickheaded [ˈθikˈhedid] (*adj.*), *F:* bête*, bas de plafond, lourdingue.

thick-skinned [ˈθikˈskind] (*adj.*), *F:* **to be t.-s.,** n'avoir pas l'épiderme *m* sensible, avoir une peau de rhinocéros; *cf.* **hide, 2; thick**[1], **4.**

thick-skulled [ˈθikˈskʌld] (*adj.*), *F:* = **thickheaded.**

thin [θin] (*adj.*), *F:* **1. t. on top,** presque chauve*, sans mousse sur le caillou. **2. to have a t. time (of it),** s'ennuyer*, s'embêter, se morfondre. **3. that's a bit t.!** c'est peu convaincant! *Voir aussi* **ice**[1], **5; thin-skinned.**

thing [θiŋ] (*noun*). **1.** *F:* **to have a t. about s.o., sth.,** avoir qn, qch., qui trotte sur le ciboulot. **2.** *F:* **it's not the (done) t.,** ça ne se fait pas, c'est peu conforme aux règles, ce n'est pas canonique. **3.** *F:* **the t. is ...,** le fait est... **4.** *F:* **just the t.,** exactement ce qu'il faut. **5.** *F:* **it's just one of those things,** on ne peut rien y faire. **6.** *F:* (*a*) **to know a t. or two,** être malin*, avoir plus d'un tour dans son sac; (*b*) **I could tell you a t. or two,** je pourrais vous en conter, je pourrais vous en dire des vertes et des pas mûres. **7.** *F:* **to see things,** avoir des visions *f.pl.* **8.** *F:* (*a*) **hello, old t.!** bonjour mon vieux! salut mon pote!; (*b*) **he's a nice old t.,** c'est un bien brave homme*. **9.** *F:* (*a*) **to be on (to) a good t.,** avoir le filon, être sur un bon filon; (*b*) **he makes a good t. out of it,** ça lui rapporte pas mal; il en fait ses choux gras. **10.** *F:* **do your (own) t.!**

* L'astérisque indique que le mot marqué de ce signe figure comme entrée dans le Répertoire.

exécutetoi! fais ton boulot! **11.** *P:* pénis*, outil *m.* **12.** *F:* **how's things?** comment ça va? *Voir aussi* **first.**

thingamy ['θiŋəmi], **thingamybob** ['θiŋəmibɔb], **thingamyjig** ['θiŋəmidʒig], **thingum(e)bob** ['θiŋəm(ə)bɔb], **thingummy** ['θiŋəmi] (*noun*), *F:* chose *m*, machin *m*, machin-chose *m*, machin-chouette *m*, truc *m*, bidule *m*.

think[1] [θiŋk] (*noun*), *F:* **you've got another t. coming!** tu peux toujours courir! tu te mets le doigt dans l'œil!

think[2] [θiŋk] (**to**), *F:* **1. I don't t.!** sûrement pas! et mon œil! **2. just t. of that!** ça, c'est pas banal! qui l'eût cru!

think-box ['θiŋkbɔks], **thinker** ['θiŋkər] (*noun*), *F:* cerveau *m*, ciboulot *m*; **to use one's t.,**faire travailler ses méninges *f.pl.*

think-in ['θiŋkin] (*noun*), *F:* colloque *m*, séminaire *m*, groupe *m* d'études.

thinking-cap ['θiŋkiŋkæp] (*noun*), *F:* **to put one's t.-c. on,** aviser à ce qu'on doit faire, réfléchir, méditer sur qch.

think-piece ['θiŋkpi:s] (*noun*), *F:* **1.** = **think-box. 2.** qch. qui fait réfléchir, remue-méninges *m*.

think-tank ['θiŋktæŋk] (*noun*), *F:* (*a*) réunion *f* d'une société savante; (*b*) des réservoirs *m.pl.* d'idées.

thin-skinned ['θin'skind] (*adj.*), *F:* **to be t.-s.,** avoir l'épiderme *m* sensible, être susceptible (*ou* chatouilleux).

thrash[1] [θræʃ] (*noun*), *P:* **1.** coït*, dérouillage *m*. **2.** réjouissances*, boum *f*, noce *f*, nouba *f*.

thrash[2] [θræʃ] (**to**), *F:* = **plaster (to), 1, 2.**

thrashing ['θræʃiŋ] (*noun*), *F:* = **plastering, 1, 2.**

thread [θred] (**to**), *P:* coïter* avec (une femme), enfiler.

threads [θredz] (*pl. noun*), *P:* = **vines (vine, 2).**

threepenny-bits ['θrupni'bits] (*pl. noun*) (*R.S.* = *tits*), *P: voir* **tit, 1;** *cf.* **Bristols; fit**[2]**, 4; tale, 3; trey-bits.**

thrill [θril] (*noun*), *P:* spasme provoqué par l'héroïne.

throat [θrout] (*noun*), *F:* **1. to ram sth. down s.o.'s t.,** rabattre les oreilles à qn de qch.; **we're always having it rammed down our throats that we've never had it so good,** on nous rabat les oreilles en répétant que tout est au mieux. **2. he's cutting his own t.,** il travaille à sa propre ruine; il creuse sa tombe. *Voir aussi* **cut-throat; jump**[2] **(to), 11.**

throne [θroun] (*noun*), *P:* siège *m* de W.C.*, trône *m*.

throne-room ['θrounru:m] (*noun*), *P:* W.C.*, cabinets *m.pl.*

through[1] [θru:] (*adv.*), *F:* **1. to get t. to s.o.,** faire comprendre qch. à qn, faire piger. **2. to be t.,** (*a*) avoir terminé qch., en avoir vu la fin; (*b*) être fichu (*ou* foutu). **3. to be t. with s.o.,** rompre avec qn, couper les ponts.

through[2] [θru:] (*prep.*), *F:* **he's been t. it,** il en a vu de dures, il en a vu des vertes et des pas mûres, il en a bavé, il en a vu de toutes les couleurs.

throw [θrou] (**to**), *F:* **1. I trust him as far as I can t. him,** je n'ai pas la moindre confiance en lui. **2. to t. a party,** donner une réception. **3.** étonner, estomaquer. **4. to t. a fight,** se laisser battre volontairement, se coucher. *Voir aussi* **bathwater; book**[1]**, 1; mud, 7.**

throw about (*or* **around**) ['θrouə'baut, 'θrouə'raund] (**to**), *F:* **to t. (one's) money a.,** dépenser* sans compter, faire valser le fric; **he doesn't t. his money a.,** il n'attache pas son chien avec des saucisses.

throwaway[1] ['θrouəwei] (*adj.*), *F:* **a t. line, remark,** un aparté.

throwaway[2] ['θrouəwei] (*noun*), *F:* prospectus *m*.

thrower-out ['θrouə'raut] (*noun*), *F:* = **chucker-out.**

throw in ['θrou'in] (**to**), *F:* **to t. i. the towel** (*or* **the sponge**), (*a*) (*sports*) abandonner la lutte (*ou* la partie); (*b*) s'avouer vaincu, quitter le dé. *Voir aussi* **end, 13.**

throw-out ['θrouaut] (*noun*), *F:* un laissé pour compte, rebut *m*.

throw up ['θrou'ʌp] (**to**), *F:* vomir*, dégobiller.

thrush [θrʌʃ] (*noun*), *P:* réjouissances*, bamboche *f*, nouba *f*.

thrust [θrʌst] (*noun*), *P:* amphétamine *f* (*drogues**).

thumb [θʌm] (*noun*), *F:* **1. to be all thumbs,** être lourdaud (*ou* pataud); **his fingers are all thumbs,** il a la main malheureuse, il est gauche, c'est un brise-tout. **2. thumbs up!** bravo! victoire! **3. to twiddle one's thumbs (and do nothing),** se tourner les pouces.

* An asterisk indicates that the word so marked is included as a head-word in the Appendix.

4. **it stands** (*or* **sticks**) **out like a sore t.**, ça saute aux yeux, ça crève les yeux. *Voir aussi* **green**[1], **5**; **Tom**, **4**.

thump [θʌmp] (**to**), *F:* battre*, tabasser, rouster (qn).

thumping [ˈθʌmpiŋ] (*adj.*), *F:* (*a*) gros* et grand, excellent*, maousse, bœuf; (*b*) = **thundering.**

thunderbox [ˈθʌndəbɔks] (*noun*), *P:* cuvette *f* (de cabinets).

thundering [ˈθʌndəriŋ] (*adj.*), *F:* du tonnerre; **to win with a t. majority,** l'emporter avec une majorité écrasante; **he's a t. nuisance,** il est assommant au possible.

thunder-mug [ˈθʌndəmʌg] (*noun*), *P:* pot *m* de chambre.

tich [titʃ] (*noun*), *P:* = **titch.**

tichy [ˈtitʃi] (*adj.*), *P:* = **titchy.**

tick[1] [tik] (*noun*). **1.** *P:* individu* méprisable, salaud *m*, saligaud *m*. **2.** *F:* crédit *m*, croum(e) *m*; **on t.**, à crédit, à croum(e). **3.** *F:* moment *m*, instant *m*; **hang on a t.!** (attends) une seconde!; *cf.* **jiff(y)**; **mo**; **sec**; **shake**[1], **1**, **2**.

tick[2] [tik] (**to**), *F:* **I'd like to know what makes him t.**, je voudrais bien savoir ce qui le pousse.

ticker [ˈtikər] (*noun*), *F:* **1.** cœur*, palpitant *m*; **to have a dicky t.**, avoir le cœur branlant. **2.** montre*, pendule *f*, tocante *f*.

ticket [ˈtikit] (*noun*), *F:* **that's (just) the t.!** exactement ce qui colle! **2.** contravention *f*, papillon *m*; **to get a parking t.**, se faire coller un biscuit. **3.** (*U.S.*) liste électorale; **to vote a straight t.**, voter pour toute la liste; **to vote a split t.**, faire du panachage; **the Republican t.**, le programme du parti républicain. **4. to give s.o. a round t.**, donner carte blanche à qn. *Voir aussi* **meal-ticket.**

tickety-boo [ˈtikitiˈbuː] (*adj.*), *F:* excellent*, parfait, bœuf, au poil, aux pommes.

ticking-off [ˈtikiŋˈɔf] (*noun*), *F:* réprimande *f*, savon *m*, engueulade *f*; *cf.* **tick off (to).**

tickle[1] [ˈtikl] (*noun*), *F:* de la chance*, coup *m* de pot; **to make a t.**, faire une touche. *Voir aussi* **slap**[2], **2**.

tickle[2] [ˈtikl] (**to**), *F:* **1. to t. s.o., to t. s.o.'s fancy,** amuser qn. **2. to be tickled pink,** être ravi, être aux anges. **3. to be tickled to death,** se tordre de rire*, se boyauter. *Voir aussi* **ivories, 4**.

tickler [ˈtiklər] (*noun*), *F:* **1.** moustache*, charmeuses *f.pl.* **2.** martinet *m*, fouet *m*. *Voir aussi* **rib-tickler.**

tick off [ˈtikˈɔf] (**to**), *F:* réprimander*, attraper, enguirlander; **to get ticked off,** être réprimandé*, écoper, recevoir un savon; *cf.* **ticking-off.**

tick over [ˈtikˈouvər] (**to**), *F:* **1.** (*commerce, etc.*) suivre son petit bonhomme de chemin. **2.** (*auto, machines, etc.*) bien marcher, tourner rond.

tidderly push [ˈtid(ə)liˈpuʃ] (*adv.*), *F:* **. . . and t. p.**, et patati et patata.

tiddle[1] [ˈtidl] (*noun*), *F:* (*langage enfantin*) urine *f*, pipi *m*; **to have a t.** = **tiddle**[2] **(to).**

tiddle[2] [ˈtidl] (**to**), *F:* (*langage enfantin*) uriner*, faire pipi.

tiddler [ˈtidlər] (*noun*), *F:* **1.** petit poisson, friture *f*. **2.** petit garçon, môme *m*, moutard *m*. **3.** pièce *f* d'un demi-penny.

tiddl(e)y[1] [ˈtidli] (*adj.*), *F:* **1.** légèrement ivre*, pompette, éméché. **2.** très petit, minuscule.

tiddl(e)y[2] [ˈtidli] (*noun*), *F:* **a drop of t.**, un petit coup d'alcool*, une goutte de gnôle.

tiddl(e)y push [ˈtidliˈpuʃ] (*adv.*), *F:* = **tidderly push.**

tide-mark [ˈtaidmɑːk] (*noun*), *F:* ligne *f* de crasse autour du cou *ou* sur la baignoire.

tide over [ˈtaidˈouvər] (**to**), *F:* **I borrowed a pound to t. me o.**, j'ai emprunté une livre pour pouvoir tenir le coup (*ou* pour me dépanner).

tidy [ˈtaidi] (*adj.*), *F:* **a t. sum,** une somme rondelette; **a t. fortune,** une jolie fortune.

tie on [ˈtaiˈɔn] (**to**), *P:* **to t. one o., to t. o. a load,** s'enivrer, se biturer, prendre une cuite, se piquer le nez.

tie up [ˈtaiˈʌp] (**to**), *F:* **1. I'm rather tied up at the moment,** pour le moment je suis pas mal occupé, j'ai pas mal à faire. **2. that ties up with what I've just said,** cela correspond à ce que je viens de dire. **3. our firm is tied up with yours,** notre entreprise a des accords avec la vôtre.

tiger [ˈtaigər] (*noun*), *P:* **t. in the sack,** amoureux déchaîné, chaud *m* de la pince.

tight[1] [tait] (*adj.*), *F:* **1.** ivre*, saoul,

* L'astérisque indique que le mot marqué de ce signe figure comme entrée dans le Répertoire.

rétamé, raide; **to get t.**, prendre une cuite; *voir aussi* **newt. 2.** avare*, serré, ladre, dur à la détente. 3. (*en parlant d'argent*) à court. *Voir aussi* **squeeze[1], 2.**

tight[2] [tait] (*adv.*), *F:* **to sit t.**, (*a*) voir venir, serrer les fesses; (*b*) ne pas bouger, ne pas se laisser ébranler.

tight-fisted [ˈtaitˈfistid] (*adj.*), *F:* = **tight[1], 2.**

tightwad [ˈtait-wɔd] (*noun*), *F:* avare *m*, radin *m*, grigou *m*.

tike [taik] (*noun*), *P:* = **tyke.**

tile [tail] (*noun*), *F:* **1.** chapeau*, bitos *m*; haut-de-forme *m*, gibus *m*. **2. to have a t. loose,** être un peu fou*, onduler de la toiture. **3. he spends his nights on the tiles,** il traîne dehors toute la nuit.

time [taim] (*noun*), *F:* **to do t.**, être en prison*, purger sa peine. *Voir aussi* **all-time; big-time; day, 3; good-time; short[1], 2; small-time.**

timothy [ˈtiməθi] (*noun*) (*Austr.*), *P:* bordel*, boxon *m*.

tin[1] [tin] (*adj.*), *F:* **1. t. hat** (*or* **lid**), casque *m* (de soldat). **2. that puts the t. lid on it,** c'est le comble, c'est la fin des haricots. **3. little t. god,** individu* qui se croit sorti de la cuisse de Jupiter, esbrouf(f)eur *m*, poseur *m*. **4. t. fish,** torpille *f*.

tin[2] [tin] (*noun*), *P:* argent*, galette *f*, pognon *m*, fric *m*.

tinker [ˈtiŋkər] (*noun*). **1.** *F:* petit diable, vilain *m*. **2.** *P:* **I don't care** (*or* **give**) **a t.'s** (*or* **a t.'s cuss** *or* **a t.'s toss**), je m'en fiche, je m'en bats l'œil, je m'en soucie comme de l'an quarante (*ou* de ma première chemise).

tinkle[1] [ˈtiŋkl] (*noun*), *F:* **to give s.o. a t.**, téléphoner (*ou* passer un coup de fil) à qn.

tinkle[2] [ˈtiŋkl] (**to**), *F:* (*langage enfantin*) uriner*, faire pipi.

tinkler [ˈtiŋklər] (*noun*), *P:* pot *m* de chambre, Jules, Thomas.

tinned [tind] (*adj.*), *F:* **t. music** = **canned music** (**canned, 2**).

tin-pan alley [ˈtinˈpænˈæli] (*noun*), *F:* **1.** quartier *m* des éditeurs de musique populaire. **2.** les compositeurs *m.pl.* de musique populaire.

tinpot [ˈtinˈpɔt] (*adj.*), *F:* inférieur, de second ordre, camelote.

tiny [ˈtaini] (*adj.*), *F:* **you must be out of your t. mind,** tu es en train de perdre le peu de raison que tu avais.

tip [tip] (**to**). **1.** *F:* donner*, passer, lancer (qch. à qn). **2.** *P:* coïter* avec (une femme), envoyer en l'air. *Voir aussi* **fin, 1; flipper; wink.**

tip-off [ˈtipɔf] (*noun*), *F:* renseignement*, avertissement *m*, tuyau *m*.

tip off [ˈtipˈɔf] (**to**), *F:* avertir, affranchir, mettre (qn) dans le coup.

tipple [ˈtipl] (*noun*), *P:* boisson corsée, très alcoolisée.

tip-top [ˈtipˈtɔp] (*adj.*), *F:* excellent*, extra, super.

tit [tit] (*noun*). **1.** *V:* sein*, nichon *m*, téton *m*. **2.** *V:* **to get on s.o.'s tits,** taper sur le système à qn. 3. *P:* individu bête*, idiot *m*, crétin *m*; **you big t.!** grand imbécile! sacré crétin! *Voir aussi* **arse, 4; Tom, 3.**

titch [titʃ] (*noun*), *P:* petit* individu, bas-du-cul *m*, astèque *m*.

titchy [ˈtitʃi] (*adj.*), *P:* petit, crapoussin.

titfer [ˈtitfər] (*noun*) (*R.S.* = *tit-for-tat* = *hat*), *P:* chapeau*.

titty [ˈtiti] (*noun*) (*pl.* **titties**), *V:* = **tit, 1.**

titty-bottle [ˈtiti-bɔtl] (*noun*), *P:* biberon *m*.

tizwas [ˈtizwɔz] (*noun*), *F:* **to be all of a t.**, être aux cent coups, être démonté, être affolé; *cf.* **doodah; tizzy.**

tizzy [ˈtizi] (*noun*), *F:* (*a*) affolement *m*, remue-ménage *m*, débandade *f*; (*b*) panique *f*, bile *f*, mauvais sang; **to be in a t.**, être affolé.

toast [toust] (*noun*), *F:* **to have s.o. on t.**, avoir qn à sa merci, tenir qn.

toby [ˈtoubi] (*noun*), *P:* **the t.**, la grande route*, le grand trimard.

tod, Tod [tɔd] (*noun*) (*R.S.* = *Tod Sloan* = *alone*), *P:* **to be on one's t.**, être tout seul, être seulabre.

toddle[1] [ˈtɔdl] (*noun*), *F:* petite promenade, balade *f*.

toddle[2] [ˈtɔdl] (**to**), *F:* **1.** se balader, se baguenauder, déambuler. **2.** = **toddle off (to).**

toddle along (*or* **off**) [ˈtɔdl-əˈlɔŋ, ˈtɔdl-ˈɔf] (**to**), *F:* partir*, se trotter, se carapater.

to-do [təˈduː] (*noun*), *F:* remue-ménage *m*; **what a t.-d.!** quelle affaire! quelle histoire!

toe [tou] (*noun*), *F:* **1. to tread on s.o.'s toes,** marcher sur les pieds de qn, offenser qn, froisser qn. **2. to be on one's toes,** être alerté, être sur le qui-vive, ouvrir

* An asterisk indicates that the word so marked is included as a head-word in the Appendix.

l'œil. 3. **to turn up one's toes,** mourir*, casser sa pipe, avaler sa chique.

toehold [ˈtouhould] (*noun*), *F:* **to get a t.,** avoir une prise précaire.

toe-ragger [ˈtou-rægər] (*noun*) (*Austr.*), *P:* prisonnier *m* de courte durée, enschibé *m* d'une courte.

toey [ˈtoui] (*adj.*) (*Austr.*), *P:* inquiet, anxieux, bileux.

toff [tɔf] (*noun*), *F:* rupin(os) *m*, cossu *m*, milord *m*; **the toffs,** le grand monde, le gratin.

toffee [ˈtɔfi] (*noun*), *F:* **he can't play for t.** (*or* **for t. apples** *or* **for t. nuts**), il joue comme un pied.

toffee-nose [ˈtɔfi-nouz] (*noun*), *F:* snob *m*, crâneur *m*, poseur *m*.

toffee-nosed [ˈtɔfi-nouzd] (*adj.*), *F:* prétentieux*, bêcheur, pincé.

together [təˈgeðər] (*adv.*), *F:* sans mousse, pénard.

tog out [ˈtɔgˈaut] (**to**), *F:* **to t. (oneself) o.,** se mettre sur son trente et un.

togs [tɔgz] (*pl. noun*), *F:* vêtements*, nippes *f.pl.*, frusques *f.pl.*

tog up [ˈtɔgˈʌp] (**to**), *F:* **to t. (oneself) u.** = **to tog (oneself) out.**

toke[1] [touk] (*noun*), *P:* 1. pain*, bricheton *m*, larton *m*. 2. bouffée *f*.

toke[2] [touk] (**to**), *P:* tirer, traîner, remorquer.

toke up [ˈtoukˈʌp] (**to**), *P:* allumer (une cigarette*).

tokus [ˈtoukəs] (*noun*), *P:* 1. fesses*, pétrus *m*, pétrousquin *m*. 2. anus*, troufignon *m*.

Tom, tom [tɔm] (*noun*). 1. *F:* **any T., Dick, or Harry,** Pierre et Paul, n'importe qui, le premier venu. 2. *P:* **Tom Mix,** (*a*) (*R.S.* = *fix*) piqûre *f* de narcotique; (*b*) *voir* **bingo (6).** 3. *P:* **T. Tit, t. tit** (*R.S.* = *shit*): **to go for a t. tit,** aller déféquer*, aller faire caca. 4. *P:* **T. Thumb** (*R.S.* = *rum*), rhum *m*; *cf.* **kingdom-come, 3; touch-your-bum.** 5. *F:* (=*tom cat*) matou *m*. *Voir aussi* **Uncle, 9.**

tomato [təˈmeitou] (*noun*) (*U.S.*). 1. *F:* jolie fille*, fleur *f*, pépée *f*, poulette *f*. 2. *P:* prostituée*.

tommy[1] [ˈtɔmi] (*noun*). 1. *P:* pain*, provisions *f.pl.*; nourriture*. 2. *F:* **t., T. (Atkins),** soldat* anglais, Tommy *m*.

tommy[2] [ˈtɔmi] (**to**) (*Austr.*), *P:* s'enfuir*, décamper, filer.

tommy-rot [ˈtɔmiˈrɔt] (*noun*), *F:* bêtises*, tissu *m* d'âneries.

ton [tʌn] (*noun*), *F:* 1. = **ton-up.** 2. **tons of...,** une abondance* de..., une tripotée de...; **to have tons of money,** avoir beaucoup d'argent*, avoir des masses d'argent*, avoir de l'argent* à gogo; **to have tons of time,** avoir largement le temps. 3. cent livres *f.pl.* sterling. 4. **to weigh a t.,** peser lourd, peser des mille et des cents. *Voir aussi* **come down (to), 3.**

tongue [tʌŋ] (**to**): **to t. a woman,** (*a*) *P:* filer une langouse à une femme; (*b*) *V:* sucer une femme (*coït* buccal*).

tongue-kiss [ˈtʌŋkis] (*noun*), *F:* = **French kiss (French**[1]**, 1).**

tongue-pie [ˈtʌŋˈpai] (*noun*), *F:* **to get a slice of t.-p.,** se faire dire ses (quatre) vérités *f.pl.*, en prendre pour son grade.

tonk [tɔŋk] (*noun*), *P:* pénis*, tringle *f*. *Voir aussi* **honky-tonk.**

ton-up [ˈtʌnʌp] (*noun*), *F:* **to do a t.-u.,** faire cent milles (160 km) à l'heure (en moto); **the t.-u. boys,** les motards *m.pl.* bolides.

toodle-oo [ˈtuːdlˈuː] (*excl.*), *F:* 1. au revoir, ciao. 2. *voir* **bingo (22).**

toodle-pip [ˈtuːdlˈpip] (*excl.*), *F:* = **toodle-oo, 1.**

tool [tuːl] (*noun*), *P:* 1. pénis*, outil *m*. 2. pickpocket *m*, tire *m*, tireur *m*, fourche *f*, fourchette *f*. 3. (*pl.*) attirail *m* de camé.

tool along [ˈtuːləˈlɔŋ] (**to**), *F:* se balader, se baguenauder.

tool off [ˈtuːlˈɔf] (**to**), *P:* partir*, se barrer.

tooth [tuːθ] (*noun*) (*pl.* **teeth**), *F:* 1. **to have a sweet t.,** aimer les sucreries *f.pl.* 2. **to be long in the t.,** n'être plus jeune, avoir de la bouteille. 3. (*Austr.*) **on the t.,** (*a*) affamé; (*b*) de bon goût, savoureux, succulent. 4. **to get one's teeth into sth.,** se mettre pour de bon à qch., s'acharner à faire qch. 5. **to knock s.o.'s teeth in,** battre* qn, rentrer dans le chou à qn, amocher le portrait à qn. 6. **to go at it t. and nail,** travailler* d'achar. *Voir aussi* **dress up (to), 2; fed up, (*a*).**

toothy-peg [ˈtuːθi-peg] (*noun*), *F:* (*langage enfantin*) petite dent* d'enfant, quenotte *f*.

tootle [ˈtuːtl] (**to**), *F:* corner, klaxonner.

* L'astérisque indique que le mot marqué de ce signe figure comme entrée dans le Répertoire.

tootle along [ˈtuːtl-əˈlɔŋ] (**to**), *F:* suivre son petit bonhomme de chemin.

toots [tuts] (*noun*), *F:* chéri(e), mon petit, ma petite; **hello, t.!** bonjour (*ou* salut) coco, cocotte!

tootsie [ˈtutsi] (*noun*). **1.** *F:* = **toots. 2.** *P:* lesbienne*, gouchotte *f.* **3.** (*pl.*) *F:* = **tootsie-wootsies.**

tootsie-wootsies [ˈtutsiˈwutsiz] (*pl. noun*), *F:* (*langage enfantin*) pieds*, petons *m.pl.*, paturons *m.pl.*

tootsy [ˈtutsi] (*noun*), *F:* = **toots; tootsie.**

tootsy-footsy [ˈtutsiˈfutsi] (*noun*), *F:* = **footsy.**

top[1] [tɔp] (*noun*), *F:* **1. to go over the t.,** exagérer*, y aller fort. **2. to blow one's t.,** se mettre en colère*, éclater, sortir de ses gonds; *cf.* **flip**[3] (**to**), 2. **3. the t. of the morning to you!** je vous souhaite le meilleur des bonjours! **4. off the t.,** la première réaction, (le mouvement) d'instinct. **5. t. of the shop:** *voir* **bingo** (**90**). *Voir aussi* **copper-top; heap, 2** (*a*); **rag-top; tail**[1]**, 6; thin, 1.**

top[2] [tɔp] (**to**), *P:* pendre*, exécuter, agrafer; **topped (and chopped),** pendu, exécuté.

top-flight [ˈtɔpˈflait], **top-hole** [ˈtɔpˈhoul] (*adj.*), *F:* excellent*, foutral, le dessus du panier, le bouquet.

top-knot [ˈtɔpnɔt] (*noun*), *P:* tête*, bobèche *f*, plafond *m.*

topless [ˈtɔplis] (*adj.*), *F:* torse nu, seins* nus.

top-line [ˈtɔpˈlain], **top-notch** [ˈtɔpˈnɔtʃ] (*adj.*), *F:* = **top-flight.**

top-liner [ˈtɔpˈlainər], **top-notcher** [ˈtɔpˈnɔtʃər] (*noun*), *F:* as *m*, expert *m* (dans sa profession), crack *m.*

top off [ˈtɔpˈɔf] (**to**) (*Austr.*), *P:* **1. to t. s.o. o.,** rabrouer qn, remettre qn à sa place. **2.** dénoncer*, servir d'indicateur* de police.

topper [ˈtɔpər] (*noun*), *F:* **1.** le dessus du panier, le bouquet, la crème, la fleur des petits pois. **2.** chapeau* haut de forme, gibus *m.*

topping [ˈtɔpiŋ] (*adj.*), *F:* excellent*, formid(able), épatant.

topping-out [ˈtɔpiŋˈaut] (*noun*), *F:* cérémonie qui marque la terminaison de la construction de la grosse œuvre d'un bâtiment.

tops [tɔps] (*noun*), *F:* **the t.,** le dessus du panier, la crème.

torch [tɔːtʃ] (*noun*) (*U.S.*), *F:* **1. to carry the t. for s.o.,** aimer* qn qui ne vous aime pas, soupirer en vain. **2.** pyromane *m*, incendiaire *m*, pétroleur *m.*

torch-song [ˈtɔːtʃsɔŋ] (*noun*) (*U.S.*), *F:* chanson *f* d'amour déçu, lamentation *f* d'amour.

torch up [ˈtɔːtʃˈʌp] (**to**), *P:* = **toke up (to).**

torn [tɔːn] (*p.p.*): *voir* **tear**[2] **(to).**

torpedo [tɔːˈpiːdou] (*noun*) (*U.S.*), *P:* but(t)eur *m* de louage.

tosh [tɔʃ] (*noun*). **1.** *P:* individu*, mec *m*, type *m.* **2.** *F:* bêtises*, sornettes *f.pl.*, blague *f.*

tosher [ˈtɔʃər] (*noun*), *P:* = **tosh, 1.**

tosh-light [ˈtɔʃlait] (*noun*), *P:* feu pris à une autre cigarette.

toss-off [ˈtɔsɔf] (*noun*), *V:* acte *m* de masturbation, moussage *m* maison.

toss off [ˈtɔsˈɔf] (**to**). **1.** *V:* **to t. (oneself) off,** se masturber*, se faire mousser. **2.** *F:* **to t. o. a pint,** boire*, s'enfiler un verre, écluser un godet.

toss-pot [ˈtɔs-pɔt] (*noun*), *F:* ivrogne*, vide-bouteilles *m.*

toss-up [ˈtɔsʌp] (*noun*), *F:* (*a*) une chance sur deux, chance égale, pile ou face; (*b*) affaire* à issue douteuse.

tote[1] [tout] (*noun*), *F:* (*turf*) totaliseur *m*, totalisateur *m* (des paris), le pari mutuel, le P.M.U.

tote[2] [tout] (**to**), *F:* **1.** porter, trimballer, transbahuter; **to t. a gun,** être armé (*ou* flingué). **2. to t. for business,** chercher à faire des affaires, quémander du travail.

tote-bag [ˈtoutbæg] (*noun*), *F:* (sac) fourre-tout *m.*

tother, t'other [ˈtʌðər] (*adj. & pron.*) (=*the other*), *F:* l'autre; **you can't tell one from t., you can't tell t. from which,** ils sont du pareil au même, on ne peut les distinguer l'un de l'autre, ils se ressemblent comme deux gouttes d'eau.

touch[1] [tʌtʃ] (*noun*). **1.** *P:* **to make a t., to put the t. on s.o.,** emprunter* de l'argent à qn, taper qn. **2.** *F:* **it was t. and go, it was a near t.,** cela ne tenait qu'à un fil; *voir aussi* **touch-and-go. 3.** *F:* **soft t.** = **easy mark (easy**[1]**, 3).**

touch[2] [tʌtʃ] (**to**). **1.** *P:* **to t. s.o. for money** = **to make a touch (touch**[1]**, 1). 2.** *F:* **to t. lucky,** avoir de la chance*, être veinard. **3.** *P:* arrêter*, épingler, alpaguer. *Voir aussi* **rock**[1]**, 4; wood, 1.**

* An asterisk indicates that the word so marked is included as a head-word in the Appendix.

touch-and-go [ˈtʌtʃənˈgou] (*adj.*), *F:* (*a*) très incertain, douteux, dans la balance; (*b*) hasardeux, chanceux, aléatoire; *voir aussi* **touch**[1], **2.**

touched [tʌtʃt] (*adj.*), *F:* **t. (in the head),** fou*, toqué, timbré.

touch up [ˈtʌtʃˈʌp] (**to**), *P:* **to t. u. a girl,** peloter une fille.

touch-your-bum [ˈtʌtʃjəˈbʌm] (*noun*) (*R.S.* = *rum*), *P:* rhum *m*; *cf.* **kingdom-come, 3; Tom, 4.**

tough[1] [tʌf] (*adj.*), *F:* **1. a t. nut** (*or* **guy**), un dur (à cuire), un coriace. **2. he's a t. customer,** il est peu commode. **3.** difficile*. **4. t. luck, a t. break,** malchance*, déveine *f*, guigne *f*.

tough[2] [tʌf] (*noun*), *F:* **1.** vaurien*, voyou *m*. **2.** brute *f*, crapule *f*, fripouille *f*, sale type *m*. **3.** gangster *m*, criminel *m*, saigneur *m*.

toughie [ˈtʌfi] (*noun*), *F:* **1.** = **tough**[2], **1, 2, 3. 2.** problème *m* difficile à résoudre, casse-tête *m*.

tousing [ˈtauziŋ] (*noun*), *F:* = **roasting.**

towel [taul, ˈtauəl] (**to**), *P:* battre*, rosser, dérouiller.

towelling [ˈtau(ə)liŋ] (*noun*), *P:* raclée *f*, peignée *f*, dérouillée *f*.

town [taun] (*noun*), *F:* **1. to go to t.,** (*a*) faire la bombe (*ou* la foire *ou* la noce); (*b*) réussir, arriver, percer; (*c*) dépenser* sans compter, mettre le paquet. **2. to go on the t.** = **to go to town** (*a*). **3. to go to t. on s.o.,** réprimander* qn, engueuler qn. *Voir aussi* **red**[1], **3.**

townified [ˈtaunifaid], **towny** [ˈtauni] (*adj.*), *F:* urbain, citadin.

track[1] [træk] (*noun*). **1.** *F:* (=*sound track*) piste *f* sonore (d'un film). **2.** *F:* disque *m*. **3.** *F:* **to have the inside of the t. with s.o.,** l'emporter sur qn, avoir le dessus, tenir le bon bout. **4.** *F:* **to hit the t., to make tracks,** partir*, se mettre en route, plier bagage, mettre les bouts, se tailler; **to make tracks for home,** rentrer chez soi, regagner le bercail. **5.** (*pl.*) *P:* trous *m.pl.* (de piqûres hypodermiques). *Voir aussi* **dirt-track.**

track[2] [træk] (**to**) (*Austr.*), *F:* **to t. with a girl,** faire la cour à une fille. *Voir aussi* **backtrack (to).**

trad[1] [træd] (*adj.*), *F:* (=*traditional*) traditionnel; **t. jazz,** jazz *m* Nouvelle-Orléans et ses dérivés.

trad[2] [træd] (*noun*), *F:* (=*traditional jazz*), jazz traditionnel.

trade[1] [treid] (*noun*). **1.** *F:* **to take it out in t.,** se faire payer en nature plutôt qu'en argent. **2.** *P:* clientèle *f* (d'une prostituée *ou* d'un pédéraste); miché *m*, micheton *m*. **3.** *F:* **he knows all the tricks of the t.,** il la connaît dans les coins.

trade[2] [treid] (**to**). **1.** *F:* **to t. punches,** échanger des coups*, se crêper le chignon. **2.** *P:* chercher des rapports sexuels, faire le trottoir.

trade-in [ˈtreidin] (*noun*), *F:* (article *m* de) reprise *f*.

trade in [ˈtreidˈin] (**to**), *F:* **to t. i. a car,** acheter une voiture avec reprise, donner une auto en reprise.

trading-in [ˈtreidiŋˈin] (*noun*), *F:* vente *f* en reprise.

trail [treil] (*noun*), *F:* **to hit the t.** = **to hit the track (track**[1], **4).**

train [trein] (*noun*), *P:* fille* qui suit les bandes de garçons, les groupes de pop, *etc.*; groupette *f*; **to pull a t.,** (*pour une fille*) coïter* avec une succession de garçons, caramboler à la file. *Voir aussi* **gravy, 1; milk-train; puffer(-train).**

tramp [træmp] (*noun*), *P:* femme* facile, chaude lapine, baiseuse *f*.

trap [træp] (*noun*). **1.** *P:* bouche*, gueule *f*; **shut your t.!** tais-toi! (*se taire**), ferme-la! ferme ton clapet!; **to keep one's t. shut,** taire sa gueule, la fermer; *cf.* **rat-trap. 2.** *P:* agent* de police, flic *m*. **3.** (*pl.*) *F:* vêtements*, fringues *f.pl.* **4.** (*pl.*) *F:* possessions *f.pl.*, affaires *f.pl.*, effets *m.pl.*, armes et bagages; **to pack up one's traps,** plier bagage. *Voir aussi* **bug-trap; flea-trap.**

trash [træʃ] (*noun*) (*U.S.*), *P:* mendiant*, clodot *m*, mangav *m*.

travel-agent [ˈtrævəlˈeidʒənt] (*noun*), *P:* fournisseur *m* de LSD (*drogues**), agent *m* de voyage.

traveller [ˈtræv(ə)lər] (*noun*), *F:* romanichel *m*, manouche *mf*.

trawler [ˈtrɔːlər] (*noun*) (*Austr.*), *P:* car* de police, panier *m* à salade, fourgon *m*.

treacle [ˈtriːkl] (*noun*), *P:* opium *m* (*drogues**), noir *m*.

tread [tred] (*noun*), *P:* **to do** (*or* **chuck**) **a t.,** coïter*, faire l'amour, faire un carton.

* L'astérisque indique que le mot marqué de ce signe figure comme entrée dans le Répertoire.

treat[1] [triːt] (a) (*adv.*), *F:* agréablement, extrêmement bien; **that whisky went down a t.**, ce whisky a fait du bien par où il a passé.

treat[2] [triːt] (*noun*), *F:* **to stand t.**, offrir la tournée; **I'm standing t.**, c'est moi qui régale.

tree [triː] (*noun*), *F:* **1. up a t.** = **up a gum-tree. 2. they don't grow on trees,** on n'en trouve pas à la douzaine. *Voir aussi* **apple-tree; Christmas-tree; palm-tree.**

tremble [ˈtrembl] (*noun*), *F:* **to be all of a t.**, avoir la tremblote.

tremendous [triˈmendəs, trəˈmendəs] (*adj.*), *F:* **1.** énorme, immense; **a t. decision,** une décision très importante. **2.** passionnant, palpitant; **a t. game of tennis,** une partie de tennis formidable.

tremendously [triˈmendəsli, trəˈmendəsli] (*adv.*), *F:* énormément, démesurément; **he is t. popular,** il jouit d'une immense popularité.

trendiness [ˈtrendinis] (*noun*), *F:* nouvelle mode, dernier cri.

trendy[1] [ˈtrendi] (*adj.*), *F:* à la mode, dans le vent.

trendy[2] [ˈtrendi] (*noun*), *F:* qn à la mode, dandy *m*, gandin *m*.

trey [trei] (*noun*), *P:* colis *m ou* paquet *m ou* sachet *m* de stupéfiants.

trey-bits [ˈtreibits] (*pl. noun*) (*Austr.*), *P:* = **threepenny-bits.**

tribe [traib] (*noun*), *F:* enfants *mf.pl.* d'une même famille, rejetons *m.pl.*, smala(h) *f*; (toute) une kyrielle (d'enfants).

trick[1] [trik] (*noun*). **1.** *F:* **how's tricks?** quoi de neuf? **2.** *F:* **he doesn't miss a t.**, rien ne lui échappe; il est roublard. **3.** *F:* **that should do the t.**, ça fera l'affaire. **4.** *P:* **to turn a t.**, (*d'une prostituée*) trouver un client, faire une passe. **5.** *F:* **to be up to all sorts of tricks,** faire les cent coups. *Voir aussi* **bag**[1]**, 6, 7; funny**[1]**, 2; trade**[1]**, 3.**

trick[2] [trik] (**to**), *P:* coïter* avec (une femme), godiller, pinocher.

trick-cyclist [ˈtrikˈsaiklist] (*noun*), *P:* psychiatre *mf*.

trig [trig] (*noun*) (*abbr.* = *trigonometry*), *F:* la trigo(nométrie).

trigger-happy [ˈtrigəhæpi] (*adj.*), *F:* **to be t.-h.**, être rapide à la gâchette, avoir la gâchette facile.

trigger-man [ˈtrigəmæn] (*noun*), *P:* (*a*) assassin*, professionnel *m* de la gâchette; (*b*) but(t)eur *m*, flingueur *m*; (*c*) garde *f* du corps, gorille *m*.

trilbies [ˈtrilbiz] (*pl. noun*) (*Austr.*), *P:* jambes*, gambettes *f.pl.*

trim [trim] (**to**), *P:* coïter* avec (une femme), fourailler.

trip[1] [trip] (*noun*), *P:* **1.** mesure *f* de LSD (*drogues**). **2. to take** (*or* **make** *or* **go on**) **a t.**, (*a*) être sous l'effet du LSD, être du voyage; (*b*) purger sa peine en prison*, faire sa taule.

trip[2] [trip] (**to**), *P:* = **to take a trip** (**trip**[1]**, 2** (*a*)).

tripe [traip] (*noun*), *F:* **1.** bêtises*, sornettes *f.pl.*, fichaises *f.pl.* **2.** camelote *f*, quincaillerie *f*.

tripehound [ˈtraiphaʊnd] (*noun*), *P:* vaurien*, charogne *f*.

tripperish [ˈtripəriʃ], **trippery** [ˈtripəri] (*adj.*), *F:* envahi de touristes, popu(lo), populmiche.

tripy [ˈtraipi] (*adj.*), *F:* camelote, gnognot(t)e; **a t. novel,** roman *m* sans valeur, navet *m*.

trizzer [ˈtrizər] (*noun*) (*Austr.*), *P:* W.C.*, chiottes *f.pl.*

trog [trɔg] (*noun*), *P:* **1.** spéléologue *m*, troglodyte *m*. **2.** individu vieux jeu, collet monté, vieux tableau, vieille baderne.

trolley [ˈtrɔli] (*noun*) (*U.S.*), *F:* **off one's t.** = **off one's rocker** (**rocker, 2**).

trot [trɔt] (*noun*). **1.** *F:* **on the t.**, (*a*) à la suite, coup sur coup; **to win four times on the t.**, gagner quatre fois de suite; (*b*) (*après s'être échappé de prison*) en fuite, en cavale. **2.** *F:* **to keep s.o. on the t.**, faire trotter qn, actionner qn. **3.** *P:* prostituée*, marcheuse *f*, roulure *f*. **4.** *P:* **the trots,** diarrhée*, courante *f*.

trotter [ˈtrɔtər] (*noun*), *P:* **1.** déserteur *m*, franc-fileur *m*. **2.** individu recherché par la police, décarreur *m*. **3.** (*pl.*) pieds*, trottinets *m.pl.*

trouble [ˈtrʌbl] (*noun*). **1.** *F:* **to get a girl into t.**, rendre une fille enceinte*. **2.** *P:* **t. and strife** (*R.S.* = *wife*), épouse*.

trousers [ˈtrauzəz] (*pl. noun*), *F:* **to wear the t.**, (*d'une épouse*) porter la culotte; *cf.* **pants, 7.**

trouser-snake [ˈtrauzə-sneik] (*noun*) (*Austr.*), *P:* **one-eyed t.-s.**, pénis*, anguille *f* de calecif.

trout [traut] (*noun*), *P:* vieille femme*,

* An asterisk indicates that the word so marked is included as a head-word in the Appendix.

vieille savate, vieux trumeau, vieille guenon, vieille rombière, charogne *f*.

truck-driver [ˈtrʌkdraivər] (*noun*), *P*: = **driver, 2.**

trump [trʌmp] (*noun*), *F*: **1.** brave homme*, chic type *m*. **2. to turn up trumps,** (*a*) réussir mieux que l'on espérait, avoir de la chance*; (*b*) rendre service donner un bon coup de main. *Voir aussi* **card, 7.**

trusty [ˈtrʌsti] (*noun*), *F*: prisonnier *m* à qui l'on donne certains privilèges, un sûr, un prévot.

try [trai] (*noun*), *F*: **just (you) have a t.!** = **just (you) try it on!** (*voir* **try on (to)**).

tryanthewontigong [ˈtrai-ænθiˈwɔnti-gɔŋ] (*noun*) (*Austr.*), *F*: = **thingamy.**

try-on [ˈtraiɔn] (*noun*), *F*: **1.** ballon *m* d'essai. **2.** (coup *m* de) bluff *m*.

try on [ˈtraiˈɔn] (**to**), *F*: **don't (you) t. it o. with me!** ne cherche pas à me bluffer (*ou* à me mettre dedans)! il ne faut pas me la refaire!; **just (you) t. it o.!** chiche! vas-y qu'on voit!

try-out [ˈtrai-aut] (*noun*), *F*: premier essai, essai préliminaire (*ou* préalable).

tub [tʌb] (*noun*), *F*: **1.** gros ventre*, bedaine *f*. **2. old t. (of a boat),** raf(f)iot *m*.

tube [tju:b] (*noun*), *F*: **1. it's my tubes** [miˈtju:bz], c'est mes bronches. **2. the T.,** le Métro; **we came by T.,** nous avons pris le Métro. *Voir aussi* **test-tube.**

tub-thumper [ˈtʌbθʌmpər] (*noun*), *F*: = **soapbox orator.**

tuck [tʌk] (*noun*), *F*: (*école*) friandises *f.pl.*, sucreries *f.pl.*; *cf.* **tuckshop.**

tuck away [ˈtʌkəˈwei] (**to**), *F*: **1.** mettre à gauche. **2. to t. it a.,** boire* et/ou manger*, s'en mettre derrière la cravate, s'en mettre jusque-là, se caler les côtes.

tucker [ˈtʌkər] (*noun*) (*Austr.*), *F*: nourriture*, mangeaille *f*. *Voir aussi* **bib.**

tuckered [ˈtʌkəd] (*adj.*), *P*: fatigué*, éreinté, vanné.

tuck-in [ˈtʌkˈin] (*noun*), *F*: repas faramineux, gueuleton *m*, bombance *f*; **to have a good t.-i.** = **tuck in (to).**

tuck in [ˈtʌkˈin] (**to**), *F*: manger* de bon cœur, s'en mettre jusqu'au menton, s'en mettre plein la lampe; **t. i.!** vas-y, mange!

tuck into [ˈtʌkˈintu:] (**to**), *F*: **to t. i. a meal,** manger* un repas à belles dents, faire bonne chère.

tucks [tʌks] (*pl. noun*), *F*: **to be in t.,** se tordre de rire*, se fendre la bouille, être plié en deux.

tuckshop [ˈtʌkʃɔp] (*noun*), *F*: (*école*) annexe *f* de la cantine où se vendent les friandises *f.pl.*; *cf.* **tuck.**

tumble[1] [ˈtʌmbl] (*noun*), *F*: **to have a t. with** = **tumble**[2] **(to), 1.**

tumble[2] [ˈtʌmbl] (**to**), *F*: **1. to t. (a woman),** culbuter (une femme). **2. to t. to sth.,** comprendre qch. tout à coup, entraver qch.

tummy [ˈtʌmi] (*noun*), *F*: (*a*) ventre*, bide *m*, bidon *m*; (*b*) bedaine *f*.

tummy-ache [ˈtʌmi-eik] (*noun*), *F*: mal *m* au ventre.

tune [tju:n] (*noun*), *F*: **1. to the t. of...,** pour la somme (pas mal salée) de... **2. to change one's t.,** changer de ton (*ou* de langage), chanter sur une autre note. *Voir aussi* **old, 5.**

tune in [ˈtju:nˈin] (**to**), *F*: **1.** se mettre au diapason. **2.** être pris dans l'engrenage *m*.

tune up [ˈtju:nˈʌp] (**to**), *F*: se conditionner, s'entraîner.

tup [tʌp] (**to**), *P*: coïter* avec (une femme), calecer, caramboler, sch(e)-nailler.

tuppence [ˈtʌp(ə)ns] (*noun*) (=*twopence*), *F*: **I don't care t.,** ça m'est bien égal, je m'en fiche pas mal; **it's not worth t.,** ça ne vaut pas deux sous, ça ne vaut pas chipette.

tuppenny [ˈtʌp(ə)ni] (*adj.*) (=*twopenny*), *F*: **I don't give** (*or* **care**) **a t. damn** (*or V*: **fuck**), je m'en contre-fiche, *V*: je m'en fous pas mal; *cf.* **damn**[3].

tuppenny-ha'penny [ˈtʌp(ə)niˈheip(ə)-ni] (*adj.*) (=*twopenny-halfpenny*), *F*: insignifiant, piètre, de quatre sous.

tupp'ny [ˈtʌpni] (*adj.*) = **tuppenny.**

turd [tə:d] (*noun*), *P*: **1.** étron*, colombin *m*. **2.** saligaud *m*, salaud *m*, fumier *m*. **3. to skin a t.,** être avare*, être constipé du morlingue.

turd-burglar [ˈtə:dbə:glər], **turd-snipper** [ˈtə:d-snipər], *V*: pédéraste*, qui est de la bague (*ou* du rond).

turf [tə:f] (*noun*) (*U.S.*), *P*: **to be on the t.,** racoler*, faire le bitume (*ou* le trottoir *ou* le pavé).

* L'astérisque indique que le mot marqué de ce signe figure comme entrée dans le Répertoire.

turf out ['tə:f'aut] (**to**), *F:* flanquer dehors, balancer, envoyer dinguer.
turk, Turk [tə:k] (*noun*), *F:* (**little**) **t.**, petit démon, sale gosse *m*, vermine *f*.
turkey ['tə:ki] (*noun*). **1.** *P:* **cold t.**, sevrage *m* de drogues. **2.** *F:* **to talk t.**, parler* sérieusement, en venir au fait.
turn [tə:n] (*noun*), *F:* **1.** (*a*) **it gave me quite a** (**nasty**) **t.**, (tout) mon sang n'a fait qu'un tour; (*b*) **you gave me such a t.!** vous m'avez fait une belle peur*! vous m'avez retourné le sang! **2. she had one of her turns yesterday,** hier elle a eu une de ses crises (*ou* attaques).
turn-about-face ['tə:nəbaut'feis] (*noun*), *F:* volte-face *f*.
turned on ['tə:nd'ɔn] (*p.p. & adj.*), *F:* = **switched on, 1, 2, 3.**
turn in ['tə:n'in] (**to**), *F:* **1.** se coucher*, se pieuter. **2.** rendre, rapporter (qch.); **to t. oneself i.** (**to the police**), se constituer prisonnier, se faire coffrer.
turniphead ['tə:niphed] (*noun*), *P:* individu bête*, cruche *f*, ballot *m*.
turn-on ['tə:nɔn] (*noun*), *P:* une séance particulière de drogues.
turn on ['tə:n'ɔn] (**to**) = **switch on** (**to**), **1, 2, 3.**
turnout ['tə:naut] (*noun*). **1.** *F:* assemblée *f*, foule *f*, assistance *f*, auditoire *m*, public *m*. **2.** *F:* vêtements*, tenue *f*, uniforme *m*. **3.** *P:* coït* d'un groupe avec une seule fille ou femme; dérouillage *m* à la une.
turnover ['tə:nouvər] (*noun*), *P:* perquisition *f*, fouille *f*.
turn over ['tə:n'ouvər] (**to**), *P:* **1. to t. s.o. o.,** voler*, refaire qn, rouler qn. **2. to t. o. a cell,** fouiller une cellule.
turn-up ['tə:nʌp] (*noun*), *P:* **1. that's a t.-u.** (**for the book**), c'est une sacrée surprise. **2.** chahut *m*, tapage *m*, boucan *m*, chambard *m*.
turn up ['tə:n'ʌp] (**to**), *F:* **1.** arriver* (à l'improviste), débarquer, faire une apparition. **2.** arriver, se passer, se produire. **3.** découvrir*, trouver, dégot(t)er. **4. that turns me up,** ça m'écœure, ça me soulève le cœur. **5. t. it u.!** arrête (les frais)! c'est marre! *Voir aussi* **nose, 6; toe, 3.**
turps [tə:ps] (*noun*) (=*turpentine*), *F:* (essence *f* de) térébenthine *f*.
turtles ['tə:tlz] (*pl. noun*), *P:* (*R.S.* = *turtle-doves* = *gloves*) gants *m.pl.*

twack [twæk], **twam(my)** ['twæm(i)] (*noun*), *P:* = **twat, 1.**
twang [twæŋ] (*noun*) (*Austr.*), *P:* opium *m* (*drogues**), touffiane *f*.
twat [twɔt] (*noun*). **1.** *V:* vagin*, con *m*, con(n)asse *f*. **2.** *P:* individu bête*, idiot *m*, con *m*, connard *m*.
twee [twi:] (*adj.*), *F:* (*a*) gentil, mignon; (*b*) (*péj.*) maniéré, mignard.
tweetie(-pie) ['twi:ti('pai)] (*noun*), *F:* = **sweetie(-pie).**
twenty-five ['twenti'faiv] (*noun*), *P:* LSD *m* (*drogues**), vingt-cinq *m*.
twerp [twə:p] (*noun*), *F:* individu bête*, ballot *m*, crétin *m*.
twiddly ['twidli] (*adj.*), *F:* **t. bits,** (*a*) (*musique*) enjolivure *f*; (*b*) fanfreluche *f*, colifichet *m*.
twig [twig] (**to**), *P:* comprendre, saisir, piger; **now I t. it!** j'y suis maintenant!
twink [twiŋk] (*noun*), *P:* pédéraste*, homme efféminé, chochotte *f*, chouquette *f*.
twinkle ['twiŋkl] (*noun*), *P:* **1.** pénis* (d'enfant), zizi *m*. **2. to have a t.,** uriner*, pisser.
twirl [twə:l] (*noun*), *P:* **1.** gardien* de prison, maton *m*, matuche *m*. **2.** clef*, passe-partout *m*, carouble *f*. **3.** cigarette*, cibiche *f*.
twirp [twə:p] (*noun*), *F:* = **twerp.**
twist[1] [twist] (*noun*), *P:* **1. to go round the t.** = **to go round the bend** (**bend**[1], **1**). **2.** cigarette* de marijuana (*drogues**), stick *m*. *Voir aussi* **knickers; tassel, 2.**
twist[2] [twist] (**to**), *F:* **1.** escroquer*, frauder, filouter. **2. he likes to have his arm twisted,** il aime se faire prier. *Voir aussi* **burn**[1], **1** (*a*); **finger**[1], **8.**
twisted ['twistid] (*adj.*), *P:* chargé, défoncé (par les drogues).
twister ['twistər] (*noun*), *F:* **1.** faux bonhomme, faux jeton, fripouille *f*, filou *m*. **2.** casse-tête (chinois).
twisty ['twisti] (*adj.*), *P:* malhonnête, fripouille, filon.
twit [twit] (*noun*), *P:* individu bête*, ballot *m*, con(n)ard *m*; **he's a hopeless t.,** il en a une couche.
twitter ['twitər] (*noun*), *F:* **1. to be all of a t.** (*or* **in a t.**), être sens dessus dessous, être dans tous ses états. **2. to have the twitters,** avoir la tremblote (*ou* la trouille).

* An asterisk indicates that the word so marked is included as a head-word in the Appendix.

twitty [ˈtwiti] (*adj.*), *P:* bête*, stupide, con(n)ard.

two [tuː] (*numeral adj. & noun*), *F:* **1. to put t. and t. together,** tirer (*ou* en déduire) ses conclusions. **2. all the twos:** *voir* **bingo (22).** *Voir aussi* **one-two; thing, 6.**

two-bit [ˈtuːˈbit] (*adj.*) (*U.S.*), *F:* insignifiant, à la manque, à la gomme.

two-fisted [ˈtuːˈfistid] (*adj.*), *F:* = **ham-fisted.**

twopenny-halfpenny [ˈtʌp(ə)niˈhei-p(ə)ni] (*adj.*) = **tuppenny-ha'penny.**

two-piece [ˈtuːpiːs] (*noun*), *P:* testicules*, paire *f*.

twot [twɔt] (*noun*) = **twat, 1, 2.**

two-time [ˈtuːˈtaim] (**to**), *F:* **1.** tromper (qn) (en amour), être infidèle. **2.** duper*, tromper.

two-timer [ˈtuːˈtaimər] (*noun*), *F:* **1.** mari qui trompe sa femme *ou* femme infidèle. **2.** dupeur *m*, roustisseur *m*.

tycoon [taiˈkuːn] (*noun*), *F:* grosse huile, ponte *m*, grand manitou.

tyke [taik] (*noun*), *P:* **1.** natif *m* du comté du Yorkshire. **2.** malotru *m*, rustre *m*, rustaud *m*. **3.** vilain chien*, sale cabot *m*.

* L'astérisque indique que le mot marqué de ce signe figure comme entrée dans le Répertoire.

U

ugly ['ʌgli] (*adj.*) (*U.S.*), *F:* abject*, dégueulasse, salingue. *Voir aussi* **cut up (to)**, 3; **plug-ugly.**

umpit(t)y ['ʌmpiti] (*adj.*), *F:* en colère*, de mauvaise humeur, en rogne, à cran.

umpteen ['ʌmpti:n, ʌmp'ti:n] (*adj.*), *F:* je ne sais combien; **he has u. children,** il a je ne sais combien d'enfants; **to have u. reasons for doing sth.,** avoir trente-six raisons de faire qch.

umpteenth ['ʌmpti:nθ, ʌmp'ti:nθ] (*adj.*), *F:* trente-sixième, ennième.

umpty ['ʌm(p)ti] (*adj.*), *P:* un peu malade*, mal fichu, pas dans son assiette.

'un [ən] (*pron.*) (=*one*), *F:* individu*, quelqu'un, type *m*, mec *m*; **a little 'un,** un petiot; **a wrong 'un,** un fripon, un coquin, un chenapan.

unchubb ['ʌn'tʃʌb] (**to**), *P:* ouvrir*, faire jouer la serrure, débloquer, débrider; *cf.* **chubb in (to)**; **unmiln (to).**

Uncle, uncle ['ʌŋkl] (*noun*). **1.** *P:* agent* de police, flic *m*. **2.** *P:* indicateur* (de police), ma tante. **3.** *P:* **U. Dick** (*R.S.*), (*a*) (=*prick*) pénis*; *cf.* **dick**[1]; (*b*) (=*sick*) malade*. **4.** *P:* **U. Ned** (*R.S.*), (*a*) (=*bed*) lit*; (*b*) (=*head*) tête*. **5.** *F:* prêteur *m* (sur gages), tante *f*; **at (my) u.'s,** chez ma tante, au clou. **6.** *F:* **U. Sam,** l'oncle Sam, les États-Unis d'Amérique. **7.** *P:* receleur*, fourgueur *m*. **8.** (*U.S.*) *P:* = **Sam, 2.** **9.** (*U.S.*) *F:* **U. Tom,** noir *m* qui s'insinue dans les bonnes grâces des blancs, Oncle Tom. *Voir aussi* **Bob**[2]; **Dutch**[1], **5.**

uncool ['ʌn'ku:l] (*adj.*), *P:* = **cool**[1], **5.**

under ['ʌndər] (*prep.*), *F:* **to be u. the doctor,** être en traitement, être sous surveillance médicale.

undergrad ['ʌndəgræd] (*noun*) (=*undergraduate*), *F:* étudiant(e) (qui n'a pas encore ses diplômes).

underground ['ʌndəgraund] (*adj.*), *F:* révolutionnaire, contestataire.

under-the-counter ['ʌndəðə'kauntər] (*adj.*), *F:* au marché noir. *Voir aussi* **counter.**

undies ['ʌndiz] (*pl. noun*), *F:* sous-vêtements feminins, lingerie *f*, dessous *m. pl.*

unflappable ['ʌn'flæpəbl] (*adj.*), *F:* flegmatique, calme, qui ne s'affole pas.

un-get-at-able ['ʌnget'ætəbl] (*adj.*), *F:* inaccessible.

unglued ['ʌn'glu:d] (*adj.*) (*U.S.*), *P:* **1.** frénétique, forcené, affolé. **2.** fou*, loufoque, piqué.

unhitched ['ʌn'hitʃt] (*adj. & p.p.*), *F:* **to get u.,** divorcer, se séparer, se démaquer; *cf.* **hitch**[2] **(to), 2.**

unlucky ['ʌn'lʌki] (*adj.*), *F:* **u. for some:** *voir* **bingo (13).**

unmiln ['ʌn'miln] (**to**), *P:* = **unchubb (to).**

unscramble ['ʌn'skræmbl] (**to**), *F:* (*a*) débrouiller (un message); (*b*) **I'll try and u. my appointments,** j'essaierais de remanier mes rendez-vous*.

unscrewed ['ʌn'skru:d] (*adj.*) (*U.S.*), *P:* = **unglued, 1, 2.**

unstuck ['ʌn'stʌk] (*adj. & p.p.*), *F:* **to come u.,** (*a*) (*d'un projet, etc.*) s'effondrer, s'écrouler, se disloquer; (*b*) (*d'une personne*) (i) tomber sur un bec, faire un bide; (ii) s'effondrer, faire la culbute.

unwashed ['ʌn'wɔʃt] (*adj. & p.p.*), *F:* **the Great U.,** les prolétaires *m.pl.*, les prolos *m.pl.*, les pouilleux *m.pl.*

up[1] [ʌp] (*adj.*), *F:* **1.** euphorique dû à la drogue, high, défoncé, planant. **2. u. drugs,** drogues stimulantes psychiques; *cf.* **down**[1]. **3.** heureux, en pleine forme.

up[2] [ʌp] (*adv.*). **1.** *F:* **to be u. against it,** avoir la malchance* (*ou* la guigne *ou* la déveine). **2.** *F:* **to be u. to sth.,** fabriquer qch., mijoter qch. **3.** *F:* **it's all u., the game's u.,** c'est fichu (*ou* flambé); *voir aussi* **all**[2], **1.** **4.** *F:* **what's u.?** que se passe-t-il? qu'y a-t-il? **5.** *P:* en coït* (avec une femme), en mise. *Voir aussi* **move**[1], **2.**

up[3] [ʌp] (*noun*). **1.** *F:* **to be on the u. and**

* An asterisk indicates that the word so marked is included as a head-word in the Appendix.

u., (*a*) être en bonne voie, prospérer, faire son beurre; (*b*) être honnête (*ou* correct *ou* impec). 2. *P:* = **upper**[2]. 3. *F:* **to give s.o. a quick u. and down,** jauger qn, faire le tour de qn. *Voir aussi* **high-ups.**

up[4] [ʌp] (*prep.*), *P:* 1. **u. yours!** colle (*ou* fous) ça dans la poche (et ton mouchoir par-dessus)!; tu peux te le mettre (*ou* te le fourrer) quelque part! *cf.* **arse, 6; flue, 2; gonga; jacksie, 1; jumper, 1; Khyber.** 2. en coït* avec (une femme). *Voir aussi* **creek; spout**[1], **1, 3.**

up[5] [ʌp] (**to**). 1. *F:* **to u. sticks,** déménager, décaniller, bouger ses bois *m.pl.* 2. *P:* (*a*) se lever d'un bond; **then he upped and left the room,** puis d'un bond il se mit debout et quitta la pièce; (*b*) agir avec élan; **so I ups and tells him what I think,** et je me suis lancé et lui ai dit exactement ce que je pensais.

up-and-downer [ˈʌpənˈdaunər] (*noun*), *F:* querelle*, prise *f* de bec, engueulade *f*, attrapage *m*.

upbeat [ˈʌpbiːt] (*adj.*), *F:* pétillant, fringant, pimpant, euphorique; *cf.* **downbeat.**

upholstery [ʌpˈhoulstəri] (*noun*), *P:* = **shelf-kit;** *cf.* **well-upholstered.**

upper[1] [ˈʌpər] (*adj.*), *F:* 1. **u. storey,** tête*, cerveau *m*, ciboulot *m*; **to be weak in the u. storey,** avoir une araignée dans le plafond. 2. **u. bracket,** tête *f* de liste. 3. **u. crust,** les huiles *f.pl.*, la crème, le gratin, le dessus du panier. *Voir aussi* **lip, 2; ten, 1.**

upper[2] [ˈʌpər], **uppie** [ˈʌpi] (*noun*), *P:* amphétamine *f* (*drogues**); *cf.* **downer, 1; downie.** *Voir aussi* **uppers.**

uppers [ˈʌpəz] (*pl. noun*), *F:* **to be down on one's u.,** être très pauvre*, être dans la purée noire, marcher à côté de ses pompes. *Voir aussi* **upper**[2].

uppish [ˈʌpiʃ] (*adj.*), *F:* = **uppity, 1.**

uppity [ˈʌpiti] (*adj.*), *F:* 1. prétentieux*, arrogant, rogne, crâneur, hautain. 2. (*U.S.*) (nègre américain) qui réclame ses droits. 3. féroce, brutal, sauvage.

ups-a-daisy! [ˈʌpsəˈdeizi] (*excl.*), *F:* hoop-là!

upset [ˈʌpset] (*noun*), *F:* querelle*, remue-ménage *m*.

upsides [ˈʌpsaidz] (*adv.*), *F:* **to be u. with s.o.,** être quitte avec qn, rendre la pareille à qn.

upstage[1] [ˈʌpˈsteidʒ] (*adj.*), *F:* prétentieux*, snob, bêcheur, plastronneur.

upstage[2] [ˈʌpˈsteidʒ] (**to**), *F:* 1. (*th.*) mettre (un autre acteur) à l'ombre du public, retirer le haut des planches à (un autre acteur). 2. remettre (qn) à sa place, faire semblant de ne pas voir (qn).

upstairs [ˈʌpˈstɛəz] (*adv.*), *F:* **to have sth. u.,** avoir le ciboulot bien rempli, être intelligent. *Voir aussi* **kick upstairs (to).**

upsy-daisy! [ˈʌpsiˈdeizi] (*excl.*), *F:* = **ups-a-daisy!**

uptake [ˈʌpteik] (*noun*), *F:* (*a*) **to be quick on the u.,** comprendre (*ou* savoir) vite, avoir l'esprit vif (*ou* éveillé), avoir la comprenette facile; (*b*) **to be slow on the u.,** avoir la comprenette difficile.

uptight [ˈʌpˈtait] (*adj.*), *F:* 1. tendu, ému, agité. 2. survolté. 3. (*U.S.*) connu à fond, su sur le bout du doigt, notoire. 4. complexé, inhibé. 5. fielleux, rancunier.

urger [ˈəːdʒər] (*noun*) (*Austr.*), *P:* = **shill(aber).**

us [ʌs,əs] (*pron.*) (=*me*), *F:* moi; **give u. a kiss!** alors on m'embrasse!; **let's have a look!** laisse-moi regarder!

use [juːz] (**to**). 1. *F:* exploiter, tirer parti de (qn), abuser de (qn). 2. *F:* prendre plaisir à, profiter de (qch.); **I could u. a cup of tea,** une tasse de thé me ferait plaisir. 3. *P:* se droguer*, se camer.

used up [ˈjuːzdˈʌp] (*adj. & p.p.*), *P:* très fatigué*, crevé, claqué.

useful [ˈjuːsful] (*adj.*), *F:* efficace, habile; **he's pretty u. with his fists,** il sait bien jouer des poings.

user [ˈjuːzər] (*noun*), *P:* drogué*, camé *m*, toxico *m*.

usual [ˈjuːʒu(ə)l] (*noun*), *F:* **the u.,** ce que l'on a (*ou* prend) d'habitude, l'ordinaire.

V

vac [væk] (*noun*) (*abbr. = vacation*), *F:* vacances *f.pl.*; **the Long V.**, les grandes vacances.

vamoose [vəˈmuːs] (**to**), *P:* s'enfuir*, décamper, filer.

varieties [vəˈraiətiz] (*pl. noun*), *F:* **all the v.:** *voir* **bingo (57)**.

varmint [ˈvɑːmint] (*noun*), *F:* (*a*) vermine *f*; (*b*) **young v.**, verminard *m*, petit polisson.

varnish[1] [ˈvɑːniʃ] (*noun*), *P:* mauvais alcool*, camphre *m*, cogne *f*.

varnish[2] [ˈvɑːniʃ] (**to**), *P:* **to v. the cane,** se masturber*, s'astiquer la colonne.

varsity, Varsity [ˈvɑːsiti] (*noun*), *F:* l'Université *f*, la Faculté, la Fac.

veep [viːp] (*noun*) (*U.S.*), *F:* vice-président *m*.

velvet [ˈvelvit] (*noun*). **1.** *P:* **blue v.**, drogues* (parégorique et antihistamine). **2. black v.**, (*a*) *F:* mélange *m* de champagne et de stout; (*b*) *P:* négresse *f*, bougnoul(l)e *f*. **3.** *F:* **to be on v.**, (*a*) jouer sur le velours; (*b*) vivre comme un prince, mener la vie de château. **4.** *F:* (*a*) bénéfice*, velours *m*, gâteau *m*; (*b*) argent*, galette *f*, galtouze *f*.

verbal [ˈvəːbəl] (*noun*), *P:* **the v.**, bavardage *m*, bavette *f*.

vet[1] [vet] (*abbr.*), *F:* **1.** (*=veterinary surgeon*) vétérinaire *mf*. **2.** (*U.S.*) (*= veteran*) ancien combattant.

vet[2] [vet] (**to**), *F:* **1.** examiner, soigner, traiter (une bête, qn) (médicalement). **2.** revoir, corriger, mettre au point.

vibes [vaibz] (*pl. noun*) (*abbr.*), *F:* **1.** (*jazz*) vibraphone *m*, vibraharpe *f*, *etc.* **2.** (*=vibrations*) vibrations *f.pl.*

vice [vais] (*noun*) (*abbr.*), *F:* **1.** (*=vice-president, vice-chairman*) vice-président *m*, sous-Mec *m*. **2.** (*=vice-chancellor*) recteur *m* (d'une université), recto *m*. **3.** (*=deputy*) substitut *m*, délégué *m*, sous-Mec *m*.

villain [ˈvilən] (*noun*), *F:* **1.** bandit *m*, scélérat *m*. **2.** coquin *m*, garnement *m*; **you little v.!** petit polisson!

villainy [ˈviləni] (*noun*), *F:* **to do a v.**, (*a*) cambrioler*, faire un fric-frac; (*b*) commettre un crime, faire un acte criminel.

vim [vim] (*noun*), *F:* vigueur *f*, force *f*, énergie *f*, vitalité *f*.

vine [vain] (*noun*). **1.** *P:* **the v. = the grapevine. 2.** (*pl.*) *P:* vêtements*, fringues *f.pl.*, frusques *f.pl.* **3.** *F:* **clinging v.**, femme* possessive, pot *m* de colle.

vino [ˈviːnou] (*noun*), *P:* vin*, gros rouge, pinard *m*.

V.I.P. [ˈviːaiˈpiː] (*abbr. = very important person*), *F:* personnage important, grosse légume, huile *f*; **to give s.o. V.I.P. treatment,** recevoir qn avec la croix et la bannière.

viper [ˈvaipər] (*noun*) (*U.S.*), *P:* (*a*) drogué* à la marijuana; (*b*) fourgueur *m* de marijuana.

visit [ˈvizit] (*noun*), *F:* **to pay a v.**, aller faire pipi, aller faire sa petite commission.

vocab [ˈvoukæb, vəˈkæb] (*noun*) (*abbr. = vocabulary*), *F:* vocabulaire *m*.

vocals [ˈvoukəlz] (*pl. noun*), *P:* **to give with the v.**, chanter*, pousser une goualante, y aller de sa goualante.

voyager [ˈvɔiədʒər] (*noun*), *P:* drogué(e)* au LSD, voyageur *m*; *cf.* **trip**[1], **2** (*a*).

* An asterisk indicates that the word so marked is included as a head-word in the Appendix.

W

wack [wæk] (*noun*), *P:* **1.** fou *m*, fêlé *m*, cinglé *m*, détraqué *m*. **2.** excentrique *m*, original *m*, farfelu *m*. **3.** = **wacker.**

wacker [ˈwækər] (*noun*), *P:* ami*, copain *m*, pote *m*.

wacky [ˈwæki] (*adj.*), *P:* **1.** fou*, fêlé, cinglé, détraqué. **2.** excentrique, original, farfelu. **3.** de qualité inférieure, camelote.

wad [wɔd] (*noun*), *F:* **1.** (*a*) petit pain; (*b*) sandwich *m*; **tea and a w.**, casse-croûte *m*. **2.** liasse *f* de billets* de banque, matelas *m* de faf(f)iots. **3.** abondance*, une bardée (de...), un tas (de...). **4. to shoot one's w.**, risquer le tout pour le tout, parier sa chemise. *Voir aussi* **tightwad.**

wade in [ˈweidˈin] (**to**), *F:* s'attaquer à qch., intervenir, s'interposer.

wade into [ˈweidˈintuː] (**to**), *F:* **1. to w. i. s.o.**, (*a*) attaquer* qn; agrafer qn; (*b*) critiquer* qn sévèrement, cafarder, éreinter qn. **2. to w. i. sth.**, entamer un travail, s'y mettre.

waffle[1] [ˈwɔfl] (*noun*), *F:* verbosité *f*, verbiage *m*, fariboles *f.pl.*

waffle[2] [ˈwɔfl] (**to**), *F:* **1.** épiloguer, écrire (*ou* parler) dans le vague. **2.** dire des bêtises*, sortir des niaiseries *f.pl.* **3.** bavarder*, dégoiser, jaboter.

waffle on [ˈwɔflˈɔn] (**to**), *F:* = **waffle**[2] **(to), 3.**

waffler [ˈwɔflər] (*noun*), *F:* **1.** baratineur *m*. **2.** épilogueur *m*, individu verbeux.

wag[1] [wæg] (*noun*), *F:* **to hop the w.**, vagabonder, faire l'école buissonnière.

wag[2] [wæg] (**to**), *F:* **to w. it** = **to hop the wag (wag**[1]**).**

wag(g)on [ˈwægən] (*noun*), *F:* **1. to be on the (water) w.**, s'abstenir de boissons alcooliques, être buveur d'eau, être au régime sec; **to be off the w.**, s'adonner à la boisson. **2.** (*U.S.*) **to fix s.o.'s w.**, se venger sur qn, avoir qn au tournant. *Voir aussi* **bandwagon; cop-wagon; holler-wag(g)on; meat-wag(g)on; milk-wag(g)on; paddy-wag(g)on.**

wag out [ˈwægˈaut] (**to**), *P:* devenir défoncé par la drogue, glisser dans le high.

wake-up [ˈweikʌp] (*noun*), *P:* **1.** première piqûre de drogues du matin. **2.** amphétamine *f* (*drogues**). **3.** dernier jour de prison*.

wakey(-wakey)! [ˈweiki(ˈweiki)] (*excl.*), *F:* **1.** réveille-toi! debout! au jus! **2.** secoue-toi! secoue tes puces!

walk [wɔːk] (**to**), *F:* **1.** (*sports*) **to w. it**, arriver dans un fauteuil. **2.** (*d'un article*) disparaître, passer à l'as. *Voir aussi* **jaywalk (to).**

walk-about [ˈwɔːkəbaut] (*noun*), *F:* bain *m* de foule.

walk-away [ˈwɔːkəwei] (*noun*), *F:* = **walkover.**

walk away [ˈwɔːkəˈwei] (**to**), *F:* **1. to w. a. with sth.** = **to walk off with sth. 2. to w. a. from a competitor**, semer un concurrent.

walkie-talkie [ˈwɔːkiˈtɔːki] (*noun*), *F:* walkie-talkie *m*, talkie-walkie *m*.

walking-sticks [ˈwɔːkiŋ-stiks] (*pl. noun*), *F:* *voir* **bingo (77).**

walk into [ˈwɔːkˈintuː] (**to**), *F:* attaquer* (qn), enguirlander (qn).

walk off [ˈwɔːkˈɔf] (**to**), *F:* **to w. o. with sth.**, voler* qch., faucher qch., ratiboiser qch.

walk-out [ˈwɔːkaut] (*noun*), *F:* grève *f*, mise *f* à bas.

walk out [ˈwɔːkˈaut] (**to**), *F:* **1.** se mettre en grève. **2. to w. o. on s.o.**, abandonner* qn, lâcher qn, plaquer qn.

walkover [ˈwɔːkouvər] (*noun*), *F:* victoire *f* facile (*ou* dans un fauteuil *ou* les doigts dans le nez), promenade *f*.

walk over [ˈwɔːkˈouvər] (**to**), *F:* **to w. all o. s.o.**, agir abominablement envers qn, traiter qn par-dessus la jambe (*ou* comme du poisson pourri).

wall [wɔːl] (*noun*), *F:* **1. to be up the w.**, (*a*) (*d'une personne*) être fou*, être cinglé; (*b*) (*d'une chose*) être trompeur. **2. to drive s.o. up the w.**, rendre qn fou*, taper sur les nerfs (*ou* le système) à qn.

* L'astérisque indique que le mot marqué de ce signe figure comme entrée dans le Répertoire.

3. **to go to the w.,** (*a*) succomber; (*b*) perdre la partie; (*c*) faire faillite. 4. **to go over the w.,** s'échapper de prison*, faire le mur. 5. **to hit** (*or* **knock** *or* **run**) **one's head against a (brick) w., to come up against a blank w.,** ne rien tirer de qn; se heurter contre une porte de prison, se buter à l'impossible. 6. **he can see through a brick w.,** il a le nez fin. 7. **you might just as well talk to a brick w.,** autant vaut parler à un sourd. *Voir aussi* **back**[2], 7.

walla [ˈwɔlə] (*noun*), *F:* = **wallah.**

wallaby [ˈwɔləbi] (*noun*), *F:* Australien *m.*

wallah [ˈwɔlə] (*noun*), *F:* 1. individu*, homme*. 2. (*av.*) **ground w.,** rampant *m*; **ground wallahs,** personnel *m* de terre.

wall-eyed [ˈwɔːlˈaid] (*adj.*), *P:* ivre*, raide, rétamé.

wallflower [ˈwɔːl-flauər] (*noun*). 1. *F:* fille qui, à un bal, n'est pas invitée à danser; **to be a w.,** faire tapisserie. 2. (*U.S.*) *P:* = **bar-fly,** 2.

wallop[1] [ˈwɔləp] (*adv.*), *F:* **smack** (*or* **slap**), **bang, w.!** pan, vlan, boum!; *voir aussi* **slap-bang(-wallop).**

wallop[2] [ˈwɔləp] (*noun*). 1. *F:* gros coup*, torgn(i)ole *f.* 2. *F:* **and down he went with a w.!** et patatras, le voilà par terre! 3. *P:* bière *f*; *cf.* **codswallop,** 2.

wallop[3] [ˈwɔləp] (**to**), *F:* 1. battre* (qn), rosser (qn), flanquer une tournée à (qn). 2. vaincre, écraser, griller (qn).

walloping[1] [ˈwɔləpiŋ] (*adj.*), *F:* énorme, fantastique, phénoménal.

walloping[2] [ˈwɔləpiŋ] (*noun*), *F:* **to give s.o. a w.,** (*a*) donner une volée de coups* à qn, donner une roulée (*ou* une raclée) à qn; (*b*) battre qn à plate(s) couture(s).

wally [ˈwɔli] (*noun*), *P:* pénis*, frétillard *m.*

waltz into [ˈwɔlsˈintuː] (**to**), *F:* 1. se taper dans (qn *ou* qch.). 2. = **wade into** (**to**), 1 (*a*).

waltz off [ˈwɔːlsˈɔf] (**to**), *F:* partir*, déhotter, jouer rip.

wampum [ˈwɔmpəm] (*noun*) (*U.S.*), *P:* argent*, fric *m.*

wangle[1] [ˈwæŋgl] (*noun*), *F:* moyen détourné, truc *m* malhonnête, manigance *f.*

wangle[2] [ˈwæŋgl] (**to**), *F:* 1. cuisiner, resquiller. 2. obtenir par subterfuge, manigancer, carotter. 3. pratiquer le système D, se débrouiller.

wangle-dangle [ˈwæŋglˈdæŋgl] (*noun*), *P:* = **dingle-dangle.**

wangler [ˈwæŋglər] (*noun*), *F:* fricoteur *m*, carotteur *m*, resquilleur *m.*

wangling [ˈwæŋgliŋ] (*noun*), *F:* fricotage *m*, resquille *f.*

wank[1] [wæŋk] (*noun*), *V:* **to have a w.,** se masturber*, tirer son coup, se l'astiquer, se branler.

wank[2] [wæŋk] (**to**), *V:* **to w. (oneself off)** = **to have a wank (wank**[1]**).**

wanker [ˈwæŋkər] (*noun*), *V:* 1. masturbateur *m*, branleur *m.* 2. **w.'s doom,** masturbation excessive.

wanna [ˈwɔnə] (**to**) (=*want to*), *F:* vouloir.

want [wɔnt] (**to**), *F:* 1. **you don't w. much, do you!** (*iron.*), tu ne doutes de rien! 2. (*a*) **to w. in,** vouloir participer à qch., vouloir être dans le coup; (*b*) **to w. out,** vouloir se retirer, retirer ses marrons du feu.

war [wɔː] (*noun*), *F:* **to be in the wars,** être malmené, être tarabusté.

warb [wɔːb] (*noun*) (*Austr.*), *P:* 1. ouvrier *m*, prolétaire *m*, prolo *m.* 2. personne sale* *ou* désordonnée, souillon *m*, salope *f*, cochon *m.*

warby [ˈwɔːbi] (*adj.*) (*Austr.*), *P:* sale*, désordonné, salingue, crado, craspignol.

war-horse [ˈwɔːhɔːs] (*noun*), *F:* **an old w.-h.,** (*a*) un vieux soldat*; (*b*) un vétéran de la politique.

warm [wɔːm] (*adj.*), *F:* 1. **to be (getting) w.,** être sur le point de trouver qch., brûler. 2. **to make things** (*or* **it**) **w. for s.o.,** punir qn, en faire baver à qn. 3. riche*, flambant, galetteux.

war-paint [ˈwɔː-peint] (*noun*), *F.* maquillage *m*, badigeon(nage) *m*; **to put on the w.-p.,** se maquiller*, faire le (*ou* son) ravalement.

war-path [ˈwɔː-pɑːθ] (*noun*), *F:* **to be on the w.-p.,** être sur le sentier de la guerre, chercher noise; **the boss is on the w.-p.,** le patron* est d'une humeur massacrante.

wash[1] [wɔʃ] (*noun*), *F:* 1. **to hold up in the w.,** tenir à l'usage. 2. **to come out in the w.,** (*a*) être révélé un jour ou l'autre; (*b*) se tasser. *Voir aussi* **belly-wash; eyewash; hogwash; pigwash; whitewash**[1].

wash[2] [wɔʃ] (**to**), *F:* **it won't w. with me,**

* An asterisk indicates that the word so marked is included as a head-word in the Appendix.

cela ne prend pas, cela ne passe pas. *Voir aussi*, **linen; whitewash**[2] **(to)**.

washed out [ˈwɔʃtˈaut] (*adj.*), *F:* **1.** = **washed up, 1.** **2.** annulé, supprimé.

washed up [ˈwɔʃtˈʌp] (*adj.*), *F:* **1.** fatigué*, exténué, vanné, lessivé. **2.** mis au rancart, fichu en l'air.

washer-upper [ˈwɔʃəˈrʌpər] (*noun*), *F:* qn qui fait la vaisselle, plongeur *m.*

washing [ˈwɔʃiŋ] (*noun*), *F:* **to take in one another's w.**, se rendre mutuellement service.

washout [ˈwɔʃaut] (*noun*), *F:* **1.** échec*, fiasco *m.* **2.** raté *m*, propre à rien, fruit sec.

wash out [ˈwɔʃˈaut] **(to)**, *F:* **you can w. that right o.**, il ne faut pas compter là-dessus, barre cela de tes tablettes; **the best thing is to w. o. the whole business,** mieux vaut passer l'éponge là-dessus.

wasp [wɔsp] (*noun*) (*U.S.*), *P:* (=*white Anglo-Saxon Protestant*) parpaillot *m.*

watch [wɔtʃ] **(to)**, *F:* **w. it!** attention! fais gaffe! acré! gare!

water [ˈwɔːtər] (*noun*), *F:* **1. to pour cold w. on sth.**, jeter une douche froide sur qch. **2. to keep one's head above w.**, réussir tant bien que mal, surnager, se maintenir sur l'eau. **3. to hold w.**, avoir du sens, tenir debout. **4. to be in low w.**, (*a*) être sans le sou, être dans les eaux basses; (*b*) être déprimé, être dans le troisième dessous. *Voir aussi* **bath-water; bilge-water; bridgewater; dish-water; ditchwater; duck**[1]**, 8; fire-water; hell, 17; hot, 14; jerkwater; wag(g)on, 1.**

waterworks [ˈwɔːtəwəːks] (*pl. noun*), *F:* **to turn on the w.**, (*a*) se mettre à pleurer*, ouvrir les écluses *f.pl.*, gicler des mirettes *f.pl.*; (*b*) uriner*, faire pipi.

wavelength [ˈweivleŋθ] (*noun*), *F:* **on the same w.**, sur la même longueur d'ondes; *cf.* **beam, 1.**

wavy ˈ[weivi] (*adj.*), *F:* **the W. Navy** (*W.W.II = Royal Naval Volunteer Reserve*), réservistes *m.pl.* de la Marine.

wax [wæks] (*noun*), *F:* accès *m* de colère, crise *f*, rage *f.*

waxy ˈ[wæksi] (*adj.*), *F:* en colère, en rogne.

way[1] [wei] (*adv.*) (=*away*), *F:* **it was w. back in 1900,** cela remonte à 1900.

way[2] [wei] (*noun*), *F:* **1. all the w.**, (*a*) complètement, sans réserve, à bloc; **I'll go all the w. with you on that,** là-dessus, je te soutiendrai jusqu'à la gauche; (*b*) jusqu'à une complète satisfaction sexuelle; **to go all the w.**, casser la canne jusqu'au bout. **2.** (*a*) **to go for s.o., sth., in a big w.**, s'emballer follement pour qn, qch.; (*b*) **to do sth. in a big w.**, mettre les petits plats dans les grands. **3. to know one's w. about** (*or* **around**), être malin*, être roublard (*ou* démerdard). **4. to put s.o. out of the w.**, se débarrasser* de qn, virer qn, vider qn. **5. down our w.**, chez nous. **6. no w.**, balpeau, des clous, que dalle, que pouic. **7. any w. round:** *voir* **bingo (69)**. *Voir aussi* **family, 1.**

way out [ˈweiˈaut] (*adj.*), *F:* **1.** anti-conformiste, outré. **2.** original, excentrique. **3.** dans l'erreur, gour(r)é, fichu dedans.

weapon [ˈwepən] (*noun*), *P:* pénis*, carabine *f*, arbalète *f.*

wear[1] [wɛər] (*noun*), *F:* **to feel the worse for w.**, avoir la gueule de bois.

wear[2] [wɛər] **(to)**, *F:* admettre, tolérer, fermer les yeux sur; **he won't w. it.**, il ne consentira pas, il ne marchera pas.

weasel out [ˈwiːzlˈaut] **(to)**, *F:* se défiler, se rétracter.

weather [ˈweðər] (*noun*), *F:* **under the w.**, (*a*) malade*, patraque; (*b*) déprimé, qui n'a pas le moral. *Voir aussi* **fair-weather; heavy**[1]**, 3.**

weave [wiːv] **(to)**, *F:* **to get weaving,** s'y mettre, se lancer; **get weaving!** vas-y!

wedge [wedʒ] (*noun*), *P:* LSD *m* (*drogues**).

wee [wiː] (*noun & verb*), *F:* = **wee-wee**[1,2].

weed [wiːd] (*noun*), *F:* **1.** (*a*) cigare*; (*b*) cigarette*; (*c*) tabac*, perlot *m.* **2.** marijuana *f* (*drogues**), chiendent *m*, herbe *f*; **to be on the w.**, être esclave des cigarettes* de marijuana, marcher au chiendent; *voir aussi* **giggle, 4; love-weed.** **3.** personne étique (*ou* malingre *ou* chétive); chiffe *f.*

weedhead [ˈwiːdhed] (*noun*), *P:* habitué(e) de la marijuana.

weed-tea [ˈwiːdˈtiː] (*noun*), *P:* marijuana *f* (*drogues**), thé (vert).

week [wiːk] (*noun*), *F:* **to knock s.o. into the middle of next w.**, donner à qn un fameux coup*, envoyer valdinguer qn.

weener [ˈwiːnər] (*noun*), *P:* = **weeny**[2].

* L'astérisque indique que le mot marqué de ce signe figure comme entrée dans le Répertoire.

weeny[1] [ˈwi:ni] (*adj.*), *F:* minuscule, menu; *cf.* **teeny-weeny.**

weeny[2] [ˈwi:ni] (*noun*), *P:* pénis*, petit frère.

weepers [ˈwi:pəz] (*pl. noun*), *F:* favoris *m.pl.* (*barbe**), côtelettes *f.pl.*, pattes *f.pl.* de lapin.

weeping [ˈwi:piŋ] (*adj.*), *P:* **w. willow** (*R.S.* = *pillow*), oreiller *m.*

weepy [ˈwi:pi] (*noun*), *F:* film (livre, *etc.*) larmoyant.

wee-wee[1] [ˈwi:wi:] (*noun*), (*langage enfantin*) *F:* pipi *m*; **to do w.-w.** = (**go**) **wee-wee**[2] (**to**).

wee-wee[2] [ˈwi:wi:] (**to**), (*langage enfantin*) *F:* **to** (**go**) **w.-w.**, uriner*, faire pipi.

weigh in [ˈweiˈin] (**to**), *F:* arriver*, s'amener.

weigh off [ˈweiˈɔf] (**to**), *P:* juger, condamner, gerber, saper; *cf.* **Follies.**

weight [weit] (*noun*), *F:* **to take the w. off** (**one's feet**), s'asseoir, poser ses fesses*. *Voir aussi* **chuck about** (**to**), **2**; **lightweight.**

weirdie [ˈwiədi], **weirdo** [ˈwiədou], **weirdy** [ˈwiədi] (*noun*), *F:* individu étrange, excentrique *m*, olibrius *m*, drôle *m* de coco.

welcome-mat [ˈwelkəmˈmæt] (*noun*), *F:* **to put out the w.-m. for s.o.**, accueillir qn à bras ouverts.

well-endowed [ˈwelenˈdaud], **well-equipped** [ˈweliˈkwipt] (*adj.*), *F:* **1.** (homme) riche en génitoires *m.pl.* (*ou* en bijoux de famille). **2.** (femme) aux seins* développés, à la belle devanture; *cf.* **well-stacked, 2; well-upholstered, 1.**

well-fixed [ˈwelˈfikst], **well-heeled** [ˈwelˈhi:ld] (*adj.*), *F:* riche*, plein aux as, rupin, galetteux.

wellies [ˈweliz] (*pl. noun*), *F:* bottes *f.pl.* en caoutchouc.

well-lined [ˈwelˈlaind] (*adj.*), *F:* = **well-fixed.**

well-off [ˈwelˈɔf] (*adj.*), *F:* **1. to be w.-o.**, être riche*, avoir de quoi. **2. you don't know when you're w.-o.**, vous ne connaissez pas votre bonheur. **3. to be w.-o. for sth.**, être bien pourvu de qch.

well-stacked [ˈwelˈstækt] (*adj.*), *F:* **1.** = **well-fixed. 2.** = **well-endowed, 2.**

well-upholstered [ˈwelʌpˈhoulstəd] (*adj.*), *F:* **1.** = **well-endowed, 2**; *cf.* **upholstery. 2.** grassouillet, bien rembourré.

welsh [welʃ] (**to**), *F:* partir* sans payer, se refuser à payer une dette, poser une ardoise, planter un drapeau; **to w. on s.o.**, manquer à une obligation, chier dans les doigts à qn.

welsher [ˈwelʃər] (*noun*), *F:* tire-au-cul *m*, tire-au-flanc *m.*

welt [welt] (**to**), *P:* battre*, rosser, flanquer une raclée à (qn).

wench [wentʃ] (*noun*), *F:* **1.** fille*, gaillarde *f.* **2.** prostituée*, traînée *f.*

wencher [ˈwentʃər] (*noun*), *F:* = **wolf**[1], **1.**

west [west] (*adv.*), *F:* **to go w.**, (*a*) mourir*, casser sa pipe; (*b*) (*vêtements*) s'user, être fichus; (*c*) (*d'une affaire*) faire faillite, passer en lunette; (*d*) **that's another fiver gone w.**, encore un billet (*ou* un faf(f)iot) de claqué.

wet[1] [wet] (*adj.*). **1.** *F:* **he's a bit w.**, il est plutôt bête*, c'est une vraie nouille. **2.** *F:* **w. blanket**, rabat-joie *m.* **3.** *F:* à l'eau de rose. **4.** (*U.S.*) *F:* qui a la permission de vendre de l'alcool. **5.** *F:* **to be w. behind the ears**, être né d'hier, être né de la dernière pluie; *cf.* **dry, 2. 6.** *F:* **w. sock**, main* molle et flasque. **7.** *F:* **to be all w.**, se fourrer le doigt dans l'œil. **8.** *P:* **the w. season**, menstrues*. *Voir aussi* **dream**[2], **2; rag**[1], **11.**

wet[2] [wet] (*noun*), *F:* **1.** individu bête*, nouille *f*, andouille *f.* **2. to have a w.**, boire* un coup, se rincer la dalle.

wet[3] [wet] (**to**), *F:* **to w. the baby's head**, arroser la naissance d'un bébé; boire* un coup, prendre un pot. *Voir aussi* **whistle**[1], **1.**

wet-head [ˈwethed] (*noun*), *F:* = **wet**[2], **1.**

whack[1] [(h)wæk] (*noun*). **1.** *F:* coup*, taloche *f*, torgnole *f.* **2.** *F:* **to have a w.**, tenter, faire un essai. **3.** *F:* **to get a good w.**, avoir un bon salaire, toucher un bon paquet. **4.** *P:* = **wack, 1, 2. 5.** *F:* part *f*, portion *f.*

whack[2] [(h)wæk] (**to**). **1.** *F:* battre*, rosser, bourrer de coups*. **2.** *F:* battre, rouler (une équipe, *etc.*); vaincre, défaire. **3.** *P:* partager, répartir.

whacked [(h)wækt] (*adj.*), *F:* fatigué*, éreinté, vanné.

whacker [ˈ(h)wækər] (*noun*), *F:* **1.** qch. de colossal; énormité *f*, mastodonte *m.* **2.** gros mensonge*, sacré bourrage de crâne; **what a w.!** en voilà une (d'un peu) forte! *Voir aussi* **bush-whacker.**

* An asterisk indicates that the word so marked is included as a head-word in the Appendix.

whacking[1] [ˈ(h)wækiŋ] (*adj.*), *F:* énorme, maousse, bœuf.

whacking[2] [ˈ(h)wækiŋ] (*noun*), *F:* rossée *f*, raclée *f*, volée *f* de coups*.

whacko! [ˈ(h)wækou] (*excl.*), *F:* magnifique! épatant! formid!

whack up [ˈ(h)wækˈʌp] (**to**). **1.** *F:* **to w. u. the pace,** aller plus vite*, forcer (*ou* allonger) le pas. **2.** *F:* augmenter (prix, *etc.*). **3.** *P:* diviser et partager en parts égales. **4.** *P:* distribuer un butin* *ou* un gain, fader le barbotin.

whacky [ˈ(h)wæki] (*adj.*), *P:* = **wacky, 1, 2, 3.**

whale [(h)weil] (*noun*), *F:* **1. we had a w. of a time,** on s'est follement amusé. **2. to be a w. at sth.,** être un as (*ou* un crack) à qch. **3. to have a w. for sth.,** être engoué (*ou* enthousiasmé) par qch.

wham [(h)wæm] (**to**). **1.** *F:* battre*, frapper fort, botter, assaisonner. **2.** *P:* coïter* avec (une femme), envoyer en l'air.

wham-bam [ˈ(h)wæmˈbæm] (*noun*) (*U.S.*), *P:* coït* rapide et sans tendresse; bourre *f*.

whammy [ˈ(h)wæmi] (*noun*), *F:* **1. a w. of a smile,** un large sourire, un sourire éclatant. **2.** (*U.S.*) **to put the w. on,** mettre des bâtons dans les roues.

whang[1] [(h)wæŋ] (*noun*), *P:* pénis*, berdouillette *f*.

whang[2] [(h)wæŋ] (**to**), *P:* **1.** frapper fortement, mettre en pièces. **2.** = **bung**[2] **(to), 1, 2.**

whank [(h)wæŋk] (*noun & verb*), *V:* = **wank**[1, 2].

what-all [ˈ(h)wɔtɔːl] (*noun*), *F:* **... and I don't know w.-a.,** ... et je ne sais quoi encore.

whatcha(ma)callit [ˈ(h)wɔtʃə(mə)ˈkɔːlit], **what-do-you-call-it** [ˈ(h)wɔtdjuːˈkɔːlit], **what-d'ye-call-it** [ˈ(h)wɔtdjəˈkɔːlit] (*noun*), *F:* machin *m*, chose *m*, machin-chose *m*.

what-for [ˈ(h)wɔtˈfɔːr] (*noun*), *F:* **to give s.o. w.-f.,** réprimander* qn, laver la tête à qn, flanquer une bonne raclée à qn.

what-ho! [ˈ(h)wɔtˈhou] (*excl.*), *F:* **1.** eh bien! eh alors! **2.** salut!

whatnot [ˈ(h)wɔtnɔt] (*noun*), *F:* = **whatcha(ma)callit.**

what's-(h)er-name [ˈ(h)wɔtsəneim] (*noun*), *F:* Madame Machin-Truc.

what's-(h)is-name [ˈ(h)wɔtsizneim] (*noun*), *F:* Monsieur Machin-Truc.

whatsit [ˈ(h)wɔtsit] (*noun*). **1.** *F:* = **whatcha(ma)callit. 2.** *P:* **Willie's w.:** *voir* **bingo (1).**

what-you-may-call-it [ˈ(h)wɔtʃəməˈkɔːlit] (*noun*), *F:* = **whatcha(ma)callit.**

wheel[1] [(h)wiːl] (*noun*), *F:* **1. there are wheels within wheels,** les rouages (de la chose) sont très compliqués. **2. big w.** = **big shot (big**[1]**, 1). 3. to take (over) the w.,** prendre la barre, prendre les commandes. **4. it greases the wheels,** cela fait marcher les affaires, cela graisse les roues. *Voir aussi* **cartwheel.**

wheel[2] [(h)wiːl] (**to**), *F:* **to w. and deal,** brasser des affaires plus ou moins louches.

wheeler-dealer [ˈ(h)wiːləˈdiːlər] (*noun*), *F:* brasseur *m* d'affaires louches, arrangeman *m*.

wheeze [(h)wiːz] (*noun*), *F:* ruse *f*, artifice *m*, truc *m*.

wheezy [ˈ(h)wiːzi] (*adj.*), *F:* poussif.

whelk [wilk, welk] (*noun*), *P:* crachat*, glaviot *m*.

wherewithal [ˈ(h)wɛəwiðɑːl] (*noun*), *F:* **the w.,** argent*, le Saint-Fric.

whet [(h)wet] (*noun*), *F:* **to have a w.** = **to have a wet (wet**[2]**, 2).**

whiffy [ˈ(h)wifi] (*adj.*), *P:* = **nifty, 3;** *cf.* **niffy.**

whing-ding [ˈ(h)wiŋdiŋ] (*noun*) (*U.S.*), *P:* = **wing-ding.**

whinge [(h)windʒ] (**to**) (*Austr.*), *F:* grogner*, bougonner, râler.

whingy [ˈ(h)windʒi] (*adj.*), *F:* geignard, grincheux, grognon.

whip[1] [(h)wip] (*noun*), *F:* **1. to get a fair crack of the w.,** avoir sa (bonne) part, en tirer un bon parti; *cf.* **shake**[1]**, 3. 2. to hold the w. hand** (*U.S.:* **handle**), avoir le dessus. **3.** (*Austr.*) **whips of ...** = **tons of ... (ton, 2). 4. to crack the w.,** montrer le fouet, faire preuve d'autorité.

whip[2] [(h)wip] (**to**). **1.** *F:* battre*, rosser, dérouiller, passer à tabac. **2.** *P:* voler*, faucher, piquer. **3.** *F:* vaincre, battre à plate(s) couture(s), tailler en pièces. **4.** *P:* **w. it to me!** = **sock it to me! (sock**[2] **(to), 2).**

whipcracker [ˈ(h)wipkrækər] (*noun*), *F:* individu* à po(i)gne pète-sec *mf*.

whipped [(h)wipt] (*adj.*), *F:* très fatigué*, vanné, occis.

* L'astérisque indique que le mot marqué de ce signe figure comme entrée dans le Répertoire.

whipper-snapper [ˈ(h)wipə-snæpər] (*noun*), *F:* freluquet *m*, paltoquet *m*.

whippy [ˈ(h)wipi] (*adj.*), *F:* agile, leste, preste.

whip-round [ˈ(h)wipˈraund] (*noun*), *F:* **to have a w.-r. for s.o.,** faire une collecte (*ou* un appel) en faveur de qn, faire la (*ou* une) manche à qn.

whip through [ˈ(h)wipˈθruː] (**to**), *F:* faire (qch.) rapidement, bâcler, liquider.

whip up [ˈ(h)wipˈʌp] (**to**), *F:* **1. to w. u. a meal,** préparer (*ou* fricoter) un repas rapidement, faire un repas à la va-vite. **2. to w. u. one's friends,** rallier ses amis.

whirl [(h)wəːl] (*noun*), *F:* **to give sth. a w.,** essayer qch., faire l'essai de qch.

whirly-bird [ˈ(h)wəːlibəːd] (*noun*) (*U.S.*), *F:* hélicoptère *m*, battoir *m* (à œufs).

whirly-boy, -girl [ˈ(h)wəːlibɔi, -gəːl] (*noun*), *F:* pilote d'hélicoptère.

whisker [ˈ(h)wiskər] (*noun*), *F:* **1. to win (a race) by a w.,** gagner dans un mouchoir. **2. to have whiskers,** être vieux jeu, être vieux comme Hérode. *Voir aussi* **cat, 8.**

whistle[1] [ˈ(h)wisl] (*noun*). **1.** *F:* gorge*, avaloir *m*, gargoulette *f*; **to wet** (*or* **whet**) **one's w.,** boire*, s'humecter le gosier, se rincer la dalle. **2.** *P:* **w.** (**and flute**) (*R.S.* = *suit*), complet *m* (pour homme). **3.** *P:* **to blow the w. on s.o.,** dénoncer* qn, vendre la mèche. *Voir aussi* **clean, 1; wolf-whistle.**

whistle[2] [ˈ(h)wisl] (**to**). **1.** *F:* **you can w. for it!** tu peux te fouiller (*ou* te brosser)! **2.** *V:* **to w. in the dark** = **muff**[2] (**to**), **3.**

whistle-stop [ˈ(h)wisl-stɔp] (*noun*) (*U.S.*), *F:* (*a*) halte *f* de chemin de fer; (*b*) patelin *m*, trou *m*, bled *m*; **w.-s. tour,** campagne électorale menée du wagon d'un train.

white[1] [(h)wait] (*adj.*). **1.** *P:* **w. cross** (*or* **stuff**), (*a*) cocaïne *f* (*drogues**), coco *f*, (fée) blanche *f*, neige *f*; (*b*) héroïne *f* (*drogues**); (*c*) morphine *f* (*drogues**); *voir aussi* **white**[2], **4. 2.** *F:* honnête, intègre, estimable; **to play the w. man,** se bien conduire, agir en «honnête homme». *Voir aussi* **angel, 4; lily-white; snow-white.**

white[2] [(h)wait] (*noun*), *P:* **1.** cinq livres *f.pl.* sterling et au-dessus. **2.** platine *m* (*bijouterie*), blanc *m*, blanquette *f*. **3.** pièces *f.pl.* d'argent*, blanchettes *f.pl.*; *voir aussi* **phon(e)y**[1], **2** (*b*). **4.** (**old lady**) **w.,** (*a*) = **white cross** (*b*) (**white**[1], **1**); (*b*) amphétamine *f* (*drogues**); (*c*) Benzédrine *f* (*marque déposée*).

white-collar [ˈ(h)waitˈkɔlər] (*attrib. adj.*), *F:* **w.-c. worker,** employé de bureau, gratte-papier *m*.

white-headed [ˈ(h)waitˈhedid] (*adj.*), *F:* **the w.-h. boy,** le chouchou de la famille.

white-livered [ˈ(h)waitlivəd] (*adj.*), *F:* = **yellow-bellied;** *cf.* **lily-livered.**

white-slaver [ˈ(h)waitˈsleivər] (*noun*), *F:* souteneur*, mangeur *m* de blanc (*ou* de brioche), marchand *m* de barbaque (*ou* de bidoche *ou* de viande).

whitewash[1] [ˈ(h)waitwɔʃ] (*noun*), *F:* (*sports*) défaite *f* à zéro.

whitewash[2] [ˈ(h)waitwɔʃ] (**to**), *F:* **1.** blanchir, disculper, réhabiliter. **2.** (*sports*) **to w. one's opponents,** battre ses adversaires sans qu'ils aient marqué un point.

whitey, whitie [ˈ(h)waiti] (*noun*), *P:* **1.** homme blanc. **2.** amphétamine *f* (*drogues**).

whittled [ˈ(h)witld] (*adj.*) (*Austr.*), *P:* ivre*, rétamé.

whiz(z)[1] [(h)wiz] (*attrib. adj.*). **1.** *P:* **w. gang,** bande* de pickpockets, flèche *f* de fourchettes. **2.** *F:* **w. kid,** jeune cadre *m* qui monte en flèche, jeune coq *m*.

whiz(z)[2] [(h)wiz] (*noun*), *F:* **1. to be a w. at sth.,** être un as (*ou* un crack) à qch. **2.** dynamisme *m*, entrain *m*, vitalité *f*.

whiz(z)[3] [(h)wiz] (**to**). **1.** *F:* aller très vite*, bomber, gazer, filer à plein tube. **2.** *P:* voler* à la fourchette (*ou* à la tire).

whizz-bang [ˈ(h)wizˈbæŋ] (*noun*), *P:* **1.** (*a*) obus *m* à vitesse accélérée; (*b*) feu *m* d'artifice. **2.** mélange *m* de morphine et de cocaïne; un bang; piquouse-bang *f*.

whizzer [ˈ(h)wizər] (*noun*), *P:* = **dip**[1], **1.**

whizzing [ˈ(h)wiziŋ] (*noun*), *P:* vol *m* par une bande de pickpockets.

who [huː] (*pron.*), *F:* **you know w.,** qui-vous-savez.

whodunit [huːˈdʌnit] (*noun*), *F:* roman policier, série noire, polar *m*.

whole [houl] (*adj.*), *F:* **there's not a w. lot you can do about it,** tu ne peux pas y faire grand-chose.

whole-hogger [ˈhoulˈhɔgər] (*noun*), *F:* (*a*) qn qui s'engage à fond, qn qui fonce tête baissée; (*b*) partisan *m*, supporte(u)r acharné; *cf.* **hog**[1], **2.**

* An asterisk indicates that the word so marked is included as a head-word in the Appendix.

whole-hoggism [ˈhoulˈhɔgizm] (*noun*), *F:* jusqu'au-boutisme *m.*
whoopee![1] [ˈwuˈpiː] (*excl.*), *F:* youpi! youp!
whoopee[2] [ˈwupiː] (*noun*), *F:* **to make w.,** (*a*) fêter bruyamment, faire du chahut, faire la noce; (*b*) bien s'amuser.
whoops-a-daisy! [ˈ(h)wupsəˈdeizi] (*excl.*), *F:* oup-là (boum)! debout!
whoosh [(h)wuʃ] (**to**), *F:* conduire très vite*, rouler *ou* voler à plein gaz.
whop [(h)wɔp] (**to**), *P:* = **whack**[2] **(to), 1, 2.**
whopper [ˈ(h)wɔːpər] (*noun*), *F:* = **whacker, 1, 2.**
whopping[1] [ˈ(h)wɔpiŋ] (*adj.*), *F:* **1.** = **whacking**[1]. **2. w. lie** = **whacker, 2.**
whopping[2] [ˈ(h)wɔpiŋ] (*noun*), *P:* volée *f* de coups*, rossée *f*, raclée *f*, dérouillée *f*, trempe *f*.
whore[1] [hɔər, hɔːr] (*noun*), *P:* **dirty w.:** *voir* **bingo (34).** *Voir aussi* **forty-four.**
whore[2] [hɔər, hɔːr] (**to**), *P:* putasser, courir la gueuse.
whore-house [ˈhɔː(ə)haus] (*noun*), *P:* bordel*, baisodrome *m.*
whoring [ˈhɔː(ə)riŋ] (*noun*), *P:* putasserie *f*, dragage *m.*
whore-shop [ˈhɔː(ə)ʃɔp] (*noun*), *P:* = **whore-house.**
wibbly-wobbly [ˈwibliˈwɔbli] (*adj.*), *F:* branlant, chancelant.
wick [wik] (*noun*), *P:* **1. to get on s.o.'s w.,** taper sur les nerfs (*ou* le système) à qn. **2. to dip** (*or* **bury**) **one's w.,** coïter*, mouiller le goupillon; *cf.* **Hampton.**
wicked [ˈwikid] (*adj.*), *P:* = **groovy.**
widdle [ˈwidl] (*noun & verb*), *F:* = **piddle**[1,2].
wide [waid] (*adj.*). **1.** *F:* malin*, roublard, marloupin, retors; **a w. boy,** un affranchi, un débrouillard, un fortiche. **2.** *P:* **w. world,** (*courses hippiques*) la pelouse. *Voir aussi* **berth, 1.**
wide-awake [ˈwaidəˈweik] (*noun*), *F:* chapeau* de feutre à larges bords, capeline *f*.
wife [waif], **wifey** [ˈwaifi] (*noun*), *F:* **the w.,** l'épouse*, la bourgeoise, la ménagère.
wig [wig] (*noun*), *P:* **to blow** (*or* **flip** *or* **lose**) **one's w.,** être très en colère*, fulminer, sortir de ses gonds, piquer une crise. *Voir aussi* **bigwig.**
wigging [ˈwigiŋ] (*noun*), *F:* réprimande *f*, engueulade *f*, verte semonce, savon *m*; **to get a good w.,** se faire réprimander*, se faire laver la tête.
wiggle [ˈwigl] (*noun*), *F:* **to get a w. on,** se dépêcher*, se dégrouiller, faire vinaigre.
wiggy [ˈwigi] (*noun*), *F:* (*langage enfantin*) pénis*, zizi *m.*
wig out [ˈwigˈaut] (**to**), *P:* = **freak out (to).**
wild [waild] (*adj.*), *F:* **1.** en colère*, furibard. **2. to be w. about s.o.,** être emballé pour qn. **3.** = **fun**[1]. **4.** passionnant, palpitant, captivant. *Voir aussi* **woolly.**
wildcat [ˈwaildkæt] (*adj.*), *F:* **1.** téméraire, risqué, douteux. **2. a w. venture,** une entreprise risquée (*surtout* au point de vue financier). **3. a w. strike,** une grève non-officielle, grève sur le tas.
Willie [ˈwili] (*pr. noun*), *P:* **1.** pénis*, petit frère. **2. W.'s whatsit:** *voir* **bingo (1).**
willies [ˈwiliz] (*pl. noun*), *F:* **to give s.o. the w.,** donner la chair de poule (*ou* la tremblote) à qn; **to have the w.,** avoir peur*, avoir la trouille.
win [win] (**to**). **1.** *F:* **you can't w. (can you)!** *c.p.*, tu auras toujours tort! **2.** *F:* **you can't w. them all,** *c.p.*, on ne peut pas plaire à tout le monde. **3.** *P:* voler*, rouler, soulever.
wind [wind] (*noun*), *F:* **1. to raise the w.,** se procurer de l'argent*, battre monnaie. **2.** (*a*) **to get the w. up,** avoir peur*, avoir les foies *m.pl.*; (*b*) **to put the w. up s.o.,** faire peur* à qn, ficher la frousse à qn. **3. to be all w. (and water),** être comme une bulle de savon. **4. to be full of w.,** mentir*, mener en barque. **5. to sail close to the w.,** (*a*) friser l'illégalité, l'insolence, l'indécence, *etc.*; (*b*) faire des affaires* douteuses. **6. there's something in the w.,** il y a anguille sous roche, il se manigance quelque chose. *Voir aussi* **bag**[1], **3; load, 7; sail; sheet, 1.**
wind up [ˈwaindˈʌp] (**to**), *F:* **to w. u. on the scrap-heap,** finir sur la paille (*ou* en décrépitude); **to w. u. in prison,** finir en prison*.
windy [ˈwindi] (*adj.*), *F:* **to be w.,** avoir peur*, avoir le trac (*ou* la frousse).
wing [wiŋ] (*noun*), *P:* bras*, aile *f*, aileron *m.* *Voir aussi* **ping; sprout (to).**

* L'astérisque indique que le mot marqué de ce signe figure comme entrée dans le Répertoire.

wing-ding [ˈwiŋdiŋ] (*noun*) (*U.S.*), *P:* **1.** attaque *f*, crise *f* d'épilepsie, digue-digue *f*. **2.** accès *m* de folie dû aux drogues, le flip. **3.** prétendue crise (pour s'attirer la sympathie). **4.** coup *m* de colère*, rage *f*. **5.** réjouissances* bruyantes, réunion pleine de bruit*, chahut *m*, ramdam(e) *m*, boum déchaînée.

wink [wiŋk] (*noun*), *F:* **to tip s.o. the w.,** avertir qn, faire signe de l'œil à qn, lancer une œillade à qn, faire le châsse à qn. *Voir aussi* **forty.**

winkers [ˈwiŋkəz] (*pl. noun*), *F:* clignotants *m.pl.*

winking [ˈwiŋkiŋ] (*noun & pres. part.*), *F:* **1.** **(as) easy as w.,** simple comme bonjour. **2.** **like w.,** en un clin d'œil, en rien de temps.

winkle [ˈwiŋkl] (*noun*), *P:* pénis*, frétillard *m*, frétillante *f*.

winkle-pickers [ˈwiŋkl-pikəz] (*pl. noun*), *F:* chaussures *f.pl.* à bout pointu.

winner [ˈwinər] (*noun*), *F:* (*a*) réussite certaine, succès assuré; (*b*) roman (pièce, *etc.*) à grand succès.

wino [ˈwainou] (*noun*), *P:* ivrogne*, sac *m* à vin.

win out [ˈwinˈaut] (**to**), *F:* surmonter les difficultés *f.pl.*, arriver au but.

wipe[1] [waip] (*noun*), *P:* **1.** mouchoir*, tire-jus *m*. **2.** = **swipe**[1], **1.**

wipe[2] [waip] (**to**), *P:* **1.** **to w. the floor with s.o.,** (*a*) fermer le bec à qn; (*b*) battre qn à plate(s) couture(s), n'en faire qu'une bouchée; (*c*) réprimander* qn, agonir qn de sottises *f.pl.*, incendier qn. **2.** battre*, flanquer une raclée à (qn).

wipe out [ˈwaipˈaut] (**to**), *F:* **1.** liquider, passer l'éponge sur (qch.). **2.** tuer*, nettoyer, ratatiner, lessiver (qn); **the whole lot were wiped out,** toute la bande a été zigouillée.

wire [waiər] (*noun*). **1.** *F:* **to give s.o. the w.,** donner un tuyau à qn, mettre qn dans le coup. **2.** *P:* **to pull one's w.,** se masturber*, se l'allonger; *cf.* **wire-puller; wire-pulling, 2.** **3.** *F:* **a live w.,** un malin, un dégourdi, un débrouillard. **4.** *F:* télégramme *m*, petit bleu. **5.** *F:* **to get in under the w.,** arriver* au dernier moment, s'abouler pile. **6.** *F:* **to get one's wires crossed,** se tromper, se gour(r)er, s'embrouiller, se mettre le doigt dans l'œil. **7.** *P:* pickpocket *m*, fourlineur *m*, fourchette *f*. **8.** *F:* **to pull (the) wires,** tirer les ficelles *f.pl.*, faire jouer le piston.

wired [ˈwaiəd] (*adj.*), *P:* (*a*) adonné à une drogue; (*b*) (*drogues*) défoncé, high.

wire into [ˈwaiəˈrintuː] (**to**), *P:* = **wade into (to), 1** (*a*).

wire-puller [ˈwaiə-pulər] (*noun*). **1.** *F:* intrigant *m*, manœuvrier *m*. **2.** *P:* masturbateur *m*, branleur *m*; *cf.* **wire, 2.**

wire-pulling [ˈwaiə-puliŋ] (*noun*). **1.** *F:* l'art *m* de tirer les ficelles *f.pl.*, intrigues *f.pl.* de couloir *m*, manigances *f.pl.* **2.** *P:* masturbation *f*, allongement *m*, astiquage *m.*; *cf.* **wire, 2.**

wise [waiz] (*adj.*), *F:* **to get w.,** se mettre à la coule, se dessaler; se dégourdir; **to get w. to sth.,** s'apercevoir de la vérité; saisir qch.; **to put s.o. w.,** affranchir qn, mettre qn à la page; **put me w. about it,** expliquez-moi ça. *Voir aussi* **guy**[1], **1.**

wisecrack[1] [ˈwaizkræk] (*noun*), *F:* **1.** bon mot, mot spirituel, boutade *f*. **2.** riposte impertinente, coup *m* de langue, pointe *f*, rosserie *f*.

wisecrack[2] [ˈwaizkræk] (**to**), *F:* faire de l'esprit, aiguiser un trait.

wise up [ˈwaizˈʌp] (**to**), *F:* (*a*) = **to get wise;** (*b*) **to w. s.o. u.** = **to put s.o. wise.**

wish [wiʃ] (**to**), *F:* **it's been wished on me,** c'est une chose que je n'ai pas pu refuser.

wisher [ˈwiʃər] (*noun*) (*U.S.*), *P:* = **fed**[2], **2.**

wishy-washy [ˈwiʃiwɔʃi] (*adj.*), *F:* fade, insipide, lavasse.

with [wið] (*prep.*), *F:* **1.** (*a*) **to be w. it,** être dans le vent (*ou* dans le mouvement *ou* à la page); (*b*) **to get w. it,** se mettre dans le bain, se mettre au diapason. **2.** **I'm not w. you,** je ne comprends pas, je ne pige pas, je n'y suis pas.

with-it [ˈwiðit] (*attrib. adj.*), *F:* **w.-i. gear,** des vêtements* dernier cri.

without [wiˈðaut] (*prep.*), *F:* **w. any,** sans alcool*, au régime sec.

wizard [ˈwizəd] (*adj.*), *F:* excellent*, épatant, au poil.

wodge [wɔdʒ] (*noun*), *F:* (*a*) gros morceau, bloc *m*, quartier *m*; (*b*) liasse *f* (de papiers).

wog [wɔg] (*noun*), *P:* (*péj.*) **1.** Levantin *m*, Égyptien *m*, Arabe *m*, bico(t) *m*, bougnoul(l)e *m*. **2.** un étranger.

* An asterisk indicates that the word so marked is included as a head-word in the Appendix.

wolf[1] [wulf] (*noun*). **1.** *F:* séducteur *m*, coureur *m* de cotillons (*ou* de jupons *ou* de gueuses), juponneur *m*, homme *m* à femmes. **2.** *F:* **to keep the w. from the door,** se mettre à l'abri du besoin (de nourriture). **3.** *P:* pédéraste* actif, loup *m* de Sibérie, chien *m* jaune. **4.** *F:* **lone w.,** (*a*) = **loner;** (*b*) célibataire endurci, vieux bouc.

wolf[2] [wulf] (**to**). **1.** *F:* manger* abondamment, s'empiffrer, dévorer, se goinfrer. **2.** *P:* séduire la femme d'un autre, griller.

wolfish [ˈwulfiʃ] (*adj.*), *P:* plein de convoitise, allumé.

wolf-whistle [ˈwulf(h)wisl] (*noun*), *F:* sifflement admiratif à l'adresse d'une femme.

woman-chaser [ˈwumən-tʃeisər] (*noun*), *F:* coureur *m* de jupons, dénicheur *m* de fauvettes.

woman-crazy [ˈwumənˈkreizi], **woman-mad** [ˈwumənˈmæd] (*adj.*), *F:* qui a les femmes dans la peau; *cf.* **man-crazy; man-mad.**

wonder[1] [ˈwʌndər] (*noun*), *F:* **1. wonders will never cease!** *c.p.*, il y a toujours des miracles! c'est un prodige! **2. no w.!** pas étonnant!

wonder[2] [ˈwʌndər] (**to**), *F:* **1. I shouldn't w.,** cela ne me surprendrait pas. **2. I w.,** j'en doute, j'ai des réserves *f.pl.*, que tu dis.

wonk [wɔŋk] (*noun*) (*Austr.*), *P:* pédéraste*, empapaouté *m*.

wonky [ˈwɔŋki] (*adj.*), *P:* **1.** titubant, chancelant, branlant, zigzaguant. **2.** hésitant, vacillant, oscillant. **3.** mal fichu, patraque. **4.** (*Austr.*) homosexuel.

wood [wud] (*noun*), *F:* **1. touch** (*U.S.* **knock on**) **w.!** touche du bois! **2. you can't see the w. for the trees,** *c.p.*, on se perd dans les détails *m.pl.*; les arbres empêchent de voir la forêt. **3. he's w. from the neck up,** il est bouché à l'émeri, il a une tête de bûche. *Voir aussi* **bird-wood.**

woodbine [ˈwudbain] (*noun*), *P:* **African w.,** cigarette* de marijuana (*drogues**).

wooden [ˈwudn], *F:* **to win the w. spoon,** arriver le dernier (*ou* à la queue), faire la lanterne rouge; **the w. spoon goes to X,** X fermait la marche. *Voir aussi* **overcoat.**

woodshed [ˈwudʃed] (*noun*), *F:* **there's something nasty in the w.,** on nous cache quelque chose, il y a un cadavre dans la grange.

wool [wul] (*noun*). **1. to lose one's w.,** (*a*) *P:* se mettre en colère*; **keep your w. on!** ne te frappe pas! calme-toi!; (*b*) *F:* = **to lose one's thatch. 2.** *F:* **to pull the w. over s.o.'s eyes,** jeter de la poudre aux yeux de qn. *Voir aussi* **cotton-wool.**

woolie, wooll(e)y, woollie [ˈwuli] (*noun*), *F:* (*a*) tricot *m*; lainage *m*, paletot *m* de laine; **put your w. on,** mets ta laine; (*b*) **winter woollies,** sous-vêtements chauds.

woolly [ˈwuli] (*adj.*), *F:* (**wild and**) **w.,** (*a*) ignare, inculte, mal léché; (*b*) hirsute, hérissé.

woozy [ˈwu:zi] (*adj.*). **1.** *F:* étourdi, qui a le vertige, dont la tête tourne. **2.** *P:* ivre*, blindé, chargé.

wop [wɔp] (*noun*), *P:* (*péj.*) Italien *m*, macaroni *m*.

work[1] [wə:k] (*noun*), *F:* **a nasty piece of w.,** un sale type, une peau de vache. *Voir aussi* **bodywork; cut out (to), 3, 4; homework; legwork; works.**

work[2] [wə:k] (**to**). **1.** *F:* arranger, manigancer, machiner, trafiquer; **to w. a fiddle,** manigancer une combine. **2.** *P:* coïter* avec (une femme), bourrer.

working over [ˈwə:kiŋˈouvər] (*noun*), *P:* **to give s.o. a w. o. = to work s.o. over.**

workout [ˈwə:kaut] (*noun*). **1.** *F:* essai *m*, tentative *f*, ébauche *f*. **2.** *P:* volée *f* de coups*, raclée *f*, tabassée *f*.

work over [ˈwə:kˈouvər] (**to**), *P:* **to w. s.o. o.,** battre* qn, passer une peignée à qn.

works [wə:ks] (*pl. noun*). **1.** *P:* **to give s.o. the w.,** (*a*) battre* qn, tabasser qn, passer qn à tabac; (*b*) tuer* qn, zigouiller qn, faire son affaire à qn. **2.** *P:* **the w. = the business** (**business, 4** (*a*), (*d*), (*e*)). **3.** *F:* **the whole w.,** tout le bataclan, tout le bazar; *cf.* **boiling; caboodle; shebang, 1; shoot**[1]**, 1.** *Voir aussi* **foul up (to); gum up (to); shoot**[2] **(to), 8; spanner; waterworks.**

work up [ˈwə:kˈʌp] (**to**). **1.** *P:* exciter sexuellement, émoustiller. **2.** *F:* mettre (qn) en colère, échauffer, affoler; **don't get worked up (about it),** ne t'emballe pas, ne te monte pas le bourrichon. *Voir aussi* **lather**[1]**; sweat**[1]**, 3.**

* L'astérisque indique que le mot marqué de ce signe figure comme entrée dans le Répertoire.

world [wə:ld] (*noun*), *F:* **1. to feel on top of the w.,** être en pleine forme, être au septième ciel. **2. out of this w.,** mirifique, transcendant, sensas(s). **3. to think the w. of s.o.,** estimer hautement qn, porter qn aux nues. *Voir aussi* **come down (to), 4; dead**[1], **7; wide, 2.**

worry [ˈwʌri] **(to),** *F:* **1. not to w.!** faut pas s'en faire! **2. I should w.!** ce n'est pas mon affaire! c'est le cadet de mes soucis!

worryguts [ˈwʌrigʌts] (*U.S.:* **worry wart** [ˈwʌriwɔ:t]) (*noun*), *P:* bileux *m,* qn qui se met martel en tête (*ou* qui se fait des cheveux).

worth [wə:θ] (*adj.*), *F:* **1. for all one is w.,** de toutes ses forces. **2. was she w. it?:** *voir* **bingo (76).**

wotcher! [ˈwɔtʃə] (*excl.*), *P:* **w., mate! w., cock!** comment ça gaze, mon vieux?

wow![1] [wau] (*excl.*), *F:* oh la la! héhé!

wow[2] [wau] (*noun*), *F:* succès *m* formidable (*ou* du tonnerre *ou* à casser la baraque). *Voir aussi* **pow-wow.**

wow[3] [wau] **(to),** *F:* stupéfier, époustoufler, en mettre plein la vue.

wowser [ˈwauzər] (*noun*) (*Austr.*), *F:* rabat-joie *m,* trouble-fête *m.*

W.P.B., w.p.b. [ˈdʌblju:ˈpi:ˈbi:] (*abbr.* = *waste paper basket*), *F:* corbeille *f* à papier.

wrap [ræp] **(to),** *F:* **1. w. yourself round that!** mange* (*ou* bois*) cela! tape-toi cela! mets-toi ça derrière la cravate! **2. he wrapped his car round a tree,** il a encadré un arbre.

wrap-up [ˈræpʌp] (*noun*), *P:* **1.** résumé *m,* topo *m.* **2.** colis *m* contenant des drogues.

wrap up [ˈræpˈʌp] **(to). 1.** *P:* se taire*, la fermer, la boucler; **w. u.!** ta gueule! la ferme! **2.** *F:* terminer, achever, boucler; **it's all wrapped up,** tout est arrangé (*ou* bouclé).

wringer [ˈriŋər] (*noun*), *P:* **to put s.o. through the w.,** en faire voir des vertes et des pas mûres à qn, passer qn à la casserole.

wrinkle [ˈriŋkl] (*noun*), *F:* **1.** tuyau *m,* truc *m,* combine *f;* **to know all the wrinkles,** la connaître dans les coins, connaître les ficelles. **2.** nouveauté *f,* idée originale, novation *f;* **that's a new w.,** c'est du neuf.

wrist [rist] (*noun*), *V:* **1. limp w.,** pédéraste*, chouquette *f,* chochotte *f.* **2. one off the w.,** masturbation *f,* un astiquage maison, un branlage maison.

write [rait] **(to),** *F:* **it's nothing to w. home about,** cela n'a rien d'extraordinaire, cela ne casse rien.

write-off [ˈraitɔf] (*noun*), *F:* individu désemparé, épave *f.*

wrong[1] [rɔŋ] (*adj.*), *F:* **to get on the w. side of s.o.** = **to be in w. with s.o.** (**wrong**[2], **2**). *Voir aussi* **bed**[1], **2; end, 11.**

wrong[2] [rɔŋ] (*adv.*), *F:* **1. to get s.o. in w. with s.o.,** disgracier qn aux yeux de qn d'autre. **2. to be in w. with s.o.,** ne pas être dans les bonnes grâces (*ou* les petits papiers) de qn, être mal vu.

wrongheaded [ˈrɔŋˈhedid] (*adj.*), *F:* bête*, demeuré.

* An asterisk indicates that the word so marked is included as a head-word in the Appendix.

Y

yabber[1] [ˈjæbər] (*noun*), *F*: bavardage *m*, bavasse *f*, jactage *m*.
yabber[2] [ˈjæbər] (**to**), *F*: bavarder*, bavasser, jacter.
yack[1] [jæk] (*noun*), *F*: = **yackety-yack.**
yack[2] [jæk] (**to**), *F*: (*a*) bavarder*, jacasser; (*b*) ragoter, papoter; (*c*) caqueter, dévider.
yackety-yack [ˈjækətiˈjæk] (*noun*), *F*: caquetage *m*, jacasserie *f*, bla-bla *m*; *cf.* **clackety-clack.**
yahoo [jɑːˈhuː, jəˈhuː] (*noun*), *F*: **1.** homme* bestial, brute *f*, sauvage *m*. **2.** (*U.S.*) (*a*) paysan*, petzouille *m*, croquant *m*, cul-terreux *m*; (*b*) buse *f*, niguedouille *mf*.
yak[1] [jæk] (*noun*), *F*: = **yackety-yack.**
yak[2] [jæk] (**to**), *F*: = **yack**[2] (**to**).
yammer [ˈjæmər] (**to**), *F*: bavarder*, bavasser, dégoiser.
yancy [ˈjænsi] (*adj.*) (*U.S.*), *F*: = **antsy;** *cf.* **yantsy.**
yang [jæŋ] (*noun*) (*U.S.*), *P*: pénis*, zobi *m*.
yank[1] [jæŋk] (*noun*), *F*: secousse *f*, saccade *f*, coup sec.
yank[2] [jæŋk] (**to**). **1.** *F*: tirer d'un coup sec; **to y. the bedclothes off s.o.,** découvrir qn brusquement **2.** (*U.S.*) *P*: arrêter*, agrafer.
Yank[3] [jæŋk], **Yankee**[1] [ˈjæŋki] (*adj.*), *F*: américain, amerlo(que), yankee, ricain.
Yank[4] [jæŋk], **Yankee**[2] [ˈjæŋki] (*noun*), *F*: **1.** habitant *m* de la Nouvelle Angleterre ou d'un des états du nord des États-Unis. **2.** Américain *m*, Amerlo *m*, Amerloque *m*, Yankee *m*, Ricain *m*.
yankeeism [ˈjæŋkiːiz(ə)m] (*noun*), *F*: (*a*) mot américain; (*b*) américanisme *m*, amerloche *m*.
yantsy [ˈjæntsi] (*adj.*) (*U.S.*), *F*: = **antsy;** *cf.* **yancy.**
yap[1] [jæp] (*noun*), *P*: **1.** (*a*) bavardage bruyant, caquetage *m*; (*b*) bouche*, goule *f*. **2.** (*U.S.*) individu bête*, gourde *f*, crétin *m*, navet *m*.
yap[2] [jæp] (**to**), *P*: **1.** grogner*, bougonner, rouspéter. **2.** parler* beaucoup, déblatérer, en dégoiser, japper.
yapper [ˈjæpər] (*noun*), *P*: bavard*, jacasseur *m*.
yapping [ˈjæpiŋ] (*noun*), *P*: bavardage *m*, dévidage *m*, jactage *m*.
yard[1] [jɑːd] (*noun*), *F*: **words a y. long,** mots longs d'une toise; **statistics by the y.,** statistiques *f.pl.* à gogo; **a face a y. long,** visage* long d'une au(l)ne. *Voir aussi* **bone-yard; churchyard.**
yard[2] [jɑːd] (**to**), *P*: **to y. s.o.,** coïter* avec qn de tout à fait étranger.
yardbird [ˈjɑːdbəːd] (*noun*) (*U.S.*), *F*: = **jailbird.**
yard-dog [ˈjɑːddɔg] (*noun*) (*U.S.*), *P*: malappris *m*, chien galeux.
yarn[1] [jɑːn] (*noun*), *F*: (*a*) histoire *f* (*ou* conte *m*) de matelot; (*b*) longue histoire; **to spin** (*or* **pitch** *or* **pull**) **a y.,** (*a*) raconter (*ou* débiter) une histoire; (*b*) mentir*, raconter des histoires *f.pl.*, bourrer le crâne à qn.
yarn[2] [jɑːn] (**to**), *F*: débiter des histoires *f.pl.*
yarra [ˈjærə] (*adj.*) (*Austr.*), *F*: (**stone**) **y.,** fou*, loufoque.
yatter[1] [ˈjætər] (*noun*), *P*: bavardage *m*, baratin *m*, déblatérage *m*.
yatter[2] [ˈjætər] (**to**), *P*: bavarder*, baratiner, déblatérer, tenir le crachoir.
yawny [ˈjɔːni] (*adj.*), *F*: ennuyeux*, rasoir, qui fait bâiller (à s'en décrocher la mâchoire).
yawp [jɔːp] (**to**) (*U.S.*), *F*: = **yap**[2] (**to**), **1.**
yeah [ˈjɛə, ˈjɛəː] (*adv. & excl.*), *F*: (*a*) oui*, gy, gygo; (*b*) **oh y.?** et alors? et après?
year [jiər, jəːr] (*noun*), *F*: **to put years on s.o.,** donner du mal à qn, donner des cheveux blancs à qn. *Voir aussi* **donkey, 3.**
yegg [jeg] (*noun*) (*U.S.*), *P*: **1.** coffioteur *m*, déboucleur *m* (*ou* casseur *m*) de coffiot. **2.** voleur*, caroubleur *m*.

* L'astérisque indique que le mot marqué de ce signe figure comme entrée dans le Répertoire.

yell [jel] (*noun*), *F:* **it's a y.** = **it's a scream** (**scream**[1], **2**).

yellow [ˈjelou, ˈjelə] (*adj.*), *F:* **1.** lâche, couard; **to have a y. streak,** être poltron* (*ou* froussard), avoir les foies *m.pl.* (*ou* les grolles *f.pl.*), ne rien avoir dans le ventre. **2. the Y. Press,** presse *f* qui vise à la sensation, journaux* à scandales. *Voir aussi* **dirt**[1], **7**; **jack**[1], **13**.

yellow-bellied [ˈjelou-belid, ˈjelə-belid] (*adj.*), *F:* qui a peur*, déballonné, flubard; **to be y.-b.,** avoir les foies (blancs).

yellow-belly [ˈjelou-beli, ˈjelə-beli] (*noun*), *F:* froussard *m*, trouillard *m*, foie blanc (*ou* bleu).

yellow-jacket [ˈjelou-dʒækit, ˈjelə-dʒækit] (*noun*), *P:* pilule *f* à base de barbital, barbiturique *m* (*drogues**).

yellow-livered [ˈjelou-livəd, ˈjelə-livəd] (*adj.*), *F:* = **yellow-bellied.**

yen[1] [jen] (*noun*). **1.** *F:* désir ardent et obsédant, appétit *m*. **2.** *P:* = **yen-yen.** *Voir aussi* **pen-yen.**

yen[2] [jen] (**to**), *F:* désirer ardemment, en vouloir.

yen-shee [ˈjenˈʃiː] (*noun*), *P:* = **pen-yen.**

yen-yen [ˈjenjen] (*noun*), *P:* besoin *m* de la drogue, guêpe *f*, guenon *f*.

yep [jep] (*excl.*), *P:* = **yeah** (*a*).

yer [jəːr] (*pron.* = *you*), *P:* tu, vous; **will y. or won't y.?** veux-tu ou veux-tu pas?

yesca [ˈjeskə] (*noun*), *P:* marijuana *f* (*drogues**).

yes-girl [ˈjesgəːl] (*noun*), *P:* fille facile, Marie-couche-toi-là, fille qui se couche quand on lui dit de s'asseoir.

yes-man [ˈjesmæn] (*noun*), *F:* individu* qui dit oui à tout, béni-oui-oui *m*.

Yid [jid] (*noun*), *P:* (*péj.*) Juif *m*, Youpin *m*.

ying-yang [ˈjiŋjæŋ] (*noun*) (*U.S.*), *P:* = **yang.**

yippee! [ˈjiˈpiː] (*excl.*), *F:* bravo! hourrah!

yippie [ˈjipi] (*noun*), *F:* hippie turbulent et tapageur.

yob [jɔb] (*noun*), *P:* **1.** (*péj.*) gars *m*, fiston *m*. **2.** rustre *m*, lourdaud *m*, paltoquet *m*.

yobbo [ˈjɔbou] (*noun*), *P:* = **yob, 2.**

yogs [jɔgz] (*pl. noun*), *F:* longtemps, des années*, des berges.

Yorkshire [ˈjɔːkʃə] (*pr. noun*), *P:* **to come** (*or* **put**) **Y. on** (*or* **over**) **s.o.,** escroquer*, posséder, rouler qn.

you-and-me [ˈjuənˈmiː] (*noun*) (*R.S.* = *tea*), *P:* thé *m* (*boisson*).

yours [jɔːz, jɔəz] (*pron.*), *F:* **1. what's y.?** qu'est-ce que tu prends? **2. y. truly,** moi-même, mézigue, bibi. *Voir aussi* **up**[4], **1.**

yow [jau] (*noun*) (*Austr.*), *F:* **to keep y.** = **to keep nit** (**nit, 2**).

yowly [ˈjauli] (*adj.*), *F:* pleurnicheur, geignard.

yuck! [jʌk] (*excl.*), *F:* pouah!

yucky [ˈjʌki] (*adj.*), *F:* **1.** odieux, dégueulasse. **2.** à l'eau de rose, mauviette.

yummy [ˈjʌmi] (*adj.*), *F:* très bon, délicieux, du nanan, de derrière les fagots.

yum-yum! [ˈjʌmˈjʌm] (*excl.*), *F:* du nanan!

* An asterisk indicates that the word so marked is included as a head-word in the Appendix.

Z

zany ['zeini] (*adj.*), *F:* bouffon, gugusse, gourdiflot.

zap [zæp] (**to**) (*U.S.*), *P:* **1.** tuer* d'un coup de feu, zigouiller. **2.** battre à plate(s) couture(s), anéantir. **3.** se dépêcher*, se décarcasser.

zazzle ['zæzl] (*noun*), *P:* désir sexuel, tracassin *m.*

zazzy ['zæzi] (*adj.*), *F:* appétissante, bien roulée, qui a du chien.

Z car ['zedkɑːr] (*noun*), *F:* voiture *f* de police, voiture pie.

Zen [zen] (*noun*), *P:* **instant Z.**, LSD *m* (*drogues**).

zing [ziŋ] (*noun*), *F:* vitalité *f*, vigueur *f*, énergie *f*, dynamisme *m.*

zingy ['ziŋi] (*adj.*), *F:* plein de vitalité *f* (*ou* d'entrain *m*), qui pète le feu.

zip [zip] (*noun*), *F:* **1.** énergie *f*, entrain *m*; **put some z. into it!** mets-y du nerf! secoue-toi! **2.** = **zipper.**

zip along ['zipə'lɔŋ] (**to**), *F:* aller très vite*, aller à toute pompe.

zipper ['zipər] (*noun*) (=*zip-fastener*), *F:* Fermeture *f* Éclair (*marque déposée*), fermeture *f* à curseur.

zippy ['zipi] (*adj.*), *F:* vif, plein d'allant, dynamique; **look z.!** grouille-toi! magne-toi (le train)!

zip up ['zip'ʌp] (**to**), *F:* **will you z. me u.?** veux-tu fermer ma Fermeture Éclair?

zit [zit] (*noun*) (*U.S.*), *P:* bouton *m* (de l'épiderme), bourgeon *m.*

zizz[1] [ziz] (*noun*), *F:* petit somme *m*, roupillon *m.*

zizz[2] [ziz] (**to**), *F:* dormir*, faire dodo, piquer un roupillon (*ou* une ronflette).

zombi(e), zomby ['zɔmbi] (*noun*), *F:* **1.** individu* sans force de caractère, lavette *f*, chiffe *f*, avachi *m.* **2.** individu bête*, duschnock *m.*

zonk [zɔŋk] (**to**), *P:* = **zap** (**to**), **1, 2, 3.**

zonked (out) ['zɔŋkt('aut)] (*adj.*), *P:* (*a*) ivre* mort, cuit, rétamé; (*b*) (*drogues*) défoncé à zéro, complètement ivre.

zoom [zuːm] (*noun*), *P:* amphétamine *f* (*drogues**), speed *m.*

zoom up ['zuːm'ʌp] (**to**), *F:* **to z. u., to come zooming up,** arriver en trombe.

zoot [zuːt] (*adj.*), *F:* (*a*) voyant, criard; (*b*) à la mode, (au) dernier cri; **z. suit,** complet *m* d'homme avec veston long et pantalon étroit; costume *m* zazou.

zosh [zɔʃ] (*noun*) (*U.S.*), *P:* femme* (*péj.*), tarderie *f*, rombière *f.*

* **L'astérisque indique que le mot marqué de ce signe figure comme entrée dans le Répertoire.**

Répertoire alphabétique de synonymes argotiques et populaires

(*N.B.—Ce répertoire offre un choix de synonymes et de termes analogiques pour tous les mots suivis d'un astérisque dans le Dictionnaire.*)

abandonner: balancer, balanstiquer, bouler, débarquer, déposer, foutre à la cour, lâcher, laisser choir (*ou* courir *ou* glisser *ou* tomber), laisser en carafe (*ou* frime *ou* panne *ou* plan *ou* rade), larguer, plaquer, quimper, scier, semer, virer.

Voir aussi **débarrasser de, se.**

abîmer: amocher, bousiller, esquinter, fusiller, rangemaner, saboter.

abject (*adj.*)**:** cradingue, crado, débectant, dégueulasse, dégueulbif, salingue.

abondance *f*: aboulage *m*, bardée *f*, bottée *f*, des bottes *f.pl.*, charibotée *f*, chiée *f*, flanquée *f*, flopée *f*, flottes *f.pl.*, foul(e)titude *f*, des mille et des cents, potée *f*, ribambelle *f*, secouée *f*, séquelle *f*, suée *f*, tapée *f*, tas *m*, tassée *f*, tinée *f*, tirée *f*, trimbalée *f*, tripotée *f*.

accord, d' (*excl.*)**:** banco, ça biche, ça boume, ça colle, ça gaze, ça marche, dac, d'acc, gy, O.K.

accoucher: abouler, chier (*ou* faire) un lard (*ou* un lardon *ou* un môme *ou* un salé), débouler, larder, pisser sa (*ou* une) côtelette (*ou* son os), pondre.

adultère *m*: carambolage *m* en douce, char *m*, coup *m* de canif (dans le contrat), découchage *m*, doublage *m*, galoup *m*, impair *m*, mise *f* en double, paille *f*, paillons *m.pl.*, queues *f.pl.*

adversité *f*: bouillasse *f*, bouillie *f*, cerise *f*, confiture *f*, choux *m.pl.*, emmerdement *m*, emmouscaillement *m*, guigne *f*, limonade *f*, marmelade *f*, mélasse *f*, merde *f*, mouise *f*, mouscaille *f*, panade *f*, purée *f*, schkoumoun *m*.

affaire *f*: balle *f*, blot *m*, boulot *m*, combine *f*, coup *m*, filon *m*, flanche *m*, fric(-)frac *m*, parcours *m*, travail *m*, truc *m*, turbin *m*.

agent *m* **de police:** bourrin *m*, cogne *m*, condé *m*, fachiste *m*, flic *m*, flicard *m*, gardien *m* (de la paix), mannequin *m*, maton *m*, matuche *m*, pélerin *m*, raper *m*, sergot *m*, tige *f*.

agent cycliste: cyclo *m*, hirondelle *f*, raper *m*, roulette *f*.

Voir aussi **policier.**

agent *m* **en moto:** mobilard *m*, motard *m*.

agression *f*: accrochage *m*, braquage *m*, colletage *m*, cravate *f*, mise *f* en l'air, serrage *m*.

aimer: s'amouracher de, avoir à la bonne (*ou* à la chouette), avoir dans les globules (*ou* dans la peau), avoir un (*ou* le) béguin pour, avoir un pépin pour, se casquer de, se chiper de, se coiffer de, en croquer pour, s'enticher de, être chipé pour, être entiché (*ou* pincé *ou* toqué) de, gober, étre mordu pour, en pincer pour, raffoler de.

alcool *m*: blanche *f*, camphre *m*, casse-gueule *m*, casse-pattes *m*, cogne *f*, cric *m*, élixir *m* de hussard, fil *m* en quatre, ginglard *m*, gn(i)ole *f*, gnôle *f*, goutte *f*, pousse-au-crime *m*, raide *f*, schnap *m*, schnick *m*, tafiat *m*, tord-boyau(x) *m*, vitriol *m*.

alibi *m*: berlanche *f*, berlue *f*, chauffeuse *f*, couverte *f*, couverture *f*, couvrante *f*, parapluie *m*, pébroc *m*, pébroque *m*.

Allemand *m*: alboche *m*, boche *m*, chleu(h) *m*, doryphore *m*, fridolin *m*, friscou *m*, frisé *m*, fritz *m*, frizou *m*, prusco(t) *m*.

amant *m*: coquin *m*, dessous *m*, doublard *m*, gigolo *m*, gigolpince *m*, Jules *m*, matou *m*, matz *m*, mec *m*, miché *m*, micheton *m*.

ami *m*: aminche *m*, amunche *m*, camerluche *m*, cop(a)in *m*, fiston *m*, frangin *m*, frelot *m*, gonze *m*, gonzier *m*, pote *m*, poteau *m*, vieille branche, zig(ue) *m*.

(très) amusant (*adj.*)**:** à se crever de rire, astap(e), bidonnant, bolant, boyautant, cocasse, crevant, drôlichon, fendant, gondolant, impayable, marrant, pilant, pissant, poilant, rigolard, rigolboche, rigouillard, roulant, tire-bouchonnant, tordant.

an *m*, **année** *f*: berge *f*, carat *m*, gerbe *f*, longe *f*, pige *f*.

anus *m*: anneau *m*, bagouse *f*, bague *f*, boîte *f* à pâté, chevalière *f*, chouette *m*, croupion *m*, échalote *f*, entrée *f* des artistes, fias *m*, fion(ard) *m*, foiron *m*, motte *f*, œil *m* de bronze, oignon *m*, pastille *f*, pot *m*, petit guichet, rond *m*, rondelle *f*, rondibé *m*, trou *m* (de balle *ou* du cul), troufignard *m*, troufignon *m*, troufion *m*.

argent *m* (*monnaie*): ardèche *f*, artiche *m*, aspine *f*, auber *m*, aubère *m*, avoine *f*, beurre *m*, blanc *m*, blé *m*, boules *f.pl.*, braise *f*, bulle *m*, caire *m*, carbi *m*, carbure *m*, carme *m*, carmet *m*, dolluche *m*, douille *f*, ferraille *f*, fifrelin *m*, flouse *m*, flouze *m*, fric *m*, galette *f*, galtouze *f*, grisbi *m*, kope(c)ks *m.pl.*, lovés *m.pl.*, mitraille *f*, mornifle *f*, oseille *f*, osier *m*, pécune *f*, pépètes *f.pl.*, pépettes *f.pl.*, pèse *m*, pésètes *f.pl.*, pésettes *f.pl.*, pèze *m*, picaillons *m.pl.*, po(i)gnon *m*, quibus *m*, radis *m.pl.*, rond *m*, rotin *m*, Saint-Fric *m*, soudure *f*.

billet(s): biffeton *m*, faf *m*, faf(f)iot *m*, la grosse artillerie, image *f*, papier *m*, taffetas *m*, talbin *m*.

argot *m*: arguemuche *m*, jar(s) *m*, largongi *m*.

arrêter (*procéder à une arrestation*): accrocher, agrafer, agricher, agriffer, alpaguer, arquepincer, baiser, bicher, ceinturer, cercler, chauffer, chiper, choper, coffrer, coincer, cravater, croquer, cueillir, emballer, embarquer, embastiller, embourmaner, engerber, entoiler, épingler, fabriquer, faire (marron), friser, gauf(f)rer, gauler, grouper, harponner, lever, mettre (*ou* jeter *ou* poser) le grappin sur, mettre la main sur l'alpague de, paumer, pincer, pingler, piper, piquer, poisser, poivrer, quimper, rafler, ramasser, ratisser, sauter, secouer, serrer, servietter, sucrer.

être arrêté: être baisé (*ou* bon *ou* fabriqué *ou* fait *ou* marron *ou* propre *ou* têtard), se faire bondir, se faire faire, se faire piger.

Voir aussi **emprisonner.**

arriver: s'abouler, amener sa graisse, s'amener, s'annoncer, débarquer, débouler, rabattre, radiner, rappliquer.

assassin *m*: but(t)eur *m*, flingueur *m*, metteur *m* en l'air, repasseur *m*, saigneur *m*, scionneur *m*, surineur *m*, tueur *m*.

assassiner: arranger, bousiller, but(t)er, crever, dégommer, démolir, descendre, dessouder, dézinguer, escoffier, effacer, estourbir, expédier, faire avaler son bulletin de naissance à, faire la peau à, ficher (*ou* flanquer *ou* foutre) en l'air, flinguer, gommer, lessiver, liquider, mettre en l'air, nettoyer, ratatiner, rectifier, refroidir, repasser, saigner, suriner, zigouiller.

assez (en avoir): arrêter les frais, en avoir sa claque, en avoir par-dessus la tête, en avoir plein les bottes (*ou* le derche *ou* le dos), en avoir (plus que) marre, en avoir quine, en avoir ras (le bol), en avoir soupé.

assez! (*excl.*): arrête les frais! barca! basta! ça va comme ça! c'est class(e)! c'est marre! écrase! flac! passe la main! quine! rideau!

attaquer: agrafer, chabler dans, harponner, râbler, rentrer dans le lard (*ou* le mou) à, rentrer dedans, sauter dessus, serrer, tomber dessus, tomber sur l'alpague (*ou* le paletot *ou* le poil) de.

attendre: compter les pavés, draguer, faire le pied de grue, faire le poireau, se faire poser un lapin, moisir, poireauter, poser, prendre racine.

avare (être): avoir un cactus dans la poche, avoir un oursin dans la fouille, coucher dessus, être chien (*ou* dur à la desserre *ou* dur à la détente), être grigou (*ou* grippe-sou *ou* pignouf *ou* pingre *ou* radin *ou* rapiat *ou* rat), être constipé du crapaud (*ou* du morlingue), les lâcher avec un lance-pierre, les planquer, ne pas les lâcher (avec des saucisses), ne pas les sortir.

avocat *m*: bavard *m*, baveux *m*, cravateur *m*, débarbot *m*, débarbotteur *m*, menteur *m*, perroquet *m*.

avouer: accoucher, s'affaler, s'allonger, blutiner, casser (le morceau), cracher (dans le bassin), déballer ses outils, déballonner, se déboutonner, dégorger, dégueuler, lâcher le paquet, manger le morceau, se mettre à table, ouvrir les vannes, vider son sac.

bagarre *f*: badaboum *m*, baroud *m*, bigorne *f*, castagne *f*, chambard *m*, chambardement *m*, cognage *m*, cogne *f*, coup *m* de chien, crêpage *m* de chignon(s) (*ou* de tignasse(s)), grabuge *m*, razzia *f*, rififi *m*, serrage *m*, torchage *m*, torchée *f*.

balle *f* (*armes à feu*): bastos *f*, bonbon *m*, dragée *f*, pastille *f*, praline *f*, prune *f*, pruneau *m*, valda *f*.

bande *f* (*groupe d'individus*): action *f*, brigade *f*, équipe *f*, flèche *f*, gang *m*, soce *f*, tierce *f*, tribu *f*.

barbe *f*: artichaut *m*, bacchante *f*, barbouze *f*, foin *m*, piège *m*.

battre: abîmer le portrait à, amocher, aplatir, aquiger, arranger, assaisonner, astiquer, attiger, avoiner, battre comme plâtre, bigorner, botter (le cul à), bourrer de coups, brosser, carder le cuir à, casser la gueule à, cogner, crêper (le chignon *ou* la tignasse à), décrasser, démolir, dérouiller, encadrer, étriller, filer (*ou* foutre) une avoine (*ou* une danse *ou* une pâtée) à, se frotter, moucher, passer à tabac, passer une peignée (*ou* une raclée *ou* une trempe) à, ramponner, rentrer dans le chou (*ou* le lard) à, rentrer dedans, rosser, rouster, sataner, scionner, sonner, tabasser, talmouser, tamponner, tarter, tatouiller, tisaner.

battre, se: s'amocher (le citron *ou* la gueule *ou* le portrait), se bagarrer, se bigorner, se bouffer le blair, se bûcher, se châtaigner, se colleter, se coltiner, se crêper le chignon (*ou* la tignasse), se crocheter, se filer des toises, se flanquer (*ou* se foutre) sur la gueule, se flanquer (ou se foutre) une peignée, se frotter, se peigner, se riffer, se torcher.

bavard *m*: baratineur *m*, bavasseur *m*, jacasse *f*, jacasseur *m*, jacteur *m*, jaspineur *m*, mitraillette *f*, pie *f*, tapette *f*, vacciné *m* à l'aiguille de phono.

bavarder: avoir une platine, baratiner, bavacher, bavasser, baver, blablater, caqueter, dégoiser, dévider, jaboter, jacasser, jacter, jasper, jaspiner, musiquer, palasser, papoter, pomper de l'air, potiner, rouler, tailler une bavette, en tailler une, tenir le crachoir, user sa salive.

Voir aussi **parler.**

beau, belle (*adj.*): badour, bath, baveau, bavelle, bœuf, choucard, chouctose, chouettard, chouette, chouettos, girofle, girond(e), impec, jojo, juteux, lobé, mirobolant, nickel, au poil, ridère, riflo, roulé(e) au moule, schbeb, soin-soin, soua-soua, du tonnerre, urf.

beaucoup (*adv.*): bézef, bigrement, bougrement, lerche, vachement.

bébé *m*: criard *m*, gluant *m*, ourson *m*, petit salé.

bénéfice *m*: affure *f*, bénef *m*, beurre *m*, gants *m.pl.*, gâteau *m*, gras *m*, gratouille *f*, gratte *f*, rab(e) *m*, rabiot *m*, velours *m*.

bête (*adj.*): andouille, ballot, baluchard, baluche, bas de plafond, bébête, bec d'ombrelle, bêta, bidon, bille, bouché (à l'émeri), bourrique, branque, buse, carafon, cave, cavé, con, con(n)ard, con(n)asse, con(n)eau, cornichon, couillon, crétin, cruche, cruchon, cul, culcul, déphosphaté, déplafonné, duschnock, empaillé, empaqueté, emplâtré, empoté, enflé, fada, gourde, gourdiflot, lavedu, lourdingue, moule, navet, niguedouille, noix, nouille, oie, panard, patate, pied, plat de nouilles, pocheté, pomme, saucisse, schnock, serin, à tête de linotte, tourte, truffe, veau.

bêtise *f*: de la balançoire, des balançoires *f.pl.*, bidon *m*, blague *f*, bourdes *f.pl.*, connerie *f*, eau bénite de cour, eau *f* de bidet, fadaise *f*, faribole *f*, fichaise *f*, focard(e) *f*, focardise *f*, focardité *f*, foutaise *f*, pommade *f*, salades *f.pl.*, sornettes *f.pl.*, sottise *f*.

bévue *f*: boulette *f*, bourde *f*, cagade *f*, caraco *m*, char *m*, connerie *f*, gaffe *f*, galoup(e) *f*, impair *m*.

billets: *voir* **argent.**

blennorragie *f*: castapiane *f*, chaude-lance *f*, chaude-pince *f*, chaude-pisse *f*, chtouille *f*, coulante *f*, schtouille *f*.

blesser: abîmer, allumer, amocher, aquiger, arranger, attiger, jambonner, maquiller, moucher, servir.

blesser au couteau: faire des boutonnières à, mettre les tripes à l'air à, piquer, poser un portemanteau dans le dos de, rallonger.

bluffer: *voir* **exagérer.**

boire: s'arroser l'avaloir (*ou* la dalle), biberonner, chopiner, écluser (un godet), s'enfiler un verre, s'envoyer un coup, en étouffer un, en étrangler un, se gargariser, se graisser le toboggan, s'humecter les amygdales, se jeter une jatte, s'en jeter un (derrière la cravate), lamper, se laver les dents, lever le coude, lécher, lichailler, licher, se mouiller la dalle (*ou* la meule), picoler, picter, pinter, se piquer la ruche, pitancher, pomper, se rincer la dalle (*ou* le fusil *ou* le plomb), siffler, siroter, soiffer, sucer, téter.

bordel *m*: baisodrome *m*, bobinard *m*, bocard *m*, bocsif *m*, boxon *m*, bric *m*, cabane *f*, clac *m*, clandé *m*, claque *m*, foutoir *m*, lupanard *m*, maison d'abattage (*ou* bancale *ou* de passe), taule *f*, tringlodrome *m*, volière *f*.

bouche *f*: accroche-pipe *m*, bec *m*, boîte *f*, claque-merde *m*, dalle *f*, égout *m*, gargoulette *f*, gargue *f*, goule *f*, goulot *m*, gueule *f*, malle *f*, margoulette *f*, marmouse *f*, micro *m*, museau *m*, porte-pipe *m*, saladier *m*, terrine *f*, tirelire *f*, trappe *f*.

bourreau *m*: arrangeur *m*, correcteur *m*, faucheur *m*, grand coiffeur, rectifieur *m*.

bouteille *f*: boutanche *f*, pot *m*, rouillarde *f*, rouille *f*.

bouteille de champagne: roteuse *f*.

bouteille de vin rouge: kilbus *m*, kilo *m*, légionnaire *m*, litron *m*, négresse *f*, pieu *m*.

bouteille vide: cadavre *m*.

boutique *f*: boucard *m*, bouclard *m*, boutanche *f*, boutoche *f*, clapier *m*, estanco *m*, piaule *f*.

boutique de receleur: moulin *m*.

bras *m*: aile *f*, aileron *m*, anse *f*, aviron *m*, balancier *m*, ballant *m*, bradillon *m*, brandille *f*, brandillon *m*, nageoire *f*.

brave (être): avoir du battant (*ou* des couilles *ou* du cran *ou* de l'estomac *ou* du poil), avoir quelque chose dans le slip, en avoir au cul (*ou* dans le bide *ou* dans le moulin *ou* dans le ventre), n'avoir pas froid aux yeux, être accroché, être d'attaque, être gonflé, être un peu là.

briquet *m*: briquetoque *m*, chalumeau *m*, flamme *f*, lance-flamme *m*.

bruit *m*: bacchanal *m*, barouf *m*, bastringue *m*, boucan *m*, bousin *m*, boxon *m*, brouhaha *m*, cacophonie *f*, casse-oreilles *m*, casse-vitres *m*, chabanais *m*, chahut *m*, chambard *m*, foin *m*, grabuge *m*, musique *f*, pétard *m*, potin *m*, raffut *m*, rafût *m*, ramdam(e) *m*, zin-zin *m*.

butin *m*: barbotin *m*, bouquet *m*, fade *m*, rafle *f*, taf *m*, taffe *m*.

cacher: camoufler, car(r)er, étouffer, mettre à l'ombre (*ou* en planque *ou* en veilleuse *ou* au vert), planquer, planquouser.

cacher, se: se carrer, se nicher, se placarder, se planquer, se planquouser.

cachette *f*: placarde *f*, plan *m*, planque *f*, planquouse *f*, trou *m*.

cadavre *m*: allongé *m*, can(n)é *m*, croni *m*, macchab *m*, macchabé(e) *m*, refroidi *m*, saumon *m*, viande froide.

café *m* (*boisson*): cafeton *m*, cao *m*, caoua(h) *m*, cahoua *m*, chaud *m*, jus *m* de chaussette (*ou* de chique *ou* de shako), maza *m*, noir *m*.

café *m* (*débit*): abreuvoir *m*, bar *m*, bistre *m*, bistro *m*, bistroquet *m*, bistrot *m*, caboulot *m*, estanco(t) *m*, tapis *m*, troquet *m*.

cambrioler: caroubler, casser, faire un baluchonnage (*ou* une cambriole *ou* un casse *ou* un fric-frac), faire du bois, fracasser, frapper, fricfraquer, mettre (*ou* monter) en l'air, travailler au bec de canne.

cambrioleur *m*: baluchonneur *m*, cambrio *m*, caroubleur *m*, casseur *m*, chevalier *m* de la lune, fracasseur *m*, lourdeur *m*.

Voir aussi **voleur.**

campagne *f*: bled *m*, bouse *f*, brousse *f*, cambrousse *f*, parpagne *f*, patelin *m*, savane *f* au vert.

caprice *m*: béguin *m*, dada *m*, foucade *f*, pépin *m*, toquade *f*.

car *m* **de police**: car *m*, familiale *f*, fourgon *m*, panier *m* à salade, porte-poulaille *m*, poulailler ambulant, voiture *f* de mariée, voiturin *m*.

caresses *f.pl.*: chatouilles *f.pl.*, chouteries *f.pl.*, mamours *m.pl.*, pattes *f.pl.* d'araignées (*ou* de velours), papouilles *f.pl.*, patouilles *f.pl.*, pelotes *f.pl.*

cartes *f.pl.* **à jouer**: bauches *f.pl.*, biftons *m.pl.*, brèmes *f.pl.*, cartons *m.pl.*, papiers *m.pl.*, poisseuses *f.pl.*

casquette *f*: bâche *f*, deffe *f*, gapette *f*, gaufre *f*, grivelle *f*, guimpe(tte) *f*.

cercueil *m*: boîte *f* à dominos, caisse *f*, paletot *m* (*ou* redingote *f*) de sapin, pardessus *m* sans manches.

chambre *f*: cabine *f*, cambuse *f*, carrée *f*, case *f*, crèche *f*, garno *m*, gourbi *m*, guitoune *f*, niche *f*, piaule *f*, planque *f*, quatre murs *m.pl.*, strasse *f*, taule *f*, turne *f*.

chance (avoir de la): avoir du baraka (*ou* du bol *ou* du cul *ou* du fion *ou* du gluck *ou* du pot *ou* du proze *ou* du vase *ou* de la veine), être beurré (*ou* bidard *ou* chançard *ou* cocu *ou* doré *ou* veinard *ou* verni).

chanter: dégosiller, l'envoyer, gargouiller, goualer, la pousser, pousser la goualante, y aller de sa goualante.

chapeau *m*: bada *m*, bibi *m*, bitos *m*, bloum *m*, capet *m*, doul(e) *m*, doulos *m*, galurin *m*, papeau *m*, pétase *m*, toiture *f*.

chapeau haut de forme: cylindre *m*, décalitre *m*, gibus *m*, huit-reflets *m*, lampion *m*, tube *m*, tuyau *m* de poêle.

chaussures *f.pl.*: bateaux *m.pl.*, boîtes *f.pl.* à violon, crocos *m.pl.*, croquenots *m.pl.*, écrase-merde *m.pl.*, flacons *m.pl.*, godasses *f.pl.*, godilles *f.pl.*, godillots *m.pl.*, grôles *f.pl.*, lattes *f.pl.*, pompes *f.pl.*, ribouis *m.pl.*, rigadins *m.pl.*, savates *f.pl.*, sorlots *m.pl.*, targettes *f.pl.*, tartines *f.pl.*, tatanes *f.pl.*, tiges *f.pl.*

chauve (être): avoir une boule de billard (*ou* le caillou dégarni *ou* un crâne de limace *ou* un mouchodrome *ou* le melon déplumé *ou* la tête comme un genou *ou* une tête de veau), avoir une perruque en peau de fesse, n'avoir plus de chapelure (*ou* de cresson *ou* de mousse) sur le caillou, n'avoir plus de cresson sur la fontaine, être dégazonné (*ou* déplumé *ou* jambonneau *ou* zigué).

chemise *f*: bannière *f*, drapeau *m*, limace *f*, lime *f*, limouse *f*, liquette *f*, sac *m* à lard (*ou* à puces).

cher, chère (*adj.*) (*coûteux*): chaud, chérot, grisole, lerche, lerchem, salé.

cheval *m*: bidet *m*, bique *f*, bourdon *m*, bourrin *m*, bousin *m*, canard *m*, canasson *m*, carcan *m*, carne *m*, dada *m*, gail(le) *m*, hareng *m*, rossard *m*, rosse *f*, tréteau *m*.

cheveux *m.pl.*: cresson *m*, crins *m.pl.*, douilles *f.pl.*, gazon *m*, plumes *f.pl.*, tiffes *m.pl.*, tifs *m.pl.*, tignasse *f*.

couper les cheveux à quelqu'un: épiler la pêche à quelqu'un, tiffer quelqu'un, varloper la toiture à quelqu'un.

chien *m*: azor *m*, bougnoul(e) *m*, cabot *m*, cador *m*, chien-chien *m*, clébard *m*, clebs *m*, oua(h)-oua(h) *m*, toutou *m*.

cigare *m*: churchill *m*, long *m*.

gros cigare: barreau *m* de chaise.

petit cigare: clou *m* de cercueil, crapulos *m*.

cigarette *f*: baluche *f*, cibiche *f*, cousue *f*, grillante *f*, pipe *f*, pipette *f*, sèche *f*, taf *f*, taffe *f*.

cigarette à filtre: périodique *f*, tampax *f*.

cigarette papier maïs: chinois *m*.

Voir aussi **drogues: cigarette de marijuana.**

cimetière *m*: boulevard *m* (*ou* jardin *m*) des allongés, champ *m* des refroidis, chez les têtes en os, jardin *m* des claqués, parc *m* des cronis.

clef *f*: carouble *f*, gerbière *f*, tournante *f*.

clitoris *m*: berlingot *m*, berlingue *f*, bouton *m* (de rose), clicli *m*, clito(n) *m*, flageolet *m*, framboise *f*, grain *m* de café, haricot *m*, noisette *f*, praline *f*, soissonnais *m* (rose).

clochard *m*: cloche *m*, clodo(t) *m*, traîne-lattes *m*, traîne-patins *m*, traîne-sabots *m*, traîne-savates *m*, trimardeur *m*, zonard *m*.

Voir aussi **vagabond.**

cœur *m*: battant *m*, horloge *f*, palpitant *m*, grand ressort, toquant *m*.

coït *m*: baisade *f*, baisage *m*, bourre *f*, carambolage *m*, chique *f*, coup *m* d'arbalète, crampe *f*, crampette *f*, criquon-criquette *m*, dérouillade *f*, dérouillage *m*, fouraillage *m*, frottage *m*, giclée *f*, mise *f*, partie *f* de balayette (*ou* d'écarté *ou* de jambes en l'air *ou* de piquet), passe *f*, pelée *f*, politesse *f*, soupe *f* à la quéquette, torpillage *m*, tringlage *m*, tronchage *m*, tronche *f*, truc *m*, yensage *m*, zizi-panpan *m*.

coït anal: **1. pratiquer la pédérastie active (sur)**: (*a*) (*intransitif*) baiser à la riche, casser coco, casser le pot, prendre de l'oignon, tourner la page, tremper la soupe; (*b*) (*transitif*) caser, dauffer, emmancher, empaffer, empaler, empapaouter, empétarder, emproser, encaldosser, enculer, enfifrer, enfigner, miser, planter.

2. pratiquer la pédérastie passive: (*intransitif*) filer de la jaquette, lâcher de l'anneau, *etc.* (*voir* **anus**), ramasser des épingles, se faire taper dedans.

faire un coït buccal: (*a*) (*intransitif*) bouffer la chatte (*femme*), brouter (le cresson) (*femme*), se le faire allonger, se faire croquer, faire mimi (*femme*), faire minette (*femme*), faire un pompier, se laver les dents, prendre la pipe, rogner l'os, souffler dans la canne (*ou* le mirliton *ou* le tube), tailler une plume; (*b*) (*transitif*) dévorer, manger, pomper, prendre en poire, sucer.

coïter: I. (*intransitif*) aller à la bourre (*ou* aux cuisses *ou* au cul *ou* au taponard), aller au mâle (*femme*), amener le petit au cirque, arracher un copeau (*ou* un pavé), asperger le persil, besogner, casser la canne, cracher dans le bénitier, cramper, décrasser les oreilles à Médor, se dégraisser, dérouiller (son petit frère *ou* Totor), effeuiller la marguerite, s'envoyer (en l'air), s'envoyer une femme, le faire, faire l'amour, faire la bête à deux dos, faire ça, faire un carton, faire criquon-criquette, faire une partie de jambes en l'air, faire zizi-panpan, se farcir du mâle (*femme*), se farcir une femme, filer un coup d'arbalète (*ou* de brosse *ou* de patte *ou* de sabre *ou* de tromblon), fourailler, foutre un coup de brosse (*ou* de manche de plumeau *ou* de rouleau), godailler, godiller, se mélanger, le mettre, mettre la cheville dans le trou, nettoyer son verre de lampe, niquer, planter le mai, pousser sa pointe, prendre du mâle (*femme*), tirer sa chique (*ou* son coup *ou* sa crampe *ou* sa crampette), tirer son (*ou* un) coup, voir la feuille à l'envers.

coïter avec...: 2. (*transitif*) aiguiller, baiser, biquer, bit(t)er, bourrer, bourriner, bourriquer, brosser, calecer, caramboler, caser, chevaucher, coller, coucher avec, égoïner, enfiler, enjamber, envoyer en l'air, fourailler, fourrer, foutre, frotter, goupillonner, grimper, guiser, limer, mettre au bout (*ou* au chaud), miser, niquer, piner, pinocher, piquer, planter, pointer, ramer, ramoner, sabrer, sauter, sch(e)nailler, tomber, torcher, torpiller, tringler, trombiner, troncher, verger, yenser.

colère *f* **(être en)**: attraper le coup de sang, l'avoir à la caille, crosser, éclater, s'emballer, être à cran (*ou* en fumasse *ou* furibard *ou* en rogne *ou* en suif), exploser, fulminer, fumer, marronner, monter à l'échelle (*ou* sur ses grands chevaux), mousser, pétarder, piquer une crise, râler, renauder, roter, rouspéter, sortir de ses gonds, voir rouge.

complice *m*: baron *m*, cheville *f*, équipier *m*, gaffeur *m*.

concierge *mf*: bignole *mf*, cloporte *mf*, lourdier *m*, pibloque *mf*, pipelet *m*, pipelette *f*. tortue *f*.

condamnation *f*: gerbage *m*, sape *m*, sapement *m*, sucrage *m*.

condamné (être): cascader, écoper, être bon(nard), être sucré, gerber, morfler, payer, saper, trinquer.

congédier: balancer, balayer, bouler, débarquer, dégommer, déposer, envoyer dinguer (*ou* paître), flanquer (*ou* mettre) à la porte, sa(c)quer, scier, sortir, vider, virer.

Voir aussi **débarrasser de, se.**

corbillard *m*: balai *m*, corbi *m*, dernier autobus, roulotte *f* à refroidis, trottinette *f* (à macchab).

cou *m*: col *m*, colbaque *m*, kiki *m*, sifflet *m*, vis *f*.

coucher, se: aller au dodo (*ou* à la dorme *ou* au paddock *ou* au page *ou* au pageot *ou* au pieu *ou* au plumard *ou* à la ronflette *ou* au schloff), se bâcher, se borgnot(t)er, se crécher, faire banette, se filer dans les toiles, se glisser dans les bannes, se grabater, mettre sa viande dans le torchon, se paddocker, se pager, se pagnoter, se pajoter, se pieuter, se plumarder, se plumer, se sacquer, se zoner.

coup(s) *m* (*pl.*): atout *m*, avoine *f*, baffe *f*, baffre *f*, beigne *f*, brossée *f*, cabachon *m*, calotte *f*, châtaigne *f*, danse *f*, décoction *f*, dégelée *f*, dérouillée *f*, fricassée *f*, frictionnée *f*, frottée *f*, gnon *m*, jeton *m*, marron *m*, passage *m* à tabac, pâtée *f*, pêche *f*, peignée *f*, pile *f*, pipe *f*, purge *f*, raclée *f*, ramponneau *m*, ratatouille *f*, rincée *f*, rossée *f*, roulée *f*, tabassée *f*, talmouse *f*, taloche *f*, tannée *f*, tarte *f*, tartine *f*, tatouille *f*, tisane *f*, torchée *f*, torgn(i)ole *f*, tournée *f*, trempe *f*, trempée *f*, trifouillée *f*, tripotée *f*, triquée *f*, valse *f*.

Voir aussi **recevoir (des coups).**

courageux: *voir* **brave.**

courir: affûter ses gambettes (*ou* ses pincettes), se carapater, cavaler, crapahuter, drop(p)er, jouer des flûtes (*ou* des guibolles), tricoter des bâtons, des gambettes, *etc.* (*voir* **jambe**).

couteau *m*: coupe-lard *m*, cure-dent *m*, lame *f*, lardoir *m*, ouvre-saucisses *m*, pointe *f*, rallonge *f*, rapière *f*, saccagne *f*, sorlingue *m*, surin *m*.

couverture *f*: *voir* **alibi.**

crachat *m*: glaviot *m*, gluau *m*, graillon *m*, huître *f*, mol(l)ard *m*, postillon *m*.

cracher: glavioter, graillonner, mollarder.

crâne *m*: caillou *m*, mansarde *f*, plafond *m*, toiture *f*.

crier: beugler, brailler, braire, donner des coups de gueule, goualer, gueuler (au charron), péter, piailler, piauler, pousser des gueulements.

critiquer: abîmer, aquijer, assassiner, bêcher, carboniser, charrier, chiner, débiner, déchirer (à belles dents), dégrainer, démolir, déshabiller, éreinter, esquinter, faire un abattage de, griller, jardiner, jeter la pierre à, vanner.

croire: couper dedans, donner dedans (*ou* dans le panneau), encaisser, gober, marcher, rendre.

danser: gambiller, gigoter, guincher, en suer une, (faire) tourner.

débarrasser de, se: balancer, balanstiquer, se décramponner de, se défarguer de, dégommer, envoyer (*ou* faire) dinguer, laisser choir, larguer, lessiver, sa(c)quer, scier, vider, virer.

Voir aussi **abandonner; congédier.**

débrouiller, se: avoir la combine (*ou* le système D), la connaître (dans les coins), se défendre, se démerder, se démouscailler, se dépatouiller, savoir s'expliquer (*ou* nager *ou* se retourner).

découvrir: dégot(t)er, dénicher, dépiauter, frimer, piger, repérer.

déféquer: aller où le Roi va à pied, caguer, chier, couler un bronze, déballer, débloquer, déboucher son orchestre, débourrer (sa pipe), déflaquer, faire caca, faire sa grande commission, faire ses affaires, faire ses grands besoins, flasquer, foirer, lâcher (*ou* poser) un colombin (*ou* une prune *ou* une sentinelle), planter une borne, tartir.

dénoncer: balancer, balanstiquer, balloter, bourdiller, bourriquer, brûler, cafarder, donner, filer, griller, moucharder, moutonner, retapisser.

dénonciateur *m*: bordille *m*, bourdille *m*, bourricot *m*, bourrique *f*, cafard *m*, cafardeur *m*, casserole *f*, chacal *m*, chevreuil *m*, croqueur *m*, donneur *m*, fileur *m*, grilleur *m*, indic *m*, mouchard *m*, mouche *f*, mouton *m*, tante *f*.

Voir aussi **indicateur.**

dents *f.pl.*: castagnettes *f.pl.*, chocottes *f.pl.*, crochets *m.pl.*, crocs *m.pl.*, croquantes *f.pl.*, dominos *m.pl.*, pavés *m.pl.*, piloches *f.pl.*, quenottes *f.pl.*, râteaux *m.pl.*, ratiches *f.pl.*, ratoches *f.pl.*, touches *f.pl.* de piano.

dépêcher, se: s'activer, allonger le pas (*ou* la sauce), se décarcasser, se dégrouiller, se déhotter, se démancher, se démerder, se dérouiller, faire fissa (*ou* vinaigre), se grouiller (les puces), se magner (le cul *ou* le derrière *ou* le popotin *ou* le train), en mettre (*ou* filer) un rayon.

dépenser: balancer (*ou* bouffer *ou* claquer *ou* croquer) de l'argent, carmer, casquer, cigler, décher, les écosser, les faire valser, les lâcher, larguer son fric.

dépensier *m*: claque-fric *mf*, décheur *m*.

dés *m.pl.*: bobs *m.pl.*, doches *m.pl.*

dés truqués: artillerie *f*, balourds *m.pl.*, bouts *m.pl.* de sucre, matuches *m.pl.*, pipés *m.pl.*, plateaux *m.pl.*, plats *m.pl.*

déshabiller: décarpiller, défagoter, défringuer, défrusquer, déloquer, dénipper, désaper, désharnacher, foutre (*ou* mettre) à l'air (*ou* à poil), trousser la cotte.

dessous *m.pl.* (*féminins*): falbalas *m.pl.*, fringues *f.pl.* de coulisses, linges *m.pl.*, mouillettes *f.pl.*, soies *f.pl.*

détester: avoir à la caille, avoir dans le blair (*ou* dans le cul *ou* dans le nez *ou* dans le tube), ne pas pouvoir blairer (*ou* encadrer *ou* encaisser), ne pas pouvoir voir en peinture.

diamant *m*: bauche *m*, bouchon *m* de carafe, caillou *m*, diam(e) *m*, éclair *m*, pierre *f*, speech *m*.

diarrhée *f*: chiasse *f*, cliche *f*, courante *f*, foirade *f*, foire *f*, foireuse *f*, riquette *f*.

difficile (*adj.*): coton, duraille, duraillon, duringue, glandilleux, turbin.

discours *m*: baratin *m*, boniment *m*, palas(s) *m*, parlotte *f*, postiche *m*, salade *f*, speech *m*.

doigt *m*: (*main*) apôtre *m*, fourchette *f*, phalangette *f*, piloir *m*; (*pied*) racine *f*, radis *m*.

donner: abouler, allonger, balancer, balanstiquer, coller, ficher, filer, flanquer, foutre, lâcher, refiler.

dormir: baisser la vitrine, dormailler, dormasser, en écraser, faire dodo (*ou* schloff), pioncer, piquer une ronflette (*ou* un roupillon), ronfler, roupiller, roupillonner, tomber dans les bras de Morphée, zoner.

dormir dehors: coucher à la belle étoile (*ou* sur la dure), être de la zone, refiler la comète.

drap *m*: bâche *f*, banne *f*, lingerie *f*, toile *f*, torchon *m*.
drogué (*adj*.): bourré, camé, chargé, défoncé, dynamité, envapé, high, junké.
drogué *m*: camard *m*, camé *m*, camelinque *m*, dynamité *m*, enschnouffé *m*, junkie *m*, toxico *m*.
droguer, se: se camer, se charger, se chnouffer, se doper, s'envaper, se piquer, se piquouser, prendre une reniflette (*ou* une respirette) (*cocaïne*), se schnouffer, tirer sur le bambou (*opium*).
drogues *f.pl.*: came *f*, chnouff *m*, narcs *m.pl.*, schnouff(e) *m*, stups *m.pl.*
amphétamines *f.pl.*: bleues *f.pl.*, bonbons *m.pl.*, rouquine *f*, serpent vert, speed *m*, topette *f*.
barbituriques *m.pl.*: barbitos *m.pl.*, balles *f.pl.* de copaille.
Benzédrine *f* (*marque déposée*): b *f*, bennie *f*, benz *m*.
cannabis *m*: *voir* **marijuana.**
cocaïne *f*: bigornette *f*, blanche *f*, la c, cécile *m*, coco *f*, dynamite *f*, fée blanche, fillette *f*, métro *m* (1 gr.), neige *f*, poison blanc, poudrette *f*, talc *m*, topette *f*.
drinamyl *m*: arbre *m* de Noël, bleuet *m*.
éphédrine *f*: Freddie *m*.
ha(s)chisch *m*: fée verte, griffs *m.pl.*, merde *f*.
héroïne *f*: boy *m*, cheval *m*, H *f*, héro *f*, horse *m*, jus *m*, naph(taline) *f*, niflette *f*, poudre *f*, shit *m*, shmeck *m*.
LSD *m*: acide *m*, D *m*, sucre *m*, vingt-cinq *m*.
marijuana *f*: bambalouche *f*, canapa *f*, chanvre *m*, chiendent *m*, dagga *m*, douce *f*, foin *m*, gania *m*, gold *m*, herbe (douce), juana *f*, juju *f*, kif *m*, Maria *f*, Marie(-Jeanne) *f*, pot *m*, thé *m* (des familles *ou* vert).
cigarette *f* **de marijuana**: bouffée *f*, drag *m*, fume *f*, joint *m*, juju *f*, pipe *f*, reefer *m*, stick *m*.
morphine *f*: lili-pioncette *f*, morph *f*.
opium *m*: bénarès *m*, boue (verte), chandoo *m*, dross *m*, fée brune, lourd *m*, noir *m*, op *m*, pavot *m*, touffiane *f*.
duper: *voir* **escroquer.**

eau *f*: bouillon *m*, Château-la-Pompe *m*, flotte *f*, jus *m* (de parapluie), lance *f*, lancequine *f*, sirop *m* de canard (*ou* de grenouille *ou* de parapluie).
échec *m*: bec *m* de gaz, bide *m*, black-boulage *m*, bouchon *m*, bûche *f*, cassage *m* de nez, chou blanc, fiasco *m*, foirage *m*, four *m*, gamelle *f*, loupage *m*, marron *m*, pelle *f*, pipe *f*, vert *m*, veste *f*.
échouer: se casser le nez, claquer, faire chou blanc, faire la culbute, faire un four, finir dans les choux (*ou* en eau de boudin *ou* en queue de poisson), foirer, louper, péter dans la main, ramasser une veste, récolter un bide, remporter une pelle, tomber dans le lac.
économiser: carrer, faire son beurre (*ou* sa pelote), garer, en mettre à gauche, planquer, planquouser.
éjaculer: *voir* **orgasme (avoir un).**
élégant (*adj*.): badour, (super-)chic, eulpif, flambard, tout flambe, gandin, en grand tralala, hiche-life, en jetant (un jus), jojo, juteux, minet, régence, rider, ridère, riflo, sur son trente et un, tiré à quatre épingles, urf(e).
embrasser: bécoter, biser, coquer un bécot à, faire un bec (*ou* un bécot) à, faire une langue (fourrée) à, lécher (*ou* se sucer) le caillou (*ou* le citron *ou* le museau *ou* la poire *ou* la pomme) à, rouler une galoche (*ou* un patin *ou* des saucisses) à.
emploi *m*: *voir* **travail.**
emprisonner: bloquer, boucler, coffrer, encager, enchetarder, enchrister, ench(e)tiber, ficher (*ou* flanquer *ou* fourrer) dedans, mettre au bloc (*ou* au clou *ou* au gnouf *ou* à l'ombre *ou* au trou), mettre derrière les barreaux, mettre en taule, remiser, serrer.
emprunter (de l'argent) à: bottiner, latter, relancer, sonner, taper, tartiner, torpiller.
enceinte (être): s'arrondir, attraper le ballon, avoir avalé le pépin, avoir du ballon, avoir sa butte, avoir un polichinelle (*ou* un moufflet *ou* un petit salé) dans le tiroir (*ou* sous le tablier), avoir sucé son crayon, être cloquée (*ou* en cloque), être dans une situation intéressante, être engrossée, être tombée sur un clou rouillé, gondoler de la devanture, travailler pour Marianne.
enfant *m*: bout *m* de zan, chiard *m*, chiot *m*, crapaud *m*, gamin *m*, gniard *m*, gosse *mf*, graine *f* de bois de lit, lardon *m*, loupiot *m*, merdeux *m*, mioche *mf*, môme *mf*, momichon *m*, momignard *m*, morbac *m*, morpion *m*, moucheron *m*,

moufflet *m*, moujingue *m*, moussé *m*, moutard *m*, niston *m*, pitchoun *m*, salé *m*, tchiot *m*, têtard *m*.

enfuir, s': *voir* **partir.**

ennuyer: assassiner, assommer, barber, bassiner, canuler, casser le bonbon (*ou* les couilles *ou* les pieds) à, cavaler, courir (*ou* taper) sur le système à, cramponner, emmerder, emmieller, emmouscailler, empoisonner, enquiquiner, faire chier (*ou* suer), raser, scier, tanner.

ennuyeux (*adj.*): accrocheur, assommant, assommoir, barbant, barbe, bassin, canulant, canule, casse-burettes, casse-burnes, casse-couilles, casse-pieds, colique, crampon, emmerdant, gluant, pot de colle, raseur, rasoir, sciant, scie, tannant.

épouse *f*: baronne *f*, bergère *f*, bobonne *f*, boulet *m*, bourgeoise *f*, gouvernement *m*, légitime *f*, ma (chère) moitié, particulière *f*, vieille *f*.

érection *f* **(être en)**: avoir le bambou (*ou* le bâton *ou* la canne *ou* la gaule *ou* le gourdin *ou* le manche *ou* le mandrin *ou* l'os *ou* le tracassin *ou* la trique), avoir des coliques cornues, l'avoir dur (*ou* en l'air), bander, bandocher, être en l'air, être triqué, goder, lever, marquer midi, présenter les armes (*ou* son offrande), redresser, répondre du starter, triquer.

escroc *m*: arnaqueur *m*, arrangeur *m*, carambouilleur *m*, carotteur *m*, dragueur *m*, empileur *m*, entôleur *m*, estampeur *m*, faisan *m*, faisandier *m*, faiseur *m*, filou *m*, floueur *m*, musicien *m*, pipeur *m*, rangemane *m*, rangeur *m*, repasseur *m*, roustisseur *m*, turbineur *m*.

escroquer: arnaquer, arranger, avoir, baiser, carotter, caver, doubler, écailler, écorcher, empaumer, empiler, endormir, enfiler, englander, engourdir, entuber, estamper, fabriquer, faisander, farcir, filouter, flouer, mener au double, monter le coup à, posséder, pigeonner, rangemaner, refaire, rouler, roustir, tirer une carotte à.

escroquerie *f*: arnac *f*, arnaquage *m*, arnaque *f*, bourrage *m*, carambouillage *m*, carottage *m*, carotte *f*, coup *m* d'arnac, doublage *m*, doublure *f*, entôlage *m*, entubage *m*, filouterie *f*, repassage *m*, resquille *f*.

estomac *m*: bocal *m*, boîte *f* à ragoût, buffet *m*, burlingue *m*, cornet *m*, estom(e) *m*, fanal *m*, fusil *m*, garde-manger *m*, gésier *m*, jabot *m*, lampe *f*, lampion *m*, tube *m*.

Voir aussi **ventre.**

étonner: abasourdir, aplatir, asseoir, en boucher un coin (*ou* une surface) à, clouer, couper la chique à, épater, époustoufler, estomaquer, occire.

étrangler: dévisser le coco à, donner le coup de pouce à, nouer la cravate à, serrer le kiki (*ou* la vis) à.

étron *m*: bronze *m*, caca *m*, colombin *m*, déflaque *f*, factionnaire *m*, orphelin *m*, pêche *f*, prune *f*, rondin *m*.

évader, s': les agiter, se barrer, (se) calter, se carapater, se casser, se cavaler, chier du poivre, décarrer, se donner de l'air, en jouer un air, jouer rip (*ou* la fille de l'air), (se) faire la malle (*ou* la valise), filer, larguer les amarres, mettre les bouts (*ou* les voiles), se mettre en cavale, riper, se tirer, se trotter.

évanouir, s': tomber dans le cirage (*ou* les frites *ou* les pommes *ou* le sirop *ou* les vapes), tomber en digue-digue, tourner de l'œil.

exagérer: attiger (la cabane), bêcher, blouser, broder, charrier, cherrer (dans les bégonias), chier dans la colle, chiquer, cravater, se donner des coups de pied, enfler des chevilles, envoyer le bouchon, esbrouf(f)er, faire de l'esbrouf(f)e (*ou* de la musique *ou* du pallas), en faire une tartine, forcer la dose, se gonfler, gonfler le mou, graisser, en installer, jardiner, majorer, se monter le job, pousser, se pousser du col, en rajouter, vanner, y aller fort.

excellent (*adj.*): à tout casser, baisant, bath, bœuf, bolide, chouette, chouettos, de première, doré sur tranche, du tonnerre, épatant, époustouflant, faramineux, formid(able), foutral, impec, meu-meu, nickel, au poil, sensas(s), soin-soin, super, terrible, wif.

---

faim (avoir): avoir un creux, avoir les crochets (*ou* les crocs *ou* la dalle *ou* la dent), avoir l'estomac dans les talons, bouffer des briques, se brosser, claquer du bec, la crever, danser devant le buffet, se mettre la ceinture, la péter, la sauter, la serrer, (se) serrer la ceinture, se taper.

faire: s'appuyer, fabriquer, ficher, foutre, fricoter, goupiller.

fatigué (être): avoir le coup de bambou (*ou* de barre *ou* de pompe), avoir son compte, être à bout (*ou* à plat), être affûté (*ou* avachi *ou* brisé *ou* claqué *ou* crevé *ou* crevetant *ou* éreinté *ou* esquinté *ou* flagada *ou* flapi *ou* fourbu *ou* foutu *ou* lessivé *ou* pompé *ou* raplapla *ou* rendu *ou* rincé *ou* rompu *ou* sur le flanc *ou* vanné *ou* vaseux *ou* vasouillard *ou* vidé), être sur les dents (*ou* les genoux *ou* les rotules).

faux (*adj.*)**:** bidon, chinetoque, toc, tocard.

femme *f* (*péj.*)**:** baronne *f*, bougresse *f*, chipie *f*, créature *f*, donzelle *f*, dragon *m*, fatma *f*, femelle *f*, fendue *f*, fumelle *f*, garce *f*, gisquette *f*, gonzesse *f*, greluche *f*, grognasse *f*, harpie *f*, hotu *f*, houri *f*, lamdé *f*, lamfé *f*, largue *f*, limace *f*, mémé *f*, ménesse *f*, mistonne *f*, moukère *f*, mousmé(e) *f*, nana *f*, nénette *f*, pépée *f*, pétasse *f*, polka *f*, poule *f*, poulette *f*, pouliche *f*, rombière *f*, souris *f*, tarderie *f*, tartavelle *f*, toupie *f*, typesse *f*.

jeune femme: bergère *f*, garce *f*, gisquette *f*, gonzesse *f*, greluche *f*, grimbiche *f*, Julie, lamdé *f*, lamfé *f*, mistonne *f*, môme *f*, mousmé(e) *f*, nana *f*, nénette *f*, palombe *f*, pépée *f*, poule *f*, poulette *f*, pouliche *f*.

(vieille) femme laide: bique *f*, carabosse *f*, carcan *f*, guenon *f*, guimbarde *f*, hotu *m*, mémée *f*, mocheté *f*, prix *m* à réclamer, remède *m* d'amour, rombière *f*, tarderie *f*, tartignol(l)e *f*, tardingue *f*, tartavelle *f*, vieille chèvre (*ou* galoche *ou* mocheté *ou* noix *ou* savate), vieux trumeau.

fesses *f.pl.***:** arrière-boutique *f*, as *m*, baba *m*, bernard *m*, cadran *m* (solaire), dédé *m*, der *m*, derche *m*, derge *m*, dossière *f*, faubourg *m*, fessier *m*, fouettard *m*, griottes *f.pl.*, joufflu *m*, lune *f*, miches *m.pl.*, montre *f*, mouilles *f.pl.*, moutardier *m*, noix *f.pl.*, panier *m* à crottes, père-fouettard *m*, pétard *m*, pétoulet *m*, pétrousquin *m*, pétrus *m*, pont-arrière *m*, popotin *m*, postère *m*, potard *m*, prose *m*, prosinard *m*, proze *m*, prozinard *m*, radada *m*, sonore *m*, tal *m*, tapanard *m*, trafanard *m*, train *m*, valseur *m*, vase *m*, verre *m* de montre.

fête *f*: *voir* **réjouissances.**

figure *f*: *voir* **visage.**

(jeune) fille *f*: benette *f*, caille *f*, frou-frou *f*, gamine *f*, gisquette *f*, gosse *f*, gosseline *f*, loulou *f*, minette *f*, mômaque *f*, môme *f*, nistonne *f*, pisseuse *f*, quille *f*, tendron *m*.

flatter: baratiner, bonimenter, bourrer la caisse (*ou* le crâne *ou* le mou) à, casser le nez à coups d'encensoir à, cirer, enduire, faire de la lèche à, faire du boniment (*ou* du flan *ou* du plat) à, lécher les bottes (*ou* le cul) à, passer la main dans le dos à, passer (de) la pommade (dans les cheveux) à, peloter, pommader.

fort (être): en avoir, être d'attaque (*ou* balèze *ou* bien balancé *ou* bien baraqué *ou* costaud *ou* fortiche *ou* mailloche *ou* malabar *ou* maousse), être un peu là, se poser là.

fou (*adj.*)**:** azimuté, branque, braque, chabraque, cinglé, cinoque, cintré, déboussolé, déplafonné, dérangé, détraqué, dévissé, dingo, dingue, fada, fêlé, focard, follingue, fondu, frappé, givré, locdu, louf, louffe, loufoque, louftingue, maboul(e), marteau, percuté, piqué, sinoc, sinoque, siphonné, sonné, tapé, timbré, tocbombe, toctoc, toqué, tordu, touché.

devenir fou: déménager, dérailler, partir du ciboulot, perdre la boule (*ou* la boussole *ou* la carte *ou* le nord), piquer le coup de bambou.

être fou: avoir une araignée au plafond (*ou* une chauve-souris dans le beffroi), avoir reçu un coup be bambou, avoir une fissure (*ou* un grain), battre la breloque, bouillir de la cafetière, se décarcasser le boisseau, être cucu (la praline), onduler de la toiture, travailler du chapeau (*ou* du cigare), yoyoter de la mansarde.

foule *f*: populo *m*, trèfle *m*, trèpe *m*, trèple *m*.

frère *m*: frangibus *m*, frangin *m*, frelot *m*, frérot *m*, moré *m*.

fromage *m*: coulant *m*, frome *m*, frometon *m*, fromgi *m*, fromtogomme *m*, puant *m*, rampant *m*, tapant *m*.

fumer: bombarder, bouffarder, en griller une, piper, sécher, tiger, tirer (sa touche *ou* sa taf *ou* sa taffe).

gagner (de l'argent): affurer, arrondir (*ou* faire) sa pelote, en amasser, en ramasser, faire du pèse, faire son beurre, prendre le paquet, se remplir (les poches), se sucrer (tant et plus).

gain *m*: affure *f*, bénef *m*, beurre *m*, bonus *m*, velours *m*.

gardien *m* **(de prison)**: gâfe *m*, gaffe *m*, maton *m*, matuche *m*.
  gardien-chef *m*: double *m*.
gendarme *m*: bédi *m*, pandore *m*, sansonnet *m*, sauret *m*, schmit *m*.
goinfre *m & adj.*: bâfreur (*m*), bec *m* à tout grain, (béni-)bouftou(t) (*m*), bouffe-la-balle (*m*), bouffe-tout (*m*), crevard (*m*), goulu (*m*), gueulard (*m*), morfal (*m*), morfalou (*m*), piffre (*m*), porc *m*.
gonorrhée *f*: *voir* **blennorragie.**
gorge *f*: avaloir *m*, cornet *m*, couloir *m*, courgnole *f*, dalle *f*, fanal *m*, gargane *f*, gargoulette *f*, goulot *m*, tube *m*.
gras (*adj.*): *voir* **gros.**
gratuit (*adj.*): au béguin, au châsse, gratis (pro Deo), à l'œil, pour la peau, pour que dalle.
grogner: bougonner, être en boule (*ou* à cran *ou* comme un crin *ou* en rogne), groumer, marronner, râler, la ramener, renâcler, renauder, ronchonner, rouscailler, rouspéter, tousser.
gros (*adj.*): bibendum, bouboule, boulot(te), dondon, gravos, mailloche, malabar, maousse (poil-poil), patapouf, pépère, plein de soupe, rondouillard, soua-soua.
guetter: avoir à l'œil, broquer, faire le gaffe (*ou* le pet *ou* la planque), gaffer, mater, zyeuter.
guillotine *f*: abbaye *f* de Monte-à-regret, bascule *f*, bécane *f*, coupante *f*, coupe-cigare *m*, faucheuse *f*, hachoir *m*, machine *f* à raccourcir, Veuve *f*.
  être guillotiné: y aller du caillou, basculer du chou (*ou* du gadin), cracher dans le panier, épouser la Veuve, éternuer dans le son, se faire décoller le cigare, se faire raccourcir, mettre la tête à la fenêtre, tirer sa crampe avec la Veuve.

habile (être): avoir le coup (*ou* le truc), la connaître dans les coins, en connaître un rayon, se démerder, être ferré (*ou* marle), savoir y faire.
habiller: fagoter, fringuer, friper, frusquer, harnacher, linger, loquer, nipper, sabouler, saper.
  mal habillé: mal fagoté, mal ficelé, fringué comme l'as de pique.
habiter: crécher, nicher, percher.
habits *m.pl.*: *voir* **vêtements.**
homme *m*: artiste *m*, asticot *m*, birbe *m*, bougre *m*, client *m*, coco *m*, escogriffe *m*, fias *m*, frangin *m*, frelot *m*, gars *m*, gazier *m*, gniasse *m*, gnière *m*, goncier *m*, gonze *m*, Jules *m*, Julot *m*, lascar *m*, loulou *m*, loustic *m*, matz *m*, mec *m*, mecton *m*, mironton *m*, moineau *m*, numéro *m*, oiseau *m*, paroissien *m*, piaf *m*, pierrot *m*, pistolet *m*, sujet *m*, tartempion *m*, type *m*, zèbre *m*, zigomard *m*, zigoto *m*, zigue *m*.
hôpital *m*: castre *m*, host(e)au *m*, hosto *m*, planque *f* aux attigés.

ignorant (*adj.*): bûche, crétin, croûte, croûton, cruche, en retard d'une rame, pas affranchi, pas à la page, pas au parfum, pas dans le coup.
imaginer, s': avoir la berlue (*ou* des visions), se berlurer, croire que c'est arrivé, entendre des voix, se faire du cinoche, se fourrer le doigt dans l'œil, se monter le bourrichon (*ou* le cou).
indicateur *m* (*police*): balanceur *m*, bordille *m*, bourdille *m*, cafeteur *m*, casserole *f*, chacal *m*, chevreuil *m*, coqueur *m*, donneur *m*, gamelle *f*, indic *m*, mouchard *m*, mouche *f*, mouton *m*.
  Voir aussi **dénonciateur.**
individu *m*: *voir* **homme.**
initier: affranchir, dessaler, éclairer (sur la couleur), mettre à la page (*ou* au parfum *ou* dans le coup).
injurier: agoniser, baptiser, engueuler, enguirlander, incendier, rembarrer.
insouciant (*adj.*): je-m'en-fichiste, je-m'en-foutiste, pas bileux, qui ne s'en fait pas, qui se les chauffe, qui se la coule (douce), qui se laisse vivre.
interdiction *f* **de séjour**: badine *f*, bambou *m*, bâton *m*, trique *f*.
interrogatoire *m*: baratin *m*, blutinage *m*, cuisinage *m*, cuisine *f*, musique *f*, saignement *m* de nez.
ivre (être): s'arrondir, avoir du vent dans les voiles, avoir pris la bit(t)ure (*ou* la cuite), avoir sa cuite (*ou* son plumet), avoir un coup dans l'aile, avoir un verre dans le nez, se bit(t)urer, être asphyxié (*ou* beurré *ou* bit(t)uré *ou* blindé *ou* blindezingue *ou* bourré (à bloc) *ou* brindezingué *ou* chargé *ou* chicoré *ou* cuit *ou* dans le cirage *ou* dans les vapes *ou* éteint *ou* fabriqué *ou* fadé *ou* fait *ou* fara *ou* gazé *ou* givré *ou* mâchuré *ou* mûr *ou* murdingue *ou* noir *ou* noircicot *ou* paf *ou* parti *ou* pion *ou* pionnard *ou* plein (comme

une bourrique) *ou* raide *ou* rétamé *ou* rond *ou* rondibé *ou* saoul (comme un Polonais) *ou* schlass *ou* soûl *ou* teinté), se pionner, se piquer le nez, ramasser une beurrée, en rouler une, en tenir une bit(t)ure (*ou* une cuite).

être légèrement ivre: avoir chaud aux plumes, avoir son aigrette (*ou* sa pointe), être allumé (*ou* attendri *ou* ébréché *ou* éméché *ou* émoustillé *ou* ému *ou* entre deux vins *ou* gris *ou* parti *ou* pompette).

ivresse *f*: beuverie *f*, bit(t)ure *f*, caisse *f*, cuite *f*, cuvée *f*, pionnardise *f*, poivrade *f*, saoulerie *f*, saoulographie *f*, soûlerie *f*.

ivrogne *m*: bibard *m*, licheur *m*, picoleur *m*, pion *m*, pionnard *m*, pochard *m*, poivrier *m*, poivrot *m*, riboteur *m*, sac *m* à vin, saoulard *m*, saouloir *m*, saoulot *m*, soiffard *m*, soiffeur *m*, soûlard *m*, soûlographe *m*, soûloir *m*, soûlot *m*, vide-bouteille(s) *m*.

jambes *f.pl.*: baguettes *f.pl.*, bâtons *m.pl.* (de chaise), bégonias *m.pl.*, béquilles *f.pl.*, brancards *m.pl.*, cannes *f.pl.*, compas *m.pl.*, flubards *m.pl.*, fusains *m.pl.*, fuseaux *m.pl.*, gambettes *f.pl.*, gambilles *f.pl.*, gigots *m.pl.*, gigues *f.pl.*, guibolles *f.pl.*, pattes *f.pl.*, pivots *m.pl.*, quenelles *f.pl.*, quilles *f.pl.*

jambes faibles: crayons mal attachés, genoux *m.pl.* en pâté de foie.

grosses jambes: colonnes *f.pl.*, poteaux *m.pl.*

jambes maigres: allumettes *f.pl.*, crayons *m.pl.*, échalas *m.pl.*, échasses *f.pl.*, fils *m.pl.* de fer, flûtes *f.pl.*, fumerons *m.pl.*, pinceaux *m.pl.*, pincettes *f.pl.*

avoir les jambes torses: avoir les jambes Louis XV (*ou* en manches de veste), faire du cheval sur un tonneau, pisser entre parenthèses.

jeter: balancer, balanstiquer, envoyer dinguer, ficher (*ou* foutre) en l'air, virer.

jeu *m*: attrape-pognon *m*, flambe *m*, flanche *m*.

jouer: flamber, flancher.

jouer aux cartes: taper le carton, taquiner les bauches (*ou* les brèmes).

journal *m*: babillard *m*, canard *m*, cancan *m*, feuille *f* de chou, menteur *m*, torchon *m*.

là (*adv.*): ladé, laga, lago, laguche.

laid (*adj.*): bléchard, blèche, blèque, miteux, mochard, moche, mocheton, pas jojo, roupie, tarde, tartavelle, tarte, tartouille, tartouse, toc, tocard.

Voir aussi **(vieille) femme laide.**

personne laide: caricature *f*, carnaval *m*, gueule *f* en coin de rue (*ou* à coucher dehors *ou* d'empeigne *ou* en fer de cheval *ou* à la manque *ou* de raie), roupie *f*.

laisser: *voir* **abandonner.**

langue *f*: battant *m*, bavarde *f*, bavette *f*, baveuse *f*, chiffe *f*, chiffon *m*, clapette *f*, langouse *f*, lavette *f*, membrineuse *f*, menteuse *f*, mouillette *f*, patin *m*, platine *m*, râpeuse *f*, tapette *f*, torche *f*, torchette *f*.

lent (*adj.*): à la bourre, à la traîne, en retard d'une rame, longin.

lesbienne *f*: éplucheuse *f* de lentilles, gavousse *f*, gouchotte *f*, goudou *f*, gougne *f*, gougnette *f*, gougnot(t)e *f*, gouine *f*, gousse *f*, marchande *f* d'ail, qui aime (*ou* tape) l'ail, vrille *f*.

lettre *f* (*missive*): babillarde *f*, bafouille *f*, biffeton *m*, lazagne *f*, lazane *f*.

lèvre *f*: babine *f*, babouine *f*, badigoince *f*, bagougnasse *f*, baiseuse *f*, baveuse *f*, limace *f*, pompeuse *f*.

lit *m*: bâche *f*, banette *f*, dodo *m*, nid *m*, paddock *m*, page *m*, pageot *m*, panier *m*, pieu *m*, plumard *m*, plume *f*, pucier *m*, sac *m* à puces.

litre *m* (*de vin*): kil *m*, kilbus *m*, kilo *m*, litron *m*, rouillarde *f*, rouille *f*.

Voir aussi **bouteille.**

logement *m*: bahut *m*, barraque *f*, bercail *m*, bocal *m*, cabane *f*, cagna *f*, cambuse *f*, carrée *f*, casba(h) *f*, case *f*, crèche *f*, gourbi *m*, guitoune *f*, niche *f*, piaule *f*, planque *f*, poulailler *m*, strasse *f*, taule *f*, tôle *f*, turne *f*.

loucher: avoir les châsses qui font du billard (*ou* qui se surveillent), avoir les mirettes qui se croisent les bras, avoir un œil qui dit merde (*ou* zut) à l'autre, bigler (en biais), boiter des calots.

lunettes *f.pl.*: berniches *f.pl.*, binocle *m*, carreaux *m.pl.*, faux quinquets, pare-brise *m.pl.*, quat-zyeux *m.pl.*, vitraux *m.pl.*

maigre (*adj.*): désossé, gras comme un cent de clous, maigrichon, maigrot, sec comme une trique (*ou* un coup de trique), sécot.

personne maigre: asperge *f*, échalas *m*, fil *m* de fer, gringalet *m*, planche *f* à pain.

main *f*: agrafe *f*, battoir *m*, croche *f*, cuiller *f*, grappin *m*, grattante *f*, louche *f*, mimine *f*, palette *f*, paluche *f*, papogne *f*, patte *f*, pat(t)oche *f*, pince *f*, pogne *f*, quintuplée *f*, toucheuse *f*.

maître-chanteur *m*: goualeur *m*, musicien *m*, musico *m*, serinette *f*.

malade (*adj.*): affûté, amoché, ayant un pet de travers, mal fichu (*ou* foutu *ou* vissé), pas dans son assiette, patraque, plombé, vaseux.

atteint de maladie vénérienne: assaisonné, attigé, ayant le panaris chinois, fadé, faisandé, lazziloffe, mangé aux vers, nase, nasebroque, naze, nazeloque, nazicoté, plombé, poivré, pourri.

Voir aussi **blennorragie; syphilis.**

très malade: cuit, fichu, flambé, foutu, fricassé, frit, paumé, qui a un pied dans la tombe, qui bat de l'aile, qui file un mauvais coton, qui marche à côté de ses pompes, qui sent le sapin, rétamé.

malchance *f*: bouillabaisse *f*, bouscaille *f*, cerise *f*, confiture *f*, guigne *f*, guignon *m*, marmelade *f*, masque *m*, moutarde *f*, pestouille *f*, pétrin *m*, poisse *f*, pommade *f*, scoumoune *f*, sirop *m*, vape *f*.

avoir de la malchance: être dans de beaux (*ou* mauvais *ou* vilains) draps.

malin (*adj.*): affranchi, à la coule, à la page, dans le train, débrouillard, dégourdi, démerdard, fortiche, mariole, marle, marloupin, roublard, sondeur.

manger: aller à la graille, becqueter, bouffer, boulotter, boustifailler, brichetonner, briffer, buffer, se caler les côtes (*ou* les joues), casser la croûte (*ou* la graine), claper, cléber, croquer, croustiller, croûter, se dérouiller les crochets, s'en donner par les babines, grailler, grainer, jaffer, lipper, mastéguer, mastiquer, morfiler, morganer, muffler, recharger les accus, se remplir le bocal (*ou* le cornet *ou* le garde-manger *ou* la lampe), se taper la cloche (*ou* la tête), tortorer.

manger abondamment: bâfrer, bouffer (à crever), s'empiffrer, se faire péter la sous-ventrière, s'en foutre plein la lampe, s'en jeter (*ou* s'en mettre) derrière la cravate, s'en mettre jusque-là (*ou* plein le fusil), se goinfrer, se graisser la gueule, morphaler, prendre une bonne ventrée, se tasser une plâtrée.

manières prétentieuses: chichis *m.pl.*, épates *f.pl.*, esbrouf(f)es *f.pl.*, magnes *f.pl.*, pal(l)as *m*, singeries *f.pl.*

maquiller, se: se badigeonner, se faire une façade (*ou* un raccord *ou* un ravalement), se plâtrer, se sucrer la fraise (*ou* la gaufre).

marchandise *f*: came *f*, camelote *f*, lamedu *m*.

marcher: affûter des pinceaux, aller à pattes, les allonger, arpenter, arquer, bagoter, battre le bitume, charrier sa viande, giguer, prendre le train onze (*ou* la voiture de Saint-Crépin), ripatonner, tricoter (des guibolles), trimarder.

mariage *m*: conjungo *m*, entiflage *m* de sec, maquage *m*, marida(t) *m*.

marin *m*: cachalot *m*, col bleu, loup *m* de mer, marsouin *m*, mataf *m*, matave *m*, mathurin *m*, pompon *m* rouge.

masturber, se: se l'agiter, se l'allonger, s'astiquer (la colonne *ou* le manche), s'astiquer le boilton (*femme*), s'en battre une, se branler (la colonne). épouser (*ou* fréquenter) la veuve poignet, étrangler Popaul (*ou* Popol), faire cinq contre un, faire glouglouter le poireau, se faire malice tout seul, se faire mousser, se fréquenter, se griffer, jouer de la mandoline (*femme*), se palucher, se pogner, se secouer le bonhomme, se taper (sur) la colonne, se taper un rassis, se tirer son (*ou* un) coup, tomber sur le (*ou* un) manche.

mauvais (*adj.*): à la noix, bidon, blèche, creux, locdu, loquedu, moche, raté, tarte, tartouse, toc, tocard.

méchant *m*: carne *f*, chameau *m*, charogne *f*, gale *f*, peste *f*, pou *m*, salaud *m*, salope *f*, salopard *m*, teigne *f*, vache *f*.

médire: bêcher, casser du sucre sur le dos (*ou* sur la tête) de, débiner, dégraisser, habiller.

mégot *m*: clope *m*, meg *m*, orphelin *m*, sequin *m*.

mendiant *m*: clodo(t) *m*, frappeur *m*, manchard *m*, mangav(eur) *m*, mendiche *m*, mendigot *m*, pied *m* de biche, pilon *m*, pilonneur *m*, quelqu'un de la cloche, tapeur *m*, torpille *f*, torpilleur *m*, tubard *m* (*mendiant du métro*).

mendicité *f*: frappe *f*, manche *f*, mangave *f*, mendiche *f*, mendigoterie *f*, pilon *m*, pilonnage *m*, tape *f*, torpille *f*.
mendier: aller à la mangave, faire la manche (*ou* le tube), frapper, mangaver, marcher à la torpille, mendigoter, pilonner, taper, torpiller.
menottes *f.pl.*: bracelets *m.pl.*, brides *f.pl.*, cabriolets *m.pl.*, cadènes *f.pl.*, cadenettes *f.pl.*, chapelet *m*, ficelles *f.pl.*, fichets *m.pl.*, manchettes *f.pl.*, pinces *f.pl.*, poucettes *f.pl.*
mensonge *m*: balançoire *f*, bateau *m*, bidon *m*, blague *f*, bobard *m*, boniment *m*, bourde *f*, bourrage *m* (de crâne), du bourre-mou, contes *m.pl.* à dormir debout, couleuvre *f*, craque *f*, doublage *m*, frime *f*, pilule *f*, van(n)e *m*.
menstrues *f.pl.*: anglais *m.pl.*, argagnasses *f.pl.*, cardinales *f.pl.*, carlets *m.pl.*, doches *f.pl.*, histoires *f.pl.*, ours *m.pl.*, rue barrée, sauce *f* tomate, trucs *m.pl.*
avoir ses menstrues: avoir ses affaires, être confiture, faire relâche, jouer à cache-tampon, marquer, pavoiser, repeindre sa grille (en rouge).
mentir: bourrer la caisse (*ou* le crâne *ou* le mou), en conter, envoyer du vent, mener en barque (*ou* en bateau), monter le cou.
mère *f*: dabe *f*, dabesse *f*, dabuche *f*, daronne *f*, doche *f*, mam(an) *f*, mater *f*, matouse *f*, vieille *f*.
mitraillette *f*: arroseuse *f*, arrosoir *m*, distributeur *m*, lampe *f* à souder, machine *f* à coudre (*ou* à percer *ou* à secouer) le paletot, mandoline *f*, moulin *m* à café, moulinette *f*, sulfateuse *f*, tititine *f*, vaporisateur *m*.
mollet *m*: jacquot *m*, molleton *m*, moltegomme *m*.
monnaie *f*: carmouille *f*, ferraille *f*, mitraille *f*, monouye *f*, mornifle *m*, vaisselle *f* de fouille.
montre *f*: bob *m*, broquante *f*, dégoulinante *f*, montrouze *f*, tocante *f*, toquante *f*, trotteuse *f*.
moquer de, se: acheter, bêcher, blaguer, chambrer, charrier, chiner, jardiner, se ficher de, se foutre de, mettre en boîte, se payer la gueule (*ou* la tête) de.
mouchoir *m*: blave *m*, tire-jus *m*, tire-moelle *m*.
mourir: avaler son acte de naissance (*ou* sa chique), boucler sa malle, bouffer (*ou* manger) les pissenlits (par la racine), cadancher, calancher, caner, cascader, casser sa pipe, clamser, clapoter, clapser, claquer, cramser, crever, cronir, la déchirer, déposer le bilan, dépoter son géranium, déramer, (la) dessouder, dévisser son billard, éteindre sa lampe, faire couic, graisser ses bottes, lâcher la rampe, se laisser glisser, oublier de respirer, partir les pieds devant (*ou* en avant), passer l'arme à gauche, perdre le goût du pain, plier bagage, quimper, remercier son boulanger, sauter le pas, souffler la veilleuse, tourner le coin.
moustaches *f.pl.*: bacchantes *f.pl.*, baffes *m.pl.*, balai *m* (à chiottes), charmeuses *f.pl.*, ramasse-miettes *m*.

nègre *m*: bamboula *m*, bougnoul(l)e *m*, canaque *m*, gobi *m*, moricaud *m*, négrillot *m*, négro *m*, noyama *m*.
nez *m*: baigneur *m*, blair *m*, blaireau *m*, blaze *m*, boîte *f* à morve, cep *m*, naze *m*, pif *m*, piffard *m*, piton *m*, pivase *m*, priseur *m*, reniflant *m*, step *m*, tarin *m*, trompette *f*.
nez épaté: patate *f*, pied *m* de marmite, truffe *f*.
grand nez: éteignoir *m*, fer *m* à souder, quart *m* de brie, step *m* à trier, tasseau *m*, tassot *m*.
nez rouge: aubergine *f*, betterave *f*, pif communard, piment *m*, tomate *f*.
nom *m*: blaze *m*, centre *m*, chouette *m*.
non (*excl.*): bernique, des bigorneaux, des clopes, des clopinettes, des clous, des daches, macache (et midi sonné), mon œil, mon zob, nib, nibe, de la peau, peau de balle (et balai de crin), que dalle.
nourriture *f*: avoine *f*, becquetance *f*, bectance *f*, bouffe *f*, bouftance *f*, boustifaille *f*, briffe *f*, croustance *f*, croustille *f*, croûte *f*, frichti *m*, fricot *m*, frip(p)e *f*, graille *f*, graine *f*, grinque *f*, jaffe *f*, mangeaille *f*, mastègue *f*, tambouille *f*, tortore *f*.
mauvaise nourriture: graillon *m*, ragougnasse *f*, rata *m*, ratatouille *f*.
nu (*adj.*): à loilpé, à loilpuche, comme un savon, (le) cul à l'air, en Jésus.
nuit *f*: borgne *f*, borgniot *m*, borgnon *m*, brune *f*, neuille *f*, sorgue *f*.

œil *m*: bille *f*, calot *m*, carreau *m*, châsse *m*, clignotant *m*, coquillard *m*, lampion *m*, lanterne *f*, lentille *f*, loupe *f*, lucarne *f*, mire *f*, mirette *f*, mironton *m*, œillet *m*, quinquet *m*, yakas *m*.

coup d'œil: coup *m* de sabord.

œil poché: coquard *m*, coquelicot *m*, œil au beurre noir, œil pavoisé, poche-œil *m*.

œillade (faire une): lancer un appel (*ou* un coup de châsse *ou* un coup de sabord *ou* son prospectus), jouer des châsses, reluquer, renoucher.

or *m*: jonc *m*, joncaille *f*.

lingot *m* **d'or:** lingue *m*, quart *m* de beurre.

oreille *f*: ance *f*, anse *f*, cliquette *f*, écoute *f*, écoutille *f*, esgourde *f*, esgourdille *f*, étagère *f* à mégot, étiquette *f*, feuille *f* (de chou), pavillon *m*, portugaise *f*, soucoupe *f*, voile *f*, zozore *f*.

grande oreille: escalope *f*, grande feuille, plat *m* à barbe.

orgasme (avoir un): y aller du voyage, balancer le jus (*ou* la purée), se balancer, briller, cracher son venin, décharger, dégorger, envoyer la came, s'envoyer en l'air, faire pleurer le cyclope, jouir, juter, lâcher sa came (*ou* une giclée *ou* le jus), mouiller le goupillon, prendre son fade (*ou* son panard), rayonner, se régaler, reluire, vider ses burettes.

Voir aussi **coïter.**

orgueilleux *m*: bêcheur *m*, cracheur *m*, faiseur *m* de magnes, frérot *m*, gommeux *m*, plastronneur *m*, poseur *m*.

oui (*excl.*): banco, ça botte, ça colle, c'est bon, dac, d'acc, gy, gygo, jave, lygodu, O.K., positif.

ouvrier *m*: bosseur *m*, boulonneur *m*, boulot *m*, bûcheur *m*, piocheur *m*, prolo *m*, pue-la-sueur *m*, turbineur *m*.

ouvrir: débâcler, déboucher, débrider, mettre en dedans.

pain *m*: bricheton *m*, briffeton *m*, brignole *f*, brignolet *m*, brignoluche *m*, larton *m*.

pain bis: brutal *m*.

pain blanc: larton savonné.

pantalon *m*: bénard *m*, cotte *f*, culbutant *m*, falzar(d) *m*, fendard *m*, flosse *m*, froc *m*, futal *m*, grimpant *m*, montant *m*, valseur *m*.

pantalon étroit: fourreau *m*, fuseau *m*, tuyau *m* de poêle.

papier *m*: faf(f)e *m*, faf(f)elard *m*, faf(f)iot *m*, papelard *m*, pelure *f*.

paquet *m*: lacson *m*, pacsif *m*, pacson *m*.

parapluie *m*: pare-flotte *m*, pare-lance *m*, pébroc *m*, pébroque *m*, pépin *m*, riflard *m*.

pardessus *m*: lardeusse *m*, lardingue *m*, lardosse *m*, pardaf *m*, pardingue *m*, pardosse *m*, pelure *f*.

parents *m.pl.*: dabs *m.pl.*, darons *m.pl.*, vieux *m.pl.*, viocards *m.pl.*, vioques *m.pl.*

paresse *f*: cosse *f*, flemme *f*, poils *m.pl.* dans la main, rame *f*.

paresser: avoir la rame, les avoir palmés (*ou* à la retourne *ou* retournés), s'endormir sur le mastic, enfiler des perles, feignasser, ne pas en ficher (*ou* foutre) un coup (*ou* une rame), flânocher, flémarder, flemmarder, ne pas se fouler (la rate), ne rien se casser, tirer sa cosse (*ou* sa flemme), tirer au cul (*ou* au flanc), se tourner les pouces, traîner les patins (*ou* la savate).

paresseux *m*: cagnard *m*, cossard *m*, feignant *m*, feignasse *m*, flânocheur *m*, flemmard *m*, ramier *m*, tire(ur)-au-cul *m*, tire(ur)-au-flanc *m*, vachard *m*.

parler: bagouler, baratiner, bonnir, déblatérer, dégoiser, dévider, jacasser, jacter, jaspiner, l'ouvrir, tailler une bavette, tenir le crachoir.

Voir aussi **bavarder.**

partir: se barrer, (se) calter, se carapater, se cavaler, débarrasser les lieux (*ou* le plancher), se débiner, déblayer le terrain, décambuter, décamper, décaniller, décarrer, déguerpir, se déhotter, démarrer, détaler, se donner de l'air, s'éclipser, s'évaporer, ficher (*ou* foutre) le (*ou* son) camp, foncer dans le brouillard, jouer (à) rip, en jouer un air, les jouer, lever l'ancre, lever le pied, mettre les adjas (*ou* les baguettes *ou* les bouts *ou* les cannes *ou* les voiles), les mettre, plaquouser, plier bagage, prendre la clef des champs (*ou* le large *ou* la poudre d'escampette *ou* la tangente), prendre ses cliques et ses claques, riper, se tailler, se tirer, se tracer, se trisser, se trissoter, se trotter.

partir sans payer: faire jambe de bois, faire une queue, laisser une feuille de chou, planter un drapeau, poser une ardoise.

patron *m*: boss *m*, chef *m*, dab(e) *m*, daron *m*, direlot *m*, dirlingue *m*, dirlot *m*, le grand manitou, latron *m*, singe *m*, taulier *m*, tôlier *m*.

patron de café: bistranche *m*, bistre *m*, bistrotier *m*, mastroquet *m*, troquet *m*.

patronne *f* **(de maison de tolérance):** bordelière *f*, daronne *f*, maquerelle *f*, maquesée *f*, marquise *f*, mère-maca *f*, mère-maquerelle *f*, rombière *f*, taulière *f*, tôlière *f*.

pauvre (*adj*.)**:** à la côte, cisaillé, crève-la-faim, dans la dèche (*ou* la mélasse *ou* la purée *ou* le ruisseau), décavé, déchard, fauché (comme l'as de pique *ou* comme les blés), fauchemane, grand schlem, lavé, lessivé, miséreux, miteux, mouisard, nettoyé, pané, panné, paumé, purotin, qui traîne les patins (*ou* la savate), raide, raqué, rincé, rôti, sec, sur la paille (*ou* le pavé), tondu, vacant, vidé, de la zone.

pauvreté *f***:** bouillabaisse *f*, débine *f*, dèche *f*, mélasse *f*, mistoufle *f*, mouise *f*, mouscaille *f*, panade *f*, purée *f*.

payer: les abouler, les aligner, aller au refil (*ou* au rembour), les allonger, allumer, arroser, banquer, carburer, carmer, casquer, cigler, cracher (dans le bassin), décher, douiller, éclairer, envoyer la valse, s'exécuter, se fendre, les lâcher, mouiller, raquer, régaler, les sortir, valser.

paysan *m***:** boueux *m*, bouseux *m*, cambroussard *m*, croquant *m*, culterreux *m*, glaiseux *m*, pécore *m*, péd(e)zouille *m*, peigne-cul *m*, péquenaud *m*, péquenot *m*, pétrousquin *m*, petzouillard *m*, petzouille *m*, plouc *m*.

pédéraste *m***:** chochotte *f*, chouquette *f*, coquine *f*, emmanché *m*, empaffé *m*, empapaouté *m*, emprosé *m*, encaldossé *m*, enculé *m*, enfifré *m*, enfoiré *m*, enviandé *m*, fagot *m*, fiotte *f*, gazier *m*, girond *m*, joconde *f*, lopaille *f*, lopart *m*, lope *f*, lopette *f*, Madame Arthur, papaout *m*, P.D. *m*, pédale *f*, pédalo *m*, pédé *m*, pédéro *m*, pédoque *m*, qui en est, qui est de la bague (*ou* du rond *ou* du zéro), qui est de la famille tuyau de poêle, qui est de la joyeuse, rivette *f*, sœur *f*, tante *f*, tantouse *f*, tapette *f*, tata *f*, travesti *m*.

pendre: agrafer, anguer, béquiller, grupper.

pendu *m***:** duc *m*, qui bénit avec ses pieds, qui garde des moutons à la lune.

pénis *m***:** andouille *f* à col roulé, anguille *f* de calecif, arbalète *f*, asperge *f*, baigneur *m*, baïonnette *f*, baisette *f*, balayette *f*, baveuse *f*, berdouillette *f*, berloque *f*, biroute *f*, bit(t)e *f*, (gros) bout *m*, bra(c)quemard *m*, canne *f*, carabine *f*, Charles-le-Chauve, chibre *m*, chinois *m*, cigare *m* à moustache, clarinette *f*, colonne *f*, cyclope *m*, dard *m*, dardillon *m*, défonceuse *f*, fifre *m* à grelots, flageolet *m*, frétillante *f*, frétillard *m*, gaule *f*, gland *m*, goupillon *m*, gourde *f* à poils, gourdin *m*, guignol *m*, guise *m*, instrument *m*, jambe *f* du milieu, macaroni *m*, mandrin *m*, marsouin *m*, mohican *m*, nœud *m*, os *m* à moelle, outil *m*, paf *m*, panais *m*, le père frappart, petit frère, pine *f*, pointe *f*, poireau *m*, polard *m*, Popaul *m*, Popol *m*, quéquette *f*, queue *f*, quique *f*, quiquette *f*, sabre *m*, Totor, tracassin *m*, tringle *f*, trique *f*, verge *f*, zeb *m*, zigouigoui *m*, zizi *m*, zob(i) *m*.

perdre (au jeu): être enfoncé (*ou* entubé *ou* lessivé *ou* plumé), se faire enfiler, manger la ferme, paumer.

père *m***:** dab*m*, daron *m*, papa *m*, papy *m*, pater *m*, paternel *m*, pépère *m*, vieux *m*.

pet *m***:** boule *f*, cloque *m*, loffe *f*, louffe *f*, pastille *f*, pastoche *f*, perle *f*, perlouse *f*, perlouze *f*, vesse *f*.

péter: annoncer son matricule, cloquer, déchirer son froc (*ou* la toile), en écraser un, fuser, en lâcher un, lâcher les gaz (*ou* une perle *ou* une perlouse), louffer, vesser.

petit individu: astèque *m*, avorton *m*, basduc *m*, bas-du-cul *m*, bout-de-cul *m*, courte-botte *m*, crapaud *m*, crapoussin *m*, demi-portion *f*, échappé *m* de bidet, fabriqué *m* au compte-gouttes, fond-de-bain *m*, inachevé *m*, merdaillon *m*, microbe *m*, mignard *m*, nabot *m*, pot *m* à tabac, puce *f*, qui est haut comme trois pommes, ras-de-bitume *m*, ras-de-mottes *m*, rasduc *m*, ras-du-cul *m*, rikiki *m*, riquiqui *m*, tom-pouce *m*.

peu (un): un (petit) bout, un chouia, pas bésef(f), pas bézef(f), pas gras, pas lerche, pas lourdingue, une larme, une miette.

peur *f***:** chiasse *f*, chocottes *f.pl.*, colombins *m.pl.*, flubes *m.pl.*, frousse *f*, fuchsias *m.pl.*, grelots *m.pl.*, pétasse *f*, pétoche *f*, pétouille *f*, taf *m*, taffe *m*, trac *m*, tracsir *m*, traquette *f*, traquouse *f*, trouille *f*.

avoir peur: avoir chaud aux fesses, avoir les baguettes (*ou* les blancs *ou* la colique *ou* les copeaux *ou* les foies *ou* les jetons), avoir les miches qui font bravo, avoir le trouillomètre à zéro, les avoir à zéro, caler, caner, chier dans son froc, se déballonner, se dégonfler, fluber, foirer, les mouiller, serrer les fesses (*ou* les miches), trouilloter.

pieds *m.pl.*: argasses *m.pl.*, arpions *m.pl.*, artous *m.pl.*, nougats *m.pl.*, panards *m.pl.*, patins *m.pl.*, pattes *f.pl.*, paturons *m.pl.*, péniches *f.pl.*, petons *m.pl.*, pinceaux *m.pl.*, pingets *m.pl.*, pingouins *m.pl.*, raquettes *f.pl.*, ribouis *m.pl.*, ripatons *m.pl.*, trottinants *m.pl.*, trottinets *m.pl.*

pince-monseigneur *f*: clarinette *f*, dauphin *m*, dingue *f*, dombeur *m*, dur *m*, jacques *m*, jacquot *m*, plume *f*, sucre *m* de pomme.

pipe *f*: bouffarde *f*, brûle-gueule *m*, chiffarde *f*, gnaupe *f*, quenaude *f*.

pleurer: baver des clignotants, chialer, gicler des mirettes (*ou* des œillets), miter, ouvrir les écluses, pisser des châsses, viauper.

pluie *f*: bouillon *m*, flotte *f*, lancequine *f*, rincée *f*, saucée *f*.

poche *f*: bacreuse *f*, ballade *f*, farfouillette *f*, fouille *f*, fouillette *f*, fouillouse *f*, glande *f*, pocket *m*, profonde *f*, vague *f*, valde *f*.

poing *m*: *voir* **main.**

poitrine *f*: armoire *f*, caisse *f*, caisson *m*, coffre *m*, plastron *m*.

police *f*: arnaque *f*, bigorne *f*, bourrique *f*, condaille *f*, flicaille *f*, maison arrangemane (*ou* bourremane *ou* cognedur *ou* parapluie *ou* pébroc *ou* poulaga *ou* poulardin *ou* poulemane), ces Messieurs, poulaille *f*, poule *f*, raclette *f*, renâcle *f*, renifle *f*, rousse *f*, volaille *f*.

policier *m*: argousin *m*, bourre *m*, chaussette *f*, cogne *m*, condé *m*, drauper *m*, flic *m*, flicaillon *m*, flicard *m*, guignol *m*, ham *m*, hambourgeois *m*, lardu *m*, matou *m*, perdreau *m*, pied-plat *m*, plancton *m*, poulaga *m*, poulard *m*, pouleminche *m*, poulet *m*, raper *m*, roussi *m*, roussin *m*.

poltron *m*: baisse-froc *m*, caneur *m*, capon *m*, chiasseur *m*, déballonné *m*, dégonflard *m*, dégonflé *m*, dégonfleur *m*, flubard *m*, foireux *m*, froussard *m*, grelotteur *m*, péteux *m*, pétochard *m*, poule mouillée, taffeur *m*, traqueur *m*, trouillard *m*, vessard *m*.

portefeuille *m*: lasagne *m*, lazingue *m*.

portefeuille plein: matelas *m*, mateluche *m*.

porte-monnaie *m*: artichaut *m*, artiche *m*, crapaud *m*, lasagne *m*, lazingue *m*, morlingue *m*, morniflard *m*, portebiffeton *m*, porte-faf(f)iots *m*, portemorfic *m*, morpion *m*, piocre *m*, toto *m*.

pou *m*: crabe *m*, galopard *m*, gau *m*, grain *m* de blé, guêpe *f*, mie *f* de pain (mécanique *ou* à ressort), morbac *m*, morfic *m*, morpion *m*, piocre *m*, toto *m*.

pourboire *m*: bouquet *m*, gants *m.pl.*, pièce *f*, pourliche *m*, poursoif *m*.

prétentieux (être): bêcher, crâner, se croire sorti de la cuisse de Jupiter, s'en croire, épater, esbrouf(f)er, faire des chichis (*ou* de l'épate *ou* de l'esbrouf(f)e *ou* des magnes), faire du vent (*ou* du zeph), se gober, se gonfler, en installer, se monter le job, plastronner, pontifier.

prêtre *m*: calotin *m*, coin-coin *m*, corbeau *m*, cureton *m*, radis noir, rase *m*, ratiche *m*, ratichon *m*, sac *m* à carbi, sanglier *m*.

prison *f*: ballon *m*, bigne *f*, bing *m*, bloc *m*, boîte *f*, cabane *f*, carluche *f*, centrouse *f*, chétard *m*, clou *m*, coffre *m*, coquille *f*, gn(i)ouf *m*, grande marmite, grosse *f*, jettard *m*, lazaro *m*, malle *f*, mitard *m*, ombre *f*, ours *m*, petit château, placard *m*, ratière *f*, schib *m*, schtard *m*, schtib *m*, schtilibem *m*, séchoir *m*, taule *f*, tôle *f*, trou *m*, violon *m*.

prostituée *f*: béguineuse *f*, bisenesseuse *f*, boudin *m*, bourrin *m*, catin *f*, chamelle *f*, chèvre *f*, essoreuse *f*, fille *f*, frangine *f*, frangipane *f*, gagneuse *f*, garce *f*, gerce *f*, girelle *f*, gisquette *f*, gonzesse *f*, goton *f*, greluche *f*, grue *f*, langouste *f*, marcheuse *f*, mistonne *f*, morue *f*, moukère *f*, mousmé(e) *f*, nana *f*, pépée *f*, péripatéticienne *f*, persilleuse *f*, ponette *f*, pouffiasse *f*, poule *f*, putain *f*, pute *f*, raccrocheuse *f*, racoleuse *f*, radeuse *f*, respectueuse *f*, rouchie *f*, roulure *f*, souris *f*, tapin *f*, tapineuse *f*, traînée *f*, truqueuse *f*, turfeuse *f*, volaille *f*, zigouince *f*.

prostituer, se: *voir* **racoler.**

provoquer: chercher la cogne (*ou* des crosses *ou* des patins *ou* du rif *ou* des rognes *ou* du suif) à, crosser.

querelle *f*: accrochage *m*, asticotage *m*, attrapade *f*, attrapage *m*, badaboum *m*, barabille *f*, baroud *m*, barouf *m*, barouffe *m*, baroufle *m*, bigorne *f*, bisbille *f*, châtaigne *f*, corrida *f*, crosse *f*, engueulade *f*, pétard *m*, prise *f* de bec (*ou* de gueule), rif *m*, rififi *m*, rogne *f*, salade *f*, savon *m*, suif *m*, tabac *m*, tapage *m*, torchée *f*.
querelleur (*adj.*): asticoteur, crosseur, crosson, mauvais coucheur, pétardier, péteur, râleur, renaudeur, saladier, suiffeur.

racoler (*prostituée*): aller aux asperges, chasser le mâle, se défendre, draguer, emballer, s'expliquer, faire le business (*ou* le bitume *ou* les boules *ou* la grue *ou* un levage *ou* le macadam *ou* le pavé *ou* le quart *ou* le raccroc *ou* le rade *ou* la retape *ou* le ruban *ou* le tapin *ou* le tas *ou* le trottoir *ou* le truc *ou* le turbin *ou* le turf), faire son persil, lever un client, michetonner, en moudre, persiller, raccrocher, en retourner, tapiner, truquer, turbiner, turfer.
rafle *f*: coup *m* de filet (*ou* de serviette *ou* de torchon), cueille *f*, descente *f*, dragage *m*, drague *f*, piquage *m*, (coup *m* de) raclette *f*.
raser, se: se gratter, se gratter (*ou* se peler) la couenne, se racler.
rasoir *m*: coupe-chou *m*, grattoir *m*, racloir *m*, rasibe *m*, rasife *m*, razif *m*.
receleur *m*: fourgat *m*, fourgue *m*, fourgueur *m*, franquiste *m*, laveur *m*, lessiveur *m*.
recevoir (*des coups ou des insultes*): déguster, dérouiller, écoper, effacer, encaisser, étrenner, palper, en prendre pour son grade.
recommencer: rebiffer, remaquiller, remettre ça, remmancher, (y) remordre, repiquer (au truc).
reconnaître: reconnobler, reconnobrer, redresser, retapisser.
regarder: allumer, bigler, borgnoter, châsser, frimer, gaffer, lorgner, loucher sur, mater, matouser, mirer, mordre, rechâsser, reluquer, remoucher, tapisser, viser, zyeuter.
réjouissances *f.pl.*: bamboche *f*, bamboula *f*, bombe *f*, bordée *f*, bosse *f*, boum *f*, bringue *f*, faridon *f*, fiesta *f*, foire *f*, foiridon *f*, java *f*, noce *f*, nouba *f*, renversée *f*, ribote *f*, ribouldingue *f*, riboule *f*, surboum *f*, vadrouille *f*, virée *f*.
rendez-vous *m*: rambour *m*, rancart *m*, rembo *m*, rencart *m*, rendève *m*.
renseignement *m*: duce *m*, rancard *m*, rencard *m*, rencart *m*, tubard *m*, tube *m*, tuyau *m*.
renseigner: affranchir, éclairer la lanterne à, embrayer sur, mettre à la page (*ou* dans le coup), parfumer, rancarder, rembiner.
réprimander: agonir, agrafer, assaisonner, attraper, casser, donner le bal à, doucher, engueuler, enguirlander, filer (*ou* flanquer *ou* passer) un savon à, habiller, incendier, laver la tête à, lessiver, mettre sur le tapis, moucher, passer une bonne engueulade (*ou* quelque chose) à, ramasser, ramoner, sabouler, secouer (les puces à), sonner les cloches à.
être réprimandé: écoper, en prendre pour son grade, recevoir une saucée (*ou* une savonnée).
revolver *m*: azor *m*, bagaf *m*, basset *m*, boukala *m*, boum-boum *m*, brelica *m*, brûle-parfum(s) *m*, calibre *m*, feu *m*, flingot *m*, flingue *m*, pétard *m*, pétoire *m*, pistolache *m*, remède *m*, ribarbère *m*, riboustin *m*, rifle *f*, riflette *f*, rigolo *m*, rigoustin *m*, soufflant *m*, tic-tac *m*.
riche (*adj.*): bourré (à bloc), calé, cousu d'or, flambant, au fric, galetteux, gonflé, gros, oseillé, péseux, plein aux as, qui a du foin dans ses bottes, qui a le sac, qui roule dans le fric (*ou* sur l'or), rempli, rupin, rupinos, tombé sur un champ d'oseille.
rien (*adv.*): balpeau, des clopinettes, des clous, des prunes, macache, de la merde, négatif, nib, niente, nix, la peau, peau de balle (*ou* de zébi(e)), que dalle, que pouic, que t'chi, du vent, zéro.
rire: se bidonner, se boler, se boyauter, se crever, se fendre le bol (*ou* la bouille *ou* la gueule *ou* la pipe), se gondoler, se marrer, s'en payer une tranche, se poiler, se pouffer, se rouler, se tenir les côtes, se tirebouchonner, se tordre (comme une baleine).
route *f*: antif(fe) *f*, bitume *m*, ruban *m*, tire *f*, trimard *m*, trime *f*.
ruiné (*adj.*): *voir* **pauvre.**
rupture *f*: lâchage *m*, largage *m*, malle *f*, mallouse *f*, plaquage *m*, valise *f*, valoche *f*.

sale (*adj.*): cochon, cracra, cradingue, crado, crapoteux, crasp, craspec, craspèque, craspet, craspignol, craspouette, craspouillard, débectant, dégueulasse, dégueulbif, merdeux, miteux, pouilleux, saligaud, salingue.

saleté *f*: crotaille *f*, crotte *f*, merdoie *f*, merdouille *f*, saloperie *f*.

séduire: chauffer, emballer, embobiner, faire des boniments (*ou* du pal(l)as(s) *ou* du plat *ou* du rentre-dedans) à, frotter, gringuer, musiquer, pal(l)asser, quimper, rambiner, tomber.

seins *m.pl.*: amortisseurs *m.pl.*, avantages *m.pl.*, avant-postes *m.pl.*, avant-scène *f*, balcon(s) *m* (*pl.*), ballons *m.pl.*, boîtes *f.pl.* à lait (*ou* à lolo), devanture *f*, doudounes *f.pl.*, flotteurs *m.pl.*, globes *m.pl.*, hémisphères *m.pl.*, loloches *m.pl.*, lolos *m.pl.*, mappemondes *f.pl.*, du monde au balcon, montgolfières *f.pl.*, nénés *m.pl.*, nichons *m.pl.*, pelotes *f.pl.*, roberts *m.pl.*, rondins *m.pl.*, ropoplots *m.pl.*, rotoplots *m.pl.*, rototos *m.pl.*, tétasses *f.pl.*, tétés *m.pl.*, tétons *m.pl.*

sentir: blairer, renifler.

sentir mauvais: boucaner, cocot(t)er, cogner, comancher, corner, foisonner, fouetter, plomber, polker, puer, refouler, renifler, rougnotter, (s)chlinguer, taper, troufigner, trouilloter.

sentir mauvais de la bouche: plomber du goulot, puer du bec, refouler, repousser (du goulot), taper du saladier, tuer les mouches à quinze pas.

sœur *f*: fraline *f*, frangine *f*, frangipane *f*, frelotte *f*, sister *f*, sistère *f*.

soif (avoir): avoir la dalle en pente, avoir le gosier sec, avoir la pépie, cracher blanc, la sécher.

soldat *m*: bidasse *m*, biffin *m*, chti *m*, déguisé *m*, deuxième pompe *f*, gribier *m*, grif(e)ton *m*, griveton *m*, grivier *m*, pioupiou *m*, tourlourou *m*, troubade *m*, trouf(f)ion *m*.

sou *m*: bourgue *m*, croque *m*, fléchard *m*, jacques *m*, kope(c)k *m*, pelot *m*, radis *m*, rond *m*, rotin *m*.

sourd (*adj.*): constipé (*ou* dur) de la feuille, ensablé des portugaises, sourdingue (comme un pot).

sous-maîtresse *f* **(d'un bordel)**: retirée *f* des banquettes, sous-baloche *f*, sous-maque *f*, sous-maquerelle *f*, sous-maquesée *f*.

souteneur *m*: Alphonse *m*, barbe *f*, barbeau *m*, broche *f*, brochet *m*, croc *m*, dauphin *m*, dos *m* (vert), estaf(f)ier *m*, hareng *m*, Jules *m*, Julot *m*, mac *m*, mangeur *m* de blanc (*ou* de brioche), maquereau *m*, marchand *m* de barbaque (*ou* de bidoche *ou* de viande), marle *m*, marlou *m*, marloupin *m*, mec *m*, mecton *m*, merlan *m*, poiscaille *m*, poiscal *m*, poisse *f*, poisson *m*, rabat *m*, rabatteur *m*, sauré *m*, sauret *m*.

sperme *m*: blanc *m*, came *f*, foutre *m*, jus *m* (de corps *ou* de cyclope), purée *f*, venin *m*.

stupéfait (*adj.*): asphyxié, assis, baba, bleu, comme deux ronds de flan (*ou* de frites *ou* de tarte), époustouflé, estomaqué, occis, sidéré, soufflé, suffoqué.

suicider, se: se but(t)er, se déramer, s'envoyer (*ou* se filer) en l'air, se faire sauter la caisse (*ou* le caisson), s'occire (la cervelle).

syphilis *f*: chtouille *f*, daube *f*, lazziloffe *f*, naze *m*, nazebroque *m*, schtouille *f*, sigma *m*, syphilo *f*, syphlotte *f*.

tabac *m*: fume *f*, gris *m*, herbe *f*, percale *m*, perle *m*, perlot *m*, pétun *m*, tref *m*, trêfle *m*.

taire, se: avoir la bouche cousue, la boucler, écraser, s'éteindre, s'étouffer, fermer sa boîte (*ou* son clapet *ou* sa gueule), la fermer, y mettre un cadenas, ne pas moufter, ne pas piper, poser sa chique, rengracier, taire sa gueule, tirer sa fermeture éclair.

faire taire: boucler la trappe à, brider, clouer (le bec à), museler, rabattre le caquet à, rembarrer, river le clou à.

tatouer: bouziller, brider, marquouser, piquer.

taxi *m*: bahut *m*, brutal *m*, fiacre *m*, hotte *f*, loche *f*, rongeur *m*, sapin *m*, taquemard *m*.

téléphone *m*: bigophone *m*, bigorneau *m*, biniou *m*, cornichon *m*, grelot *m*, phonard *m*, ronfleur *m*, télémuche *m*, tube *m*.

testicules *f.pl.*: balloches *f.pl.*, ballustrines *f.pl.*, bijoux *m.pl.* de famille, billes *f.pl.*, blosses *f.pl.*, bonbons *m.pl.*, burettes *f.pl.*, burnes *f.pl.*, claoui(e)s *m.pl.*, clopinettes *f.pl.*, couilles *f.pl.*, couillons *m.pl.*, croquignoles *f.pl.*, génitoires *f.pl.*, joyeuses *f.pl.*, montgolfières *f.pl.*, noisettes *f.pl.*, noix *f.pl.*, olives *f.pl.*, paire *f*, parties *f.pl.* (nobles), pendeloques *f.pl.*, précieuses *f.pl.*, rognons *m.pl.*, roubignolles *f.pl.*, rouleaux *m.pl.*, roupes *f.pl.*, roupettes *f.pl.*, roupignolles *f.pl.*, roustons *m.pl.*, valseuses *f.pl.*

tête *f*: baigneur *m*, balle *f*, bille *f*, binette *f*, bobèche *f*, bobéchon *m*, bobine *f*, bougie *f*, bouille *f*, bouillotte *f*, boule *f*, bourrichon *m*, boussole *f*, burette *f*, caberlot *m*, caboche *f*, cabochon *m*, cafetière *f*, caillou *m*, carafe *f*, carafon *m*, cassis *m*, chou *m*, ciboulot *m*, cigare *m*, citron *m*, citrouille *f*, coco *m*, coloquinte *f*, fiole *f*, gadin *m*, gourde *f*, nénette *f*, patate *f*, plafond *m*, poire *f*, pomme *f*, sinoquet *m*, siphon *m*, terrine *f*, tétère *f*, téterre *f*, théière *f*, tirelire *f*, tomate *f*, toupie *f*, tranche *f*, trogne *f*, trognon *m*, trombine *f*, tronc *m*, tronche *f*.

tirer (*une arme à feu*): défourailler, envoyer (*ou* lâcher) la fumée (*ou* la purée *ou* la sauce), flingot(t)er, flinguer.

tomber: aller à dame, aller valser dans les décors, se casser la figure, chuter, faire une valdingue, se ficher (*ou* se foutre) la gueule en l'air (*ou* par terre), partir à dame, prendre (*ou* ramasser) un billet de parterre (*ou* une bûche *ou* un gadin *ou* une pelle *ou* un traînard *ou* une valdingue), quimper.

tracasser, se: se biler, se cailler, se casser la tête, être aux cent coups, s'en faire, se faire de la bile (*ou* des cheveux (blancs) *ou* des crins *ou* du mauvais sang *ou* du mouron *ou* de la mousse), se monter le bourrichon, se turlupiner.

travail *m*: bibelotage *m*, bis(e)ness *m*, boulot *m*, bricolage *m*, charbon *m*, coltin *m*, coltinage *m*, flambeau *m*, flanche *f*, gâche *f*, gratin *m*, groupin *m*, job *m*, placarde *f*, truc *m*, turbin *m*.

travailler dur: bosser, boulonner, bûcher, buriner, se cailler, se casser (le cul), se décarcasser, en donner (une secousse), s'échiner, s'éreinter, s'esquinter, s'expliquer, en ficher (*ou* en foutre) un coup (*ou* une secousse), se fouler la rate, gratter, marner, pinocher, piocher, pisser du sang, suer (sang et eau), taper dans la butte, trimer, turbiner, usiner.

travailleur *m*: *voir* **ouvrier.**

tricher: arnaquer, arrangemaner, biseauter, doubler, échauder, empalmer, escan(n)er, étriller, faisander, maquiller, quiller, rangemaner.

tricheur *m*: arnaqueur *m*, arrangeman *m*, biseauteur *m*, empalmeur *m*, entôleur *m*, faisandier *m*, faiseur *m*, graisseur *m*, maquilleur *m*.

triste (*adj.*): bourdon, cafardeux, dépon(n)é, fouille-merde, tout chose.

tromper: arnaquer, arranger, avoir, bidonner, blouser, carotter, charrier, doubler, empiler, endormir, enfiler, enfler, enfoncer, entôler, entuber, faire (à l'oseille), ficher (*ou* foutre) dedans, gour(r)er, jobarder, maquiller, mettre dedans, posséder, quiller, ranger, refaire, rouler, roustir.

trottoir *m*: bitume *m*, pavé *m*, ruban *m*, turf *m*.

trouver: *voir* **découvrir.**

tuer: *voir* **assassiner.**

uriner: aller faire sa petite commission, faire pipi, faire son petit besoin, lâcher l'eau (*ou* l'écluse *ou* un fil), lancecailler, lancequiner, lansquiner, lisbroquer, lispoquer, ouvrir les écluses, pisser, renverser la vapeur; (*homme*) changer son poisson d'eau, égoutter son colosse (*ou* son cyclope *ou* sa sardine), se l'égoutter, faire pleurer le colosse, jeter de la lance, prendre une ardoise à l'eau, tenir l'âne par la queue, verser de l'eau; (*femme*) arroser le persil, humecter sa fourrure, mouiller son gazon.

urinoir *m*: ardoises *f.pl.*, lavabe *m*, pissoir(e) *m*, pissotière *f*, pissotoire *f*, tasse *f*, théière *f*.

vagabond *m*: cloche *f*, clodo *m*, clodomir *m*, clodot *m*, grelotteux *m*, mouisard *m*, refileur *m* de comète, traîne-lattes *m*, traîne-patins *m*, traîne-pattes *m*, traîne-sabots *m*, traîne-savates *m*, trimard *m*, vacant *m*.
Voir aussi **clochard.**

vagin *m*: *voir* **vulve.**

vantard *m*: baratineur *m*, blagueur *m*, bluffeur *m*, bourreur *m* de crâne, chiqueur *m*, cracheur *m*, cravateur *m*, esbrouf(f)eur *m*, fort *m* en gueule, fumiste *m*, grande gueule, gueulard *m*, musicien *m*, rambineur *m*.

vaurien *m*: affreux *m*, apache *m*, bon-à-rien *m*, bordille *f*, (sale) bougre *m*, bourdille *f*, canaille *f*, charognard *m*, charogne *f*, copaille *f*, couillon *m*, crapule *f*, dur *m*, fan *m* de pute, fias *m*, fils *m* de pute, fripouillard *m*, fripouille *f*, fumier *m*, gale *f*, gouape *f*, locdu *m*, loquedu *m*, malfrappe *m*, mange-punaise *m*, mauvaise graine, muf(f)e *m*, mufle *m*, ordure *f*, peau *f* de vache, poisse *f*, pourriture *f*, pute *f*, raclure *f*, rien-du-tout *m*, salaud *m*, sale coco *m*, saligaud *m*, salopard *m*, salope *f*, varlot *m*, (sale) vicelard *m*.

ventre *m*: ballon *m*, balourd *m*, baquet *m*, battant *m*, bedaine *f*, bedon *m*, bide *m*, bidon *m*, bocal *m*, boîte *f* à ragoût, brioche *f*, buffedingue *m*, buffet *m*, bureau *m*, burlingue *m*, caisse *f*, fusil *m*, gras-double *m*, panse *f*, sac *m* à tripes, tiroir *m*.

Voir aussi **estomac.**

verre *m* **à boire**: auge *f*, baquet *m*, canon *m*, chope *f*, godot *m*, guindal *m*, pot *m*.

veste *f*: alezingue *f*, alpague *f*, alpingue *f*, pelure *f*, vestouse *f*.

vêtements *m.pl.*: fringues *f.pl.*, frip(p)es *f.pl.*, frusques *f.pl.*, harnais *m.pl.*, linges *m.pl.*, loques *f.pl.*, nippes *f.pl.*, pelure *f*, sapes *f.pl.*, vêtures *f.pl.*

viande *f*: barbaque *f*, bidoche *f*, carne *f*, charogne *f*, crigne *f*, crignolle *f*, criolle *f*.

vieillir: avoir (*ou* prendre) de la bouteille (*ou* du flacon), être bon pour la casse (*ou* la refonte), faire d'occasion, se fossiliser, prendre un coup de vieux, sentir la fin de saison, vioquer.

vieux (*adj.*): bibard, bléchard, blèche, croulant, périmé, schnocke, viocard, vioque.

vieux *m*: bonze *m*, croulant *m*, fossile *m*, mironton *m*, périmé *m*, son-et-lumière *m*, vestige *m*, vieille baderne (*ou* noix), vieux birbe (*ou* croûton *ou* jeton *ou* rococo), vioc *m*, viocard *m*, vioquard *m*, vioque *m*.

vin *m*: jaja *m*, pinard *m*, pive *m*, piveton *m*, pivois *m*, tutu *m*; (*blanc*) blanquette *f*, savonné *m*; (*rouge*) anti-dérapant *m*, aramon *m*, brutal *m*, décapant *m*, gobette *f*, gorgeon *m*, du gros (qui tache), gros bleu, gros *m* rouge, petit velours, pichetegorne *m*, pichtogorme *m*, pichtogorne *m*, picolo *m*, picrate *m*, picton *m*, reginglard *m*, reguinglet *m*, rouquemoute *mf*, rouquin *m*, rouquinos *m*, sens *m* unique, tumec *m*, vinasse *f*.

visage *m*: balle *f*, bille *f*, binette *f*, bobine *f*, bougie *f*, bouille *f*, bouillotte *f*, boule *f*, burette *f*, cerise *f*, fiole *f*, fraise *f*, frime *f*, frimousse *f*, frite *f*, gaufre *f*, gueule *f*, hure *f*, margoulette *f*, museau *m*, poire *f*, pomme *f*, portrait *m*, terrine *f*, tirelire *f*, trogne *f*, trognon *m*, trombine *f*, trompette *f*, tronche *f*.

vite (*adv.*): à bride abattue, à fond de train, à plein(s) tube(s), à tout bersingue (*ou* berzingue), à toute blinde, à toute barre, à toute bombe, à toute(s) pompe(s), comme un zèbre, dare-dare, en cinq secs, en moins de deux, en quatrième vitesse, fissa, presto, quatre à quatre, rapidos, rapio.

aller vite: bomber, bousculer les bornes, brûler le pavé (*ou* la route), foncer, gazer, se magner le train, rouler à plein(s) gaz (*ou* à plein(s) tube(s) *ou* à toute pompe).

(vieille) voiture *f* (*auto*): bagnole *f*, bahut *m*, berlingot *m*, bouzine *f*, charrette *f*, chignole *f*, chiotte *f*, guimbarde *f*, guinde *f*, hotte *f*, tacot *m*, tape-cul *m*, tarare *f*, tine *f*, tinette *f*, tire *f*, tombereau *m*.

voler: accrocher, acheter à la foire d'empoigne, aller (en) chercher, arranger, asphyxier, barbot(t)er, bichotter, calotter, chaparder, chauffer, chiper, choper, chouraver, dégraisser, doubler, écorcher, empiler, emplafonner, emplâtrer, engourdir, enquiller, escan(n)er, estamper, étouffer, étourdir, fabriquer, faire, faire sauter, faucher, gauler, grapper, grappiner, griffer, grincher, lever, pégrer, piquer, plumer, poirer, poisser, raboter, ratiboiser, ratisser, refaire, rincer, roustir, secouer, soulever, sucrer, tirer.

Voir aussi **cambrioler.**

voleur *m*: barbot(t)eur *m*, carotteur *m*, chapardeur *m*, chipeur *m*, chopeur *m*, doubleur *m*, encanneur *m*, faucheur *m*, filou *m*, gauleur *m*, grinche *m*, leveur *m*, pégriot *m*, piqueur *m*, roustisseur *m*.

Voir aussi **cambrioleur.**

vomir: aller au refil(e) (*ou* au renard), bader, débagouler, dégobiller, dégoupillonner, dégueuler, évacuer le couloir, gerber, lâcher une fusée, refiler, remesurer, renarder.

vulve *f*: abricot *m*, baba *m*, barbu *m*, baveux *m*, bénitier *m*, bijou *m* de famille, boîte *f* à ouvrage, bonbonnière *f*, bréviaire *m* d'amour, chagatte *f*, chat *m*, chatte *f*, cheminée *f*, cicatrice *f*, con *m*, con(n)asse *f*, crac *m*, cramouille *f*, craque *f*, craquette *f*, crevasse *f*, didi *m*, didine *f*, étau *m*, fente *f*, figue *f*, fri-fri *m*, grippette *f*, millefeuille(s) *m*, mimi *m*, minet *m*, minou *m*, motte *f*, moule *f*, nénuphar *m*, pâquerette *f*, pince *f*, portail *m*, tabernacle *m*, tirelire *f*.

W.C. *m.pl.*: azor *m*, cabinces *f.pl.*, chiards *m.pl.*, chiottes *f.pl.*, débourre *f*, débourroir *m*, garde-manger *m*, gogs *m.pl.*, goguenots *m.pl.*, gogues *m.pl.*, lieux *m.pl.*, ouatères *m.pl.*, petit coin, tartiss(es) *m.pl.*, tartissoires *m.pl.*, téléphone *m*, tinettes *f.pl.*, vécés *m.pl.*

yeux *m.pl.*: *voir* **œil.**

DEC 1 1978

LIBRARY
FLORISSANT VALLEY COMMUNITY COLLEGE
ST. LOUIS, MO.

SPRING '83

COMPLETED